W9-ATR-422

THE LIBRARY
ST. MARY'S COLLEGE OF MARYLAND
ST. MARY'S CITY, MARYLAND 20686

Harvard Historical Studies, 125

Published under the auspices
of the Department of History
from the income of the
Paul Revere Frothingham Bequest
Robert Louis Stroock Fund
Henry Warren Torrey Fund

From the Other Shore

Russian
Social
Democracy
after 1921

André Liebich

Harvard University Press

Cambridge, Massachusetts, and London, England   1997

Copyright © 1997 by the President and Fellows of Harvard College
All rights reserved
Printed in the United States of America

Library of Congress Cataloging-in-Publication Data

Liebich, André, 1948–
    From the other shore : Russian social democracy after 1921 /
André Liebich. — (Harvard historical studies ; 125)
        p.   cm. — (Harvard historical studies ; 125)
    Includes bibliographical references (p.   ) and index.
    ISBN 0-674-32517-6 (cloth : alk. paper)
    1. Mensheviks—History.   2. Rossiĭskaia sotsial-demokraticheskaia
rabochaia partiia—History.   3. Socialist parties—Soviet Union—
History.   I. Title.   II. Series.
DK265.9.M45L54   1997
947.084—dc20   96-41417

Modern Man, that melancholy *Pontifex Maximus*, only builds a bridge—It will be for the unknown man of the future to pass over it. You may be there to see him . . . But do not, I beg, remain on *this shore* . . . Better to perish with the revolution than to seek refuge in the almshouse of reaction.

The religion of the coming revolution is the only one that I bequeath to you. It has no paradise to offer, no rewards, except your own awareness, except conscience . . . When the time comes go and preach it amongst us *at home;* my language was once loved there and perhaps they will remember me.

Alexander Herzen

Acknowledgments

This book has been in the making, off and on, for well over a decade. At the end of a long road it is therefore a great source of satisfaction to be able to acknowledge some of the many debts I have incurred along the way.

The project was conceived during a sabbatical year at Harvard's Russian Research Center in 1979–80 and continued at a subsequent sabbatical there in 1986–87. On both occasions I found the congenial atmosphere that I had known earlier as a graduate student. In 1983–84 I worked on this project at Stanford, formally as a visiting scholar at the Hoover Institution. All my thanks in that period, however, go to the Stanford University History Department and its then-chairman James Sheehan, who extended a much-appreciated welcome. The Kennan Institute of Advanced Russian Studies in Washington, D.C., kindly offered me a short-term grant in 1985 and then a visiting scholarship in 1987, allowing me to take advantage of its unique ambience and facilities.

The principal source of material support for this project was the Social Sciences and Humanities Research Council of Canada, which provided two sabbatical fellowships, a research grant in 1981–82, and a time research stipend in 1983–84. Canadian academics are truly fortunate to have such a remarkable national institution which unflaggingly supports research purely on the basis of scholarly considerations. My home university at the time, the Université du Québec à Montréal, kindly supplemented other grants at crucial moments, confirming the commitment to research made by its rector, and my colleague, Claude Corbo.

As I now know from both ends, teachers are teachers for life. Over the years Adam Ulam continued to give me the steady support which I had enjoyed as his graduate student, and he brought his unparalleled knowledge of Soviet history to bear on my final manuscript. Judith Shklar initially chided me, in her inimitable way, for taking up the study of emigrés, but she read the early chapters of the manuscript attentively and reacted enthusiastically. Her last writings were on the political responsibilities of exiles, and I wish she had lived to receive this book.

I have been extraordinarily fortunate in the generous support of several senior colleagues whom I met in the course of this research. Daniel Bell urged me on vigorously and offered judicious advice. This book might not have appeared in the present form without his counsel. Alexander Dallin helped in ways both practical and intellectual, from sharing his office and his library to reading the final manuscript. Leopold Haimson offered encouragement as I was embarking on the project and put his vast collection of materials at my disposal. Walter Laqueur expressed his keen interest in the book on several occasions. It is because of him that a modified version of part of Chapter 8 was published in the *Journal of Contemporary History* 30 (1995) and that my manuscript was put forward for the Fraenkel Prize. Marc Raeff responded unfailingly to my queries, sharing his knowledge of the subject and carefully reading and commenting on all that I sent him, including the final manuscript. These individuals and so many others, unfortunately too numerous to list by name, have been faithful correspondents, willing interviewees, counselors, and friends. So long as there are academics of their ilk, the Republic of Letters thrives.

Scholars are helpless by themselves, and I must therefore thank a veritable army of librarians and archivists in half a dozen countries, in particular Susan Gardos, Hilja Kukk, and A. V. N. Van Woerden. I also thank my two assistants at the Kennan Institute, Dorothea Hanson and Zoe Heineman, as well as Faina Burko and Helen Solanum, who read Yiddish materials to me.

And of course Rayya, Nadya, and Hayat, who were with me throughout and without whom life would have been incomplete.

Contents

Illustrations

Following page 202.

Mensheviks with L. Deich on the occasion of his return from America, 1917

L. Martov and Fedor Dan, Petrograd, 1917

LSI Executive Committee Meeting, Zurich, 1926

Lidia and Fedor Dan vacationing, France, 1927

A Menshevik picnic in the forest, Berlin, 1927

The Menshevik patriarch and his friends, Berlin, ca. 1927

Mensheviks traveling to the LSI Congress, 1928

Soviet caricature of Raphael Abramovitch, 1931

Boris Nicolaevsky, Berlin, 1932

Twenty-fifth anniversary celebrations of *Sotsialisticheskii vestnik,* New York, 1946

Note on Spelling

The Mensheviks abroad altered the spelling of their names according to the usage of their countries of exile. In the text I have used their own English versions of their names (thus Abramovitch, not Abramovich or Abramowitsch; Dallin, not Dalin; Nicolaevsky, not Nikolaevskii or Nikolajewsky). In the notes I have given the names as they appear in the original source (for example, Abramowitsch for German-language or Nikolaevskii for Russian-language publications or correspondence). All versions of a given name are cross-referenced in the index. Regarding other Russian names, I have used Library of Congress transcription except for standard deviations such as Trotsky rather than Trotskii.

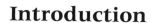

Introduction

The years 1921 and 1922 marked the end of the legal existence of the Russian Social Democratic Labor Party, the Mensheviks. Russian social democracy, however, did not disappear at that time. For several years the party continued to function underground in Soviet Russia. For an entire generation it existed abroad, in the West, represented by its "Foreign Delegation." Throughout the interwar period the Mensheviks were prominent members of the Labor and Socialist International (LSI), remaining closely in touch with the leaders of Western social democracy. For over forty years, successively in Berlin, Paris, and New York, they published *Sotsialisticheskii vestnik,* a unique and respected journal of Soviet developments and socialist theory.

This book is a study of Russian social democracy as it existed after 1921. I have been drawn to the subject, on the one hand, through an interest in the nature and influence of exile movements and, on the other, through a reflection on the fate of Marxism in the aftermath of the Russian Revolution. In the course of my work I found myself dwelling specifically on the way in which Soviet "reality" and Soviet history have been interpreted in the West. It may be useful at the outset to consider the nature and relevance of these concerns.

Scholarly neglect of the phenomenon of exile movements reflects a deplorable lack of historical imagination.[1] Historical and social studies seem unable to adopt any perspective other than that defined by outcome, considered as the only possible outcome. Success at a given time is taken as success for all time, and the victorious cause is equated with the cause of truth and virtue. Recent historical inquiry has introduced previously neglected collective actors, but, in a manner corresponding to the outlook of mass societies, it has substituted numbers for success as a criterion of significance.

Neither traditional nor new social studies has managed to overcome a

1

deeply ingrained disregard for exile movements. As a key actor in this study puts it, such disregard is "only a peculiar form of that contempt which any well-ordered bourgeois with a checkbook experiences in regard to a man without a current account in the bank."[2] It is a form of intellectual philistinism which makes scholars prisoners of events as they have occurred, deprives them of a basis for critical evaluation by excluding the possibility of alternative developments, and blurs the ability to make moral judgments by removing criteria other than that of success. Ultimately, such an approach undermines even its own validity. By resorting to anticipation, that is, by examining phenomena only in light of their future success, one is unable to see a historical process from inside. In short, one is unable to attain understanding even of the specific phenomena one has chosen to examine at the exclusion of others.

Considerations of this sort would suggest that the study of exile movements might serve as a corrective to conventional, one-dimensional ways of looking at social movements and historical experiences. Such a suggestion may not require much demonstration in the case of movements that found their way back to their homeland: German Social Democrats or Communists during the Third Reich, Russian Bolsheviks before the Revolution, even Spanish Republicans under Franco. In these cases, however, we are witnessing the retrospective application of the criterion of success: the exile movement is deemed worthy of attention only to the extent that it ceases to be an exile movement. In fact, movements which never succeeded in transcending exile have been significant in themselves and deeply influential. Polish history of the nineteenth century is incomplete without the Great Emigration after 1830, just as the recent history of that country cannot be explained independently of the cultural role of the post–World War II Polish emigration. Even those movements that seem to have vanished into the past without leaving a significant trace constitute an integral part of a given historical period and milieu. There may be few remains of the unsuccessful Jacobite movement, but the history of eighteenth-century Britain cannot be written without taking account of the hopes and fears this movement raised.

Exile movements, and particularly exile politics, have also been neglected because of the ungratifying nature of the enterprise. Much of exile politics is marked by futile endeavor, frustration, factionalism, and pettiness.[3] In fact, however, most differences between exile politics and politics *tout court* are differences of degree. Factionalism among Bolsheviks did not cease once they became a ruling party, and personal rivalries among them were not necessarily different in Zurich from what they were later in the Kremlin. Even the phenomenon of ideological and political degeneration, seemingly so typical of exile movements, is in fact a manifestation of the process of entropy which affects all ruling parties, governing regimes, and dominant ideologies. In short, some of the peculiarities of exile movements are actually acute manifestations of familiar processes. If the task of studying these movements is not a comforting one, it is nonetheless worthwhile. Indeed, it would be sheer scholarly irresponsibility to shirk this task and to forgo the insights that might be garnered from the study of exile movements because one chose to shun the company of the defeated and the forgotten.[4]

Studying the post-1917 Russian emigration can certainly be justified on its own terms. Produced by one of the most momentous events of the early part of this century, it dispersed more than a million people of all classes over five continents. For more than a generation Russian emigré colonies existed as a self-contained worldwide society. They enjoyed a rich and vibrant cultural and intellectual life rivaling that of the Soviet Union and regularly impinging on the emigrés' host countries. Twentieth-century culture cannot be imagined without Stravinsky, Kandinsky, Diaghilev, Nabokov, and Berdyayev. This century's debates on communism and totalitarianism owe much of their force and arguments to the contribution of emigrés from Bolshevik Russia.

Among Russian emigrés, the Mensheviks were intellectually incisive and coherent witnesses to their own fate. In this sense the history of the Mensheviks after the Revolution is the history of a group that understood and accepted the reasons for its own defeat. Moreover, it is they who posed, in the clearest possible fashion, the question of the fate of Marxism, which is the second major concern behind this study.

The crisis of Marxism preceded 1917, but it came to be seen largely as the crisis of the Revolution. For a whole generation "the hopes and fears of revolutionaries were inseparable from the fortunes of the Russian Revolution."[5] The unexpected and unorthodox seizure of power by Marxists in a backward country sent the deepest tremors throughout Marxist parties. The failure of revolution on the Bolshevik pattern elsewhere led to the elaboration of variants of Marxism which deprecated the proletariat as revolutionary agent. Eventually the jagged course of the Soviet experience with its staggering toll led to selfinterrogation concerning the costs of socialist construction in Soviet Russia, the congruence of means and ends, and ultimately the legitimacy of the enterprise launched in Petrograd in November 1917.

The Mensheviks stand at the very heart of the crisis of Marxism. They were the first Marxists to lose in a socialist revolution. Contrary to some widespread impressions, they were neither doctrinal revisionists nor dogmatists. As committed to Marxism as other members of the Second International, Bolsheviks included, and no less creative in their application of Marxism, they lost the Revolution without losing their Marxist convictions; indeed, many found confirmation of their beliefs in the course of Soviet development. The disenchantment with Marxism of some Mensheviks in the 1940s and 1950s only mirrored a process that was equally pervasive within other Marxist parties.

The Mensheviks thus belong to the mainstream of Marxism. By the very nature of their predicament, they were forced to pose, earlier and more acutely than other Marxists, a number of questions about Soviet Russia, socialism, and Marxism. What was the nature of the Bolshevik Revolution? Could the order that emerged from the Revolution be considered progressive, and did revolutionaries owe allegiance to it? Could one have a workers' state without a workers' democracy? Or, to paraphrase Rosa Luxemburg, could barbarism lead to socialism? Finally, to put the question polemically, is there a logic to Marxism which leads toward the Gulag?

This study is further focused on two issues: Menshevik perceptions of the Soviet Union and their influence on Western attitudes. These perceptions show both the possibilities and the limitations of Marxist theory, and they provide an answer to a recurrent question: What would be the content of a critique of the Soviet Union from the left? Trotsky's reply is best known, but the Mensheviks' answer is more credible and more thoroughly considered inasmuch as it was developed in debate among themselves and with foreign socialists, and it remains, in fact, paradigmatic.

The basic Menshevik position, known as the "Martov Line," can be described as revolutionary vis-à-vis Western capitalism but reformist vis-à-vis the USSR. It represents the search for a third way, a course between bolshevism and bourgeois reformism, attempted at different times by other parties, such as Austro-Marxists with whom the Mensheviks had so much in common and, much later, by those parties that styled themselves "Eurocommunist." Its difficulties emerge readily enough from a study of the Mensheviks. In the conditions of the 1920s and 1930s, to what extent could one refuse to make the stark choice, demanded both by the Bolsheviks and by their opponents, between approval or condemnation of the Soviet experience? Then, as later, to what extent could one criticize the Soviet Union without making common cause with its ideological enemies?

The Menshevik Left argued that the party could not separate its support for the Revolution and for the Russian working class from support for the outcome of that Revolution and for the first regime—not only in Russia but worldwide—that commanded the allegiance of a significant part of the working class. The barbaric forms of Soviet development did not annul its positive achievements, and in the face of the bankruptcy of Western capitalism and bourgeois ideology, socialist hopes had to remain focused on the Soviet Union.

The Menshevik Right declared that democracy and socialism were indivisible, and it excoriated attempts to compromise principles in favor of accommodation with the Soviet regime, regarding such attempts as founded on self-delusion about the nature of Bolshevik power and the probable course of its evolution. What was the coherence and credibility, asked the Right, of a policy that condemned dictatorship over the working class but tolerated dictatorship over other classes? How would the working classes, of both Russia and the West, interpret Russian social democracy's support for the Soviet regime, which was practicing terror upon, among others, workers and socialists?

The dialectic between Right and Left characterized the Menshevik analysis of the Soviet experience. In addition to its paradigmatic value, this analysis was itself a formative influence on the definition of Western socialist attitudes toward the Soviet Union.

In the broadest terms, the question of the influence of Menshevik ideas and policies concerns the effectiveness of a political party with no visible political base. The problem is common to all exile phenomena, and it is particularly acute in the case of political movements: What can be the power of a political party cut off from all the conventional trappings, instruments, and foundations of power? The case of the Mensheviks suggests that such a group can indeed exert a certain type of power or influence by virtue of its ability to define the terms of debate, to set agenda (whether literally or metaphorically), to provide information to decision makers, to obstruct policies, or even to obtain a veto power over certain options.[6]

In all these respects Mensheviks in exile proved adept politicians. They painstakingly maintained a network of personal relations with Western socialist leaders through assiduous correspondence, personal exchange, and various forms of literary and political cooperation. They also successfully exploited their bureaucratic and ideological position in the Labor and Socialist International. As a founding member party, represented in the LSI Bureau and Executive, the Mensheviks enjoyed a significant audience. Their arguments were buttressed by their unique ideological value to the International: the presence of Russian social democrats among their Western counterparts demonstrated that the traumatic division of the working class caused by the Russian Revolution was an anomaly. The Mensheviks were guarantors of "another Russia," or, at the very least, of the possibility of another socialism in Russia. They provided balm to the conscience of those Western parties that smarted under accusations of having betrayed the working class.

In large measure the Mensheviks' strength was based on their command of information about the Soviet Union. As knowledge about conditions in Russia was fragmentary and confusion reigned concerning the Bolsheviks, reliable information and the ability to process it were a powerful political weapon. Mensheviks abroad were able to reconstruct and interpret what was happening in Russia through communications from home as well as through an informed and meticulous reading of Soviet sources. The flagship of this vast information campaign was *Sotsialisticheskii vestnik,* but the campaign also included a regular bulletin in German and frequent contributions to the Western socialist press. The wealth and reliability of this information, combined with a readiness to supply information on demand to Western comrades and to enter into public debate on the Russian Question, placed the Mensheviks among the leading interpreters of the Soviet Union. It would be no exaggeration to describe them as the first generation of sovietologists, who marked out many of the paths their successors were to follow.[7]

The question of the Menshevik analysis of the Soviet Union and of the influence of that analysis opens up broader areas of inquiry concerning the history of the Soviet Union and the way that history has been written. Not all Menshevik hypotheses regarding the major stages and issues of Soviet history can withstand the test of time, but they all offer a contemporary view of events that can be used to measure our present understanding or rival interpretations. As well as providing a perspective on the "commanding heights" of Soviet history, an examination of Menshevik sources offers a unique insight into the microhistory of the Soviet regime, into daily life under Lenin and Stalin. Year after year *Sotsialisticheskii vestnik* published communications from anonymous correspondents who reported on living and working conditions, on the mood among rank-and-file Bolsheviks and ordinary people, on labor unrest, and on repression. Given the dearth of firsthand, grassroots information of this sort, it is surprising that Western academics have not exploited this source.[8]

Finally, reconstructing Soviet history through Menshevik eyes leads one to reflect on how the history of the Revolution has been written in the West. As prominent observers of an increasingly distant historical event, the Mensheviks found a ready academic and journalistic audience for their historical reminiscences. In general, this activity brought very positive results, counteracting precisely the sort of success-oriented writing of history that I have already criticized and winning the admiration of even the severest critics. Remarkably, however, there has been little inclination to examine these Menshevik historians themselves. Such an examination is surely imperative in the case of historians describing their own experience after an interval marked by momentous historical events.[9]

A number of methodological problems are involved in a study of this kind.

With respect to the Menshevik analysis of the Soviet Union, the most straightforward question is that of its priority and accuracy: What did the Mensheviks say that had not been previously known, and how does the Menshevik analysis compare with what we now know? Once the question is put in this way, it is possible to find an answer. For example, *Sotsialisticheskii vestnik* was the first to publish part of Lenin's "Testament" in 1924; and thirty-two years later Khrushchev's secret speech on the crimes of Stalin confirmed that the Mensheviks' information was indeed accurate.[10]

At the same time it should be recognized that even a collection of such cases could not establish the value of the Mensheviks' analysis, for two reasons. First, many of the facts they presented have not been fully elucidated, and consequently it is not possible to verify them conclusively. For instance, the "Letter of an Old Bolshevik" is the most important document published by *Sotsialisticheskii vestnik* in the 1930s and is potentially one of the most important sources on that period. Yet controversy about its accuracy and reliability continues to this day and may never be resolved. Second, much of the Menshevik analysis involves not stark facts but trends and attitudes which do not allow cut-and-dried pronouncements about their correctness. For instance, if the Mensheviks comment on the growing wealth of the kulaks under the New Economic Policy (NEP), part of their statement can be verified factually. In all likelihood, however, their comment is formulated in terms of a tendency and is invoked in order to make a point about, say, the growing assertiveness of the kulaks. At this moment the analysis is no longer descriptive but becomes predictive, raising a host of new problems.

Any attempt to evaluate the Menshevik analysis in terms of its predictive accuracy rests on a misunderstanding both of the nature of this analysis and of predictive statements. The Mensheviks certainly did not consider themselves prophets. It is worth noting, too, that they did not indulge in the exercise, popular among journalists, diplomats, and emigrés, of repeatedly announcing the imminent downfall of the Soviet regime. To be sure, they did make the occasional outright prediction, for instance, on the fall of Trotsky (which proved right) or a takeover by the generals in the 1930s (which proved wrong). For the most part, however, they couched their "predictive" statements in conditional and open-ended terms. For instance, the Mensheviks insisted (correctly) that there were insoluble contradictions inherent in the practice of the New Economic Policy (NEP). They concluded (incorrectly) that the Bolsheviks would be forced to make basic concessions in the direction of democratization. The premise behind this conclusion was that any alternative to NEP would jeopardize the leadership of the Bolshevik Party and many of the achievements of the Revolution.

This analysis may be considered a case of wishful thinking and a symptom of the inability to face the possibility of Stalinist ruthlessness. Let it be said that such an inability was shared by a great many Bolsheviks in power. Above all, however, a condescending attitude toward such an analysis can be based only on retrospective knowledge. Social psychologists have warned of the tendency to confuse foresight with hindsight.[11] In this case it is assumed that "Russian communism *had* to turn out as it has because it now can be seen to have turned out as it has."[12]

One might add that excessive significance should not be attributed to predictions when they do turn out to be correct. One can get a prophecy right for the wrong reasons, that is, foresee an outcome but mistake its causes; or one can fail to act according to one's own prophetic insight. The literature on Russian social democracy before 1917 is replete with references to the "brilliant premonitions" of various key figures. Yet the "brilliant premonitions" of, for example, Trotsky regarding the inevitable Bolshevik reduction of party life to one-man rule did not prevent him from throwing in his lot with the Bolsheviks or from identifying with bolshevism even after his defeat.[13] As Tolstoy remarked with reference to the events of 1812, the explanation would seem to be that individuals are likely to make numerous incompatible predictions; it is therefore not possible to heed even all one's own predictions.

It may already be obvious that in addition to the problems derived from attributing premonitions to historical actors, there is a further question regarding the reading of anticipations into an account of the past. To what extent can one read back outcomes into initial positions? To take an example, one might be inclined to say that the psychological makeup of the Menshevik leader Fedor Dan and the attitudes he displayed throughout the 1920s (rather than, say, changes in objective circumstances in the 1930s and 1940s) give us grounds to anticipate the Sovietophilia of his last years. At the same time, however, the evolution of another leader, Raphael Abramovitch, toward Sovietophobia does not seem to be foreshadowed by his psychological and political point of departure. In this study I have not tried to draw any definitive conclusions on the question of anticipations; I have, however, sought to explore this issue, especially since it is one to which some Mensheviks themselves proved sensitive and which stands at the very center of Menshevik historiography.

If methodological problems raised by the attempt to evaluate the Menshevik analysis of the Soviet Union are many, questions regarding Menshevik influence on Western perceptions of the Soviet Union are more easily stated but even more intractable. How does one demonstrate that given actors actually determined or contributed to determining a given choice? To provide an irrefutable demonstration would require showing that, without their contribution, another choice would have been made. This leads to a thorny path—an impasse, in fact—of counterfactual statements, by their very nature unprovable.

Such problems can be addressed only in terms of plausible lines of causality and of relationships. I approach the problem of Menshevik influence from various vantage points: through analysis of policy outcomes; through analysis of participation in political processes and public debates; through a "positional" analysis of relations between Mensheviks and various decision-makers as revealed in private correspondence and other sources; and, finally, through a "reputational" analysis, that is, in terms of the perceived authority of the Mensheviks.[14]

This last element merits particular consideration because of its unique relevance to the case. It might be noted that the authority of the Mensheviks was directly enhanced by Bolshevik polemical invocation of the category of menshevism. In a sense, therefore, the Mensheviks were propped up by the importance that the Bolsheviks attached to them. Bolshevik efforts to discredit the Mensheviks thus wrought the opposite effect, as Mensheviks, in what may be called a complicity of deception, exploited Bolshevik charges to increase the bases of their influence in the West. This curious phenomenon may serve as a final illustration of the difficulties encountered in this study as well as the value of pursuing this subject.

1

The Menshevik
Family

A Group Portrait

In addition to being a study of a political movement, this book is also a collective biography. It is an account of a group of men and women whose personal fate is inseparable from momentous historical events of which they were witnesses and participants. The members of this group shared a common revolutionary past, a common party allegiance, and a common exile. Their lives were so intertwined for so long that they referred to themselves as the "Menshevik family," with all that the term implies, including intimacy and even long-standing quarrels.[1]

To a large extent, therefore, the Mensheviks in exile constitute a single collective subject. Their principal achievement, the journal *Sotsialisticheskii vestnik*, is remarkable precisely as a collective organizer, much like the legendary *Iskra* at an earlier period. At the same time, the individual actors in this account must be identified. The outer edges of the group are fluid, but its hard core is well defined. It includes, above all, the two party leaders, Fedor Dan and Raphael Abramovitch, as well as Boris Nicolaevsky, David Dallin, and Solomon Schwarz. It also comprises a second string, so to speak, made up of other members of the "Foreign Delegation" and the prominent women of the party. Other figures wend their way in and out of the account. It includes Mensheviks who attained prominence in foreign socialist parties without cutting ties to their party of origin and those who kept their distance from the party organization but not always from its politics. On a ridge, as it were, casting their shadow on the party in exile, stand the party's historic leaders.

The Mensheviks considered here are a remarkably homogeneous group, both chronologically and sociologically. Almost without exception they were born in the decade of the 1880s. They reached political consciousness in the first years of this century and entered the social democratic movement at about the time the party split into Bolshevik and Menshevik factions in 1903. They attained maturity in the Revolution of 1905, and with the ebb of the revolutionary tide in the following years, most found themselves too deeply involved to withdraw.[2]

As these Mensheviks were entering the revolutionary movement, several intraparty doctrinal struggles against reformism had already been won at a time when the split of 1903 had barely occurred.[3] Thus, for them the question of reformism was an *affaire classée;* they felt inured to its temptations and, for the next half-century, indignantly rejected the accusation of having succumbed to it. At the same time, the division of the party was something of a fact of life. These Mensheviks regretted the division, and many hoped to overcome it, but for the most part, almost until 1917 the existence of Menshevik and Bolshevik wings within a single party was taken as a given, an important fact but not the paramount one. Indeed, several Mensheviks in our group were themselves at one time Bolsheviks, and it was only years later—in some cases decades later—that they elaborated an image of themselves and their opponents that made menshevism and bolshevism into utterly incompatible and contradictory options.[4]

The significance of the generational factor is brought out, *a contrario,* in the example of two Mensheviks who stand outside this chronological framework. Fedor Dan was born a decade earlier than most other members of the group. His formative experiences were the great industrial strikes of the 1890s, and in these years he worked directly with Martov and Lenin in combating reformism. Dan proudly recalled bringing into Russia (in the false bottom of a suitcase) the first copies of Lenin's classic polemic against reformism, *What Is To Be Done?* It was Dan, too, who was responsible for subverting earlier initiatives so that the Second Congress of the Russian Social Democratic Labor Party (RSDRP) could be dominated by *Iskra* centralizers.[5] For the rest of his life he remained acutely watchful for any hint of reformism, and he never reconciled himself to the division of the party.[6] For some of his contemporaries, such as the slightly senior Aleksandr Potresov, the inability to accept the division took the form of a violent and personal anti-Leninism; for Dan it meant a steady inclination, if not always directly toward bolshevism, then toward a belief in the possibility of a compromise with it and toward a conception of the party that incorporated bolshevism.

At the other end of the chronological spectrum stands David Dallin, who entered the revolutionary movement sometime between 1907 and 1910 and was soon acclaimed as one of the party's promising young figures. Dallin's political curriculum followed an unexceptional course until 1921. Then, however, he published an analysis of the postwar situation as one of stabilization, which put him sharply at odds with the Menshevik group abroad.[7] In 1933 he withdrew entirely from political activity, disheartened by what he saw as the futility of the effort to keep the party alive. Although he returned to the Menshevik Foreign Delegation in 1940, his later efforts were directed primarily at building up a personal reputation in the United States as a sovietologist. He separated once again from the majority of the Menshevik group in 1948, advocating a new political formation that would integrate the postwar Soviet emigration and unite various, even nonsocialist, emigré organizations. The psychological factors in Dallin's position should be duly considered, though one cannot escape the impression that the growing gap between Dallin and most of his party comrades can be explained to some extent as a generation gap on the part of an individual who never participated in the process of building up the party in the first years of this century, and who was not tied to the group through the common experience of the Revolution of 1905.

In addition to forming a single, well-defined generation, the Menshevik family was also a socially homogeneous group. Most of its members represented that peculiar and remarkable phenomenon, the Russian Jewish intelligentsia.[8] The term resists breakdown into its component elements, since members of this stratum did not think of themselves as primarily Jewish or Russian, and they shared only some of the traditional traits of the intelligentsia. Nevertheless, the complex and unique character of the phenomenon can best be measured, and the group under examination better understood, in terms of these elements.

With a single exception, that of Boris Nicolaevsky, all members of the Menshevik Foreign Delegation (until 1943) were Jewish, but this fact is not as straightforward as one might imagine. All were largely assimilated, having cut their ties to the Jewish religion and tradition. To be sure, the degree of assimilation varied: some, notably those who came to menshevism through the Jewish Labor Bund, had worked among the Jewish masses and knew Yiddish; for most Mensheviks, however, such specifically Jewish experience was marginal. Common to them all was a profound hostility to anything that smacked of Jewish nationalism and an aversion to singling out the Jewish Question for any special consideration. Just as the Mensheviks were to be reluctant to invoke strictly moral arguments against the Soviet regime in order to avoid playing into the hands of bourgeois moralists, so too were they opposed to dwelling on the injustices suffered specifically by Jews so as not to provide support for Jewish nationalism or separatism. This attitude is prefigured as early as 1903 by Martov's arguments in favor of combating Zionism more vigorously than antisemitism. Later it is exemplified in the Mensheviks' attitude toward the assassination of the Ukrainian leader S. V. Petliura in 1926; as soon as it became evident that the assassin had acted out of Jewish nationalist considerations, Menshevik plans to help in the legal defense of the assassin evaporated.[9]

At first glance there seems to be no evidence that the Mensheviks were repressing their Jewishness. Even as they heaped scorn on Jewish nationalism, they invoked (often in a bantering manner) their own Jewishness; they appealed to Jewish organizations for help; and they moved largely among other Jewish intellectuals and activists. In the 1930s Raphael Abramovitch saw nothing incongruous in asking that Dan, who had never been a Bundist, be included among the beneficiaries of a fund for veterans of the Jewish labor movement. Dan was a deserving champion of the proletariat—that was qualification enough. To be sure, one Menshevik, Grigorii Aronson (significantly, a Bundist by origin), recounts his guilt at having once unknowingly traveled on Yom Kippur in his early revolutionary days, but for most Mensheviks such an incident would have been a source of amusement. It is noteworthy that the Menshevik who expressed the deepest anguish at the treatment of Jews in occupied Europe during World War II was a gentile, Vera Alexandrova, who "passionately wish[ed] that every socialist wear on his sleeve the yellow star of David" in solidarity with the Jews.[10]

The Menshevik attitude toward the Jewish Question was so unselfconscious that, initially, it does not even seem to have been a source of tension. Several Mensheviks, however, eventually came to abandon their original position, to emphasize their Jewishness, and to reverse their longstanding antipathy to Zionism.[11] Beginning in the 1930s, the group became increasingly dependent on the Jewish labor movement in the United States, first financially and then, after 1940, in personal and other ways as well. Although the original Menshevik attitude resisted transformation even through the Holocaust, the Mensheviks were to turn increasingly to specifically Jewish themes after the creation of the state of Israel. This reorientation was a response to the increasingly narrow Menshevik "constituency," then consisting largely of Jewish labor veterans who read *Vestnik* in the United States and in Israel. To what extent, one may ask, was this also a subjectively determined reorientation involving the discovery of long-unacknowledged roots and the development of long-suppressed potential? The fact, for instance, that so thoroughly Russified a Menshevik as Solomon Schwarz chose, at the age of almost ninety, to go to Israel to die (taking the ashes of his gentile wife with him) leaves one pensive.[12]

Just as the Mensheviks kept their distance from Jewish nationalism, they also remained impervious to the appeal of Russian nationalism. In the pre-revolutionary context, the appropriation of nationalist themes by reactionary forces and the autocratic regime, as well as disabilities suffered by many Mensheviks as Jews and revolutionaries, were reason enough to reject Russian nationalism. This rejection was further reinforced by the Mensheviks' strictly orthodox Marxism, with its accompanying idealization of the West and its proletarian internationalism, by their lack of contact with the Russian countryside, and by their lengthy sojourns abroad.

In the post-1917 period, however, the Mensheviks found themselves in a different situation. The Russia they were dealing with was a revolutionary regime, and, especially during the Allied intervention, it was difficult to reject wholly any identification with the Russian state. Most significantly, the Mensheviks emerged as representatives of *Russian* social democracy within the Socialist International. They chafed against the contemptuous attitude toward Russia exhibited by some Western socialist parties. They defended the territorial integrity of their country within the councils of the International against the claims of Ukrainians and other nationalities.[13] In short, the Mensheviks had a national role thrust upon them, and in their postrevolutionary migration they accustomed themselves to acting as spokesmen for Russia.

This is not to say that the Mensheviks abandoned their characteristically internationalist outlook. Indeed, the basic reason for their alienation from the other Russian emigrés was not their deep-seated difference in social outlook but rather their refusal to espouse out-and-out nationalism. This defiance persevered even against the patriotic tide unleashed among emigrés by Soviet victory in World War II. Nevertheless, one can identify a growing Russian nationalist inclination among certain Mensheviks. The examples of Boris Nicolaevsky and Fedor Dan suggest that those who did not develop a Jewish consciousness in emigration did develop a Russian national consciousness.

It is not altogether surprising that Nicolaevsky was more susceptible to Russian nationalism than other Mensheviks. He was an ethnic Russian and a descendant of state serfs and of eight generations of village clergy. Moreover, until his exile to Berlin in 1922, Nicolaevsky had never traveled abroad; while other Mensheviks were in Paris, Geneva, or cosmopolitan Petersburg, Nicolaevsky spent years in internal exile at remote locations of the Russian Empire, often among the peasants with whom he instinctively sympathized. Finally, and somewhat unexpectedly for a historian so well known in the West, Nicolaevsky never really mastered any foreign languages; in contrast to most party comrades, even after decades of emigration he could function comfortably only in Russian.[14]

Nicolaevsky's thorough Russianness did not preclude an awareness of the "national question." Indeed, Nicolaevsky was the exiled Menshevik most interested in establishing contacts with the Soviet minority nationalities. Was it foreseeable that such efforts would come to naught? National minorities existed in Nicolaevsky's distant home province of Ufa, but these were not Jews and Poles, whose national consciousness could compete with that of Russians, but rather Tatars and Chuvash. As a child Nicolaevsky sometimes sided with Tatar underdogs in street fights against Russian boys, but such gestures could not change the pattern of Russian dominance, which he accepted early in life. Although Nicolaevsky maintained warm relations in exile with some Georgian socialists, notably Iraklii Tsereteli, much more indicative was his hostility to Ukrainian nationalism.[15] Nicolaevsky's efforts in regard to minority nationalities were therefore received as the expression of an anachronistic Great Russian paternalism, which they probably were.

Nicolaevsky's nationalism was thus deeply rooted. When Stalin deprived the Mensheviks of citizenship in 1932, Nicolaevsky grieved bitterly that one more thread tying him to the homeland had snapped. Consolations offered by fellow Mensheviks, who coolly belittled the significance of the gesture, were unavailing, and to the end of his life he refused to take out any other nationality.[16] Yet Nicolaevsky's nationalism was not without its nuances and paradoxes. His most fundamental attachment was to the Russian nation, to the Russian masses in their flesh and blood, and the concreteness of this attachment made him immune to any bedazzlement at the grandeur of the Soviet state. In 1919 Nicolaevsky moved left after witnessing the treatment inflicted on the peasants under Admiral Aleksandr Kolchak's counterrevolutionary rule. In the 1930s he broke with the Martov Line and joined the right wing of the Foreign Delegation because of his repulsion at the human horrors of collectivization. After World War II Nicolaevsky abandoned the majority of his party comrades to stretch out a welcoming hand toward new Soviet emigrés; even though they had fought in German uniforms and were politically totally unappealing, they represented a new surge of that Russian nation from which Nicolaevsky could not bear to be separated.[17]

In exile Dan and Nicolaevsky were the Mensheviks most eager to return, physically, to Russia, but their nationalism was different. Whereas Nicolaevsky's was simple in its origins and complex in its expression, Dan's was complex in its origins and simple in its expression. Although Nicolaevsky's nationalism can be explained in terms of his social origins, Dan's background in an assimilated Petersburg Jewish pharmacist's family gives no grounds for similar conclusions. Dan's nationalism is explicable in terms of proclivities and function: of all the Mensheviks Dan was most attuned to bureaucratic and state power, and, as leader of the exiled Mensheviks, he felt a statesman's historic responsibility toward Russia. As a result, while Nicolaevsky's nationalism focused on the people, the *narod,* Dan's was oriented toward the Russian state. In the 1920s Dan, too, combated Ukrainian separatism, and, unlike Nicolaevsky, he even broke with one of his closest and oldest political allies, Tsereteli, over the national question.[18] In the following years Dan was drawn toward admiration for the achievements of the Soviet regime, first only weakly and indirectly, but then, after 1941, openly and wholeheartedly. Russian nationalism, which led Nicolaevsky to abandon all hope of positive evolution in the Soviet Union and to welcome those who had fought against the Soviet regime, also led Dan to focus all his hopes on the Soviet Union and to make partial peace with Stalin's Russia.

Whatever the evolution of individual Mensheviks—toward Jewish nationalism or even, in the peculiar case of Vladimir Woytinsky, toward American nationalism—this group can be described in social terms as a late and, in some ways, incongruous offshoot of that legendary stratum, the intelligentsia of Old Russia.[19] Inasmuch as the intelligentsia was primarily defined by its oppositional attitude to the existing regime, the Mensheviks discussed here did not differ from their predecessors. They were nurtured on the same classics of Russian literature; they developed a similar sense of guilt and responsibility toward the toiling masses; they cultivated the same romantic hopes of a revolutionary transformation; and many maintained, throughout their lives, something of the selfless youthful outlook of student rebels. As if their own disabilities as Jews, or as the offspring of the impoverished lower middle classes, or as inhabitants of culturally desolate provincial towns were insufficient, these Mensheviks also voluntarily absorbed the bad conscience of the traditional Russian intelligentsia. It may not be surprising to read that Petr Garvi felt like a repentant nobleman paying his debts to the poor; but this attitude is poignant in the case of Garvi, who was disqualified from higher education for both legal and financial reasons and was barely eking out a living.[20]

At the same time, the Mensheviks differed from the rest of the intelligentsia in several, perhaps contradictory, ways. First, for all their revolutionary qualities, they were ideologically conservative. They remained untouched by the crisis that shook the intelligentsia in the early years of this century, a crisis involving a profound reorientation away from secular rationalism.[21] Only two members of our Menshevik group stand apart here: Grigorii Bienstock, who developed an interest in mysticism and oriental religions, and

Vera Alexandrova, who passed through Petersburg's philosophical-religious circles before joining the party. Generally speaking, our Mensheviks were the last generation to succumb to the "cosmopolitan attraction of Marxism," to radical rationalism, and to unadulterated Westernism.[22] Moreover, in contrast with the remains of the Russian intelligentsia that found itself in emigration after 1917, the Mensheviks did not quickly abandon their social radicalism, their rationalist faith, or their Marxism. In this sense it may be said that the end of menshevism in exile also marked the death of the traditional Russian intelligentsia.

Subjectively, therefore, the Mensheviks absorbed the ethos of that traditional intelligentsia so thoroughly that they clung to it even after it had been abandoned by others. Objectively, however, the situation of the Mensheviks was very different from that of the Russian intelligentsia. The days when it was composed of "repentant noblemen" with vast cultural and material resources were over, but being an *intelligent* continued to imply a higher education and a way of life free from professional preoccupations and political discipline.

A few Mensheviks did meet such criteria: Dallin and Schwarz both came from wealthy families and, in traditional fashion, earned doctoral degrees in the social sciences from foreign universities. Abramovitch and Dan studied for professional degrees (in engineering and medicine, respectively) but did not practice their professions. Most of the Mensheviks, however, were self-educated, having been excluded from institutions of higher learning for ethnic, material, or political reasons. The erudite Nicolaevsky never attended a university; in describing his prerevolutionary terms in jail and internal exile as his university years, he summarizes the experience of many comrades.[23] As autodidacts, the Mensheviks were not unique in turn-of-the-century Russia. There were so many similar cases that commentators, then and now, have spoken of a "half-intelligentsia" or, in the kinder expression of a recent author, of a "junior order of intellectuals."[24]

Nor did our Mensheviks satisfy the definition of an *intelligent* as someone ready to follow the voice of conscience, unfettered by social ties. Such independence was denied to individuals who had to work for their living, albeit in the "free" professions. Before 1914 one Menshevik, Stepan Ivanovich, wrote extensively on this very problem: the demise of the traditional *intelligent* in an era when large-scale capitalist enterprise was taking over even the press.[25] Ivanovich himself came from a poor family of Jewish artisans in Kishinev, and after having been initiated into Russsian culture through the revolutionary movement, he was enjoying a successful career as a journalist in Petersburg. His case demonstrates how participation in the revolutionary movement and adoption of the intelligentsia outlook were factors of mobility in Russia; his reflections are an illustration of the limits to that mobility.

For Ivanovich and other Mensheviks the solution to the demise of the traditional intelligentsia lay in the creation of a "workers' intelligentsia." They hoped that, with time, intellectuals in workers' organizations would be replaced by a new stratum of "advanced workers" who had come to an understanding of Marxist doctrine without losing ties to their own class.[26] In fact, such a workers' intelligentsia proved difficult to create in the years before 1914 and impossible to save from decimation during the succeeding years of war, revolution, and civil war. Nevertheless, for many years even after the Revolution, the Mensheviks continued to pin their hopes on, and seek their raison d'être in, the existence of a workers' intelligentsia. Even so, the Menshevik Foreign Delegation after 1921 included only one worker, the printer Mark Kefali-Kammermacher.

An ultimate constraint that separated these Mensheviks from the traditional intelligentsia with its free, conscience-dictated activity lay in their organizational discipline. For some Mensheviks, including Ivanovich and Garvi, the road to creation of a workers' intelligentsia lay in the movement called liquidationism *(likvidatorstvo)*, the abandonment of conspiratorial activity in favor of legal work. Among the effects of liquidationism was that of converting party activists and intellectuals into functionaries of trade unions, cooperatives, and other voluntary organizations. Even those Mensheviks who rejected liquidationism were subjected to the bureaucratic organizational rules of a social democratic party, moreover, one based on the Sozialistische Partei Deutschlands (SPD), a party of almost legendary bureaucratization. To be sure, the Mensheviks were not unique in this respect; the constraints of party discipline were shared by other groups, most notably the Bolsheviks. In short, the Mensheviks did not enjoy the traditional individual autonomy of the classic intelligentsia. In this respect, therefore, they were not only the last generation of intelligentsia (albeit of an atypical sort) but also a first generation of organization men (and women), organized revolutionaries whose time had come.

Upon reflecting on the social position of these representatives of the Russian Jewish intelligentsia, one finds that the term "alienation" persistently comes to mind. Alienated from the Jewish community in which they had originated, from the Russia for which they struggled, from the intelligentsia into which they were partially molded, these Mensheviks would seem to correspond to the traditional image of the socially marginalized and deracinated revolutionary.[27] In fact, the Mensheviks took their "alienation" firmly in stride. Any person of ideals and integrity was alienated from the tsarist regime; all the intelligentsia, Russian as well as Jewish, was alienated from the Russian masses. Certainly, exile after 1921 underscored the Mensheviks' essential homelessness. In contrast with the majority of the Russian emigration, firmly anchored in the realities and myths of a lost homeland, the Mensheviks had lost a homeland that had never been entirely theirs. Against this homelessness, however, they enjoyed a sense of belonging wherever the socialist banner flew, in a wide and warm community extending from the centers of socialist life in western Europe to the Lower East Side of New York. This sense set the Mensheviks at ease in kindred circles abroad, although inasmuch as they defined themselves as *Russian* socialists, it precluded wholehearted integration into new lands of residence.

Albert Hourani's celebrated definition of a Levantine as one who lives in two worlds or more without belonging to any can be applied to the Mensheviks. Such a situation has its tragic aspects, captured in Stepan Ivanovich's aphoristic description of an emigré (and he must mean the Menshevik emigré) as one who accustoms himself with difficulty to a foreign land and easily disaccustoms himself from his own land.[28] It can also be an element of strength. The Mensheviks' homelessness, their "in-betweenness" in several worlds, was so deeply rooted that they accepted it as essential to their identity. This acceptance can explain in part their ability to resist the discouragement of decades of separation from Russia. It can also explain their zealous activity in the Socialist International and the close ties they formed with one another.

It is in the light of these considerations that one can understand the strangest characteristic of the Menshevik Party in exile, its refusal to accept as a member anyone who had not been a member of the party in Russia, either in the prerevolutionary period or in the Soviet underground.[29] There are rational reasons for this policy: security against infiltration, protection against becoming a purely emigré party with no ties in Russia. There are also unstated reasons rooted in the party ethos, or what might be called the party mystique: anyone who has not shared in the experience of party work in Russia has not lived in one of the worlds common to the Menshevik family and thus cannot attain that particular equilibrium that characterizes its members.

One of the party's last survivors, groping for a term which would convey the nature of membership in the group, called the exiled Mensheviks a "church" or "religious order."[30] This image imparts a sense of their dedication, but, it seems to me, serves principally to bolster the legend of the Mensheviks as political innocents, victims of their own virtue. He also described Mensheviks in exile as a *kruzhok*, one of those intimate and intense circles so characteristic of nineteenth-century revolutionary Russia. The term applies to the inner life of the group—the Mensheviks discussed here are indeed the last *kruzhok*—but it is misleading in regard to its public activities and its longevity. No *kruzhok* existed as long, in so many different countries, and in such varied circumstances as the Mensheviks. Ties among exiled Mensheviks were such that perhaps the most appropriate term is the one I have already used, that of the "Menshevik family." In place of the blood ties that unite a family are historical and ideological ties, no less deeply rooted and exclusive.

As party activity in Russia petered out in the 1920s and emigration came to a standstill, it became clear that the policy of limiting membership in the party to those who had proven themselves in Russia meant the biological extinction of the Menshevik Party. It is a testimony to the uniqueness of the group, and to its consciousness of its own uniqueness, that most of its members accepted this consequence stoically.

A Portrait Gallery

Fedor Il'ich Dan's titles, chairman of the Foreign Delegation of the RSDRP and co-editor of *Sotsialisticheskii vestnik,* do not indicate fully the extent to which leadership of the party abroad rested with him.

Dan joined the revolutionary movement not in the enthusiasm of adolescence, like most of his comrades, but as a medical school graduate, having shown no radical proclivities in his student days.[1] Although his introduction to the Petersburg revolutionary milieu was facilitated by his first wife, Dan was drawn by a vision of a rationally organized society, and his involvement came about as a result of abstract considerations. Immediately he became a rare phenomenon in the movement's ranks: a businesslike party organizer, an adroit committee man far more at home in formulating resolutions than in theoretical musings.

Dan might be expected to have cast his lot with the Bolsheviks. There was a strong bond of affinity between Dan and Lenin, both in personal characteristics and in their approach to party matters; they shared a common anti-"Oblomovism," a crusading antipathy toward the stereotype of the dreamy and impractical would-be Russian reformer. This bond was further nurtured by their close collaboration on *Iskra* before the party split of 1903. Indeed, Lenin is reported to have expressed disbelief that Dan "with his strong character" should have chosen the Menshevik side and its "weak intellectuals" over his own Bolshevik wing.[2]

Even in retrospect it is difficult to explain why Dan chose menshevism over bolshevism. An unflattering explanation is that, realizing how similar his own talents and propensities were to Lenin's, he feared that his prospects for leadership in the Bolshevik faction would be limited. This explanation is not intended to present Dan in a cynical light. It merely reflects the fact that personal, and often whimsical, reasons played a large part in deciding which faction individual Social Democrats would adhere to.

Another suggestion is that Dan was "repelled by Bolshevism chiefly because of its amoralism."[3] This view finds support in one account which maintains that Lenin, who was very much counting on Dan's support after the split, gave him a file containing nasty and purely personal gossip about the Menshevik leader Martov's relations with a woman. Dan refused to look at the file, saying that if Lenin considered it necessary to acquaint him with this sort of filth, then they had nothing to discuss. In spite of this incident, however (recounted by Martov's sister Lidia, who was to become Dan's wife), the idea that Dan was so shocked by Lenin's petty intrigues that he would have made the most momentous decision of his life on this basis strikes one as implausible.[4] Neither before nor after the split did Dan show any extraordinary scruples about the back-room maneuvers of party life. Unlike other Mensheviks, he never explained his adherence to menshevism in moral terms. In fact, this moral explanation fits far too neatly with the self-image and the image of Lenin developed retroactively by other Mensheviks. In all likelihood Dan's reaction to Lenin's proposition suggests that he had already made up his mind.

The incident does, however, strike a note of verisimilitude in one respect. It has been suggested that Dan's admiration for Martov was the leitmotiv guiding his actions for most of his life.[5] It would be difficult to imagine a greater contrast in character. Martov was undisciplined, impractical, and disorganized.[6] Indeed, Martov was precisely that species of "weak intellectual" whom Lenin had contrasted with the strong and practical Dan and whose kind Lenin (and Dan) professed to scorn. Yet Martov exerted an extraordinary attraction on both these strong men. Lenin shook off this attraction in 1903, though perhaps not fully. In later life traces of Lenin's "love" of Martov (the term is Lenin's wife's) resurfaced. In 1910 and 1914 Lenin rejoiced that he and Martov appeared to be again in the same camp, and on his deathbed Lenin seemed haunted by the idea that Martov, too, was dying.[7]

Dan, by contrast, continued to experience strongly Martov's influence and attraction. As so often happened in the Russian revolutionary milieu, political ties were reinforced by personal ones. Dan married Martov's favorite sister and thus found himself welcomed into the bosom of their family, with its numerous revolutionaries. For Dan, whose home life had been unhappy, such emotional support must have been of some importance.[8] After 1903 Martov and Dan, who had already worked together previously on *Iskra*, collaborated ever more closely. Dan usually yielded to Martov intellectually, and when they disagreed, he generally came around to recognizing that Martov had been correct. Indeed, it has been suggested that Dan's leftist orientation in emigration after 1923, his adherence to what was called, significantly, the Martov Line, can be explained in terms of his guilt at having chosen a position in 1917 in opposition to Martov's, and having belatedly realized that Martov had been correct.[9]

In spite of Martov's influence, Dan remained a very Leninist sort of Menshevik. A caricature from 1904 already depicts him as a little Lenin.[10] In years to come, exiled Mensheviks, chafing under the iron hand of "Danovian autocracy," referred to "our Il'ich" as a Lenin.[11] Dan himself supported this assessment in avowing to an old party comrade in the 1930s that if he were a young man again, he would be a Bolshevik.[12] The judgment of another Menshevik, however, is perhaps more accurate: "Dan is a half-Jacobin, and to be one entirely he lacks only the necessary unscrupulousness and coherence [*Konsequenz*]. Moreover, he is a Jacobin who is forced to play the role of a Girondin."[13]

Dan's enemies were many, both inside and outside the party. His self-certitude bordered on smugness. On meeting Dan in 1907, Maksim Gorky remarked that "little Theodor Dan spoke like a man whose relationship to the authentic truth was that of father to daughter."[14] Dan's unromantic and unpoetic disposition must have jarred many in his later entourage, such as the closet poet Petr Garvi, or Grigorii Aronson, a fan of the Polish novelist Sienkiewicz, or the party aesthetes Iurii Denike and Anatolii Dubois. Dan's extreme formalism irritated even his closest party comrades. When the February 1917 Revolution began, Martov was outraged (and others were amused) that Dan would not leave the place of work assigned him by the no-longer-existing tsarist government until he had received a formal discharge.[15]

Such characteristics may explain the especially vituperative treatment accorded Dan in a milieu where invective was a staple. The fact that he chose not to exercise his profession as a doctor, preferring instead, as he put it, "to cure mankind," drew caustic comments.[16] Even on the festive occasion of his sixtieth birthday, a commemorative article presented Dan as the archtypical Petersburger—that city of fog and bureaucracy—lacking sharpness and color, elegant and polished but dominated by paper formulas and routine.[17]

When Petr Garvi, one of Dan's long-standing party rivals, poured out decades of resentment, he concluded his diatribe by insisting that he, Garvi, and not Dan had been loved in the party.[18] In fact, Dan was not courting popularity, and his certitude carried little trace of personal vanity. In exile, bereft of the trappings of power and patronage, possessed of a distant and doubtful mandate, Dan saw himself as a servant of the proletariat but also as leader of his party. His chief resources were his political adroitness and the strong-willed control he was prepared to exercise over that party.

Although the exiled Mensheviks chafed at Dan's rigorous control, most accepted it for a very long time, and many developed an almost filial relationship to their leader. In some cases this relationship satisfied individual psychological needs. Vera Alexandrova, who had been an ardent correspondent of V. V. Rozanov's religious-philosophical circle, transferred some of her devotion to Dan. Aaron Iugov, "the faithful shadow of Dan," expressed an almost abject submission to his master, even though he was not above attempts to manipulate him.[19] This image of Dan as father figure in emigration is complemented by that of his wife, Lidia, who, having left one child in Russia and lost the other in 1917, lavished her maternal feelings on the children of party members. In the final analysis Dan's role as father figure can perhaps explain the difficulty that most members of our Menshevik group had in breaking with him and the trauma they suffered when, after 1940, he broke with them.

In his *Origins of Bolshevism* Dan remarks more than once on the ironic fact that the historical roles of menshevism and bolshevism had been reversed. He might also have remarked on another reversal of roles: Dan, with his keen appreciation of state power and strong sense of party discipline, would have made an outstanding Soviet commissar or Communist Party secretary. Instead he died an exile in New York. This reversal went even further: the hardheaded Dan, who was the very antithesis of romanticism, ended his last work with a romantic and wistful vision. He saw a world, led by a Soviet Russia in the process of democratization, where the ideals of both freedom and socialism were being realized.

In many ways Dan's talents were complemented by those of Raphael Rein Abramovitch. Whereas Dan, the consummate politician, managed the affairs of the party, Abramovitch, with peerless diplomatic skill, represented the party to the outside world. An urbane, witty, and cosmopolitan polyglot, Abramovitch deployed boundless energy in cultivating contacts with foreign socialists, political leaders, and opinion makers. His efforts won him a place on the innermost councils of the LSI, where, for almost twenty years, he sat as a formal equal with the socialist leaders and ministers of the great powers and acted as spokesman for Russia.

A particularly important aspect of Abramovitch's responsibilities was his role as fund-raiser and "fixer." As early as 1903, the twenty-three-year-old Abramovitch had successfully raised significant sums of money from the Petersburg Jewish bourgeoisie for pogrom victims.[20] During the next sixty years he continued to exercise these skills on behalf of his party, which meant, after 1920, on behalf of the Mensheviks in exile. Time and again Abramovitch's efforts kept *Vestnik* alive and ensured for various Mensheviks the visas, work permits, jobs, and funds on which their lives and livelihood depended.

In spite of these many services, Abramovitch's position among the Mensheviks was not commensurate with his practical importance. He could not match the stature of Dan, who had participated personally in the heroic beginnings of the Russian social democratic movement. Moreover, he was subjected to the condescending Menshevik attitude toward ex-Bundists such as himself.[21] Abramovitch's very urbanity often worked against him. His enemies insulted him as "a traveling salesman of dirty and slanderous wares."[22] Menshevik comrades accused him of cowardice, even as foreign socialists remarked on his personal courage in pursuing his work in spite of ill health and increasing blindness.[23] Abramovitch had been closer politically than Dan to Martov in the years of war and revolution, and it was Abramovitch who accompanied Martov out of Russia in 1920 to represent the Mensheviks and found *Sotsialisticheskii vestnik*. Nevertheless, on Martov's death the mantle of leadership passed directly to Dan, and Abramovitch accepted his own subordinate position without demurral.

Throughout the 1920s Abramovitch fulfilled with good grace his role as number two within the party. Differences with Dan did occasionally emerge, for instance, about the possibilities and effectiveness of emigré politics.[24] Nonetheless, he unhesitatingly put all his contacts, particularly with Jewish labor organizations in America, his position as correspondent for the powerful New York *Forverts* (Jewish Daily Forward), and his talents as a speaker, especially in Yiddish, at Dan's disposition. In the early phases of the debates of the 1930s that were to split the Mensheviks, Abramovitch's first instinct was to express solidarity with Dan. In the course of that decade, however, Abramovitch began to create some distance between them, first by trying to mediate between the Dan-led left wing of the party and its right wing, and then by assuming leadership of the opposition to Dan.

After 1940 Abramovitch replaced Dan as chairman of the Foreign Delegation and was acknowledged as the Menshevik patriarch.[25] Yet, in his last two decades he was a very different man. His one witty and ironic style became increasingly shrill and sarcastic. Although he never repudiated Marxism, his commitment to it became questionable. Eventually his anti-Sovietism could hardly be distinguished from the unnuanced anticommunism against which he himself had previously inveighed. Even his book *The Soviet Revolution,* published shortly before his death in 1963, was something of a disappointment. The tributes it received were addressed to the author as veteran of the Russian Revolution and the socialist movement. It failed to establish Abramovitch either as a scholar or as a theorist, as he had hoped it would.

Boris Ivanovich Nicolaevsky was not a leader of the Mensheviks in the same way Dan and Abramovitch were. He was, above all, the historian and archivist of the party. For long periods he remained aloof from questions of party policy. At other times he entered into party intrigues with gusto, but with little success. And yet, *ars longa, vita brevis*, Nicolaevsky's reputation and importance to the party may well prove more lasting than those of its political leaders.

Nicolaevsky was a passionate, indeed obsessive, collector. As a child he collected things.[26] As an adult he collected history. Although his interests were encyclopedic, his political stance naturally led him to focus on the history of the revolutionary movement, in Russia and in western Europe. By the time of his death in 1966, Nicolaevsky had amassed, lost, and reamassed a peerless personal collection of documentary materials. His interests were not merely antiquarian, however. He knew his collections intimately and worked on them himself. His research—on Marx, on the First International, on Russian revolutionaries, and on the murky underground of tsarist police agents—produced innumerable scholarly articles and several books. Mastery of his materials eventually made Nicolaevsky an indispensable reference for anyone writing in the vast historical arena he had marked out for himself.

"You cannot imagine what connections these book fanatics have!" Abramovitch marveled.[27] And indeed, Nicolaevsky succeeded in creating a network that transcended political differences. Political opponents, both of the Right and of the Left, confided their archives to him. Both the SPD and Trotsky's son entrusted him with their most precious materials, certain that he would appreciate and safeguard them.[28] Moreover, Nicolaevsky discovered that erudition was a marketable commodity. In the 1920s, as a political exile from Soviet Russia, Nicolaevsky was a salaried foreign representative in Berlin of the Moscow Marx-Engels Institute, headed by David Riazanov, himself a former Menshevik. In the 1930s he was director of the Paris branch of the Amsterdam Institute of Social History. In his very last years he was able to sell his collections to the Hoover Institution and to Indiana University, proving that his archives constituted not merely intellectual but material capital as well.[29]

Nicolaevsky was both the most unworldly and the most worldly of the Mensheviks. In contrast with the sophisticated Abramovitch or the bon vivant Dan, there was something clumsy and retiring about him. Gluttony and bibliomania were his principal vices. He would much rather edit an unknown letter of Marx than issue a party proclamation; and although the demeanor of this huge, bearlike man did not conform to the image of an ascetic scholar, his style of life was almost a caricature of it. A Paris police report of the 1930s portrays Nicolaevsky's life as revolving around his office and the hotel room which was his permanent residence; his only distraction was an occasional evening of chess with old friends such as Iraklii Tsereteli.[30] Not surprisingly, Nicolaevsky remained a bachelor until his very last days. Then, in California, he married his collaborator of many years and the life-long companion of the recently deceased Tsereteli, Anna Bourguina. He did so, in part, out of the same kindness he had shown in the past. In part, however, Nicolaevsky married out of concern for his archives.[31]

In spite of his apparent unworldliness, Nicolaevsky was not politically un-astute or disinterested. Throughout the Revolution and in the years that fol-lowed, disgust at what he saw as his party's ineptitude led him to take refuge in scholarly pursuits. In the 1930s, however, Nicolaevsky entered the fray of Menshevik Party politics, and in the 1940s he plunged headlong into cold war and emigré politics in the United States. Various grandiose schemes to mobilize the emigration for anti-Bolshevik struggle under American auspices came to naught. Nevertheless, he discovered that he was able to translate his scholarly skills into political assets, and this he did in two important ways.

First, Nicolaevsky became a prominent practitioner of the art or technique of Kremlinology. Ever the scholarly detective, he applied his long experience of shifting partial evidence and dissecting obscure texts to the task of inter-preting ongoing political events in the Soviet Union. The result—exemplified in hundreds of articles, almost a hundred in the *New Leader* alone—was an approach to Soviet politics that has been widely imitated.[32]

Second, in becoming "the fairy godfather of students of the Russian revo-lutionary movement," Nicolaevsky also became an arbiter of historiographic trends in the study of revolutionary Russia.[33] Although he eschewed *partii-nost'*, or partisanship, he was the very last to underestimate the political im-pact of scholarship, and his historical research was linked to a vision of the past and present.[34]

As one examines more closely the individuals discussed here, one might well conclude that Dan was a Bolshevik manqué, Abramovitch was primarily a Bundist, and Nicolaevsky should have been a populist. At the same time, they were all indisputably Mensheviks.[35] This conclusion in itself leads to a reflection on the character of menshevism as well as to an inquiry into the nature of the ties which could outweigh all other divergences and consider-ations.

1903–1921

2

Mensheviks and Bolsheviks

A Phenomenology of Factions

It is an open question whether the Mensheviks' outlook after 1921 and divergences among them were the continuation of an ideology and of differences already firmly established earlier. It is hardly beyond doubt, however, that the prerevolutionary period constituted a crucial reference point for them as historians and interpreters of Soviet reality. In this chapter I concentrate on their early experience, particularly on the relationship between menshevism and bolshevism.

Most accounts give the impression that menshevism and bolshevism fed on each other from their very inception. The two terms are so inextricably tied that they have become mirror images, each garnering meaning from its inverted reflection in the other. Minds attuned to dialectical thinking have sharpened these images by weaving a net of opposition and complementarity. This has become a tight web of interdependence, not only in the literal sense in which a minority *(men'shinstvo)* and a majority *(bol'shinstvo)* presuppose each other, but also in the sense that each side finds self-definition and self-understanding only by confronting the other. Ultimately, the terms "menshevism" and "bolshevism" have been hypostasized so that each stands for a complex of principles, and their conflict assumes primordial proportions.

At a formal level there is surprising similarity in the characterization of menshevism and bolshevism by Soviet and Western historians, by Mensheviks and Bolsheviks; the factions are defined not by their policies but by a series of ahistorical, abstract attitudes. Curiously, the descriptions sometimes coincide: Bolsheviks and Mensheviks accuse each other of "splitterism," factionalism, opportunism, of being intelligentsia- rather than worker-oriented

29

(whether in outlook or social composition), of pandering to the undeveloped class instincts of the masses. To be sure, the similarity of epithets often dissolves on analysis: the charge of undeveloped class instinct usually implies reformism when applied to Mensheviks and adventurism when applied to Bolsheviks. Sometimes a common term splits under differing interpretations. The accusation of centralism cast by Mensheviks at Bolsheviks is defined by the accusers as "bureaucratic centralism" and by the accused as "democratic centralism."[1] In other cases each group accepts, more or less, the label attached to it by its opponent. Thus, "hard" and "narrow" Bolsheviks confront "soft" and "broad" Mensheviks.[2] Even labels hurled as accusations can be picked up as badges of honor; in Lenin's eyes the charge of jacobinism becomes a mark of pride.[3]

In most cases attributes imputed to each faction by its opponent (and by itself) postulate a permanent and unbridgeable chasm. One would almost believe that menshevism and bolshevism existed as ontological categories, psychological types, or moral options before there were any Mensheviks or Bolsheviks. Bolshevism is seen by its adversaries as conspiratorial, militaristic, hierarchic, elitist or dictatorial, power hungry, amoral and unscrupulous, or even immoral and lawless.[4] In return, menshevism is presented by its opponents as isolated from the masses, duplicitous, inept, irresolute, pusillanimous, and even craven.[5] At the same time, the self-images of each group reinforce negative assessments of the other. As in a morality play, the distribution of vice and virtue brooks no ambiguity. Each faction sees itself as the party of an independent proletariat versus an organization of petty bourgeois intelligentsia leaders who seek tutelage over the masses, exploiting their passivity and immaturity, and who pursue erroneous, nay, pernicious policies. Not surprisingly, other deformities of mind and character flow easily from the negative image of the opponent.[6]

The gulf between the two factions is further reinforced as their opposition is read back into the past and forward into the future. Each faction discovers a genealogy for itself or, even more significantly, for its opponent. Bolsheviks become the lineal descendants of the terrorist group Narodnaia Volia and of the Russian Jacobin Petr Tkachev, or the anarchist Mikhail Bakunin, in addition to their Western ancestors, such as Louis-Auguste Blanqui and the French Jacobins.[7] Mensheviks are depicted as the heirs of reformist revisionists who betrayed revolutionary Marxism. The debate between menshevism and bolshevism is even seen as the continuation of the controversy between Westernizers and Slavophiles.[8]

Anachronistically the division between menshevism and bolshevism is interpreted (by Mensheviks and some Western historians) as a clash between totalitarianism and democracy. Thus, confrontation is transferred from the plane of historical analogy, a continuation of the struggle between Jacobins and Girondins, to the plane of historical anticipation.[9] Bolshevism is seen as essentially totalitarian from its very inception; its struggle against menshevism is therefore a prefiguration of all later struggles. Future opposition between communism and social democracy or the separation of democracy from socialism is thus seen as implicit in the early history of the two factions.[10]

Even though Marxists are involved, there is not much effort at class analysis of the opponent. This is particularly true of the Mensheviks and their sympathizers, who, for the most part, insist on Lenin's personal role in the constitution of bolshevism. Looking beyond Lenin's personal characteristics—iron will, ruthlessness—these Mensheviks see *vozhd*ism (that is, the leadership principle), exemplified by Lenin, as central to bolshevism.[11] When combined with the moral differences separating the two factions, the thesis that Stalinism represents the continuation of Leninism requires no further proof.[12] Bolsheviks and Soviet historians are more inclined to seek a class interpretation of their adversary. But by contenting themselves with reference to Mensheviks as representatives of the petty bourgeoisie or the "intermediate" classes (an accusation, incidentally, which the Mensheviks also made against the Bolsheviks), they blur, quite intentionally, the differences between the Mensheviks and other non-Bolshevik socialists—SRs (members of the Socialists-Revolutionaries Party), for example.[13] Moreover, they fail to paint a recognizable portrait of the Mensheviks and their constituency or to provide any insight into the problem of the division of the working class, in Russia and on a world scale, so fundamental to understanding the labor movement in this century.

Surprisingly, the overall picture of polar opposition between menshevism and bolshevism is contradicted by what emerges (sometimes in the same source) from any detailed examination of policies or relations. The whole does not correspond to its parts; the "macro" analysis of bolshevism and menshevism does not tally with "micro" analyses. In many cases the same historians who have postulated fundamental, unbridgeable differences between menshevism and bolshevism uncover affinities on innumerable issues.[14] Historians sometimes even trace an astounding reversal of roles, whereby Mensheviks act or preach in a way generally identified with bolshevism and Bolsheviks embrace Menshevik tenets or attitudes.[15]

Often enough, such confusing ambiguities and paradoxical reversals can be clarified by departing from abstract characterizations and favoring close attention to historical periodization. This must be done, for instance, if we are to explain properly how menshevism and bolshevism stood in relation to some central themes of Russian Marxism, the question of "consciousness" versus "spontaneity," and the problem of the "democratic" or "bourgeois" revolution versus the "socialist" or "proletarian" revolution.[16] Indeed, a major thesis of Fedor Dan's *Origins of Bolshevism* is that each group's relation to questions of consciousness and spontaneity, socialism and democracy, evolved until it embraced the position it had previously shunned. This fact, however, is even more complex than one might suppose.[17] In one sense the Mensheviks were early partisans of spontaneity: they believed in the inherent revolutionary capacity of the working class more firmly than the Bolsheviks, who emphasized the need for outside guidance (from party or intelligentsia). In another sense it was the Mensheviks who were advocates of consciousness. In the prerevolutionary period they sought to build up a class-conscious workers' party, unlike the Bolsheviks, who were prepared to rely on a more heterogeneous, elemental *(stikhiinyi)* movement. In the Revolution and its aftermath, however, it was the Bolsheviks who put socialist—that is, class—tasks on the agenda, and it was the Mensheviks who focused on democratic tasks.[18]

By proceeding historically, one is less surprised to find each faction not only straddling the border with the other's ideological "field" but even reversing itself. Dan has sought to explain this phenomenon by referring to menshevism and bolshevism as "Siamese twins."[19] This is a potent image which captures the essence of the relationship between the two factions in the prerevolutionary period and even, to a certain extent, later. It does not, however, convey a sense of the mobility of ideas, and even of individuals, between the two factions, nor does it do justice to the variety of positions within each faction. It fails to explain, for example, how some Menshevik groups could find themselves closer at times, both tactically and ideologically, to groups within the Bolshevik camp than to certain Menshevik comrades.

As a working hypothesis it may be fruitful to view the relations between bolshevism and menshevism in terms of a broad continuum, each end of which is defined by a Bolshevik or Menshevik ideal type, but where the real historical actors find themselves cutting across the continuum at different angles and different points.[20] Viewed in this light, the fluidity of each group's tactical and ideological position can be taken in stride. Similarly, the affinities between, say, right Bolsheviks and left Mensheviks or the paradox of some Mensheviks standing farther "left"—even in the Soviet period—than certain Bolsheviks are more easily comprehensible.[21]

The image of a Menshevik-Bolshevik continuum may be of only limited value to any overall history of Russia on the eve of the Revolution or during the Revolution, but in the context of this study it provides a useful framework in which to examine the development of menshevism vis-à-vis bolshevism. It throws light on the ideology of the Menshevik group under discussion even as it casts doubt on the historiography promoted by these Mensheviks. This framework will be tested as we follow the relations between the two factions from 1903 to 1921.

The Second Congress and Its Aftermath

The split between bolshevism and menshevism dates back to the Second Congress of the RSDRP held in Brussels and London in July–August 1903. The Congress is therefore the locus classicus of all discussion on the relation between bolshevism and menshevism.

The more hostile an account is to one of the party factions, the more likely it is to insist on the importance of the Second Congress. Soviet historians and Western commentators least sympathetic to bolshevism stand in substantial agreement on the depth of the division which occurred at the Second Congress.[1] The opposite formulation does not necessarily hold. Some authors who minimize the importance of the Second Congress do not insist any less on the depth of division but attribute its origin to another, earlier or later, period.[2] All in all, however, there has been an overwhelming tendency to see the Second Congress as a milestone not only in the history of the Russian revolutionary movement but in world history as well.[3]

This emphasis on the Second Congress has been achieved at the cost of considerable inconsistency. Commentators and even protagonists have called into question their own contention regarding the importance of the congress.[4] They have described the random or secondary nature of disagreements among emerging congress factions.[5] They have given accounts of the further development of the RSDRP which show that any basic differences between the two factions emerged later and that these differences were by no means the only ones, sometimes not even the most significant ones, within the ranks of the RSDRP. Finally, both Mensheviks and Bolsheviks have borne witness to the fact that the depth of their differences was in no way evident to the protagonists themselves in 1903.[6]

And yet the temptation to read back basic divergences into the Second Congress is so strong that it has established something of a consensus. This affirms that although the meaning of the Bolshevik-Menshevik division was not apparent at the time of the congress, it was indeed there that the seeds of division were planted.[7] This view is defended by Soviet historians in the name of an inevitable and objective *(zakonomernyi, gesetzmässig)* process; bourgeois historians (and their Menshevik counterparts) are criticized for stressing the subjective or personal elements that led to division.[8] Such criticism is unfair to the extent that even those Western historians who dwell on subjective elements also agree that they were part of an objective process which had to culminate in a complete split.[9]

In the light of subsequent developments, it is difficult to dispute that the seeds of factional division were sown at the Second Congress. This statement, however, remains problematic and somewhat disturbing. Not only is it based on an uneasy organic metaphor and an anticipatory logic, but also it suggests a teleological view of history, even among those who reject such a view in principle.[10] It discounts all contingent factors by postulating a historic necessity which brushes aside the expressed intentions of the protagonists and makes light of the actual processes at work.[11] Indeed, it is an expression of the tendency, already questioned here, to present bolshevism and menshevism in abstract terms as the personification of moral qualities.[12] Only when seen as the confrontation between vice and virtue can the inevitability of the final split between bolshevism and menshevism be anticipated. Here I shall examine the the Second Congress in the light of its contingent elements.

In his *History of Russian Social Democracy*, Martov refers, rather blandly, to the great successes enjoyed by the *Iskra* organization in preparing for the Second Congress.[13] Somewhat unkindly, Martov's statement might be translated as acknowledgment that the Second Congress was, in fact, "packed." This impression is confirmed by the scholarly literature, both Soviet and Western: the Second Congress was convened, to borrow a later expression, as a "Congress of Victors." Its purpose was to affirm the triumph of Iskrite centralizers who had succeeded in subordinating elected local committees and imposing themselves on the fledgling Russian social democratic movement.[14] Above all, Martov's remarks bring out the extent to which his views before the Second Congress were closely aligned with Lenin's and the degree to which the future Bolshevik-Menshevik split was preceded by, and for a long time overshadowed by, an equally profound Iskrite–non-Iskrite division.

The question of Martov's views stands at the very heart of Menshevik historiography and illustrates the tendency to see bolshevism and menshevism in moral terms. No doubt because one of Lenin's defining characteristics is considered to be his amoralism, Lenin's opponents are assumed to possess all the moral qualities he lacks. The main beneficiary of such reasoning has been Martov, although another historic leader, Pavel Axelrod, has benefited too. Among exiled Mensheviks after 1921 (and, to a certain extent, even earlier), Martov acquired icon status. The cult of Martov—one would be tempted to say the cult of his personality, if this term did not carry ominous overtones—was founded on the person of Martov rather than on his policies: many Mensheviks contested the "Martov Line" though few denied that he represented an overwhelmingly positive moral personality.[15]

Martov's scrupulous biographer shows a rare indulgence of his subject's peccadillos.[16] Moreover, Martov's aura of moral superiority has illuminated the Menshevik movement as a whole. From the point of view of the internal life of the party in exile, Martov-as-icon served as a potent integrating symbol. For over forty years the masthead of *Sotsialisticheskii vestnik* proudly carried the inscription "Founded by L. Martov." In relation to foreign socialists, too, the image of Martov was a powerful instrument: it touched the conscience of foreign comrades, leaving them vulnerable to moral pressure from the Mensheviks; it raised the prestige of the Menshevik Party, the party of Martov, in the Socialist International.[17] Indeed, the image of Martov contributed significantly to the widespread assumption that the defeat of the Mensheviks in 1917 was proof of their moral superiority.[18]

Of course, one reason why Martov has been considered a more attractive moral personality than Lenin is that he indeed was such. A massive body of hagiographic literature, mostly from the Soviet Union, extolls Lenin the man, and some Mensheviks, too, have commented favorably on Lenin's human qualities.[19] Indisputably, however, it is Martov who possessed a force of moral attraction that seduced even his opponents.[20] The problem with claims advanced in favor of Martov's moral superiority is not that they are false—although they tend to be one-sided and exaggerated—but that they minimize the areas of agreement between Martov (and the Mensheviks) and Lenin (and the Bolsheviks). At the very least, they suggest that Martov's early collaboration with Lenin was a temporary mental and moral impairment on Martov's part; once this impairment had been removed, presumably at the Second Congress, the full extent of preexisting, implicit opposition between Martov and Lenin, menshevism and bolshevism, could come out into the open.[21]

Such claims are not supported by events preceding, or even during, the Second Congress. The pillars of the unified *Iskra* group were Lenin and Martov. They (with A. N. Potresov) had founded *Iskra* in 1901 to regain control over Russian social democracy against the rising tide of reformist Economism. After they had been joined on the editorial board by the most seasoned leaders of Russian Marxism—Pavel Axelrod, Vera Zasulich, and Georgii Plekhanov—friction emerged. The veterans objected to Economism primarily for its belittling of Marxist doctrine; the young editors emphasized the ineffective organizational structures toward which Economism gravitated.[22] A (perhaps inevitable) generational division thus arose, further aggravated by the veterans' personalities. Above all, the overbearing and vain Plekhanov proved to be an impossible collaborator. Historians have so emphasized Lenin's negative personality traits that Plekhanov's have been overshadowed. In fact, if one can describe Dan's character as a milder version of Lenin's, then Lenin's character may be called a milder version of Plekhanov's.[23]

The young editors of *Iskra* thus rallied together. They set up editorial offices away from Switzerland, where the veterans resided. They relied increasingly on one another and on their intimate circle, including Lenin's wife and Martov's sister and her future husband, Fedor Dan. Even within the close troika of young editors, however, Potresov—more formal and reserved than his comrades—stood apart.[24] No such division existed between the other two young editors, Lenin and Martov. Their editorial talents complemented each other; in all other respects they were inseparable.

The intimacy and unanimity of the editorial troika survived until 1903. Lenin's blueprint for a centralized workers' party, *What Is To Be Done?* was endorsed enthusiastically by the other young editors. Even Potresov, who later fought Leninism so vigorously that he set himself outside the Menshevik Party, gushed about a "superlative" impression.[25] Discussion about *Iskra*'s proposed party program pitted Lenin against Plekhanov and other members of the board against one another. Eventually, however, differences were overcome in favor of a compromise program.[26] This was duly adopted at the Second Congress and, more surprisingly, was to remain the common program of both the Mensheviks and the Bolsheviks until 1919.

As the Second Congress approaches, one searches for signs of a nascent rift between Martov and Lenin.[27] Lidia Dan suggests that relations between the two in London (just before the congress) were not as warm and spontaneous as they had been earlier in Munich.[28] If so, this did not impinge on the common Iskrite line. Martov inveighed against the elective principle and against majority rule in local organizations, as did Lenin. Martov's very notion of democracy as mass support for the party rather than control of the party from below showed his closeness to Lenin.[29] If anything, Martov chafed more (or perhaps more vocally) than did Lenin under the heavy hand of the older editors.[30] It is therefore likely that the question of replacing some of the other editors—which was to provoke Martov's break with Lenin at the Second Congress—had been raised earlier. If so, Martov might be supposed to have given his implicit agreement to such a move.[31]

When the Second Congress opened, *Iskra* controlled at least thirty-three of the fifty-one votes. These figures represented not the relative strength of the various organizations but the success of *Iskra*'s strategy. Significantly, however, success did not mean the disappearance of non-Iskrite forces. For decades to come the division between Iskrite and non-Iskrite was to persist within the ranks of Russian social democracy. Two decades later David Riazanov, an anti-Iskrite who had been denied admission to the Second Congress, later a Menshevik, and by then a Bolshevik, spoke with tears in his eyes about the ill-treatment of his former Menshevik comrades in Soviet prisons: "It's all those damned Iskrites!" he complained.[32] Given the preparation for the congress, the proceedings might have been expected to be anticlimactic. And, indeed, the main task of the congress, the adoption of the party program, passed with little difficulty. *Iskra*'s draft was endorsed early on, after much rhetoric but in virtual unanimity and with only a few insignificant amendments.[33] Rear-guard attacks on the Iskrist hegemony, such as those by a future member of the Menshevik Foreign Delegation, the Bundist I. K. Aisenstadt-Iudin, proved unavailing.[34]

Nevertheless, in the light of later historical events, commentators have not resisted the temptation to read back anticipations of future issues even into those aspects of the congress on which dissent was minimal. Thus, during the debate on the program, one Posadovskii is credited with having posited the choice between absolute democracy and its subordination to party interests. Posadovskii did indeed pose such an alternative, but in a sense opposite to that which has been imputed to him. It is safe to surmise that he had no inkling of the significance of what he was saying, nor did his future behavior suggest that he himself ever appreciated the insight others have attributed to him.[35]

As every student of the Russian Revolution has learned, disagreements at the Second Congress arose in discussion of article 1 of the party statutes, the definition of a party member. This fact is so well known that even Soviet party history has found it necessary to emphasize that the actual division into Mensheviks and Bolsheviks took place not over this article (on which the Mensheviks obtained satisfaction), but over elections to the leading party organs (here the Bolsheviks acquired a majority, owing to a walkout by non-Iskrite delegates).[36] As a leading non-Iskrite delegate has pointed out, assertions by Mensheviks that they supported all the program's principles but disagreed with the organizational principles of its chief author, Lenin, were unconvincing. Not only were differences between the broader (Menshevik) and narrower (Bolshevik) definition of a party member minor and of little practical import (at least in the context of 1903 Russia), but also as this delegate put it, "What is a program for if it does not determine even such basic, decisive events in the life of a party as the choice of the organizational principle?"[37]

Although disagreement between future Mensheviks and Bolsheviks arose over the party statutes, the actual division took place over matters of personnel.[38] First at a meeting of the *Iskra* caucus and then before the entire congress, Martov and Lenin, with increasing vehemence, waged a "battle over places." Lenin's henchmen, to use a loaded term, were unsavory types; Martov's protégés were suspected of being wavering Iskrites.[39] The battle reached its spasmodic culmination when Lenin proposed a drastic reorganization of the *Iskra* board which would eliminate three editors while maintaining Martov. Martov not only fought this proposal but, after having been defeated, refused to accept his place on the new board. The partnership between Lenin and Martov, and the unity of *Iskra,* had been dealt a mortal blow.

There are several excellent accounts of the Second Congress.[40] Whichever side they espouse, they all paint a dramatic but sorry picture. The two major protagonists, Lenin and Martov, emerge as overwrought, even hysterical figures for whom it is difficult to summon much sympathy.[41] Martov's sister has explained Martov's vehemence and bitterness by the fact that he hated "to be made a fool of" (and, indeed, who would not hate it?).[42] Later, Martov tried to rehabilitate himself by expressing regret at his admittedly brutal behavior at the congress up to the split; his excuses were heard with skepticism by his non-Iskrite victims.[43] Lenin, too, tried to patch up the quarrel by insisting that the disagreement was not fundamental. His efforts were met with hostility by his defeated opponents.[44]

It should be noted that the future evolution of the quarrel between Martov and Lenin, the Mensheviks and the Bolsheviks, did not replace but added to the prior division between the Iskrites and non-Iskrites. For this reason traces of a common outlook and of mutual ties persisted among former Iskrites, whether in the Bolshevik or Menshevik camp. This is illustrated by reactions of members of our future Menshevik group to the party split, reactions all the more significant in light of their future role as historical witnesses to the division between bolshevism and menshevism.

A "bolt out of the blue" is how Trotsky *(primo voto* a Menshevik) described the split.[45] If this was the reaction among prominent party leaders, one can imagine the utter incredulity and bewilderment among more remote party members. Several future Mensheviks—Abramovitch, the Garvis, Valentinov-Volsky—arrived in Geneva soon after the congress and tried to glean what had transpired. The issues at stake seemed so obscure and so petty that these individuals, like others, found themselves choosing sides on the basis of considerations which had nothing to do with the events of the congress themselves.[46] They drifted into the emerging opposing camps for reasons connected with their pre–Second Congress sympathies or for personal or purely formal reasons.

Among those opting on the basis of earlier affinities were Petr Garvi and his wife, Sofia, née Fichtman. The Garvis had begun their revolutionary work in an Economist-oriented Odessa organization. It was anti-*intelligent*, very hesitant about political work, and committed to elective rather than hierarchical principles. Interestingly, Garvi admits that even here it proved impossible to put the elective principle into practice or to install a worker at the head of the organization. Consequently, the practical differences between this group and the *Iskra* line proved insignificant. Nevertheless, the Garvis were not Iskrites, and Lidia Dan has expressed Iskrite scorn for that sector of the revolutionary movement from which the Garvis came.[47] In addition, Sofia Garvi was a personal disciple of David Riazanov, the anti-Iskrite would-be delegate to the Second Congress.[48]

Even with this background Petr Garvi hesitated before choosing between the Menshevik or Bolshevik side. He listened sympathetically to the views of a Bundist who claimed that all Iskrites were from the same mold, that they were all imperialists and centralists, that Martov was no better than Lenin. He declined the proposal of O. A. Ermanskii, the former Economist, future Menshevik, and, ultimately, Bolshevik, to found a non-Bolshevik, non-Menshevik faction. The most Garvi could bring himself to state was, "It became clear to me I was not a Bolshevik."[49]

Eventually the Garvis did become Mensheviks. Presumably they did so on the grounds that "soft" Iskrites were, all in all, preferable to "hard" Iskrites, and that the leadership principle, which Petr Garvi abhorred, weighed less heavily on the Mensheviks. Once their choice was made, the Garvis described themselves as "100 per cent Mensheviks," and although they were pained by "ugly fractional behavior among [their] own Menshevik leaders," they opposed any conciliationist tendencies.[50] In justifying their menshevism, Sofia Garvi recounts Lenin's cynical and sarcastic reply to her question about a party member's morality.[51] Her objection may have been valid, but it is unlikely that her question was raised in a "comradely" fashion; on another occasion the impetuous Mrs. Garvi threw a beer mug at her debating partner.[52] At the very least some sympathy can be summoned for Lenin, who, at a time when he was fighting desperately to hold on to his gains at the Second Congress, found himself challenged by an obscure and impassioned *collégienne* barely out of her teens.

Given the party background of the Garvis, their adherence to menshevism may be thought understandable. Some more prominent anti-Iskrites—Ermanskii, Martynov, Riazanov—made the same choice but went over to the Bolsheviks after 1917. If the choice of factions was not always easy for non-Iskrites, it was downright difficult for former *Iskra* sympathizers or for those who had not yet taken sides before the Second Congress. The factors involved in an individual's choice of faction were so contingent and so personal that one can only examine them individually.

Among Menshevik leaders the case of Fedor Dan has already been considered: Dan was the prototypical "hard" Iskrite on whom Lenin counted and whom he tried to woo to his cause—without success. The case of Raphael Abramovitch is also instructive: he defined himself as an Iskrite in political questions but a Bundist in the national question.[53] After the Bund walked out of the Second Congress (hounded out by Martov at Lenin's behest), Abramovitch, figuratively speaking, followed. In the aftermath of the congress, Abramovitch remained a Bundist, refusing to identify himself as either a Menshevik or a Bolshevik. In 1906, upon the Bund's reentry into the RSDRP, Abramovitch fought hard to obtain better conditions for the Bund; on the same occasion most Mensheviks voted against the Bund's reentry, presumably because of its closeness to the Bolsheviks at that time.[54]

Echoes of Abramovitch's indecision between menshevism and bolshevism are evident in the example of several other former Bundist members of our Menshevik group. Boris Dvinov entered the Bund a few months after the Second Congress expressly because he could not make up his mind whether to be a Bolshevik or a Menshevik.[55] For Grigorii Aronson, Bundism became a transitional phase between his early bolshevism and his later menshevism.[56]

Boris Nicolaevsky joined the RSDRP in Russia at the end of 1903 as a Bolshevik, having already served a prison term for participating in a vaguely ecumenical revolutionary organization. Nicolaevsky explains that he was impressed by the mass character of social democracy; presumably he means the mass character of German social democracy (which he had not witnessed at first hand) or of Russian social democracy *in potentia,* since the RSDRP hardly qualified then as a mass party. Nicolaevsky states, too, that he found the Marxist worldview grander and more structured than its populist alternative. Surprisingly, therefore, in marked contrast with most other Russian Marxists—including many members of our Menshevik group—Nicolaevsky claims not to have been impressed by the writings of the father of Russian Marxism, Plekhanov.[57]

Nicolaevsky also cheerfully admits that on joining the party he had not read Lenin's *What Is To Be Done?* Nevertheless, when confronted with the choice between menshevism and bolshevism, Nicolaevsky chose the latter for what can be called "formal" reasons. As he saw it then, Mensheviks were "splitters" who were "being difficult." They had refused to respect the decisions of the Second Congress and were trying to drive Lenin from his position, confirmed by the congress, on the editorial board of *Iskra* and on the Central Committee. In emphasizing such formal considerations, Nicolaevsky was typical. Nikolai Valentinov-Volsky invokes the same reasoning.[58] Even within Martov's own family there was a certain malaise about his behavior. Although all his kin eventually became Mensheviks, Martov's brother and sister-in-law Sergei Ezhov and Konkordiia Zakharova originally inclined toward bolshevism.[59] The devoted Lidia Dan also continued to find fault with her brother for his actions at the Second Congress and for his subsequent attitude toward Lenin.[60]

Above all, Nicolaevsky saw himself as a conciliator.[61] Local revolutionary traditions in Ufa encouraged such an outlook. Social democrats and SRs cooperated well there; when Nicolaevsky joined the former, he did not isolate himself from the latter (who had previously courted him). In later years Nicolaevsky continued to look beyond party labels. In the 1920s he caused consternation among fellow Mensheviks by appearing on a platform with SRs, Kadet Liberals, and other non-Mensheviks. In the 1940s he vigorously encouraged unification attempts among the remaining exiled parties.

It is not surprising, therefore, that in the early prerevolutionary years Nicolaevsky was also a conciliator with respect to the split between the Bolsheviks and the Mensheviks. This propensity to conciliation survived his switch from bolshevism to menshevism in 1906. It even continued to manifest itself in different forms into the 1930s, until Stalin's purges eliminated the Old Bolsheviks. As a conciliator Nicolaevsky was not unique, either in Menshevik or in Bolshevik ranks. Within our Menshevik group, Iurii Denike, initially a Bolshevik, was also a conciliator.[62] Among the prominent Bolshevik conciliators were the future Marshal K. E. Voroshilov and Lenin's successor as Soviet prime minister, A. I. Rykov. Nicolaevsky's conciliationism was based on disregard for party labels rather than on temperament; if anything, his obstinate and willful character was an obstacle to conciliation. In the case of most other members of our Menshevik group (and probably many other social democrats at the time), however, temperament was the key to a conciliationist or nonconciliationist attitude and even to the choice of factional label.

The importance of temperament seems to be particularly pronounced among the many Mensheviks who first opted for bolshevism. One after another they all stress the same theme: bolshevism represented energy, initiative, daring, will, decisiveness, radicalism, and true revolutionary spirit.[63]

Some Menshevik ex-Bolsheviks explain their susceptibility to these qualities by invoking youth and impatience; others mention quirks such as "my temperament inherited from generations of cossacks, fighting men and empire builders."[64] In large part this image of bolshevism as more revolutionary was the result of an incipient cult of Lenin, which affected even those who later claimed they were not really impressed by Lenin's person.[65] In 1903–4, when these revolutionaries were choosing bolshevism, this ideology had not yet proved its revolutionary mettle. Its reputation was based only on its title as the party of Lenin, the author of *What Is To Be Done?* and the true heir of the *Iskra* tradition.[66]

Beyond the element of temperament, pettier considerations played a role in the choice of factions. Valentinov-Volsky became a Bolshevik when he learned that a comrade with whom he was at loggerheads had chosen menshevism.[67] In his case, however, this was but one factor among others. Volsky was an admirer of *What Is To Be Done?* and an adventurous personality. It was, he suggests, only natural that he should have gravitated toward Lenin and, after having met Lenin, that he should have fallen under his spell.[68] In other cases personal likes and dislikes are evoked only to be discarded as a factor. O. A. Ermanskii writes that he had always had difficult relations with Dan. "This should have driven me to the Bolsheviks," writes Ermanskii without further explanation, "but the opposite happened."[69] A future Bolshevik stalwart states woodenly, "My personal sympathies were with the minority [the Mensheviks]," but "I endorsed the organizational structure of the party advocated by Comrade Lenin."[70] Of course, people are far less hesitant to impute personal motives in the choice of factions to individuals other than themselves.

The picture that emerges from these individual cases is hardly one of coherence. The split between bolshevism and menshevism even divided couples: E. M. Aleksandrova, Martov's protégée at the Second Congress, naturally enough chose Menshevism; her husband, M. S. Ol'minskii, became a Bolshevik.[71] Almost all party members, including Lenin, were distressed by the split; most were confused by it as well.[72] Very few, especially among the Bolsheviks, imagined that the division would last long.[73] Even among the Mensheviks, Lidia Dan still considered the Economists a greater enemy than the Bolsheviks. Among the most intransigent Mensheviks was G. V. Chicherin, the future Bolshevik commissar of foreign affairs.[74]

Despite the confusion a lighthearted view could on occasion prevail. Petr Garvi describes a carnival parade in Geneva in 1904.[75] The Russian social democratic colony organized a float with three figures representing Lenin, Plekhanov, and Trotsky (or Martov) holding musical instruments. The legend on the float was a citation from Lenin: "We need a great orchestra of counterbass, violoncello, and fiddle." There is no record of how the good burghers of Geneva interpreted this float. For emigré Russians its meaning was clear: the split between the Bolsheviks and the Mensheviks could still be the subject of humorous depiction; surely it could not have portentous significance.

Revolutionary Rehearsal

After the Second Congress the process of factional self-definition and mutual demarcation proceeded apace. Although the terms Menshevik and Bolshevik came into general use in 1904, the uppermost party echelons dictated this process.[1] Several leaders—Axelrod, Lenin, Trotsky, Martynov—published the first of innumerable attempts to formulate factional differences in theoretical terms.

Pavel Axelrod's contribution to the self-definition of menshevism focused on the central dilemma of Russian social democracy. The universal task of social democracy lay in developing the independent activity of the working class. This task was complicated in Russia by the immaturity of the working class and the despotic character of the state, with twofold implications. First, the Russian revolutionary intelligentsia found itself either substituting for or exercising a tutelary role over whatever proletariat existed. Second, Russian social democrats confronted simultaneously the distinct tasks of fostering proletarian independence and of promoting basic bourgeois rights. As a result of these peculiar conditions, Axelrod argued, Russian social democracy had deviated from its proper path. Within the party, bureaucratic centralism reigned triumphant. The party functioned like a quasi-military organization in which intelligentsia officers plotted political strategies on behalf of a passive proletariet and the party machine functioned for its own sake.[2]

Axelrod's definition of the Russian social democratic dilemma endured. He was not the first to point to the problem of domination of the proletariat by the intelligentsia, the substitution of party organization for proletarian activity, or the conflict between a workers' revolution and a bourgeois revolution.[3] Nonetheless, it was his juxtaposition of "class" goals and "democratic" goals that served as the leitmotiv of Fedor Dan's *Origins of Bolshevism* decades later. Like Axelrod, Dan was to see in the duality of tasks facing the party the major cause of its division. Unlike Axelrod, Dan found in this duality a justification for the division and a validation of both menshevism and bolshevism. As Dan put it, each faction was right, "each in its own way, because with all its one-sidedness each . . . was expressing a certain essential need of Russian political life."[4]

If Axelrod's schema was to dominate Dan's understanding of his party's history almost a half-century later, it is not surprising that Axelrod's articles should have impressed other party members earlier. Petr Garvi saw in them a "dazzling" light and believed them to mark the moment when menshevism became conscious of itself, understood the schism, found its ideology, and hoisted its banner.[5] True, Garvi, an almost filial disciple of Axelrod, was paying homage to him two decades after the events he described had occurred. Nevertheless, Garvi's comments were echoed by a less partial source, albeit also at a late date. Martov, in a new edition of his *History of Russian Social Democracy* in 1923, praised Axelrod for having shown that "bolshevism is the struggle against the class independence of the proletariat, the desire to dissolve the proletarian movement in a popular general revolutionary movement."[6]

In fact, Axelrod's articles do not fully bear out such claims. The immediate target of his criticism (though nowhere mentioned) was Lenin. But the true object of the articles was Iskrism itself. Axelrod, as the most hesitant member of the original *Iskra* editorial board, was engaging in self-criticism. The ills he detected, especially bureaucratic centralism, culminated in the Second Congress. The victory of bureaucratic centralism, which Axelrod rued, occurred when Iskrites managed to seize control of the party. In his view bolshevism's emergence out of that victory was an unfortunate outcome of an inherent Iskrite tendency and of a tragic Russian dilemma.

Lenin's rage at these articles can therefore be explained by the fact that they went deeper than a critique of incipient bolshevism. Axelrod was repudiating his own and Lenin's common Iskrite past.[7] Similarly, Garvi's elation was founded on these articles' critique of Iskrism. And yet, Martov's interpretation of them suggests that he was either too prone to forget his own contribution to Iskrism before the Second Congress or too keen to attribute to bolshevism alone the negative heritage of Iskrism.

The extent to which the critique of bolshevism merged with a critique of Iskrism is underscored by the fact that one of the strongest attacks on Lenin came from Aleksandr Martynov, an anti-Iskrite still smarting from humiliation at the Second Congress. Martynov took as his point of departure Lenin's defiant statement that a "Jacobin tied to the organized, conscious proletariat and knowing its class interests is a revolutionary social democrat."[8] In fact, argued Martynov, jacobinism and social democracy were diametrically opposed. Lenin's identification of the two betrayed a dangerous streak of Blanquism, which could be traced to the Russian populist and terrorist Petr Tkachev. Above all, Lenin's endorsement of jacobinism confirmed Axelrod's warnings: the current of Russian history was such that it chased Russian social democracy in the direction of bourgeois revolutionism of the Jacobin type.

Mensheviks have seen Martynov's brochure as a landmark because of its dichotomous vision (Bolshevik Jacobins versus Menshevik Social Democrats), because of its discovery of a non-Marxist genealogy for Lenin's views (Lenin as pupil of Tkachev), and because of its apparently prescient references to the problem of power.[9] If social democracy is unlike jacobinism, then the Jacobin strategy of seizing power at the first opportunity and holding onto it against all odds is unsuitable for social democrats. Instead, Martynov argues, social democrats should remain the party of extreme opposition right up to the socialist revolution. It is not that social democrats are "afraid of power." Rather, they realize that premature or isolated seizure of power would lead only to discredit and defeat for social democracy.

Martynov's position was, in fact, more flexible than one might imagine. He also envisioned the possibility that social democrats might be brought to power, independently of their will and by the inner dialectic of the revolution, even when national conditions for socialism had not yet matured.[10] In this case, Martynov affirmed, social democrats must not "lag behind." They would have to break out of the narrow national framework of their own revolution and push the West in the direction of revolution, just as revolutionary France pushed the East a century before. Moreover, once in power, social democrats would have no right to hold out from fulfilling all their socialist obligations.[11]

Such intensive discussions concerning self-definition and tactics might be expected to have prepared Russian social democrats for the Revolution of 1905. In fact, quite the opposite is true. The outbreak of the Revolution took both social democratic factions utterly by surprise. The Mensheviks, under the leadership of Dan and Axelrod, and against Bolshevik objections, had been concentrating on a propaganda campaign among the liberal local authorities, or *zemstva*.[12] The Revolution reduced this issue to insignificance. Instead, "fairy-like and fantastic revolutionary events erupted in Russia and captured the attention of all Social Democrats."[13] They erupted, however, without any social democratic presence.[14] Even the Petersburg Soviet, although at first presided over by a (future) Menshevik, may well have arisen through the efforts of former Economists, not of social democrats.[15] Moreover, in the face of revolutionary events, differences between the Bolsheviks and Mensheviks, painstakingly expounded in the polemical literature of 1904, dwindled or were replaced by others. The forced, hothouse nature of factional division became glaringly evident as the Revolution unfolded without much regard to that division.

On a practical level both factional leaderships were subjected to intense pressure to unite. The party rank and file saw no reason for continued wrangling among the intelligentsia.[16] The urgencies of the moment brought Mensheviks and Bolsheviks together, on the streets, on the barricades, or in the factories. On a theoretical level, however, the party succumbed to a new and more intense process of division as the basic factional positions collapsed.

The incoherence and inconsistency of the Menshevik position is most striking. The Mensheviks seem to have been "floundering" on the most important issues: the question of an armed uprising, the prospects of a seizure of power, the possibility of a link with revolution in the West, the nature of the soviets, the policy of class alliances, the relation between an immediate bourgeois revolution and a more distant—or perhaps not so distant—proletarian revolution.[17] Each of these important questions found different and contradictory replies, sometimes in the same resolution, sometimes from the same individual.

Initial contradictory reactions to the events of 1905 eventually crystallized into new positions. Closest to the original social democratic position stood Martov and Axelrod. Although early in 1905 Martov had toyed with the idea of calling for a seizure of power, he came to concentrate instead on the development of a strong workers' movement, via the soviets, within a classic bourgeois revolution. Even Lenin's position could be seen as a variant, however far-fetched, of the basic social democratic position: rejecting the bourgeoisie as unreliable, he called for an alliance of workers and (petty bourgeois) peasants which would carry out bourgeois democratic tasks.[18]

The greatest departure from doctrine resulted from a third tendency. This approach saw the possibility of pursuing a purely workers' revolution in Russia by linking up with simultaneous revolution in the West. Russia could thus be spared the need to await completion of its bourgeois revolution before embarking on its own proletarian revolution.[19] It should be noted that this radical doctrinal innovation was elaborated by a then-Menshevik, Trotsky, and won the adherence of prominent Mensheviks such as Martynov and Dan. It may be traced to one of the ambiguous resolutions adopted by the Menshevik Party Conference of 1905. Nevertheless, it runs so completely against the grain of Menshevik thinking that it can only underscore the ideological havoc wrought by the Mensheviks' first confrontation with revolution, even as it belies the image of Menshevik doctrinal rigidity.

As the smoke settled over charred revolutionary hopes, the social democrats found themselves staring at a disastrous balance sheet. All strategies, all different tendencies, had come to grief. Neither a "Menshevik" soviet-oriented strategy in Petersburg nor a "Bolshevik" insurrectionary strategy in Moscow, neither Lenin's call for the capture of power nor Martov's vision of expanding areas of revolutionary self-government, had succeeded. Neither the peasants nor the Western proletariat nor the Russian bourgeoisie had proved worthy allies.

Decades after the catastrophic outcome of the Revolution of 1905, Mensheviks writing about these events were unable to avoid apologia, recrimination, or embarrassment. Valentinov-Volsky and Garvi, later right wing Mensheviks, explain their own participation in the Bolshevik-inspired Moscow uprising in terms of "solidarity" or "forgetfulness."[20] Dan quite rightly makes fun of such "forgetfulness." In 1905, however, he describes himself as living in a state of intoxication, and in his last book he also leaves himself open to criticism by complaining peevishly that the peasants and the bourgeoisie failed to play the role assigned to them.[21] Perhaps another Menshevik was thinking of such attitudes when he noted aphoristically: "The problem with revolutions is that they always occur at inopportune moments."[22]

The Mensheviks' attempts to overcome embarrassment at their incoherence and failure in 1905 emerge even in Solomon Schwarz's scrupulous study of that revolution. Schwarz does not conceal the confusion prevailing in social democratic ranks, and he often brings out the numerous similarities between Bolsheviks and Mensheviks. Nevertheless, whenever possible, and at the risk of anachronism, Schwarz attempts to show that the theoretical characteristics commonly attributed to each faction (open versus closed, organization versus initiative) were operative in 1905. When Schwarz's study was published with a preface by an American historian who referred to Menshevik tactics as "talmudic" in their complexity, one of the last surviving Mensheviks attacked the use of this term, insisting that the Mensheviks were no more "talmudic" than the Bolsheviks.[23]

Even failed revolutions can be rich in lessons and may weigh heavily on the consciousness of participants. The Revolution of 1905 left an indelible imprint on the Mensheviks, particularly on that generation with whom we are concerned, and even on those Mensheviks who were Bolsheviks in 1905. In spite of their failures and mistakes then, our Mensheviks saw 1905 as a heroic moment in their lives. In exile after 1921 they reminisced more readily about this period than about later days and continued to pay tribute to the heroes of 1905.[24]

The lessons of the Revolution are problematic. The events of 1905 have been seen—by all concerned—as a "dress rehearsal" for those of 1917.[25] Formal parallels abound: both revolutions break out spontaneously under the stress of war and engender soviets as revolutionary alternatives to the existing state apparatus; and many of the same actors, both individual and collective, appear in both revolutions. Even when divergences occur, they are sometimes mirror images of each other. In 1905 Lenin's strategy called for convocation of a provisional government and his own entry into it; in 1917 his action was premised on rejection of the provisional government. In 1905 Martov stood isolated from many of his closest collaborators by refusing to follow the radical revolutionary path taken by Martynov, Dan, and others; in 1917 he cut himself off from the party majority through his own radicalism.

In spite of these parallels, the lessons of 1905 were to prove treacherous in 1917. From the Menshevik point of view, the single dominant lesson of 1905 seemed to be that excessive radicalism, abandonment of the doctrine of bourgeois revolution, and isolated action of the proletariat spelled disaster. After 1905 remorse over doctrinal infidelity in that year reinforced a natural tendency to interpret new facts in the light of familiar truths, that is, those of 1905.[26] Russian (and other) revolutionaries have regularly harked back to the events of 1789, 1848, and 1870–71. What could be more normal than that they should also reach back to those of 1905, which they themselves had experienced? Indeed, as one observer has written, "[Revolutionary leaders are] like actors who, when improvising a piece, cannot emancipate themselves from the memories of a familiar text."[27] In this case the Mensheviks of 1905 had learned the wrong lines for 1917.

After the Revolution (1905)

Sometime between 1903 and 1917 the Menshevik and Bolshevik factions within Russian social democracy became two parties. The indeterminacy of this statement is intentional. Commentators who see the Second Congress in 1903 as a clash between two worldviews consider it the birth, albeit unknown to themselves, of two distinct parties. Others see two parties emerging out of different factional responses to the failures of the Revolution of 1905. From this standpoint the factions acquired their distinctive identity in 1907 when hopes of reigniting the Revolution disappeared, at least among Mensheviks.[1] Equally plausible is the view that two parties developed out of the inability to execute a formal reunification agreement concluded in 1910.[2] A more clear-cut moment of rupture occurred in 1912, when first the Bolsheviks and then the Mensheviks held separate conferences purporting to be all-party bodies.[3] Yet, up to 1913, Bolshevik and Menshevik parliamentary (Duma) factions cooperated closely, only to be split by an agent provocateur under the Bolshevik label.[4] Nevertheless, World War I and the February Revolution in 1917 brought about such realignments that hopes of reunification flared up again and endured, perhaps even beyond the October Revolution.[5]

Whatever one's judgment on the definitive break between the factions, two points should be made. First, common ground between the Mensheviks and the Bolsheviks persisted throughout their quarrels and beyond the successive points of rupture. Second, the Menshevik-Bolshevik division was not the only, and at times not even the preeminent, division within Russian social democracy. Multiple strands continued to connect or separate individual social democrats.[6]

An empirical study of the RSDRP up to 1907 reveals comparable social origins for members of both factions.[7] There were differences in occupational structure: the Mensheviks included more professionals, intelligentsia, and skilled workers. There was no overall difference in education. Menshevik leaders were generally older and more likely to have come to Marxism from populism. Bolshevik leaders were, for the most part, Great Russians, whereas Jews and Georgians were more prominent among the Mensheviks. For our purposes these differences are not significant; other cleavages within the RSDRP did not coincide with factional divisions.

The Mensheviks complain that the party lost its intimate character between 1907 and 1914.[8] Some add that the party lost its very best members—democratic, idealistic professionals who went off to pursue nonparty work—and that it, or rather its Bolshevik faction, drew instead the most unsavory, plebeian elements.[9] It is true that the party as a whole suffered huge losses of members, of public support, and of morale after the 1905 Revolution and the reactionary coup of 1907. Reversals affected both factions, even though modes of response to these reversals differed. Those responses covered positions ranging from liquidationism (the dissolution of the underground party and its replacement with more modest legal activity) to armed expropriations. Individuals at extreme ends of the spectrum would not stay in the party long: an individual totally dedicated to working within the legal framework had no use for the party; nor would a guerrilla leader long accept party discipline. Between the extremes of this spectrum, however, a certain consensus existed.

The core of consensus lay in common ideological premises. Not only were both factions Marxist, but also they both stood on the same side in the great debates raging within European Marxism. Even extreme liquidators considered themselves orthodox rather than reformist in the European sense.[10] Neither faction rejected unconditionally opposing tactics. Thus, mainstream menshevism sought to combine the open, legal work of liquidators with an underground and emigré network.[11] The Bolsheviks, after having denounced their opponents' involvement in trade unions, made a successful effort to capture these same unions.[12] In spite of stormy disagreements, both the Mensheviks and the Bolsheviks eventually came around to accepting Duma participation.[13] Perhaps the most telling link was the fact that the party program adopted in 1903 remained common to both factions until after the 1917 Revolution. Less significantly but more paradoxically, in 1907 the Mensheviks voted for adoption of that version of article 1 of the party statutes that Lenin had proposed against Martov in 1903 and that had done so much to precipitate the factional division.[14]

Even in their disagreements the Mensheviks and Bolsheviks came together. After the mass defections among both factions following 1905, ex-Mensheviks were more likely to maintain contact with former comrades, for example, through common participation in social organizations, but both ex-Mensheviks and ex-Bolsheviks were, temporarily or permanently, lost to the party. Party cadres remained subject to repression in the form of censorship, internal and foreign exile, or imprisonment, regardless of faction. Even the deepest differences between the factions rested on similar assessments. Both Mensheviks and Bolsheviks feared an "embourgeoisement" of the party. For the Mensheviks, however, embourgeoisement meant domination by the intelligentsia; for the Bolsheviks it meant trade unionist tactics and mentality. Similarly, both Mensheviks and Bolsheviks were disappointed in the behavior of their class allies in 1905. Neither the bourgeoisie nor the petty bourgeoisie, that is, the peasantry, had fulfilled revolutionary expectations. Conclusions drawn from this assessment, however, were different. The Bolsheviks evolved toward a policy that was to culminate in a revolutionary seizure of power by a proletariat that dominated the peasantry and disregarded the bourgeoisie. The Mensheviks sought to develop the internal strength of the working class so that it might meet future challenges more adequately, regardless of the behavior of its allies.

Thus, after 1905 the party was still united in many formal ways and tied together by a host of ideological, practical, and personal connections. Divisions other than that between Bolsheviks and Mensheviks, however, complete the picture of a movement in which positions have been staked out but definitive lines have not yet been drawn. Most surprising in light of the future total identification between Lenin and bolshevism is the fact that, at various moments, Lenin found himself in a minority among the Bolsheviks. This was the case briefly in 1905 when he disagreed with his faction over supporting the soviets, and it was to be the case later. After 1905 he steered a difficult course between "right" and "left" Bolshevik groups. On the one hand, tendencies aiming at conciliation with the Mensheviks probably enlisted a majority of Lenin's faction. On the other hand, Lenin fought against left Bolsheviks who defied him after he had changed his mind to favor Duma participation. In this context one might expect left Mensheviks to ally themselves with right Bolsheviks. This is what happened in 1909, when some left Mensheviks under Plekhanov made common cause with right Bolsheviks, including Lenin, against Bolshevik "recallists" opposed to Duma participation and Menshevik liquidators. The following year right Bolsheviks and left Mensheviks were cooperating, in a common antidisciplinarian spirit, at a party school in Bologna. At that time left Bolshevik attacks on Lenin were no less vehement than earlier Menshevik attacks.[15]

Within the Menshevik camp divisions are less easily defined in terms of bipolar dichotomies. Rather, divisions revolve around the issue of liquidationism and are expressed in numerous, sometimes only slightly differentiated nuances of policy and attitude. Liquidationism thus appears in a variety of degrees, and shades off imperceptibly into orthodox menshevism. Indeed, some Mensheviks and some historians have denied that liquidationism ever really existed.[16] They are correct to the extent that liquidationism was, above all, a Bolshevik term of abuse.[17] Even those Mensheviks considered wholesale liquidators saw themselves as amphibians, creatures of both land and water who worked in both party and trade union organizations, amenable therefore to a retreat underground if conditions should so dictate.[18]

There is a bewildering array of positions within the RSDRP, not even considering centrist, nonfactional groups such as those led by Trotsky and Plekhanov. No wonder the two Menshevik historians of this period, (Nicolaevsky and Valentinov-Volsky, were unable to bring their studies to a conclusion. A question that has provoked contradictory responses asks which faction showed a stronger will to unity. Among the Mensheviks it is an article of faith that Lenin was working for a complete rupture from very early on. Historians point to the existence of a secret Bolshevik center.[19] They are reluctant to acknowledge the formation of a secret Menshevik bureau as early as 1903. Indeed, Dan is so discreet about this organization (to which he belonged) that he claims he is incapable of ascertaining its membership.[20] Lidia Dan maintains that, at least after 1905, neither her husband, Fedor Dan, nor her brother, Martov, had any illusions about unity, though Bolsheviks in general and Lenin in particular did. Martov's animus against Lenin was especially strong, far stronger than his hostility to bolshevism.[21] Whether one accepts the reproach of Martov's biographer that Martov was halfhearted in his struggle against Lenin or the opposite reproach that he willfully frustrated reunification, it must be remembered that Martov was himself embattled within his faction and could not choose his course freely.[22]

The aborted attempt at reunification in 1910 illustrates the problem of attributing responsibility for the failure of reconciliation. A plenary meeting of the party's Central Committee managed to hammer out an agreement which depended on cooptation into the Central Committee of three Menshevik liquidators, including Petr Garvi. When these individuals declined the invitation, the Bolsheviks considered themselves freed from the agreement. Writing in 1923, Dan seems to justify the decision of the three liquidators; twenty-some years later he is much harsher.[23] The change lies in the evolution of Dan's attitudes toward bolshevism and toward the Menshevik right wing represented by Garvi.

As the factions maneuvered, what were the members of our future Menshevik group doing in the years after 1905? Fedor Dan was the Menshevik "stage manager." His phlegmatic manner—"Wood" was one nickname—and taste for back-room politicking made him admirably suited for the task of brokering factional interests.[24] These qualities brought Dan to the pinnacle of the party at the Stockholm "Reunification" Congress of 1906. He authored almost all of the resolutions that were adopted. Only he and Lenin appeared on all three ballots for election to the party presidium. He and Plekhanov received the greatest number of votes, whereas Lenin narrowly escaped defeat. During debates on the agrarian question, Dan easily put the obscure Georgian Bolshevik Iosif Dzhugashvili (Stalin) in his place.[25] The outcome of the congress—formal reunification of the party and, for the first time, Menshevik domination of it—was largely Dan's work.

In later years Dan worked indefatigably on behalf of the Menshevik faction. Although harsh toward liquidationism, he advocated participation in the Duma earlier than others, thus incurring Lenin's accusations of bargaining with bourgeois politicians under the guise of a "private meeting for a cup of tea."[26] In 1908 Dan and Martov founded the newspaper *Golos Sotsialdemokrata*, first based in Geneva and later in Paris. Dan was able to parry Martov's desire to use it primarily for anti-Bolshevik campaigns, making it instead an instrument, though not a very successful one, for reconciliation between liquidators and whatever remained of the underground party.[27] At the ill-fated reunification plenum of 1910, Dan guided the work of the Social Democratic, later Menshevik, Duma faction.

None of our other Mensheviks came close to sharing Dan's prominence in this period, a fact that partly explains his later long domination over the exiled Mensheviks. Raphael Abramovitch was elected to the Central Committee at the Stockholm Congress of 1906, entering it with Bolshevik support, as a representative of the Bund, courted by both Bolsheviks and Mensheviks. The focus of Abramovitch's previous concerns had been, to his later remorse, narrowly Jewish.[28] Although now in the upper echelon of the Russian party, he continued to act, to use his own term, as a Bundist "commis-voyageur," making speeches and giving lectures. Politically, in spite of his earlier insistence on the identity of Bundist and Bolshevik organizational principles, Abramovitch became the first Bundist liquidator. He was at pains to point out that Bundist liquidators were, in fact, different from Menshevik ones in that Bundists did not completely abandon illegal work.[29] As we have seen, this corresponds entirely to the self-description of such a typical Menshevik liquidator as Garvi.

Petr Garvi was another prominent party professional in these years, one of the *praktiki* (as opposed to theorists) who stood at the center of the controversy over liquidationism. Garvi's description of the post-1905 climate applies to a great many party members, not only liquidators. He writes vividly of his intense relief at being able to surface, to take permanent lodgings rather than to flit from one hiding place to another, and to set up his books and anticipate uninterrupted studies. He also stresses the effects of the changed social climate on a party member's ability—or will—to continue clandestine life. Before 1905 the underground revolutionary had a refuge in every intelligentsia home; now society, disillusioned with revolution, was keeping its distance, treating the revolutionary not as a hero but as an anachronism.[30]

Garvi is indeed the ultimate liquidator, particularly in his organizational views and in his suspicion of Bolsheviks. He is unenthusiastic about efforts to restore the old underground apparatus and relieved when efforts to appease the Bolsheviks fail.[31] Curiously, Garvi's memoirs do not mention his role in blocking the reunification agreement of 1910. He does write, however, about the Vienna Conference of 1912, a Menshevik and centrist meeting called in response to a Bolshevik meeting in Prague. Garvi expresses his suspicion of the main conference organizer, Trotsky, and his mistrust of Dan, who promised Trotsky that he would publicly denounce the liquidators if they sabotaged the conference. Garvi's reluctance to countenance cooperation with other factions also comes out in his memoirs, as does his resentment of the liquidators' bad press among foreign socialists.[32] Garvi clearly feels that liquidationism has been vindicated by events but that it has not found the recognition it deserves, especially from his party comrades.

Among other members of our group, many former Bolsheviks became Mensheviks after 1905. This move was perhaps facilitated in Petersburg by the fact that the local party committee managed to unite the factional organizations. Even Bolsheviks, such as Woytinsky, who only transferred their factional allegiance to the Mensheviks much later (1917 in Woytinsky's case) were impressed by their contact with the Petersburg Mensheviks.[33] Other Bolsheviks, such as Nicolaevsky, changed factions either out of exasperation at the Bolsheviks' inability to adjust to new conditions or out of indignation at the new Bolshevik policy of armed expropriations.[34]

The further evolution of these former Bolsheviks was anything but uniform. Some, such as Valentinov-Volsky and Denike, left party work altogether until 1917 or later. Others—Dubois and Bienstock, for example— became out-and-out liquidators. Still others, such as Nicolaevsky, opposed liquidationism. All that can be said is that an individual Menshevik's political origin (as Bolshevik or Economist, for example) was no indication of position in this period. Nor was one's position now a guide to future choices. The two right wing Mensheviks in the Foreign Delegation after 1921, Aronson and Kefali, began their careers as Bolsheviks. Mikhail Uritskii, the future head of the Soviet secret police, the Cheka, was the very model of Bolshevik conciliationism, and Martynov, the former Economist and antiliquidator Menshevik, ended up, after 1917, a Bolshevik.[35]

Despite the multiplicity of strands within the RSDRP, common ground existed. A sense of unity is well documented with respect to the party rank and file: ordinary party members saw no sense to the ideological wrangling. They adopted positions in response to local considerations; their party consciousness was stronger than their factional consciousness. This sense of unity reached the party leadership as well. True, the factionalist attitude of Garvi, for instance, was not an isolated one, and it was supported by party patriarchs such as Potresov and even by Axelrod. Nevertheless, the sense of unity is vividly conveyed by a brief memoir.

In the summer of 1910 the French town of Arcachon was the vacation spot chosen by Ekaterina Kuskova and her husband, Sergei Prokopovitch, both leading Economists; by the Dans; and also by the Bolshevik leader Lev Kamenev and his wife, then a passionate Menshevik who was also Trotsky's sister: three factions practically under one roof! It seemed to be a recipe for a poisoned summer, writes Kuskova, but in fact the situation was not in the least strained. Debates were sharp, but they turned on the question of the relation of forces within the coming Revolution, not on the Revolution itself. Kuskova tells of meeting the Kamenevs' young son and, before kissing him, asking, "Which cheek is Menshevik and which cheek is Bolshevik?" The boy answered, laughingly, "I won't let you kiss either. Mensheviks are our people, too, but you are a liberal."[36]

Into the Great War

On the eve of World War I the tempo of historical change in Russia quickened. This fact is not in dispute. Historians, however, are deeply at odds over their interpretations of this change. Many Western historians emphasize the stabilizing social and political effects of Russian economic development in the last peacetime years of the old regime.[1] In the wake of economic upswing came a surge in workers' self-confidence as an ever more mature working class, increasingly like that of the advanced industrial countries, focused on winning freedom of coalition. This emphasis has appealed particularly to Menshevik historians inasmuch as it vindicates Menshevik policies since 1905.[2]

Doubts about this interpretation have arisen, even among Mensheviks. Such a quintessential example of Menshevik historiography as Raphael Abramovitch's *Soviet Revolution* (1962) opens with a bright picture of prewar Russia moving quickly toward industrialization and democracy.[3] Abramovitch's correspondence, however, reveals that he was long skeptical about Russia's possibilities for evolutionary development. "It was beautiful to behold," he writes privately, "but unfortunately it was already dead."[4] Abramovitch's doubts may have been overcome by Nikolai Valentinov-Volsky. This old comrade argued the so-called Menshevik vision of history forcefully, and he was commissioned by Abramovitch, now nearly blind, to prepare materials for the opening chapter of *Soviet Revolution*. The interpretation that emerged was largely Volsky's.[5]

Boris Nicolaevsky, too, in his American years voiced doubts about the direction in which Russia had been heading before 1914. These doubts were expressed in his criticism of the liquidators: their simplistic devotion to open nonparty organization meant that they had given up the party "shingle" to the Bolsheviks, allowing Lenin to use the rise in labor activity on the eve of the war to his own advantage.[6] Writing to Volsky, Nicolaevsky was much more explicit: as he traveled throughout Russia in the years before the war, he perceived a growing gulf between the expectations and attitudes of the intelligentsia and the workers; only the intelligentsia was oriented toward evolution.[7]

Menshevik doubts about the evolutionary, stabilizing course of Russian history before 1914 lead directly to the alternative interpretation of that period. In this version the Russian labor movement's powerful upsurge in the last prewar years was revolutionary, not evolutionary. It expressed itself not in an orderly campaign for freedom of coalition but in massive, savage strikes. The beneficiaries of this movement were not Mensheviks but Bolshe-viks.[8]

Statistics do indeed show a sudden dramatic swell in the number of strikes from 1912 on. Most significant, the Mensheviks begin to lose control to the Bolsheviks of the very labor organizations they had founded and nurtured, including the insurance councils and the Union of Printers, where future members of our Menshevik group were active leaders (Schwarz in the former, Kefali in the latter). The tide of events was clearly moving against the Mensheviks. Some scholars have argued that the decline of the Mensheviks benefited centrist groupings—such as Trotsky's "nonfactionalist" social democrats and Plekhanov's party Mensheviks—rather than the Bolsheviks.[9] Trade union electoral results, however, indicate that the Bolsheviks were very much an ascendant force.

At issue remains the extent to which the Bolsheviks were initiators and not merely beneficiaries of this revolutionary upsurge of labor militancy. The most that can be said with certainty is that in 1912–1914, as in 1917, the Bolsheviks proved capable of riding the crest of the revolutionary *stikhiia*—the elemental, spontaneous, maximalist forces that swelled up from the depths of Russian society like a powerful force of nature. Although the Mensheviks adopted *stikhiinost'*, in the sense of spontaneity, as their principle, when confronted with the *stikhiia* they recoiled. In years to come Mensheviks would point to their failure to take account of the *stikhiia* as the cause of their defeat.[10]

As their strength in Russia ebbed, the Mensheviks could take comfort in their advances on the international arena. Ever since 1903 Bolsheviks and Mensheviks had been competing for the approval of their foreign comrades, particularly the Germans, who acted as arbiters of orthodoxy within the international socialist movement. Initially this contest tended toward a stalemate, and it was only on the eve of World War I that the Mensheviks scored decisive advances.

The difficulties of recruiting foreign socialists to support the Menshevik or Bolshevik side are reflected in Karl Kautsky's vacillating attitudes. As high priest of Marxism and editor of the leading Marxist journal, *Neue Zeit*, Kautsky was in a position to throw considerable weight on behalf of either faction. Both courted him, although the Mensheviks had an initial advantage in Kautsky's long-standing friendship with Axelrod.[11] Generally speaking, Kautsky resisted being drawn into the dispute on the grounds that it was not his business, that he was not familiar enough with the issues involved, or even that the issues separating the factions were too insignificant to be taken seriously. With time, however, Kautsky's studied indifference turned to outright irritation at both factions. He, like other foreign socialists, was shocked by the venom, bad faith, and sordidness of the Russian quarrels. At various times Kautsky cast plagues on both Martov and Lenin. Much later, in 1925, after having been the object of savage Bolshevik denunciations, and in spite of his close relations with exiled Mensheviks, Kautsky acknowledged his admiration for the Bolsheviks in 1905. His remark provoked anguished recriminations from Axelrod, just as his initial wavering on the Bolshevik-Menshevik split had aroused Axelrod's reproaches in 1903–4.[12] The remark, however, underlines the problem inherent in the attempt to appropriate the pre-1917 Kautsky entirely to the Menshevik side, as the Mensheviks have been tempted to do.[13]

In spite of vicissitudes, by 1914 the correlation of forces within the councils of international socialism was turning in favor of the Mensheviks. The Bolsheviks' trump card vis-à-vis their foreign comrades had been their steadfast revolutionary attitude and revolutionary élan in 1905.[14] The value of this card diminished as the years passed and the situation in Russia evolved. As the Bolsheviks emerged from underground to capture the trade unions and the Mensheviks staked out initiative groups (that is, embryonic underground organizations supplementing legal positions), the Bolsheviks' advantage, already undermined by their expropriationist antics, was diminished further in the eyes of foreign socialists. Instead of comparing revolutionary zeal, by 1914 foreign socialists were judging Russian factions in terms of a single question: Which one was more inclined to seek and restore the unity of the Russian Social Democratic Labor Party?

It was to resolve the question of unity that the Bureau of the Socialist International called a conference of all Russian factions in Brussels in July 1914. Whatever the conference's prospects, its preparations and proceedings augured well for the Mensheviks. The Bolsheviks stood almost completely isolated, and Lenin himself, whether out of desperation or defiance, did not even appear in person. The Bolsheviks' resistance to the resolution calling for unity identified them squarely in the eyes of all, Russians and foreigners, as the obstacle to party peace, with all the opprobrium this implied. Indeed, it has been suggested that the Brussels Conference set the stage for an outright expulsion of the Bolsheviks from the International at the congress to be held in Vienna the following month.[15] Of course, history intervened, pushing the Menshevik victory at Brussels, real or illusory, deep into the background.

3

From Exile
to Exile

War

Recollections of the atmosphere in Russia on the eve and at the outbreak of World War I differ. Fedor Dan remembers the mounting wave of strikes and demonstrations quelled only a few days before the beginning of mobilization by vigorous measures of repression. Grigorii Aronson describes society, including workers' circles, as sleeping an "unawakeable" sleep. It follows that for Dan the war marked a halt to social ferment, whereas for Aronson it stimulated the social movement. Observers outside the Menshevik camp, too, have recorded very different perceptions: one bourgeois politician comments on the patriotic fervor that gripped the same masses who had just been demonstrating against the government; another notes the depth of popular opposition to the war.[1] The only conclusion one can draw is that radical shifts and swings were occurring in the population's mood; these were to continue through 1917.

The war created new lines of divergence within the social democratic movement, superseding or perhaps superimposing themselves over earlier divisions.[2] As in other belligerent countries the fundamental opposition lay between defensists and internationalists, distinguished by the priority accorded to national or class values. In Russia, however, the defensist position was never as dominant among socialist leaders as it was elsewhere.[3] Moreover, this basic division concealed an entire gamut of opinion. Unconditional defensists, led by the venerable Plekhanov and the ex-Bolshevik Duma deputy Alexinsky, threw their wholehearted support into the anti-German campaign. Potresov's more moderate defensist group resolved to continue the struggle against tsarism without hindering the conduct of the war. As internationalists, Martov was guided by the spirit of the Socialist International's

58

earlier resolutions denouncing all belligerents in an imperialist war, while Lenin adopted a defeatist postion in regard to Russia.[4]

These divergences reverberated within each of the factions and even within families. David Dallin became an internationalist, whereas his brother Simon Wolin was a moderate defensist. Martov emerged as the leading Menshevik internationalist; his brother Vladimir Levitskii became an extreme defensist, and another brother, Sergei Ezhov, moved from defensism to internationalism. At the same time, these divergences opened up prospects of realignment. Generally speaking, Mensheviks might be expected to have inclined toward defensism, Bolsheviks toward internationalism.[5] In fact, anti-German defensist sentiment prevailed among both Mensheviks and Bolsheviks in Berlin in 1914, as described by Alexandra Kollontai, then a Menshevik, later a Bolshevik and a Soviet ambassador.[6] Subsequently in Paris an internationalist newspaper appeared which gathered together eminent Mensheviks such as Axelrod and Martov, Mensheviks who later became Bolsheviks, Bolshevik conciliators, and the undefinable Trotsky.[7]

Hopes of transcending factional estrangement surged. Lenin inquired anxiously about Dan's position, and heaped uncharacteristic praise on Martov, who initially responded to these overtures favorably.[8] Partisans of unity took heart in the fact that the Menshevik and Bolshevik Duma factions, which had split the previous year, now issued a common declaration before walking out of the Duma together rather than voting for war credits. This common action may reveal the Bolsheviks' disarray more than a will to unity. Apparently, Bolshevik deputies asked to subscribe to the declaration worked out by a Menshevik committee, including notably Petr Garvi and Eva Broido, without reading the text of the declaration.[9] At the very least, however, these developments suggested that the course of events was depriving earlier divisions of their relevance.

In later years it was often assumed that factional lines of continuity ran from the prewar to the postrevolutionary period, encompassing the war years as well.[10] Menshevik liquidators might be expected to have rallied to defensism in 1914 before emerging as right wing Mensheviks after 1917. Such was the case, for example, for Potresov and Levitskii as well as for one of the two right wing members of the future Foreign Delegation, Mark Kefali, and for the prominent extraparty right wing Menshevik, Stepan Ivanovich. Exceptions abound, however. The other rightist on the Foreign Delegation, Grigorii Aronson, had conducted characteristically liquidationist-type work before the war but in 1914 joined the internationalists. Raphael Abramovitch had defined himself as a liquidator but emerged as the only internationalist on the Bund's Central Committee, before adopting the left wing Menshevik position after the Revolution and in emigration.[11] Solomon Schwarz, a liquidator and a defensist, clung to the left wing Menshevik position in emigration far longer than did Abramovitch. By contrast, Axelrod turned from internationalism to right wing menshevism.

Generalizations are thus barely tenable, and yet wartime allegiance became a central component of subsequent individual and factional self-definition. Owing to the outcome of events, after 1917 an internationalist past inspired respect among Russian socialists whereas defensism fell into disrepute. Internationalism, like bolshevism earlier, was now seen as the more active, vigorous, and uncompromising current within social democracy.[12] The beneficiaries of this reputation were the Bolsheviks and the internationalist Mensheviks under Martov. Indeed, it was partly the prestige acquired through their wartime stance that allowed Martov's internationalists to wrest control of the Menshevik Party after the October Revolution and to impose their views, in many ways the continuation of their wartime views, on the party through many years of emigration.

Our Mensheviks were not only divided politically during the war years; they were also widely scattered and isolated from one another. Some, finding themselves in the West at the outbreak of the war, continued the familiar patterns of emigré life in Paris or in Switzerland. Some emigré defensists enlisted under French command.[13] Martov, Axelrod, Abramovitch, and other internationalists in the West sought to re-create the Socialist International (or, in Lenin's case, to create a new International) and to put an end to the war. Several of our Mensheviks—David Dallin, Grigorii Bienstock and his wife, Judith Grinfeld—joined other socialists, including Bolsheviks, in Copenhagen. Here they worked as researchers in a mysterious Institute for the Study of the Social Consequences of the War, run by the equally mysterious Alexander Helphand-Parvus, socialist millionaire, collaborator of Trotsky's in 1905, and later German agent. The institute's academic work influenced later thinking on economic planning, but its contribution to Parvus's hopes of bringing about revolution through Russian defeat was probably disappointing.[14]

In Russia some future members of our Menshevik group, including both Lidia and Fedor Dan, Eva Broido, and Boris Nicolaevsky, were arrested in 1914 and sent into internal exile. Here they emerged as members of a distinct political tendency known as Siberian Internationalism or Siberian Zimmerwaldism, led by Iraklii Tsereteli and Fedor Dan, whose collaboration was to continue throughout 1917. The Siberian group also included Vladimir Woytinsky, still nominally a Bolshevik, whose confused version of internationalism eventually gave way to acceptance of Tsereteli's position. By 1917

Woytinsky was a Menshevik in all but name and decided, on Tsereteli's ad-vice, to remain in the Bolshevik party only in order to propagate Tsereteli's view within it.[15] Initially, to the great relief of all concerned, it appeared that there were no divergences between Siberian internationalists and their Martovite counterparts in the West. With time, however, differences emerged, and in 1917 they ripened into fundamental opposition, pitting Martov against the now "revolutionary defensist" leaders, Tsereteli and Dan, whose attitude toward the war had changed with the fall of the tsarist re-gime.[16]

Those Mensheviks who had managed to escape arrest in Moscow and Pe-tersburg in 1914 found themselves constrained within an even more limited sphere of activity. The workers' press and organizations had already suffered the severest repression in the few weeks before war broke out, and such measures now multiplied with the further arrest and exile of social demo-crats.[17] Defensists survived more easily than internationalists, and if one adopts the thesis of continuity between liquidationism and defensism, one might even say that the war gave a new lease on life to liquidationism.[18] In fact, only a very few defensists managed to survive the entire war period at liberty in the two capitals.

Given the pitifully narrow scope of activity available to socialists in war-time conditions, an initiative undertaken by some Russian industrialists ac-quired enormous significance. In 1915 politicians of the Duma's "progressive bloc" established a network of war industries committees with the participa-tion of industrialists intent on improving production and perhaps influencing war policies. An invitation from the committees' first congress to send work-ers' representatives stirred up the sharpest disagreements in socialist ranks.[19] Naturally, most internationalists found the proposal abhorrent, while de-fensists tended to see merit in it. Above all, the proposal opened up once again the old issue of exploiting legal means of struggle and showed that there was no more agreement now on this question than there had been before the war.

Among the Mensheviks divergence over worker participation in the war industries committees partly took the form of an opposition between émigré Mensheviks and party workers at home.[20] The Menshevik Organizational Committee's Foreign Secretariat, which included Martov and Axelrod, ex-pressed its support for that committee's desire to participate "in the widest possible area of struggle," but drew the line at participation in the war indus-tries' committees.[21] Siberian internationalists, including Dan, applied similar logic to support participation. Among our Mensheviks several individuals actually took part in the committees. These included Petr Garvi, then a prom-

inent member of the Menshevik organizational committee in Petersburg/
Petrograd, and Solomon Schwarz, secretary of the Moscow committee's
workers' group.[22] Their activity came to an end in the summer of 1916, when
Garvi was exiled to Astrakhan province and Schwarz was punitively con-
scripted into the army. As for the workers themselves, their reaction to participation varied from one factory to another and was sometimes inconsistent
within the same factory.[23]

In retrospect, the issue of workers' participation in the war industries committees may be seen as having laid the groundwork for some of the developments of 1917. From the outset the issue was identified as one of socialist
collaboration with the bourgeoisie, and thus opened up hoary questions regarding the configuration of class forces in Russia and the role of a working-
class party in a country that had not yet experienced its bourgeois revolution.
For these reasons Nicolaevsky could affirm that "the struggle around the
question of participation in the war industries committees became the fundamental struggle which split menshevism and prepared the groupings of the
year 1917."[24] The workers' groups of the war industries committees acquired
importance for another reason as well. Thinking back to 1905, some socialists
saw the groups as a step toward the convocation of a general workers' congress or toward the formation of soviets, especially since the electoral system
adopted for choosing delegates to the workers' groups was modeled directly
on that of the 1905 Petersburg soviet. To a certain extent these expectations
were not disappointed. In February 1917 members of the workers' groups
were among those who met in the Tauride Palace to convoke the Petrograd
Soviet of Workers' Deputies.[25]

Revolution

When the revolutionary events of 1917 began, the Mensheviks were perhaps
the strongest political party in Russia. They immediately achieved leadership
of the Executive Committee of the newly formed Petrograd soviet, and,
though sharing numerical preponderance with the SRs, they obtained de
facto leadership of the soviet as well.[1] In all likelihood the Menshevik-SR
bloc could have seized power.[2] Instead, in conformity with their own revolutionary strategy, the Mensheviks bestowed governmental power on a progressive bourgeois cabinet. This first government, like its successors, proved
utterly dependent on the support of the Menshevik-SR bloc within the soviet. When the soviet and the government clashed over a soviet peace manifesto, it was the government that collapsed. In May, hesitantly and reluc-

tantly, two Mensheviks entered a first coalition cabinet in the realization that without such participation, no government could muster credibility.[3]

The Menshevik Party's fortunes continued to rise during the spring of 1917, amidst growing chaos and increasing economic difficulties. Perhaps the most telling sign of Menshevik ascendancy was Bolshevik acquiescence in Menshevik policies and the powerful calls for unification that seized Bolsheviks and Mensheviks from the grass roots to the highest level. There was no Bolshevik opposition to the formation of a bourgeois government or to the Menshevik-sponsored peace manifesto. The Bolsheviks even reprinted thousands of copies of Dan's 1905 brochure concerning a constituent assembly.[4] When Lenin arrived in Petrograd in April, he found the soviet Bolshevik faction meeting with its Menshevik counterparts to establish terms of unification. As Trotsky put it, with disgust, "Stalin and Kamenev, who led the party in Lenin's absence, carried Bolshevism in March 1917 to the very boundaries of Menshevism."[5]

At the First All-Russian Congress of Soviets in June, the Menshevik-SR bloc commanded more than five times as many delegates as the Bolsheviks, and the Menshevik Party emerged with a plurality of seats on the new Central Executive Committee. Even as the congress was being held, however, a manifestation of support for the soviet majority turned into a pro-Bolshevik rally. In the following weeks the fiasco of an ill-fated military offensive launched by the soviet-supported provisional government was offset by the government's success in quelling an equally ill considered Bolshevik insurrection. In late August, however, an abortive coup d'état by General L. G. Kornilov succeeded in swinging mass opinion toward Bolshevik positions, and the Petrograd soviet adopted a Bolshevik resolution on worker and peasant power. Thereafter, increasingly frantic efforts to shore up the provisional government by forcing it to adopt decisive measures to counter the Bolshevik advance proved unavailing. The Second Congress of Soviets opened with 300 or more Bolshevik deputies out of a total of 650; the Mensheviks managed to muster only 70 votes.[6] Meanwhile, on the eve of the congress a Bolshevik uprising in Petrograd had effectively overthrown the provisional government. The crushing decline of the Mensheviks was confirmed in the weeks that followed by the results of the long-awaited Constituent Assembly elections: the Mensheviks polled somewhat more than 1 million votes, half of them in the Caucasus, in comparison with the SRs' 16 million and the Bolsheviks' 9 million.

Every member of our Menshevik group experienced the tumultuous months of 1917. Martov, as leader of the Menshevik internationalists, took a stance in opposition to the party majority. Martov's injunctions from Switzerland to party leaders in Russia during the first months of the Revolution remained unheeded (much like Lenin's similar injunctions to the Bolsheviks). Upon his arrival in Russia in May, Martov was confronted with the very situation against which he had been inveighing: Menshevik minority participation in a largely bourgeois coalition government. At that time Martov had more in common with the Bolsheviks than with most of his own Menshevik comrades. He exchanged greetings with the Bolsheviks, and, in the flurry of unification activity, it even seemed possible that Martov might cast his lot with them as Trotsky was on the point of doing. Instead, Martov accepted election to the Menshevik Central Committee, although he insisted on the right to "criticize the Party's decision to the masses."[7] This was hardly a coherent position, particularly for a leader who was to impose iron discipline on the Mensheviks after his own faction had obtained a majority in the post-October period. Even such Martovites as Raphael Abramovitch and Martov's brother Sergei Ezhov dissented from Martov on this issue.

As the revolution lurched toward its Bolshevik denouement, Martov's calls for an all-democratic, that is, socialist, government and his emphasis on immediate peace—policies superficially similar to those of the Bolsheviks—acquired increasing respect. They did not acquire a larger mass following, however, precisely because they resembled positions defended more forcefully by the Bolsheviks. When the Mensheviks withdrew from the Second Congress of Soviets in protest against the Bolshevik coup, Martov remained in the hall for a few more hours, thus symbolizing his intermediate position between the Bolsheviks and the Menshevik majority.[8]

Fedor Dan incarnated mainstream menshevism in 1917. As was the case with other Siberian Zimmerwaldists such as Tsereteli and Woytinsky, Dan's earlier internationalism gave way to revolutionary defensism, a policy that combined the search for peace in the international arena with pursuit of war for the sake of safeguarding the revolution in Russia. This policy permitted partial reconciliation between former defensists and internationalists. In the first months it seemed to correspond to the attitude of the soviet majority and to the mood of the soldiery. Just as earlier—and later—Dan linked his political fate to that of Martov, Dan in 1917 emerged as the indispensable lieutenant of the Soviet's first charismatic leader, Iraklii Tsereteli. As vice-chairman of the Petrograd soviet and editor of its journal, *Izvestiia*, Dan exercised his considerable political skills with an adroitness acknowledged even by some of his detractors.[9] Although Dan was at least partially responsible for the June demonstration which turned into a pro-Bolshevik rout, he was also instrumental in thwarting the Bolshevik show of force in July. Only on the very eve of the October Revolution did Dan summon sufficient doubts about his earlier position to lay down an ultimatum to the head of the provisional government, Alexander Kerensky.[10] Dan's challenge proved unavailing, and at the opening of the Second Congress of Soviets, it was Dan who ceded the chairmanship of the meeting to the representative of the new Bolshevik majority.

Notwithstanding their political divergences in 1917, Dan and his brother-in-law Martov lived under the same roof in Petrograd. Axelrod occupied a room behind the kitchen; several other Martov relatives of different political complexions, including the extreme defensist and secretary to Plekhanov, Fedor Dnevnitskii, also lived in the same apartment, as did Nicolaevsky and another houseguest, the Austrian socialist Otto Bauer. Tsereteli was a frequent visitor. Some disagreements were ironed out at evening tea, but the strain in the house was considerable. Tension reached its highest point in the wake of the Bolshevik coup attempt in July. Dan's concern was to put an end to the reigning disorder; Martov, too, did not approve of people riding through the streets shooting indiscriminately but saw them as primarily socialists, not hooligans. As Lidia Dan (who sided more with her brother than with her husband in 1917) also put it, Martov never thought that order could be useful; Dan, by contrast, was shocked by the murder even of the disreputable Rasputin.[11]

As a result of the political estrangement between Martov and Dan, it was Raphael Abramovitch who, among our Mensheviks, stood closest to Martov in 1917. Abramovitch's internationalist position during the war served him as a bridge from bundism to menshevism and as a strong bond with Martov personally. Abramovitch returned to Russia with Martov—and other Menshevik and Bolshevik leaders—in a second trainload of emigrés sponsored by the German government (Lenin returned in the first train). He became editor of the Yiddish language *Arbeitershtime* and a prominent member of the Soviet Executive Committee as well as of the Menshevik Central Committee. Indeed, Abramovitch's prominence was such—and such was the confusion at mass meetings—that at the Second Congress of Soviets a speech by the defensist Henryk Erlich was attributed, in the press and later in John Reed's classic work, to the internationalist Abramovitch, who had spoken in favor of Martov's opposing proposition.[12] Abramovitch's energetic politicking as well as his political style earned him his share of enemies, then and later.

Another Menshevik attained prominence in 1917, though not quite to the degree portrayed in his own memoirs. Vladimir Woytinsky served first as a member of the Soviet Executive Committee, as well as a staff member of *Izvestiia,* and then as a political commissar on the northern front. It may not be surprising that in March the Menshevik chairman of the Petrograd soviet should have offered Woytinsky, still nominally a Bolshevik, the chief editorship of *Izvestiia*, but it is astonishing to read that after October 1917 Lenin should have asked Woytinsky, by then a Menshevik, to join the new Council of People's Commissars as war minister and supreme commander.[13] Notwithstanding such delusions of grandeur, it is true that Woytinsky played an important role in summoning army support against the Bolsheviks, successfully in July and unsuccessfully in October.[14] Commentators, however, have been less impressed by his achievements than by the completeness of his reorientation in 1917.[15] After having sat as a Bolshevik on a joint Bolshevik-Menshevik committee on the question of the war in early April, at the height of cooperation between the two factions, Woytinsky became more anti-Bolshevik than majority Mensheviks such as Dan. His personal antipathy toward Dan, already pronounced in 1917, would push him later to the fringe of the Menshevik exile group.

Our Mensheviks were scattered ideologically, geographically, and professionally in 1917. Several held responsible positions in Petrograd under a Menshevik minister of labor; Anatolii Dubois, a lawyer by training, served as deputy minister of labor. Solomon Shwarz, as deputy chairman of the soviet's labor division, represented the soviet in the ministry and later headed its social insurance section, an area in which he was an acknowledged expert. Naum Jasny, later a prominent agricultural economist in the West, sat on the All-Union Food Board and represented the Soviet as deputy commissar in the Ministry of Agriculture.[16] Boris Nicolaevsky, a member of the Soviet Executive Committee, represented it on a commission investigating the tsarist Okhrana Police Archives, a foretaste of what was to be his life's work. Grigorii Bienstock was one of the closest collaborators of the future Soviet planner Iurii Larin, but did not follow him into the Communist Party.

Some members of the future Menshevik Foreign Delegation—Eva Broido and David Dallin (also employed in the labor ministry)—first entered the Menshevik Central Committee at the party's Unification Congress in August 1917. Others experienced the Revolution in the provinces. Grigorii Aronson became chairman of the Vitebsk soviet; Iurii Denike was vice-chairman of the Kazan' soviet. Boris Dvinov served in the Moscow soviet and recounts that a soldiers' meeting actually proposed to elect him tsar! In contrast, Vera Alexandrova (not yet a party member) worked quietly as an editorial assistant for the Moscow soviet's *Izvestiia;* she spent the critical October days reading H. G. Wells's *War of the Worlds.*[17]

In the aftermath of the Revolution, the exiled Mensheviks could hardly escape reflecting on the causes of their vertiginous decline during 1917 and of their defeat. Indeed, such self-interrogation began in the Menshevik press on the very morrow of the Bolshevik seizure of power and at the Menshevik Party's Extraordinary Congress in late November 1917.[18] In years to come the Mensheviks continued the debate over 1917.[19] Their explanations and interpretations afford a wealth of insight into both the events of the Russian Revolution and the attitudes of its actors.

One may distinguish several levels to the Mensheviks' explanation for their defeat. A first level concentrates on Menshevik policies. It pits those who see the Mensheviks' error in their "doctrinairism" against those who see error in their readiness to "compromise."[20] The divergence reflects a right-left division within the Menshevik camp and, indeed, within the non-Menshevik historiography of the Revolution.[21] "Doctrinairism" in right wing parlance here means ideological rigidity, an unwillingness to abandon a schematic and a priori vision of the Revolution's supposed course, an inordinate suspicion of potential allies such as the liberal bourgeoisie, and a reluctance to support fully the provisional government, particularly in its efforts to stem the growing disorder. For the Left, "compromise" signifies dilution of revolutionary class consciousness, timidity or procrastination in relation to urgent reforms, self-effacement before bourgeois elements in the provisional government, and tolerance of overtly counterrevolutionary tendencies.[22]

An unacknowledged common thread in both points of view is that they both put into question Marxism itself. To legitimize its collaboration with nonsocialist elements, the Menshevik Right appealed to the fundamental Marxist tenet that the Russian Revolution was a bourgeois revolution. The Left rejected such collaboration, also in the name of Marxism, by invoking the principle of defending the Russian working class. Both perspectives led the Mensheviks into an impasse. The result was an implicit critique of Marxism as an erroneous guide to action; such a critique can be sensed in the 1931 Berlin lecture by Anatolii Dubois, who moved from the Right of the party in 1917 to its Left in the 1940s. The uproar created by the lecture demonstrates the Mensheviks' extreme reluctance to probe the foundations of their beliefs.[23]

Such reluctance contributed to the search for an explanation for the Menshevik defeat at a second level of analysis, the juxtaposition of "subjective" and "objective" factors. Many Mensheviks and others saw the fatal error in faulty "psychology."[24] According to this view, the Mensheviks lacked the "will to power."[25] They feared the masses, scorned the peasantry, and shrank from state power.[26] Alternatively, it has been argued that the Mensheviks were so blinded by the danger of counterrevolution that they underestimated the danger from the Left.[27] In opposition to such subjective explanations, other Mensheviks have maintained that the configuration of objective circumstances and social forces in 1917 made the Mensheviks' defeat inescapable.[28] Given the prevailing war-weariness and the peasants' hunger for land, it was inevitable that the most demagogic political party would win ascendancy. Here, the division between Right and Left is not clear-cut. Some Mensheviks who shared power in 1917, such as Dan, would favor objective explanations, whereas those who stood in opposition (but not only those) would stress subjective factors, thus generalizing their criticism of party leaders already expressed in 1917.

The third level of explanation is, from a theoretical point of view, the least interesting. Caricaturing only slightly, it opposes Menshevik virtue and good faith in 1917 to Bolshevik conspiracy and betrayal of promise and principle.[29] This analysis elaborates on the preceding subjective explanation by removing the reservations of moral judgment. Some ambivalence persists: it is only a small step from virtue to naïveté and from naïveté to sheer political stupidity. This may explain why imputations of Menshevik virtue are occasionally rejected even by Mensheviks themselves.[30] Right wing Mensheviks appeal to this explanation to found their contention that the October events were not a revolution but an overthrow.[31] In its boldest form this explanation has the merit of simplicity. In more nuanced formulations it wins the assent even of the Menshevik left wing: the Mensheviks did not follow the course adopted by the Bolsheviks because they were aware of its disastrous long-term consequences.[32]

Of course, these explanations are not mutually exclusive. Together they satisfy the Mensheviks' need to understand their defeat. If we look at the specific issues of 1917, however, even the most coherent of such interpretations gives way to an echo of what was also Lenin's plaint on his deathbed: "What else could we have done?"[33]

There is little doubt that the main reason for the Mensheviks' loss of popularity and credibility in 1917 was their failure to put an end to the war.[34] Nonetheless, even so ardent an opponent of the war as the Menshevik internationalist Nikolai Sukhanov admits that abandonment of the war effort early on would have provoked civil war and would have been considered by the army itself as a betrayal of the troops at the front. Moreover, even later, when antiwar sentiment was rife, none of the antiwar parties had a coherent plan to disengage Russia. All parties, including the Bolsheviks, considered the formula of a separate peace to be a disaster for the Revolution, thus tacitly conceding the revolutionary defensists' argument that a separate peace would in fact mean collaborating with imperial Germany in waging war against the Allies. Lenin himself did not dare preach outright defeatism, and his formula of "fraternization" between Russian and enemy soldiers proved to be no solution. Even after the Bolshevik seizure of power, the Brest-Litovsk Treaty, in fact a separate peace, was presented as a pause for breath rather than a capitulation. Moreover, the treaty caused such division in Bolshevik ranks that Lenin had to mortgage all his personal authority to win acceptance for it. As for the Menshevik internationalists, their opposition to revolutionary defensism stemmed less from opposition to the defensists' policies—after all, the internationalists did not have a solution to the war either—than from the consequences of these policies, that is, that they made the socialists hostages to militarist elements and paralyzed all radical reform.[35]

It is even more difficult to fault Menshevik policies in 1917 when they are considered individually rather than globally. In reply to Trotsky's charge that the socialists should have seized power in February, Dan and others have argued cogently that such a move would have isolated the working class and rallied all intermediate social elements against the Revolution. In a historical analogy that other socialists found persuasive, Dan suggested that socialists had to avoid repeating the experience of the Paris Commune of 1871, a workers' movement crushed by a coalition of national forces.[36] In respect to the other major issue of 1917, the question of land, the Mensheviks have recognized the heavy costs of their own peasantophobia.[37] The best response they have been able to make is that such antipeasant attitudes also existed among the Bolsheviks, and that the Bolsheviks themselves did not understand their own party's agrarian program.[38] Here, too, there is a persuasive logic to Menshevik policies: majority Mensheviks gave priority to ensuring the flow of food supplies to the army and to the cities. Any agrarian disturbances would have put this policy into jeopardy, leading to starvation or, at the very least, to mass dissatisfaction, which would provide fertile terrain for counterrevolutionary agitation.

The question of Menshevik responsiblity for the defeat of non-Bolshevik forces in 1917 remains contentious, and the debates sometimes sidestep the central issues. For instance, Woytinsky seems convinced that if only the provisional government had not tried to send troops from the Petrograd garrison to the front, the Bolshevik seizure of power might have been averted. An inordinate amount of debate has focused on symbolic issues, such as the question of German subsidies.[39] For Martov, abolition of the death penalty in 1917 was a particular hobbyhorse.[40] Dan, Abramovitch, and Woytinsky have gone out of their way to defend their respective stands in this matter, although the differences are of little consequence in the final outcome of events.[41]

Recent historiography of the Revolution has tended to move away from many of the Menshevik explanations discussed here.[42] By considering the sentiments of the worker masses, however, it has once again focused attention on the elemental forces *(stikhiinost')* which figure so prominently in Menshevik reflections. The question posed by Dan—whether it is justifiable to oppose oneself to the elemental strivings of the working masses when these strivings are clearly leading workers toward their own destruction, or at best into an impasse—remains as acute as ever.[43] Moreover, in insisting on the importance of impersonal social forces, recent historiography has vindicated Dan's insistence, over sixty years ago, on objective explanations. It has done so without putting an end to the debates in which the Mensheviks and others have so long engaged.[44]

Facing Bolshevik Power

Bolshevik seizure of power did not end the divisions that had characterized the Menshevik Party, to its own detriment, in 1917. All Mensheviks condemned the Bolshevik coup and sought to reverse the situation. Consensus within the party, however, did not extend further. The Mensheviks were divided between those who saw the Bolshevik seizure of power as a reckless, suicidal "adventure" and those who considered it an outright "crime."[1] Although these assessments occurred within hours of the event, they defined a fundamental line of division well into the future.

The Menshevik Central Committee first issued an ultimatum excluding any overtures to the Bolsheviks. Two days later it voted, by a majority of one, to concentrate all efforts on "averting the danger of civil war among workers."[2] Henceforth this formulation was to be a code term for a policy of rapprochement and compromise with the Bolshevik regime. Among the reasons for this reversal was a visit from a Petrograd workers' delegation who described their fear and indignation at the news of counterrevolutionary troops marching against the capital.[3] The pivotal role in the reversal was played by several revolutionary defensists, including Fedor Dan, who now cast their lot with the internationalist minority. The depth of the continuing schism was demonstrated by the fact that remaining defensists, including Petr Garvi, resigned in protest from the Central Committee, if only for a few days. Mensheviks have been accused of indecisiveness and contradictory policies during the period of the provisional government, but never before or after would they display these woeful qualities as glaringly as in the last week of October 1917.

Shortly thereafter the Mensheviks participated in several progressively less ambitious schemes to counter Bolshevik power with another independently constituted authority. On the very day of the Bolshevik insurrection, a Committee for the Salvation of Fatherland and Revolution sprang up, with a mixed membership representing bodies as diverse as the Petrograd Duma, the pre-Bolshevik Soviet Executive Committee, and the socialist parties, including both Menshevik defensists and internationalists. The committee hoped both to succeed the defunct provisional government and to replace the newly formed Council of People's Commissars. Instead, it found itself acting unwittingly as a shield for an abortive anti-Bolshevik military operation.[4]

Menshevik historians, with the exception of right wingers, have had very little to say about this Committee for Salvation.[5] They have, however, attached enormous significance to the so-called Vikzhel initiative. Under the aegis of the All-Russian Executive Committee of the Railroad Union (Vikzhel), representatives of all socialist parties, including the Bolsheviks, sought to broaden the new government. As negotiations continued through the first days of November, participants' hopes rose, particularly because of the conciliatory attitude of the Bolshevik delegation, headed by Lev Kamenev and including the ex-Mensheviks David Riazanov and S. A. Lozovskii. Kamenev announced the creation of an all-socialist government, and Raphael Abramovitch informed his neighbors that the crisis was over.[6] But the Bolshevik Central Committee countermanded Kamenev's concessions. Lenin would not accept that he and Trotsky were to be excluded from government, and in any case the military danger to the new regime was subsiding. With the collapse of the Vikzhel initiative, the best opportunity for arriving at a solution that corresponded to the wishes of many socialists, including numerous Bolsheviks, disappeared.[7] Nevertheless, for some Mensheviks, such as Abramovitch, who had thrown themselves wholeheartedly into the Vikzhel negotiations, this episode retained paradigmatic significance.[8] For years to come, the Mensheviks continued to hope that under the pressure of working-class organizations, the Bolsheviks might be induced to broaden the basis of their regime by sharing power with other socialist parties.

In early 1918 a powerful grass-roots movement of opposition to the Bolsheviks emerged among industrial workers calling for an all-Russian assembly of factory representatives (*upolnomochennye:* plenipotentiaries).[9] Just as, in 1917, the Bolsheviks had managed to entrench themselves in factory committees when they were still in a minority in the soviets, so in 1918 the Mensheviks sought to establish new political footholds outside the soviets through the factory representatives. In contrast with the Vikzhel initiative, however, the factory representatives' movement was largely the initiative of the Menshevik right wing. Originating at least partly in the Printers' Union, where the future Menshevik Foreign Delegation member Mark Kefali played a leading role, this movement rapidly came to represent an alternative to participation in the soviets, now seen as corrupted by a Bolshevik monopoly of power.[10] The movement was thus looked on with suspicion by Martov and Dan. With ill grace Dan declined to speak at a meeting of factory representatives; Abramovitch accepted the invitation without asking for party permission.[11] Reservations were both principled and strategic: as a rival to the soviets, the factory representatives' movement threatened to create divisions within the working class; moreover, as prospects for Menshevik gains in the soviet elections of spring 1918 improved, Menshevik leaders concentrated on the soviet arena.[12] Consequently, when confronted with a workers' initiative corresponding to the sort of workers' "self-activity" they so often invoked, Menshevik leaders drew back because of the movement's right wing coloring and its anti-soviet stance. The factory representatives' movement was crushed in a series of mass arrests in the summer of 1918.

Between the collapse of the Vikzhel talks and the emergence of the factory representatives' movement, the All-Russian Constituent Assembly was elected, convened, and dispersed. A constituent assembly had been such a long-standing demand that one might expect the Mensheviks to have focused their hopes on this institution. In fact, their attitude to the Constituent Assembly can best be described as tepid.[13] Before the assembly met, Martov expressed doubts about whether it would be allowed to function, and of all Menshevik deputies from the Caucasus (the only region where the Mensheviks enjoyed substantial electoral support) only Tsereteli bothered to come to Petrograd for the assembly's first—and, as it turned out, last—session.[14]

The Mensheviks participated in demonstrations in January 1918 protesting the dispersal of the Constituent Assembly and called for reconvocation of the assembly for several months. At no time, however, did most Menshevik leaders display enthusiasm for this idea. Indeed, they had effectively abandoned it within weeks of the assembly's dispersal when they reentered the Central Executive Committee, the Soviet alternative to a constituent assembly.[15]

One can suggest several reasons for the Mensheviks' lukewarm attitude toward the Constituent Assembly. Given the Mensheviks' dismal electoral performance, their criticism of the Constituent Assembly elections as inherently vitiated would seem to be self-serving, as would the argument that the election results reflected only an ephemeral constellation of forces.[16] Their reservations regarding reconvocation of the Constituent Assembly, however, also rested on suspicions that this slogan was being improperly exploited by the SRs, the uncontested victors of the elections. Suspicions were confirmed when an alternative SR government in Samara, set up as a committee of the Constituent Assembly in the summer of 1918, gave way to an overtly counterrevolutionary junta.

Fundamentally, however, the Menshevik leaders kept their distance from the Constituent Assembly because they saw a clear choice between the assembly and the soviets. Choosing the assembly implied alliances to the Right, with SR representatives of the peasant petty bourgeoisie and perhaps even with remnants of the liberal bourgeoisie. Choosing the soviets meant keeping faith with the working class, even though it had been manifestly led astray by the Bolsheviks. Given such an option between general democratic and specific class values, the Mensheviks opted for the latter, overcoming misgivings and objections expressed by their own right wing. The choice may have embarrassed them, given the importance their Western sympathizers attached to the Constituent Assembly, but it dictated Menshevik policies for many years to come.[17]

This choice was facilitated by the fact that most Mensheviks, and even some Bolsheviks, believed that the new regime's days were numbered. Before the expected Bolshevik uprising in October 1917, Abramovitch had been so confident of its failure that he worried about excesses occurring in its suppression.[18] Solomon Schwarz told his future wife in November that the Bolsheviks would not hold out for two weeks; tactfully, she refrained from reminding him of his prediction when they met again several months later.[19] Amid such confidence, Dan's hint at the Party Congress in November that the present situation might continue for as long as ten or twenty years sounded unduly somber.[20] Martov may have been the only Menshevik leader who felt that the new regime could survive for long, and even he confined such views to private correspondence.[21]

If one saw the Bolshevik regime as ephemeral, the main problem was to prevent it from giving way to overtly counterrevolutionary forces, even if this meant indirectly supporting the Bolsheviks. A counterargument was already being formulated on the right wing of the party: that the Mensheviks' task was to spare social democracy from discredit, so the Mensheviks must not be put in a position where they would be obliged to share responsibility for Bolshevik crimes, especially if Bolshevik power was to be short-lived.[22] Nevertheless, the party majority rallied around those who proposed to stand behind the working class, right or wrong, rather than to embrace correct principles ignored by an erring working class. In short, even after having heard the counterarguments, the Mensheviks preferred the soviets to the Constituent Assembly.

As various attempts at countering Bolshevik power collapsed, the Menshevik Party's position at the edge of the political arena became ever more precarious. For the next three years the RSDRP operated in a twilight zone of repression and concessions, where dim boundaries between the permissible and the forbidden were continually fluctuating. Indeed, the only constant during this period was the incoherence of Bolshevik policies toward the Mensheviks. Such incoherence was caused by the Bolsheviks' uncertainty as to how to deal with a socialist opposition, as well as by the unsteadiness of Soviet power in large parts of the country. It also reflected the fact that the new government was, as often as not, simply reacting in some desperation to conditions which escaped its control.

Formally, the RSDRP remained a legal organization. Only between June and November 1918 were its few representatives—including Martov, Dan, and Abramovitch—expelled from the Central Executive Committee of Soviets; local soviets received recommendations to follow suit. In contrast with measures taken against the SRs, these recommendations were not universally applied. As a result, within weeks of his dramatic ejection from the Central Executive Committee, Martov became a member of the Moscow soviet.[23] Even earlier, the Menshevik Party had itself ordered its members to boycott the presidia of the soviets, thus partially anticipating the Bolshevik initiative.[24] Strictly speaking, the expulsion decree did not amount to a ban on the party. Indeed, at no time, then or later, was the RSDRP formally delegalized.

The Mensheviks clung to legality tenaciously, even ferociously, until 1922. As they saw it, legal status offered some protection from the worst excesses of police arbitrariness. Once arrested, Mensheviks could invoke police violation of Soviet norms to appeal to higher authorities. Often such calculations proved well founded, since they provided Bolshevik leaders with grounds for intervening on behalf of Mensheviks, whether for personal reasons or for reasons of principle. Exasperated, the Cheka instructed its agents to find suitable criminal grounds, such as speculation or neglect of professional duties.[25] A Menshevik chronicler proudly notes that no such charges could ever be pinned on a party member, though numerous Bolsheviks were being arrested for these crimes.[26] At the very least, the Mensheviks' adherence to legality won them public sympathy, even as it exposed the contradictions of Bolshevik power. Above all, the attachment to legality expressed the Mensheviks' own image of themselves as an opposition party within the Soviet system and as a continuing participant in the ongoing revolutionary process.

The policy of adhering to legality exerted a heavy toll. It imposed limitations which drastically reduced the effectiveness of the party and even forced it into a suicidal stance. Until late 1922 Mensheviks were forbidden to deny party membership in police interrogations under pain of expulsion from the party. Nor would they resist or escape arrest, leading the Cheka head to quip that "Mensheviks can be arrested by telephone."[27] Party leaders continued to speak freely on tapped phones. Party meetings were held openly and announced in advance in the Soviet press, thus multiplying the chances of being disrupted. The party insisted that members who traveled abroad do so only with valid Soviet travel documents and on the assumption that they would soon be returning to Russia. In 1921 the Moscow Menshevik leadership even requested use of the Soviet Foreign Ministry's radio to inform the West of mistreatment of Menshevik prisoners. Astonishingly, the request was granted.[28]

The Mensheviks continued to participate in soviet elections until the autumn of 1922, although under increasingly difficult conditions. In 1919 there were numerous Mensheviks in local soviets, particularly in the South, where freer conditions prevailed. In late 1920 there were still 45 Mensheviks among the 1,800 members of the Moscow soviet; there were only 18 by the summer of 1921.[29] At the Seventh Congress of Soviets in December 1919, Menshevik representatives were invited as guests with the right to speak. On this occasion Dan pledged support of Soviet power, whereas Martov indicted the regime, reflecting not any disagreement between them but rather the double-edged nature of Menshevik policy.[30] This invitation may be explained by the Bolsheviks' need to garner maximum support during the Civil War. To their own surprise, however, the Mensheviks were also invited to the Eighth Congress of Soviets in December 1920, after the Civil War had ended, where they shared the podium with Bolshevik dignitaries.[31]

Participation in the process of deliberation within the soviets did not imply self-censorship in criticizing Bolshevik policies. On the contrary, whether on ceremonial occasions or in local soviets, the Mensheviks took full advantage of the forums available. Sometimes Menshevik speakers were hissed and threatened, but they were also applauded, and occasionally the time allotted to them was prolonged at the insistence of the audience over the objections of presiding officers.[32] The Mensheviks' impact was certainly out of proportion to their paltry numbers. They provided practically the only challenge to the government, and inasmuch as many Bolsheviks felt that the soviets should be loci of debate, some soviet chairmen welcomed Menshevik participation.[33] Even those Bolsheviks who thought otherwise, including Lenin, found themselves responding involuntarily to Menshevik challenges.[34]

Although Mensheviks continued to appear on public platforms until 1921–22, the Menshevik press suffered repression very early. Within days of the Bolshevik seizure of power, Menshevik newspapers in Petrograd were being raided by bands of sailors dispatched from Bolshevik headquarters.[35] The several hundred Menshevik publications that had sprung up throughout Russia between February and October 1917 suffered a similar fate. At the same time, in a curious but not atypical manifestation of the prevailing atmosphere, Bolshevik Commissar of Internal Affairs Alexei Rykov would obligingly call up the Menshevik Central Committee to warn Mensheviks of a possible attack on their central organ, *Rabochaia Gazeta*.[36]

The Mensheviks at first proved resilient in the face of harassment, moving their printing presses and changing the banner on their newspapers to avoid detection. The cat-and-mouse game continued even when the Bolsheviks introduced censorship and other formal means of control. Indeed, the Mensheviks managed to turn to their own advantage the judicial efforts at muzzling their press. In Odessa the trial of *Iuzhnyi Rabochii* staff members, including co-editor Petr Garvi, turned into an anti-Bolshevik workers' demonstration, and in Kharkov a similar trial had to be adjourned because of workers' protests.[37] The most famous press trial in the spring of 1918 pitted Stalin against Martov on charges of the latter's having slandered Stalin's party past. Although Martov was eventually censured for disrespect toward Soviet power, Stalin's case was dismissed on the grounds that it lay outside the court's competence. The main result of the affair was to cause embarrassment to the Bolshevik leadership.[38]

In July 1918 the Bolsheviks decided to put an end to such sparring by closing down the social democratic press entirely. With the exception of a brief period in early 1919, the press was to remain permanently closed, thus depriving the party of its most effective voice. The Mensheviks did have substantial support within the Printers' Union, but because of their devotion to legality, they were reluctant to utilize such support to establish an underground press. At most they put out flyers and proclamations, largely containing the texts of party resolutions. As a result, until the launching of *Sotsialisticheskii vestnik* abroad in February 1921, the main platforms for Menshevik propaganda were meetings of the soviets, as well as trade union and other congresses.[39]

The arrival of foreign labor delegations in Russia, made possible by the end of civil war in 1920, briefly provided the Mensheviks with an international audience at home. Vis-à-vis foreign visitors, the Soviet government was rather proud of its socialist opposition. Thus, during the Second Comintern Congress it allowed the Mensheviks to meet foreign delegates and distribute materials. In May 1920 it invited the Menshevik Central Committee to attend a gala welcome for a British delegation, where Raphael Abramovitch took the floor. The delegation also attended a meeting of the Printers' Union which ended in an uproar when SR leader Viktor Chernov emerged out of hiding in disguise, addressed the several thousand people present, and disappeared before Cheka agents in the hall could lay hands on him.[40] Bolshevik retribution was swift and lasting. This was, indeed, in the words of a Menshevik commentator, "the last big oppositional meeting in the history of the Revolution."[41]

Within the Party

In January 1920 Martov could tell Kautsky that the Menshevik Party was not being persecuted and that, in a sense, it was even tolerated. As its sphere of activity shrank, however, the party turned inward. It evolved toward what it had been in the past and what it was to become again in exile: a network of circles, or *kruzhki,* consisting of dedicated activists who met in party clubs. As Martov lamented, the party was becoming "a propaganda society."[1]

Even in its weakened state the Menshevik Party was still capable of inspiring concern in the Bolshevik leadership. The Cheka complained that although there was nothing to prevent the party from functioning entirely legally, the Mensheviks were cultivating an ambiguous half-legal situation. They were spreading malicious proclamations and successfully exploiting the difficult economic situation.[2] Lenin denounced the Mensheviks repeatedly as the main danger, and Trotsky was particularly prompt to describe all opposition as "menshevism."[3] Such attacks did not preclude overtures to individual Mensheviks: Fedor Dan was approached to become deputy chairman of the Supreme National Economic Council, and rumors proliferated concerning Martov's candidacy for the position of foreign commissar.[4]

Pressure on the Menshevik Party took its toll. At the end of 1917 Menshevik local committees could invite workers to lodge their complaints, and they could intervene on their behalf before Soviet institutions.[5] In the spring of 1918 the Mensheviks could hope that their successes in local soviet elections would put a dent in the Bolshevik monopoly of power.[6] By mid-1918, however, there was a glaring gap between the party's self-defined role as defender of working-class interests and its capacities, a gap as fatal as that between Menshevik policies and mass aspirations in 1917.

The situation led to deep discouragement among all but the strongest activists. Menshevik party membership fell from 200,000 at the Unification Congress in August 1917 to 120,000 at the Extraordinary Congress in December, to something between 60,000 and 90,000 in May 1918, and plummeted further thereafter.[7] Rank-and-file members left because of disenchantment or Bolshevik pressure or a change of heart. Some Menshevik leaders also left the party, and one might well inquire why they changed allegiance whereas others, including members of our group, elected to suffer a life of imprisonment and exile on account of their party membership.

Some Menshevik leaders left because of policy or philosophical disagreements with the party.[8] Others defected in response to psychological needs: they could not bear to stand in opposition to a regime that defended Russian national interests and that proclaimed itself proletarian. Some Mensheviks, including Andrei Vyshinskii, later notorious as prosecutor in the 1930s Moscow trials, joined the ruling party on the premise that change could only be effected from within.[9] Almost invariably, however, there was a strong element of personal ambition. In the cases of Osip Ermanskii and Aleksandr Martynov this may have been the only element. Even among others, substantial career rewards enjoyed by former Mensheviks overcame lingering scruples.[10] As the following examples demonstrate, right wing Mensheviks were as likely to join the Bolsheviks as left wingers.

Both personal ambition and policy disagreements drove Ivan Maiskii, a right wing member of the Menshevik Central Committee, to abandon the party. In the summer of 1918 he accepted a ministerial post in an SR-sponsored government in Samara, initially maintaining that this was compatible with his Menshevik Party status. The Samara government had been set up under the slogan of reconvening the Constituent Assembly, at a time when this goal was still formally endorsed by the Mensheviks. Maiskii argued that since Mensheviks viewed the Revolution as a democratic one, they should continue to support its democratic institutions, and the stronger the Menshevik role in the anti-Bolshevik camp, the better the chances that an overthrow of the Bolsheviks would lead to a democratic outcome. Maiskii also claimed that party resolutions did not forbid participation in territorial governments but, rather, left the matter to be decided by the regional party, which in this case had approved his decision. None of these arguments convinced Martov, although they did win Maiskii sympathy on the right flank of the Menshevik Party.[11] Maiskii was thus duly read out of the RSDRP, and the party's suspicions appeared confirmed when the Samara government was easily overthrown in a right wing military coup. Ironically, though the Menshevik charge against him was that of rightist deviation, Maiskii soon found his way into the Communist Party and made a brilliant career as a Soviet ambassador.[12]

Another right wing member of the Menshevik Central Committee, Aleksandr Troianovskii, also made a complete turnabout by going over to the Bolsheviks in 1921. Troianovskii confused the issue by pretending to leave for "left" reasons and then confidentially telling his Menshevik comrades that he was concealing the true grounds for his conversion out of "conspiratorial considerations." This was not Troianovskii's first change of heart; he had the curious distinction of having served on both the Bolshevik and Menshevik Central Committees. In Troianovskii's case, as in Maiskii's, personal ambitions proved a powerful stimulus. After leaving the Mensheviks, Troianovskii first tried to win leadership of the nonparty deputies' bloc in the Moscow soviet but failed because of the deputies' unwillingness to follow an individual with such a checkered past.[13] He fared better later as vice president of Gosplan, and ambassador to Japan and to the United States. An additional factor in Troianovskii's conversion was his strong Russian nationalism. When another Menshevik, Anatolii Dubois, met his old friend Troianovskii in Paris in the 1930s on the latter's way to Washington, Dubois asked him point-blank whether he now thought there was socialism in Soviet Russia. "It's not a question of socialism at all," answered the ambassador, implying that Russian national interests were foremost in his mind, and perhaps in that of the Soviet leadership.[14]

Lev Khinchuk, a prominent Menshevik defensist at the Second Congress of Soviets, found that he "could not sit with arms folded while a proletarian revolution was going on." Khinchuk left the Mensheviks abruptly and, to their utter astonishment, published a statement affirming that he had long been disappointed with menshevism. He was rewarded with the chairmanship of the Central Union of Cooperatives and later with the posts of commissar for commerce and ambassador to Germany. When Khinchuk ran into Menshevik Foreign Delegation member Boris Dvinov in Berlin, he tried to persuade Dvinov to join the embassy staff as a trade representative. Khinchuk's argument was hardly lofty: "Formerly, I traveled abroad with a false passport and feared any gendarme; now gendarmes stand at attention before me."[15]

Defections of longtime comrades weakened the Menshevik Party further and wounded Martov personally.[16] The Bolsheviks exploited such defections by publishing testimonials of former Mensheviks and by organizing a movement of *byvshie,* or former Mensheviks, headed by Martynov, with its own publications and congresses. One such testimonial typically argued that the Mensheviks were generals without an army and prophets of doom, waiting for the "inevitable crash" and busying themselves with criticism as workers went about the task of building communism.[17]

The Menshevik Party responded by denouncing all these "renegades, deserters, ordinary traitors, careerists."[18] Martynov was described as a "Bolshevik midwife for receiving the redeemed souls of repentant Mensheviks."[19] Martov attacked another defector, Iurii Larin, as a "contemptible adventurer." As *Sotsialisticheskii vestnik* put it, "There have been worse times but there have been none as foul."[20] Nevertheless, many ex-Mensheviks maintained personal relations with their former comrades even when the latter had gone into exile; Ermanskii was even offended that the Menshevik Party refused his offer to act as a courier.[21] In the 1920s former Mensheviks were to become a leading source of information for *Sotsialisticheskii vestnik*. Interestingly, they seem to have survived Stalin's purges more easily than Old Bolsheviks.

Those Mensheviks who remained witnessed an unprecedented process of *Gleichschaltung* (homogenization) within the Menshevik party itself. As policies aimed at coming to terms with the new regime failed, proponents of such policies gained the upper hand. In part this occurred because opponents of accommodation, first Plekhanovites and then Potresovites, were leaving the party organization in protest. Above all, the uniformization of party policy occurred because, after having gained ascendancy at the November 1917 Party Congress, Martov, now seconded by new allies such as Dan, pushed his advantage to the utmost. Mensheviks who disregarded party policy "put themselves outside the party."[22] This was the fate of rightist deviationists such as Martov's brother Vladimir Levitskii, who participated in an anti-Bolshevik uprising in Iaroslav in 1918, and of less serious offenders. Iurii Denike has spoken of a purge and of a police regime in the party, and in 1920 the Central Committee undertook a reregistration of party members, never fully carried out, to exclude automatically those party members who disagreed with the controversial new party platform.[23] Petr Garvi had ample grounds to complain that "the organizational bolshevization of the party took place under war communism."[24]

Martov's insistence on strict party discipline is surprising in view of his antiauthoritarian reputation and of his own, very recent invocation of the right to dissent when his own group had been a minority. Perhaps this insistence was a reassertion of underlying Iskrite instincts. It may have been simply an act of self-preservation dictated by the fact that, as Martov himself admitted, Menshevik supporters were more rightist than the party—that is, more than the party leadership.[25] Party discipline was thus a substitute for party democracy.

The Mensheviks were also reacting to two very different organizational models displayed by kindred parties. The SRs, factious and unruly, split into increasingly incompatible wings, confirming the Bolshevik view of "petty bourgeois" parties as vacillating and undisciplined. The Bolsheviks, by contrast, after having experienced their share of splits, were reinforcing party discipline and acquiring internal coherence, however distasteful its nature. Martov opted for the Bolshevik organizational model just as he had earlier opted to seek rapprochement politically with the Bolsheviks rather than with the SRs. Although the new party discipline was a cause of resentment, it was also to be a source of strength under increasingly difficult conditions of semilegality, clandestine work, and exile.

As the party's main activity consisted of "trying through resolutions and declarations to give its appraisal of current events," it is in party documents that one can trace the growing imprint of Martov's views.[26] A Menshevik Central Committee resolution of November 1917 compared Bolshevik power to the worst days of tsarism, even though there had not yet been any terror directed at the Mensheviks.[27] A year later, however, a party conference declared that the present (disastrous) situation resulted from Bolshevik policies *and* from the equally ruinous policies of petty bourgeois democrats who were fostering counterrevolution. In April 1920 a party conference rejected "abstract" democracy, recognized the inevitability of a temporary dictatorship, and affirmed that preconditions for a worldwide social revolution inaugurating socialism had been created.[28] The leftward drift of these party documents is unmistakable.

The underlying vision of the Bolshevik regime in these Menshevik Party documents is fluid. Its policies are described as "maximalist," a designation coinciding linguistically with "Bolshevik" and implying out-and-out radicalism.[29] Most frequently these policies are condemned as "utopian," a negative term in Marxist parlance suggesting ignorance of historical laws but not necessarily disagreement on ultimate goals. The class nature of the Bolshevik regime emerges as petty bourgeois or, better still, plebeian. Historical references are borrowed to describe the ethos of the regime: praetorian, caesarist, bonapartist.[30] A curious but perhaps not necessarily self-contradictory description is that of the regime as both "anarchic" and "bureaucratic."[31] Significantly, most of the terms later applied to the Soviet Union are already present in the immediate aftermath of the Revolution. Then as later, Menshevik analysis shows a willingness to experiment with a wide variety of concepts to characterize the Soviet phenomenon.

Martov did not impose one interpretation of the Bolshevik regime on his party (although he did impose one strategy), but his views were highly influential. In an oft-cited assessment, Martov denounced Bolshevik efforts as senselessly utopian. Above all, he expressed disgust at the coarseness of Soviet "socialism," which brought out the foulest *meshchanstvo*, or petty bourgeoisie, with its specifically Russian vices of *nekul'turnost'*, base careerism, venality, parasitism, dissipation, and irresponsibility. The resultant discrediting of the very idea of socialism could only lead, via anarchy, to some sort of "caesarism."[32]

In early 1919 Martov wrote a series of articles, later published as *World Bolshevism*. Tracing the origins of the "Bolshevik mentality," Martov defined "world bolshevism" as a movement of soldier masses composed of déclassé and uprooted elements. The soldiery was characterized by its antiparliamentarianism, its ignorance of the laws of social production, its destructive and essentially parasitic "consumer communism," its maximalism or naive social optimism, and its tendency to resolve all political issues by armed force. Such an outlook existed, he wrote, in all countries which had experienced the war; only in Russia had its representatives succeeded in seizing and holding power. Here, bolshevism as an "ideology of contempt for spiritual and material culture," engendered by bourgeois militarism and born of the working classes' disillusion with prewar socialist organization, had reached its apogee.

Martov devoted much of his *World Bolshevism* to debunking the idea that the soviets represented a higher, much less an ultimate, form of democracy. In fact, soviet democracy was but a new variant of jacobinism, the power of a revolutionary minority defending the interests of a majority which had not recognized the regime as its own. Martov was prepared to make some allowances for soviet democracy. The fact that it limited suffrage did not automatically make it nondemocratic; even so-called universal suffrage excluded certain groups, such as women and youth. Elsewhere Martov condoned even more explicitly the principle of a revolutionary dictatorship as a necessary phase of the revolution. He described Soviet dictatorship as a "surgeon's knife with which history, with profuse expenditure of blood and energy, has extracted our present bourgeois society," albeit under the socialist banner.[33] The road to socialism lay through democracy, but stages had to be traversed, and dictatorship was one such stage.[34] The fundamental question was whether dictatorship was to be permanent or transitory; the fundamental defect of the Bolshevik regime was that it had abandoned democracy even *within* the limits of the Soviet system.

Martov's most celebrated and most influential pronouncement on the nature of the Bolshevik regime took place abroad in October 1920. Here Martov dwelt on the "sickness" of the Russian Revolution. Its symptoms were militarism and, above all, terror; its causes lay in the "utopian and religious folly" unleashed among backward masses by self-proclaimed Marxists who were, in fact, followers of that destructive genius Bakunin. This emotionally charged analysis fired even the imagination of those who did not share Martov's Marxist premises. His speech eventually found its way into the U.S. *Congressional Record.*[35]

Although Martov did not seek to impose his view of bolshevism on his party, he did insist on adherence to the policy implications of his view. It was these policy guidelines and the reasoning behind them that became known as the "Martov Line." The fundamental injunction consisted of avoiding participation in any attempts to overthrow the Bolshevik regime by force. As Martov stressed, this was based not on "the sentimental idea that revolt against a government made up of socialists or revolutionaries is inacceptable" but on two well-argued considerations.[36]

First, the Bolsheviks were supported by a significant minority (or, in another formulation, by significant strata) of the working class and exerted effective influence among the broad proletarian masses. Although working-class support for the Bolsheviks was proof of utopianism or immaturity, the RSDRP as "flesh of the flesh and bone of the bone of the proletariat" could not break faith even with an erring proletariat by joining its enemies. Nor could the party initiate a civil war within the proletariat by pitting Menshevik against Bolshevik workers, however "criminal and self-destructive" Bolshevik policies happened to be.[37]

Second, although the Bolshevik regime was distasteful in almost every way, in the present circumstances the foreseeable alternatives could only be worse. In part this was the fault of the Bolsheviks themselves. By discrediting the idea of socialism, they were pushing broad strata of the population into the arms of counterrevolution. By destroying the country's productive forces, they were weakening the working class, strengthening the peasantry and new petty bourgeoisie, and thus preparing a colossal historical defeat for the proletariat. Since the choice lay between bolshevism and counterrevolution, the Mensheviks should not be afraid to say that they opposed the "democracy" (in quotations) of the anti-Bolsheviks and they supported the tyranny (without quotations) of Lenin and Trotsky.[38]

Martov's position was thus based on the premise, contested by right wing Mensheviks, that the Bolsheviks enjoyed at least some proletarian support as well as on the unprovable premise that any regime that replaced the Bolsheviks by force would be worse than the present one. The logical consequence of Martov's position was for the Mensheviks to try to act as a "loyal opposition" within the Soviet system. The frustration of displaying loyalty to a regime under which one was suffering persecution may explain Martov's emphasis on the inevitability and historical role of the "Bolshevik phase of the Revolution." According to him, history had assigned to a proletarian party, that is, the Bolsheviks, the task of carrying out an eighteenth-century revolution of the peasant petty bourgeoisie. In realizing this task, the Bolsheviks entered into conflict with their own aim of expressing the class interests of the proletariat. On an optimistic note, however, Martov concluded that the vast and costly contradictions into which the Bolsheviks had driven the Russian Revolution were surmountable, and the Mensheviks' mission was precisely to point a way out of the impasse and to prod the Bolsheviks in that direction.[39]

The Martov Line was the guiding tenet of the Menshevik Party for over twenty years. In spite of objections from the Menshevik Right and growing reservations within the Menshevik majority, it remained the cornerstone of party policy, in Berlin and in Paris exile, throughout the years of NEP, Stalin's revolution, and the purges of the 1930s. The split within the Menshevik Foreign Delegation in 1940 occurred over the Martov Line, which Dan continued to defend and most other former Martovites by then rejected. Given the aura surrounding Martov, it is not surprising that those who rejected the Martov Line should seek to show that in his last days Martov himself became disillusioned with it.

The first effort to disassociate Martov from the Martov Line was undertaken by the extraparty right wing Menshevik Stepan Ivanovich soon after Martov's death in 1923.[40] Subsequent efforts from the center of the party came only in the 1950s, when David Dallin drew a portrait of Martov in his last days as a man who had lost hope. As Dallin writes, it was not acceptable in their milieu to talk of one's doubts, so all the Mensheviks were troubled when a newcomer from Moscow remarked, "Who knows, perhaps it was all in vain, perhaps it is time for another life of drinking Tokay wine and kissing beautiful women." For party leaders, continues Dallin, there was no way out, even if they had already lost faith in the triumph of their cause. Martov continued to write; he waited avidly for news from Russia; he remained a lively debating partner; but sometimes he would fall inexplicably silent.[41]

Dallin's reminiscences were reinforced by party historian Boris Nicolaevsky, who dates the beginning of Martov's reorientation to the Polish-Soviet War of 1920, which "revealed to Martov new characteristics of bolshevism that called for significantly changing the behavior of the party."[42] Nicolaevsky also suggested that the notoriously leftist April theses of 1920, the most radical formulation of the Martov Line ever adopted as a party platform, had been amended in a leftist direction by some Kharkovite Mensheviks against Martov's will.[43] Dallin's and Nicolaevsky's campaign to disassociate Martov from the Martov Line came to fruition in the work of Martov's biographer. According to Israel Getzler, Martov's struggle to "straighten out" the Revolution "ended only in 1922, when Martov at last [!] began to write off the Bolshevik régime as a Bolshevik perversion of the revolution."[44]

Notwithstanding the personal and scholarly qualifications of its advocates, the claim that Martov changed his opinion radically in his last days remains problematic. For example, the article that Getzler cites to prove his point contains supporting elements but also considerable evidence in favor of the contrary position. Martov does admit here that recent changes—the end of civil war, the waning of revolutionary prospects in the West, the introduction of NEP—make it imperative to revise the Menshevik economic program of 1919 and the political theses adopted in April 1920. He acknowledges that, economically, the scope for nationalization of Russian industry is far smaller than the Mensheviks previously supposed. Politically, the obligation—"which tied our hands so strongly"—to support Soviet power in the face of external danger ceases to be a main plank of Menshevik policy, and it is now possible to strive directly for the establishment of a democratic republic.[45]

At the same time, Martov reminds his readers that the Mensheviks never believed in the imminence of a socialist transformation in Russia. Acknowledging that Russia's reconstruction would have to take place along basically capitalist lines does not therefore negate earlier expectations. Politically, the Bolshevik party is "still far from having lost its roots in the Russian working class," even if its ties to this class are weakening. Above all, the strategic injunction which flows from the Martov Line stays constant: the Menshevik party remains unconditionally hostile to the slogan of a revolutionary overthrow of Soviet power, and the party's main goal has to remain that of preventing the transformation of the Red dictatorship into a bonapartist one.

The continuity in Martov's views was confirmed by his very last articles. In a biting polemic against Stepan Ivanovich, Martov lambasts those socialists who entertained "democratic illusions" about the adequacy of democratic institutions without independent proletarian ones and who placed their trust in a peaceful passage from bourgeois democracy to socialism.[46] It is clear that Martov was not making any concessions to "liberal socialism" or offering any overtures to the Right. Martov's last article was a reply to those right wing Mensheviks who saw his call for revision of the party platform as an acknowledgment of earlier mistakes and as an acceptance of some rightist theses. Martov denied his critics' claim that the party's leftist orientation had been predicated on the expectation of revolution in the West. He defended the fact that during the Civil War the Mensheviks had called for equal rights for all socialist parties but not for bourgeois parties. He stood by his earlier commitment to *trudovlastie*, the principle of "toilers' democracy," which meant the disenfranchisement of some formerly privileged groups, as exemplified in the Soviet system. Martov again denied that such limitations represented a negation of democracy (France denied women the vote yet was considered a democracy). Bolshevik claims that the Soviet system was a higher form of democracy were spurious, Martov concluded, but that did not mean the Soviet system was undemocratic.[47]

One may argue that after Martov's death his followers, and Fedor Dan in particular, simplified and schematized the Martov Line beyond recognition. One may also speculate that if Martov had lived to see Stalinism, he would have disowned the Martov Line. The fact remains that, however discouraged Martov may have been by the evolution of the Bolshevik regime, he never repudiated the strategy that bore his name. One must therefore inquire into the reasons, psychological and other, that lead commentators to ascribe to Martov a change of heart which never took place.

David Dallin would seem to be transferring his own doubts about the Martov Line to the person of Martov. Already in 1918–1920 Dallin demurred from the party majority by insisting more firmly than others on the slogan "back to capitalism." In 1921 and again in 1922 Dallin collided head-on with Martov by suggesting that capitalism had recovered its long-term equilibrium and that the period of postwar social revolution was therefore definitely over.[48] Such pessimism led Dallin in the 1930s to leave the Menshevik Foreign Delegation precisely out of the sort of discouragement he attributed to Martov. It is impossible to verify the feelings Dallin imputes to Martov, but there is no doubt they were Dallin's own.[49]

In the case of other commentators on Martov's last days, the impulse for their argument would seem to be the conviction that Martov can be portrayed as a liberal democrat with whom an enlightened, non-Marxist Western opinion could sympathize. Nicolaevsky's contribution here is unconvincing since his argument rests on Martov's purported discovery of Bolshevik militarism and aggressiveness in 1920; as we have seen, Martov had already identified these qualities in 1919 as essential characteristics of bolshevism without revising his views. Getzler's case is more solidly grounded, but it too leads to reinforcement of a schematic view whereby Martov and the Mensheviks appear as the polar opposites of Lenin and the Bolsheviks.[50]

The mainsprings of Martov's and the Mensheviks' attitude to Bolshevik power are brought vividly into view in their reaction to the Kronstadt sailors' uprising of March 1921.[51] This event proved to be a milestone in the history of the Russian Revolution, not because it led to NEP, as is sometimes claimed, but because Kronstadt marked the first time that elements loyal to the Revolution rose up against it.[52] Kronstadt marked a milestone for the Mensheviks, too, because it was the defeat of this uprising, more than any other single event, that convinced them of the durability of Soviet power. Moreover, Kronstadt confirmed Lenin's will to initiate unprecedented repression against the Menshevik Party, thus effectively obliterating the vestiges of its public existence.

The Mensheviks' initial attitude toward the Kronstadt Uprising was very circumspect. In Moscow their Central Committee condemned it. According to one account this was because depletion of the Central Committee allowed one member, Aaron Iugov, the overly zealous and sometimes slavishly loyal left wing follower of Martov and Dan, to impose his own projection of his leaders' views.[53] The Petrograd Menshevik Committee, by contrast, put out a resolution condemning only the bloodshed and calling for negotiations between the government and the rebels.[54] Abroad, Dallin, writing for a foreign audience, described the events as a classically spontaneous revolt launched in favor of free soviets rather than against the Soviet system. Dallin, however, saw a danger in the fact that the revolt was led by a general (a claim which later proved untrue) rather than by a political party; it was "possible, even probable," he feared, "that bonapartism would grow out of this."[55] An even greater danger lay in the possibility that the uprising would lead to foreign intervention.

Sotsialisticheskii vestnik's initial reaction appeared under the heading "A Terrible Warning." The editorial reiterated Menshevik rejection of armed struggle against the Bolsheviks, not for reasons of abstract principle but because such struggle would inevitably turn into fratricidal war within the working class. Although it absolved the Kronstadt rebels of charges that they were counterrevolutionary, *Vestnik* did not put much hope in the success of their enterprise. It predicted that Kronstadt was but a foretaste of what was to come if the Bolsheviks failed to carry out the reforms that the Mensheviks had long been urging: an end to terrorist dictatorship, abandonment of utopian economic policies, and accord with other socialist parties.[56]

Fedor Dan seems to have been even more skeptical about the prospects for the Kronstadt Uprising.[57] He emphasized the enormous difference between the mass movements of early 1917 and the workers' disturbances in Petrograd which immediately preceded the Kronstadt events. In 1921 the working masses were disorganized and exhausted by four years of suffering and deprivation. They had lost faith in their own struggle and had no clear political goals. In the absence of a strong party organization, they could easily be bought off by the regime through the immediate satisfaction of material demands. There was no possiblity of creating the powerful mass pressure which alone could have widened the uprising to bring about positive changes.

Martov's comments on the Kronstadt Uprising appear more favorable than Dan's or Dallin's. Two months after the crushing of the uprising he summarized its significance: the masses that formerly supported the regime had now revolted; even though the Mensheviks had no influence among the rebels, the slogans they invoked were Menshevik ones; finally, the rebels had refused to use terror even against a terrorist regime. The uprising's defeat, Martov concluded, was due to the fact that it had been forced into taking an armed form, but defeat did not diminish its historical significance. One might suggest, however, that Martov's assessement was an obituary to a lost cause. In this respect his attitude toward the Kronstadt Uprising was peculiarly reminiscent of Marx's attitude toward the 1871 Paris Commune (which Martov compared to Kronstadt). For both Marx and Martov a popular social movement, such as the Commune or Kronstadt, provoked reservations while it was occurring because of its spontaneous nature and the weakness of Marxist elements within it. Only in defeat did these movements win praise before passing into glorious legend.[58]

Personal Itineraries

For our Mensheviks, the years spent in Russia under Soviet power represent a kaleidoscope of experiences. In spite of the party's formal legality, they confirm the Russian proverb, "There is no escaping prison and misery." Even in persecution, however, the Mensheviks enjoyed a curiously privileged position. Not only was repression against them tardy, but it was attenuated by their own courage and the forbearance of the authorities. Their experiences thus give a sense both of the ordeals of the socialist opposition and of the ambiguity of Soviet attitudes toward it.

In a sense, Martov was invulnerable. Few other figures shared his standing as a Marxist theoretician and a founder of the Russian workers' movement. Lenin's personal feelings for Martov were known to all and shared by many. Martov himself felt no compunction to reciprocate such feelings. He avoided referring to Lenin as "comrade" and, when asked to write an article in *Izvestiia* for Lenin's fiftieth birthday recalling their early common struggle, replied that the only article which interested him was Lenin's obituary. Nevertheless, Martov remained at liberty, only occasionally confined to house arrest. Moreover, he was appointed an academician, which assured him better food rations than for anyone else. When Martov petitioned to leave Russia in the summer of 1920 with the avowed intention of arguing against the Comintern in western Europe, his request was granted, at Lenin's insistence.[1]

Other Mensheviks found themselves in and out of prison. When at liberty, they served the Soviet government conscientiously. In 1919, after three months in Butyrki prison, Fedor Dan was mobilized into the Commissariat of Health as head of the section of surgical supply procurement. For almost a year he coaxed and bribed state institutions and the few remaining private firms to obtain materials. His main problem was warding off Cheka crackdowns on hoarding and speculation, which, if successful, would have cut off the trickle of medical supplies entirely.[2]

The strain of Dan's work and the anomaly of his position explain his sudden decision to resign. A chance newspaper item accusing Mensheviks of poisoning wells stung him to the core, perhaps because the article contrasted Mensheviks with patriotic tsarist generals, perhaps because it echoed ritual antisemitic accusations. Dan insisted on a transfer to ordinary medical service, in spite of entreaties from superiors who dismissed the accusations as Chekist rubbish.[3]

Dan's first assignment, to Ekaterinburg, was boring and depressing. Absence of reading material "made even *Pravda* and *Izvestiia* seem attractive." Police surveillance and occasional arrests, combined with the apathy of local workers, stifled virtually all party activity. Dan requested transfer to the front and was reassigned to Minsk. Here he ascertained that the outlook of the Red Army officer corps had not changed from tsarist times. He also explained to his own satisfaction the enthusiasm of local workers for communism.[4]

After months of lobbying by both the Commissariat of Health and the Menshevik Central Committee, Dan received permission to return to Petrograd, rather than to Moscow, where the Cheka warned the commissar of health that Dan would be arrested immediately. Dan's native city, which he continued to call Petersburg, impressed him as a marble tomb. Not a single shop was open, but in the shadow of magnificent buildings dusty wares were being sold, even as the Bolsheviks tore down market installations.[5] In this city of the dead, Dan obtained a sinecure as a medical doctor in a sports club. He was arrested again during the workers' disturbances that preceded the Kronstadt Uprising in February 1921.

Some Mensheviks enjoyed more interesting careers. After three months in prison in early 1918, Iurii Denike found work in the Commissariat of Enlightenment. He suffered material deprivation, even losing his nails and half his teeth during the cold, hungry winter of 1918–19. As a right winger he was ostracized and finally eased out of the Menshevik Party, although he insisted on declaring himself a Menshevik (even on official questionnaires).[6]

Eventually Denike's situation improved. He was elected to a teaching position at Moscow University, and was appointed to head a section of the Socialist Academy. Here, Denike shared an office with Bukharin, and apparently
the two became the fastest of friends, with Bukharin recounting to his of-
ficemate details of daily lunches with Lenin.[7]

Boris Dvinov, too, looked back to the early 1920s in Russia as happy days.
As one of the longest-surviving and most vocal Menshevik deputies to the
Moscow soviet, he relished the "David and Goliath" nature of his mandate.
Whenever possible Dvinov would enliven the proceedings of the soviet with
public revelations of Bolshevik iniquities.[8] He invested his remaining considerable energy in the Union of Cooperatives (to whose board he was nomi-
nated by the Bolshevik-controlled soviet), in service to his soviet constituency, the Union of Shop Clerks, and in Menshevik Party work. At length,
Dvinov emerged as principal liaison between the party at home and in exile,
as well as chief distributor of *Sotsialisticheskii vestnik* in Russia.

Other Mensheviks managed as best they could. Mark Kefali, head of the
Moscow Printers' Union, had to flee to Siberia to escape the repression that
followed the dramatic Printers' Union meeting attended by the British labor
delegation in May 1920. Even his close ties with Soviet trade union chief
Mikhail Tomskii could not save him.[9] By constrast, Aaron Iugov, secretary
of the Menshevik Central Committee, held on until 1922 to the chairmanship of Mosselprom, a prestigious official organization created to foster trade
between city and countryside. He even appointed another Menshevik, Samuel Estrine, to head Mosselprom's economic division.[10] Iugov's wife, Olga
Domanevskaia, after April 1921 no longer a Menshevik Party member, edited the journal of the National Economic Council, where Vera Alexandrova
was an editorial assistant. Alexandrova's husband, Solomon Schwarz, held
various jobs: after having been one of the organizers of the civil servants'
strike in Petrograd just after the October Revolution, he worked in the Moscow sick funds administration, was mobilized into the Red Army, acted as
a Red Cross administrator, and, at the moment of his arrest in February 1921,
was employed in the legal section of the Revolutionary-Military Soviet.[11]
Other Mensheviks found a niche on the staffs of trade unions—primarily
the unions of chemists, printers, or functionaries—or in politically untainted
institutions. Much as prerevolutionary *intelligents* had flocked to *zemstvo* social organizations, Mensheviks now sought out cooperatives, voluntary organizations, or welfare offices. Lidia Dan, for example, worked in the Political
Red Cross and then in the Soviet for the Protection of Children. In addition,
until the end of the Civil War in 1920, able-bodied male Mensheviks were
mobilized into the Red Army, with the participation of Menshevik-staffed
induction commissions.

The Mensheviks thus tried to lead normal lives in abnormal times. This undertaking was facilitated by their defiant, sometimes even brazen, attitude. For instance, when Boris Dvinov was disqualified from membership in the Moscow soviet by its mandate commission in the summer of 1921, he simply refused to give up his identity card and kept attending soviet meetings. Moreover, he would bring copies of *Sotsialisticheskii vestnik*, provoking the rage of the chairman.[12] The veteran Menshevik Isaak Iudin used the reading room of the Socialist Academy for impromptu conferences with other Mensheviks, leading an official to complain to Denike: "Iudin has created a Menshevik *iavka* [a conspiratorial meeting place] here. I can't make remarks to someone like [Iudin], but please talk to him in a comradely fashion."[13]

Mensheviks could function fairly freely also as a result of Cheka inefficiency. Cheka lists of Menshevik Party members and addresses were usually out of date.[14] It was not difficult to hide one's identity, either. Denike, for example, took a false Jewish identity, counting on the assumption that no one who falsified his identity would choose a Jewish one. When, at the suggestion of his office superior, Denike sought to recover his true identity, the police proved very cooperative, since they assumed he had obtained his false papers under the tsarist regime. The Cheka also lacked perseverance. It was sometimes enough to lie low for several weeks until the Cheka turned to other victims. Some Mensheviks were able to work and move about for months while a warrant was out for their arrest.[15]

Above all, the Mensheviks benefited from the protection extended by high Bolshevik officials and from the rivalry between state or party institutions and the Cheka. Dan claimed there was not one mass arrest of party members in Moscow about which he and Martov had not been warned in advance by anonymous well-wishers. Sometimes this protection came only at the eleventh hour. Raphael Abramovitch escaped the firing squad by a hair in 1918 during the terror that followed the assassination of Cheka official Mosei Uritskii.[16] The Bolshevik leadership was evenly divided between those favoring execution, such as Trotsky and Stalin, and those opposed, including Lunacharskii and Lenin's wife, Nadezhda Krupskaia. In this as in similar cases, David Riazanov lobbied energetically on behalf of former Menshevik comrades. During the Kronstadt Uprising, Dan found himself in a similarly perilous position in Petrograd's Petropavlovsk fortress. Friends in Moscow lobbied furiously with no assurance that even a phone call from Lenin could avert tragedy. In this case it was Gorky's and Lunacharskii's intervention that proved decisive.[17] Even Cheka head Feliks Dzerzhinskii was known to have visited imprisoned socialists to assure them that a decree categorizing them as hostages had not been intended seriously.[18]

Sooner or later all our Mensheviks (with the exception of Martov) were subjected to imprisonment. The certainty of arrest was mitigated by an expectation of more or less prompt release. At a meeting of the Moscow Social Democratic Club in February 1921, over 150 Mensheviks came *zaarestovat'-siia* (to get arrested). One latecomer even entered after having seen the Cheka surround the building. When the arrest order was read out, some Mensheviks began to sing the "Internationale"—and demanded that the Chekists take off their hats, which they did unwillingly. As some went on singing, other Mensheviks frantically destroyed documents; one comrade swallowed a newly written proclamation. Two-thirds of the group had already been arrested at least once under the Bolsheviks, and two-thirds had known arrest under the tsarist regime. The next day the Cheka offered to release the workers in the group, as well as members of the Menshevik Central Committee. They refused to be set free unless all their other comrades were released as well.[19]

The Mensheviks displayed the same defiant attitude inside prison.[20] Grigorii Bienstock amused himself by trying to persuade a Cheka officer that the latter was, in fact, completely dependent on his prisoner: "If it were not for us," Bienstock teased him, "you would not be here."[21] Dan delighted in recounting examples of Cheka stupidity, such as his interrogator's suspicion that Dan's real name was "Menshikov," or petty venality, for instance, how members of the Cheka tribunal would buy and sell among themselves the cigarettes they had just confiscated on grounds of "speculation."[22]

The Mensheviks felt sheltered even in prison. Dzerzhinskii was personally sympathetic to socialist prisoners, and declared that "their conditions of detention should not bear a punitive character."[23] He intervened to improve prison conditions for Martov's brother Vladimir Levitskii, accused of taking up arms against the Soviet regime. Even Dzerzhinskii's rigid successor, Iosif Unshlikht, who imposed much harsher conditions, sent his personal car to take Dan home on his release from prison.[24] The lower Cheka echelons also treated Menshevik prisoners deferentially, whether out of earlier comradely ties or a bad conscience. Denike claims that a guard hanged himself upon realizing that they had been in the same Bolshevik Party organization in 1905.[25]

Prison life for the Mensheviks in the first years of Soviet power was light years away from the grim prison realities that later reigned. Denike claims that one ate better in prison than outside, thanks to food packages, and guards bent prison regulations to allow Dan to enjoy unlimited electricity.[26] There were prison choirs and theaters, historical lectures, and a "living newspaper." Someone quipped that Nicolaevsky was publishing the proceedings of the "Butyrki [prison] Academy."[27] Indeed, prisoners did write pamphlets for distribution outside as well as declarations signed by imprisoned soviet members for transmission to their soviet through the good offices of the prison director. Prisoners regularly received books, newspapers, including foreign ones, and even *Sotsialisticheskii vestnik*.[28]

Prisoners were grouped according to political factions. Each group had its food commune, elected its "elders," and, generally speaking, ran its own affairs; cells were left open, and guards were told to go away when they intruded on a Menshevik meeting.[29] The Bolshevik faction was the most privileged. It enjoyed control over the prison grand piano and received visits from regime dignitaries. The high position of Mensheviks in this curious pecking order is confirmed by the fact that when the Communists expelled one of their number, he was accepted, with some distaste, in the Menshevik corridor.[30]

Mensheviks are not being entirely ironic when they speak of their "prison privileges" and "well-being" or even of their "prison paradise."[31] They emphasize, however, that such advantages were maintained through constant pressure on the authorities, including hunger strikes. Over time these acquired self-destructive momentum and lost their effectiveness. Indeed, the Mensheviks' "happy days" in prison were numbered. The heaviest blow came in April 1921, when political prisoners in Butyrki prison were brutally beaten and deported to the provinces. Public protests on an international scale and the prisoners' organized resistance eventually brought improved conditions and a return to Moscow. The earlier "prison republic" appeared restored, complete with a humorous prison journal, cartoons on the walls, and animated games. Now, however, everyone waited nervously for new shocks.[32]

The Mensheviks' experience recalls the truism that the freest members of an unfree society are those in prison. Even relatively benign imprisonment, however, takes a heavy psychological toll.[33] The Mensheviks remained undaunted, owing to their mutual support system and to two other factors. First, they were convinced that the Russian terror was not supported by the Russian masses. In contrast with the example of revolutionary France, Russian terror was ambivalent and hypocritical; its executions were carried out not to popular applause but in secret.[34] Second, the Mensheviks treated their situation in prison as a paradigm of their overall predicament. Both inside and outside prison they sought to enlarge the sphere of freedom available within the limits of the system. They did not try to overthrow the regime or to flee the country any more than they sought to overpower their jailers or to escape from prison. Eventually, however, the decision to leave Russia was made for them.

In the first days of 1922, imprisoned Mensheviks learned that they had been condemned to internal exile in the remotest corners of Russia, far from any city or even any railway station; ordinary party members were sentenced to one year, Central Committee members to two. Forty-five individuals reacted with a hunger strike. The Bolshevik Politburo voted, by a majority of one and against Trotsky's insistence, to make concessions. It accepted Dan's proposition that the regime offer at least the same choice the tsarist regime used to offer, that is, between internal exile and exile abroad for an equivalent period. Within a few days strikers were being released to prepare for their departure, although some chose to stay in prison a day longer to celebrate Christmas with their remaining comrades.[35]

Dan initially opted for internal exile. On reentering Moscow, however, he was shocked by the "thick atmosphere of venality and corruption . . . the absence of even an iota of economic progress and the galloping moral and political disintegration." The new commercial freedom was serving the interests only of nouveaux riches, who were flaunting their wealth while misery and famine spread. Unemployment and prostitution were rampant. For the first time in years one heard the *ancien régime* term *barin* (sir).[36] In disgust, and perhaps in desperation, Dan changed his mind and chose exile abroad.

Bolshevik authorities were very eager to have the Mensheviks leave quickly, before forthcoming elections to the Moscow soviet. Each exile was given thirteen dollars and a Soviet passport. A few who lacked Latvian visas were turned back at the border. Because of a similar technical delay, Martov's brother Sergei Ezhov stayed in Russia. He spent most of his remaining years in internal exile in Kazakhstan. Like most other socialist internal exiles, he was shot by Soviet authorities when Germany invaded Russia in 1941.[37]

There was considerable reluctance within the party to allow its members to go abroad, even though no one spoke as yet of emigration, and, in principle, the exiles were entitled to return in one or two years.[38] Nicolaevsky, sick with scurvy after his hunger strike, obtained party permission to go abroad only after promising to circle the world and return with a report on conditions in the Russian Far East.[39] Some Mensheviks had left earlier. Woytinsky, who had accompanied Tsereteli to Georgia in January 1918, was in western Europe, having represented the Georgian Republic as a diplomat until that Menshevik state's forcible absorption into Soviet Russia in 1921. Axelrod and Bienstock had gone to the West in 1918 to participate in conferences of the Socialist International, although Bienstock had returned to Odessa in 1920–21 before being arrested and expelled. Martov and Abramovitch had left in 1920 and, by January 1922, had been editing *Sotsialisticheskii vestnik* in Berlin for a year. Other Mensheviks were to leave later. Boris Dvinov and the Garvis accepted an offer of exile in 1923. Defiant to the end, they refused to pay the passport fee of twenty rubles on the grounds that they were not leaving of their own free will. In 1926 and 1930, respectively, Denike and Valentinov-Volsky defected from postings at Soviet offices in Berlin and Paris. Dallin's brother Simon Wolin escaped abroad from internal exile in 1927.[40]

The largest single contingent of Mensheviks—Dan, Schwarz, Nicolaevsky, Aronson, and others, with their families—left in February 1922. Dan describes the hideous atmosphere in the train which took them from Moscow's Riga Station to the Latvian border and into foreign banishment, "experienced so many times under tsarism and now so unexpected in the fifth year of the Revolution."[41] One wonders whether they suspected that none of them would ever see Russia again.

1921–1933

4

Inside and Outside

Settling into Exile

The Mensheviks did not choose emigration. Martov and Abramovitch went abroad in August 1920 to attend the German socialist congress in Halle and prolonged their stay awaiting more favorable conditions in Russia.[1] They were the original members of the Foreign Delegation which expanded its membership as other Central Committee members made their way to Berlin. These, too, left Russia legally and, in their minds, temporarily. For years they regularly renewed their Soviet passports in order to maintain their formal right to return.

All political emigrés leave their homeland with the expectation of returning. In this case, however, such expectations did not appear unrealistic. In contrast with the mass of Russian exiles, the Mensheviks were awaiting not the overthrow of the Bolshevik regime but merely its evolution toward normalcy. Moreover, with the end of civil war in 1920 and the introduction of the New Economic Policy in early 1921, the Mensheviks could discern undeniable signs of such evolution. It did not seem foolhardy or unduly optimistic to believe that the worst was already over.[2] Finally, the survival of the party, however beleaguered, in Russia and the persistence of ties with it encouraged the exiled Mensheviks' hopes of an imminent return to normal party activity at home.

In retrospect, the creation of *Sotsialisticheskii vestnik* in Berlin marked a milestone in the transformation of the RSDRP into an exile party. This was not immediately apparent, however. The first issue of *Vestnik*, dated 1 February 1921, proclaimed that "its tasks [were] modest": "to serve the needs of the social democratic movement in Russia, presently deprived, thanks to the policies of the Bolshevik government, of its press organ, and to inform western European socialist public opinion about the development and problems of the Revolution and of the proletarian movement in Russia." Neither the staff of *Vestnik* nor its readers suspected that this journal would continue to appear for almost forty-five years in over seven hundred issues and that it would migrate from Berlin to Paris and across the Atlantic to New York. Nor could anyone suspect that *Vestnik* would soon become the center of party activity and, finally, the only manifestation of the party's existence. Indeed, the journal outlived the party.

Even if their exile was to be temporary, the Mensheviks had to cope with the practical question of earning a living in a new environment. Incongruously, two Foreign Delegation members, David Dallin and Boris Dvinov, became successful businessmen. In Dallin's case, a prerevolutionary family import-export lumber business allowed him to invest in Berlin real estate. Dvinov was an entirely self-made commercial entrepreneur. Even the impractical Martov revealed unexpected business instincts in his willingness to play the stock market. In the autumn of 1921 Martov believed, contrary to general opinion, that the mark would fall, and he urged his comrades, unsuccessfully, to put some party money into industrial stocks. "Fortunately," comments one comrade, "we spent our money before we could lose it."[3]

All the Mensheviks tried their hand at journalism and political or scholarly writing. Most successful was Raphael Abramovitch, who became Berlin correspondent of the biggest Yiddish-language daily in the world, the New York *Forverts* (Jewish Daily Forward). Not only did this position provide a readership of over a quarter of a million, but also it ensured a regular dollar income, an especially precious asset as inflation raged. In later years several other Mensheviks made careers as authors, columnists, or editors. Iurii Denike (pseudonym Georg Decker) was assistant editor of the *Gesellschaft,* the leading theoretical organ of German social democracy, edited by Rudolf Hilferding, and he published widely in the German socialist press. Another latecomer, Menshevik whiz kid Alexander Shifrin (pseudonym Max Werner), was an editor of the *Mannheimer Volksstimme* before he turned thirty as well as a prolific columnist. Later Shifrin and Grigorii Bienstock won recognition as best-selling authors on international military and geopolitical matters.[4]

Others were not as proficient in German, as talented, or as lucky. Nor were they helped by Menshevik Party policy, which forbade party members from writing in the nonparty press. Only occasionally was this rule bent, for example, in favor of Boris Nicolaevsky, whose temperament, interests, and contacts made him a difficult individual to control. It was also ignored in the case of Grigorii Aronson, who wrote for various emigré newspapers. Aronson's position as an official spokesmen for the party's right wing and, perhaps most significantly, his desperate financial plight allowed him to defy party policy.[5]

Fortunately, the Mensheviks enjoyed a powerful and far-reaching institutional protector in the German Social Democratic Party. The exiled Mensheviks' long-standing personal ties with prominent German Social Democrats gave a strong stimulus to the solidarity expected between socialists in power and those in distress. Owing in particular to Alexander Stein, the influential journalist and head of the SPD Culture and Education Office, a Russian socialist who had emigrated to Germany after 1905, some Mensheviks found themselves on the staff of the SPD or its affiliates.

For example, Petr Garvi was hired as a Russian specialist in the SPD Secretariat.[6] Vladimir Woytinsky became a highly paid economic adviser to and head of the statistical department of the General Federation of German Labor Unions (ADGB), which represented 80 per cent of German organized labor. Woytinsky's appointment was somewhat different from others since it was due less to political patronage than to his impressive personal talents. Soon Woytinsky quarreled with the leading socialist economic theoretician and sometime minister of finance, Rudolf Hilferding. Woytinsky's "proto-Keynesian" proposals were criticized as inflationary, and the SPD rejected his public works projects with the argument that the unemployed were the problem of the parties for which they voted, that is, the Communists and Nazis.[7] SPD patronage even embraced members of the extraparty right wing such as Stepan Ivanovich.[8]

Soviet institutions were another important source of material support for the exiled Mensheviks. Several were employed in the Soviet trade and diplomatic missions in Berlin.[9] When this drew complaints from Moscow, Soviet plenipotentiary N. N. Krestinskii retorted that Mensheviks, unlike his other employees, could be trusted not to steal.[10] Naum Jasny wrote for the journal of the Ukrainian Commissariat of Foreign Trade; the Soviet trade representative, himself a former Menshevik, paid Jasny one dollar a page. Later, Jasny joined the staff of the Soviet trade mission's grain branch in Hamburg as its expert on world grain markets before going on to a German research institution in a humbler capacity.[11]

Literary ventures involving Soviet publishers provided authors' royalties for Martov, Dan, Nicolaevsky, and the party patriarch Pavel Axelrod, too old and ill to earn his living.[12] For a time the publisher Z. O. Grzhebin acted as a bridge between Moscow and Berlin. Woytinsky contracted with him for his memoirs, and Grzhebin's *Letopis' revoliutsii* counted as its editors Martov and Nicolaevsky in Berlin, Sukhanov in Moscow, and Maxim Gorky, who straddled both worlds.[13] Owing to the efforts of David Riazanov, several Mensheviks, most notably Nicolaevsky but also Dan, worked as Berlin-based researchers for Moscow's Marx-Engels Institute.[14]

A few exiled Mensheviks lived in modest comfort. Most, however, particularly those with families to support, could barely eke out a living. Subject to all sorts of economic fluctuations, they were forced to fall back on whatever menial or humdrum jobs they or their spouses could find. Among the Gourevitches (not to be confused with Boris Dvinov-Gurevitch), family members in internal exile in Russia described their miseries to their relatives in Berlin, who wrote back about "illusions" concerning life in the West.[15] For a time Anna Gourevitch was the only provider for a family of six. Lidia Dan continued her work with children, now in a Berlin kindergarten. Material anxieties took their toll: Petr Garvi was continually "so worried about his material position that he [couldn't] sit down to write."[16]

The daily life of a Menshevik family in Berlin is chronicled in Anna Gourevitch's recollections. Her husband, Azrail, worked for several years in a partly Soviet-owned enterprise. Anna herself, trained in medicine, held a low-ranking office job in a Soviet foreign trade agency. Both lived in fear that their activities as Mensheviks would come to the attention of Soviet police authorities. This did not prevent them from attending all Menshevik Club meetings, even when they believed themselves to be under surveillance. By 1927 both Gourevitches had been dismissed from their jobs. Even thereafter, Anna Gourevitch's superior, a Bolshevik Central Committee member who was aware of her identity, sought to extend what help he could. At his behest, and with the additional intervention of an old friend in a high position in Moscow, she managed to obtain a Soviet passport even though she had left Russia illegally. The same Soviet official commissioned her husband for various ghostwriting assignments. Several Soviet notables engaged Azrail Gourevitch to tutor their children. By the end of the decade, however, he could only find work as a taxi driver, a job which he carried out to the point of utter exhaustion.[17]

Naum Jasny, too, has described his family's appalling living conditions in Berlin in 1923–24: they occupied a string of cells in a former prison, where floods would bring several inches of sewage into the corridor.[18] Yet Jasny was fortunate enough to be gainfully employed without interruption. As foreigners Mensheviks were not permitted to rent unfurnished appartments; the Gourevitches lived in fifteen different places over a period of ten years.[19] It would not have been much comfort for the exiles to know that their material situation would worsen with the onset of the depression in Germany and decline even further in Paris.

Although material hardships weighed on them, the Mensheviks found compensation in other aspects of life in Berlin. As Woytinsky put it, "We were aliens but no longer outsiders." Owing to their proximity to the German socialist milieu, the Mensheviks observed the struggles of the Weimar Republic from inside.[20] They witnessed social dislocation caused by uncontrollable inflation and the seething resentment born of the Allies' reparation and occupation policies; here the Mensheviks' sympathies lay with the Germans against the Allies. They also witnessed the twin specters of revolution from the left and from the right. Their outlook did not allow them then to see these two dangers as comparable, though they tended to merge in later memories. At the height of the multiple crises in 1923, Dan considered the Mensheviks' position in Germany so precarious that he turned to a Swedish comrade for asylum for the whole group.[21]

Because of the SPD and kindred organizations, the Mensheviks were able to satisfy partially their need for political activity. Maintaining contact with the party in Russia, with visiting Soviet officials, and with Soviet institutions, the exiles did not feel entirely cut off from their homeland either. Above all, they found intellectual and emotional satisfaction as well as a mutual support system in the collective life of their group, with its common devotion to a cause, its social exchanges and familial relations, its formal meetings and publications. In the decade that the Mensheviks spent in Berlin, these ties tended to outweigh political divergences.[22]

There is a tendency toward introversion in every exile group, if only for reasons of collective self-preservation and identity. The extraparty right wing Menshevik Stepan Ivanovich commented caustically on the Mensheviks' politics of isolation and their "aristocratic-Marxist disdain for the whole world, except for the proletariat, which is presently not in the party."[23] In one respect in particular the Mensheviks did adopt an attitude of utter isolation: they would have nothing to do with the vast, culturally vibrant, and politically active Russian emigration. In part this isolation was imposed on them. As socialists and Jews they were ostracized by the overwhelmingly right wing and nationalist emigré community. In large part, however, their isolation was self-imposed. Not only did the Mensheviks differ radically from the "White" emigration in outlook, but also they were keen to emphasize their differences. In some ways they were as scornful of the emigration as were the Bolsheviks.[24] The result was that they constituted, as Garvi put it, "an emigration within the emigration."[25]

At the heart of the Mensheviks' outlook lay the fact that their experience of the Revolution was fundamentally different from that of other Russian emigrés. Most Mensheviks had lived in Russia for several years after the Revolution. Many had worked as Soviet functionaries and had served in the Red Army. Above all, they had stood firmly within the Red camp in the Civil War. Years later even those Mensheviks who had by then abandoned the Martov Line still defended unconditionally their parti pris in favor of the "Reds" against the "Whites."[26] If, as some historians have argued, the Civil War represents the Bolshevik Party's and the Soviet regime's essential formative experience, it is significant that in this experience the Mensheviks were aligned with the Bolsheviks rather than against them.[27]

Individual Menshevik exiles managed as best they could, but the party organization also required material means to survive. Contributors to *Vestnik* were not remunerated. Some issues were consigned to a cheap printer who could be reached only by a two-hour train ride followed by a six-kilometer walk.[28] At all times the party's only salaried employees were its chairman, Fedor Dan, and its elderly secretary, Isaak Iudin, appointed to ensure him a livelihood. Nevertheless, income from membership dues and from the sale of *Vestnik* and other publications was inadequate to cover even the party's modest needs abroad, much less allow transfer of funds to Russia to support underground activity there or to help needy comrades living illegally, in prison, or in internal exile.

Money problems were thus a constant preoccupation. Rumors persisted that Lenin was secretly financing *Vestnik*, probably in order to receive the Menshevik reaction to his policies.[29] According to one version, when *Vestnik* editors discovered that a German intermediary was buying seven hundred copies of each issue, they proposed to the Soviet trade mission that it buy these copies outright, and the ensuing agreement held until Lenin's death.[30] To an extent that remains obscure to this day, the party was able to draw on some contributions from western European socialist parties, either directly or through the Socialist International.[31] In addition, the party counted heavily on money collected among sympathizers, particularly in America. At a single banquet in New York organized for 650 participants by the Jewish Socialist Verband, the incomparable fund-raiser Raphael Abramovitch collected $6,250.[32]

Until 1928 *Vestnik* published a "funds received" column, divided into an account for the party journal and one for relief in Russia. Headings suggest these were special funds over and above regular income. Generally speaking, funds received increased over the years, from some $6,000 in 1921 to over $30,000 in 1927 (in today's dollars). Most striking is the diversity of sources. Individuals (sometimes anonymous) from Bulgaria to China sent modest sums. Foreign socialist groups contributed, including the Finnish and Czech-German Social Democratic parties, the Central Committee of the Bulgarian

Social Democrats, a group of Lithuanian social democrats in Chicago, and workers in German factories. Contributions came from otherwise unknown Russian social democratic groups in Rome and Basel and from the distant Far Eastern *oblast'* committee of the RSDRP. They were donated by unrelated organizations, such as Russian student groups in Padua and Bonn, the Political Red Cross in Paris, and the Relief Society for Socialist Prisoners in Soviet Russia, centered in New York. As a whole these accounts provide eloquent testimony, certainly not to the wealth of the Mensheviks but to the wide sympathy they enjoyed.

In addition to ensuring its financial base, the party also sought to set up the most effective party structures possible in exile conditions. It adopted a restrictive organizational model that resembled more closely the sort of party suggested in Lenin's *What Is To Be Done?* than traditional Menshevik organizations. There was a sharp distinction between, on the one hand, party organizations proper, limited to individuals who had been party members in Russia, "who [knew] the party line and [were] ready to adhere to it," and, on the other, party auxiliary or support groups consisting of party sympathizers, as well as "comrades who because of long separation from Russia or by virtue of earlier divergences with the party find themselves on the road to defining their political views."[33] Formal party meetings were usually limited to members, and only party members and invited foreign socialists could contribute to the party press.[34] Not only were there no attempts at recruitment abroad, but applications from old party members were carefully vetted, with particular scrutiny paid to those who claimed membership only in the Soviet period. Party membership could be revoked or suspended by the Foreign Delegation in cases of misbehavior or infringement of party rules.[35] Even the offspring of long-standing party members were directed away from the RSDRP to the socialist parties of their countries of adoption.

The Foreign Delegation sought to keep close watch and control over all party structures abroad, as well as to monopolize contacts with the party in Russia. It was firmly in charge of the main Menshevik organization, the Martov Club, which functioned in Berlin with a stable party membership of about seventy individuals. This represented approximately twice the membership of the next most important organization, the Paris club, which disposed of the prewar RSDRP's quarters and its historic library on the rue des Gobelins. The Paris group was active, but it was viewed with suspicion from Berlin because of the rightist sympathies of some of its members, and it sometimes stepped out of line. When Paris Mensheviks organized a celebration of the tenth anniversary of the February Revolution jointly with SRs, they received a rebuke from the Foreign Delegation.[36]

The Menshevik organization in London proved short-lived. It was effectively allowed to die after having been heavily censured by Martov for insubordination and rightist deviationism.[37] In Riga a Russian section of the Latvian Social Democratic Party served as a substitute for a local Menshevik chapter. Riga Social Democrats, both Latvian and Russian, were especially supportive of the Foreign Delegation. As a governing party in a country situated on the Soviet border, Latvian Social Democrats, themselves members of the RSDRP when Latvia was part of the Russian Empire, were able to help their Russian comrades in many concrete ways.[38] There was also a small but sporadically active party organization in Geneva.[39] Other groups existed at various times in places as diverse as Chicago, Bern, and Liège. Finally, ephemeral Menshevik groups would spring up in university towns such as Heidelberg or Toulouse whenever a few Menshevik students came together.[40]

In New York the large and influential group of Russian social democrats stood out from other Menshevik organizations, both ideologically and organizationally. Founded in the 1890s as the Russian section of the Socialist Party of America and later of the Social Democratic Federation, the organization had evolved into the Plekhanoff New York Russian Social Democratic Group. It was thus older than the RSDRP itself and enjoyed an uninterrupted existence until 1941. Throughout its life the Plekhanoff Group was led by its original founders, Sergius Ingerman, a member of the legendary Emancipation of Labor Group in the 1880s, and Iakov Lupolov-James, another pioneer of Russian social democracy.[41] Moreover, the Plekhanoff Group was bolstered by numerous kindred organizations, notably the Workmen's Circle (Arbeiter Ring), the Jewish Socialist Verband led by Sol Levitas, and David Dubinsky's powerful International Ladies' Garment Workers' Union (ILGWU).

The strength, wealth, and continuity of the New York social democratic community, in addition to the distance between New York and Berlin, and the different composition of the New York group (made up largely of people who had emigrated before 1917), strained relations between the Foreign Delegation and New York. Strains were also grounded in ideological divergences. After an initial bout of pro-Bolshevik feeling immediately after the October Revolution, the New York Mensheviks turned sharply right. Their strident antibolshevism led to tension with Martov and his followers and to open support for the extraparty right wing. In the 1920s such tensions had practical consequences for party peace and for the party's coffers, but they did not yet threaten the unity of the party.[42]

The Political Economy of NEP

Within weeks of publication of the first issue of *Sotsialisticheskii vestnik* in Berlin, momentous changes took place in Russia which dictated the course of Soviet development over the next decade. On 21 March 1921 a Soviet decree confirmed the Tenth Communist Party Congress's decision to replace the requisition of peasant produce with a tax in kind. This measure, which removed the cornerstone of previous Soviet policy toward the peasant, heralded the disintegration of the entire structure of war communism. Soon, Russia restored a monetary economy, introduced enterprise accountability *(khozrashchet)*, revived private trade, and partially denationalized industry. Recognition of native capitalist elements and promotion of foreign-run concessionary enterprises, envisaged earlier, became pillars of Soviet economic policy. What emerged was a mixed economic system in which private, cooperative, and state sectors coexisted as did markets and attempts at central planning. The ensemble of such measures and the economic reality they produced came to be known as the New Economic Policy.[1]

Following Lenin, Soviet historians have insisted that introduction of NEP represented fulfillment of Lenin's original plans, interrupted between 1918 and 1921 by the Civil War, with its attendant emergency economic measures.[2] In fact, although Lenin had advocated some NEP-like measures in the spring of 1918, he was still intensifying policies of war communism after the Civil War had ended.[3] As late as December 1920, the Eighth Congress of Soviets witnessed a dramatic confrontation between Lenin and Dan in which Dan advocated proposals of economic liberalization, including the tax in kind, and Lenin refuted these proposals as capitulationist.[4] Moreover, such proposals had already been presented in the Menshevik program of July 1919, "What Is To Be Done?"[5] The Mensheviks thus had good reason to see NEP as an expropriation of their own ideas; indeed, Martov accused the Bolsheviks of having literally stolen their program with some confiscated Menshevik Central Committee documents. *Vestnik*'s first editorial on NEP, titled "Lenin Retreats," described Lenin's concessions as ones "which our party has been teaching the Communists for three years."[6]

The Mensheviks followed the course of NEP avidly but critically. Observers have been at a loss to explain the apparent contradiction between Menshevik support of the idea of NEP and rejection of NEP itself.[7] Indeed, the strength of the Menshevik analysis lies in the fact that it represents a critique from within a shared set of goals. The Mensheviks were in agreement with the Bolsheviks on objectives: industrialization, productive agriculture, harmonious exchange relations between city and countryside, and ultimately a planned socialist economy. Their critique was based on the argument that NEP policies would fail to attain these objectives. It stated openly what many Soviet economists, and even certain leaders, suspected.

Menshevik writings do not provide a periodization of NEP. Instead of the pattern of orderly, stage-by-stage development portrayed by Soviet historians, the Mensheviks recorded a confused and irregular process.[8] They noted Lenin's promise that there would be no new retreats, that is, no intensification of NEP, and they cited the Soviet leaders' belief by 1924 that NEP had exhausted its possibilities.[9] A year later, however, the situation had turned around, as *Vestnik* recorded the inauguration of a "neo-NEP."[10] Within six months the neo-NEP, too, appeared exhausted and on the point of abandonment. As David Dallin predicted, this chaotic course of alternating advances and retreats was to continue until NEP's final demise.[11]

The Mensheviks identified vacillation as the primary characteristic of NEP. In Aaron Iugov's words, "As if under the influence of some mysterious spell, the Soviet government precipitates itself now in one direction, now in another."[12] Such zigzags produced deplorable effects on the Soviet economy, but these were largely inevitable. The economic system itself was founded on an inherently unstable amalgam within which the imperatives of pragmatism conflicted at every moment with the desiderata of utopianism, the principles of privatization clashed with statism, and radicalism sought common ground with moderation. The already poor, taut, and battered Soviet economy was being tugged leftward and rightward in self-immobilizing and even self-destructive fashion. Indeed, such were the frustrations of NEP that one Menshevik even expressed nostalgia for the period of war communism: at least there was method in that madness.[13]

Underlying the NEP zigzags lay the essential "planlessness" of the Soviet economy, a concept developed in particular by Iugov. From the very outset the Bolsheviks had dreamed of establishing a "teleological" economic system, that is, an economy governed by a rational plan. With the introduction of NEP, they had renounced direct control over a large part of the economy, but they still maintained the goal of organizing economic life in accordance with a central plan. By 1924 the formal mechanisms of such planning were in place: Gosplan elaborated long-term (fifteen-year) and medium-term (five-year) guidelines by balancing inputs and outputs throughout the various sectors of the economy as well as among these sectors on the basis of control figures. As socialists, the Mensheviks could only applaud the principle of planning. In this case, however, they considered attempts at planning to be self-deluding. The question was not whether a plan was needed but whether the leadership had the capacity, under given social and cultural conditions, to carry it out.[14]

As Iugov and other Mensheviks saw it, the Russian economy lacked all the necessary premises for planning. First, Soviet planners lacked essential information. The rudimentary level of Soviet statistics meant that official prognoses were nothing but vague estimates, if not outright guesses. Second, even those economic sectors that were largely state controlled were dependent on uncontrollable outside factors, such as the world market. Above all, the largest sector, the peasant economy, escaped the control of planners altogether. Thus, planners were unable to impose their guidelines on the main consumers of industrial products and on that part of the economy that accounted for two-thirds of the raw materials supplied to industry. For example, in 1925–26 planners overestimated peasant crops by 30 percent, even as they overestimated the peasants' willingness to hand over their crops at low purchase prices. In 1925 peasant demand for industrial products was underestimated by 20 to 25 percent. But the following year, instead of demonstrating the expected significant rise in "hunger for commodities," the peasants purchased less, provoking a crisis of marketing. By the time the state had adjusted its industrial supplies, the economy was suffering once again from a lack of commodities.[15]

Just as NEP was disappearing into history, Iugov modified slightly his pessimistic assessment of the prospects for Soviet planning. He now argued that by trying to embrace all economic life, the planners had been hindered from concentrating on the necessary and practicable regulation of the principal branches of the economy. It is not clear why Iugov thought that such partial planning would not be open to the same objections he had previously raised. Moreover, Iugov did not address an implicit contradiction in his views: if planning could be successfully carried out only under socialism, as he maintained, then any attempts at using planning to bring about socialism were doomed to failure. Planning thus emerged as both a necessary characteristic of socialism and an essential but impossible precondition for establishing it.[16]

In any case, it was clear to the Mensheviks that Soviet "pseudo-planning" had not solved any economic problems. How could it succeed, given its blatant disregard for the principles of equilibrium and its adoption of methods which, instead of building on actual economic processes, consisted of fixing goals to be attained and then searching for the requisite means?[17] As proof of failure, they pointed to the repeated crises of the Soviet economy, including market crises of a distinctly capitalist sort.[18] It was not the plan but the elemental forces of the Russian economy and the iron laws of economics that were dictating Russia's development, argued the Mensheviks. Their studies highlighted both the errors of the Bolsheviks and the inherent dilemmas of Soviet development.

All observers recognized that agriculture constituted the linchpin of the Russian economy. Agriculture had to be revived in order to feed the cities, to supply industry, and to provide exportable products. Yet Bolshevik rule in the countryside in the 1920s was akin to that of "an army of occupation in hostile territory." A field study undertaken by some young Mensheviks in 1924 confirmed that there was no *vlast'* (government authority) there.[19] NEP thus represented a recognition that Soviet power could not be stabilized, perhaps not even maintained, without the willing collaboration of the peasantry. Initially the NEP wager proved fruitful. Although Iugov had declared Russian agriculture technically "petrified," in the early NEP years it revived with extraordinary speed.[20] As of 1923, however, the pace of reconstruction slackened. With an area under cultivation as large as that before World War I, the amount of produce marketed declined, in part because of increased peasant consumption but, above all, because of disincentives to production caused by low state purchase prices.

The Soviet government reacted to its agricultural problems with a mixture of coercive measures and incitements. In 1924, partly in response to peasants' efforts to satisfy their tax obligations by dumping spoiled or inferior produce on the state, the government replaced the tax in kind with a money tax; it thus abolished one of the last reminders of the moneyless economy of war communism.[21] In 1925 the government made further concessions, especially to the prosperous peasantry. Leasing of land and use of hired labor by individual peasants were made easier.[22] In response to peasant unrest, manifested in the murder of village officials and the militancy of peasant organizations, the government broadened the electoral law and sought to breathe life into village soviets.[23] Meanwhile, marketing of peasant produce was increasingly concentrated in the hands of the state, making the peasantry ever more dependent on low state prices.[24]

As the Mensheviks pointed out repeatedly, the measures that were undertaken did not penetrate to the roots of peasant malaise. The Bolsheviks had wagered successively on the poor peasant *(bedniak)* under war communism, on the middle peasant *(seredniak)* in the early years of NEP, and finally on the rich peasant, or kulak, even as they had tried, unsuccessfully, to regulate the process of differentiation within the peasantry.[25] At no time, however, had they managed to resolve the "scissors crisis," that is, the discrepancy between high industrial and low agricultural prices. The basic contradiction of NEP was that high industrial prices aggravated the crisis and intensified the exploitation of the peasantry, but lower prices brought about greater deficits and a crisis of turnover capital.[26] After having reached dramatic proportions in 1923 and then having narrowed somewhat, the scissors crisis was widening once again by 1926.[27] Given the overriding political and economic considerations that underlay the Bolshevik policy of cheap food supplies, there was no prospect of closing the scissors significantly.[28]

In these circumstances the Mensheviks rightly suspected that the peasantry would prove increasingly reluctant to hand over produce to the state at low prices.[29] Above all, the peasantry would not become a productive and responsible economic actor so long as it lacked security.[30] The zigzags of Soviet policy and continuing long-term uncertainty over issues such as land tenure had left the peasantry suspicious, even of favorable state initiatives, and had made it unwilling to improve techniques or to increase production beyond what it required for its own needs. As the Mensheviks never tired of repeating, the security of the peasantry could be guaranteed only in a democratic state. Without democracy, no promises or threats could obtain peasant cooperation with the workers' state.[31]

The problems of industry were even more staggering. Industry had experienced a far sharper decline than agriculture and proved much slower in recovering its prewar level of output. Costs of industrial production were extraordinarily high during the NEP period. Initially this was due to the fact that enterprises were recovering from disruption and not yet working at full capacity.[32] Even in 1924 production costs remained so high that in some factories outputs for salaries exceeded the entire value of products. Later, production costs rose because of the failure to renew and repair capital stock.[33] Throughout NEP, industry was bedeviled by organizational and managerial problems, by lack of skilled workers (along with massive unemployment of the unskilled), and, sporadically, by shortages of fuel and raw materials. By 1927–28 industry had recovered to the level not only of prewar output but also of prewar productive capacity. At this point, however, it had exhausted all preexisting reserves and required massive capital inputs to obtain any further growth. Indeed, Iugov warned of an impending catastrophe unless new capital was forthcoming.[34]

Nationalized industry, deficit-ridden and starved for capital, thus constituted a severe drain on the economy.[35] As Dallin pointed out, subsidizing state enterprises through the private sector meant that the existence of the nationalized sector was dependent on the profitability of the private sector.[36] The Bolsheviks pinned their hopes on leasing enterprises to individuals and granting concessions to foreign companies, as provided by NEP legislation. In fact, such measures attracted fewer entrepreneurs than expected, and even these tended to invest in speculative, short-term, and commercial ventures or in existing industrial concerns rather than in new productive projects. The entrepreneurs' caution proved well founded. Within months of the denationalization ordinance of August 1921, a new decree broadened the extent of nationalization.[37] From 1923 on there were regular campaigns against the private trader, and from 1925 private industry was increasingly restricted.[38]

Although the Mensheviks had expressed concern in 1925 about Russia's "deindustrialization," they viewed with misgiving the post-1925 industrialization campaign.[39] The tempo of industrialization was both too slow and too fast. On the one hand, the rate of investment compared unfavorably with that of tsarist times, and industrialization plans were insufficient to solve problems such as mass unemployment. On the other hand, these plans were too ambitious in relation to the investment capital available, and they imposed an intolerable tax burden on the peasantry. Finally, the very limited capital available was being squandered on ill-considered experiments because of ignorance and mismanagement.[40]

According to the Mensheviks, the only realistic solution lay in attracting massive amounts of foreign capital. Iugov saw some encouraging signs of Bolshevik realism in this direction at the very end of the NEP period. He welcomed a July 1928 decree liberalizing policies on concessions, although he was more circumspect in regard to a decree the following month that granted special privileges to private capital, both Russian and foreign, in building houses.[41] Iugov was forthrightly critical with respect to a government proposal to broaden denationalization, denouncing it as a "disorderly retreat" which would "auction off" even those enterprises which had been publicly owned in tsarist Russia. Like other Mensheviks who approved the principle of concessions or foreign loans but castigated the Soviet government for selling off Russian industries and for "thinking of nothing but loans at 6 percent," Iugov rejected simplistic formulas.[42] The fact that industrialization and nationalization were desirable goals did not mean that all measures promoting them were wise or progressive.

Whatever decrees or policies were proclaimed, the key to raising capital and to promoting industrialization lay in the creation of stable and secure political conditions. Earlier, the Bolsheviks had fantasized that they could realize communism in a backward land by means of terror and bureaucracy; now their illusion was that they could introduce capitalism without democracy. The arbitrary use of power paralyzed all initiatives and eliminated all hopes of overcoming corruption, of motivating technical and scientific workers, and of limiting the caprice of industrial satraps.[43] Just as peasants would not increase production beyond their own needs and cooperate with the state as long as rights to land and produce were not guaranteed, native and foreign capitalists could not be expected to invest under conditions of political uncertainty. The complete absence of political guarantees in respect to NEP's durability had always been its weakness. At the outset of NEP the Mensheviks had warned that the absence of democracy would "kill in the bud all rational measures of economic policy." At NEP's close they were even more convinced that this position was valid. With unwitting prescience Iugov affirmed that, under conditions of dictatorship, the vast capital required for industrialization could be obtained only by openly expropriating the peasants and the private traders among whom some accumulation was taking place.[44] Such a policy, he concluded, would be absolutely ruinous for the peasantry and for the country as a whole. For him and other Mensheviks it was simply unthinkable.

Contrary to some critics' views, the contradiction in Menshevik thinking on the political economy of NEP does not lie in the opposition between support of NEP principles and rejection of NEP reality. Rather, it lies between the Mensheviks' Marxist belief in the universal iron laws of economic development and their insistence on the overriding importance of political conditions. The NEP experience demonstrated that objective forces of production did not flow freely as dictated by history. Their course might be diverted, at least temporarily, by subjective factors. Sound economic policies were fruitless without sound political conditions. The lesson the Mensheviks drew was therefore that of the primacy of politics. It was a lesson the Bolsheviks had learned earlier and one the Mensheviks would have occasion to reflect on in anguish as NEP gave way to Stalin's "Great Turn."

The Nature of NEP Russia

Underlying Menshevik discussions of NEP policies was the quest for a theoretical explanation of Soviet events. As interpreters of Soviet developments, the Mensheviks sought to describe ongoing processes in terms familiar to themselves and recognizable to Western readers. As Marxists, the Mensheviks were concerned to fit Soviet developments into classic Marxist patterns, in order both to understand these developments more fully and to confirm the validity of these patterns. Indeed, the Mensheviks' search for a theoretical perspective on Soviet Russia represents the longest sustained effort to confront Marxist theory with Soviet reality.

The character of the Russian Revolution, understood as a continuing process, was the point of departure for reflection. Martov had spoken of a "petty bourgeois national revolution decked in the proletarian garb of an extreme

Communist utopianism," and others made this formula even more explicit: the Revolution was dual in nature—proletarian only in ideology, petty proprietory in nature.[1] In Dallin's formulation, the Revolution was objectively bourgeois but subjectively heterogeneous. It had accomplished the bourgeois task of destroying an ancien régime but had done so in the name of immediate socialism. It had practiced socially reactionary utopianism and terror but had defended the real conquests of a peasant revolution. Well after NEP had ended, Dallin still saw the essential characteristic of the "Bolshevik period of the Revolution" in the struggle between realism and utopia, between Marxism and fantasy.[2]

The dual character of the Revolution created contradictions which NEP did not resolve. One Menshevik in Russia described bolshevism as a regime in which "one hand beats socialists in the Solovki [prison]; the other hand brings a new edition of Marx into the Sverdlov University auditorium."[3] As Marxists, the Mensheviks believed that contradictions could be vehicles of historical progress. The Bolsheviks' fault lay in their failure to recognize that the unraveling of present contradictions would inevitably crush the Revolution.[4]

Another fateful fault lay in the Bolsheviks' efforts to disguise these contradictions. History had organized a gigantic masquerade by confiding to a socialist party the task of destroying vestiges of feudalism. Perhaps this masquerade was necessary to induce the proletariat to carry out the agrarian revolution and to expropriate the gentry on behalf of a bourgeoisie which had defaulted in its historical task.[5] After all, proletarians would not have shed their blood to bring about instauration of a bourgeois order. During the Civil War, history had made the Bolshevik Party the defender of the foundations of the Revolution against the armed forces of reaction. Under NEP normalcy, however, in a country where nine-tenths of the population—that is, the peasantry—dreamed of becoming petty bourgeois proprietors, the force of necessity was reasserting itself. The bourgeois tide was now overpowering the Communist utopia, but the Bolsheviks refused to recognize this fact.[6] As one Menshevik put it, "Bolsheviks set out for Communist India but discovered bourgeois America. They are not yet convinced that this is America but still think it is India."[7]

The Mensheviks thus saw their theoretical mission as that of unmasking the true nature of the Revolution and the society emerging from it. They asked whether the Russian Revolution was the last bourgeois revolution or the first socialist one and concluded that, in spite of the rule of a proletarian party, it was essentially the revolution of the petty bourgeois strata of a backward land.[8] In 1921 Dallin affirmed that the new course in Russia did not yet amount to capitalism, but a year later he defined NEP as "capitalism under communism."[9] In the struggle between "subjective" and "objective" factors, the latter were gaining the upper hand, perhaps because Marxist doctrine decreed that it must be so.

It is psychologically difficult for socialists to acknowledge that capitalism is the order of the day in their country. Belief in the inevitability of capitalism, however, had long constituted the raison d'être of Russian Marxism in its opposition to populism. True, Russian Marxists had not dwelt on the possibility of constructing capitalism after a successful proletarian revolution, but from Plekhanov to Martov, they had recognized that the bourgeois revolution need not be led by the bourgeoisie.[10] In his *Posle voin i revoliutsii* Dallin could appeal to the authority of his mentors when he declared that the political power of the proletariat was compatible with capitalism, that workers' parties should be prepared to govern a bourgeois state without destroying capitalism, and that the capitalist class still served a valuable function.[11] Nevertheless, Dallin's sanguine views shocked his fellow Mensheviks, many of whom awaited the onset of capitalism in Soviet Russia, however inevitable, with unease and foreboding.

Menshevik exasperation with Bolshevik attempts to disguise the capitalist nature of NEP intensified as Soviet leaders elaborated the notion of "state capitalism," a concept advanced before 1917 by the German social democratic theorist Rudolf Hilferding, who spoke of "organized capitalism," and by the Bolshevik theorist Nikolai Bukharin.[12] Lenin himself had stated in 1918 that "state capitalism would be a step forward as compared with the present state of affairs."[13] In the context of NEP, however, the concept acquired an elasticity which eventually deprived it of any precise meaning. In the narrowest sense, NEP state capitalism referred to the concessionary enterprises leased out by the Soviet state to private capitalists. In the broader sense, it came to encompass all collaboration with capitalist elements, including traders and the peasantry. Finally, Lenin himself ceased to use the concept.[14]

Menshevik attacks on the Soviet invocation of "state capitalism" were two-pronged. First, they ridiculed the Soviet use of the term as a sleight of hand. Lenin's affirmation that state capitalism was capitalism "that we will be able to restrict" reflected wishfulness rather than analysis.[15] It rested on the premise that if a government is Communist, then the capitalism over which it presides must be state capitalism. The assumption was that even the most unregenerate capitalism was somehow uplifted by the fact that it was developing within a political order that chose to call itself socialist.[16] As Dallin pointed out, the corollary of this flimsy thesis was that if the government changed, then one would return, without any further ado, to capitalism *tout court*. Could any serious Marxist base the description of an economic order on such subjective criteria?[17]

The second objection was more fundamental. The Mensheviks were prepared to call the state sector of the economy in Soviet Russia "state capitalist," as they would in the case of any other country. The Bolsheviks, however, insisted on calling their state sector "socialist." For the Mensheviks this was no mere semantic divergence. Rather, it epitomized both Bolshevik ignorance and Bolshevik deception. The Bolsheviks would have the world believe that the mere nationalization of industry amounted to socialism. Moreover, they would not acknowledge that relations of production in the "socialist" sector of the Soviet economy were still marked by all the defects of capitalism. Russian workers in state factories were subject to the same discipline, lack of control over their own production, job insecurity—in short, to the same exploitation—as their capitalist counterparts.

Mensheviks also quarreled with Bolsheviks over the degree of state capitalism (or "socialism," in Bolshevik parlance) that existed in Soviet Russia. Under NEP, state ownership shrank to pitiful proportions. In 1923 fewer than 1.5 million workers out of a total population of 130 million remained in the state or "socialist" sector.[18] Martov had warned that some measure of state ownership must be ensured if the country was to avoid agrarianization. Instead, the Bolsheviks had capitulated before capitalism to a far greater degree than necessary, sacrificing even sectors that had been publicly owned before the Revolution.[19] The remaining state sector was so isolated and weak that it was not viable. In Dallin's words, it was like an English lord's park or an American millionaire's garden: a pseudo-productive, idle luxury with no economic justification.[20]

Ambiguity persisted as Mensheviks and Bolsheviks discussed "state capitalism" among themselves. G. E. Zinoviev, the head of the Comintern, tacitly endorsed Menshevik theses by suggesting that Soviet "socialist" industry was part of a state capitalist economic arrangement.[21] A Menshevik Central Committee document echoed Lenin in declaring that the reign of state capitalism had begun in Russia.[22] Confusion over terms reflected a deep-seated uncertainty about Russia's economic course. A "state capitalist" economy was to be a transitional economy, but a transition toward what? Would implementation of state capitalism prepare the way for socialism, as the Bolsheviks claimed, or would it usher in capitalism, as the Mensheviks predicted? What, too, would be the worldwide implications of an unsuccessful socialization of production in Russia? If socialization led to a fall in productivity here, how would socialism elsewhere recover from this devastating blow to its force of attraction?[23] The awkwardness of the terms available to describe the nature of NEP Russia raised questions about the country's future evolution as well as about the adequacy of classic Marxist economic categories. In stating that the Soviet economy was neither capitalist nor socialist but sui generis, Dallin in 1925 unwittingly prefigured later answers to these questions.[24]

In puzzling over a satisfactory definition of NEP Russia, the Mensheviks turned, as other Marxists would, to a class analysis of this new society. Already in 1920 Martov had affirmed that if the Menshevik critique of bolshevism was not to be a simple imitation of Bolshevik style, it should be founded on an analysis of the social nature of bolshevism.[25] His Menshevik followers proved faithful to this injunction as they sought to identify the social forces making up NEP society.

From the Menshevik point of view, the most important social actor was the Soviet working class. As Martov put it, the Mensheviks were not the only working-class party in Soviet Russia, but they were the only exclusively working-class party.[26] The political logic of Menshevik policies was therefore dictated by an assessment of this class and its potential. The Mensheviks' readiness to welcome pseudo-capitalist conditions in Soviet Russia rested on the premise that political emancipation of the proletariat had to take place through struggle against capitalism (in this way it was analogous to the earlier Menshevik readiness to accept the instauration of capitalism in tsarist Russia). Similarly, Menshevik reluctance to undertake action which might lead to overthrow of the Bolshevik regime was motivated by a realization of the weakness of the working class and fear that working-class interests would be disregarded in any political overturn. At the same time, however, the Mensheviks maintained that the persistence of Bolshevik dictatorship impeded the strengthening of the working class.

The situation of the Russian working class was indeed pitiful. Dan calculated that the number of workers on the eve of NEP was about one-quarter of what it had been before World War I. The fall in wages was even more vertiginous, sinking to as low as 10 percent of prewar levels. Moreover, one-quarter of even these paltry wages was never paid out because of enterprise insolvency. Even highly qualified workers could not find employment; coffin building was one of the few thriving industries. There was virtually no provision for the unemployed; the very few workers on the unemployment insurance rolls received less than half, sometimes as little as 6 percent, of a regular salary. In these circumstances, observed Dan, the slogan "He who does not work neither shall he eat" acquired a completely new, antiworker meaning.[27]

The situation of the working class improved under NEP. By 1928 numbers had reached prewar levels and, if we take account of social services, real wages stood at a higher level than in 1913. Conditions were still extremely harsh; most improvement in wage levels was attributable to overtime work, which gave the lie to Soviet pride at introducing legislation of the eight-hour day.[28] Above all, the composition of the working class changed. A small, highly qualified working class, which had first been decimated in the Revolution and the Civil War and then depleted to fill bureaucratic needs, was replaced by a "massive, illiterate, unreliable and fluctuating class of semi-peasants, semi-workers."[29]

The Mensheviks saw their task, in part, as that of struggling for an improvement in the living and working conditions of workers. Above all, however, it centered on the call for independent workers' organizations. They argued that the strength of other classes lay in their acquisitive capacity, and, hence, other classes could thrive without freedom. The working class, however, was by its very nature democratic, and therefore freedom was essential to it. The strength of the working class lay in its independent class organization, and the greatest crime of the Bolshevik regime was that it had deprived workers of the possibility of organizing.[30] Thus, the battlefield on which the Mensheviks proposed to engage the Bolsheviks was that of the struggle for freedom of coalition, an area in which the Bolsheviks were particularly vulnerable. Any Menshevik successes in this area threatened the legitimacy of the Bolshevik dictatorship without putting into question the Soviet order. The emphasis on worker organization thus turned out to be the logical application of the overall Menshevik policy of putting pressure on the Soviet regime from within.

Clarity on the attitude to take toward the working class did not preclude doubts on another issue: What were the links between the Bolshevik Party and the working class? Martov himself gave contradictory replies to the question whether the Bolshevik Party had "lost its roots in the Russian working class."[31] This ambivalence persisted, producing disagreement among the Mensheviks themselves and hampering their ability to define a coherent attitude toward both the Bolshevik Party and the working class.

As the working class dwindled, the peasantry grew in numbers and importance. Bolsheviks and Mensheviks agreed that the fate of NEP would be decided in the countryside. Raphael Abramovitch quoted Soviet premier A. I. Rykov approvingly to this effect as he reflected on the feasibility of a NEP strategy of controlling the "commanding heights" of the economy while leaving agriculture to its own petty capitalist ways.[32] Abramovitch recalled that this strategy had already been suggested by Kautsky and Bauer for western Europe. In Russia, Abramovitch contended, it could not succeed because the socialized urban economy would be swamped by the peasant masses.[33] The nature of these masses and social trends among them thus became a prime preoccupation for the Mensheviks as they were for Bolshevik leaders. Indeed, one has the impression that the Mensheviks were stating openly what many Bolsheviks suspected and what left wing Bolsheviks were arguing in their own party debates.

In terms of class consciousness, the fundamental Marxist truth about the peasantry was that it tended to constitute a reactionary mass. The Mensheviks were prepared to entertain the notion that the peasantry, even in Russia, might demonstrate democratic instincts. Basically, however, the peasants had been "communists" for only one brief moment—in 1917. Since then, objective tendencies pointed to increasing differentiation among them, and this new inequality only reinforced antidemocratic elements. As Dallin put it, there was no sociological law that a strong peasantry must be necessarily a bearer of reaction, but in most cases it was indeed so.[34]

In spite of this harsh evaluation, the Mensheviks could not "write off" the peasantry. Excessive insistence on its benighted character undermined one of the Mensheviks' chief criticisms: that the *soglashenie* (agreement) between town and country proclaimed by Lenin merely masked the shameless domination and exploitation of the latter by the former.[35] Psychologically and strategically, too, the Mensheviks could not adopt a position which pitted them unconditionally against the overwhelming mass of the Russian population. For these reasons, the Mensheviks were prepared to moderate their judgment. Dallin revised his earlier views to suggest that the basic characteristic of the peasantry was not its reactionary nature but the fact that it could not act independently. It had to ally itself either to the Right or to the Left, and in present Soviet circumstances, it was more likely to ally itself to the Right.[36]

Menshevik suspicion of the peasantry was founded on hostility to an even broader category, the petty bourgeoisie, or, in a native Russian variant, the *meshchanstvo*. Whereas the petty bourgeoisie is an identifiable social stratum consisting of peasant proprietors and numerous nonproletarian urban elements, *meshchanstvo* refers as much to an attitude as to a specific social group. The Russian term is generally pejorative, and Menshevik use of the term is particularly negative. Indeed, in their contempt and their vehemence, Menshevik characterizations of *meshchanstvo* exceed their descriptions of either the Bolsheviks or the former possessing classes. *Meshchanstvo* is defined, above all, by its pettiness.[37] Its spirit could corrupt any class, and, under Soviet conditions, it was corrupting even the working class; the adjective *mesh-*

chanskii partially supplanted the earlier term "plebeian" as a negative description of the Russian worker. *Meshchanstvo* was rampant in the villages, too, as rural inequalities bred a new class of village proprietors. Above all, *meshchanstvo* was incarnated in a new bourgeoisie, a term which some Mensheviks used in an uncharacteristically loose way.

In every European country a new bourgeoisie had emerged from the tumult of war, its fortunes founded on speculation and shady dealings. Nowhere was this bourgeoisie as new, as vulgar, and as lawless as in Russia. Here it consisted of deserters, thieves who had enriched themselves in requisitions, peasants who sold at the highest prices, functionaries who took bribes, and specialists who charged stiff fees for their services. In other words, it was made up of riffraff, "people of all ranks and classes, . . . without mothers or fathers."[38] Indeed, Dallin waxes nostalgic in comparing these swindlers, rascals, and adventurers to the solid, contract-respecting bourgeoisie of the past. This new bourgeoisie had quickly sunk its roots in postrevolutionary Russia. One of its spawning grounds was the Cheka, where confiscation was an instrument of self-enrichment. Even under war communism, in 1919, a decree allowing state firms to place orders with private suppliers obliquely recognized the existence of this new class, and NEP represented nothing less than the new bourgeoisie's Magna Carta.[39]

The Mensheviks explained the emergence of the new bourgeoisie by the fact that conditions for economic equality were lacking in Soviet Russia. Scarcity as well as lack of culture, or *nekul'turnost'*, made such negative phenomena inevitable, and NEP gave them a push forward. Nevertheless, the Mensheviks insisted, even at the end of NEP, that this postrevolutionary bourgeoisie was only in the process of formation.[40] Just as the Mensheviks were wary of calling NEP Russia capitalist, preferring to speak of capitalist tendencies, so too were they leery of describing these beneficiaries of NEP as a full-blown bourgeoisie. In both cases, the Mensheviks allowed their Marxist framework, with its emphasis on the criterion of formal ownership of the means of production, to direct their analyses and their sentiments.

A particular breeding ground of *meshchanstvo* was the Soviet bureaucracy. On the eve of NEP one out of two adults in Moscow and Petrograd worked in a Soviet office, constituting a huge mass of irresponsible petty functionaries and a depraved upper bureaucratic stratum. Clawing their way upward from the social depths where they originated, bereft of any culture or schooling, these former sailors, noncommissioned officers, postmen, kulaks, and clerks eagerly chose management of the state over productive work. In the absence of elective organs, of a free press, and of *glasnost'*, bureaucratic tendencies toward careerism, intrigue, and nepotism flourished. Bureaucrats were chosen for political reliability rather than professional competence, but they were rewarded for being apolitical, for renouncing their civic rights, and for practicing servility toward their superiors. The terror they administered was no longer impulsive, as in the early phase of the Revolution; it was now cold and calculating.[41] In Kafka's words, the Revolution evaporated, leaving behind only the slime of a new bureaucracy.

At the same time, in contrast with anarchist and syndicalist currents among workers, even within the Bolshevik party, the Mensheviks did not believe that bureaucracy could be dispensed with altogether. All bureaucracies were wasteful and incompetent, but it was utopian to believe that bureaucracy could be abolished, or even reduced numerically, as the state assumed control of a country's productive apparatus. Thus, the Mensheviks were not surprised at Soviet admission that nationalized enterprises had more management personnel than their prewar equivalents. But they countered the Soviet argument that these new managers were paid lower salaries by pointing to "invisible" compensations and concluded that, in terms of its implications for the accumulation of capital, the personal consumption of managers was hardly less than it had been in the past.[42]

Admitting the inevitability of some sort of bureaucracy, the Mensheviks attempted to differentiate within the bureaucracy itself. Polemically they might equate the entire state administration with the Cheka, but they also sought to contrast non-Communist and Communist elements within the bureaucracy. In Martov's analysis, Lenin, having concluded that NEP could not be implemented by Communist utopians, emerged as the defender of the non-Communist part of the bureaucracy, the specialists and intelligentsia "hangers-on" to Soviet power, against radicals such as Bukharin and Trotsky.[43] Other Menshevik analyses agreed that it was perfectly logical for a pseudo-capitalist NEP to require a bureaucracy that was bourgeois rather than Communist in spirit, but they stressed the loss of that honest Communist rank and file "which had not lost its faith in the force of the masses, which contained the huge kernel of democratism present in classical bolshevism [!] and which felt at ease in congresses, committees, and elections rather than among officers, subcommissars, Chekists, and gendarmes."[44] Indeed, one of the ills of bureaucratization was that it corrupted the party, transforming bolshevism into a party of peasants who held administrative posts.[45]

In drawing up their tableau of NEP society, the Mensheviks rounded out their analysis of the economic nature of NEP. A pseudo-capitalist system such as NEP did not necessarily produce the social aberrations they were describing. Rather, as the Mensheviks insisted time and again, it was the conjunction of pseudo-capitalist conditions and the absence of democracy that dictated the deformed development of Soviet Russia. The political pendant to the phenomena they were describing can be summarized in two terms borrowed from the French Revolution, which recur almost obsessively in Menshevik discussions: "bonapartism" and "thermidor."

In the Marxist vocabulary bonapartism refers primarily to a situation in which the state apparatus has emancipated itself from its social basis. As Marx wrote, bonapartism is the "only form of government possible at a time when the bourgeoisie has already lost, and the working class has not yet acquired, the faculty of ruling the nation."[46] Its historical prototype was the regime established by Louis Napoleon Bonaparte. In Marx's analysis this "little Napoleon" gained power by manipulating the peasantry, and held it by playing off social classes against one another. In fact, however, he was using his vast state machine to create favorable conditions for capitalist development.

In the background of this analysis stood the image of the first Napoleon, the revolutionary general who turned his cannon against the Revolution to create a new postrevolutionary order. In a wider sense, bonapartism thus also came to stand for the danger of a military takeover of the Revolution. It was in this sense that the term was used by Lenin to discredit Kerensky in 1917 and by Trotsky's rivals to discredit the political ambitions of the founder of the Red Army.[47] Borrowing loosely from the same historical model, "thermidor" became a shorthand reference to the moment of emergence of bonapartism. It could refer to a specific event, typically a coup which brought a military leader to power. More problematically, it might refer to the general process of halting and eventually reversing the course of the Revolution.

All these elements were present as the Mensheviks discussed Russia's political future. Without claiming originality, the Mensheviks gave these terms unprecedented currency and elasticity.[48] In their usage bonapartism meant a "despotically ruled bureaucratic state" animated by the "antisocialist violence of the peasant masses and of the bearers of a new capitalism."[49] Above all, it pointed to a novel and peculiar phenomenon. Bonapartism was an original "synthesis of tsarism and peasant revolution." It was an autocracy, but one "with the passive approval of the people."[50] Consequently, bonapartism was not merely a conventional reactionary despotism. Its revolutionary roots provided it with a residue of popular support and limited the extent to which it could openly repudiate its original ideals. Just as Napoleon I did not restore the ancien régime but built his new order on lip service to revolutionary ideals, forces of bonapartism in Russia could not readily free themselves entirely from their revolutionary origins. In short, bonapartism was a deviation rather than a retreat from revolution.

Some Mensheviks emphasized the capitalist character of bonapartism more than others.[51] Disagreements arose concerning the agents and the timing of the phenomenon. Generally speaking, right wing Mensheviks assumed that Bolsheviks themselves would carry out the bonapartist transformation and that the thermidorian moment of bonapartization was imminent or even that it had already occurred.[52] In support of this view, Petr Garvi, for example, distinguished between an economic thermidor and a political thermidor and between an existing "social bonapartism" and an emerging "bourgeois bonapartism."[53] Left wing Mensheviks stressed obstacles to bonapartism posed by bolshevism's class character, its past, and its ideology, and they tried to identify alternative agents of bonapartization.[54] In the same vein, they thought of thermidor as a possibility, a sort of *terminus ad quem* toward which the Bolshevik regime was tending. As critics pointed out, however, this meant that left wing Mensheviks treated thermidor as a permanently receding horizon, ever present but never attained.

The Mensheviks thus spent the NEP years recording signs of thermidor and bonapartization. They scrutinized the social forces vying for the crown of a collective Bonaparte: army, peasantry, state bureaucracy, new bourgeoisie, the Bolshevik Party itself. As late as March 1928 Dallin wrote that the Bolshevik regime was evolving very slowly. Neither he nor his comrades realized that Russia was on the verge of seismic transformations that would make the notions of bonapartism and thermidor quaint anachronisms.[55] At the very most, the Mensheviks would have the bitter satisfaction of knowing that although they had not foreseen these transformations, their general analysis had proven correct: a petty bourgeois, utopian revolution which had veered onto a pseudo-capitalist course of development without making any concessions to democracy could not put the Revolution back on the right track.[56] Quite the contrary, by unleashing dangerous new forces and repressing democracy, it had created insurmountable contradictions. The Russian Revolution was heading toward catastrophe.

The Party Underground

As NEP evolved, the Menshevik Party changed. So long as the RSDRP existed in Russia, Mensheviks abroad could insist they were not an emigré party. Its point of gravity, however, moved toward Berlin, and at the end of 1922 the party in Russia went underground. Although it had not been made illegal, the fiction of legality to which its members clung was simply untenable.

The Menshevik Central Committee transferred most functions to the Foreign Delegation, and its remains in Russia reconstituted themselves as the Bureau of the Central Committee. The rank and file no longer had to declare party affiliation under interrogation, party cadres dropped out of public view, and party cells changed into clandestine bodies. The party reassumed something of its prerevolutionary aspect in the vastly transformed conditions of postrevolutionary Russia.[1]

Curiously, perhaps perversely, the Bolsheviks contributed substantially to maintaining the image of the Mensheviks as an effective political party. Lenin himself took the lead in warning of a Menshevik danger; in 1921–1923 he returned to this theme in over seventy articles, sometimes in bloodcurdling language.[2] In reply to a hypothetical Menshevik's plea, ''You are now retreating; I have been advocating retreat all the time . . . let us retreat together,'' Lenin declared: ''For the public manifestation of menshevism our revolutionary courts must pass the death sentence, otherwise they are not courts but God knows what.'' This judgment was only slightly qualified later: ''The application of the death sentence should be extended (commutable to deportation) . . . to all forms of activity by Mensheviks, SRs, and so on.''[3] In comparison, some of Lenin's other statements on the subject sound mild. In an important article initiating NEP he accepted, almost philosophically, that revival of cooperatives would bring to the fore ''more business-like, economically more advanced elements'' such as Mensheviks and SRs. Commenting on nonparty conferences, he affirmed that these were ''valuable if they help us come closer to the impassive masses . . . [T]hey are harmful if they provide a platform for Mensheviks and SRs, masquerading as 'nonparty men.' '' His conclusion was that ''the place for Mensheviks and SRs, avowed or in nonparty guise, is not at a nonparty conference but in prison (or on foreign journals, side by side with White Guards; we were glad to let Martov go abroad).''[4]

These statements were made *before* the Mensheviks went underground. They represented calls for vigilance in the relatively relaxed conditions of NEP, and in making them Lenin sought to counter the still widespread assumption, even among Communist workers, that Mensheviks were ''half-Bolsheviks'' and should be seen as potential allies.[5] The statements also expressed Lenin's frustration with the last remnants of an organized opposition. Some Mensheviks saw in the virulence of these remarks signs of impending mental disequilibrium.[6] Others suggested that they were intended to appease the Bolshevik left wing at a time when the Bolshevik Party was turning sharply rightward.[7] Whatever the meaning of Lenin's remarks they sanctioned a particularly combative attitude toward the Menshevik Party. In years to come this attitude legitimized exchanges of accusations of "menshevism" among all contenders for Lenin's succession. It transformed the term into a catchall epithet for completely unrelated phenomena.[8] Indeed, *Sotsialisticheskii vestnik* suggested early on that charges of "menshevism" simply concealed struggles among Bolsheviks; this practice was to be generalized recklessly in the future.[9]

Lenin's inveighings against menshevism also served as the basis for a systematic party campaign which promoted the Mensheviks to the status of the "main danger" facing the Bolshevik regime.[10] A Communist Central Committee circular of June 1923 sent to all provincial organizations described the Menshevik Party as the only organization seeking to spread its work over the whole country and "the most significant force on our political arena working in the direction of bourgeois counterrevolution." Its actual recommendations were rather mild: the circular called on party organizations to "categorically forbid Mensheviks from giving lectures in party schools and circles" and to strengthen party work wherever Menshevik influence was felt. A subsequent circular in January 1924 signed by Molotov made it clear that the Bolsheviks put high hopes in the *byvshie* movement to "liquidate" the Menshevik Party, thus allowing it to be said that the party had dissolved itself.[11]

Above and beyond such efforts, the Moscow Communist Party's agitation bureau *(agitcollegium)* decided to send a copy of *Sotsialisticheskii vestnik* to all its district organizations, and the Petrograd provincial committee created a special commission on the struggle against menshevism. State organs provided the requisite follow-up owing to the Cheka's very active Second Section for Menshevik affairs. *Pravda* expressed satisfaction at the "disintegration of Mr. Dan's party," but the Menshevik problem refused to go away. A Communist Central Committee resolution of 1926 noted the attempts of "petty bourgeois parties" to reestablish their influence, and in 1927 *Pravda* still considered it important to continue its anti-Menshevik campaign.[12]

In the face of such pressure, Menshevik organizations in Russia proved remarkably resilient. Reports from the Bureau at home to the Foreign Delegation in Berlin capture the striking contrast between a somber reality and the buoyant mood of party workers. At Christmas 1923 Raphael Abramovitch echoed these reports in a letter to Kautsky: "News from Russia is sad as far as the party in the *narrow* sense of the word is understood: prison, banishment, suicide in prison, hunger strikes. But, politically, we seem to be at a turning point. The proletariat is gradually awakening from its earlier lethargy." Four Christmases later, Fedor Dan was even more sanguine. As he read reports of the revival of political activity among old Mensheviks and of the inclination of many young Communists (Komsomols) toward social democracy, his principal fear was that the "optimism of our comrades in Russia" might move them to undertake tasks which exceeded their capacities. He did not doubt that he was witnessing the beginnings of authentic *political* struggles in Russia. Even the grimmest letters, which spoke of "truly monstrous conditions of terror, of general demoralization," stressed that "raging repressions [have] failed to kill us altogether and *potentially* we are strong."[13]

To a certain extent such affirmations represent "official optimism" meant to keep up party morale and to impress foreign socialists. With the wisdom of hindsight, one can dismiss as grotesque a letter to Russia dated 1929—as collectivization and industrialization were under way—which expresses pleasure at information received on the rebirth of party activities.[14] Nevertheless, party correspondence and reports in the "Po Rossii" (Throughout Russia) and "Iz partii" (From the Party) columns of *Sotsialisticheskii vestnik* confirm that party life went on under the most arduous circumstances. In 1925 the Foreign Delegation claimed, with legitimate pride, that "comrades in Russia have managed to maintain a well-conducted party machinery which functions without interruption, is in contact with numerous local party organizations and groups, possesses a secret printing press of its own, and keeps up regular intercourse with the party abroad." In 1928 the Menshevik Foreign Delegation still reported the existence of at least ten local organizations in Russia.[15] Soviet authorities did intercept some Menshevik communications from Berlin to Russia. For the most part, however, these were articles and statements intended for public distribution. Individual names in the intercepted letters remained disguised or were left blank.[16]

The Mensheviks' success in setting up an underground apparatus in Russia was due in part to the energy and determination of the head of the illegal Russian Bureau, Georgii Kuchin-Oranskii. In 1917 Kuchin, "a young lieutenant with a gentle pink face, nearsighted eyes and blond whiskers," had been a prominent spokesman for troops at the front.[17] Thereafter he served as a volunteer in the Red Army during the Polish-Soviet war and continued legal party work until his arrest and banishment to Central Asia in 1921. After his escape and return to Moscow the following year, Kuchin took charge of the party in Russia until his final arrest in 1925. During the intervening years, not only did he manage to crisscross the country without being detected, but in 1924 he even traveled to Berlin and Vienna (and back to Russia) to participate in party deliberations and in LSI meetings. Sentenced to five years' imprisonment, Kuchin was put in solitary confinement. He launched a hunger strike which received international publicity. Then, at the expiration of his prison term, Kuchin, like virtually all other social democrats who had served a prison sentence, was banished to a distant part of the Soviet Union.[18]

Much of the optimism and enthusiasm which radiate from reports sent by the party in Russia can be attributed to the emergence of a Social Democratic Youth League (its motto was "The future belongs to us"). This movement arose spontaneously, in defiance of a party ban on such separate organizations. Most members were students, old enough to have witnessed as adolescents the Revolution of 1917 and the political ferment of the first Soviet years. They were more radically anti-Bolshevik than their elders, more zealous in plunging into illegal activity, and more daring in their party work. Their numbers cannot be determined precisely, but they amounted to at least several hundred individuals, 120 to 150 in Moscow alone. They operated under the strictest conspiratorial cover, divided into circles of five to seven members, only one of whom would be in touch with representatives of other circles. The youth movement published its own pamphlets and occasional periodicals, in cooperation with the party but with an intensity of its own.[19]

Andrei Kranikhfeld, leader of the Social Democratic Youth League and Martov's nephew, provided the same inspiration for his young comrades as Kuchin did for their elders. Described as a *narodnik*-like personality of the 1870s, upright, uncompromising, and fearless, Kranikhfeld almost seemed to enjoy playing cat and mouse with the police as he underwent arrest and escaped, twice, from his jailers.[20] Kranikhfeld's ambition was to establish a countrywide youth organization. Although the constituent meeting did take place in September 1923, the delegates were all arrested just as the meeting ended. Shaken but undaunted, the youth movement continued its activities for at least another two years. Its chronicler attributes its ultimate demise not simply to repression, which had not become noticeably harsher, but also to the disappearance of that particular generational group and attitudes that had given birth to the movement. By 1926 passivity, conformism, and weariness with politics dominated all age groups. Moreover, universities, the movement's prime recruiting ground, were being filled with graduates of "workers' faculties" *(rabfaktsy)*, ambitious and upwardly mobile youths entirely formed under Soviet conditions and loyal to the regime.[21] Thereafter, the youth movement lived on only in the prisons, camps, and places of internal banishment to which its members were confined.

The frustrations of life underground were sometimes more difficult to bear than its dangers. Kuchin complained that the deeper the party apparatus went underground, the more petty became the difficulties they encountered. The tasks of finding safe meeting places even for the smallest group, of sheltering party cadres, and of storing documents and publications proved all-absorbing. The party's main printing press had to be established in Petrograd rather than in Moscow because it proved impossible to find a secure apartment in the capital. Boris Dvinov once had to flee his home and spend a night roaming the streets in the rain with two heavy batches of party archives under his arm until a friendly neighbor took him in.[22] Above all, financial problems weighed constantly on the party, limiting its already narrow room for maneuver.

In spite of these difficulties, the Foreign Delegation in Berlin and the party in Russia managed to remain in contact almost without interruption. The flow of publications and a steady exchange of views continued throughout the 1920s. Copious reports of the situation in urban centers and in various factories sent from Russia by individual party members persisted well into the 1930s. Even an unsympathetic observer acknowledges that these reports were unique inasmuch as they were based on living ties with Russia.[23] The reports were frequently utilized or reprinted in whole by the emigré press and by foreign newspapers; they also found their way into the chancelleries of foreign powers.

To this day, channels used by the Mensheviks to maintain communications with Russia have not been fully divulged.[24] Available information suggests there were four separate channels. The first required the services of "honorable, honest smugglers, as in the old days." The smugglers alleged, however, that the import of illegal literature was far more dangerous than in the past, and they raised the price of their services accordingly.[25] The second was the Latvian embassy in Moscow. As a Latvian socialist put it, the Latvian Social Democratic Party was "actually a Menshevik party"; it was also the strongest party in the country. The Latvian diplomatic pouch carried several hundred copies of each issue of *Sotsialisticheskii vestnik* to Moscow, where the secretary of the embassy distributed them to representatives of Menshevik organizations. Moreover, forged travel documents were provided by the Latvians to Eva Broido, and perhaps to other Mensheviks as well.[26] A third channel may have been the German embassy in Moscow whenever the SPD was in the government.[27] Even less is known about the fourth channel.[28]

In addition to these clandestine means of communication, the Mensheviks also added messages in invisible ink to family letters. In contrast with other channels, such messages were not coded, which suggests that there were few fears of detection. Presumably this particular channel became unusable by the end of the 1920s, when the very fact that one received (even innocent) letters from abroad could become cause for arrest.[29] Finally, a certain amount of information, although probably not much written material, could be transmitted by the occasional traveler in either direction who, for reasons of family, friendship, or conviction, would agree to act as a go-between.

Sotsialisticheskii vestnik constituted the bulk of Menshevik traffic from Berlin to Russia. For the Foreign Delegation, the illegal distribution of several hundred copies of a sixteen-page newspaper every two weeks represented a formidable logistical challenge.[30] They met this challenge so successfully that not until the early 1930s did they feel the need to facilitate the penetration of *Vestnik* into Russia by printing a special miniature version of the paper. It is impossible to ascertain the readership of *Vestnik* within Russia or the efficiency of the internal distribution network. As Dvinov put it dryly, only in prison could one keep statistics on readership. Each copy, however, was passed from hand to hand and was read by numerous individuals, "literally until the holes form."[31]

Sotsialisticheskii vestnik was therefore not simply the main link between the party on the inside and outside. It was the fundamental expression of the party's continued existence and the measure of its vitality. For the Mensheviks in Berlin, publication of *Vestnik* justified the decision to go abroad inasmuch as party opinion (and individual conscience) sanctioned foreign exile only in the interest of party work, not for personal reasons. The interaction between the two sectors of the party in the pages of *Vestnik*, with its exchange of opinion and information from Berlin to Russia concerning international developments and from Russia to Berlin concerning Soviet ones, validated the Mensheviks' claims that they were not an exile group but a functioning party. Indeed, the readership of *Sotsialisticheskii vestnik* may be seen as the real constituency of the RSDRP after 1921–22.

The journal was no less vital for the party at home. For the Mensheviks in Russia, *Vestnik* was a lifeline. Its initial arrival has been compared to the restoration of speech to a mute or to the cross that wards off the devil. The Mensheviks felt that "all those around us judge the extent of our activity by the regularity and breadth of distribution of *V*." So long as *Vestnik* kept arriving, Mensheviks underground could feel that they enjoyed a window onto the outside world, that their voice could be heard abroad and even, indirectly, at home as well. In their letters to the party leadership they repeatedly demanded greater coverage of the western workers' movement in *Vestnik*. They showed avid interest in its numerous discussions. They also used it as a bulletin board concerning the fate of individual party members.[32]

Although *Sotsialisticheskii vestnik* constituted a focus for the party's energies and a strong link between the party at home and abroad, it did not resolve tensions between the two. For instance, when Eva Broido, as a member of the Foreign Delegation, asked what the party at home was doing on behalf of women, her question was derided as proof that Berlin's Mensheviks had no appreciation of the conditions of party work in Russia.[33] Certain tensions concerned the paper itself. Some Mensheviks, in general those abroad, considered *Vestnik* a "combat instrument," whereas others saw it as a theoretical organ.[34] If we can judge by samplings, the underground press in Russia was less theoretically sophisticated and more *ouvrieriste* than *Vestnik*. A number of Mensheviks, mostly in Russia, objected to the designation of *Sotsialisticheskii vestnik* as the central organ of the RSDRP.[35] Eventually, even its success was a cause for concern among some underground party members. As one frustrated member put it, reading *Vestnik* had turned from an instrument into a goal in itself.[36]

Behind these issues stood the question of who should define the party's orientation. The Foreign Delegation was better equipped, practically and perhaps also intellectually, to assume leadership. The Bureau in Russia was better placed to judge the party's needs. It was also in a stronger moral position: the party in Russia was considered by all Mensheviks to be the very raison d'être for the organization abroad, and the sufferings of the party in Russia put it on a superior moral plane. Quite rapidly, however—and in spite of Kuchin's fulminations against the emigré *stikhiia*, or psychosis—initiative in all party matters passed entirely to the Foreign Delegation.[37] This was not simply because of continuing repression in Russia but also because of the party's initially tacit recognition of a new role. As soon as the party ceased to see itself as a mass organization embroiled in open political struggle, its self-definition changed. The criterion of success resided no longer in factors such as party membership but in the ability to disseminate its views. The party became important not as a political force but as the expression of a political possibility. Mensheviks in exile could play this role more easily and more fully than those in Russia.

The ascendancy of the emigré wing of the Menshevik Party recalls similar emigré dominance within the original RSDRP at the turn of the century. Indeed, the organizational structure of menshevism after 1922 would seem to have been borrowed directly from that earlier period. According to the plan drawn up by Lenin in 1902, the party was to have two controlling centers, an intellectual and a practical one. The central organ, *Iskra*, played the role of the former, owing to its location abroad, far from "Russian gendarmes"; the Central Committee in Russia, which was "always in accord with the central organ in all essentials," played the role of the latter.[38] It is not surprising that Martov and Dan, who had been directly involved in these earlier plans, should have adopted them again. It is puzzling, however, that they should have been indifferent to the possible consequences of such a structure, especially since they had for so long denounced the consequences of Lenin's organizational scheme. Lenin's plan had been designed to ensure emigré hegemony over party workers at home. In spite of protests that it remained a party within Russia, the structures of the Menshevik Party after 1921 also ensured primacy to the emigrés.

Kuchin realized the irony of the fact that his party had chosen a Bolshevik solution to the organizational question. He may also have felt, justifiably, that it was sound strategy to adopt the battle formations of one's (victorious) enemies. For older Mensheviks the temptation to fall back on familiar solutions from the party's early days was insurmountable. One longtime party member declared in 1931 that what was needed in present circumstances was a "collective Plekhanov," a body which would trace the paths down which the country was heading. By that late date, as in the distant past, such a body could exist only abroad.[39]

In addition to other sources of tension, one must take account of the division between right and left Mensheviks which cut through the party organization at home and abroad. At a prison meeting just before leaving Russia in early 1922, Grigorii Aronson was entrusted by like-minded comrades with the task of establishing a right Menshevik organ in the West. After having assessed the situation abroad, and particularly the reigning pro-Soviet attitudes among foreign socialists, Aronson concluded it would be preferable to work within existing structures. From then on the struggle to recognize the right wing viewpoint in information published in *Vestnik* became a major preoccupation of the party minority. The two right wing members of the Foreign Delegation, Mark Kefali and Aronson, demanded that the business of maintaining practical ties with Russia not be left in the hands of Iugov and Nicolaevsky, who were responsible for editing reports for publication in *Vestnik*.[40] In an inconclusive quarrel each side accused the other of seeking to impose censorship. The quarrel was never resolved but was merely exhausted with the severing of ties to Russia in the 1930s.

The attempt to enlist the underground party on the side of one of the Foreign Delegation factions (or on the side of the extraparty right Mensheviks) encountered resistance at home. "Let them consider us heroes, as long as they do not consider us fools" was Kuchin's attitude toward pressure from Berlin.[41] Not only was Kuchin unwilling to act as the instrument of emigré party factions, or even as the prize over which they were fighting, but also his own views were virtually unclassifiable in terms of the traditional Menshevik spectrum. It might be said that Kuchin began as a right Menshevik in the early 1920s (he had been a defensist during the war and something of a liquidator previously) to become eventually a left Menshevik. In fact, his position was peculiarly pragmatic. Kuchin believed, as did the Menshevik right wing, that there was no point in talking of socialist possibilities in Russia. The course of future development was resolutely capitalist, whatever the rhetoric of the Bolsheviks. Kuchin, however, also advocated defense of the regime, and he continued to express optimism about the prospects for revolution in the West longer than most of his comrades.[42]

It was Kuchin who, out of pessimism, insisted that the party go underground in 1922, but it was also he who worked hardest to propagate party work in these unfavorable conditions. He consistently criticized the party leadership, usually in the bluntest terms, reproaching it for earlier illusions, exemplified in the radical left theses of April 1920, as for later efforts to formulate a new party platform (which he dismissed as an attempt to "put a top hat on a naked man"). He offended the Right of the party by adopting a strictly class-conscious position and by mocking "liberal sobs about the 'horrors of terror'" even as he disappointed the Left by scoffing at the notion that "significant" strata of the proletariat stood behind the regime and by repudiating hopes of any sort of agreement with the regime.[43]

Surveying the situation of the Mensheviks in Russia, one notes a group which might be called, paradoxically, nonparty Mensheviks. These were party members who had drifted away from the RSDRP without joining the Bolshevik Party and usually without publicly repudiating their views. They were particularly numerous among the specialists serving the Soviet state in nonpolitical institutions. *Sotsialisticheskii vestnik* judged these Menshevik specialists severely. It saw them as nourishing the illusion that one could develop the country's economic base without touching its political superstructure. It explained their attitude as founded on impotence: since these specialists were given wide discretion in the economic field but were not admitted to political work, they concluded that politics was "just a noble sport for the aristocracy," that all Russia's problems lay in its backwardness, and that salvation was to be found in attracting capital to Russia.[44] Nonparty Mensheviks reciprocated this disdain. They were convinced that NEP offered significant possibilities for a "healthy evolution of Soviet power" and found confirmation in the statistics they compiled (the Soviet statistical apparatus was one of their bastions). Indeed, they concluded that the Russian people, in the cities and in the countryside, had never lived as well as they were living at the height of NEP.[45]

The basic quarrel between nonparty Mensheviks and *Sotsialisticheskii vestnik*, however, centered not on the issue of whether conditions in Russia had improved (on which there was substantial agreement for a brief period), but on the question of capitalism. Given the nationalization of land, forests, and mineral resources and the extent of state ownership in heavy industry, transport, banking, and wholesale commerce, nonparty Mensheviks adamantly denied that NEP could be characterized as capitalism. They also refused to concede that the Soviet worker was subjected to capitalist-type exploitation. Given their prominence in the Soviet planning apparatus, it is not surprising that they also rejected the theses of emigré Menshevik economists concerning the essential planlessness of the Soviet economy.[46]

These disagreements dictated political divergences. Nonparty Mensheviks were dismayed that the RSDRP's analysis should coincide with, even if its political conclusions differed from, that of the Bolshevik left wing opposition. As one of them put it, "*Sotsialisticheskii vestnik* only said crudely what Trotskyists and Zinovievites expressed euphemistically." They reacted strongly to this failure to appreciate NEP's positive potential and to the tacit support given to factional Bolshevik elements among whom one could discern "not a grain of democracy."[47] Even thirty years later Abramovitch was not able to convince their spokesman, Valentinov-Volsky, that *Vestnik*'s position had been justified. According to Abramovitch, *Vestnik* was not anti-NEP and certainly not Trotskyist, as Volsky had insinuated. Rather, its contributors saw their duty as that of pointing out the political danger of NEP, the divorce between NEP policies and the "dictatorship of the proletariat," and the likelihood that dictatorship plus NEP would lead to bonapartism. As for Volsky's implied accusation that the Berlin Mensheviks had failed to support the best chance for a happy outcome in Soviet Russia, Abramovitch conceded that they did not foresee the ensuing "bacchanalia of communization," but, he added, the nonparty Mensheviks had also proven wrong in their expectations.[48]

Valentinov-Volsky's memoirs of his years as a Soviet specialist provide an unrepentant defense of the nonparty Mensheviks' stance and a unique insight into Soviet political and bureaucratic life under NEP.[49] Sporting a bowler hat (which he wore precisely because it was an unfashionable and even a subversive item), Volsky worked as de facto editor of *Torgovopromyshlennaia gazeta* (Commercial-Industrial Journal), the organ of the Supreme Economic Council (VSNKh) throughout the 1920s. Here, this former companion of Lenin and later fiercely right wing Menshevik watched the leading Bolsheviks and listened in on some of their debates. As might be expected, Trotsky, G. L. Piatakov, and E. A. Preobrazhenskii struck him as petty or sectarian or lacking judgment. In fact, Volsky—and others like him—gladly supported Stalin over Trotsky.[50]

A Bolshevik who merited Volsky's unstinting praise was the creator of the

Cheka, Feliks Dzerzhinskii, by then head of the Supreme Economic Council. When the radical Bolshevik planner Iurii Larin accused the council of being in the hands of Mensheviks, Dzerzhinskii retorted that he could only wish that other commissariats were in their hands as well. According to Volsky, Dzerzhinskii was eager to bring about rapprochement between Communist and non-Communist industrial cadres; he protected specialists from arrest and even wanted to provide them with some sort of protective "constitution." All the positive campaigns of the Supreme Economic Council—in favor of lowering industrial prices, increasing the productivity of labor, and reconstituting the metal industry, among others—were attributable to Dzerzhinskii himself. In 1925, during his tenure as head of the Supreme Economic Council, NEP reached its apogee, Russia attained an unprecedented level of social harmony and prosperity, and the council itself hummed busily as it planned the country's economic future.[51] Dzerzhinskii's untimely death the following year, just hours after he delivered a passionate speech attacking bureaucratism and poor administration, was mourned by all nonparty specialists. It was only a partial coincidence that his death marked the decline of their privileges and hopes.

Among the revelations of Volsky's memoirs is the description of an unusual secret club consisting mainly of nonparty Mensheviks, including some who had been prominent before the Bolshevik takeover and others who held responsible positions in Soviet institutions. Dubbed half-jokingly by its members "Liga nabliudatelei" (League of Observers), this club met from 1922 to 1927 in the manner of a traditional Russian *kruzhok*. Members discussed questions of ideology and politics and exchanged impressions of current developments. There was nothing subversive about the club. Its members were convinced of the durability of the Soviet regime; they were committed to NEP; and the club itself had no ties to Mensheviks underground or abroad.[52]

Volsky himself shunned contact with the Mensheviks to such an extent that when he found himself temporarily in Berlin, he avoided meeting with them, though he spent his time there reading *Sotsialisticheskii vestnik*—at the Soviet mission. In spite of his disdain for *Vestnik*'s views, which comes out clearly even in memoirs written many years later, Volsky admits that he was amazed at *Vestnik*'s awareness of what was going on in the very highest Soviet spheres. His readings in Berlin made him realize that the press section of the Bolshevik Central Committee had been withholding some issues of *Vestnik* even from high-ranking Communists. It was only in Berlin that he became acquainted with Lenin's "Testament" and was able, on the basis of Trotsky's letters leaked to *Vestnik*, to make sense of rumors he had heard earlier in Moscow.[53]

Volsky's curiosity concerning the Mensheviks' informers had still not been satisfied when he was writing his memoirs in the mid-1950s. Only through his later correspondence with Abramovitch did he learn that one informer had been V. G. Groman, a member of the Liga nabliduatelei who, whatever else he revealed, also gave the Berlin Mensheviks details about the Liga itself. Another nonparty Menshevik who had taken advantage of official Soviet missions to Germany to make contact with the party abroad was A. M. Ginzburg, a man, according to Volsky's memoir, so hostile to the Menshevik line that he "refused to even look at *Sotsialisticheskii vestnik.*"[54]

Both Ginzburg and Groman were to be defendants in the Menshevik trial of 1931. In light of Abramovitch's revelation and of Volsky's description of the subculture of nonparty Menshevik specialists, one can reconstruct something of the background to that trial. The nonparty Mensheviks served NEP policies enthusiastically even as they worked on the first drafts of a long-term economic plan. When Soviet policies changed radically at the end of the 1920s, the nonparty Mensheviks aroused suspicion on all counts. They were identified with now-repudiated NEP policies; their cautiously formulated draft plans were treated as sabotage attempts; and breakdowns in the realization of the plan were imputed to them. Ties with the Menshevik Party confirmed these suspicions, although, interestingly, Groman's confession of such ties at his trial was based on the inventions of his interrogators, and no mention of the Liga nabliudatelei was ever made. As for Volsky, on learning of Groman's arrest in 1930 and realizing that NEP was definitely over, he left his new position at the Soviet trade mission in Paris to become an emigré and, much later, a contributor to *Sotsialisticheskii vestnik.* One of his last services to the Soviet state, just before he defected, was to write an article for *Izvestiia* on how to attract tourists to the USSR.[55]

To return to the mainstream of the Menshevik Party, as the party's organization shifted abroad, its rank and file in Russia found themselves living increasingly within the world of prison, labor camp, and internal exile. One Menshevik estimates that 2,500 to 3,000 socialists were subjected to repression in the second half of the 1920s, with Mensheviks representing the largest group. This includes so-called "minuses": internal exiles excluded from living in a specific number of urban centers or provinces. For example, "exile minus five" meant that one could not live in Moscow, Leningrad, Kharkov, Kiev, or Odessa.[56]

This surprisingly low estimate by a party member is an indication of the party's ambivalence toward the repression it was enduring. The Mensheviks felt an instinctive repugnance at having their plight treated in purely humanitarian terms, for such treatment failed to distinguish them from bourgeois enemies of the Revolution, belittled their role as a political opposition, and engendered pity rather than respect. As a rule, accounts of "how socialists sat and suffered" were viewed by Mensheviks as unworthy.[57] The exception was the Mensheviks' willingness to focus on mistreatment of party members in Russia to appeal to foreign public opinion. Here, straightforward humanitarian arguments proved to be most effective, even vis-à-vis foreign socialists, because they spoke to basic human decency and bypassed all political disagreements.[58] In this way the Mensheviks hoped that their imprisoned comrades, held as hostages of sorts by the Bolsheviks, would be turned into hostages vis-à-vis international public opinion so that the Bolshevik government could become, to some extent, the hostage of its own hostages.

Repression of Mensheviks in the 1920s has found its chroniclers in more recent times and outside the ranks of the party. *Lenin and the Mensheviks,* written by Vera Broido, the daughter of Menshevik Foreign Delegation member Eva Broido, covers this aspect of party life thoroughly and sympathetically. It is an open question how Mensheviks themselves would have reacted to its martyrological emphasis. In all likelihood indignation aroused in one Menshevik survivor by Solzhenitsyn's annals of the Gulag would probably have been shared by many.

According to T. I. Til', Solzhenitsyn both overstates the advantages enjoyed by political prisoners and understates the degree of socialist resistance within the Gulag. Solzhenitsyn is faulted for failing to see that designation as a political prisoner was not "granted" by the GPU (successor to the Cheka) but won by prisoners after hard struggle. Solzhenitsyn's claims that political prisoners demanded special food rations and received extra cigarette rations are also refuted in detail. The only privileges accorded socialist prisoners were those of isolation, in some prisons, from common law convicts and a certain "self-management" of their material affairs. Prison authorities allowed elected party "elders" to allocate individual food packages among all imprisoned party members. Similarly, political prisoners could pool their money and transfer it from one party member to another so that on liberation each individual had at least some funds to help pay for the return home.[59]

Underpinning disagreements on points of detail between these two chroniclers of the Gulag is a fundamental divergence in ideological vision. Til' is visibly irritated by Solzhenitsyn's underlying implication that socialists were partial or unwitting accomplices to the evils which befell Russia and that they therefore somehow shared responsibility for their own miseries and those of others. In reply to Solzhenitsyn's rhetorical question as to why socialists who used to escape from prison as a matter of course under the tsars should have lost their nerve under the Bolsheviks and accepted their fate meekly, Til' provides a reasoned answer. He points out that a number did escape—Leo Lande escaped four times, the last time abroad—and that successful prison escapes required conditions, such as the existence of safe hiding places, which were absent under the Soviet system. This answer, however, also casts light on the dilemma of the Mensheviks in the new, postrevolutionary circumstances. As he puts it, flight is not an art practiced for its own sake. One can flee for the sake of a cause, but "when there is no longer a cause," one can only flee abroad, and the prospect of leaving Russia entirely was unacceptable to many Mensheviks. As for Solzhenitsyn's resentment of the superior attitude adopted by the Mensheviks to "KRs" (counterrevolutionaries), Til' reciprocates Solzhenitsyn's contempt by arguing that KRs were incapable of any struggle in prison. KRs—even White officers whose profession was combat—lacked the requisite political traditions to continue their struggle after they had been disarmed.[60] In a sense, the mixture of defiance and resignation in this rebuttal only adds grist to Solzhenitsyn's accusations.

It is true that some deprivations suffered by Mensheviks seem mild in comparison with the horrors portrayed by Solzhenitsyn. At times, the Mensheviks continued to benefit from the contradictions of Soviet policy. Martov's brother Sergei Ezhov and Eva Broido had their memoirs published by state publishing houses (and Ezhov was awarded a pension), even as Ezhov experienced internal exile and Broido was imprisoned.[61] Internal exiles received foreign newspapers, and some kept sufficiently abreast of literary developments to request the latest Western novels. Such amenities helped them endure the hardships of life in forlorn places of exile.[62] Psychologically they softened the burden of the exiles' status as *lishentsy*, that is, as individuals deprived of electoral and other rights, including even that of having their children admitted to school. Of course, imprisoned Mensheviks were far worse off than those in exile. By 1928 prisoners in *politisolator*s were allowed to correspond with and receive books from only their closest relatives; walks were reduced to a minimum; and they were forbidden to receive goods such as sweets, dried fruits, and vegetables from outside. Moreover, humiliations and deprivations intensified from year to year.[63]

Even as some Mensheviks at home, moved both by prudence and by a peculiar political pudency, preferred not to dwell on their own sufferings (otherwise the correspondence pages of *Sotsialisticheskii vestnik* would have contained little else), Mensheviks abroad gathered and transmitted with the utmost avidity the reports of ordinary workers' conditions which first flowed and then trickled in from Russia.

A striking aspect of these reports is the deep-seated distaste for NEP among workers. Volsky has noted that his mistake, and that of other non-

Communist specialists in Soviet Russia, was to underestimate the revulsion against NEP at the grass roots of the Communist Party. Had he been more familiar with the sentiments of Menshevik and nonparty workers, he would have found the same attitudes. Dubbing NEP "the New Gastronomic Policy" and "New Exploitation of the Proletariat," large segments of the working class were as repelled by the successes of NEP as by its failures and its hypocrisy. A correspondent from Moscow described the shameless luxury of certain restaurants and cinemas (owned by cooperatives, no less) and added that one Old Bolshevik, V. D. Bonch-Bruevich, had a bookstore where he sold religious books found in various warehouses. Another correspondent wrote sarcastically about the "grandiose life" trumpeted by the Bolsheviks: "Prices are grandiose, trusts are grandiose, theft is grandiose, banditry is grandiose, hunger is grandiose, shootings are grandiose, gluttony and drunkenness are grandiose."[64]

Descriptions of shop floor conditions make arresting reading. Not only were wages repeatedly lowered, but also wage payments were delayed, sometimes for months, either because funds were depleted or, in some cases, because management sought to exploit the fall of the ruble. Workers reacted by striking and, in at least one instance, by murdering a manager. In this case authorities retaliated by killing eight workers, setting off disturbances at other factories. Most reports describe individual conflicts, but occasionally, as in the period July–September 1924, entire waves of strikes were noted as well. In this case *Sotsialisticheskii vestnik* enjoyed the satisfaction of having its information confirmed by no less an authority than *Pravda* itself.[65]

Politically, too, workers proved difficult to subdue. A particularly vivid account in *Vestnik* describes politics within the Comintern printing shop. Elections held there in mid-1922 resulted in the victory of a Social Democratic slate. The local Communist cell had the election results canceled and called for new elections immediately so that its opponents would not have time to present their slate of candidates. The maneuver failed, and three separate slates—Communist, Social Democratic, and nonparty—found themselves again in confrontation. The Communists brought in heavyweight speakers, including Andrei Vyshinskii, to point out the "dangers" (such as loss of jobs) of electing a Menshevik slate. When such threats proved insufficient, the Communists withdrew their candidates and called on all workers to vote for the nonparty list. Nonetheless, the nonparty slate drew only sixty votes against ninety-six for the Social Democrats. Authorities confirmed the election results but sought to exclude the printing shop workers from the cooperative of Comintern employees. This move aroused such indignation among Communist workers themselves that the move was rescinded.[66]

Such stories belong only to the earliest period of NEP. The prevailing atmosphere then may be gauged by the fact that official trade unions were still known to intervene on behalf of rebellious workers. Before the end of NEP open defiance and support from official bodies were no longer possible. By 1924 Communist workers were being expelled from the party solely for advocating wage hikes.[67] A memoir recounts how, in 1929, managers of a factory obtained unanimous support for a Communist-sponsored resolution one afternoon, only to find the inside of the factory plastered with posters denouncing the same resolution the next morning.[68] Only in this sullen fashion could workers express their dissent.

Worse than repression in the workplace, worse than terror, was the problem of unemployment. "In overall living conditions, what hits us even harder [than terror] is the monstrous, utterly uncommunicable, absolutely hopeless . . . unemployment."[69] The fear of being cast out on the street weighed on both workers and *inteligenty* and served as the surest instrument of political conformity. Instead of dealing with unemployment, the authorities reduced the number of people on the unemployment rolls. Inspectors visited homes and removed individuals from the rolls if they were not satisfied with their origins or if they discovered the least trace of luxury in the home. The presence of a soft sofa might be sufficiently damning evidence, even if it was a hand-me-down from previous owners. In spite of such measures, the number of registered unemployed rose. In Moscow, for example, the figure almost doubled in a few months.[70] Only one-third of those registered as unemployed received any benefits at all, and in any case, the benefits were insignificant.

Lassitude and demoralization thus took a heavier toll than political oppression. The curious custom of applying the names of Bolshevik leaders to various vices suggests, however, that the connection between politics and social decay was clear to all. Drunkenness, boosted by the reintroduction of vodka sales in 1924, was associated with Rykov. His heavy drinking led to his name being popularly conferred on a thirty-proof vodka. Black market speculators were referred to as "relatives of Zinoviev," and Tsvetnoi Boulevard in Moscow, a main center for prostitution, was dubbed Bukharinskii Boulevard. It is not known whether the bands of unemployed who wandered the streets poking into chic shops and casinos attached to themselves the name of any particular leader.[71]

As the 1920s advanced, Menshevik correspondence from Russia suggested ever more forcefully that the contradictions of NEP society were becoming intolerable. A report from Moscow on preparations for the tenth anniversary of the Bolshevik Revolution explained that "beautification of the capital" consisted of sending special police units to pick up and expel beggars and other homeless elements. Within the city talk was of war, including civil war between the city and the countryside, and there were fears of famine. As *Vestnik's* informant noted, the rumor that lack of food was caused by the presence of foreign guests attending anniversary celebrations only added an element of xenophobia to the usual antisemitism. An earlier report denied that there were any special fears among the population, but spoke of "a certain tense atmosphere," a growing sense of unease, explicable only in part by the fact that imports of food into the city were falling and it was becoming ever harder to make ends meet.[72]

Psychologically the population seemed to be reaching a breaking point. As one Menshevik put it, for a long time people had tried with all their strength to "carry themselves forward." They had combed, washed, organized, participated in social initiatives and self-improvement schemes. Now, all these people had given up, and the formerly hidden dirt and slime of Moscow had slithered out onto the street. In the aftermath of the tenth anniversary celebrations, a *Vestnik* correspondent wrote that previously it had looked as if an economic revival might be possible. This was no longer the case; ruin was seen as inevitable. Private food stores were closing, and bread lines were ever longer and more ominous. In the thirteenth year of the Revolution ration cards were being reintroduced, but this new "commodity" was not a part of NEP. It was a product of Soviet industrialization and served as one signal among others that NEP was over.[73]

Watching the Kremlin

Objective factors would determine the future of Soviet Russia. The Mensheviks were so convinced of this Marxist truth that they were inclined to express disdain for contingent considerations such as the jostling for power among the Bolsheviks. As the leadership struggle in the Kremlin continued throughout the 1920s, however, several Menshevik attitudes evolved. Initially, the Mensheviks treated dissent among the Bolsheviks simply as proof of the degeneration of the regime. In time some came to see groupings within the Bolshevik, now Communist, Party as bearers of different class interests, while others sought in them a wedge for introducing social democratic influence into Communist ranks. Slowly and reluctantly most Mensheviks began to adopt the position that the outcome of the factional struggle was not a matter of indifference to the future of the Revolution.

Although the Mensheviks tended to minimize the significance of clashes among Communist chieftains, they were particularly well qualified to report on them. The identity of Menshevik sources at the top of the Soviet hierarchy has never been fully elucidated. It is clear that there were a number of highly placed individuals willing and able to transmit privileged information to the RSDRP Foreign Delegation. One might speculate that among these sources was ex-Menshevik Central Committee member Troianovskii, who remained well disposed toward his former comrades and who, before being appointed ambassador to Japan in 1927, worked in the Kremlin as an archivist.[1] It is probable, too, that David Riazanov, director of the Marx-Engels Institute and head of the Central Archives, leaked information. Not only was Riazanov consistently friendly toward the Mensheviks, but also he was regularly in touch with those in Berlin, in connection with scholarly projects. Sentiment, conscience, and frustration also moved other prominent Soviet functionaries, such as Groman, to unburden themselves of secrets in the course of conversations with Mensheviks at home or abroad.

Nicolaevsky has indicated that Lenin's successor as chairman of the Council of People's Commissars, A. I. Rykov, was one of *Sotsialisticheskii vestnik's* informers.[2] Rykov's conciliatory attitude toward the Mensheviks in the past, their convergence on certain issues, and his growing isolation within the Soviet leadership support this suggestion, and his family ties with Nicolaevsky reinforce it.[3] On the basis of ideological and personal ties, one might suspect that the Soviet trade union head M. I. Tomskii kept some Menshevik contacts open. If such highly placed sources for *Vestnik's* information are plausible, it can be taken for granted that there were also lower-ranking individuals within the Soviet establishment who were willing, for a variety of reasons, to divulge gossip, information, or simply hints which could help the Mensheviks piece together what was happening in the Kremlin.[4]

The willingness of prominent Bolsheviks and otherwise loyal Soviet officials to share their views and information with Mensheviks abroad opens questions regarding disinformation and manipulation. A confidential report to the French authorities by a prominent Soviet defector (in all probability Boris Bazhanov) states that the Politburo deliberated on several occasions what measures should be taken to halt the flow of the Mensheviks' "excellent information concerning events occurring in the Bolshevik center." Stalin let the matter drop, however, because the facts presented by the Mensheviks, true though they were, appeared in such distorted form that he felt they could do no harm. Indeed, continues the report, Stalin was very pleased that *Sotsialisticheskii vestnik* was exaggerating its information on struggles among party chiefs "because this only served to camouflage the real mechanics of power in Russia."[5]

This anonymous informant's credibility is undermined by his or her eagerness to prove that any talk of differences among Bolsheviks was a Stalinist trick intended to deceive the outside world about the absolute nature of Stalin's power (this as early as 1923–24).[6] The testimony does beg the question, however, to what extent the Mensheviks served as a conduit for Bolshevik leaks, allowing Bolshevik factions to put forth their views anonymously, and outside the Soviet press. The Berlin Mensheviks, particularly Nicolaevsky and Iugov, who put together *Vestnik*'s "From Russia" columns, were alert for any penetration by Soviet agents, but they seem to have been relatively indifferent to the possibility of unconscious complicity in the Bolshevik leadership struggle.[7]

Every document published in *Vestnik* in the 1920s relating to the intra-Bolshevik struggle has proven authentic.[8] Some were picked up by Western media.[9] Inexplicably, however, Western historians have been inconsistent in recognizing Menshevik priority and the reliability of Menshevik sources. A key study of Lenin's "Last Struggle" fails to mention that the bulk of the documents on which it is based could be found in *Vestnik* decades before they appeared in the Soviet publications on which the study relies.[10] Suspicion of Menshevik information would not seem to be an explanation here since, elsewhere, the same historian accepts the authenticity of a more controversial Menshevik source from the 1930s.[11] Similarly, two historians who have written sympathetically of the Mensheviks credit only the American ex-Trotskyist Max Eastman with first divulging Lenin's "Testament."[12] In fact, Eastman himself wrote that the information in his sensational book *Since Lenin Died* came from "official documents stolen by counter-revolutionists and published . . . in the *Sotzialistichesky Viestnik* [sic]." As he puts it, this "remnant of Menshevism publishes a good deal of nonsense and irresponsible rumor about Russia," but there is "no doubt" about the authenticity of these documents.[13]

Beyond the authenticity of documents, it is more difficult to assess the value of Menshevik analyses and predictions concerning the leadership struggle. *Sotsialisticheskii vestnik*'s articles have certainly withstood the test of time better than contemporary Western journalistic reports. A *New York Times* article compared Stalin the "autocrat" and Trotsky the "democrat," claiming that "their differences are the same as those between the governmental conceptions of Hamilton and Jefferson [!]." The article concluded that Trotsky must show that he has no connection with ultraleft tendencies in the Comintern, "which experience shows really play the game of Menshevism." In any case, "no one thinks the struggle between the two conceptions of government will lead to anything more than a party quarrel."[14]

With the wisdom of hindsight, certain scholars see the Mensheviks' running comments as either self-evident or ill founded. Thus, E. H. Carr refers condescendingly to *Sotsialisticheskii vestnik* as "belatedly" reporting, in September 1923, that Trotsky's self-effacement at the Twelfth Congress was seen as a tactical maneuver and, in October 1928, that Bukharin had joined the new Right opposition.[15] In fact, Carr acknowledges that the 1923 *Vestnik* report was well informed, and he does not offer any other source, earlier or later, for his information. As for the 1928 report, the only earlier sources he invokes are the Trotsky archives, which did not became available until the 1950s. Moreover, Bukharin's biographer emphasizes that the moment when the Stalin-Bukharin coalition fell apart is obscure, and issues dividing the coalition crystallized only in mid-1928.[16] It is true that in the late 1920s Trotskyist groups forming in the West rivaled the Mensheviks as Kremlin watchers, but *Sotsialisticheskii vestnik* was prompt to glean and complete the information published by these groups.[17]

The Mensheviks did not become victims of disinformation in their reports; it is less clear that they they sought to avoid becoming instruments in the Bolshevik leadership struggle. Indeed, they nourished a complicity of illusion in the exchange of epithets.[18] The term "menshevism" was so elastic that it was used by the Bolshevik Central Control Commission to describe the ultraleft "Workers' Truth" group, by Bukharin as a synonym for "formal democratism," by Rykov as an epithet for the party opposition, and by Zinoviev as a description for any criticism of the party line.[19] Karl Radek concluded that Stalin's disastrous policy in China in 1927 was Menshevik and he supported his insight by accusing the former Mensheviks Martynov and Rafes of having imposed this policy on the Comintern. Dan's praise for Martynov's position only confirmed the accusation.[20] No wonder that the *New York Times* would headline an article on the struggle between Trotsky and the Stalin–Zinoviev–Kamenev triumvirate "Dispute Keeps Alive Controversy between Bolsheviki and Mensheviki Factions."[21]

Although the Mensheviks' commentaries on factional infighting multiplied after Lenin's death, their initial position had been defined earlier. In February 1921 *Sotsialisticheskii vestnik*, treated the "Workers' Opposition" at the recent Communist Congress as the manifestation of an inexorable process. Where parties are outlawed, wrote *Vestnik*, factional divisions are inevitable.[22] As for the demands of the "Workers' Opposition," *Vestnik* considered them suspiciously syndicalist, halfhearted, and naive. In patronizing terms it expressed the conviction that partisans of "workers' democracy" would come to realize that calls for freedom within the Communist Party would have to be extended to Social Democrats, SRs, and other democratic parties (excluding, implicitly, bourgeois parties).

The same attitude appeared two years later in Dallin's assessment of the dissident "Workers' Truth" manifesto published in *Vestnik*.[23] The dissidents, he said, were partisans of independent trade unions but were "afraid to use a term identified with Mensheviks." Their complaint that the Communist Party was "turning into a party of bourgeois dictatorship" was superficial. Rather, the Communist Party was a vessel in which the most diverse social strata of postrevolutionary Russia were planting the seeds of their future political organization. Above all, it was contradictory to accuse the Communist Party of being bourgeois and yet to call for a restoration of the power of this same party. As the title of the article—"It Must Be Thought Through to the End"—suggests the logic of the situation would force these dissidents to deepen their analysis and reach more daring conclusions.

Splits within the ruling party were thus seen as inevitable, and Lenin's death could only accelerate them. The Mensheviks were generous in their obituary to the founder of the Soviet state. They paid tribute to him as a co-founder of their own party, forever linked to Martov "like two poles of the same movement." They had no kind words for any of Lenin's successors. As the Russian proverb puts it, "The fish begins to stink from the head," wrote Garvi, and the stench of disintegration at the top of the Bolshevik party could not be disguised.[24]

As the Mensheviks saw it, Trotsky was the only Bolshevik leader with the moral authority to replace Lenin. During Lenin's illness the ruling troika had carefully kept Trotsky at a distance; as a contender for power, he had been content to keep his hands free. By the time of Lenin's death, Mensheviks believed that Trotsky had been effectively, if not formally, removed from leadership.[25] In refuting rumors that Trotsky had been arrested, Dan asked ironically, "Why should he be arrested when he has already committed political suicide?"[26] Abramovitch pointed out that Trotsky had always remained an outsider among the Bolsheviks, with the result that the one point on which the party apparat could agree was the need to neutralize Trotsky. Above all, however, it was character that destroyed him. Commenting on the quarrel over the pamphlet "Lessons of October," in which Trotsky accused Zinoviev and Kamenev of cowardice in 1917, Dan wrote, "The only lessons of October that Trotsky drew [in 1924] were those of his own superiority to the other pretenders for dictatorship."[27]

As in their evaluation of other oppositionists, the Mensheviks tended to present Trotsky's struggle as a vehicle for their own ideas. Trotsky, they said, was dimly aware of the need to transform the economic NEP into a political NEP, but he was incapable of acknowledging this as, they insisted, Lenin would have done. In this respect Trotsky's opposition was symptomatic of the malaise within the Communist Party. His outbursts, his opportunism, and his inconsistencies provided a barometer of the confused mood of the party masses. Trotsky's opposition, however, had no independent significance. His efforts to create a distinct line had failed before the Revolution and they would fail now. There could not be any "Trotskyism" because there could be no intermediate forms between communism and social democracy.[28]

Having written Trotsky off as a contender for power, *Sotsialisticheskii vestnik* nonetheless followed his declining fortunes. In early 1924 it was plausible that Trotsky might still play some sort of political role, and rumors suggested that he would become foreign commissar, replacing Chicherin, who was to be sent to London, and that Stalin would take over the War Commissariat.[29] By 1925 Trotsky was being identified first as a potential ally of Stalin and then of Zinoviev against Stalin.[30] The following year, reporting the creation of a united bloc consisting of Trotsky, Zinoviev, and Kamenev, *Vestnik* remarked that the new bloc's slogan of struggle with the kulak opposition was logical for Trotsky but not for Kamenev and Zinoviev. In fact, the new opposition, formed on the basis of Trotsky's positions of 1923–1924, soon came to grief. As late as the end of 1928, the Mensheviks were reporting rumors that Trotsky had been in Moscow to negotiate with Stalin but that Trotsky had been unwilling to concede anything.[31]

Sotsialisticheskii vestnik continued to record the ebb and flow of Trotsky's personal popularity, even though this was no gauge of his political prospects. At the Thirteenth Congress, held just after Lenin's death, it reported that Trotsky was alone but enjoyed great popularity. He was applauded enthusiastically at a lecture presented by Zinoviev (much to Zinoviev's embarrassment) but barely succeeded in getting elected to the Central Committee, as fifty-first of its fifty-two members. Trotsky's popularity rose after the failure of Stalin's China policy and especially during the war scare of 1927; it fell as economic hardships inflamed antisemitism and dissatisfaction with the radical policies then being pursued by the leadership but still identified with Trotsky and the opposition.[32] Talk of excluding Trotsky from the party and reports on the persecution of his supporters grew more persistent. Persecution included the creation of a special security police (GPU) section to hunt down Trotskyists, a successor perhaps to the earlier anti-Menshevik Second Section of the Cheka. Indeed, by the end of the decade Trotskyists shared the lot of Mensheviks: their political action consisted of clandestine meetings, anonymous distribution of illegal pamphlets, and the transfer of party activity abroad.[33]

Who defeated Trotsky? The Mensheviks' initial response was to point to an impersonal force. It was the apparatus that triumphed, a party machine made up of obedient cogs who realized that defeat of the opposition opened up career opportunities.[34] The name of Stalin was barely mentioned. Previous experience, as well as Stalin's provincialism and his lack of intellectual qualities, led the Mensheviks to share Trotsky's (and, no doubt, many Bolsheviks') disdain for the rising general secretary.[35] The Mensheviks also underestimated Stalin because of what they considered his moderate and centrist tendencies. Unlike Trotsky, however, they did not view these tendencies reproachfully.

Throughout the leadership struggles in the 1920s, *Sotsialisticheskii vestnik* noted that Stalin consistently defended Trotsky against the extreme reprisals proposed by other members of the Bolshevik majority. During the early phase of the struggle, in contrast with Trotsky, and even in contrast with his own ally Zinoviev, Stalin represented the voice of realism. "Lenin only understood the need for NEP after Kronstadt, Stalin understands the need for a neo-NEP without a second Kronstadt," affirmed *Vestnik* in 1925.[36] Even Stalin's espousal of the call for accelerated industrialization, a slogan previously identified with the party opposition, did not disturb the Mensheviks. After all, they too believed that industrialization was a vital necessity for Russia and for the salvation of the Revolution.

Signs that Stalin was acquiring hegemony within the leadership were thus greeted, initially, with relative equanimity. Stalin's declarations about the construction of socialism in Russia were harmful, mainly because they nourished illusions among the European proletariat. For the moment, however, the Mensheviks did not see anything ominous in his statement that "socialism cannot be built with white gloves."[37] In mid-1925 *Vestnik* noted that portraits and busts of Stalin were appearing everywhere. He was being described as Lenin's sole pupil and his position was strengthening every day.[38] There was no doubt, predicted *Vestnik,* that the forthcoming Party Congress would mark his full triumph.

Stalin's leadership, however, was not yet permanently assured; not only his political line but also his status within the leadership was fluctuating. In autumn 1925 he seemed to suffer a momentary eclipse, to the advantage of Kamenev. Several months later *Vestnik* still saw Stalin as sharing power, this time with Dzerzhinskii, "dictator of the administrative apparatus," just as Stalin was "acknowledged dictator on the party line." By 1927, when there could no longer be any doubt that Stalin was supreme, *Vestnik*'s emphasis shifted from Stalin's relations with his opponents to the nature of his power. Stalin had strengthened his position within the state and party apparatus to such an extent that it was no longer even possible to fight against him. As *Vestnik* put it, Stalin was an uncontested autocrat.[39]

The Mensheviks did not foresee much of a future for the United Opposition of Trotskyists and Zinovievites, an inherently contradictory combination (including Kamenev and, for a time, Lenin's widow, Krupskaia), which emerged in April 1926. They condemned as unrealistic this new opposition's program of expropriating the peasantry in the interests of socialist industry even as they endorsed its critique of Stalin, who was promoting industrialization without explaining where the necessary capital would come from.[40] When defeat of the United Opposition came, the Mensheviks attributed it to three factors: among Bolsheviks the apparat decided everything, and Stalin controlled the apparat; within the Bolshevik Party all tendencies feared discussion; and the opposition was handicapped by the fact that all its leaders were Jews.[41] In any case, who won or lost was of little importance, *Vestnik* claimed. All factions would necessarily tend toward identity so long as they called for the preservation of the dictatorship.[42]

The feeling that the warring factions were morally equivalent (and a plague upon all of them) was deeply anchored in Menshevik sentiment. Yet a competing impulse to search for significance in the internecine struggle also existed. The radical utopianism of left Communist groups received attention, as a caricature of the utopianism of the regime and as an expression of its deepest crisis.[43] Behind the "monstrous mask of party quarrels" one could make out the "true face of class struggle." The party conflicts thus reflected, albeit in a distorted way, a struggle in which petty bourgeois realism and the interests of capital and of the state opposed proletarian utopianism, self-deception, and anarchy.[44] Because of objective laws of development, the Mensheviks were convinced that the former tendencies would gain the upper hand; Stalin's ascendency over the left-leaning opposition confirmed this conviction.

Emergence of a right opposition under Bukharin, Rykov, and Tomskii in 1928, as Stalin moved left, transformed these basic assumptions. The Mensheviks argued, as they had earlier, that it was simply a Leninist habit to adopt the ideas of one's defeated opponents. Stalin's assumption of a left course had originally been a tactical move, covering up the fact that his coalition had no positive program.[45] The Mensheviks now sensed, however, that a new situation was emerging. Stalin's zigzags were bearing ever more consistently, as well as ever more radically, leftward. For the first time it was the Communist opposition that was staking out a position to the right of the party leadership.[46] Realism had moved to the opposition side; utopianism was in power.

The Mensheviks had previously shown no partiality for the leaders of the now-emerging right opposition. There was no reason to prefer them on personal or moral grounds, and their demands only deepened the danger of bonapartism, particularly since the state apparatus, a cradle of bonapartism, was solidly on their side. Nonetheless, they evoked more sympathy than any previous oppositional grouping. Fedor Dan went so far as to state that the Communist rightists' program resembled that of the Mensheviks in many ways: both favored a return to NEP, and both counted on capitalist stabilization. Even though return to NEP was impossible without other significant changes, most important a passage to a "political NEP," the struggle was indeed one between "NEP" and "anti-NEP." Stalin was perfectly correct in showing that the right wing's program meant the complete ideological capitulation of bolshevism to petty bourgeois elements, but "the logic of life and the needs of the country" were on the side of the right opposition, with its calls for concessions to the peasantry and revocation of Stalin's revolutionary measures.[47]

Stalin continued to perplex his Menshevik observers. Some persisted in referring to his line as "centrist" and insisted that he might still change his course. After all, "the wager on the kulak" and "peaceful growing into socialism," now considered the main heresies, had only recently constituted "Lenin's most sacred legacy."[48] In January 1929 the Mensheviks reported rumors that Stalin had made his peace with the right opposition and would apply its line. Soon the tone of *Vestnik* correspondence turned skeptical: Stalin had no sly plan up his sleeve; if he did make a turnabout it would be only because there was no other way out of the crisis. The only certitude was that Stalin did not want to share power with anybody.[49]

"The right deviation exists but it is difficult to tell who is in it," complained David Dallin at the end of 1928.[50] The increasingly murky atmosphere of the intraparty struggle was reflected in contradictory reports coming from Russia. *Vestnik* correspondents successively suggested that Bukharin was playing the role of intermediary between the "Stalin and the Rykov groups," and that the right opposition contained two tendencies, Rykovite and Bukharinite, the former so radical as to constitute its own party and the latter fearful of becoming the nucleus of a petty bourgeois party. In spite of contradictions, the Mensheviks' information was still sound. They accurately analyzed the defeat of the right opposition at the Sixteenth Party Conference, and they even provided a speaker-by-speaker account of the preceding Central Committee plenum.[51]

By mid-1929 *Sotsialisticheskii vestnik* was reporting that right Communist circles believed Stalin intended to stay his course for a long time. Even they no longer believed that once he had defeated the Right, he would adopt their policies. Menshevik attention shifted to the fate of the "most 100 percent" Bolshevik whom Stalin had been able to drive out, his most recent ally, Nikolai Bukharin.[52] First indications came when Bukharin almost failed to get elected to the Leningrad Academy and when the volume of the *Bol'shaia sovetskaia entsiklopedia* containing his article on the Communist Party was withdrawn from circulation.[53] At the same time, reports announced prematurely that the Stalinists had already decided several months earlier to remove Bukharin, Rykov, and Tomskii from the Politburo at its next plenum.[54] A *Vestnik* correspondent wrote that he did not think much of Bukharin as a theoretician but he was disgusted by the humiliations Bukharin was enduring at the hands of young upstarts.[55] Although Bukharin made his peace with Stalin and served in high government posts for several more years, by 1930 *Vestnik* was describing Bukharin and his allies as politically dead, serving Stalin as "hostages." As an article titled "The Last Bolshevik Theoretician" put it, Bukharin "not only had to live through his own funeral; he did not even get a worthy obituary."[56]

Henceforth, speculation about leadership matters centered solely on Stalin. *Vestnik* noted that a new formula had emerged at the Sixteenth Congress, where the only basic political question was that of Stalin's unlimited personal dictatorship.[57] One no longer spoke about the "Leninist Central Committee" but about the "Leninist Central Committee *under the leadership of Comrade Stalin.*"[58] Rumors flew: friction was developing between Stalin and the GPU; Stalin was about to be removed because even his closest collaborators were dissatified; Stalin had suffered a heart attack.[59] Indeed, there was talk of nothing but conspiracies within the Communist Party. Meanwhile, *Vestnik* recorded the first use of one of its favorite later designations for Stalin: Genghis Khan.[60]

The Mensheviks saw themselves not only as political observers—Kremlinologists *avant la lettre*—but as political actors. In spite of their efforts to remain "above the fray," they were tempted to intervene in intra-Bolshevik struggle and to express a preference for one faction over another. Fedor Dan led in this respect, in spite of his affirmation that social democrats differed from Communists in seeking explanations in social processes rather than in "correct leadership." Addressing the party organization in Russia, Abramovitch complained that during the period after Martov's death, Dan and his disciples had been creating illusions about the possibility of a split within the Communist Party, as well as about the role of the Trotskyist and Workers' Opposition. "Fortunately," remarked Abramovitch in an ironic tone, the "evolution of Bolsheviks in the direction of Bolshevism" was so pronounced that it overcame such differences among *Vestnik* editors.[61]

Abramovitch himself could not remain indifferent to the leadership struggle. He began to read objective significance into personal rivalries, explaining to Friedrich Adler that the struggle between Zinoviev and Stalin was between "Bolshevik ideology" and "Russian reality." Even the intransigent Menshevik patriarch Pavel Axelrod acknowledged privately that not he but Dan seemed to have been correct in foretelling and in attaching importance to the "internal evolution (if this term can be used in the given case)" of the Bolsheviks. "The inner party squabble among the Bolsheviks fills me with optimism," wrote Axelrod, adding that perhaps in the coming transitional period "we shall be able to come home and work as in Horthy's empire. (What have we come to?)"[62]

It is not surprising that the quickening tempo of the intra-Bolshevik struggle should have excited the Mensheviks. Ironically, however, the Mensheviks' inclination to search for the signs of political revival grew as this struggle was winding down. "Politics are returning by crooked paths into the social life of Russia," declared *Vestnik* as it reported the unexpected demonstration that accompanied the removal from Moscow of the leftist leader I. T. Smilga in June 1927. Under the heading "The Great Eve," Dan announced that the fierce struggles within the party were only a prelude to real struggles. Soon the military and security apparati would come into play, leading first to bonapartism but ultimately to a reactivation of the masses.[63] Even as *Vestnik* predicted that the approaching Fifteenth Congress would seal the fate of the opposition, it added that the struggle of different Bolshevik factions was turning into an open political one: "Out of the bowels of the ruling Communist Party come the sparks of political rebirth."[64]

The Menshevik Foreign Delegation's discussions concerning factional conflicts within the Kremlin continued until—and even beyond—the disappearance of open factions. Two documents from 1929 provide an epilogue to these discussions and an illustration of the role they played in demarcating the increasingly irreconcilable left, center, and right wings among the exiled Mensheviks themselves.[65]

Dan's left wing position was that the Mensheviks should appeal to democratic elements within all Bolshevik groups. Bolshevik factionalism played a positive role by undermining faith in the infallibility of the Communist Party; whatever their specific oppositional programs, these factions became temporary poles of attraction for all dissatisfied social forces. In every faction, he argued, there were sincere elements who could not be ignored.

Dallin, speaking for a Menshevik center which included Nicolaevsky and Abramovitch, demanded that Bolshevik factions be judged not by their programs but by their capacity to break with the principle of minority dictatorship. There was no chance of alliance with the Bolshevik Left since this was the faction most hostile to social democracy. Bolshevik centrists had no independent political line; their only principle was preservation of party unity. The Bolshevik Right, who correctly saw no possibility of socialist construction in present circumstances, was halfhearted and opportunistic: the aim of the RSDRP should be to support the rightists' positive demands while remaining vigilant against those rightist elements oriented toward the bourgeoisie and the reactionary part of the peasantry.

Kefali and Aronson, on behalf of the Menshevik right wing, declared flatly that Stalin was pursuing not a centrist but a leftist course, having isolated the Soviet Union and created a war psychosis in order to deflect intraparty opposition and the discontent of the masses. The Bolshevik Right had some understanding of the dangers of conflict with the peasantry, but it preferred bonapartism to democracy. All in all, the intraparty struggle was merely a fight among insignificant cliques, which showed the incapacity of the Bolshevik dictatorship to evolve. Any alliance with one of these cliques would merely drag the RSDRP into palace coups and isolate it from the popular democratic movement.

By 1928–29 the question whether to support Bolshevik factions, and if so which ones, was in fact moot. Indeed, the undertone of futility to these Menshevik debates underscores a deep irony: it was precisely at the time that the Mensheviks were best informed of Kremlin struggle that they mistook the ebb of factional fighting for its flow and proved least able to predict its outcome. Behind this miscalculation lie a number of fundamental weaknesses in the Mensheviks' position. First, they tended to consider the very existence of disputes within the Communist Party as evidence of degeneration, thus raising the question of their understanding of party democracy. Second, they adopted some of the political attitudes of the left Communist opposition and important elements of its critique of NEP trends, but they favored the economic platform of the Communist leadership (in the years 1923–1927) and the victory of the right opposition thereafter. Third, the Mensheviks' hopes regarding factional struggles were mixed with fears that these struggles would lead the Revolution not forward but backward. Such miscalculations, ambivalences, and contradictions were not unique to the Mensheviks. They were shared by many Bolsheviks, who, to their own misfortune, proved no better able to predict political outcomes than the Mensheviks.

5

Mensheviks and the Wider World

Into the International Arena

As the Menshevik Party in Russia faded, its visibility in the arenas of international socialism remained undiminished. The international role of the RSDRP had been at the heart of the party's preoccupations from the outset of its postrevolutionary exile, and its importance only increased over time.

Like other socialists, but to an even greater extent because of their particular circumstances, the Mensheviks defined themselves in the first instance as members of an international workers' movement.[1] Looking back into their own history, they stressed the connection between the birth of Marxism in Russia and the rise of a powerful workers' movement in the West. Looking forward from their defeat in 1917, they continued to see the cause of world revolution and the Russian Revolution as indivisible.

This internationalism was not incompatible with the RSDRP's immediate interests. Menshevik leaders sensed that handicaps imposed on the party by exile and by its destruction at home might find compensation in its ability to function within the world of international socialism. Indeed, the Mensheviks who had proved such ineffectual politicians at home turned out to be adroit actors on the international socialist scene. They pursued their advantage here in the belief that international working-class support might serve as a lever to exert pressure on the Soviet government.[2] In pursuit of this goal, and ultimately as a substitute for its attainment, they forged a role for themselves as authoritative spokesmen for Russia and as prime interpreters of Russian events within the international socialist movement.

The international role of the RSDRP provided the original impulse to the transfer of party activities abroad. In the summer of 1920 Martov and Abramovitch, the nucleus of the future Foreign Delegation, responded to an invitation from leaders of the German Independent Social Democratic Party (USPD) with whom Martov had met during the Second Comintern Congress in Moscow. The two Menshevik leaders applied to leave Russia for the purpose of attending a crucial USPD congress and with a view to establishing an RSDRP representation abroad. Although Axelrod had filled the role of representative abroad in the first years after the Revolution (with the assistance of junior comrades such as Grigorii Bienstock and Samuil Shchupak), divergences between him and the party leadership in Russia had left the party without an authoritative spokesman in the West. The Soviet authorities acceded to Martov's request after he had sent copies of his passport application (or, in Abramovitch's version, an open letter) to foreign delegates attending the Comintern Congress.[3]

Soviet acquiescence was motivated by various longer-term considerations. The Soviet leaders were keen to rid themselves of a vocal opposition leader, but at least some may have been moved by humanitarian considerations. Lenin in particular was sufficiently concerned by Martov's declining health to overrule a majority opinion of the Bolshevik Politburo.[4] The decision also involved shrewd political calculation. Martov's departure served as proof of Soviet generosity and maturity. Whatever else Martov did abroad, he could be counted on to support the fundamental aim of Soviet foreign policy at that time, the international recognition of Soviet Russia. Thus, in September and October 1920, respectively, Martov and Abramovitch left Russia with an anomalous travel document: a Soviet passport stamped "traveling on behalf of the Central Committee of the RSDRP."[5]

The USPD, toward whose congress at Halle Martov was heading, stood at its most critical juncture. The party had grown from its original status as the antiwar faction of the SPD into a powerful party which boasted such luminaries as Kautsky and Hilferding as well as almost a million members and the support of almost 5 million voters.[6] At the same time, the USPD, like virtually all socialist parties in that era, found itself divided into a pro-Bolshevik and an anti-Bolshevik orientation. The USPD delegation to the Comintern Congress was composed of an equal number of representatives of both factions, but, to Martov's regret, it was only anti-Bolshevik delegates who met with the Mensheviks. At the forthcoming Halle Congress the question of USPD adherence to the Comintern was to be posed, and both sides were mustering all the strength they could gather. Martov was persuaded that his presence could make a difference, perhaps that it could even sway the vote, and this was certainly one reason for his agreeing to leave Russia.[7]

Several accounts bring out the drama of the Halle Congress.[8] The collision between two incompatible strands of socialism was enacted on the congress stage, where Grigorii Zinoviev, head of the powerful Comintern, confronted Martov, leader of a doomed opposition. In a hall festooned with pro-Soviet slogans, Zinoviev, a masterly orator fluent in German, kept the congress enthralled for over four hours (even though the time limit for foreign guests was supposedly set at thirty minutes). No one could fail to note the contrast between the robust and self-confident Zinoviev and the mortally ill Martov, already so weakened by throat cancer that his speech had to be read out for him (by Alexander Stein). Rarely could the David and Goliath nature of the conflict between Bolsheviks and Mensheviks have been as stark as at that moment. It is a tribute to Martov's moral authority even among a largely hostile audience that he was listened to at all.

Zinoviev compared the congress to those held in the RSDRP before the split of the party. He could have compared it equally well to clashes that took place at key moments of the Russian Revolution. Certainly the stakes were seen by many to be as high as those fought over in Petrograd in 1917. The immediate issue here was the allegiance of a significant part of the most conscious and mature working class in Europe, the German proletariat. Behind this issue stood the choice between what Zinoviev himself called "international menshevism" and "international bolshevism."

Both sides presented sweeping arguments. Zinoviev painted a picture of revolutionary successes and called on German workers not to waver but to join in the imminent and inevitable triumph of communism. The argument was calculated to appeal to a working class ashamed of its unrevolutionary stances in the past and frustrated at the failure of its own revolution. Martov denounced Russian hegemony within the Comintern, but the thrust of his speech concerned Bolshevik terror against socialists and their families. Such an insistent emphasis on terror might have been seen by the audience as merely the complaint of the weak and fainthearted. In Martov's hands it became a powerful indictment. The passion of his speech transcended theoretical considerations, challenging the Bolsheviks on the emotional level where they usually dominated, and where the Mensheviks were generally loath to engage them.

Beneath the drama of this verbal duel the results of the Halle Congress were foreordained. Delegates came to Halle with binding mandates, and, although there was only limited enthusiasm for the Comintern's "twenty-one conditions" of adherence, most delegates were committed to having their party enter the Comintern.[9] Even at the rhetorical level Martov's speech was not, strictly speaking, a reply to Zinoviev. This task fell to Rudolf Hilferding, who expressed his skepticism at Zinoviev's revolutionary prognostics and argued that an era of capitalist stabilization was dawning.[10] Although one Menshevik scholar has argued that Martov's appearance was decisive in preventing the entire USPD from going over to the Comintern, the more accurate view seems to be that the Halle Congress only formalized an earlier split.[11] The result of the congress was the immediate departure of the party minority from the hall and the subsequent merger of the USPD majority with the German Communist Party. Foreign guests, such as the French socialist Jean Longuet, whose party was standing on the threshold of a decision similar to that facing the USPD, also remained unmoved by Martov's arguments. The rump USPD, now in the hands of its right wing, resolved to publish 100,000 copies of Martov's speech immediately.[12] Even this project failed to come to fruition.

In spite of these reverses the Halle Congress has passed into history as a victory for the Mensheviks and their German allies. As Hilferding put it, "In Halle was won the great battle between bolshevism and European socialism; it was there that bolshevism suffered its decisive defeat in the European labor movement." Perhaps one should allow for the circumstances in which this statement was made—an obituary for Martov—but its sentiments can be traced to Hilferding's assertions at the Halle Congress itself. There, Hilferding had attributed martyrlike qualities to Martov, concluding that "between socialism and Bolshevism there is an unbridgeable, not only ideological but also moral gulf."[13]

In making such claims Hilferding was staking out, on behalf of the Mensheviks and on the international level, the same moral high ground which the Mensheviks already claimed for themselves. The notion that the difference between bolshevism and menshevism was fundamentally a moral one had been developing steadily since 1903, though as late as 1914 it was still a novel idea in international socialist circles. The added notion that moral victory was the complement of political defeat had been growing since the October Revolution. As Marxists, the Mensheviks must have felt somewhat uneasy with the idea: it seemed to be a surrender to abstract moralism, disconnected from the workings of historical reason as expressed in political victory.

And yet, the moral aura which the Mensheviks assumed, and which foreign socialists were prepared to confer on them, represented a political weapon of immeasurable strength. Inasmuch as international socialism, regardless of Marxist and other positivist accretions, never lost its original moral impulse, the Mensheviks' moral superiority endowed them with unique authority. As Hilferding put it at Halle, "No more powerful protest could be raised [against Bolshevik methods of terrorism] than the pallid, emaciated visage of comrade Martov suddenly appearing on the tribune."[14]

The specter of Martov's suffering, collectively transferred to his party, continued to haunt international socialism for years to come.

After Halle, Martov could turn to the issue which concerned him most: the reconstruction of international proletarian unity, broken by the old Social Democratic parties in 1914 and further ruptured by Bolshevik establishment of the Comintern. In autumn 1920 the situation of international socialism was chaotic. The reformist Second International was shaken and, in the eyes of many socialists, discredited. Nevertheless, it still included the two largest workers' parties in Europe, the German SPD and the British Labour Party. Some parties had already joined the Comintern, and others were debating adherence. Within months of the USPD congress at Halle, the French and Italian socialist parties also split. Many socialist leaders showed an aversion to accepting the Comintern's "twenty-one conditions" but still expressed readiness, real or feigned, to enter a Communist-led International and continued to refuse any dealings with Second International reformism.[15]

These circumstances seemed propitious to Martov for the realization of a cherished plan. As early as May 1919 the Menshevik Central Committe, in denouncing both anarcho-Bolshevik and class-collaborationist tendencies within the European proletariat, had called for a conference of Marxist parties opposed to both communism and reformism.[16] Indeed, the underlying purpose of Martov's and Abramovitch's departure for the West was to reinforce this project of a conference of "centrist parties." In the aftermath of the Halle Congress, the right wing remnant of the USPD was particularly amenable to such propositions. The way out of disarray for German comrades—Martov compared them to Mensheviks, an "avantgarde without masses"—lay in regrouping with those other parties or factions of parties that refused both the London-based and the Moscow-based Internationals.[17]

The Mensheviks' conception of a new, centrist grouping of socialist parties was not identical with that of their allies. The USPD and others seem still to have hoped that such a grouping could negotiate a new deal with the Comintern, leading eventually to organizational unity. Many western European socialists saw their problems with the Comintern as organizational rather than ideological. The Mensheviks were less sanguine. They envisaged the emerging centrist organization as a new International alongside the existing ones. It would serve not as a broker for merger but as a rallying point for parties uncommitted to either of the existing Internationals. The result would be coexistence rather than fusion. Ultimately this could lead to a situation on the international level similar to that which the Mensheviks had sought, unsuccessfully, in Russia during the brief Vikzhel negotiations in 1917: a working coalition of socialist forces to act as a constraint on Bolshevik ambitions and abuses.

The Mensheviks were an essential pillar of a new centrist organization. For western European centrist socialist parties, the RSDRP constituted their strongest available link to the Russian Revolution. At the same time, the Mensheviks' position was fragile. They were weakened by lack of a political base at home and by repeated, even obsessive, Bolshevik accusations against them.[18] For this reason they could not afford to set themselves too strongly apart from their allies and were constantly obliged to reaffirm their own revolutionary credentials.

Martov was able to transform a personal invitation to attend a preparatory meeting of the new centrist grouping in Bern in December 1920 into an invitation to his party. He may also have been instrumental in securing a Menshevik monopoly as sole Russian representatives at the meeting, even though Left SRs had expressed interest. When Axelrod and other right wing Mensheviks grumbled at the meeting's manifesto describing Russian Communists as "the avantgarde of the international revolution," Martov retorted that foreign socialists could not be expected to see Bolsheviks in any other terms.[19] The Mensheviks had to accept this as a statement of the mood of the Western masses, just as they had accepted the pro-Bolshevik enthusiasm of a significant part of the Russian working class.

Beyond their bow in the direction of Moscow, the seven parties gathered at Bern adopted other principles perfectly palatable to the Mensheviks. They condemned British and American imperialism as well as French militarism. They pronounced themselves against the blockade of revolutionary Russia. Most significantly, they affirmed that the strategy of the proletariat could not be limited either to parliamentary methods or to the revolutionary methods employed in Russia but depended on specific national conditions. Finally, the conference convoked an international socialist meeting to be held in Vienna in February 1921.[20]

It was at this meeting that a formal union of centrist parties—referred to henceforth as the Vienna Union or the $2^{1}/_{2}$ International—took shape. Twenty parties from twelve countries attended, with the original Bern group dominating and the Mensheviks as active at the conference as they had been in its preparation. Especially prominent was Abramovitch. In his double capacity as RSDRP delegation member and Latvian Bund representative, Abramovitch seemed ubiquitous as he spoke and lobbied tirelessly at the conference. He was not always successful. In the mandate commission Abramovitch was unable to block entry of the socialist Zionists (Poale Zion) or to challenge the distribution of Russia's votes between the newly arrived Left SRs and the Mensheviks. On the congress floor Abramovitch was more successful, as he refuted the Left SR claim that the soviet system was an intrinsically superior form of democracy. Moreover, he added for good measure, it was Mensheviks not Bolsheviks who had created soviets both in 1905 and in 1917.[21] Owing to his visibility, his energy, his linguistic and diplomatic skills, and his association with Martov, Abramovitch emerged as one of the recognized leaders of the Vienna Union, thus ensuring the Mensheviks a voice in the future organization.

The founding of the Vienna Union satisfied a long-standing Menshevik project. Not surprisingly, it was immediately attacked from Moscow as a Menshevik plot.[22] The orientation of the new organization caused some unease among the Mensheviks. During the Vienna meeting, news arrived of the Soviet overthrow of the Menshevik government of Georgia. Instead of condemning the Soviet invasion, as the Mensheviks proposed, the congress chose to reserve its judgment until it had more information. Even as the Vienna Union was showing itself to be insufficiently firm vis-à-vis new Bolshevik misdeeds, its revolutionary qualities were being diluted by the entry of parties that had broken with reformism only recently, and perhaps not entirely.[23]

In spite of such weaknesses deplored by the Mensheviks, the Vienna Union seemed to be making headway toward its goal. The London International took the initiative of proposing talks with it even though the Union criticized London's reformism much more harshly than Moscow's maximalism. Soon the Comintern, too, showed itself open to a common meeting. The centrist organization thus found itself courted on both sides. In fact, the Second and the Third Internationals were seeking to expose each other's bad faith; as events unfolded, they succeeded only in exposing their own.[24]

The immediate upshot of these developments, however, was highly gratifying to the Vienna Union. In April 1922 it saw its efforts come to fruition as a preliminary conference of representatives of the three Internationals opened in Berlin. Friedrich Adler, speaking on behalf of the Vienna Union, warned it was not yet possible to speak of organizational unity; at most, groundwork for common action might be laid. Even such modest expectations were threatened as the Vienna Union's guests jockeyed for advantage. Most menacing was an ultimatum from the Second International, whose members threatened to leave the meeting unless three preliminary conditions were satisfied: an end to Communist subversion in the member parties and unions of the Second International; the appointment of a commission of inquiry into the Bolshevik takeover of Georgia; and the liberation of all political prisoners in Russia.[25]

The crisis was resolved largely because of the intervention of Menshevik leaders. Inasmuch as the demand that political prisoners be freed concerned their own party, the Mensheviks were in a uniquely strong position to argue that this particular demand should not be made a precondition of dealings with the Comintern. The Mensheviks' readiness to subordinate their own interests to the cause of international unity created a strong impression on representatives of the Second International. In fact, their willingness to sacrifice immediate party interests, on this and on other occasions, was one of their strongest weapons. It added to their moral capital by underscoring their internationalism and their revolutionary credibility, and it transformed their weakness into a source of strength. In this case the Mensheviks prevailed, and the Second International agreed to put off satisfaction of its demands until a follow-up meeting, to be held the following month.[26]

The test case for Comintern intentions with respect to political prisoners in Russia was to be the fate of arrested SR leaders whose trial was pending in Moscow. At the April meeting in Berlin, Comintern delegate Karl Radek gave a commitment that the other Internationals could send advocates to the SR trial and that, in any case, no death sentences would be carried out. The Menshevik Foreign Delegation threw itself wholeheartedly into this cause. Martov, who insisted on a formal repudiation of the death penalty (whereas Dan sought only a private commitment from Radek), even considered returning to Moscow to serve as a defender of the SRs. The Menshevik Central Committee in Russia was more reserved. It feared that excessive Menshevik association with the case would identify the party too closely with the SRs, thus tarnishing the Mensheviks with SR misdeeds during the Civil War. Although Mensheviks abroad shared such mistrust, even to the point of blocking SR membership in the Vienna Union, in this case they aligned themselves with their foreign allies rather than with their comrades at home. At this juncture it was especially important that the Menshevik Party not be seen as obstructing the common position of Western socialists. Internal party considerations again yielded before the obligations of internationalism.[27]

In spite of such efforts, all hopes of reaching agreement among the three Internationals floundered. When their representatives met again in Berlin, an acrimonious exchange of accusations took place. Communists claimed that member parties of the Second International were sabotaging efforts at unity with the Comintern. They had failed to respect their promise to hold common May Day demonstrations with Communists in western European countries. The representatives of the Second International affirmed that the Comintern had not satisfied any of the conditions previously presented to it, even those to which it had agreed. Lenin had repudiated the commitment regarding the SR trial made by Radek, and it was clear that Western advocates at the trial would not be able to carry out their task. Although there were no Mensheviks present at the meeting, they were invoked by both sides. Ramsay MacDonald, representing the British Labour Party, quoted Lenin's statement that Mensheviks should be shot. Radek, who complained that the SPD-led Prussian government was obstructing his movements in Germany, was asked if Martov had been able to travel to Russia to report on the previous Berlin conference. Radek retorted by quoting Abramovitch to support his claim that member parties of the Second International were obstructing moves toward unity out of electoral considerations.[28]

The meeting adjourned in utter failure. Its collapse dashed all hopes of calling a world workers' conference, which had been the main item on its agenda. More significantly, its breakdown marked the death knell of the Vienna Union. Although it continued to attract new member parties in the coming months, the 2½ International had lost its raison d'être. The Mensheviks were prepared to come to terms with the coexistence of three Internationals until the Russian Revolution had been "straightened out." Most other member parties, however, saw the Vienna Union as a direct and rapid bridge toward unity with a more amenable Comintern. When it became clear that unity was not attainable, these parties found themselves rudderless in the international arena.

The beneficiary of these developments was the Second International. The Vienna Union, as heir to the revolutionary Zimmerwald tradition of wartime internationalism, had originally been far more hostile to the Second International, with its record of reformism and and wartime impotence, than to the Comintern. Its bitter experience with the Comintern, and no doubt the waning of the revolutionary tide in Europe, led it to reconsider its position. Like a once-rejected suitor who renews his suit as a rival's courtship flags, the Second International pushed forward its advantage.[29]

The signal for the impending merger of the Vienna Union and the Second International was given by the reunification of the rump USPD and the SPD. Even as ardent a champion of the Vienna Union as Martov, who only a few months earlier had reacted indignantly to Dallin's thoughts about a merger, now recognized its inevitability. Martov published an unusually hard-nosed article that sought to dispel illusions about the progressive nature of the merger and to put forward the minimal conditions required to salvage something positive. Neither the "Moscow wolves" nor the "London lambs," he wrote, had any intention of giving up their instincts. The Vienna Union therefore had to renounce hopes of real unity and content itself with partial and purely mechanical unification. He did, however, define two conditions for the new International to be something more than a "discussion club": it would have to function in war as in peace, and it would have to be recognized by member parties as the highest authority in all "national questions."[30]

Martov could find comfort in the fact that the Vienna Union had stood by its principles vis-à-vis the Comintern. This it had been able to do largely owing to information transmitted by Mensheviks concerning the situation in Russia, their concern for the question of political prisoners, and their intransigence in the face of the Comintern's "twenty-one conditions." The Mensheviks had thus contributed to denying the centrist parties to the Comintern, but it now appeared that they had done so only to see these parties turn to the Second International. According to Martov, the result was a step backward for the working class, albeit an inevitable one. He dismissed optimism about the centrist parties' influence on reformists within a united International and about the "moral" effect of unification on the working class. Repudiating or ignoring the role which his party, and he himself in particular, had played, Martov scoffed at the tendency among his allies to "replace the lack of real success with illusory 'moral' successes."[31]

Martov's blessing for the impending marriage between the two Internationals was thus a reluctant one, but it was a blessing nonetheless. It allowed the Vienna Union to proceed toward self-liquidation with the acquiescence of one of its most prestigious theoreticians and one of its most committed parties. Moreover, Martov's conditions gave an orientation to the negotiating process already under way. Finally, Martov's endorsement ensured that his party would not become marginal to the international socialist movement. The Mensheviks thus escaped the fate of the other Russian party within the Vienna Union, the Left SRs, who refused the merger.[32] Henceforth, however, the Mensheviks would have to share the task of representing Russia in a new International with the Second International's Russian spokesmen, the SRs.

The Mensheviks now undertook a campaign to minimize the costs of merger. Within the Vienna Union's select negotiating committee, Abramovitch intervened repeatedly. He was unsuccessful in his original proposition that the two Internationals preserve their own identity and confine themselves to creating a common action committee. He was also unsuccessful in having Martov's conditions for unity adopted as preconditions for a merger. Perhaps other centrist parties considered Martov's insistence on broad supremacy for the International too reminiscent of the Comintern's "twenty-one conditions," which they had repudiated.[33] Martov's conditions were to be incorporated, however, albeit in diluted form and in Abramovitch's formulation, in the statutes of the new Labor and Socialist International (LSI).[34]

The Mensheviks came to the founding congress of the LSI in Hamburg in May 1923 in a position of weakness. In general, the balance of power at the congress favored the parties of the Second International over those of the former Vienna Union. Moreover, German and Austrian Social Democrats, to whom the Mensheviks were particularly close, found themselves at a disadvantage with respect to the parties of the victorious Allied powers. The postwar revolutionary situation, insofar as there had ever been one, was definitely over, and the mood among those workers' parties, such as the RSDRP, which considered themselves revolutionary rather than reformist was despondent.[35]

The position of the Mensheviks was even more precarious than that of other Vienna-affiliated parties. Only a few weeks earlier they had suffered an irreparable loss with the death of Martov. At the congress itself, the RSDRP was threatened on two sides. On the one hand, Beatrice Webb, representing the British Labour Party, contested the membership application of people, such as Mensheviks and SRs, who were "fighting against a socialist government in their own country."[36] On the other hand, the right wing *Zaria* group of Russian Social Democrats, led by Stepan Ivanovich (Portugeis), was demanding representation at the congress, first within the RSDRP delegation and then as an independent party. The Menshevik majority, embarrassed by the damage that *Zaria*'s interventionist position could do to the credibility of the RSDRP, proved utterly uncompromising. The extraparty right wing Mensheviks, successfully excluded from the Hamburg Congress, never forgot or forgave this repression of their views.[37]

On the congress floor, too, the Mensheviks had to wage a defensive battle. To their chagrin, the congress agenda failed to include a separate item on the "Russian Question," confining this issue uncomfortably within one labeled "Struggle against International Reaction." The RSDRP's Russian rivals, the SRs, gained the limelight with a dramatic announcement that their designated delegates could not attend the congress because they were under a death sentence in Moscow prisons. As the congress was deliberating, it learned of the Curzon ultimatum, a threat by the British Conservative government to sever relations with Soviet Russia.[38] The immediate reaction was a wave of sympathy for the Soviets. Meanwhile, outside the congress hall German Communists—who had launched an unsuccessful insurrection in Hamburg two months earlier—demonstrated noisily, obliging the congress to mount a protective guard of one thousand volunteers. Among the Communists' least offensive tactics was the sale of a book by the former Menshevik Martynov, titled *From Menshevism to Communism*.[39]

In the face of such adversity, the Mensheviks managed to have their attitude toward the Soviet Union prevail. Abramovitch, as co-chairman of the congress session at which the Curzon ultimatum was announced, immediately associated his party with protests against the British threat to revolutionary Russia, thus establishing the RSDRP's anti-interventionist credentials.[40] The following day Abramovitch's main speech, a critique of the Bolshevik regime, was not seriously challenged from the floor, although it displeased a number of delegates.[41] In effect, the congress tacitly acknowledged Menshevik authority in matters related to Soviet Russia.

The emerging role of the Mensheviks as policy makers on Soviet matters within the LSI was underscored when they presented a separate resolution on the Russian Question alongside the general resolution prepared by the congress commission on the struggle against international reaction. Whereas the commission, under the leadership of Otto Bauer and Beatrice Webb, thought it untimely to condemn the Soviet government in view of the threat from the Curzon ultimatum, the Mensheviks both condemned intervention and called for an end to Bolshevik terror and to persecution of Russian socialists. In spite of the mood of the congress, "the majority of the delegates felt nevertheless that Congress could not throw out a resolution which embodied fundamental democratic Socialist principles."[42] The appeal to socialist conscience prevailed. The Menshevik resolution was adopted, although, unlike other congress resolutions, it was passed by a majority rather than unanimously, with two minor parties dissenting and, more significantly, with the British abstaining.[43]

From the Menshevik point of view, the balance sheet of the Hamburg Congress was mixed. The LSI was born as an excessively loose union, dominated by reformist parties and unlikely to inspire the proletarian masses. It did, however, recognize the class struggle (a code term for Marxist principles), and its congress had given support to the Menshevik position on the Russian Question. In the long term, the most significant consequence of the congress was that the RSDRP, in the person of Abramovitch, obtained one of two seats reserved for Russia in the Executive and the only Russian seat in the nine-member Bureau of the LSI. The RSDRP's international legitimacy was substantially reinforced by these appointments.[44]

The founding of the LSI inaugurated a new chapter in the life of international social democracy. Its establishment did not satisfy the hopes that Martov and Abramovitch had carried with them out of Russia in 1920. Nonetheless, largely as a result of their commitment and political skills, it did not confirm their worst fears. The Mensheviks now had a new institutional base for the pursuit of their international mission.

Menshevik Foreign Relations

Exile is the pursuit of politics by other means. The internal life of a party organization driven into exile continues as before with its debates about policy, its competition among factions, its leadership struggles. The national dimension of party politics, however, ordinarily predominant, recedes as party life erodes in the homeland and exiles compete for the uncertain allegiance of a distant population or of the emigré community which acts as its substitute. In these circumstances the foreign relations of a political party come to the forefront. The exile party, operating on foreign soil, confronts foreigners daily without the benefit of its own state structure. It turns to them for the support which it cannot draw on among its own people as it appeals to the outside world to legitimize its cause.

For the RSDRP in exile, foreign relations were all the more important because it disdained the resources of the Russian emigration. Even as the RSDRP sought to maintain links to its natural constituency, the Russian working class, it developed its broader constituency, world socialist opinion. It did so by defining a worldview which situated the principal preoccupation of the Mensheviks, the Russian Question, within the broad concerns of world socialism. The "foreign policy" of the RSDRP in exile consisted of seeking outside support for this worldview and lending support to those who shared it.

The Hamburg Congress of the LSI and a German-language pamphlet, also in 1923, offered the world a classic statement of Menshevik views.[1] The Russian Revolution, Raphael Abramovitch explained, was a successful peasant—that is, (petty) bourgeois—revolution carried out by Bolsheviks as an unsuccessful proletarian revolution. Given the low level of productive forces and the weakness of the Russian working class, capitalist development was inevitable, regardless of the subjective intentions of the Bolsheviks. The only relevant question was whether it would develop in conditions of despotism or democracy. For the moment, the Bolsheviks were doing everything to stifle democratic possibilities. Not only was the constitution a sham, but even within the ruling Communist Party there was no freedom. The Bolshevik regime rested on a new bourgeoisie, a new peasantry, a new military apparatus, and a new bureaucracy, with the Cheka as its strongest pillar.

Abramovitch drew on themes abundantly covered in *Sotsialisticheskii vestnik*. When he addressed a foreign audience, however, the usually tentative nature of Menshevik reflections gave way to starker formulations. There was little sense here of internal Menshevik debates over the degree to which one could already speak of a reestablishment of capitalism in Soviet Russia or of a full-blown new bourgeoisie. Nuances and interrogations disappeared before the imperatives of persuasive political discourse. Moreover, applying a technique which the Mensheviks were to perfect over the years, Abramovitch used Soviet statistics and statements abundantly to lend authority to his arguments in the eyes of a foreign audience. It was this combination of clearly defined theses and uncontestable sources that gave his statements their persuasive power.

Beyond the question of the Russian Revolution, a main focus of Menshevik concern was the attitude of the great powers toward revolutionary Russia and, in particular, the call for diplomatic recognition.[2] The Mensheviks did not consider recognition of the regime by the greatest enemies of the Revolution as conferring any moral status. It was simply the basic condition, indeed a precondition, for the normal development of the Revolution in Russia and the only way of definitively liquidating the dangers of intervention. For this same reason the Mensheviks approved the Riga peace treaty between Russia and Poland, even though they considered it unfair to Russia. Such treaties were the international counterparts to NEP, strategic retreats for the sake of the Revolution's survival.[3]

The Mensheviks noted that recognition of the Bolshevik regime was connected with an interest in weakening Russia.[4] Great Britain welcomed the respite which a weak Bolshevik Russia gave to Britain's imperial position in Asia. Germany needed to integrate Russia into its economic sphere in order to overcome its own economic crisis. Only France, because of fears of Germany, and the United States, because of concern about Japan's influence in Asia, wanted a strong Russia and, for this reason, sought to replace the Bolsheviks with an effective (and antirevolutionary) regime. Even if recognition served imperialist interests, however, it was sure to have the opposite effect. As for the fact that international capitalism could not come to terms with a Communist regime, this was undoubtedly true. Given the contradictory nature of the capitalist system, however, individual capitalist countries would support the Bolshevik regime for their own purposes.[5]

As the Mensheviks looked outside Russia, they perceived the Versailles peace as the source of instability in Europe. The creation of a belt of small states in central and eastern Europe was economically regressive unless it was accompanied by federative elements (although the right to self-determination was progressive).[6] The onerous conditions imposed on the defeated powers subverted the foundations of bourgeois democracy in these countries—not, as the Bolsheviks maintained, in favor of socialism but in favor of militarism. In adopting a thoroughly anti-Entente position, the Mensheviks were aligning themselves with their closest international allies, the German and Austrian socialists, even supporting the call for *Anschluss*.[7] Overall, the Mensheviks approved the idea of a coalition of defeated powers even as they feared that it would turn to Soviet Russia for support, with negative results for both Russia and Europe.

Like other socialists, the Mensheviks believed in the peaceful solution of international conflicts. They were most skeptical, however, about instruments such as the League of Nations.[8] The Mensheviks did take part in the Hague Peace Conference in December 1922 which brought together a broad array of progressive elements. One suspects they participated mainly to assert themselves on the international scene and to counter the Bolshevik presence at the conference. They also successfully used this forum to raise the question of socialist prisoners, an issue sure to win the sympathy of the gathering. Forty years later Abramovitch recalled with gusto his oratorical exchanges at the conference with Comintern representative Karl Radek. He saw these as a further round in the verbal duel which had pitted Martov against Zinoviev two years earlier. If so, it was a final round, since there was never again to be a public exchange between Bolsheviks and Mensheviks before an international audience.[9]

From the Hamburg Congress in 1923 to the fall of France in 1940, the principal multilateral forum for the promotion of Menshevik views was the LSI. I have already noted that the Mensheviks were able to exert influence in this body through their membership in its Executive and Bureau. They were also fortunate in having a close ally in the perennial secretary of the LSI, Friedrich Adler. Unlike Menshevik ties with Karl Kautsky, which went back to the prewar period, or with Otto Bauer, dating to 1917, when Bauer lived in the Tsederbaum-Dan household in Petrograd, the association with Adler was more recent. Martov, Dan, and especially Abramovitch cooperated closely with him in the Vienna Union between 1921 and 1923. Thereafter, bonds of ideological sympathy, reinforced by friendship with Adler's Russian wife, were further nurtured by a common nostalgia for the ideals of the $2^{1}/_{2}$ International.[10]

Adler stood at the head of a current within the LSI that was determined to resist the reformist tendencies of the new International's majority and to give revolutionary Marxism pride of place. In this respect the Mensheviks were his most zealous supporters, and eventually their efforts and Adler's bore fruit.[11] By the time of the Second Congress in Marseilles in 1925, Otto Bauer could write that "our fears" about the LSI have proven unfounded.[12] After the Third LSI Congress in Brussels three years later, Dan, as skeptical in regard to the LSI as Bauer, even expresed "satisfaction and pride" at what it had managed to accomplish.[13]

The price of such gains was the further weakening of an already feeble International. The aloof and disinterested British Labour Party allowed Adler and his Continental allies to get the upper hand in the LSI out of indifference.[14] Neither the Germans nor the French proved strong enough to replace the British. Lacking leadership, and hampered by its origins as a compromise body, the LSI was unable to inspire the authority its prewar predecessor or its Communist counterpart enjoyed. The strongest interest in the LSI came from its weakest parties, such as the RSDRP. Consequently, although the LSI moved toward the revolutionary Marxist phraseology of its left wing, it found itself unable to give substance to its rhetoric.

The weakness of the LSI was particularly evident in its position on the Russian Question. Generally speaking, the LSI tended to give the Mensheviks "jurisdiction" on this issue in order to contain and "specialize" a problem which could reveal deep divergences within the International as a whole.[15] The Mensheviks, as victims of bolshevism, as defenders of the Russian Revolution, and as revolutionary Marxists posing no threat to the LSI's reformist members, were well qualified to assume this responsibility. By the same token, they were limited in their ability to exercise their "jurisdiction." Even Adler resisted their attempts to have the International adopt a binding and effective position on the Russian Question in order not to endanger its unity.[16]

Divergences on the Russian Question took as their point of departure positions staked out by Karl Kautsky and Otto Bauer. For all members of the International, with the exception of the British, these two theoreticians were the indispensable reference points for any serious consideration of the Russian issue. For the Mensheviks they were the standards against which to measure their own views.

Kautsky condemned the Soviet experience unreservedly in the name of an unsurmountable opposition between democracy and dictatorship.[17] Notions such as "barracks socialism," "bonapartism," and "state capitalism" figured as prominently in Kautsky's writings as they did in *Sotsialisticheskii vestnik.* These convergences of vocabulary were based on common premises concerning the immaturity of Russian conditions for a socialist experiment and the weight of the peasant factor in the Russian Revolution. Divergences between Kautsky's views and those of the Menshevik majority lay in the categorical nature of the former and the tentative nature of the latter. Whereas Kautsky affirmed that a new bureaucratic class had already founded a bonapartist and state capitalist order in Russia, the Mensheviks would assert only that there existed a tendency in that direction. The Mensheviks believed this tendency could be countered by the establishment of democracy, even if limited to the working classes, and they expressed the hope that such a countertendency might yet emerge. Kautsky insisted on full democracy, and he was confident that the fall of the Bolsheviks was the necessary precondition to democracy in Russia. These divergences could be traced back to the dissolution of the Constituent Assembly in 1918, an event which horrified Kautsky but left the Mensheviks only moderately perturbed. They deepened in later years, with Kautsky referring to Soviet Russia as reactionary or counter-revolutionary even as the Mensheviks were describing it as a deformed but still revolutionary regime.

Kautsky's position did not win the assent of most Mensheviks, but he was treated cordially and respectfully.[18] To the embarrassment of the Menshevik Foreign Delegation, Kautsky's views were shared, discreetly, by the patriarch of the party, Pavel Axelrod, and openly by another founder of the RSDRP, Alexander Potresov. They were also invoked most vociferously by the Menshevik right wing, both inside and outside the party, even though Kautsky would not allow himself to be used for factional infighting. Kautsky's negative role, from the point of view of the Menshevik majority, was partially redeemed by the fact that he confirmed a basic Menshevik premise: it was indeed possible to criticize Soviet Russia, even very harshly, and yet remain an authentic Marxist.

The other pole of opinion on the Russian Question was represented by Otto Bauer. His point of departure was the same as Kautsky's and, for that matter, the same as the Mensheviks'. Bauer pointed to the immaturity of Russian conditions to conclude that socialism, in any generally accepted sense, was impossible. Terror, despotism, and other aberrations of the Bolshevik regime were the inevitable price of its utopian experiment. As for the Sovietophilia so prevalent among the European masses, this was an understandable phenomenon based on the illusions and frustrations of a proletariat whose own revolutionary hopes had been disappointed. In a letter to Kautsky, Bauer wrote that it was necessary to "immunize" people in the West against Moscow.[19] This telling image, taken literally, suggests that Bauer was prescribing an "injection" of bolshevism—but only in measured doses—into the western European workers' movement if its health was to be restored.

Bauer's views found a sympathetic echo among most Mensheviks. His argument that Russia could not yet afford full democracy reiterated the more radical variant of the Menshevik position.[20] At the same time, Bauer's distinction between west European and Russian roads to socialism disturbed the Mensheviks. Axelrod had already complained in 1921 that this distinction expressed a condescending attitude toward Russia and undue indulgence toward the Bolsheviks.[21] Indeed, if Bauer's distinction was adopted integrally, it undermined the foundations of Menshevik activity within the International. What basis could there be for calling the Bolsheviks to order if Russia's situation was so sui generis that it could not be subjected to the scrutiny of international socialism? In the mid-1920s this problem remained below the surface of discussion.[22] Only in the 1930s was it to emerge as a key obstacle to enlisting international socialist opinion on the Menshevik side.

Throughout the 1920s the Mensheviks managed to maneuver successfully between the two poles represented by Kautsky and Bauer. They kept the question of political prisoners at the forefront of LSI concerns by dramatizing news about mistreatment, with the camps on the Solovetskii Islands a particular cause célèbre. The Mensheviks prevailed on the LSI to set up a commission for the investigation of the condition of political prisoners, and the fact that it covered all nondemocratic countries—that is, including right wing dictatorships—only underlined the element of reprobation.[23]

Even as they kept an LSI spotlight on Bolshevik persecution of socialists, the Mensheviks remained vigilant against anything which might smack of interventionism or support for a forcible overthrow of the Soviet regime. A particularly vivid example of such vigilance was Menshevik reaction to a discussion memorandum submitted to the LSI Executive by Kautsky in 1924. The memorandum suggested that if spontaneous peasant uprisings should occur in Soviet Russia, as they well might, the LSI should not condemn them outright. In the meantime, member parties of the LSI should put pressure on their own governments to make loans and agreements with the Soviets conditional on improvement of the condition of socialists in Russia.[24]

The Mensheviks were appalled by the content of the memorandum and even more so by the prospect that it would be discussed within the LSI and perhaps adopted as official policy.[25] In private they also admitted their concern that the discussion would provoke a confrontation between the LSI's two Russian parties, the SRs and the RSDRP. Given the tenor of Kautsky's memorandum, such a confrontation would probably be detrimental to the Mensheviks, perhaps even leading to their expulsion from the LSI or their forced fusion with the SRs. Finally, the majority of the Menshevik Foreign Delegation feared that Kautsky's memorandum would be used by right Mensheviks to bolster their own position, a fear which proved well founded.[26]

The Mensheviks first tried to convince Kautsky personally that his propositions were ill advised. When this approach failed, they managed to delay discussion by not sending in their own draft of a corresponding resolution. Finally, they effectively killed the memorandum by persuading the LSI Bureau to omit discussion from the agenda of the forthcoming Executive meeting and to shelve it thereafter. Dan declared that the problems raised in the memorandum were really an internal matter for the Russians, and in any case, the issue was too important to be subjected to a haphazard vote. In this instance the Mensheviks were successful in utilizing to their own advantage the LSI's unwillingness to take a firm stand on the Russian Question.[27]

In various ways—persuasion, agenda manipulation, moral pressure, control of information—the Mensheviks were able to retain control over the Russian Question within the LSI. They could not always bring this issue to the forefront, and they were unable to enforce unanimity around their viewpoint. At the very least, however, they wielded a veto power in this matter. Moreover, their authority on Russian questions acquired a monopoly character by the end of the 1920s as internal disputes among the SRs reduced the voice of this rival party.[28] The impotence of SRs, whose claim to speak on behalf of Russia rested on their incomparably stronger showing in the elections to the Constitutent Assembly, gave the Mensheviks some satisfaction. It not only favored the more nuanced Menshevik approach to Soviet Russia, but also from an internal party view, it vindicated the iron discipline which the Menshevik leadership imposed on its own troops.

At successive LSI congresses the Mensheviks fared well. At the Marseilles Congress in 1925, as at Hamburg two years earlier, the Russian Question was subsumed under a more general issue. A resolution, "Dangers of War in the East," spread blame for international tensions equally among imperialist powers, primarily Great Britain, and Soviet bolshevism. The resolution was contested, in particular by SRs but also by representatives of Russia's border states and even by some Western parties, as insufficiently emphatic with respect to "Red imperialism." Nevertheless, largely because of the joint efforts of Mensheviks and the relevant commission's rapporteur, Otto Bauer, the resolution was adopted easily.[29]

At the LSI Brussels Congress in 1928, held in an atmosphere marked by apparent stabilization of capitalism, the LSI reaffirmed its commitment to the defense of Soviet Russia against imperialist onslaughts even as it stressed the deep organizational gulf between bolshevism and social democracy, a gulf it traced back to the division between bolshevism and menshevism in 1903. Dan remarked with satisfaction that whereas the Hamburg Congress in 1923 had tried to circumvent the Russian Question by limiting itself to a protest against terror, and the Marseilles Congress had approached it as a problem of Soviet government policies, the Brussels Congress had at last posed the question correctly as one that concerned the Russian working-class movement.[30]

In spite of the pressure they were able to exert via the International, the Mensheviks were unable to control some untoward socialist initiatives, such as the multiplication of "delegations" to Soviet Russia.[31] When a British Trades Union delegation in 1924 returned from Russia and Georgia with a glowing report, the Mensheviks reacted as best they could.[32] No longer able to make their presence felt on the spot, they refuted returning delegates' factual claims and cited reaction from Mensheviks underground in Russia.

They managed to have the LSI formally condemn the delegation.[33] They also protested vigorously against a casual British comment regarding "Menshevik support for French capitalism," and even launched (and lost) a lawsuit against a German Communist newspaper that had slandered the RSDRP on the basis of this comment.[34]

The Mensheviks also devised a strategy for limiting the damage done by these delegations. They encouraged Friedrich Adler to prepare a rebuttal of the British report decrying the fact that none of the delegates spoke Russian or knew much about Russia.[35] The report was actually prepared, he claimed, by "a few pensioned bureaucrats of the Diplomatic Service" accompanying the delegates as advisers.[36] In order to avoid such distortions, the Mensheviks proposed that future workers' delegations include members of the RSDRP as advisers and interpreters. None of these delegations did, in fact, succeed in having a Menshevik accompany them. Several, however, requested permission of the Soviet authorities to do so. Denial of the request embarrassed the Soviets and, at the very least, ensured that delegates left for Russia forewarned of the limits of Soviet tolerance and more critical of what they might encounter.[37]

Fraternal Parties

In addition to "multilateral" diplomacy in the LSI, exiled Mensheviks also cultivated bilateral relations with individual Western parties. At this level, too, the Mensheviks served to authenticate others' hopes for Russia. They also profited from the tendency among political groupings to promote their foreign counterparts. Naturally, the Mensheviks were the weaker party in such relations. Wherever a symbiotic relationship developed, however, as with the Germans and the French, they acquired some leverage. Wherever they were unable to step outside their role of supplicants, as in their dealings with the Austrians and, above all, with the British, they remained impotent.

The Mensheviks' closest relations were with their German hosts. There, a few uniquely bicultural individuals drew Russian socialists and their Western counterparts together. Foremost among these was Alexander Stein, a multilingual native of Riga introduced to Marxism by then-Bundist Raphael Abramovitch. Initially a Bolshevik, Stein worked with future foreign commissar Maxim Litvinov in smuggling *Iskra*. After the 1905 Revolution Stein moved to Germany, where he attained prominence in the social democratic press, largely as an expert on Russia. By 1920 Stein was an editor of the USPD organ *Freiheit*. It was he who organized the contacts which brought

Martov and Abramovitch to Germany, and it was he who read Martov's speech at the Halle Congress.[1]

Throughout the 1920s Stein facilitated the exiled Mensheviks' penetration into the German socialist milieu. *Sotsialisticheskii vestnik* was registered in his name to comply with German legal requirements, and he put the technical facilities of the main SPD daily, *Vorwärts,* at *Vestnik*'s disposition. As an editor of *Vorwärts* and of *Sozialistische Bildung und Bücherwarte,* he opened the German press to his Russian comrades. After 1933 Stein shared the life of an exile in Prague, Paris, and New York; it was his Menshevik friends who now interceded on his behalf.[2]

If Stein was a German socialist of Menshevik origin, others remained Mensheviks even after becoming German socialists. Iurii Denike, known in Germany as Georg Decker, left his post at the Soviet mission in Berlin only when he was sure, thanks to SPD contacts, that he would be able to "become part of German life." He found the thought of living in an emigré ghetto unbearable. Denike succeeded in making a career in the SPD very quickly as a publicist. Like Stein before him, he soon became right-hand man to Rudolf Hilferding, the prominent theoretician and politician. In this capacity Denike edited the SPD's main theoretical journal, *Die Gesellschaft.*[3]

Grigorii Bienstock also joined in German socialist life. He worked for the Cultural Commission of the SPD Executive Committee (Parteivorstand) as a lecturer, was active in the local Berlin-Wedding SPD orgnization, and in 1933 joined the radical left SPD group Zukunft.[4] For Bienstock, as for Denike, engagement in German socialist politics was a way of breaking out of the isolation of exile and that imposed by party discipline. For both men, isolation was all the more acute because they stood on the right flank of the Menshevik Party. They were thus isolated not only from Russia but also from their own Russian party's leadership. Significantly, however, within the SPD Bienstock and, to a lesser extent, Denike adopted left wing positions which again put them into a minority. They thus remained mavericks in both worlds. Similar in their political trajectory (both Bienstock and Denike began as Bolsheviks before moving toward right menshevism), similar in pursuing tastes and interests unusual in their milieu (Denike was an aesthete, and Bienstock dabbled in esotericism), they both defied conventional categories of ideology and party.

Individuals helped cement ties between the SPD and the RSDRP in exile, but bonds were dependent on other factors as well. While German social democracy was divided between the USPD and SPD, the Mensheviks identified entirely with the former. Its disappearance within the SPD fold in 1922 was therefore a further defeat for them. Yet antibolshevism was so important to the internal unity of the SPD that the party could not afford to disregard exiled antibolshevik Russian comrades.[5] The fact that these Russian exiles were more orthodox in their Marxism than the Germans only made them more valuable to the huge and powerful German party.

Help extended by the SPD was vital. Berlin's Mensheviks could not have adapted to exile without the jobs, commissioned articles, introductions, invitations, committees and press campaigns in support of socialist prisoners in Russia, and other less tangible SPD means of promotion. Occasionally they found themselves playing a mediating role within the German party or the International on German matters.[6] In general, however, the Mensheviks retained a critical distance with respect to the SPD.[7] Independently of their own interests, too, they could not approve the evolution of the German party away from revolutionary Marxism, as expressed, for instance, in SPD willingness to serve in bourgeois governments.[8] They analyzed the weaknesses of the Weimar Republic and warned of the fascist danger at a very early (perhaps too early) stage.[9] It was this combination of sympathy and critical distance that made the Mensheviks such acute observers of the German scene, more accurate perhaps in their analysis of Germany than of Russia.[10]

Relations between exiled Mensheviks and Austrian socialists were paradoxical. The leading Austrian socialist, Otto Bauer, was the Mensheviks' principal ally in the International and closer to the Menshevik leadership in his analysis of Soviet Russia than any other Western socialist.[11] Bauer's party, however, and even Bauer himself, remained deaf to Menshevik appeals. Unlike other social democratic parties, the Austrians refused to set up a committee for the defense of political prisoners in Russia, and their party organ, the *Wiener Arbeiterzeitung*, tended to omit critical or unfavorable reports on Russia.

The Mensheviks complained repeatedly, mostly in private, to Friedrich Adler in his capacity as LSI secretary and as a member of the Austrian party leadership.[12] They complained about the *Arbeiterzeitung*, about the Austrian workers' delegation to Russia, about not being invited to a party congress (in contrast with the courtesy invitations they received from other Western social democratic parties), about Bauer's refusal to organize a demonstration on the tenth anniversary of the October Revolution, about Bauer himself. They blamed Sigmund Kunfi, the left-leaning exiled Hungarian socialist in Vienna, who, according to them, "reigned" over the *Arbeiterzeitung*. More philosophically, they expressed understanding that "the ten-year existence of the Soviet government weigh[ed] psychologically," comparing readiness to come to terms with Soviet Russia to the indulgence shown by a socialist such as George Bernard Shaw toward Mussolini's dictatorship.[13] They did not seem to understand Bauer's reasoning. Pressed by Sovietophile and leftist sentiment, which survived longer in the Austrian party than elsewhere, governed by an intense attachment to the ideal of proletarian unity, and convinced that Moscow would change course as Europe overcame its own postwar crises, Bauer sought to restrain the Menshevik comrades with whom he basically agreed.[14]

The Austrians' attitude could not be a matter of indifference. Although Austria was small and weak, its Social Democratic Party was disproportionately strong, both inside the country and in the international arena. Not only did it enjoy prestige and leadership, but also in spite of Austria's impoverishment, it even aided other parties materially. The French Socialist Party (SFIO), for example, received financial help from the Austrians, but the Mensheviks did not. The Austrian attitude was also an embarrassment to the Menshevik leadership vis-à-vis its own right wing members. Perhaps most discouraging was the fact that, fundamentally, the Mensheviks admired Otto Bauer, his party, and its program.[15] Although they made headway in obtaining recognition for their views, the battle was uphill and one they ultimately lost.[16]

If relations with the Austrians were less harmonious than expected, those with the French developed better than might have been anticipated. Although France was the strongest power on the Continent, the French Socialist Party had been particularly debilitated by the division between pro-Communists and anti-Communists.[17] The SFIO emerged from its Tours Congress in December 1920 even weaker than the USPD after the Halle Congress three months earlier. Not only did the vast majority of French socialists go over to a newly formed Communist Party at Tours, but also, even among remaining socialists, an important faction found itself outside the Communist Party only because it had been denied entry. Jean Longuet, leader of the centrist faction and a guest at the USPD Halle Congress, had withheld any expression of support for Martov there because he was negotiating conditions of adherence to the Comintern. Longuet now joined Léon Blum and right wing socialists such as Paul Renaudel in a small and impoverished rump socialist party.

The Mensheviks had no particular entrée into the SFIO. Their pro-German and anti-Entente attitudes worked against rapprochement. Their attempt to put out a French edition of *RSD*, the party's foreign-language bulletin, failed after only two issues. After Martov's death the Russian socialists best known in France were Iraklii Tsereteli and Pavel Axelrod, and only Tsereteli lived there. Tsereteli had reassumed a Georgian identity, so although until 1928 he maintained friendly personal relations with the Russian Menshevik leadership (to the chagrin of more nationalist Georgian socialists), he now represented a separate party; moreover, his political views were further to the right than those of the RSDRP. Axelrod (who lived in Berlin) stood outside party activity, he did not speak French, and his views also diverged from those of the Menshevik leadership.[18] As in Berlin, but unlike in Vienna, the Mensheviks had a party organization in Paris. Unlike in Berlin, however, there were no internationally known personalities among Parisian Mensheviks.

It may well have been the weakness of the SFIO that opened it up to the views of the exiled RSDRP and to the support the Russian party could offer. French socialism could not afford the condescension which powerful Germans or Austrians sometimes showed their Russian comrades. Moreover, the French did not claim expertise on Russian matters. Finally, the attitude adopted toward Soviet Russia by Léon Blum, soon the dominant figure in the party, coincided closely with Menshevik positions. Blum, too, tried to separate problems posed by the Comintern, bolshevism, Soviet Russia, and the Russian Revolution. In a sense, such distinctions demarcated right from left socialists everywhere. Nonetheless, Blum's position—defense of the Russian Revolution but repudiation of bolshevism—was particularly compatible with that of the Mensheviks.[19] Upon Martov's death the French party organ, *Le Populaire,* praised him in terms which it could have bestowed on itself: "He never confused the Russian Revolution with bolshevism; nor did he believe they could be entirely disassociated."[20]

The French socialists' willingness to accept Menshevik information and interpretations can be gauged by their prominence in the SFIO's *Populaire,* where the Menshevik Oreste Rosenfeld acquired authority.[21] This daily covered the question of socialist prisoners in Russia in great detail. It relied on *Vestnik*'s "Po Rossii" column for descriptions of Soviet social conditions and, in particular, for analyses of leadership struggles within the Bolshevik Party. The theoretical trappings of Menshevik analysis, with its use of concepts borrowed from the French Revolution, were also favorably received by the French. On the tenth anniversary of the October 1917 Revolution, *Le Populaire* ran a front-page article by Fedor Dan presenting the Bolshevik Revolution as but one phase of the Russian Revolution and recognizing its achievements, even as it denied any credit for them to the dictatorship. Dan recalled Marx's warnings about a premature seizure of power by the proletariat and declared that the Bolsheviks, having exhausted their revolutionary role, were transforming their rule into that of a supraclass bureaucratic apparatus.[22] These were classical Menshevik analyses; they were shared by the SFIO.

The French socialists not only opened their publications to the Mensheviks but also formally consulted them. Largely owing to Abramovitch's efforts, intensified after the socialists' electoral surge in 1924, members of the RSDRP Foreign Delegation were invited to Paris to address the Central Committee and the parliamentary faction of the SFIO. Dan was initially skeptical about the possibilities of influencing the French, perhaps because of an earlier rowdy reception there.[23] He changed his opinion after a handsome welcome by the SFIO leadership, which quizzed him on specialized questions.[24] During the Georgian insurrection in 1924, the Mensheviks were asked whether French socialist deputies should take a firm position and risk bringing down the Herriot government. They counseled moderation, thus allowing their French comrades to remain inactive in good conscience.[25]

The SFIO also solicited the views of Mensheviks on the attitude to adopt toward the question of French credits for Russia. One may assume that they welcomed Dan's nuanced position: encouragement of means that would help Russia economically and thus foster the rebirth of a strong Russian working class; rejection of any support for the Soviet political regime. The SFIO was advised to demand *glasnost'* in all negotiations and to reject all attempts at "securing" loans by concessions or monopolies since such measures would lead straight to sanctions and intervention. Once again, such advice also served a moral purpose. It allowed the SFIO to condone rapprochement with Soviet Russia without compromising its principles.[26]

The Mensheviks also observed with satisfaction that French socialist opinion was evolving favorably on the crucial issue of terror against socialists in Russia. In 1924 the Menshevik Club in Paris reported that "until last year, French workers simply did not believe terror existed in Russia," but a complete turnaround had occurred.[27] A committee for the defense of revolutionaries imprisoned in Russia had been formed by anarchists and dissident socialists. It imputed to all political parties, including socialists, the sins of the Bolsheviks, and its real goal was to counter Communist influence in the French trade union movement. Nevertheless, it gave the Mensheviks an audience and opened a wedge for them among French workers. Very soon, the SFIO picked up this theme and placed it squarely in the public forum.[28]

The electoral successes of their French allies in 1924 and 1928 pleased the Mensheviks but had few practical consequences. The chronic financial problems of the SFIO meant that it could not even aid the Mensheviks materially. Only when the Menshevik Foreign Delegation was forced to flee from Berlin to Paris in 1933 did the ties established earlier acquire overriding importance. Unknowingly, the exiled Mensheviks had been preparing their next port of refuge.

In contrast with their experience with the French, the Mensheviks encountered nothing but frustration in their dealings with the British. Abramovitch raged at the insulting behavior of the Labour Party, this "bulwark of bolshevism."[29] At the same time, he sought frantically to multiply contacts with the British, particularly after formation of the first Labour government in 1924. Through the intermediation of Friedrich Adler, who also tutored him on how to deal with the British, Abramovitch tried, with various degrees of success, to get himself invited to address party congresses, trade unions, or parliamentary groups. He was even prepared to go to meetings without an invitation and to "make noise" publicly, but Adler dissuaded him.[30] Even when Abramovitch was able to make himself heard in a public forum in Britain, his appearances were to little avail.

The Mensheviks' inability to pierce the British shield resulted from a profound difference in outlook. British Labour was as insular as menshevism was internationalist. The LSI, such a central Menshevik concern, was utterly marginal for the British, and they were disdainful of emigrés.[31] Moreover, the British were in no way impressed by the Mensheviks' mastery of Marxist theory. Such prowess not only aroused suspicion but actually made them incomprehensible to the British. Both literally and figuratively, the Mensheviks and the British spoke different languages.[32]

The British attitude toward Soviet Russia followed directly from these traits. The British were neither the Bolshevik bulwark nor the hopeless reformists that the Mensheviks, quite inconsistently, made them out to be. Their attitude was truly sui generis. They rose to the defense of Soviet Russia because British Conservatives were attacking it.[33] They let themselves be attracted by romantic visions of the Revolution although they had no thought of following the Russian example.[34] At the same time, they prided themselves on their pragmatism; one could work with the Russians without compromising one's principles. Finally, British Labour leaders had no quarrel with Marxism in Russia, even as they repressed Marxist tendencies in their midst.

British smugness, double standards, and incoherence exasperated the Mensheviks. British Labour was philistine in dealing with the Soviets on a businesslike basis.[35] It was derelict in its socialist duties by disregarding the problems of terror against Russian socialists.[36] It was hypocritical in invoking financial constraints to avoid participation in the LSI's commission of inquiry into political prisoners. It was cowardly in turning a blind eye to internal Russian matters for fear that the Soviets would raise thorny questions such as the Indian situation. The Mensheviks could only console themselves with Friedrich Adler's remark that "the English [Labour] government is not an iota more of a workers' government than the Russian government."[37]

The Mensheviks' predicament vis-à-vis the British was compounded by the fact that they did not have a personal foothold in England. Whereas in Germany their cause was well served by Alexander Stein, in England they had only Anatolii Baikalov. This picaresque figure landed in England in 1919, via China and Japan, with fifteen years as a Bolshevik, twelve arrests under the tsar, and, as he put it, generations of martial cossack ancestry behind him. Baikalov was a prominent member of the London Group of Russian Social Democrats so swiftly dissolved by Martov for its rightist deviation.[38] Thereafter he had few formal links with the official party; only Boris Nicolaevsky kept up a comradely and business correspondence. Instead, Baikalov moved in the circle of extraparty right wing Mensheviks and among SRs. Indeed, his agrarianist views put him at home among SRs, but he continued to define himself as a social democrat.[39]

Baikalov made it his personal mission to inform the British public of the true nature of bolshevism. As an enterprising individual he set about the task with gusto. Over the years, in spite of faulty English, he published, lectured, and lobbied extensively.[40] Expansive by nature and impervious to British reserve, Baikalov sought out eminent personalities (whom he had never met) and remained undaunted by rebuffs.[41] When Sidney Webb, replying to Baikalov's offer to help the Webbs with their book on Russia, wrote back, "Thank you for your offer to try to save us from error in our survey of Soviet communism," Baikalov contentedly informed Nicolaevsky that the *starik* (old man) had sent him a kind answer inviting him to come to the country for the day.[42]

Baikalov's activities required doggedness, bravado, and luck. One such lucky break came when Walter Citrine, general secretary of the Trades Union Council (TUC), invited Baikalov to undertake surveys of the Russian press. Citrine was particularly eager for information on interference of the Red Trade Union International or of the Communist Party (Soviet or British) in British trade union affairs. Baikalov was to choose items which were directly relevant or had not been reported in the general press. He was to be paid fifteen shillings per thousand words of translation and a guinea per summary.[43]

Citrine's attitude toward Baikalov was standoffish. He frequently turned down Baikalov's requests for an appointment and would not allow him to acknowledge help from the TUC in his books. Nevertheless, Baikalov could not resist boasting of his new position and inflating its importance. Even before Citrine's invitation, Baikalov wrote Kerensky that the TUC had decided to put him at the head of a newly created Russian subdivision in the International Department and that he was to be the editor responsible for Russian items in the TUC *Bulletin*.[44]

Baikalov's perseverance was further rewarded in later years. He bragged to Nicolaevsky that he knew "long and well" William Gillies, Labour Party international secretary, who consulted him on matters such as Ukraine.[45] Even the TUC general secretary mellowed, and by and by Baikalov was addressing him as "Dear Citrine." Above all, Baikalov succeeded in winning the confidence of the duchess of Atholl, the first woman to hold office in a British Conservative government. He sent the duchess translations of articles from *Sotsialisticheskii vestnik,* assisted her in various projects, and addressed parliamentary committees on Russian economic subjects.[46] Even *Pravda* took note of Baikalov's activities, denouncing him as a "white bandit" forging documents on behalf of oil magnate Henri Deterding's Anglo-Russian Committee.[47]

Although a Labour Party member, Baikalov was entirely bipartisan in his approach. He had no qualms about asking Karl Kautsky to write an introduction to the book of a Conservative member of Parliament (a request Kautsky politely declined).[48] After World War II Baikalov continued to counsel the Conservative duchess. He offered his advisory services both to Viscount Craigavon, chairman of the Fighting Fund for Freedom, an organization opposed to "evils like Nationalization and Communism," and to Dennis Healey, then secretary of the Labour Party's International Department.[49] In establishing contacts with antisocialist groups such as the Russian Solidarists, Baikalov was merely intensifying his earlier antibolshevism. During the cold war this evolution was not unusual, but, blessed to the end with few inhibitions, Baikalov went farther than most of his Menshevik comrades.[50]

Although Germany, Austria, France, and Britain were the countries that mattered most to exiled Mensheviks, at times their attention turned to the United States, for quite specific reasons. They had no hope of influencing the U.S. government, and they followed American socialist politics with only mild concern. In its first five years *Sotsialisticheskii vestnik* published only one substantial article about the United States; it dealt with the presidential candidacy of Robert La Follette.[51] Menshevik interest in the American socialist movement lay rather in its potential as a source of funds for the RSDRP's activities. As the Foreign Delegation's coffers emptied, even to the point of endangering publication of *Sotsialisticheskii vestnik,* the delegation accepted an invitation to send a party leader on a speaking tour of the United States.

The Jewish Socialist Verband, representing the antibolshevik minority of the American Socialist Party's Jewish Federation, stood at the center of a large network of Jewish labor institutions, including the Arbeiter Ring, a wealthy mutual aid society described as the Red Cross of the Jewish labor movement.[52] The Verband also enjoyed the support of influential leaders in powerful trade unions such as the International Ladies' Garment Workers'

Union (ILGWU). Soviet developments were of prime concern in this milieu, particularly since most Jewish American workers had roots in Russia. The Verband was thus keen to receive a Yiddish-speaking Russian socialist leader who could bolster the struggle with its procommunist rivals.[53] Abramovitch, with his flawless Yiddish, his Bund credentials, and his oratorical talent, was the natural choice for this mission. Consequently, in early 1925 he spent three months crisscrossing the United States and Canada, making some sixty public appearances. There seem to have been few places which Abramovitch did not visit. All in all he addressed some twenty-five thousand people and collected over twenty thousand dollars for his party.

American Communists correctly saw the Abramovitch visit as a challenge and responded aggressively. At the huge New York meeting there were three to four hundred Communist sympathizers, barely kept in tow by two hundred Verband security men. With the help of similar security measures and, in most cases, with the assistance of local police, Abramovitch managed to carry on successfully elsewhere, too, in spite of such confrontations. Only in Rochester, where local socialists refused, for reasons of principle, to set up a security system, and in Detroit, where city officials canceled the meeting out of fear of violence, was Abramovitch unable to speak.

Abramovitch remained unruffled by these attacks. He did voice astonishment that there were no antidefamation laws to restrict the unbridled press campaign against him. He also expressed surprise that he had received only one threatening letter; it stated that no one wanted to take away his freedom of speech, but if he said one word against the Bolsheviks he would be shot.[54] Even the bourgeois press, interested in "pleasant business relations" with the Soviet regime, joined the Communists in describing him as a former Soviet commissar, a German professor, a former Kerensky ambassador and minister, and even as a "young student." There were reports that he had stolen money from the Soviet regime and that he had come to America with Grand Duke Cyrill. As for the purpose of his visit, it was to prevent American recognition of Russia and to agitate on behalf of the open shop movement. At one meeting an Irish woman (who did not understand Yiddish) raised a commotion accusing Abramovitch of promoting British terror in Ireland.[55]

In spite of such altercations, Abramovitch was justified in considering his tour a success. Not only did it meet its propaganda and fund-raising goals, but also it provided some unexpected dividends. American civil libertarians, who had earlier concentrated on defending Communists, protested at the treatment meted out to him. This provided an opening for social democratic sympathizers among civil libertarians to set up a section for the defense of human rights in Russia and to hold a meeting against terror in Hungary,

Italy, Poland—and Soviet Russia.[56] Elsewhere, too, Abramovitch's visits led to resolutions of protest against Soviet terror, creation of support committees, and press attention to the fate of Russian social democracy. The august *New York Times* recorded his accusations, and the *Nation* quoted at length from a Menshevik letter describing the Solovetskii camp shootings.[57]

Finally, Abramovitch's tour allowed him to reestablish personal contact with prominent comrades such as David Dubinsky, future head of the ILGWU; Abe Cahan, editor of *Forverts;* Baruch Charney Vladeck, founder of the Jewish Labor Committee; and Sol Levitas, editor of the *New Leader.* These direct contacts by a member of the RSDRP Foreign Delegation were all the more valuable because of the rightist orientation of most local socialists. Their real value, however, was to emerge fifteen years later. In 1940 the Foreign Delegation and most other active Mensheviks landed as refugees in New York. They were received as comrades by the same individuals and organizations that had welcomed Abramovitch in 1925. As in France, Menshevik diplomacy in America in the 1920s turned out to be a wise investment for future personal and political survival.

6

Stalin's Revolution

The Great Turn

As the Bolshevik Revolution entered its second decade, Soviet Russia experienced seismic transformations. Under the twin onslaught of collectivization and industrialization the face of Russia changed irrevocably. The breadth, intensity, and violence of this new revolution altered the material base of Russian society as radically as the events of 1917 had changed its political superstructures. Stalin's "Great Turn" or "General Line" proved no less a historical event than the October Revolution.

The magnitude of Stalin's revolution commanded the attention of the Mensheviks as it did that of other contemporary observers and, thereafter, of historians. Indeed, the final chapter in the history of the Menshevik Party was to be a history of two currents which drew separate conclusions from Stalin's revolution. Before we examine these consequences, the contemporary reactions of Berlin Mensheviks to the General Line merit consideration, particularly in the light of unresolved historiographic issues: When was it possible to discern the contours of Stalin's Great Turn? Was it planned or improvised, a product of Stalin's will or of circumstances? The fact that such questions can still puzzle historians allows one to imagine the bewilderment that Stalin's revolution created in its own time, even among such close observers as the Mensheviks.

The question of timing of the Great Turn has elicited a straightforward answer. An authoritative study affirms that the "experienced observer could not have missed the shift to the left in the political thinking of the [Bolshevik] leadership" at the Fifteenth Party Congress held in December 1927.[1] This is also the reply given years earlier but decades after the events themselves by some prominent Mensheviks. For example, Naum Jasny accepts

182

the later official designation of the Fifteenth Congress as the "Industrialization Congress" and states that "NEP had ended in December 1927." Raphael Abramovitch adds, self-critically, that the Mensheviks were too preoccupied with the defeat of the party opposition, also confirmed then, to realize "what had really happened at the [Fifteenth] Congress."[2] In short, December 1927 marks the beginning of the General Line, and those who did not see it at the time should have seen it.

This formulation is deceptively simple. It assumes that adoption of Stalin's General Line flowed naturally from abandonment of NEP, and that passage from one to the other occurred in a seamless process readily pinpointed chronologically. Although this is the outlook favored both by hindsight and by Communist Party history, an examination of *Sotsialisticheskii vestnik* for the period in question suggests a different and more complex reality.

The Mensheviks had consistently argued that NEP was untenable. As we have seen, they pointed to the overall contradiction between economic liberalization and political repression as well as to the internal contradictions of economic policy. With time, and as economic indicators suggested that the pace of recovery in Russia was faltering, the Mensheviks shrilly proclaimed the exhaustion of NEP's possibilities. Although it was clear to them that NEP would not last, it was certainly not evident that the way out of the NEP impasse would lie in the radical course adopted by Stalin.

Occasionally *Sotsialisticheskii vestnik* entertained the hypothesis that the necessities of accumulation and the inability to attract foreign capital would lead the regime toward expropriation of the peasantry. David Dallin's inventory of the instruments of accumulation included inflation and an intensification of the price "scissors," that is, the discrepancy between high industrial prices and low agricultural prices; it did not include collectivization. In any case, Dallin argued, it was not easy to put new pressure on the peasantry. Consequently, significant accumulation was unlikely, and industry was condemned to slow development.[3]

Shortly before the Fifteenth Communist Party Congress a Menshevik Moscow correspondent quoted a Soviet specialist, an ex-Menshevik, who compared the impasse in industry to that in which the countryside found itself on the eve of NEP. The specialist concluded that NEP must be extended to industry, otherwise the economy could not hold out for more than one or two years. He reserved his most vigorous fulminations, however, for the "madmen from Gosplan" who were drawing up plans in which only they believed.[4]

In reporting on the Fifteenth Congress itself, *Sotsialisticheskii vestnik* recorded Stalin's declarations about a "sharp turn" in party policy only to dismiss them. No one at the congress even bothered to ask what this turn consisted of, noted the *Vestnik* editorialist, adding ironically, "Apparently, all is clear without [explanation] in this song without words." Whatever Stalinists might say about accelerating socialist construction, no one could doubt that Stalin's "halfhearted borrowings" from an incoherent, left-oriented opposition program were only another demagogic tool in the power struggle.[5]

The Mensheviks were radically wrong in their prognostications. They feared not that Russia would move too sharply left but rather that it would move right, toward thermidor. They condemned what they saw as the "self-satisfied, petit bourgeois, properly thermidorian spirit" of the Fifteenth Congress; at least, however, such a mood excluded revolutionary adventurism. Once again they sounded the alarm of "la révolution en danger," but they failed to identify the direction of this danger.[6] Like meteorologists, the Mensheviks predicted an imminent change for the worse in the climate. Instead of the expected snowstorm, however, they were confronted by a tropical hurricane.

This tragic misassessment is all the more startling because *Vestnik* itself provides indications which allow one to understand some of the forces behind Stalin's Great Turn. Even as *Vestnik* reported on the petty materialism that came to the fore at the Fifteenth Congress, it noted that the slogan of industrialization, to the extent that it did not require personal sacrifices, was popular. It also noted the country's intense economic nationalism and its hostility to foreign capital. For some Russians one difference between Trotsky and Stalin was that the former wanted to industrialize with money from abroad, whereas the latter would do so using only internal resources. Viewed in this way, Stalin was correct, for, as people asked, "why should we give our money to foreigners?" Such attitudes heightened the widespread revulsion, already noted, toward NEP. They reinforced dissatisfaction within the Communist Party at the decline of revolutionary heroism, all the more evident as heroes of the Revolution went down to defeat. They contributed to the profound mood of foreboding that hung over Moscow, attaining even the Bolshevik upper ranks, as the country celebrated ten years of Revolution.[7]

Such indications acquire weight only in retrospect, and it is hindsight which brings them to the fore. Given the Mensheviks' worldview, it is understandable that they should have refused to entertain seriously the hypothesis that the regime was definitively turning left, even when they were themselves presenting evidence for it. More surprisingly, some Mensheviks also proved reluctant to acknowledge the demise of NEP, even though they had long anticipated it. Such reluctance may also be interpreted as proof of the Mensheviks' unwillingess to recognize reality. Alternatively, and, I would argue, more plausibly, it suggests that historians' efforts to establish a clear-cut break, in December 1927 or at any other specific moment, between the end of NEP and the beginning of the Great Turn distort the nature of the transition which took place.

It must be noted that reluctance to acknowledge the death of NEP was equally pronounced in the Soviet press. *Pravda* wrote that "only Menshevik scum can speak of the self-exhaustion of NEP." Such declarations found support in some of the regime's policies. Intensification of agricultural procurement in early 1928 was launched as an "extraordinary" (hence temporary) measure, and even as industrialization accelerated without any influx of foreign capital, the regime revived its efforts at attracting foreign concessions. These inconsistencies bolstered the Mensheviks' initial hunch that they were merely witnessing a continuation of NEP zigzags. How else could one explain, for instance, the incoherence of a Bolshevik Central Committee resolution which called for industrialization but not superindustrialization, for the development of heavy industry but of light industry too, for collectivization but also for stimulation of the poor and middle individual peasant, for maintaining the struggle against left factionalism but without abandoning the struggle against the Right?[8]

It was these same inconsistencies, however, which led David Dallin to question early on the official Soviet thesis that NEP was still in force. In July 1928 Dallin compared the argument that Russia was still standing on NEP foundations even though extraordinary measures were sometimes being applied to that of a purported virgin who affirms everything is in order because she has given birth to only a very small child.[9] It fell to Dallin to defend *Sotsialisticheskii vestnik* in 1929 for the failure of its other editors to anticipate Stalin's Great Turn. Replying to a *Pravda* article which mocked the Mensheviks for their incorrect predictions, Dallin confronted the issue head-on. The answer to the question "How could we have been so wrong?" lay in the fact that the Mensheviks had underestimated the limitless adventurism and the Homeric stupidity of the Communists. Among others who had also been wrong in their predictions one would have to include Lenin, who had thought NEP would last several decades, and even Stalin, who had earlier warned against rough treatment of the peasantry. Indeed, if the Mensheviks had predicted the present state of affairs in 1928, *Pravda* would have taken the lead in denouncing them as madmen. Dallin added that he and his party never doubted that by physical strength one could chase out the NEP-men, disperse the kulaks, and expropriate the middle peasants. The question was whether this could be called success.[10]

In reviewing the question of timing, one must conclude that a reading of

Sotsialisticheskii vestnik does not suggest a specific moment at which NEP was abandoned and the Great Turn adopted. In this respect *Vestnik*'s analysis coincides with that of Trotsky, who also saw a process of zigzags rather than a clear reorientation in policy. It reinforces, too, the views of those historians who maintain that NEP went under before any clear alternative had been formulated and that there was no master plan for the economic system before it was in place.[11] As the Mensheviks realized at the time but failed to recall later on, any attempt to find order in the chaos of the Great Turn was illusory.

The question of timing is closely connected to the question whether the Great Turn was carried out as a willful decision or as a function of circumstances or the culmination of unpremeditated stopgap measures. Behind all such interrogations looms the shadow of Stalin. For historians who claim there was no preconceived economic model for industrialization and no single decision to collectivize, Stalin emerges as a great improviser, at best stealing belatedly the ideas of his defeated opponents, at worst drifting along with events. This "functionalist" (as opposed to "intentionalist") explanation would seem to defy reason by arguing that the most monumental experiment in planned transformation ever undertaken should have been carried out in an unplanned way.[12] The Mensheviks as historians in the post–World War II period have been among the most emphatic defenders of the "intentionalist" interpretation, but this was not the case while these events were taking place.

Sotsialisticheskii vestnik offered only the faintest hints that Stalin, after driving the left opposition out of the party, might make the opposition's program his own. A Moscow correspondent wrote that this had been Lenin's way of doing things, applied at the expense of the Mensheviks with adoption of NEP. The party apparatus now favored a similar maneuver, but it seemed far more likely that the realistic line of the economic apparatus calling for a deepening of NEP would prevail. In the aftermath of the Fifteenth Congress, as Stalin's "extraordinary measures" of grain procurement raged in the countryside, the Mensheviks could barely contain their astonishment. A correspondent noted that Stalin had always been reproached for his stubbornness and immobility; now, he added, we are all frightened by his flexibility and apparent eccentricity. The reaction against NEP, declared a *Vestnik* editorial, had exceeded all the demands of the opposition. It was quite incomprehensible why it was not Trotsky but Stalin who was sitting in the Kremlin.[13]

Astonishment at Stalin's turnabout prompted a gradual reevaluation of Stalin himself. Initially, the Mensheviks believed that Stalin was a centrist deftly maneuvering between Left and Right or even, with respect to industrialization, carrying out in a "left demagogic" way the "right wing aim" of raising productivity. Inconsistencies between Stalin's previous positions and present ones were explained in terms of bureacratic conflicts: Sovnarkom versus Gosplan, Commissariat of Agriculture versus Commissariat of Trade. Intrabolshevik struggles were invoked frequently. Was Stalin moving left in order to carry out a rapprochement with Trotsky? Were his later retreats from an extreme left position the price to be paid for a continued alliance with the right winger Rykov? As Stalin managed to push the throttle of the General Line back and forth, extracting a frightful price from the country at no apparent cost to himself, the image of Stalin as unprincipled and power-hungry replaced the earlier view. It would take two decades, and many subsequent horrors, for this image to reach its ultimate form.[14]

The final Menshevik response to the question of the timing and the planned or unplanned nature of the Great Turn was to be given by Raphael Abramovitch. Groping for a satisfactory explanation of Stalin's success, Abramovitch could only resort to a metaphor: "Stalin [was] the mathematical point of leverage of the General Line." A quarter of a century later, in *Soviet Revolution,* he still considered Stalin an instrument of historical destiny, "the only one of the party's leaders bold enough to steer the course which the contradictions of the New Economic Policy made necessary."[15] By then, however, Abramovitch did not doubt that Stalin's "grand maneuver" had been an act of premeditated deception, planned with great caution and long disguised by lip service to the doctrine of the Right. There was "not the least doubt" that Stalin's behavior at the time of the Great Turn could be understood only if he already knew what his subsequent steps would be.[16]

Abramovitch's espousal of an "intentionalist" interpretation of Stalin's actions at the time of the Great Turn reflects the moralizing tendencies of Menshevik historians in the 1950s. In this particular case one can also trace Abramovitch's thesis to the influence of his comrade Nikolai Valentinov-Volsky. Although they differed on questions such as Stalin's rationality, Abramovitch was impressed by Volsky's account of conversations held in the autumn of 1927. After having provoked the ire of Premier Rykov by reporting rumors that NEP would be abolished, Volsky was told by the Soviet planner V. G. Groman that Rykov was completely insignificant. Real power, claimed Groman, lay in the hands of Stalin; if he listened to anyone it was to the opposition. Stalin was now fighting Trotsky in order to appropriate Trotskyism for himself, and he would announce a program of superindustrialization at the next congress.[17]

In the heat and fury of the Great Turn historiographic questions which later exercised Mensheviks and other historians were buried under the rubble of the cataclysm. Seeking to make sense of events as they occurred, *Sotsialisticheskii vestnik* presented the General Line as a new form of war communism, with its peasant "committees of the poor," seizure of food surpluses, ration card system, liquidation of private trade, inflation, forced loans, and centralization.[18] A report from Russia rejected such comparisons as "superficial." Whereas formerly the state had requisitioned the substantial assets of an old bourgeoisie, now it could only plunder a pitiful NEP bourgeoisie with virtually nothing to confiscate. Instead of conscripting the technical intelligentsia into its service, the state was treating engineers as pariahs and wreckers, allowing an ambitious and unqualified stratum of Komsomols to rise to the top. Even workers, whose material suffering under war communism had been compensated by a sense of "mastery," were now being treated merely with benevolent neutrality—and only so long as their interests did not collide with those of the dictatorship. Finally, under war communism millions had fled from the city to the country, whereas the General Line was marked by reverse flight toward the city. Commenting on this rout of the peasantry, another Moscow correspondent declared that the food requisitions of the era of war communism were child's play when compared to the current system of expropriation.[19]

Comparisons with earlier periods persisted, in spite of reservations. Dallin invoked a Hegelian triad: the thesis of war communism, superseded by the antithesis of NEP, had now given way to a worse form of war communism which could hardly be called a synthesis, even if it claimed to be founded on superior technology. Another parallel compared the forward rush of Stalin's General Line to Lenin's retreat toward NEP in 1921.[20] Both were diametrical turnabouts, undertaken in order to forestall necessary political changes, and dictated by the exhaustion of previous policies. Mirror images of each other, the two changes in policy posed the same question: Whether the regime possessed the social forces required to survive such a radical turnabout. The difference between then and now lay in the fact that whereas NEP was a response to peasant uprisings and to the Kronstadt revolt, Stalin's Kronstadt lay in the future.[21]

As Stalin's revolution swept forward, the Mensheviks recorded its course. Earlier skepticism concerning peasants who "cold-bloodedly" withdrew their bread from the market turned to more sympathetic interest as the conflict between regime and peasantry sharpened. In early 1928 *Vestnik* recalled that Bolshevik power had already choked on the "hard peasant nut" in 1921 and 1924.[22] Now the regime was being pushed into a risky confrontation by a single front of striking peasants.[23] In response to the unusual cruelty with which bread procurement was being carried out, particularly in Ukraine, peasant disturbances erupted, soon accompanied by mass terror against village Communists.[24] At the same time, grain shortages were forcing mills to close and were raising the price of bread in the open market to astronomical heights. Soon the government was enacting desperate measures, such as forbidding transport of flour by rail, and bread was being treated as hard currency.[25]

By 1929 the Soviet regime was exercising what *Vestnik* called its "last wager in the battle for bread"—the campaign to herd the peasantry into *kolkhoze*s and *sovkhoze*s (collective farms and state farms). In denouncing this process, however, the Mensheviks refused to condemn collectivization as such. Peasants were not being expropriated in order to collectivize; rather, collectivization was taking place in order to expropriate the peasantry. Collectivization, theoretically a positive and progressive measure, was merely the form in which the regime was carrying out its mad policies of superprocurement, policies as suicidal as they were rapacious. Collectivization was thus a result of the agricultural catastrophe, not its cause.[26]

*Kolkhoze*s, a rational innovation in the west European context, were doomed in Russia from the very outset, it was argued. They were so unpopular that even rural Communists were reluctant to enter them. State credits and machinery were the main bait to attract peasants into *kolkhoze*s, but the state did not have the means to extend credit, and whatever state-supplied instruments there were passed into the hands of individual *kolkhoznik* households. Ironically, as collectivization triumphed, planted land areas contracted. In a situation where "every third cow [was considered] a socially dangerous element," peasants acted in desperation, slaughtering cattle, murdering Communists, and refusing to expand areas under cultivation.[27]

A "small civil war" was raging in the countryside. Previously the authorities would just send food units into the countryside to plunder and then disappear, never straying far from railway lines. Now Soviet power reached right into the peasant's hut and, without any respite, confiscated the last ounce of grain. In early 1930 *Sotsialisticheskii vestnik* gave a measure of the prevailing terror by publishing a secret directive to local Bolshevik organizations for the application of a government resolution concerning dekulakization: kulaks identified as counterrevolutionaries were to be shot; those who regularly used wage labor would undergo complete confiscation and be exiled to forced labor in the North; all other kulaks would have their entire property confiscated and be exiled from their district.[28] According to one *Vestnik* correspondent, the countryside looked as if it had experienced an earthquake, and a "prominent Communist" was reputed to have declared, "We must destroy 5 million people."[29]

Stalin's call, in his March 1930 article "Dizzy from Success," to ease the tempo of collectivization and de-kulakization was not seen by Mensheviks as significant. According to their correspondent, the change had been prompted by fear that the Red Army would revolt; reportedly, Voroshilov had thrown a packet of letters from disgruntled soldiers onto the table at a Politburo meeting in an angry dispute with Stalin.[30] The retreat came too late and too halfheartedly to make a difference. Cattle had already been destroyed, and fields would remain unplanted because of massive chaos and disorganization. Millions of peasants had already exchanged their former social status for a new sort of enserfment. Indeed, within a few months there were signs that the war between the peasantry and the regime was resuming with renewed fury.[31]

The miseries of collectivization were not compensated by achievements in industrialization. Even though collectivization represented an onslaught of the city against the countryside, terror spilled over into the urban classes, affecting specialists and the intelligentsia. As *Vestnik* reported, "After the countryside has been put on its hind legs, now it is the turn of the city." Pressure on workers intensified as the regime concentrated on "teaching workers how to work," a slogan the Mensheviks denounced as "the language of thermidor."[32]

"What is most characteristic for our life here is the contrast between the stormy construction of industrialization and the misery and poverty of life," wrote a *Vestnik* correspondent from Moscow in late 1929. Again, comparisons with the past came to the fore, only to force the conclusion that the situation combined the worst of war communism with the worst of NEP: the ration cards of the former coexisted with the luxurious restaurants of the latter; early faith in the strength of the Revolution was now being replaced by fatigue, apathy, and hopelessness.[33]

The Mensheviks had no difficulty explaining the crisis of industrialization. The regime had worked itself into an impasse by adopting a tempo that was too slow for the needs of the country but too fast for its capacities. Again and again they reiterated what they had been saying throughout NEP: industrialization was desirable, but past destruction and ill-advised Bolshevik policies had condemned the country to a slow tempo. Instead of recognizing these limitations, the Bolsheviks were embarking on an ill-considered and unbalanced (though purportedly "planned") industrialization campaign. They were building the "wrong things, in the wrong places, in the wrong way."[34]

The five year plan, which the Bolsheviks had put forth as the key to a successful industrialization, was itself thoroughly vitiated. On the one hand, the plan was treated as some sort of "New Testament" with everything, right down to journal subscriptions, subordinated to it. On the other hand, it was entirely subservient to political considerations. For instance, fearing criticism from the opposition at the Fifteenth Party Congress, Stalinist planners hurriedly changed their original plan in favor of one so fanstastic and arbitrary that they did not dare submit it to the congress.[35]

None of this was new. Throughout NEP the Mensheviks had denounced "teleological" planning carried out by a bureaucratic dictatorship. Now, as Russia embarked on the General Line, such a utopian and, ultimately, irrational approach was being elevated to the rank of supreme principle. On the tenth anniversary of NEP *Sotsialisticheskii vestnik* cited Martov's statement from 1921 that the dictatorship would nip in the bud any rational elements in the changes of policy it undertook. It could be comfortably assumed that what was rational in the General Line, that is, the abstract principle of industrialization and collectivization, was also condemned to failure.[36] Only very slowly and reluctantly did the Mensheviks, like others, come to acknowledge that the General Line may have succeeded, in an utterly unfamiliar and terrifying sense.

Socialist Debates

In late 1930 the Mensheviks still saw no reason to question their fundamental position. The five year plan was spawning immense industrial construction, and collectivization of agriculture was proceeding apace. These achievements, however, were being purchased at the price of terror and forced tempos. They left in their wake the annihilation of entire classes and the reinforcement of a dictatorial state apparatus. Surely this could not be labeled progress.[1]

Such Menshevik certitudes were not universally shared. Bourgeois intellectuals proved increasingly fascinated by the Soviet experience. As Abramovitch once put it, all intellectuals have a weakness for an experiment in which they can play God, particularly when they are too cowardly to undertake such an experiment at home. Even those who are indifferent to socialism are impressed by the extraordinarily interesting and bright chaps who run Russia and by evidence of order in the city streets—"Mein Liebchen, was willst Du noch mehr?"[2] The rise of such sentiments in the face of Stalin's Great Turn irritated the Mensheviks, but it failed to move them.

When Western socialists began to take an interest in Stalin's experiments, however, the Mensheviks were obliged to take notice. The initial challenge came from a familiar source and was couched in familiar terms. In 1930 Karl

Kautsky published his fifth full-length analysis of the Bolshevik order, *Der Bolschewismus in der Sackgasse*. According to the old master it was provoked by exasperation with some Western comrades' enthusiasm for collectivization and with the LSI's 1930 May Day appeal to Soviet workers and peasants.[3] The idea of such an appeal, the first direct address by the Socialist International to Soviet Russia, originated among right wing Mensheviks, but its content infuriated them, and they turned to Kautsky for redress.[4]

Particularly striking in *Bolschewismus in der Sackgasse* is the fact that it did not even address the issue of the plan. As Kautsky later put it, the idea that one could impose utter misery for five years in order to attain perfect abundance forever struck him as too naive to be taken seriously. His disregard of these new developments was so extreme that Garvi, in checking the manuscript, felt obliged to point out it was untrue that Russian industry was constantly declining.[5]

Kautsky showed remarkable consistency in his arguments. According to him, all the Bolsheviks' actions confirmed the theoretical notions he had formulated by early 1918, including the belief that bolshevism had long since become counterrevolutionary. These ideas hardened as Kautsky now affirmed that the Bolsheviks stood no higher than fascists; bonapartism was thus not a danger since it already existed in Russia, and there was no need to fear an overthrow of the Bolsheviks since no regime in Russia could be worse.[6]

Notwithstanding their respect for "Karl Ivanovich," the Menshevik leaders felt obliged to cross swords openly with him. Dan, in particular, could not accept Kautsky's call for a broad democratic alliance of all classes in Russia and for all democratic parties in the emigration to stand at the head of a peasant uprising.[7] Reliance on the fetishes of unity and democratic coalition had cost the Menshevik Party dearly in 1917 and had been the source of confusion during the Civil War. Haunted by the past, Dan would not swerve from a strictly worker-based strategy. In his view only reliance on the working class could avert bonapartism in Russia.[8] This argument, soon published in *Kampf*, confirmed that behind the disagreement about strategy lay the long-standing controversy over whether bonapartism was already a reality in Russia. As Abramovitch pointed out, it was not necessary to define bolshevism as counterrevolutionary to oppose it just as a revolutionary party did not become bonapartist simply because it repressed other revolutionaries. Bonapartism was the antidemocratic liquidation of a revolution in favor of new proprietor classes through forces produced by the Revolution. The plan and collectivization were not creating any such classes. Indeed, they were destroying whatever elements of such classes had existed under NEP. Soviet "bonapartism" thus lacked class content. Nor could collectivization be termed inherently antirevolutionary; socialists objected to it only because it was utopian and cruel, not because it was undesirable.[9]

Kautsky continued to press his arguments, but the Mensheviks paid ever less attention.[10] Indeed, the last word in this debate came from Friedrich Adler. Though writing in a private capacity, he brought his weight as LSI secretary into play as he stepped to the defense of his Russian comrades against his very close friend Kautsky. Adler admitted that Bolshevik Russia was no "hearth" of socialism. He even added that the international working class would have been much better off if the Bolshevik Revolution had never taken place. Nevertheless, the Soviet state did constitute a bastion against capitalist reaction, and its existence had forced both the bourgeoisie and the proletariat to confront the question of overcoming capitalism. Adler now compared Soviet Russia to an infant whose capacity to survive is doubtful: it was right to try to prevent the birth of such a child, but once it was born, no efforts should be spared to keep it alive.[11]

As Adler's intervention demonstrates, Kautsky did not have authoritative support within international socialism. A second challenge confronting the Mensheviks was much more threatening, however, since it represented a radical departure from the earlier, Menshevik-inspired consensus on Soviet Russia among Western socialists. Even more alarming was the fact that this challenge came from the Mensheviks' close ally Otto Bauer.

"Bauer is only the German translation of Dan, or Dan is the Russian translation of Bauer," fulminated Kautsky. Potresov referred to Dan even more stingingly as Otto Bauer's "evil genius." In fact, even Dan criticized Bauer's readiness to reject Bolshevik methods for the West but to endorse them for Russia.[12] Nevertheless, they converged politically, and their intimate personal ties dated back to 1917, when Bauer, a physician and a former prisoner of war in Russia, had cared for the Dans' daughter in her fatal illness.[13] In the last years of NEP Bauer's views seemed to be moving ever closer to those of the Mensheviks.[14] It was therefore a shock when Bauer announced in the conclusion to an important theoretical work of 1931 that the General Line was laying the foundations of socialism in the USSR. He now predicted that as the living standards of the Soviet people improved, the terrorist dictatorship would become superfluous and would be dismantled.[15]

The Mensheviks reacted with indignation. Abramovitch commented acidly that, according to Bauer, socialism was no longer Lenin's "soviet power plus electricity" but "the General Line plus the Inquisition, or the five year plan plus the gas chamber."[16] The apparent successes of the plan were largely illusory, argued Abramovitch. In the sphere of consumer and social goods the plan had met none of its objectives. Moreover, even in the area where the plan was supposed to be succeeding, its record was dismal. Disproportions, bottlenecks, shortages, and lack of coordination were undermining the production goods sector. The quality of this "planned" industry's products was so low and costs of production so high that the Soviet economic effort could only be described as a "pseudo-rationalization" of the very sort which Bauer decried under capitalism.[17]

The Mensheviks' more fundamental objections, however, did not concern the economic balance sheet of the *piatiletka* (five year plan). Rather, they centered on the fact that Bauer was once again applying a non-Marxist double standard to Russia. By arguing that socialism was being built in backward Russia, this leading Marxist critic was repudiating Marxist laws of universal historical development. As Abramovitch put it, if crudely, Bauer favored Marx for Europe, but he was choosing Bakunin for Russia.[18] It was David Dallin who brought out the most troubling implication of Bauer's thinking. Whereas formerly the socialists had believed that the failure of Bolshevik methods would bring Soviet Russia back to a socialist path, now, for the first time, they were resting their hopes on the success of these methods. It was entirely possible, added Dallin, that coercion and terror would make it possible for the self-proclaimed goals of the five year plan to be achieved. It would be tragic, however, if Western socialists accepted these goals as authentically socialist and concluded that the Bolshevik path had been vindicated.[19]

Bauer's reaction confirmed all apprehensions. In a characteristic display of self-assurance and disdain, Bauer refused to retract his opinions. Instead, he spelled out the devastating consequences of his arguments for his Menshevik friends. There was no point in denying that the plan was a success, he retorted. It would perhaps never be fulfilled entirely, but even bourgeois reports were acknowledging that life was becoming easier in Russia. The plan's successes led one to hope that as the dictatorship completed its economic tasks, it would create the preconditions for gradual democratization. If the Mensheviks wished, they could play a positive role in this democratization. If they persisted in seeing the Bolshevik regime only as a harbinger of bonapartism, they were unlikely to have any future role at all.[20]

The implications of Bauer's position were so divisive and far-reaching for Western socialism that the secretary of the LSI stepped in to mediate. Friedrich Adler commented caustically on those (presumably, bourgeois reporters on whom Bauer relied) who had been as enthusiastic in the past about Henry Ford as they were today about Stalin. He rejected, however, the Menshevik argument that Bauer was sanctioning an un-Marxist belief in the possibility of "leaping over" capitalism in Soviet Russia. The technical achievements of capitalism were being transplanted into Russia from abroad, wrote Adler, which meant that Marxist stages of history were being respected. As for the future of Russian social democracy, Adler's advice could provide only the coldest comfort to his Russian comrades. The old argument still held that whatever followed bolshevism might be worse than the present regime, Adler affirmed. He therefore urged the Mensheviks to make a "great sacrifice" and to adopt a "policy of toleration of Bolshevik rule," concentrating on "restoration of the independence of the trade unions" as their goal.[21]

The Mensheviks were thus faced with the burden of defending not only their policies but also their very existence. In a new round of rebuttals Dan and Abramovitch sought to win back the upper hand in the debate, even at the price of concessions. Dan acknowledged that far-reaching changes were taking place in the Soviet Union, but he claimed that they did not disprove the Mensheviks' belief that there was no alternative to capitalist development. Reaching back to a controversial concept, Dan suggested that Russia was now building state *capitalism*, inasmuch as capitalism's fundamental separation between owner and producer persisted. One could not assume, as Bauer did mechanistically, that political democracy could simply be superimposed on a state capitalist structure.[22]

Abramovitch, in turn, emphasized a philosophical point which had not figured prominently in earlier discussions. According to Bauer, a dysfunctional terror would gradually give way to rationality, and dictatorship would be replaced by democracy as the Soviet Union progressed. Abramovitch now asked what reasons there might be for introducing democracy if dictatorship proved beneficial. What sort of arguments could the defenders of freedom use to mobilize the masses against a successful dictatorship? As Abramovitch put it best, "If a people attains material welfare, a higher cultural level, social justice, a powerful position vis-à-vis the outside world, that is, 'welfare absolutism,' without a trace of freedom, what then is the historical function of freedom and why is it necessary at all?"[23]

Only in retrospect could one see that Dan's and Abramovitch's common rebuttals of Bauer were, in fact, founded on different premises. Dan's attitude toward the General Line was grounded in the same assumptions as Bauer's. Dan accepted the idea that dictatorship would constitute one phase of the Revolution; he only denied that it could serve as an instrument of socialist construction. Dan even argued that the technical and material achievements of the General Line would have to be safeguarded so that the working class would not be asked to pay twice for its progress.[24] This convergence between Dan and Bauer was psychological before it became ideological. Both cherished their ties to the working class and were ready to defer to the judgment of common workers. As Bauer put it, the views of such comrades were "more valuable than a dozen books."[25] The fear of losing touch with workers preyed upon both leaders, particularly on Dan, who felt acutely the pain of separation from the Russian proletariat. In reacting to changes in Russia, he sought to build a bridge to that generation that had never known social democracy and whose only pride lay in what it had succeeded in building under the dictatorship.[26]

Abramovitch's outlook was entirely different. Owing to his keen political instinct, he managed to grasp the significance of Bauer's theses and to spell out their theoretical implications. Thus, it was Abramovitch who pointed out that Bauer's faith in the potential of Stalin's course testified to a "metaphysical belief in the omnipotence of force." If this belief was justified, then Marxism had overestimated the power of the economic factor and Marxism itself would have to be revised.[27] Even earlier Abramovitch had warned that "if Bauer's premises hold, there would be no place in Russia for a Social Democratic Party and the whole protest against terror would be exclusively humanitarian—sentimental and not political or socialist—Marxist."[28] Replying to Kautsky in 1930, Abramovitch still maintained that the Mensheviks' primary objection to the Bolshevik experiment was that it could not succeed; if this were not the case, then the question of the means used to achieve it would become secondary.[29] As the perspectives of Bolshevik success loomed larger, however, Abramovitch reassessed his earlier disdain for the "humanitarian" critique of Stalinism. The moral dimension was to become increasingly important to him and, with time, to the Menshevik majority.

Vis-à-vis outside challenges from foreign socialists such as Kautsky and Bauer, the Mensheviks responded vigorously and confidently.[30] This brave mask, however, concealed deep fear and doubts. Within their own party circle issues raised by the General Line became the object of intense internal debates, setting the course of future party divisions. Thus, in 1931 Abramovitch told his Russian comrades that if the Bolsheviks succeeded, "we would have to make a bonfire not only of *Vestnik* and of our [party] platform but of all the Marixist primers which have been our guides." If it failed, the Bolsheviks would have played their last card and a palace coup would be inevitable.[31]

What should the RSDRP do in the event that a radical rupture took place in Russia under the stress of the General Line? This strategic question dominated the internal party debate and elicited competing responses. Abramovitch steered a middle course between the Menshevik Right, joined for the first time by Nicolaevsky, and the Menshevik Left, led by Dan. The former were prepared to take the risks of supporting a peasant uprising; the latter affirmed that "at the moment the Revolution is suppressed it is our duty to be among the vanquished." Abramovitch criticized this left view as another instance of the dogmatic unwillingness to "soil one's hands" which had cost the RSDRP so dearly in 1917. He acknowledged that social democrats might well find themselves among the defeated, and they should accept defeat to remain with the working class. They should not, however, strive for defeat and make it into a premise of their policy.[32]

Abramovitch's compromise evoked no sympathy. Indeed, both party wings seized the opportunity to demarcate themselves sharply from their adversaries. Garvi pointed out that Abramovitch's middle course presupposed passivity until the moment of the overthrow, a fault shared by the Right's new ally Nicolaevsky, who displayed a "will to power" but thought the party could not do anything until a "palace coup" had taken place. Garvi's alternative, stated clearly elsewhere, was that the RSDRP could accelerate an overthrow, perhaps by exerting pressure through the Socialist International. Dan retorted that the very hypothesis of a palace coup assumed a preponderance of reactionary forces, which meant that social democrats could not deviate from their opposition to such a coup. His reply also suggested, implicitly, that Mensheviks should cooperate with those elements within the Communist Party that were also interested in forestalling such an outcome.[33]

The discomfiture over the General Line gave right wing Mensheviks the occasion to press their call for a revision of the party platform. In their view the wager on a positive evolution of Bolshevik Russia had been lost. The Martov Line's assumption that even a revolution which dispensed with democracy could be an authentic revolution had proven illusory. Democracy was indivisible and indispensable. The Mensheviks should cease seeking rapprochement with one Bolshevik clique or another and instead find their true allies among democratic forces willing to do away with the Bolshevik regime altogether. Extraparty right wing Mensheviks, led by Potresov, were even more emphatic. As Stepan Ivanovich put it, "There is more contradiction between two socialists, one of whom is for dictatorship, than between two democrats, one of whom is for socialism."[34]

As the effects of the General Line impressed themselves on the exiled Mensheviks, the party's dominant and left-oriented majority also considered changes in the party platform, although not in the direction desired by the Right. According to the majority's spokesman, Fedor Dan, the Martov Line remained valid. Developments in Russia suggested, however, that this peasant-bourgeois revolution decked out in the garb of proletarian socialism was not creating a classic capitalist order as previously expected. Dan's proposition that Stalin's Russia was evolving toward a state capitalist order was attacked both from the right and from the left.[35] Right Mensheviks rejected the idea that such an evolution could be seen as positive. They argued that state capitalism could be a step toward socialism in the Western context, where political democracy existed, but in Russia it could only strengthen tyranny.[36] Underlying these and other objections was the more fundamental concern of right wing Mensheviks to block any attempt at salvaging the Martov Line.

Left Mensheviks objected that the new Soviet economy could not be considered capitalist in any way since it lacked the essential traits of capitalism: market laws, the profit motive, a capitalist class. More controversially, the Soviet power that defined the governing plan was founded on the working class, and not capitalism but socialism was the goal. These arguments reflected the impression made by the plan's achievements and, even more important, by the regime's survival. As the Right held back from endorsing Dan's position vis-à-vis Bauer, the Left went at least one step beyond Dan (and pehaps even beyond Bauer) in drawing conclusions from the course of events in Russia.

It was Vera Alexandrova, perhaps the most politically naive member of the Menshevik group, who posed the most pertinent and troubling questions: What is to be done if the overthrow does not take place? What if there is no clear boundary between bonapartism and revolution? The absence of replies, she suggested, lay in the fact that "we know this new Russia only a little, this [Russia] where some sort of new path of development has been laid out with which we cannot catch up." Alexandrova's affinities were left-oriented (she spoke in favor of collectivization since, she claimed, private peasants tended toward fascism), and her reasoning was confused, but her questions were valid for all shades of Menshevik opinion.[37] Both Right and Left were inching toward the realization that earlier expectations of Soviet development would have to be abandoned. The Bolshevik regime might well survive without experiencing either democratization or a distinct thermidorian moment, remaining indefinable as either capitalism or socialism. This would spell defeat not only for the Left, which had banked on the Martov Line, but for all Mensheviks, since it meant that history did not march according to Marx.

In the years to come some Mensheviks, led by Dan, sought to force a new unfathomable reality into their ideological framework, straining their credibility or abandoning their critical insight. Not only was Dan forced to endorse Bauer's position, but also he had to deny that this represented any incompatibility with the Martov Line.[38] Others, such as Abramovitch and Nicolaevsky, groped outside Marxism for new concepts, thus revising or even implicitly abandoning Marxism. These efforts were fruitful from a theoretical viewpoint, contributing, for instance, to a theory of totalitarianism.[39] But they led in conflicting directions, and their price was party unity. In a sense the debates launched by Bauer and Kautsky were not between those who emphasized democracy and those who favored socialism, but between those who believed that democracy must precede socialism and those who were prepared to hope that socialism would prepare the way for democracy. The RSDRP proved incapable of absorbing both positions.

The Menshevik Trial

At the Menshevik trial in 1931 fantasy and reality converged in singular fashion. The trial was expected; its course was unforeseen. The accused were not, strictly speaking, Mensheviks; real Mensheviks were not accused. Those charged were innocent of their crimes; they were guilty of charges that could not be brought. As if in a distorting mirror, the Menshevik trial caricatured the Menshevik Party. Accusers—and, sometimes, the accused—floundered in a hall of mirrors, unsure whether they were striking their adversaries or only their deformed mirror image. Menshevism emerged from the trial not as the menace which the Bolshevik prosecutors made it out to be but as a metaphor for the fears and failures of the General Line.

Could the Mensheviks have anticipated their own trial? The first spectacular show trial, that of the SRs in 1922, struck them as well. It involved a sister socialist party, which the Bolsheviks habitually put under the same heading as the RSDRP. In fact, the SR indictment mentioned Martov, Dan, and Abramovitch, albeit in the category of those against whom the case had been "suspended." In spite of reservations among Mensheviks in Russia, those abroad waged a campaign on behalf of SR defendants.[1] The prosecutor at the 1922 trial, Nikolai Krylenko, reappeared as prosecutor at the Menshevik trial, and Isaak Rubin, a Menshevik who had offered his services as counsel for the SRs (and had been imprisoned for this offer), appeared as one of the accused.

Krylenko once said, "A club is a primitive weapon, a rifle is a more efficient one, the most efficient is the court."[2] After the lull of the NEP years, the Soviet state again resorted to this most efficient of weapons with a series of show trials for economic crimes. The pattern was set by the Shakhty trial in 1928, involving over fifty engineers accused of "wrecking," or economic sabotage. By 1929 the discovery and punishment of "wreckers" was becoming a routine affair. *Sotsialisticheskii vestnik* noted the curious phenomenon of "a government that would seek to fabricate and exaggerate news of plots against itself," and commented ironically that "every season has its wreckers, just as every theater season has its star."[3]

These new arrests and trials had their peculiar logic. For Iugov they were dictated by the Bolsheviks' inability to harmonize the expertise of nonparty specialists with the reliability of Communist commissars. Several years earlier Iugov had warned that the law on economic espionage was phrased in such a way that it could not but be violated. Now this warning was being realized as the regime lashed out at its faithful but non-Communist specialists. Stalin had apparently decided, "not without reason," that these specialists were "not the proper human material for carrying out the General Line." In spite of intelligentsia illusions that the arrests stemmed only from excessive GPU zeal, the arrests continued, and by March 1930 *Sotsialisticheskii vestnik* was predicting that "a new trial of specialists [was] being prepared."[4]

When did the Mensheviks realize that they would be the object of a trial? As early as 1929 a *Vestnik* correspondent reported the mass arrests of social democrats and suspected sympathizers, including "many who left the party long ago and are now responsible Soviet personalities." Yet an anonymous comrade confidently stated that fears of a Menshevik trial were unfounded because the socialists were too hard a nut to crack; he even added that he dreamed of a trial because politically it would rebound to the socialists' advantage.[5]

The arrest in the summer of 1930 of Vladimir Groman and a handful of other prominent ex-Menshevik economists in Soviet service attracted the Mensheviks' attention. They saw these arrests not as a blow against themselves (since those arrested had left the party long ago) but as the "last trumpet call" for that sector of the intelligentsia who had believed that one could cooperate on an apolitical basis with the Bolsheviks. Groman, N. D. Kondratiev, N. N. Sukhanov, and others arrested were the most sincere and coherent representatives of such illusions; these had never been the illusions of authentic Mensheviks, however. *Sotsialisticheskii vestnik* predicted that as the old intelligentsia was replaced with Red youth, a Groman-Kondratiev trial was being prepared.[6] It was not yet clear that this would become a Menshevik trial.

The shape of the trial to come emerged from the Soviet press campaign that followed Groman's arrest and accompanied the trial of the "Industrial Party" at the end of 1930. *Pravda* editor N. N. Popov, an ex-Menshevik who had already celebrated the demise of his former party at the time of the SR trial in 1922, now revealed the existence of two organized groups of *byvshie*, that is, people with a political past.[7] The second consisted of Menshevik intellectuals, including Groman, Sukhanov, and V. A. Bazarov. Having established the existence of Menshevik plotters in Russia, subsequent articles in the Soviet press succeeded in weaving the names of Mensheviks abroad into the narrative of the ongoing "Industrial Party" trial. The defendants confessed to having plotted wrecking activities at the behest of the French general staff, with a view to armed intervention. The most prominent foreign accomplice named was French president Raymond Poincaré (who publicly refuted the charges), but in the course of the trial one name led to another. Soon, defendants were pointing to leading Western socialists such as Léon Blum, Paul Renaudel, Karl Kautsky, and, through them, to Russian Menshevik leaders in Berlin. A *Pravda* cartoon depicted an "exalted choir" of LSI socialist leaders, including Abramovitch; the best-known Russian writer, Maksim Gorky, reiterated these charges.[8]

By now the Mensheviks were asking whether the accusations would end with the press campaign or whether they were the prelude to a trial, and, if so, who would be tried. Their uncertainty was understandable; according to Roy Medvedev it was only after the "success" of the "Industrial Party" trial in December 1930 that Stalin had the idea of setting up a Menshevik trial. *Vestnik* also reported that a dossier containing the confessions of Groman, Sukhanov, and others was circulating among top Bolshevik leaders. It was not known whether these confessions were authentic, but those who had read them were shaken by their delirious and fantastic revelations. Whether coincidentally or not, the Bolshevik leader who had shown the least hostile attitude toward the Mensheviks, Rykov, was replaced as head of government by Stalin's henchman Vyacheslav Molotov.[9]

As the trial drew nearer, *Vestnik* scoffed at the prospect. It boasted that a Menshevik trial would be no more successful in breaking the RSDRP than the congress of former Mensheviks had been several years earlier. Nor would the Bolsheviks convince anyone of Abramovitch's and Dan's present interventionism by recalling that of Garvi during the Civil War. The president of the LSI even wrote to Soviet authorities vouching for the RSDRP's anti-interventionist stance. The bourgeois press quoted Dan as saying that a trial was likely, but charging socialists with sabotage was ridiculous. In spite of such brave words, *Vestnik*'s correspondents in Moscow reported panic, mass arrests, and a wave of suicides among the intelligentsia.[10]

The trial opened under the auspices of the Supreme Court of the USSR, with much pomp and solemnity, on 1 March 1931. Krylenko, prosecutor in several earlier political trials, assumed his familiar role, as did I. L. Braude, chief defense advocate in the "Industrial Party" trial and "one of the most celebrated and flamboyant lawyers in Russia." There were additional continuities with previous trials in regard to other members of the court, though not the presiding judge. To avoid embarrassment, the Soviet authorities did not reappoint Andrei Vyshinskii, once a right Menshevik and later a member of a left Menshevik group headed by a defendant in the upcoming trial, N. N. Sukhanov.[11]

There were fourteen defendants in the Menshevik trial. This numerical compromise between the fifty-odd accused at the Shakhty trial and the "Industrial Party's" mere eight proved a happy medium, and it set the norm for future proceedings. The defendants, all males aged between thirty-nine and fifty-eight, had innumerable years of party membership behind them. All but two had been RSDRP members well before the Revolution, some in the Bolshevik faction at one time or another; the principal defendant, Groman, was in the party at its inception in 1898. Only Sukhanov joined the party late, adhering to Martov's Internationalists in 1917. A. L. Sokolovskii had been a member of the Socialist-Zionist Party before joining the Bund and then the Communist Party. The inclusion of Sukhanov among the accused may have been due to his celebrity as a literary and even historical figure or to the fact that it was his diaries and his Sunday tea parties which provided the police with their roster of suspects.[12] Sokolovskii's inclusion may be explained by the fact that his professional profile corresponded to that of the other accused, or it may simply have been the mistake of an investigator who read Sokolovskii's past as that of a Menshevik. According to the indictment, all the accused but one had left the Menshevik Party, most just after the Revolution, but they had recently rejoined it in secret. Only V. K. Ikov was presented (also incorrectly) as having been a party member without interruption since 1901, perhaps an unwitting tribute to the fact that he was also the only defendant recognized as an authentic Menshevik by the Foreign Delegation.

The defendants belonged to the same professional circles. There was a (former) board member of Gosplan, a member of the managing board of the Central Consumers' Cooperative (Tsentrosoiuz), and two board members of the State Bank. From the Commissariat of Trade came a deputy head of supplies, a senior director for export standardization, and a head of the statistical and forecasting section. There were two "literary men" and two professors of political economy. The Supreme Council of the National Economy (VSNKh, or Vesenkha) was represented by one of its economists, its head of trade policies who had also been chairman of its prices bureau, and the head of its forecasting or "conjuncture" bureau who had been earlier deputy head of economic planning: in short, a constellation of some of the country's best economists in key positions.[13]

Mensheviks with L. Deich on the occasion of his return from America, 1917
L. Martov (standing second from left, back row), P. B. Axelrod (seated second from left, second row), L. Deich (seated fourth from left, second row), L. Dan and F. Dan (seated fifth and sixth from left, second row). Note also V. Antonov-Ovseenko, later a prominent Bolshevik, seated second from left, front row. (International Institute of Social History, Amsterdam)

L. Martov and Fedor Dan, Petrograd 1917
This photo suggests iconographically that the Martov-Dan relation is one
between leader and heir apparent, later successor. (International Institute of
Social History, Amsterdam)

LSI Executive Committee Meeting, Zurich, 1926
F. Adler, Secretary (at table with hat at feet), F. Dan (second from right in second row),
R. Abramovitch (sixth from right in second row, just behind Adler), I. Tsereteli
(third from right in back row). (International Institute of Social History, Amsterdam)

Lidia and Fedor Dan vacationing, France, 1927.
(International Institute of Social History, Amsterdam)

A Menshevik picnic in the forest, Berlin, 1927
Seated (L to R): F. Dan, P. Axelrod, L. Abramovitch, L. Dan, Roza Abramovitch.
Standing: B. Rubinstein, D. Dallin, S. Garvi, E. Landysheva, G. Garvi, N. Rubinstein,
T. Rubinstein, S. Schwarz, unidentified woman, Raphael Abramovitch.
(Courtesy of Lia Andler)

Opposite page, top: The Menshevik patriarch and his friends, Berlin, c. 1927
(L to R): V. Woytinsky, P. Axelrod, B. Sapir.
(International Institute of Social History, Amsterdam)

Opposite page, bottom: Mensheviks traveling to the LSI Congress, 1928
Front row (L to R): O. Domanevskaia, V. Alexandrova, S. Garvi, L. Dan, M. Kefali,
I. Denike, F. Dan. Back row: A. Iugov, P. Garvi, B. Nicolaevsky, Mme. Hertz,
Mme. Rubinstein, I. Iudin, T. Rubinstein. (Courtesy of Lia Andler)

Soviet caricature of Raphael Abramovitch, 1931
Abramovitch was a particular butt of Soviet sarcasm. The poem below is a parody of
Lermontov's *Demon* by Soviet poet Demian Bednyi. The picture portrays Abramovitch
as a fallen angel before the flame of Kautsky. The title reads "Abramovitch's vow. An
aria from a Menshevik Opera." (Reproduced in I. Vardin, *Men'sheviki interventsionisty*)

"I swear by the first day of creation,
I swear by its last day,"—
I swear by the yellow point of view,
That we shall shove aside the power of the Soviets,—
I swear by the bourgeois god
And by the Menshevik god, too,—
I swear by the torgprom threshold
To which I am admitted together with Dan,
I swear by the torgprom alms
And by that which we shall give in return,—
I swear by Kautsky's ruminations
And by Vandervelde's lies,—
I swear by true . . . mendacity,
It has been justified by struggle,—
I swear by my eternal trembling
Before an unknown fate,—
I swear if in this I shall fail!
Without a prayer let me die!—

I want to love, I want to pray
I want to believe in good!
Capitalism, by your pride
I want to live, as I lived before,
Having chosen you as my temple,
I laid my honor at your feet!"
Save me only from the blow
And all the intrigues of the Bolsheviks.
I await your love, like a gift,
And particularly in this moment
Give me a task, of any sort!
My death is light in return for your life:
I shall let myself down into the bottom of the sea,
I shall fly into the clouds,
I shall embark for Moscow again
And, unless I get stuck on the road,
Then it categorically

I SHALL UNDER OATH AGAIN RENOUNCE.

Клятва Абрамовича
Ария из меньшевистской оперы

«Клянусь я первым днем творенья,
Клянусь его последним днем», —
Клянуся желтой точкой зренья,
Что власть советов мы спихнем, —
Клянуся буржуазным богом
И меньшевистским богом тож, —
Клянусь торгпромовским порогом,
Куда я вместе с Даном вхож,
Клянусь торгпромовской подачкой
И тем, что мы в ответ даем, —
Клянуся Каутского жвачкой
И вандервельдовским враньем, —
Клянуся истинною... ложью,
Она оправдана борьбой, —
Клянусь моею вечной дрожью
Пред неизвестною судьбой, —
Клянусь — вот чтоб мне провалиться!
Без обмовенья пусть помру! —

Хочу любить, хочу молиться,
Хочу я веровать добру»!
Капитализм, твоей гордыней
Я буду жить, как прежде жил,
«Избрав тебя моей святыней,
Я честь у ног твоих сложил!
Спаси меня лишь от удара
И большевистских всех интриг,
«Твоей любви я жду, как дара»,
И особливо в этот миг.
Дай мне заданье, хоть какое!
Мне смерть за жизнь твою легка:
«Я опущусь на дно морское,
Я полечу за облака»,
Я проберусь в Москву вторично
И, коль в поездке не спекусь,
То от неё категорично
ВНОВЬ ПОД ПРИСЯГОЙ ОТРЕКУСЬ!

— Демьян Бедный.

Boris Nicolaevsky, Berlin, 1932. (International Institute of Social History, Amsterdam)

Twenty-fifth anniversary celebrations of *Sotsialisticheskii vestnik*, New York, 1946
At head table (L to R): V. Chernov, A. Lee (bending over), R. Abramovitch, B. Nicolaevsky, unidentified man, L. de Brouckère, I. Tsereteli (standing), two unidentified men. Note the banner, which reads "Proletarians of All Countries Unite! Russian Social Democratic Labor Party," and the portraits of Marx and Martov.
(International Institute of Social History, Amsterdam)

The story told at the trial was an intricate tale. It described complex and subtle wrecking exploits which disorganized production, undermined the five year plan, and wrought hardship on the Soviet people. It told of conspiracy at home with the anti-Soviet "Industrial Party" and the "Toiling Peasants' Party," as well as abroad with the Foreign Delegation of the RSDRP and, through it, the Second International, the SPD, and prominent Western socialists. It spoke of a half-million rubles funneled from abroad through these sources to finance wrecking activities and to prepare Western intervention in Russia, the Mensheviks' ultimate aim.

Alexander Solzhenitsyn writes that, as a twelve-year-old, he followed the Menshevik and "Industrial Party" trials with passionate interest, reading "the stenographic records . . . line by line" (over four hundred pages for the Menshevik trial). Solzhenitsyn claims that the "Industrial Party" trial was a better show. This judgment is based on his confirmed prejudice against socialists in general, even as victims of Soviet justice, and it shows insensitivity to the human drama involved in the Menshevik trial.[14] Unlike earlier victims, the defendants here were all Marxist old revolutionaries who had worked with dedication in Soviet institutions. At their trial they were being forced to repudiate their life's work and their very identity as socialists and revolutionaries.

The defendants' admitted to a gradual but inexorable descent into turpitude and treachery. They left the RSDRP and entered Soviet service around the beginning of NEP. Deeply pessimistic about prospects for socialist construction, they pinned their hopes on a prolonged and ever broadened NEP. As the bold new policies of the General Line emerged, the defendants came together in a community of the disappointed, renewing old political connections or politicizing existing ties. They tried to counter new Soviet policies by exercising their influence in the workplace. As these efforts proved unavailing, their passive attitude toward Soviet power gave way to active hostility, and they turned to radical measures. Disgruntlement, disorganization, wrecking, and intervention—these were the fateful steps of the march toward neo-Menshevism.

In 1928 informal "initiative groups" banded together in a "Union Bureau" of Mensheviks whose structures and communications network transformed a group of disgruntled individuals into a coordinated nerve center of conspiracy.[15] As the "Union Bureau" made contact with other anti-Soviet forces at home and abroad, Raphael Abramovitch paid a secret visit to Russia to give instructions and initiate transfer of funds from Western sources. Members of the Union Bureau did not take account of the hardships their program would cause and, recognizing their lack of broad support, did not seek a mass following. They confined themselves to exploiting their positions within the Soviet apparatus to carry out wrecking instructions which eventually developed into preparation for armed foreign intervention.[16]

The trial revealed subtle ways of carrying out wrecking operations. Thus, Tsentrosoiuz Mensheviks supplied goods which were seasonally or otherwise inappropriate; for instance, childrens' boots were sent to loggers' camps. While juggling among sectors, the wreckers were careful to respect the overall distribution plan so that their manipulation would remain unnoticed. Vesenkha Mensheviks had the option of wrecking by projecting either excessively maximal or minimal tempos of production. They chose the latter in the hope of aggravating shortages and undermining the country's defense capacity. Gosbank Mensheviks worked on disorganizing monetary circulation, misallocating credits, and sending out confusing instructions or delaying instructions to local offices.[17]

"Groman—the Old Man, the Leader! the Authority! the Organizer!" thundered prosecutor Krylenko. He was correct inasmuch as the trial was, above all, that of Vladimir Gustafovich Groman. Obese and alcoholic, graceless and uncultured, this brilliant economist exercised a charismatic effect on his entourage.[18] In 1917 he had been obsessed with the idea of a unified economic plan, declaring, "I shall not distribute a single pair of shoes until the national economy as a whole has been regulated."[19] Under NEP, having loudly repudiated his earlier obsession, Groman plunged into statistical work in Gosplan. The first sets of control figures between 1925 and 1928, foundations for the first Soviet plan, were so much an outcome of the work of Groman and his entourage that they have been called a "Menshevik product." Soon, however, Soviet economic literature denounced Groman's concentration on economic equilibrium as a ruse invoked to prove the impossibility of drastic shifts in the economy. His contributions to the study of the declining growth rate curve were considered criminal even before he was indicted.[20] As NEP gave way to the General Line, Groman insisted that the quality of work was more important than the degree of socialization, and he scoffed at "fantasies."[21] Even had he been more prudent, however, this giant figure could not have survived the debasement of his life's economic work.

Other defendants paraded across the stage in the prosecutor's summary like a veritable Noah's Ark of rogues: Sher and Iakubovich, Groman's right and left hand, both "cold and cruel fanatics"; Ikov and Rubin, a dialectical unity of opposites, the former taciturn and hardened in his hostility, the latter a babbler and a chameleon, but both united in counterrevolution; the merciless Ginzburg and his cheaper version, Zalkind, models of the new

Americanized intelligentsia. One must add Sukhanov—a "wild card," not quite an SR, not quite a Menshevik, not quite a Martovite; adroit, unprincipled and enamored of himself; host of a salon where counterrevolutionaries of all complexions met. Also Petunin, the human fox, and Finn-Enotaevskii, scientific consultant and master of ambiguity, as well as others.[22]

The prosecutor's call for maximum harshness was met by stormy applause from the spectators. Krylenko demanded "the highest measure of social protection," that is, the death penalty, for Groman and the four other members of the Union Bureau's inner leadership. He demanded the maximum term of imprisonment for six defendants but did not insist on long imprisonment for three others. The sentences handed down by the court were less drastic than those he demanded: ten years' imprisonment (with five years' limitation of civil rights) for seven defendants, eight years for four others, and five years for the remaining three.[23]

An air of hollow verisimilitude surounds this trial, as it does many similar ones. Prosecutor, witnesses, and defendants—all of whom pleaded guilty—cooperate in weaving an account of internal coherence. Instead of recording adversarial exchanges, the proceedings create a new reality, a world in which the defendants are accomplices, actors, and narrators before becoming victims. This is a fragile reality easily punctured by mistakes and inconsistencies. The world of the Menshevik trial also proved vulnerable.

The main technical flaw of the trial lay in the paucity of corroborative evidence. The court heard testimony from several prestigious witnesses who confirmed that they had conspired with the Menshevik Union Bureau. Among them was the famous economic theorist N. D. Kondratiev, leader of the newly discovered counterrevolutionary "Toiling Peasant Party"; Leonid Ramzin, star of the recently concluded "Industrial Party" trial; K. A. Gvozdev, Menshevik minister of labor in the Kerensky govenment. Their testimony was weakened, however, by the fact that they, too, were under arrest and thus hardly independent witnesses. The case was also weakened by the absence of any substantial documentary evidence. Proceedings mentioned numerous leaflets, instructions, and resolutions, but the prosecutor produced only three letters from Berlin Mensheviks to Ikov and, as *Vestnik* immediately pointed out, these appeared in a truncated form.[24] Krylenko did quote at length public documents such as the RSDRP Action Program of 1924 and numerous articles from *Sotsialisticheskii vestnik*. His *lecture de texte*, intended to sustain the charges of Menshevik interventionism, could only convince the converted.

A close reading of the proceedings casts further doubts. The defendants sometimes had to be prodded into saying what was expected of them:

Krylenko: Well, was this wrecking or not, according to you?

Berlatskii: This was a line, distinct from the line of the Soviet government and by virtue of this . . .

Chairman: Leading to . . .

Berlatskii: The restoration of capitalist relations, quite obviously . . .

At other times they played a cat-and-mouse game with the prosecutor or even, occasionally, showed defiance:

Krylenko: So the whole period to 1928 was for you a preparatory period for wrecking activity in 1928?

Sokolovskii: I have already said I consider myself an honest and conscientious Soviet worker up to 1927 . . . Thus, up to 1927 I cannot consider my activity to be wrecking. One could say all my activity, from the very moment of my birth, was preparation for wrecking.[25]

There were slips and discrepancies. Whereas the defendants were accused of (and did not deny) having received almost 500,000 rubles from abroad, Jasny has calculated that the testimony accounted for only 100.000.[26] Two key defendants contradicted each other on the issue whether the "Union Bureau" directed work among preexisting Menshevik underground cells (Sher) or whether it had no contact with them (Groman).[27] The discrepancy might simply be a case of poor coordination, or it might be traced to the trial organizers' inability to decide whether to emphasize the far-reaching tentacles of the Union Bureau or its failure to attract any broader support.

The question how long the Mensheviks had been engaged in criminal activities was never fully resolved. It was implied that their treachery was always implicitly present; nevertheless, activities actually charged as criminal had to be nailed down in time. Thus, Krylenko reprimanded one of the defendants who dated his ties to Groman's group too early. Other examples of excessive eagerness, on the part of both defendants and prosecutors, undermined the plausibility of the charges. For instance, all concerned tended to antedate the demise of NEP (and hence the "Union Bureau's" adoption of an active anti-Soviet position) beyond the earliest likely date. It is most improbable that Mensheviks in the Commissariat of Trade should have seen that NEP was being abandoned in 1925–26, as one defendant testified. As I have noted, the Bolsheviks themselves did not see it.[28]

The main slip in the trial involved the alleged visit of Raphael Abramovitch to Russia in the summer of 1928. In response to Abramovitch's immediate denial published in the Western press, the defendants confirmed their story and provided specific dates. Abramovitch counterattacked by obtaining the most foolproof alibis: a hotelkeeper, the Mecklenberg police, and respected human rights activist Kurt Grossman all swore that at the time Abramovitch was supposed to have been in Moscow, he was spending a seaside vacation at a German resort. In August, when Abramovitch was said to have been touring underground Menshevik cells throughout Russia, he was seen by hundreds and photographed for the newspapers as a prominent delegate at the LSI Congress in Brussels; even *Pravda* had reported on his activities at the congress![29]

Another curiosity of the trial was that it brought together individuals whose claim to party membership was disputed but did not include acknowledged Mensheviks in the GPU's hands. In late 1927 Menshevik Foreign Delegation member Eva Broido was sent to Russia illegally to undertake party work. She was arrested within months and sentenced, without trial, to three years' solitary confinement followed by five years' internal banishment. Ironically, even as she was serving her sentence the Soviets published her memoirs of prerevolutionary underground exploits. Broido was thus "available" for the Menshevik trial but did not appear.[30] Mikhail Braunshtein (party pseudonym Valerianov), a younger, left-oriented Berlin Menshevik, had gone to Soviet Russia in the spring of 1929, perhaps for personal reasons, and had been arrested that summer. He was portrayed at the trial as an emissary of the Foreign Delegation; the defendants described his stay among them, and he could have been expected to serve as a witness. Reportedly he was transferred from prison in the Urals to the Moscow Lubianka for that purpose, but he never appeared in court either.[31]

Gaffes, omissions, and inconsistencies spoil the numerous realistic details that mark the proceedings. The accounts of friction between the Berlin Mensheviks and the party in Russia, the difficulties of setting up a clandestine printing press, the dissatisfaction with Soviet economic policies that drove former Mensheviks back to their old party: all these have the ring of truth. A Menshevik correspondent in Moscow writes that the general public did not believe the details of wrecking and interventionism but did believe that there was some sort of Menshevik organization and that Abramovitch had traveled to Moscow. An Old Bolshevik is reported to have said that most Soviet leaders did not believe the tale of Abramovitch's trip, of subsidies from the bourgeoisie, and of intervention. They did, however, believe that the accused were "your" people, that they helped the Mensheviks abroad, distributed *Vestnik,* and wrote articles for it. Whether they were called a bureau or something else was not important.[32]

Abramovitch himself learned years later from two prominent Soviet defectors, Walter Krivitsky and Alexander Orlov, that the security police (OGPU) really did believe he had visited Russia. Abramovitch had gone to Riga (and probably to the Soviet border) to negotiate Broido's trip with local smugglers, and it was he who, with Garvi's help, had obtained a Soviet passport for Braunshtein; Abramovitch's name must therefore have figured prominently in the interrogation of the two unfortunate emissaries. One might even speculate that the error could have originated in confusion over patronymics; at the trial one of the defendants referred to Braunshtein as "Abramovich" rather than "Adamovich."[33]

To a surprising extent the Soviets were poorly informed about the Mensheviks' activities. *Vestnik* reported that when OGPU chief V. R. Menzhinskii gave a report to the Bolshevik Central Committee on the forthcoming trial and even spoke of executions, Rykov, one of the many objecting, shouted: "You should be the first to be shot for having allowed Mensheviks to blossom like weeds. What were your informers doing?" Menzhinskii could only answer that he and his Cheka predecessors did not have any informers among the Mensheviks.[34]

Looking beyond the absurdity of the stories spun in the Menshevik trial, one can identify the seeds from which Soviet suspicions flourished. Abramovitch later minimized the existence of any party activity in Russia at the time of the trial. "Our real party was in prison, camps, and administrative exile," he told an interviewer in 1956. In 1931, however, some of his comrades were full of hope for a Menshevik revival in Russia. Soviet youth was reported to be turning away from communism; contact was being reestablished with Mensheviks (like the defendant Ikov) who were returning from internal exile. Iugov, as a Foreign Delegation member in charge of correspondence with Russia, fretted that the delegation was not seizing opportunities available to reestablish ties. "We lost two months in deciding whether to organize a bureau in Russia in response to propositions received from there," he complained.[35]

Confessions of secret circles and encounters abroad between defendants and members of the Foreign Delegation were lurid embellishments of actual events. "Groman was, of course, consciously wrong about 'wrecking' conversations, but there were conversations," wrote Nicolaevsky privately in 1956. It turned out that the defendant Ginzburg, who ostentatiously shunned *Sotsialisticheskii vestnik* at home, had had long conversations with Lidia Dan in Berlin. *Vestnik* reported that in 1930 there had been two or three especially active intelligentsia "salons" in Moscow. Ironically, the one authentic secret group, Groman's "Liga nabliudatelei"—whose existence he had disclosed to the Berlin Mensheviks—was never mentioned at the trial.[36]

The verisimilitude of charges was founded, above all, on a factor on which accusers and accused agreed. As Solomon Schwarz put it, "Many of the defendants were Mensheviks in their hearts," even though they did not have a party card.[37] They were, as the Russians say, "our people." The Soviet court agreed. "Menshevism is not only a social-political concept," stated the defense lawyer. "A Menshevik is also a certain psychological type."[38]

This consciousness of belonging to the party in some higher, even undefinable sense casts light on one of the more dramatic episodes of the trial. At one point the prosecutor read aloud a telegram from the Menshevik Foreign Delegation in Berlin refuting the trial's fabrications and repudiating the defendants as provocateurs and terrorized individuals who had nothing to do with the party. The defendants replied emotionally, asking by what right the Foreign Delegation had appropriated to itself the prerogative of speaking on behalf of social democracy before history and reminding the court of their prerevolutionary underground credentials as social democrats.[39]

This episode acquired an additional dimension almost forty years later through the samizdat publication of the deposition of Mikhail Iakubovich, the only defendant who survived to tell his story. Iakubovich confirmed that the tale of the "Union Bureau" and the charges were pure fabrications. His indignation at the telegram from Berlin had been genuine, however. Even four decades later he expressed rage at the Foreign Delegation's accusations of provocation and expressed satisfaction with what he called "one of my best political speeches."[40]

Their sense of belonging to the Menshevik Party does not exhaust the question why the defendants confessed to their purported crimes. At the time of the trial, observers believed that confessions had been obtained only through psychological pressure; Volsky was still convinced of this in 1961. Iakubovich's deposition and a statement by the sister of the defendant Rubin, describing the tortures undergone by the defendants, have disproved these earlier assertions.[41]

These same documents confirm, however, that there was indeed a psychological dimension to the confessions. Iakubovich's last reservations disappeared when he learned that a man whom he respected profoundly, V. V. Sher, had named him as a co-member of the "Union Bureau." When doubts assailed him once again, Iakubovich was taken to prosecutor Krylenko, whom he had known intimately during the Civil War, and who now assured him that the party required his testimony. On hearing Krylenko demand the death sentence for him, Iakubovich writes that he was "grateful" to Krylenko for not humiliating him in his speech. Similar psychological mechanisms operated in the case of M. I. Teitelbaum. Unable to bear the shame of having been forced to confess that he had taken bribes from capitalist trading firms, Teitelbaum leaped at the investigator's offer to have his confession changed to one of participation in the fictitious conspiracy. "Take me into the Union Bureau," he begged his fellow prisoner; Iakubovich did so.[42]

The final question about the trial concerns its objectives. Like other such trials, it was an exercise in political education, but what were the lessons taught here? Granted that this was, in the words of Léon Blum, "justice in the service of propaganda," why were the Mensheviks the object of this exercise?[43]

The Menshevik trial was a funeral service for NEP. Personally and professionally, all the defendants had been identified with this now repudiated policy; Groman even publicly criticized its abandonment. The trial thus represented the burial of those who remained wedded to discarded ideas. At the same time, it underscored the Soviet leadership's break with the policies it had once pursued. As *Vestnik* put it, "By destroying Groman and the others, Stalin and his lieutenants were trying to destroy their own past."[44]

The trial castigated those who contrasted present policies unfavorably with NEP. As in 1921, when the Mensheviks were repressed for having criticized war communism and for having proposed alternatives later adopted by the Soviets, so in 1931 they were judged for having warned of the consequences of abandoning NEP and for pointing out the errors of the General Line. Once again the Mensheviks had been vindicated and hence had to be punished. The defendants' testimony regarding the incoherences and disastrous consequences of Soviet policies did not need to be prompted. It was sincere and credible, even if circumstances dictated that this analysis should be presented in the form of a confession attributing to conscious "wrecking" the ills described.[45]

The trial thus offered an explanation to the Soviet people for the hardships they were enduring. A few years later *Vestnik* reported that the major proponent of the Menshevik trial had been Moscow party secretary L. M. Kaganovich, who needed to explain away the disastrous food shortages in the capital. The Mensheviks confessed to wrecking activities which struck at the food industry, reducing supplies, raising prices, and distorting local distribution. A Menshevik correspondent noted at the time of the "Industrial Party" trial in late 1930 that "the masses really believe there is hunger in the country because specialists are guilty."[46] Several months later the masses were still hungry, and new specialists had to be found.

The trial not only judged ideas and actions; it also put in the dock a social category, the privileged specialists. The same Menshevik correspondent reported that workers who had demonstrated at the "Industrial Party" trial were genuinely outraged at these wreckers who "earned three thousand [rubles], rode around in automobiles, and wouldn't give you a piece of cloth for a shirt." As the Russian proverb says, "No matter how much you feed the wolf, he will keep looking to the forest." The court played on the same sentiments: "How is it that those best provided for in the Soviet Union suddenly turned out to be dissatisfied?" asked the judge. The defendant replied, "Those who are best provided for are often the least satisfied because they want to be even better provided for."[47] The satisfaction of seeing the privileged punished was to be a factor in other Stalinist purges as well.

A further crime of the specialists was that they were nonpolitical. They smugly believed that they enjoyed "political extraterritoriality" and behaved as if "Communists only reign but specialists govern." As the Old Bolshevik previously quoted put it, "I don't believe these social democrats are traitors, but they have not understood that at present there are only two flowers, black and red." They failed to realize that in post-NEP circumstances they could not stand aloof, and thus fell easy prey to baleful influences emanating from their own doubtful past. As their defense counsel pleaded, "A Menshevik is lack of appreciation for the possibilities contained in the working class . . . pessimism, passivity in the face of difficulties."[48] The Menshevik trial was the trial of those who lacked faith.

The trial thus served as a warning to the wavering. Like a preacher showing his congregation the fateful path that leads from temptation to damnation, the prosecutor gathered testimony showing how easy it was to slide from "nonpolitical" meetings with anti-Soviet emigrés and "professional" discussions among experts to wrecking and interventionism; how there was, ultimately, no difference between those, like the Foreign Delegation, who fought Soviet power from abroad, and those, like the defendants, who fought it from within. Karl Radek used the occasion to settle historical scores by treating the revelations of the trial as the final outcome of the historical development of menshevism. The defense counsel at the trial could only counter that "the logic of life [had] cheated the Mensheviks."[49]

Beyond its function as a grand morality play, the trial fueled intraparty squabbles among the Bolsheviks. *Pravda*'s editor claimed that Groman's group (as well as Kondratiev's "Toiling Peasant Party") were authors of the basic theories of the Bolshevik Right opposition. This identification (which corresponded to the Menshevik defendants' affinities) hung over the trial without ever being made explicit; the time had not yet come to confront the right wing Bolsheviks directly. An attempt to introduce a connection with the Trotskyist opposition failed: "The directive concerning Trotsky did not appear realistic to me. It was just an invention of emigrés and we did not carry it out," replied Sher to a leading question from the prosecutor.[50]

The trial served to settle petty scores. Jasny has pointed out that the five year plan worked out at VSNKh by defendant Ginzburg differed very little from that elaborated simultaneously at Gosplan by the Communist (although ex-Menshevik) S. G. Strumilin. One might therefore suspect that Ginzburg fell victim to personal and bureaucratic rivalry. It is in terms of personal vendetta, too, that one can explain the inclusion of I. I. Rubin among the defendants. This professorial figure was indicted in order to implicate former Menshevik David Riazanov, director of the Marx-Engels Institute, who could not easily be smeared directly but who had incurred Stalin's wrath ten years earlier.[51] Rubin's sister recounts her brother's anguish at being forced to incriminate his friend and patron, and she tells of his efforts at the trial to deflect the accusations.[52] Other defendants, too, avoided incriminating him directly even when prodded to do so.[53]

The Menshevik trial also had an important international dimension: "a trial of world menshevism in the shape of the Second International," *Izvestiia* called it. Another Soviet journalist stressed the utter insignificance of menshevism in Russia and attributed its strength entirely to the fact that it was "one of the branches of the social-fascist international."[54] One defendant testified that Petr Garvi, the interventionist of 1918, exerted enormous influence on German social democracy through his connection with Karl Kautsky, and that Iurii Denike had confided that the SPD minister Rudolf Hilferding favored intervention. The connection between the Mensheviks, the LSI, and interventionism was incarnated in the person of Raphael Abramovich, and this was certainly a factor in the story of his trip to Russia. It was he who had pushed through the LSI's 1930 May Day appeal, interpreted by Krylenko as a call for intervention. Although Krylenko acknowledged that the LSI's Marseilles Congress in 1924 had rejected interventionism, he managed to give a sinister interpretation even to this decision; a defendant who had spent long periods abroad testified that the debate about intervention had continued in the councils of the LSI, culminating in, but not ending with, the 1930 appeal. To be sure, the "Union Bureau" had adopted a policy of interventionism late, after some hesitation, but its decision was foreordained. Intervention was nothing but wrecking from abroad, just as wrecking was intervention from within.[55]

The trial attracted attention in the West, primarily to the advantage of the RSDRP. In an ironic, even perverse, sense it confirmed the Foreign Delegation's claims to represent an active, living party in Russia. In its telegram to the Moscow court the Foreign Delegation was careful to state that the RSDRP did have a bureau in Russia but that this had nothing to do with the alleged "Union Bureau." The trial also created international support born of indignation. Socialist parties closed ranks around their Russian comrades with rallies in German cities, including one in Berlin which drew 15,000 to 20,000 people. In a vote of confidence the LSI Congress in Vienna unanimously elected Abramovitch as its chairman. The Menshevik trial did not succeed in winning a new audience for the Soviet project of discrediting Western socialism, nor did it manage to sow divisions within the LSI.[56]

Tales told at the Menshevik trial received limited credence in the non–social democratic press. The exiled Trotsky accepted the confessions at face value but later acknowledged that he had taken them "too seriously."[57] Abramovitch sued for libel two German Communist newspapers which had transmitted, with insults added, the Soviet version of the trial; he obtained satisfaction on appeal. The *New York Times* garbled its account. It quoted "Herr Dan" as saying he had not been a member of the RSDRP for the last ten years since he wished to remain nonpolitical.[58]

There are a number of unanswered questions about the Menshevik trial. One is surprised at the absence of Groman's closest associate V. A. Bazarov, or of L. B. Kafengauz, a member of the "Liga nabliudatelei," who shared with two Vesenkha defendants the distinction of having been a favorite of Dzerzhinskii.[59] It is not clear why the "Union Bureau" was tried in place of the "Toiling Peasant Party," given the latter's purported 200,000 members, and the fact that its leaders were arrested before the Mensheviks. Indeed, it is not known why preparations for this trial were dropped, disrupting the plan for three interconnected cases—the "Industrial Party's," the "Union Bureau's," and the "Toiling Peasants' "—which together would have given a complete panorama of counterrevolutionary activity. It is even difficult to judge whether the Menshevik trial was a success or a failure. Solzhenitsyn claims that it encouraged Stalin, "opening his eyes" to the advantage of a similar show for his party enemies.[60] The Mensheviks have maintained that the trial was such a failure that it was first transferred from the front to the back pages of the Soviet press and then broken off rather than brought to an end.[61]

One might add a *post scriptum* concerning some individuals at the trial. The Menshevik Foreign Delegation was divided over the attitude to take toward the only authentic Menshevik, V. K. Ikov. *Vestnik* spoke more in sorrow than in anger about his testimony, noting that he had betrayed the trust of his party but that he stood out positively among the accused. Subsequently, however, the Foreign Delegation announced "on behalf of party organizations in Russia" that Ikov had been expelled from the party "for unworthy behavior at the trial."[62] Several years later Ikov wrote to the OGPU, with a smuggled copy to the Foreign Delegation, repudiating his trial testimony. Decades afterwards, however, doubts persisted as Abramovitch still wondered whether Ikov's return to party work shortly before the trial had not been an OGPU operation.[63]

News about other convicted participants filtered in. Groman, Sukhanov, and Sher were boycotted in the *politisolator* by other political prisoners for their behavior at the trial. Sukhanov applied to join the Communist Party but was rejected. He wrote bitter letters reminding the authorities of his services at the trial and of their promise that sentences would not be carried out. In 1956 *Sotsialisticheskii vestnik* reported that Groman, after serving his sentence, had spent the war years working in a Soviet institution in Vologda and had died there. Rubin and Sukhanov were still alive in 1954, somewhere in Kazakhstan.[64] Iakubovich survived until 1980, but his request for rehabilitation, submitted in 1967 to the Soviet procurator-general in the form of the deposition cited by Medvedev, was never granted.

The Menshevik trial was not the trial of an authentic party organization, but it does mark a milestone in the history of the RSDRP. *Sotsialisticheskii Vestnik* continued to publish correspondents' reports; news about the sporadic activity of a party cell occasionally reached Berlin. There were even rumors that in 1938 Stalin was preparing a second Menshevik trial (as well as a new SR trial).[65] But the difficulties of communicating with the outside world and the hazards of any political discussion in Russia became insurmountable.[66] Discouragement among the Mensheviks at home outpaced even the dangers confronting them and eventually stifled what remained of their hopes. Ironically, the fabricated trial of the wholly fictitious "Union Bureau" did indeed mark the end of recognizable Menshevik life in Russia.

1933–1965

7

Hard Times

Life in France

"I have the impression that we shall soon have to move to France," wrote Fedor Dan a week after the Nazis had become the largest party in the Reichstag. A few days earlier, following the constitutional coup d'état which proclaimed martial law in Prussia, most of his comrades had rejected the idea of resettlement. Dan undertook, through the good offices of Léon Blum, to obtain French visas for all seventy-three members of the Berlin Menshevik colony. Abramovitch opened a bank account for the Foreign Delegation in Paris, and all funds were henceforth to be directed there.[1]

Such measures were prudent, but they betrayed little sense of urgency. Like the German Social Democrats, the Mensheviks considered contingency plans without conviction. For example, the SPD began training some young party activists, including Abramovitch's son Mark Rein and Samuel Estrine, as clandestine radio operators, but the project went no further. Even after Hitler's appointment as chancellor, debate within the Foreign Delegation over whether to move continued. The decision was taken, in the face of growing repression in Germany, in mid-February 1933. The last issue of *Sotsialisticheskii vestnik* to appear in Berlin—with the serenely irrelevant headline "On the 50th Anniversary of Marx's Death: Marx, Scholar and Politician"— was dated March 4, the eve of Hitler's electoral victory. By the time the principal French police informer in these matters noted rumors concerning a possible Menshevik move, Fedor Dan was already presiding in Paris and the great "migration of peoples," as he humorously put it, was under way.[2]

The flight from Germany was relatively smooth. Nevertheless, several Mensheviks, notably those who were active in the SPD, were arrested and released or narrowly escaped arrest. Denike was saved from a concentration camp by Nicolaevsky's connections with right wing Russian emigrés in Germany.[3] The party had sent some of its archives to France in early January 1933, but Dan's and Abramovitch's personal archives were lost. Dallin and Nicolaevsky stayed longest in Berlin, the former in a vain effort to expatriate some of his fortune, the latter out of sheer pig-headedness.[4] Two months after the transfer, *Sotsialisticheskii vestnik* was again appearing, now from new offices in Paris.

The years in France were to prove difficult, but the Mensheviks' situation was already critical before they were uprooted by the Nazi takeover. By 1931–32 they were increasingly plagued by material and morale problems. With a touch of bravado they toyed with the idea of setting up a shortwave radio link with Russia. But they were forced to abandon *Russische Sozial Demokratie* (*RSD,* their German-language bulletin), and the miniature edition of *Vestnik* for smuggling into Russia, altogether a monthly saving of 600 marks. The tone of their appeals was increasingly frantic: "It would be nasty if we had to close *Vestnik,*" wrote the treasurer. "It is quite understandable that our friends have to limit their expenses to bare necessities, but I hope they consider this a necessity."[5]

In this context came the Soviet decree of February 1932 depriving the Mensheviks and other socialist emigrés, notably Trotsky and his family, of citizenship and the right to return to Russia. Most Mensheviks stoutly asserted that as their rights did not derive from Stalin, they could not be taken away by him.[6] Nevertheless, the decree underscored the unlikelihood of an imminent return home and the prospect of eking out one's days in emigration, without even a passport as a link with the past. Dan's friends multiplied their efforts to set up a pension fund for him so as to guarantee him some security in old age.[7]

Within the party leadership long-standing quarrels, intensified by disagreements concerning the General Line, had produced a complete deadlock. Dan's group could muster five votes in the Foreign Delegation; the rightists and Abramovitch's centrists together commanded another five. Rumblings against "Danovian autocracy" grew, and Nicolaevsky, increasingly estranged from Dan, expressed the widespread feeling that the party chairman was seeking to split the party and to seize *Vestnik.*[8] It was thus a sorely tried and divided party that undertook the ordeal of a new exile.

The first imperative in Paris was to make ends meet. "In the beginning was unemployment," as a chronicler put it. The Mensheviks had difficulty finding even the most menial work. They displayed an unsuspected streak of enterprise by setting up a cooperative radio assembly workshop—unfortunately short-lived—which employed a dozen Mensheviks under the financial management of party treasurer Iugov and the technical supervision of I. A. Raeff, a Kharkov Menshevik and engineer who had once worked in the Soviet Communications Commissariat. Later, Iugov and Schwarz collaborated with the French socialist deputy and academic (and later Resistance hero) André Philip, and with a Frankfurt School member, Arkadii Gurland, in publishing a statistical documentation series which also was not a financial success.[9]

Individual Mensheviks managed as best they could. After losing her first job, Lidia Dan was hired by a company belonging to the American millionaire Bundist S. S. Atran, who was later to show much compassion for the Mensheviks' plight. The Aronsons, particularly destitute and with a newborn baby, set up a kindergarten. Mark Kefali-Kammermacher could not obtain working papers and was desperate enough to consider forging some. Petr Garvi, plagued by failing eyesight and utterly demoralized by his plight, accepted unsuitable work at the radio assembly cooperative, then studied accounting while waiting for something to come up. His daughter worked "like a bull" giving language lessons to support the whole family even as she continued her own studies.[10]

Among the few who had a steady job was Abramovitch, albeit his *Forverts* stipend was cut by 25 percent. Nicolaevsky did reasonably well, with various research assignments covering his modest needs. Plans to make a film of his book about the police spy E. F. Azev floundered, but employment with the SPD archives transported to Paris and with the newly founded Amsterdam Institute of Social History allowed him to turn down a more lucrative but politically distasteful proposal to resume work with Moscow's Marx-Engels Institute. The former deputy minister of labor, Anatolii Dubois, whose name belied his ignorance of French, embarked on a new career as a sculptor and won a silver medal at the Paris International Exposition in 1937. Ironically, the poverty-stricken Aronsons loved their new Parisian environment, whereas Nicolaevsky, who changed lodgings four times in the first eight months, grumbled that he could not get used to Paris at all.[11]

"We do not meet with foreigners," wrote Abramovitch ironically, as new and difficult circumstances forced members of the Menshevik clan to fall back on one another. Old ties overcame political differences when it came to mutual aid. Thus, although Dan and Garvi were politically and personally at loggerheads, when it turned out that Garvi needed an eye operation, Dan unhesitatingly decreed that the party should take responsibility, adding, "If two thousand francs is not enough we can always find the few hundred missing francs."[12]

Abramovitch deployed prodigious energy on behalf of his comrades in soliciting jobs, visas, introductions, and commissioned articles, such as those for the *Encyclopedia Judaica,* which he was editing. His German contacts were now useless; indeed, Alexander Stein, the former patron now exiled in Prague, was soliciting his help. Abramovitch therefore relentlessly exploited his other connections in America, within the International, even among the incomprehensible British. His zeal extended beyond the Menshevik family; he even pleaded with the British Labour Party to grant Trotsky residence in the Channel Islands. Abramovitch's practical sense, too, proved invaluable. After obtaining fictitious credentials from *Forverts* for America-bound Naum Jasny, Abramovitch advised him: "Get a tourist visa, as a temporary visitor . . . Don't quarrel with the consulate. Once there, with appropriate support you will get an extension to one year. After that, problems will begin, but with connections of a technical sort, about which the old-timers know, you will succeed."[13]

Nicolaevsky also helped his comrades, as best he could, through his scholarly connections. He was pleased to place young Boris Sapir in the Amsterdam Institute (where Sapir remained, with interruptions, until his death in 1989). He encouraged the obscure Hoover Institution, as he called it "some sort of Institute of the History of the Russian Revolution," to commission studies from his comrades, not suspecting that thirty years later he would be curator of these materials. The Mensheviks were not yet "prisoners of American capital," as Stepan Ivanovich put it humorously, but they were becoming beneficiaries of American scholarship.[14]

The United States exerted an ever stronger pull, but success there did not come easily. Naum Jasny, "odd and impossible in social intercourse but a talented and profoundly decent chap," remained out of work there for two years. Samuel Estrine was jobless throughout his first year, in spite of contacts as former assistant to the International Trade Union secretary and personal ties, as a former Butyrki prisoner, to the secretary of the Jewish Labor Committee, I. H. Minkov. Vladimir Woytinsky, after leaving Paris and working with the International Labor Organization in Geneva, appeared reborn in America. "An amazingly interesting country! There is nothing more beautiful, more magnificent, more splendid than the Bol'shoi Kanion [Grand Canyon]," he gushed, and the following year he happily noted his progress in tennis. "I no longer feel any affinity with that S. Petrov who ran around factories," he wrote, referring to his Bolshevik pseudonym from the Revolution of 1905. But even in distant America, Woytinsky could not shake off his ties to the party. He wrote to old friends: "Tell me in detail who said what in the Foreign Delegation, who answered what to that, and who remained silent, and precisely why some understood this silence in one way and others in another."[15]

Not only individuals but the party, too, had to ensure its livelihood. Fraternal subsidies were ever harder to obtain. Some Danish socialists, on learning that *Sotsialisticheskii vestnik* was still coming out, sent 15,000 francs as encouragement. The Swedes, however, decided to replace their aid to the Mensheviks with a larger general grant to the LSI's Matteoti fund for exiles, for which there were now more eligible beneficiaries than ever before. To Nicolaevsky's fury, the party adopted the stopgap measure of selling the Menshevik library, including both the Berlin collection (which departed from Germany as the formal possession of the French state) and the historic library on the rue des Gobelins in Paris.[16] Nonetheless, *Sotsialisticheskii vestnik* continued to totter on the brink of collapse with a print run falling to as few as six hundred copies.

The only way out of the financial impasse was to send Abramovitch to America again. An "Emergency Relief Committee for Russian Social Democrats, Victims of Hitler's Terror," had already been established in New York at Abramovitch's prompting, but it required additional publicity. "My old Bundists will not leave me in the lurch," wrote Abramovitch, yet he was apprehensive because of the extreme tensions within the American socialist movement.[17]

Abramovitch's trip was successful. Steering a middle course among U.S. factions, Abramovitch wrote Kautsky that he felt closer to the Right, represented by his employer *Forverts,* although he considered it as narrow-minded and obstinate as the Left. He then wrote Sol Levitas that in many matters the Left was closer to him, but its "bolshevizing" prevented him from identifying with it. The "perfectly vulgar palestinism" of *Forverts* also irritated him, with its "pathos exceeding even the official Zionist press" and its subordination of all other issues to that of Jewish national interest. Abramovitch admitted, however, that the United States was much more interesting than it had been ten or thirty years ago.[18] As for the purpose of the trip, the money he collected saved *Vestnik*—for the moment—although the specter of having to close shop was never completely exorcised.

If hardship brought the Mensheviks together on a personal level, it did nothing to smooth their internal political quarrels. On the contrary, it was during the difficult Parisian years that the split within the party became public and definitive. Relationships with the extraparty right wing were already beyond repair. On the death in 1934 of Aleksandr Potresov, a dissenting Menshevik but a historic and well-loved personality, it proved impossible to bring the intraparty and extraparty Mensheviks together, even for the funeral. Dan withdrew his initial agreement to speak and put through a resolution forbidding Foreign Delegation members to participate. His apprehensions turned out to be well founded as the funeral gave Potresov's lieutenant,

Stepan Ivanovich, a platform for lashing out at right-oriented Mensheviks who were afraid of breaking with the official party organization.[19]

"Our political differences are becoming personal differences," complained Abramovitch as the two dimensions grew impossible to untangle. For example, Petr Garvi's anti-Dan campaign was indeed founded on opposite interpretations of the Bolshevik Revolution. But it also fed on Garvi's resentment at the fact that he had not been readmitted to the Central Committee (nor, consequently, to the Foreign Delegation) after having walked out in protest in 1917. Dan, somewhat patronizingly, attributed Garvi's vehemence to his nervous condition and material woes, but he made no political concessions and did not discourage evocation of Garvi's purportedly equivocal behavior in Odessa during the Civil War.[20]

Challenges to Dan's leadership multiplied as close comrades complained that he was becoming ever more cantankerous and imperious. Nicolaevsky especially found Dan insufferable. Their relations had already been strained by Dan's break in 1928 with Nicolaevsky's close friend, the Georgian Menshevik Iraklii Tsereteli, although in this case Nicolaevsky's views, if not his heart, lay with Dan. Now, Dan's pressure to have the Mensheviks adopt a position in favor of *kolhozes* repulsed Nicolaevsky, and he sought to push his centrist allies into an outright anti-Dan position. "Fedor Illich [Dan] is strutting about and demanding social revolution," grumbled Nicolaevsky shortly after the move to Paris. Dan's attacks on Trotsky for the latter's activism against Soviet power were stupid, claimed Nicolaevsky, and they were bound to be misunderstood in Russia. With grim satisfaction, Nicolaevsky reported that Dan was quarreling with everyone and that he had been overheard to say, "I must be really getting old, I can no longer control myself."[21]

The only member of the Foreign Delegation to resign and abandon politics was not Nicolaevsky, who was threatening to do so, but David Dallin. He had earlier acted as the Cassandra of the Foreign Delegation, and he now withdrew discreetly. Personal woes played a part in his decision, but above all, it was the fruit of lucid reflection. Dallin had come to the conclusion that there was no place anymore for the intermediate role which the RSDRP sought to play. If, as appeared increasingly likely, the USSR was not experiencing real progress, then the notion of defending revolutionary achievements made no sense. Moreover, the party seemed unable to define a new role for itself, if indeed there was a role for a tiny circle of emigrés. "First this was a danger I feared, then a supposition, now it is a certainty," he wrote and drew the consequences.[22]

Dallin's withdrawal destroyed the delicate balance within the Foreign Delegation at precisely the time when Nicolaevsky was losing patience with Dan and Abramovitch was chafing at what he saw as Dan's usurpation of his role as Menshevik representative in the International. Since these members—Dallin, Abramovitch, and Nicolaevsky—constituted the "center" group, the Foreign Delegation now found itself with an anti-Dan majority but with Dan and his people in command of all key party posts. In such an untenable situation it is indeed astonishing that the Foreign Delegation managed to hold together for almost another decade. This can be explained by the Mensheviks' realization, founded on the SRs' experience, that if they lost their unity, they would soon lose their position within the International. It must also be traced to the person of Fedor Dan: convinced that he represented the views of comrades in Russia, unqualifiedly self-assured in his exercise of leadership prerogatives, "our Ill'ich" was able to command the deference of his comrades in exile long after they had ceased to share his views.[23] Haunted by their own past, the Mensheviks made formal party unity a fetish and a principle of survival.

Amid their material misery and internal squabbles, the Mensheviks could take comfort in the fact that other emigrés were even worse off. "We are still in a good position; with the Germans they [French authorities] are doing the devil knows what, a real massacre of the innocents," wrote Nicolaevsky, describing the ignominious behavior of the French who had supported the losing side in the Saar plebiscite and were now denying refuge to their supporters. The reversal of fortune was so complete that German socialists expressed envy of the Mensheviks and now turned to them for advice, for instance, on producing a clandestine party press from abroad. One German ex-minister complained that the main French socialist daily, the *Populaire*, was "fundamentally an organ of the Mensheviki" and that when anything happened in Germany, it called on Dan for information.[24]

The Mensheviks were particularly well placed to act as a bridge between German socialist exiles and their French hosts. Ex-Berlin Mensheviks were dubbed "Germans" by members of the Parisian Menshevik club, and they joked about imposing some "deutsche Ordnung" on the prevailing French-Russian nonchalance. Nicolaevsky served as curator of the German Socialists' archives in Paris. Shifrin, Denike (initially in the Saarland), and Bienstock (initially in Prague) remained active in the RSDRP while attaining new prominence in the German party. Owing to previous exile experience, they adapted more readily than disoriented German politicians to new exile conditions.[25] Whereas Bienstock and Shifrin joined the radical opposition within the exiled German socialist movement, Denike coauthored with Rudolf Hilferding a fundamental document of the exiled SPD executive, the Prague Manifesto.[26] Without any formal training, Bienstock and Shifrin also established themselves as popular experts on strategic and international affairs.[27]

On the French side, the Menshevik gatekeeper was Oreste Rosenfeld. Unlike Alexander Stein, who had played a similar role in Germany, Rosenfeld was a junior figure whose influence was based more on personal connections than on official position. Born in 1891 in Astrakhan to an intelligentsia family, Rosenfeld may or may not have had the early revolutionary career attributed to him. In 1914 he was already a Menshevik Party member in Moscow, and it was then that he met the Dans, who were to be lifelong friends. The 1917 February Revolution found him in France as an officer in a Russian unit sent to the western front in a gesture of Allied solidarity. It is unlikely that as a twenty-six-year-old lieutenant he was military attaché in Paris for the Russian Provisional Government, as his biographer claims, although he may well have been employed in the embassy or military mission. Nor is there any further evidence to sustain the romantic story that Rosenfeld enlisted in the Foreign Legion as a private to protest Bolshevik Russia's acceptance of the Brest-Litovsk Treaty. In 1919–20 Rosenfeld turned up as editor of *La République russe,* a Paris-based publication which voiced Axelrod's ideas of socialist intervention in Russia.[28]

Rosenfeld, a lawyer by training, settled into French life, initially as a factory executive and later as a journalist. He remained active in the Paris Menshevik group, even serving on its board, but his interests moved toward French affairs. He wrote for *Combat socialiste* and *Revue socialiste,* made political speeches, and practiced backroom politics in the Socialist Federation of the Seine. His political breakthrough came when Léon Blum called on him to collaborate in the *Populaire.* Soon, Rosenfeld was the newspaper's foreign affairs editor, and in 1936, as he obtained his long-awaited French naturalization, he was appointed its editor.[29]

Blum took the young Russian emigré to heart completely. Although as late as 1924 they were not yet acquainted, by 1931 he was referring publicly to their "relationship of fraternal and daily intimacy, already several years old." Daily conversations continued even when Blum had left the *Populaire.* Blum stood up for Rosenfeld against French socialist critics who took exception to Rosenfeld's criticism of the first Soviet five year plan.[30] He also stood by Rosenfeld when the latter was forced briefly to take a less conspicuous position, whether because of pressure from the SFIO's new Communist allies or because Rosenfeld's foreign-sounding name "scorched the ear."[31] Rosenfeld was once the object of an antisemitic tirade in the National Assembly by a right wing deputy who complained that "important decisions of government would henceforth be made by a small Jewish coterie consisting of Blum, Blumel, Moch, and Rosenfeld." Forty years later Rosenfeld's friends were still rebutting this charge, not because it exaggerated Rosenfeld's influence but because Rosenfeld was not Jewish.[32]

Rosenfeld was a follower who always succeeded in making himself invaluable to his patron. There is a touch of venom in one characterization of Rosenfeld as a chameleon, someone whose voice changed with his allegiances. It is true, however, that Axelrod, who had considered Rosenfeld one of his own, noted disappointedly that "this bright and capable lad" possessed a "streak of opportunism." In spite of Axelrod's entreaties and Tsereteli's efforts, Rosenfeld went over to Dan's camp so thoroughly that he was dubbed "Dan's double." With respect to Léon Blum, Rosenfeld was the perfect *homme de confiance*, never faltering in his devotion. One might add that, in the 1950s, Rosenfeld was to display admirable independence of character in breaking with the French socialists to protest their colonial policy.[33]

By the end of the 1930s the little group of exiles that met socially at the Petit St. Benoît bistro had expanded to include not only the Dans and Nicolaevsky but also French-Russians such as Boris Souvarine and Oreste Rosenfeld, with his companion the Russian artist Nataliia Goncharova and the Czech newcomers Hubert Ripka and Ivo Duchacek.[34] Within this growing and varied world of Parisian exiles, the Russian Mensheviks stood out for their fortitude and resilience: they had been in exile longer than any other group—almost two decades—and they had been exiled not only from their home but from their first land of exile. They had managed to survive in the economically adverse circumstances of the 1930s and in the inhospitable French social and political environment. They had succeeded in rebuilding their organization, their journal, and their personal network. At the turn of the decade they would be called on to repeat this feat in yet another country and on another continent.

Contacts

The exiled Mensheviks' influence and prestige were enhanced by their well-placed international connections, but their legitimacy was still rooted in their party ties to Russia. In the course of the 1930s these ties became increasingly tenuous. "We have contact only with a couple dozen old comrades," wrote Abramovitch in 1936. Even relief work on behalf of exiled or imprisoned comrades became extremely difficult with the dissolution of the Political Red Cross in 1938, an organization previously tolerated by the Soviets as a favor to Gorky's former wife. Still, the Mensheviks asserted that every dollar donated reached its destination, though by increasingly roundabout routes.[1]

The Mensheviks also became wary of ties to Russia on discovering a police agent among their correspondents. "Nikolai Petrovich" was a Soviet engineer who established contact with the Foreign Delegation while on a business trip in Berlin. Pleasant, modest, and intelligent, he made an excellent impression, particularly on Dan, whose views he shared. Prudently, the Foreign Delegation would not allow Nikolai Petrovich to represent the party in Russia, but it did accept correspondence from him.[2]

Nikolai Petrovich aroused suspicion by appearing in Vienna during the LSI Congress in 1931, but Abramovitch conducted an investigation which vindicated him. When he reappeared in Paris in 1936–37, Nicolaevsky could not contain his mistrust. The Mensheviks interrogated their correspondent thoroughly and even sent a writing sample to a graphologist, who diagnosed "a master of pretense, an iron character who never loses control over himself and leads a double life." Of course, this could as easily have been a reference to his work for the Mensheviks as for the Soviets.[3]

Nevertheless, the Mensheviks broke off contact with Nikolai Petrovich, writing: "We have decided to stop our correspondence, and not to renew it until such time as all sacrifices which comrades in Russia bear are not so disproportionately great. When such time comes we shall try to get back in touch ourselves."[4] It is not clear whether this statement was a subterfuge or was relaying a decision actually taken. In any case, the Mensheviks heard nothing more of Nikolai Petrovich until they found his name among a list of several hundred people decorated by the Soviet government in 1940 "for courage."[5]

In the absence of traditional sources of information, the Mensheviks discovered new ones among prominent Soviet defectors. Fedor Dan welcomed these individuals as living proof that the Bolshevik regime was losing its most faithful supporters. Equally important, he saw them as valuable propaganda material which would be exploited by enemies of socialism if the socialists failed to use it. The Menshevik right wing sniffed at the "alliance with boyars fleeing from Muscovy," and the defectors themselves had to overcome their Soviet-based prejudices against the Mensheviks.[6]

Among the first of these new "allies" was Walter Krivitsky, a high-level spy in western Europe, though not the GPU "general" and "chief of military intelligence" he was later made out to be. Krivitsky defected in November 1937, after the murder of his friend and colleague Ignace Reiss. The lawyer of Reiss's widow put him in touch with Trotsky's son, and the latter called on the Mensheviks for assistance because of their excellent connections with the French government. Rosenfeld immediately arranged the necessary French papers (Blum was prime minister at the time), and the Dans' apartment became Krivitsky's first safe house.[7]

Krivitsky's story, though unreliable, is well known owing to the success of his memoirs. Most striking in Lidia Dan's account of Krivitsky's first days as a defector is the sense of a moral abyss separating the hosts from their guest. Krivitsky was both overwhelmed and irritated by the trust the Dans showed him. He could not understand why they had taken him in, why they did not fear for their lives. As if to break their trust, Krivitsky recounted how he had done away with a subordinate who had aroused only slight suspicion, a story which failed to find its way into his memoirs. "If the Bolsheviks get the idea of 'liquidating' Dan they will find other means, from which, in any case, there is no way of escaping," replied Lidia Dan sensibly. On hearing of Krivitsky's mysterious death in a Washington hotel room several years later, Lidia Dan was inclined to believe that it was indeed suicide. As she saw it, Krivitsky was an emotional and moral cripple, racked by paranoia and guilt. To be sure, he was being hounded by Soviet agents, but he was his own worst enemy.[8]

Anton Ciliga was another kind of source. A former Yugoslav Politburo member who knew Soviet Russia as a Communist dignitary and then as a Gulag inmate, Ciliga was soon to become famous for his 1938 exposé best known under its original French title, *Au pays du grand mensonge* (translated as *The Russian Enigma*). Although Ciliga did not consider himself a Trotskyist, his oppositionist views led him to begin publishing his account in Trotsky's Paris-based *Biulleten' Oppozitsii*. Trotsky abruptly suspended publication, ostensibly because Ciliga was also publishing in *Sotsialisticheskii vestnik* and the *Biulleten'* could "not accept having common contributors with Menshevik publications." Trotsky added, for good measure, that the revolutionary movement was full of examples of how the ultra-Left (that is, Ciliga) rejoined rightist opportunism. According to Ciliga, he was censored by Trotsky because of his calls for unity among socialists, opposition Communists, and anarchists. In any case, *Vestnik* scored a point by publishing a protest from Ciliga after Trotskyists had refused to do so. It also gained a valuable collaborator and a friend for some Mensheviks, although he was never to become a party comrade.[9]

As Ciliga's experience shows, relations between Trotskyists and Mensheviks in exile were unsatisfactory. Some individual Mensheviks gravitated toward the Trotskyist camp. Bienstock sought a personal meeting with Trotsky (in the company of the future West German chancellor Willy Brandt), and it is likely that he was among the socialists whom Ciliga approached in Prague regarding cooperation. Vera Alexandrova was intimately involved with Ciliga, and her enthusiasm for Trotskyists outlived this relationship. The most radical conversion to Trotskyism was that of Lolla Ginzburg, at that time married to Samuel Estrine, and later wife of David Dallin. In Germany, she had worked at the Soviet commercial mission, and in Paris she became Nicolaevsky's secretary. It was in the latter capacity that she met Trotsky's son, Leon Sedov, and she soon became the "pillar" of the Russian Trotskyist group, contributing to and aiding with the *Bulleten'*.[10]

Lolla Estrine's involvement with Parisian Trotskyists was to have fateful consequences. It was she who befriended and introduced into their circle Mark Zborowski, a young Polish Jewish drifter who made himself indispensable by helping out with office tasks. Only many years later, in America, did it transpire that "Étienne," as Zborowski was known among the Trotskyists, had been a Soviet agent. This revelation put several mysterious events of the 1930s into perspective. In November 1936 there had been a burglary at Nicolaevsky's office on the rue Michelet, and several boxes of Trotsky's documents confided to Nicolaevsky by Sedov were stolen. Lolla Estrine, Zborowski, and Nicolaevsky were the only individuals aware of the location of the documents. Zborowski was cleared of suspicion since at the time of the burglary he was safeguarding in his own home other, even more important documents which escaped the burglars.[11]

When Sedov fell ill it was Zborowski who called the ambulance. A few days later, after an appendicitis operation in a Parisian clinic, Sedov died in mysterious circumstances. Some people, including prominent Trotskyist publicist Victor Serge, blamed Lolla, since it was she who had recommended this clinic, where her Menshevik brother was a physician but where some White Russians also practiced.[12] Zborowski remained unsuspected, and in any case, it appears that his NKVD role was that of informant rather than executor. He knew nothing in advance of the burglary on the rue Michelet (apparently intended by the NKVD to provide Stalin a present for the anniversary of the Revolution) and, indeed, was horrified that his cover might be blown by the incident. There is even evidence that Zborowski contributed to saving Sedov's life by making sure that Sedov missed a rendezvous in Mulhouse where Soviet agents were lying in wait for him.

Lolla Estrine, who lavished maternal affection on Zborowski, even providing him with pocket money, never entertained any suspicions of him. Because of her, Zborowski acted as bodyguard for Walter Krivitsky soon after Krivitsky's defection, and she had him perform the same function later in New York for another defector, Victor Kravchenko.[13] When, during Lolla's stay with the Trotskys in Mexico, Trotsky received a warning which could have pointed to Zborowski, she persuaded Trotsky to disregard it. She sponsored Zborowski's immigration to the United States, and when the same ex-NKVD officer (Alexander Orlov) who had earlier tried to warn Trotsky told her outright that Zborowski was an agent, she refused to believe this and claimed not to know his whereabouts. Only when Zborowski himself came to her apartment to make a tearful confession, eighteen years after Sedov's death, was she fully persuaded.[14] Lolla's affection for Zborowski was almost as marked as her fidelity to the memory of the man he had betrayed. On her death in 1981 it turned out that for over forty years she had been paying the upkeep of Sedov's grave in Paris.

Efforts to establish personal connections in Paris between Trotskyists and Mensheviks were sometimes successful—witness the cordial ties between Nicolaevsky and Sedov—but all attempts at ideological rapprochement failed. The weight of historical animosity and suspicion was simply too heavy to overcome. Perhaps, too, the affinity between Trotskyist and Menshevik critiques of Soviet Russia, noted by right and left wing adversaries of both groups, was only superficial.

The presumption of affinity between Mensheviks and Trotskyists rests on their shared Marxist outlook and their common use of critical concepts such as bureaucratism, thermidor, and bonapartism. Moreover, they both explained the degeneration of the Russian Revolution in terms of Russian economic backwardness. On close examination, however, the logic of explanation and the lessons drawn differ. For the Mensheviks, Russian backwardness condemned the Revolution in advance; for Trotsky, the Russian Revolution ultimately failed because of the defeat of world revolution, itself largely owing to betrayal by Western social democracy. Bureaucratism for the Mensheviks was an outcome of the lack of intraparty democracy among the Bolsheviks; for Trotsky it was a cause, not a consequence, of the lack of democracy.[15]

There was enough common ground—and certainly enough common interests—for some Mensheviks to seek rapprochement. "Trotsky's analysis is very close to our own," stated Dallin in 1929. "Does it matter who said it first?" Five years later Shifrin declared that Trotsky had undergone "great positive evolution," adding that "if proletarian unity required another social democracy and another communism," then Trotsky represented another communism, and a new revolutionary social democracy was being born.[16] Not all Mensheviks shared such sentiments. The Menshevik Right was disgusted by the pity some social democratic leaders expressed for Trotsky's plight. It saw differences between Stalin's General Line and the Trotskyist platform as merely nuances, and viewed the Stalin-Trotsky conflict as a personal one.[17] For left wing Mensheviks, accused of trying to outdo Trotsky in revolutionary rhetoric, it was also not a matter of indifference that Trotsky was only now stating what "social democrats had been saying long ago."[18]

The prime adversary of rapprochement was Trotsky himself. As he put it in 1929, equating his attacks on the Stalinist bureaucracy with those of the Mensheviks was nothing but "stupid little charlatanism." The Mensheviks were among those "opportunists" who denounced bureaucratism when, in fact, they were complaining about revolutionary centralism. Trotsky dismissed collaboration with this "powerless emigré group with a discredited past and no future"—a description which might be uncharitably applied to him—as a "combination of opportunism and Don Quixotism."[19] He also sought to discredit them: "Who is Vyshinskii?" he wrote his son, "Mensheviks write that he came from their ranks. We must publicize this with all necessary details though I know nothing about it."[20] No doubt, in addition to the historical ballast, there was organizational rivalry. This explains why Trotsky's frequently conciliatory attitude toward foreign socialists never extended to Russians with whom he competed for a constituency at home and abroad. The fact that Trotsky's communications with Russia ceased earlier than those of the Mensheviks can only have sharpened this rivalry.[21] All in all, Trotsky was always ready to believe the worst about the Mensheviks. However, when persuaded by his son that Mensheviks had been unjustly accused in their 1931 trial, he publicly admitted his error.[22]

The Mensheviks lacked the Trotskyists' notoriety, but their contacts and information were more broadly based. They exploited every avenue—travelers, journalists, diplomats, defectors—to find out what was happening at home. They could even persuade a loyal Communist to act as messenger, as they did in 1935, when the Italian Emilio Sereni, distantly related to Abramovitch, carried a letter to Moscow on the latter's behalf (the Italian Communist Party as a whole was later reproached for this incident). Nicolaevsky, who was working on a historical study of that classic forgery the *Protocols of the Elders of Zion,* was particularly zealous at ferreting out current information: "I interview various fossilized old ladies and I am making acquaintances in church circles . . . I also began collecting materials about the secret history of the Comintern. I found many ex-activists here who tell me a lot of interesting things."[23]

Scholarship provided Nicolaevsky and others with an entrée into the world of high politics. The key to this world turned out to be the archives which Nicolaevsky had dispatched from Berlin under the eyes of the Nazis in May 1933. Nicolaevsky's merit and courage in this operation are incontestable, although Boris Souvarine later claimed responsibility for the rescue, complaining that "messieurs les menchéviks" had never shown any gratitude.[24] The operation consisted of getting the French government to purchase the Menshevik Berlin library and then removing it as French state property.[25]

The logistics of the operation were complex and nerve-racking. Nicolaevsky and a comrade packed three high-security containers. To the Menshevik materials they added the Jewish Labor Bund archives as well as SPD materials, including papers of the founding fathers of Marxism, hidden underneath other documents. As packing continued in the SPD headquarters, Nazi Sturmabteilung (SA) troops milling around the building became increasingly excited. It required the personal intervention of the French ambassador to remove the shipment, in the dead of night. The ambassador balked, however, at Nicolaevsky's request for two special railway cars and instead expedited the material with other diplomatic mail. Somehow, some documents were sent to the Czechoslovak embassy in Berlin, whence they made their way, via Prague, to Paris.[26]

Soon the French Bibliothèque de Guerre informed its minister that an examination of the cases sent from Berlin had revealed, in addition to the library purchased, Menshevik archives and SPD documents. In its view such materials had no place in an official French establishment.[27] Nicolaevsky grumbled that the documents were being expelled because the political wind had shifted, and he began searching for new storage space. Six months later he complained that he was taking the archives—which are "completely on my shoulders, especially the German ones"—to their third home.[28] Suddenly, however, after having been an encumbrance, the archives became Nicolaevsky's and the Mensheviks' most precious financial and political capital.

"I have to tell you an exciting story," wrote Nicolaevsky to a German comrade in August 1935. "Since yesterday the Bolsheviks are trying to establish contact with me. Today I found out that the cause of this unexpected attention was the following: the wish to obtain the Marx-Engels archive." The Soviets were sending emissaries to negotiate the purchase of the archives "at any price," which "could even be millions." They had assumed that the materials evacuated from Germany were in the possession of the French state and had offered in exchange a collection of Napoleon's correspondence with Tsar Alexander I, all letters of French statesmen of the Napoleonic era in Russian hands, as well as five hundred reports of Napoleon's secret agents and the whole archive of the Grande Armée. The French authorities—no doubt regretting their earlier inhospitality—could only direct the emissaries to the rightful owner, the exiled SPD, and to the curator, Boris Nicolaevsky. Shortly thereafter, Fedor Dan received a similar offer: the Soviets would buy the Menshevik Party archives along with the Marx-Engels archives on the most favorable conditions imaginable.[29]

The fabulous conditions offered aroused suspicions. The Soviets may have been willing to rehire Nicolaevsky for the Marx-Engels Institute, as they claimed, but it was not believable that they would fund a center to house Menshevik and other archives outside Paris with a Menshevik-appointed staff on their payroll.[30] Some German Social Democrats who saw their party as the legitimate heir to the founding fathers of Marxism were particularly hostile. They believed that the sudden Soviet interest in the archives was part of a charm campaign aimed at Western socialists; it would also embarrass the SPD as a party unwilling to ally with Communists but prepared to sell Marx's papers to them.

Nevertheless, negotiations began with Nicolaevsky as chief negotiator. Soviet representatives initially hinted that the deal could be concluded in "two or three weeks" at a price no higher than 18 million francs (compare the Menshevik sale of their library for 50,000 francs). Shortly thereafter, they announced that a high-level delegation was leaving Moscow with a concrete offer of 15 million francs, which was 10 million below the SPD's initial asking price. After the delegation had examined the documents with Nicolaevsky, including some in Copenhagen and in Amsterdam, it submitted a formal offer of 7 million francs, to be raised to 8 million if some missing documents were located.[31]

LSI secretary Friedrich Adler was furious and sought to break off negotiations. Instead, the Soviets asked for a counterproposal and the SPD demanded 20 million francs, possibly 10 percent less if the missing documents were not found. The Soviet delegates asked for two days to reflect (and, presumably, to communicate with Moscow) and then announced that they would continue their reflections through the Easter holiday. When discussions resumed, the Soviets were prepared to pay 10 million francs, and the SPD reduced its price to 13 million. It turned out that the Soviet sum included transport and other costs, but the gap between the two parties had narrowed considerably.

The deal was never concluded, for reasons that are still obscure. After the Soviet delegates were called back to Moscow in late May 1936, negotiations continued with a Soviet plenipotentiary. At the end of July, Nicolaevsky informed him that the SPD had agreed to sign for 7 million francs but set a firm closing date. At this point the shadow of events in the Soviet Union loomed darker, beginning with the arrest of Kamenev and Zinoviev and then of one of the archive negotiators, Bukharin. The closing date passed, and though Nicolaevsky continued desultory discussions, the deal receded beyond the horizon of reality. The long negotiations, involving not only money but also the terms of scholarly cooperation and even political conditions (regarding, for instance, political prisoners in Russia), bore no immediate direct fruit. They did, however, draw attention to the value of the archives and thus gave a spur to their eventual acquisition by the Amsterdam Institute of Social History. Finally, the negotiations provided unique occasion for meetings between prominent social democrats and Communists at a crucial time.

It is in the archive affair that one finds the source of the most important and controversial Menshevik document about the Soviet Union in the 1930s. The "Letter of an Old Bolshevik," first published anonymously in *Vestnik* in December 1936 and January 1937, describes the power struggle from the time of the oppositional Riutin platform in 1932, through the 1934 murder of Leningrad party chief Sergei Kirov, to the purges of Zinoviev and Kamenev in the summer of 1936. Given the dearth of other privileged information for this period, the "Letter's" picture of a Politburo struggle between advocates of repression and conciliators such as Kirov has long been the basis of Western interpretations of the period leading up to the great purges.[32]

Many years later *Sotsialisticheskii vestnik* revealed that the "Letter" had been composed by Nicolaevsky on the basis of conversations with Nikolai Bukharin, former Comintern head and Bolshevik Right opposition leader, during the latter's stay in Paris in the spring of 1936 as a member of the Soviet archival delegation. Several historians have questioned the verisimilitude of this claim on grounds of internal evidence. Some events described in the "Letter"—the death of Gorky, the replacement of NKVD chief Yadgoda by Yezhov, the 1936 trial of Kamenev and Zinoviev—took place after Bukharin had left Paris. Nicolaevsky admitted that he had made his own additions, to preserve both Bukharin's tone and anonymity, but he reiterated the substance of his claim.[33]

Lidia Dan, in a posthumously published chapter of memoirs, corroborates Nicolaevsky's assertion that Bukharin was particularly garrulous in Paris, eager to unburden himself before returning home. According to her, Bukharin arrived unannounced at the Dans' appartment one afternoon and spent several hours huddled with Fedor Dan. Among snatches of conversation heard which remained fixed in her mind was Bukharin's outcry regarding Stalin: "He is a petty and evil individual; no, this is not a man, this is the devil."[34]

More recently, challenges to Nicolaevsky's (and Lidia Dan's) claims have obtained powerful reinforcement in the memoirs of Bukharin's widow. Anna Bukharina, then twenty-two years old, joined her husband in Paris in the spring of 1936, and they experienced there the last happy moments of their short-lived marriage. Only after decades of prison, exile, and ostracism, was she able to publish a ringing denunciation of Nicolaevsky for allegedly having fabricated the "Letter" and for having "consciously helped Stalin tighten the noose around Bukharin's neck."[35] As for Lidia Dan's posthumously published reminiscences, Bukharina asserted they were a pure forgery.

Anna Bukharina's case rests on three arguments: first, that Bukharin and the Mensheviks did not have any tête-à-tête conversations; second, that Bukharin would not have spoken freely to Mensheviks; third, that Nicolaevsky and Lidia Dan misrepresent Bukharin's mood in Paris. None of these arguments holds. Bukharina joined her husband only after he had been in Paris (and, although she is not aware of it, elsewhere in western Europe) for a whole month, during which he negotiated archival matters with Nicolaevsky and Fedor Dan. Bukharin's indiscretions were in character for a man who had been called "nothing but a gossip" by his closest ally; moreover, there are two further confirmations of Bukharin's willingness to speak freely in Paris.[36] As for Bukharina's belief that her husband was carefree that spring, it is a tribute to his tender efforts to dissimulate, before his sick, pregnant, and very young wife, his own apprehensions.

Ultimately one can only state that there is no irrefutable proof of the "Letter's" authenticity, but challenges to it have proved unconvincing. The flourishes Nicolaevsky later added to his story do not suffice to undermine its credibility. Nor are we likely to be able to make a definitive judgment on Lidia Dan's story. Ironically, Nicolaevsky expresses skepticism about her account. Most tantalizingly, as Lidia Dan's literary executor has complained, all efforts to locate the manuscript of her memoirs in the British Museum, where it was supposed to be deposited, have proved fruitless.[37]

Finally, the example of Anna Bukharina illustrates the Mensheviks' growing inability, as the years went by, to address an audience in Soviet Russia. Anna was herself of Menshevik stock. Her adored stepfather, the Menshevik Iurii Larin, became a radical theoretician of war communism and a Bolshevik so fanatical that he changed his daughter's birthday on documents so that it would not coincide with the anniversary of Lenin's funeral. Indeed, by a strange quirk of circumstances (of which Bukharina appears unaware), Lidia Dan was—of all things—Iurii Larin's godmother.[38] Yet not the slightest grain of sympathy for the Mensheviks is expressed in Bukharina's testimony (although there is respect for Lidia Dan personally). On the contrary, Nicolaevsky is depicted not only as a liar and a fraud but also as a venal creature who, like his comrades, was interested only in the money to be made off Marx's archives.

Decades of persecution and suffering never changed Anna Bukharina's view of the Mensheviks nor brought her to question the image of them which she imbibed in Moscow in the early 1930s. Although she stands out from her contemporaries on so many other counts, her anti-Menshevik prejudices are those of her own and succeeding Soviet generations. Her example shows that, by the 1930s, the vital contact with Soviet youth sought so desperately by the Mensheviks could no longer exist, not only because of physical barriers erected by Stalin but also because of mental barriers that relegated the Mensheviks to objects of ignorant hatred and contempt.

The Totalitarian Nexus

Actors in the Bolshevik Revolution, witnesses to the Nazi seizure of power, the Mensheviks were among the first victims of both these epochal events. Dismay at the triumph of German fascism led the Mensheviks, like many other observers, to rethink their world outlook. More than anyone else, however, as they reflected on the German debacle, the Mensheviks harked back to Russian precedents. Indeed, at times they appeared to be re-posing the questions of 1917: Did the socialists lose because of a lack of revolutionary boldness? Could they have found firm allies among bourgeois democrats? Could they have defeated their enemies if they had acted earlier? Above all, in an effort to make sense of the double disaster that had befallen them in Russia and in Germany, the Mensheviks painstakingly, even reluctantly, sought to connect the Communist and fascist experiences. Over time this connection came to be grounded in the overarching concept of totalitarianism.

With disgust and incredulity the Mensheviks observed the proud German Social Democratic Party being hounded from the political scene without a whimper. "Most tragic is not that the SPD has been conquered in the most unheroic fashion," wrote Abramovitch, "but rather that it has lost and it does not know it." He predicted that even the best member of the International, the Austrian party, would probably suffer the same fate as the Germans, perhaps also without open struggle. Surely, however, it would not try to function as a loyal opposition in a 100 percent fascist state as the Germans were doing. German comrades not only lacked the courage to go underground but also were not even using the secret channels of communication that the Mensheviks and others had set up for them.[1]

It was the SPD's unshakable passivity more than its defeat that surprised the Mensheviks. Over the years they had been recording the rise of German fascism and emphasizing that a decisive confrontation was looming. In autumn 1932 Fedor Dan ended an article titled "Advance of the German

Counter-Revolution" on an optimistic note. At that time the SPD counted almost a million members and 5 million affiliated trade unionists. In the two 1932 elections it had won 20 percent of the vote. Not only was the SPD in power in several German states, including Prussia until mid-1932, but also the Brüning government had survived until that time only because of SPD toleration. Earlier, however, David Dallin had analyzed the significance of the fact that more than half of German voters had come out in favor of parties that wished to overthrow the republic. The SPD, he complained, was not doing anything to make itself the voice of growing dissatisfaction in the country.[2]

Long before fascism had become the main political issue in Germany, it had been an object of keen theoretical interest among socialists. One historian has even quipped that the socialist analysis of fascism is older than fascism itself. This analysis, like that of other Marxists, rested on the premise that "fascism [was] a superstructure for working out the economic problems of capitalism." Unlike Communists, however, socialists introduced so many reservations and qualifications that they put the basic premise into question. Thus, pioneering analyses by Italian socialist exiles explained Mussolini's success in terms of Italy's backwardness and pointed to the novelty of an alliance between the plutocracy and déclassé masses. Karl Kautsky also emphasized that fascists were recruited from the *Lumpenproletariat* and concluded that Germany could therefore not sustain a fascist movement.[3] The socialist analysis thus evolved, uncomfortably, as a list of exceptions to the basic theory that fascism represented the last stand of the declining bourgeoisie.

The Mensheviks were always alert to the inadequacies of this theory. They noted the ambiguity inherent in the fact that fascism seemed to be a bourgeois class movement without actually being one, and that fascism's victory was not a victory of the bourgeoisie, although it was a defeat for the proletariat.[4] Fascism's supporters came from all social spheres, and capital both cooperated with fascism and opposed it. At the same time, fascism was not a supraclass movement; its essence lay in the will to crush all anticapitalist forces.[5] The most controversial diagnosis came from one of the youngest Mensheviks, Boris Sapir. He incurred the ire of his elders not because of his emphasis on fascism's connection with statization and planning and on its plebeian character, but because of his insistence that socialists should learn to manipulate the mass media and master other "political techniques" as efficiently as their fascist rivals.[6]

The ambiguity over the class nature and the ideological content of fascism led to an apparently academic question: Was socialism or democracy the main enemy and antithesis of fascism? In fact, this question summarized some of the major divergences between left and right Mensheviks. For the Menshevik Right, defense of democracy was the surest bulwark against the fascist onslaught. This meant that the SPD had been correct in concentrating on the preservation of the constitutional order of the Weimar Republic, and henceforth socialists, too, should make common cause with democratic bourgeois parties. For the Menshevik Left, the socialists had opened the door to fascism by abandoning revolution in favor of reformism and by considering democracy an end in itself rather than a means toward socialism.[7]

The implications of this divergence went beyond the question of SPD strategy, and they raised a key theoretical issue. If the fundamental opposition lay between fascism and democracy, then Soviet Russia, an admittedly undemocratic regime, found itself on the wrong side of the divide. The Bolshevik regime was perhaps more akin to fascist Italy or Germany than to bourgeois France or England, and it was certainly not a regime worth defending. Left wing Mensheviks, reluctant to draw a conclusion so much at odds with the foundations of the Martov Line, first took shelter in classic Marxist categories. Thus, Fedor Dan argued that "the great clash toward which we are heading will not be one of political forms—fascism or democracy—but one of social—economic foundations—capitalism or socialism." Even Shifrin, an iconoclastic Marxist but also a left wing Menshevik, resorted to the dogmatic statement that "fascism secures big capital against the penetration of the state and the revolt of the middle classes [*Mittelstand*]."[8] This crude formulation stands at odds with Shifrin's usually nuanced and innovative analyses.

Nonetheless, the comparison between fascism and communism made headway among the Mensheviks, as it did among other observers. Some Mensheviks treated fascism as a reaction to communism, as a "movement which fed on all sins and crimes of communism." Others rejected the notion that fascism was simply a "preventive war of the international bourgeoisie against the threat of social revolution" and sought an explanation in national specifics. Bienstock saw both fascism and communism as movements aiming at overcoming the liberal state, a historical mission that belonged to socialism but had been abandoned in favor of reformism. The victory of fascism (and perhaps of communism) was thus the obverse of the degeneration of socialism.[9]

The idea that fascism and communism were similar rather than merely comparable germinated steadily. Dan polemicized against this view, promoted early by the extraparty right wing Mensheviks and supported, usually only implicitly, by Italian exiles. He could do so, however, only at the cost of multiplying concessions. True, Bolsheviks were adventurists like fascists, but even if it was the case (and it was not) that the Bolsheviks were using power merely to advance the interests of their own clique, it should be clear that they were wagering not on liquidating revolutionary processes but, on the contrary, on igniting them into a worldwide conflagration. True, fascism and communism were alike in their antidemocratic methods, in their reliance on a single party, and on their corrupt bureaucratic and military apparatus. They were different, however, in their goals, their historical origins, their social and economic foundations, and their attitude toward the revolutionary instincts of the masses.[10]

In his speech to the LSI Brussels Congress in 1928, Dan acknowledged that it was heartbreaking for a revolutionary to tax the self-proclaimed revolutionary Bolshevik dictatorship with the same horrors as the openly counterrevolutionary fascist dictatorship. Alas, Dan and the other Mensheviks had to undergo this painful experience repeatedly as the similarity between communism and fascism was brought out ever more systematically. A milestone in this process, Sapir's *Marx gegen Hitler*, distinguished enemies "from outside the proletariat," that is, reactionary forces, from enemies "from within the proletariat," among whom it counted both fascists and Bolsheviks. Another milestone was the 1934 French-language publication of Martov's *World Bolshevism*. Dan's introduction stressed that Martov had never forgotten that the Bolshevik dictatorship was a revolutionary one. It could hardly escape most readers' attention, however, that Martov's description of bolshevism—an ideology of scorn for existing material and spiritual culture imbibed by an immature and insufficiently emancipated proletariat—corresponded even more closely to the profile of fascism.

Even if communism and fascism were similar, it could not be said that they were identical. The earliest attempts to find a common framework to accommodate the two phenomena without dissolving them resorted to the familiar term "bonapartism." These attempts could claim the authority of Otto Bauer, who had argued as early as 1924 that the peculiarity of both the Soviet and Italian regimes was that they were dictatorships not *of* a class but *over* classes, like the political system founded by that earlier antiparliamentary adventurer Louis Napoleon Bonaparte. Such regimes, Bauer added wistfully, were necessarily only transitory phases in the development of the state.[11] Of course, the term bonapartism was already being used, especially by Mensheviks, to designate the Soviet regime alone. Perhaps because of this, but even more because of the shopworn flavor of the term, the search continued for a concept which which would capture the novelty and specificity of traits connecting communism with fascism.

A term which acquired increasing prominence in the course of this search was the neologism "totalitarian," and later "totalitarianism." Originating in Italian fascist doctrine, the adjective was used by Mussolini in 1924 and formalized by the Italian ideologue Giovanni Gentile. It appeared in English in 1928 to describe the fascist regime and in 1929 was first applied to the Bolshevik regime as well. Initially the term's origin as a self-interpretation of Italian fascism, picked up by German Nazi sympathizers such as Carl Schmitt, limited its extension among antifascists. Thus, German emigrés after 1933 were torn between their reluctance to apply the term to Hitler's regime, thus minimizing the horrors of Nazism by assimilating it to Mussolini's less brutal one, and their wish to underscore the universal—that is, not strictly German—character of the new German order.[12]

When socialists began to use the adjective "totalitarian," they did so in a relatively unself-conscious way. The term referred to the "total" nature of state power and, as a statement of fact, could be applied without controversy to both Russia and Germany. It was not Boris Sapir's checklist of the characteristics of the "total state"—étatization, destruction of opposition and independent social movements, use of force—that was controversial but rather his affirmation, influenced by a reading of Carl Schmitt, that the total state was neither good nor bad per se, and that the era of trade unions independent of the state was over.[13] Socialists acknowledged that the "total state" existed, but they were not prepared to welcome it.

By 1936 the term "totalitarian" was being used with reference to the Soviet dictatorship even by those left wing socialists widely considered uncritical of the Soviet Union, such as Dan and Bauer, as well as by Trotsky. Dan described the General Line as a third phase of the Bolshevik Revolution during which the dictatorship became ever more "totalitarian." Comparing this phase with Russia's Petrine era, Dan stated that "it was precisely its totalitarian character that allowed [the dictatorship] to carry out the historically indispensable task of economic reconstruction on such a grand scale and at so quick a pace." Bauer, reflecting on the various forms that the dictatorship of the proletariat could take, wrote that it could become "the 'totalitarian' dictatorship of a proletarian party, the dictatorship of a coercive party, state, and economic apparatus." Finally, Trotsky sprinkled the term throughout his indictment of the USSR as a "régime [which] had become 'totalitarian' in character several years before this word arrived from Germany."[14]

Notwithstanding such usage, neither the Mensheviks nor other socialists could be said to have formulated a theory of totalitarianism at this time.[15] The term appeared invariably as an adjective rather than as a noun, and sometimes even as an emphatic adverb, as in "totalitarian bonapartist dictatorship." Moreover, it was almost always enclosed in quotation marks, indicating some hesitation regarding its appropriateness. Above all, "totalitarian," when applied to the Soviet Union, consistently referred only to the political superstructure rather than to the all-important socioeconomic basis of the system.

It was not until 1940 that a prominent socialist unambiguously acknowledged the concept of totalitarianism as the most suitable framework for describing the essence of the Soviet system. This acknowledgment appeared in an article first published in *Sotsialisticheskii vestnik* by the most outstanding Marxist theorist alive, Rudolf Hilferding, under the title "State Capitalism or Totalitarian State Economy?"[16]

Formally, Hilferding was responding to the invitation of *Vestnik*'s editors to refute the argument that the USSR was state capitalist because, although private ownership had been abolished, the goals and methods of capitalist accumulation endured, and the Stalinist state bureaucracy was, functionally though not structurally, identical to a classic bourgeoisie.[17] Hilferding's rebuttal emphasized the differences between a capitalist or producers' economy governed by the autonomous laws of the market and a state-run or consumers' economy where prices and wages were simply the state's means of distributing social production. As sheer accumulation did not prove the existence of a capitalist economy, entrusting management of the economy to a bureaucracy did not make the bureaucracy into a capitalist ruling class. The bureaucracy possessed no class ties; its material benefits did not constitute an important proportion of the social product; and it did not enjoy an independent basis of power.

Hilferding's conclusion was that only Marxist "scholastics" would try to fit a new and original phenomenon such as the Soviet Union into the mutually exclusive categories of "capitalist" or "socialist." The overriding historical significance of the process undergone by Soviet Russia—and experienced also in countries where fascism had taken power—was that the economy had lost the primacy it enjoyed under capitalism. In Germany, Italy, or Russia politics governed economics. The state had freed itself of its economic and class base, with precedence in this process belonging to the Bolsheviks, who had "created the first totalitarian state—even before the name was invented."

Hilferding's article was the culmination of his own personal reappraisal and of prolonged debates among the Mensheviks concerning the nature of the Soviet Union. After his much-acclaimed *Finance Capital* in 1910, Hilferding had developed the notion of "organized capitalism," and, during the Weimar period, he believed that "organized capitalism" might represent a transitional stage toward socialism. The German catastrophe shattered such hopes. Henceforth, Hilferding focused on the total state as an instrument of nihilism and became increasingly wary of any statism at all. At the same time, he began to formulate doubts about the capacity of the proletariat to act as a historical subject and about the unilinearity of historical development.[18]

Hilferding, unlike Bauer or Kautsky, was not an expert on the USSR, but he was not indifferent to the course of events in Russia, any more than were other socialists. He therefore drew on Menshevik sources to satisfy his need for information, to keep abreast of theoretical debates concerning Russia, and to test his own views against lessons to be drawn from the Russian experience. A participant at an SPD congress in the 1920s recalls that when Hilferding entered the hall with his right-hand man and assistant editor of his journal, Iurii Denike, and with the brilliant young contributor Alexander Shifrin, delegates commented: "Das ist die Gesellschaft."[19] One wonders whether they realized that both these perfectly bicultural individuals were Russian Mensheviks.

Both Shifrin and Denike were highly critical of the old SPD. Shifrin, as one of the leading "young Turks" in the exiled SPD, called on the party to disown its reformist past. Denike, too, reproached the Germans for a lack of political will but counted among their sins an exaggerated reliance on class analysis and a disregard for spontaneous mass forces, "those shattered [social] elements which carried Lenin and Hitler to power and sealed the fate of both Russian and German social democracy."[20] By underlining the similarity of mistakes made in Russia in 1917 and in Germany in 1933, Denike was also underscoring the common traits of the ensuing regimes.

Outside his immediate entourage, on which he was even more dependent in the disorientation and isolation of exile, Hilferding could also turn to two other prominent Mensheviks. Grigorii Bienstock, as a radical leftist militant in the SPD Berlin organization but a right wing Menshevik, proved an ally for Hilferding in promoting a "Western orientation" within the exiled SPD.[21] Sharing an emphasis on the contrast between European values and the new Nazi barbarism, Hilferding could turn to Bienstock's identification of Nazi barbarism in the West with Bolshevik barbarism in the East to give ethical grounding to his theory of totalitarianism.

Finally, Hilferding maintained close contact with Boris Nicolaevsky. Privy to all party debates, Nicolaevsky, in his imperfect German, was best able to brief Hilferding on the evolution of the Mensheviks' discussions as they sought desperately to make sense of events in Russia. Nicolaevsky was not an impartial briefer, however. By the late 1930s he had lost patience with the Martov Line, and in the months preceding publication of Hilferding's article on totalitarianism, he was deeply at odds with Dan. It was in this context that Nicolaevsky wrote: "Hilf[erding] would be glad to write in our journal [*Sotsialisticheskii vestnik*], and the theme begs itself—a theoretical piece about state capitalism in connection with contemporary debates about fasco-Bolshevism."[22] One can surmise that Nicolaevsky not only persuaded Hilferding to enter the debate but even suggested the direction it might take.

Sotsialisticheskii vestnik published Hilferding's article in 1940 and included an editorial note stating that it would return to the questions raised. But historical events intervened. Within weeks Paris fell; the Menshevik group moved to America, and Hilferding, who had refused to emigrate, perished at the hands of the Gestapo. Years later *Vestnik,* now appearing in New York, sought to initiate a discussion of Hilferding's theme.[23] It reprinted his article, though without the opening lament on the fate of Marxism and without some of Hilferding's introductory comments. English and French versions appeared, owing to the efforts of *Vestnik*'s editors, making Hilferding's article a classic reference.[24]

By that time, fascist regimes had been destroyed and democratic socialists were no longer agonizing over what attitude to adopt toward the Soviet Union. Although the circumstances that gave rise to it had changed, the theory of totalitarianism remained the linchpin of the Menshevik interpretation of the USSR in the postwar world. Now, however, the Mensheviks were no longer isolated. In part because of their efforts, the theory of totalitarianism, once a novel response to the most pressing question of the day, had become political and academic dogma in the mainstream of Western thought.

Purges and Politics

Rarely was information from Soviet Russia as contradictory as in the 1930s. The specter of ever broadening purges collided with visions of constitutional reform and democratization: "Open terror and secret elections," as one Menshevik put it.[1] No longer was it possible to speak of the direction in which the Soviet Union was heading because it appeared to be heading in several directions simultaneously. By the end of the decade both purges and reforms had exhausted themselves, and only the figure of Stalin towered over the landscape as the focal point of reflection on the Soviet experience.

The issue of terror has dominated Western historiography of the 1930s. Spectacular trials, nightmarish purported plots, and a state deliberately turning on its founders have fascinated scholars, all the more so in the absence of reliable sources. Questions abound: Were the purges "engineered" by Stalin personally? If so, why? If Stalin did not initiate the purges, who, if anyone, did? Were they inscribed in the logic of the Soviet system, and might they have proceeded with only a minimum of conscious centralized direction? Can one even speak collectively of the purges, or were these distinct events rather than a single process? Was there a rationale to the purges, a logic whether of the victims or of the executioners? How did the purges affect Soviet society as a whole, rather than only those directly singled out?[2]

Such issues of agency, scope, and motivation also dominate the Menshevik treatment of the purges. Indeed, the Mensheviks contributed powerfully to the evolution of historiography, both as purveyors of raw information and as its interpreters. It is not (yet?) possible to confront Menshevik sources with all relevant archival data, and the rationale of the purges may continue to escape us even after the archives have been sifted. Nevertheless, one can examine the Menshevik record in terms of its internal consistency and the plausibility of its explanations.

The murder of Leningrad Communist Party chief Sergei Kirov on 1 December 1934 precipitated the purges. Bolsheviks and Mensheviks agree on this point inasmuch as the Kirov murder appears in successive trial indictments and is the centerpiece of the classic explanation of the purges contained in the "Letter of an Old Bolshevik." At the same time, prolonged debate has raged over the murder. The fantastic accusations and inventions of the show trials have been discredited, but the circumstances leading up to the murder have remained obscure.[3]

The "Letter of an Old Bolshevik" establishes an opposition between Stalin and Kirov over the issue whether Riutin, author of an oppositional "platform" in 1932, should be treated leniently, as Kirov suggested, or harshly, as Stalin wished. The "Letter" also cites Kirov's growing popularity within the party, at the Seventeenth Party Congress in February 1934, and among the population at large. It therefore establishes motives for Kirov's murder by Stalin but shies away from accusing him. It suggests, rather, that "Stalin did not directly oppose [Kirov's] line, but tried merely to limit the practical consequences arising from it," and that Kirov was not opposing Stalin but fighting for *"influence over Stalin,* a fight for his soul so to speak." One could even conclude from the "Letter" that Stalin had more to lose than to gain from Kirov's death.[4]

Sotsialisticheskii vestnik's reports in this period are a valuable supplement to the "Letter," inasmuch as they provide an account of events without any benefit of hindsight. These reports anticipate much of the "Letter's" account but diverge sufficiently from it to support the thesis that the "Letter" was based on new information from a non-Menshevik source.

Vestnik had noted Riutin's error—a rightist deviation on peasant policy—with sympathy and had described his disgrace in 1930 as "a new stage in inner party struggle." *Vestnik* was also the first to reveal the existence of the "Riutin Platform." Yet, the Menshevik account of the Seventeenth Party Congress identified only dimly those features which would later emerge as important. "This will be a historical congress but no one can tell us why it will be historic," complained a correspondent who emphasized the rising cult of Stalin and his popularity among rank-and-file Communists. *Vestnik* added cautiously that there seemed to be oppositional groups who felt that the Soviet Union had gone too far in accommodating bourgeois countries in foreign policy. There was no mention, however, of efforts to have Stalin replaced, by Kirov or others. Nor did *Vestnik*'s correspondents attach much significance to the information that in secret elections to the Central Committee the greatest number of votes went to Kalinin, with Stalin in third place.[5]

Contemporary discussion of Kirov in *Vestnik* corresponds to that in the "Letter of an Old Bolshevik," but on the most important issue it presents a curiously mirrorlike image. A year before Kirov's assassination *Vestnik* mentioned that some of Stalin's closest collaborators, including Kirov, had been put in their place for trying to maintain a certain independence vis-à-vis the dictator. In April 1934 a Menshevik correspondent identified two political lines, for and against easing the conditions of the peasantry. The former, represented by Kalinin, Voroshilov, and Molotov, was opposed by Kirov, as representative of proletarian Leningrad, with Kaganovich joining him after some hesitation. Stalin, as usual, remained neutral, though "informed people" claimed that Stalin's relations with Kaganovich had lately deteriorated and Stalin was very dissatisfied with Kirov's and Kaganovich's bravado. The Mensheviks had no reason to retract most of this information, but two and a half years later *Vestnik*'s "hard" Kirov was to be transformed into the "liberal" Kirov of the "Letter of an Old Bolshevik."[6]

On the eve of Kirov's murder, a Menshevik in Russia complained that life was so monotonous there was nothing to write about. The murder came out of the "clear blue sky," bringing this halcyon period to an abrupt end as, suddenly, "universal disarray and disbelief reigned."[7]

Vestnik's earliest speculation already contained the germ of all future hypotheses. The first Menshevik report after the murder described Kirov as a rising star who had been triumphantly applauded at the Seventeenth Congress and was on the point of moving to Moscow to replace Kaganovich as Stalin's closest collaborator. It mentioned the fact that a number of "Komsomol terrorists" given a light sentence the previous year had been executed in the wake of the Kirov murder. It did not refer, as the "Letter of an Old Bolshevik" did later, to the theory that the earlier lenient treatment of these "terrorists" had represented a victory of Kirov over Stalin. Evidence pointed, the report concluded, to the murder of Kirov as an episode in the dark backroom struggle among various Communist cliques. Simultaneously, a parallel report suggested that the murder was a personal act which Stalin then decided to exploit against the GPU. In any case, both accounts agreed that this was a "murky affair and it [was] doubtful whether we would ever learn the truth."[8]

The Mensheviks often had occasion to return to the question of Kirov's murder. They did not endorse Trotsky's immediate charges that the initiative could only have been Stalin's. Loath to make unprovable accusations, they long leaned toward the explanation that Stalin did not order the murder but exploited it for his own ends. This was implicit in their endorsement of the "Letter of an Old Bolshevik" in 1936–37 and in *Vestnik*'s quoting in 1939 one trial defendant who stated, "The murder of Kirov was our misfortune."[9]

In a private letter just after the murder, Boris Nicolaevsky expressed his suspicion that there had indeed been an "oppositional center" in Leningrad, though not a terrorist one, and that Stalin had decided to deal harshly with it as an example to others. Only in 1956 and, even more explicitly, in 1959 did Nicolaevsky point a finger directly at Stalin.[10] Nicolaevsky claimed that his new source was Khrushchev's revelations, but in fact Khrushchev, too, had stopped short of accusing Stalin. It is clear that Nicolaevsky's newfound certitude about Stalin's guilt was based not on new evidence but on a new vision of Stalin.

Whatever the truth about Kirov's murder, at the time the Mensheviks were more concerned about its consequences than about its causes. They were shaken by the murder itself, devoting to it a whole issue of *Sotsialisticheskii vestnik* and publishing an official statement of the Foreign Delegation in the international socialist press. Here they reiterated their long-standing condemnation of terrorist acts and pointed out that the murderer Nikolaev was a Communist Party member. In contrast to the "Red Terror" of earlier days, which could be explained, though not justified, by dangers to the regime, terror was now being employed for the first time against Bolsheviks in an effort to paralyze the protests spreading through the ranks of the ruling party. The ultimate tragedy of the terror, however, was that it laid the groundwork for counterrevolution in Russia and thus weakened the international struggle against fascism.[11]

Even more appalling than the murder were the ensuing reprisals, often against people already under arrest. Hopes expressed in early 1935 that this was the last outburst of terror proved unfounded as the Mensheviks recorded new waves in December 1935 and again in May 1936. As in the past, the

Mensheviks' measure of terror was the treatment of their comrades, now arrested not for illegal work but merely for "a harmful Menshevik attitude." Anticipating the worst, the Foreign Delegation launched a vigorous but unsuccessful international campaign to free Foreign Delegation member Eva Broido, a grandmother with forty years of revolutionary work to her credit, imprisoned and then banished to Siberia since her illegal return to Russia in 1927.[12]

In Russia, terror came as a shock to some and, initially, as a matter of indifference to others. Fear first struck at the top. "The old [guard] is dying, by natural or political death," *Vestnik* reported, and noted bemusedly that Stalin had become an absolute obsession with Old Bolsheviks. For them Stalin was the incarnation of evil, the central Russian, nay, world problem, and the question "Whither Stalin?" absorbed them more than any policy issue. At the same time, terror coincided with an easing of material conditions. Stalin's popularity in the countryside was growing, and complaints were directed at local authorities rather than at him. These sentiments were not necessarily shared by city dwellers, who felt unprotected after the abolition of ration coupons. Nevertheless, a deep gulf separated the panic-stricken upper strata from the masses, calmer and better fed than they had been for a long time and utterly absorbed in everyday matters.[13]

Only gradually were ordinary people drawn into the vortex. They were unruffled by the condemnation of Zinoviev and Kamenev in August 1936, perhaps, speculated *Vestnik*, because of the odiousness of these victims. After the Piatakov-Radek trial in early 1937 people talked, but they hardly seemed surprised. "They are all like that" and "We wouldn't put it past these no-goods" was the general reaction. By April 1937, however, following Stalin's call for intensified struggle against "enemies of the people," *Vestnik* announced that "the dikes are open." No longer did the regime require people just to be "good tractor drivers." Now they were required to participate in one political meeting after another; underlings who told all they knew about their bosses were heroes. Denunciations spread as petty intrigue and settling of personal accounts prevailed.[14]

The Mensheviks could only protest some of the blatant anti-Menshevik absurdities in official Soviet tales and seek out any possible propaganda advantages from the trials. They and others noted analogies with the 1931 Menshevik trial.[15] At the Piatakov-Radek trial the prosecution invoked a fictitious voyage just as clumsily as it had in 1931 with Abramovitch. At the Bukharin trial the portrayal of Dan as a German police spy fell flat.[16] Abramovitch may have been optimistic in stating, in September 1936, that the "shootings in Moscow [of Kamenev and Zinoviev]" had reversed pro-Soviet

Western attitudes dictated by Soviet economic success and the search for allies against Hitler. He was correct in anticipating, however, that Western public opinion would wonder at the "naïveté of these stories where the Gestapo proposes to escaped Jewish Communists in the first few minutes of their meeting to shoot Voroshilov."[17]

Even lies need to be explained, and behind the fantasies and falsifications of the trials, the Mensheviks sought a logic and a motive. Their explanations can be described as either "political" or "psychological," with the latter, founded on a premise of irrationality, gradually edging out the former.

Political explanations of the trials assume that there did indeed exist an opposition to Stalin and even to the regime. All Mensheviks accepted this assumption as factual. After all, their own party network in Russia had been destroyed by 1931, but its members were, for the most part, still alive, and thus the potential for re-creating an organization existed. Internecine opposition among the Bolsheviks was an uncontested fact. In commenting on the Sixteenth Party Congress in 1930 which seemed to mark a reconciliation between the Stalinist leadership and the defeated opposition, *Vestnik* wrote that "Stalin [was] perfectly right not to believe in the appearance of formal contrition. At every new campaign and difficulty the opposition [would] raise its head." It added that "the only unity in the party was that of forced silence." Three years later a correspondent confirmed that although there were no organized oppositional Communist groupings, the policies of the Bolshevik leadership were opening the party to factionalism, leading to the formation of other parties.[18]

The Mensheviks were prepared to accept that the trials revolved, in one way or another, around Trotsky. They even agreed that Trotsky *should* be at the center of the trials. "We are convinced that the Soviet Government is right in defending itself against Trotzkyism," declared Solomon Schwarz in a widely published piece. Trotskyism was pernicious, the Mensheviks explained, because it was seeking to provoke a war in order to set off a new, antibureaucratic revolution in the USSR. Such criminal adventurism deserved to be combated. The Mensheviks conceded that Trotsky would not compromise himself by carrying on a campaign of terror, as alleged in the trials, but at no point did they lend full credence to his protestations of noninvolvement.[19]

Lurking opposition and Trotskyist adventurism might not be admitted by all as sufficient explanation for purges and trials. Few people could deny, however, that there were good reasons for Stalin to be fearful. The danger of war hung over all reports coming out of the Soviet Union in these years of Nazi ascendancy, Japanese expansion, and the collapse of collective security. To those who sought to explain the purges rationally, the realignments of Soviet foreign policy between a pro-German and an anti-German line could explain at least the purge of Marshal Tukhachevskii and seven other generals in June 1937.[20]

Such utilitarian explanations were plausible but incapable of accounting for the self-destructive character of the purges, the outrageous accusations, and the incredible confessions. "Is it really true that the Soviet Union cannot live anymore without morphine injections or is it Stalin's need for revenge?" wrote Abramovitch to Kautsky in 1937. The hypothesis of the "permanent purge" as a systemic feature of Soviet reality had been proposed earlier.[21] It was now elaborated in terms of Stalin's need to eliminate all potential opponents including Old Bolsheviks, especially those mentioned in Lenin's "Testament." As the "ground disappeared under his feet," Stalin's carnage became ever broader, and the Mensheviks predicted that the purges would only continue.[22] Nor could the Mensheviks take any comfort in the purges: even if Stalin "broke his own neck," the struggle of one clique against another could not lead to anything but counterrevolution since the democratic liquidation of the dictatorship could arise only on the basis of a mass movement.[23]

References to Stalin's mental makeup as an explanation for the purges came late. Interestingly, the focus on Stalin's psychology originated not among the Mensheviks but in Bolshevik sources such as the Riutin Platform and the "Letter of an Old Bolshevik," as well as in the monumental biography of Stalin by former Bolshevik Boris Souvarine. Although their emphasis on Stalin's person increased with time, leading Mensheviks never adopted the thesis, promoted by others, that Stalin was mad. Boris Nicolaevsky, who had contributed to it by publishing the "Letter," steadfastedly insisted to the very end that Stalin was rational on his own terms.[24]

Whatever the imperatives of the Soviet system and of Stalin's psychology, they alone could not explain the abject confessions of the purge victims. Drawing on the experience of the Menshevik trial, Abramovitch suggested that such confessions were inspired by the victims' conviction that the interests of the Soviet Union required confession, and that sentences imposed would not be carried out. Subsequent events reinforced this theory, at least in part: "It is harder to understand false events and real death sentences than fictitious events and fictitious death sentences," reflected Abramovitch, as executions of the most prominent and most contrite Old Bolsheviks multiplied. Still, the underlying Menshevik thesis that confessions were not extorted but, in a peculiar sense, voluntary was well established by the time Arthur Koestler immortalized it in fiction.[25]

A less generous variant of the "last service to the party" thesis held that Old Bolsheviks had been so compromised by their subordination to the party and their fulfillment of Stalin's commands that they had no moral basis for opposing Stalin now. "Having lost their way in the labyrinth of lies, they could only continue the lie to the end," wrote a Greek journalist in *Sotsialis-ticheskii vestnik*. There was no lack of other theories, including the fanciful one that ex-Menshevik Andrei Vyshinskii stage-managed the Moscow trials as the Mensheviks' revenge against the Bolsheviks, or as a betrayal of the Bolsheviks in atonement for his earlier betrayal of the Mensheviks.[26]

At one point the horrors of the purges intersected with hopes raised by the new constitution, promulgated after lengthy preparation on 5 December 1936. A Menshevik correspondent in Russia suggested that repression was a prophylactic measure against those who would use the forthcoming constitution for anti-Soviet purposes. An alternative version maintained that Stalin had announced a new constitution under the illusion that he was becoming genuinely popular. The ensuing flurry of activity frightened him, provoking new repression.[27] Even democratization was thus inseparable from terror.

Nonetheless, the new constitution aroused deep and contradictory reactions among the Mensheviks. Why was Stalin introducing a new constitution? Was it to gain the favor of the peasantry? To create better preconditions for a united international front against fascism? Or perhaps to replace the support of the party, which Stalin was destroying, with popular support? Whatever the doubts about Stalin's reasons, Dan confided to Bauer that "the planned constitutional reform is to go much further than originally intended; the question of 'legalizing' certain parties is being considered." The following year a correspondent in Russia reported "talk of an amnesty project . . . Some Communists say there will soon be authentic democracy. Soviet power is so strong it can tolerate even Trotskyists."[28]

The Mensheviks tried hard, if not always successfully, to remain sober about the prospects for democratization. They insisted that they were not suffering from "constitutional illusions" regarding "self-liquidation" of the dictatorship. Rather, they saw the constitution as opening up opportunities which could be exploited in the struggle for democratization. Not surprisingly, it was Dan and the left wing Mensheviks who were the most optimistic.[29]

In a historical overview Dan defined the new constitution as the culmination of the historical process launched in 1917. The February Revolution had awakened the colossal revolutionary energy of the masses, and war communism had given free rein to this destructive strength. Inasmuch as NEP marked the exhaustion of the masses, the previous constitution of 1923 was the echo of a past revolutionary era. Driven forward by its own contradictions, the regime had embarked on the General Line using its totalitarian power to transform the country with vertiginous speed. Any political ambitions among technocratic beneficiaries of the General Line having been repressed, the transformation process was entering its final phase. The regime was now seeking to stabilize, by means of the constitution, emerging social relations and to draw appropriate political conclusions.[30]

Significantly, the Menshevik Right also expressed hopes regarding the constitution. Petr Garvi noted with satisfaction that it represented a move away from a workers' state to one based on equality. It eliminated the political privileges of the proletariat, raised the status of the intelligentsia, and legalized the private plots of the *kolkhozniks*. Moreover, in replacing indirect and open soviet elections with direct secret voting, the constitution marked a step toward a parliamentary regime. Ominously, however, article 126 of the constitution forbade opposition to Communist power. As in 1905, wrote Garvi of the regime, "they have given us a constitution; they have kept the dictatorship." Still, he concluded, the possibility was not to be excluded that the constitution would unleash powerful new political forces.[31]

Whatever the future of the constitution, the Mensheviks had to take a position with respect to it. In reply to those who rejoiced that it created new conditions for struggle, Abramovitch, ever mindful of Western socialist opinion, advised caution. "In the West this could be considered a declaration of war," he warned privately. "The Soviet government puts out a constitution which, as it happens, has many good sides. What do the Mensheviks do? They use it as a platform for a workers' struggle against the Soviet government." This remark would give credence to Soviet accusations that the Mensheviks wanted legality uniquely for subversive purposes.[32]

After much discussion, the Foreign Delegation put out a carefully worded declaration addressed to the Congress of Soviets. Recalling the common origins of bolshevism and menshevism, it stated that the RSDRP considered the "October overthrow" a historical inevitability conditioned by war and arising out of the mood of the peasant-worker masses. The Menshevik Party viewed the terrorist dictatorship that had outlived the Civil War as the greatest danger to the Revolution. In spite of persecution, the Mensheviks had continued to struggle for democratization of the Soviet regime, a goal now shared by all Soviet society. While welcoming the constitutional developments, the Foreign Delegation pointed to deep contradictions. Even as democratization was proclaimed, party dictatorship was being replaced with personal dictatorship, and terror was proceeding unabated. Moreover, the constitutional project failed to grant any collective right to organize, even as it guaranteed individual rights. The RSDRP asked for nothing for itself. It put all its hopes in the constitution's galvanization of the "self-activity" of the masses, as only this could save the Revolution and complete the durable socialist transformation of the Soviet Union. "Long live the free self-activity and organization of the toilers! Long live socialism!" concluded the declaration.[33]

Even the faintest Menshevik hopes regarding the constitution were soon dashed. Terror continued, and elections proved to be plebiscites in favor of Stalin. In one respect, however, the Menshevik analysis turned out to be well founded: proclamation of the constitution coincided with the crystallization of a new Soviet society. With the exception of a dwindling number of left wing optimists, most Mensheviks viewed this new society with dismay.[34] A broad stratum of technicians and organizers was asserting itself over those who were formerly privileged. As the party bureaucracy was decimated, a new nonparty state bureaucracy took its place. This Soviet aristocracy of "responsible people" was characterized by smugness and adulation of Stalin. It had no ties to the Revolution; if it looked to the past, it was to imitate the old bourgeoisie, whether in its Russian nationalist values, its treatment of women as "baby-producing machines," or its taste for hunting. As Communists met for their Eighteenth Party Congress in 1939, *Vestnik* commented: "This is . . . the congress of a new party which should be called Stalinist."[35]

Nostalgia for the old Bolshevik Party, for the party of Lenin, and perhaps even for the party of Trotsky, filters into Menshevik analyses of Soviet developments from the late 1930s on. "Lenin's party with all its authoritarian principles was still a link in the revolutionary chain. This [CPSU in 1939] is nothing but an obedient, bureaucratic, antipopular apparatus in the hands of the autocrat of the party and country," lamented *Vestnik*. When the Liubianka (security police) shot the Kremlin (the party), the game was over, added Nicolaevsky in 1940, implying that he had no faith in the former but had never entirely abandoned hope in the latter.[36]

One might conclude that the Mensheviks were fundamentally unable to understand Stalin and his Russia. Although they remained better informed than most other observers, owing to diligent exploitation of whatever sources came their way, they could not re-create their empathy with earlier Soviet leaderships, and Stalin remained a mystery to them. Later, they would come to speculate on his personal traits: absolute amorality (as opposed to Lenin's theoretical amorality), great instinct, animal cunning, iron will, insolent courage, a talent for games of chance combined with the skills of a political chess master. Or they would resort to metaphor, describing Stalin as "the mathematical point of leverage of the General Line" before dubbing him

"Genghis Khan with an atomic bomb."[37] In the final analysis, Stalin's Russia transcended not only the Mensheviks' understanding but even their imagination.

Search for Unity

Although the Mensheviks were powerless to affect the course of events within Soviet Russia, their international role increased in the years 1934–1936. As fascism strengthened and the danger of war grew, Western democracies and the USSR inched warily toward each other. Key actors in this rapprochement were the LSI and the Comintern, as well as Communist and socialist parties, particularly in France. The RSDRP Foreign Delegation found itself at the heart of this process, and not only because of its close ties to French socialist leaders and its prominence in the LSI. The search for allies against fascism rekindled hopes of overcoming twenty years of division within the working class and put the Russian Question on the agenda with new urgency. In the ensuing debate, socialists of all persuasions turned to the Mensheviks to legitimize their own positions. Among the Mensheviks themselves, the debate revealed the extent of their own division.

The German events that had driven the Mensheviks to Paris also precipitated a crisis in the French Socialist Party (SFIO).[1] It pitched the left majority, which shunned alliance with bourgeois parties, against the right minority, favorable to cooperation with the Radical Party. Both sides appealed to the lessons of the German debacle, and within a year coalition options were to change so dramatically that factional positions had become reversed. Fedor Dan, with more immediate experience of German events than any French socialist, unhesitatingly aligned himself with the French socialist Left, maintaining that compromises with bourgeois forces had undermined German social democracy. Above all, however, he expressed concern about the gulf between the right-oriented French party leadership and its left-oriented membership.[2]

The rise of proto-fascist forces in France in early 1934 accelerated the French socialist opening to the Left. Coinciding with a reorientation in Soviet foreign policy and unprecedented Communist offers of cooperation, the question of an antifascist united front emerged as the only item on the agenda of the SFIO national conference in July 1934. As invited guests at the conference, Dan and Abramovitch sat on the podium while one of the French Left's leaders, Jean Zyromsky, made an impassioned plea for alliance with the Communists. The Menshevik guests were applauded as they nodded assent to Zyromsky's assertion that "noble Russian socialists" were giving up any claim to have negotiations with Communists include the question of their imprisoned comrades in the USSR. "Who has given them [Dan and Abramovitch] a political and moral mandate to free French socialists from their duties?" fumed Stepan Ivanovich.[3] The deed was done, however, and the SFIO conference delegates who voted overwhelmingly in favor of alliance did so with a clear conscience, knowing that Russian comrades who had most reason to oppose such an alliance had endorsed it.

Within days, the Mensheviks' readiness to place international proletarian unity above other interests found a resounding echo from the USSR. The French socialist press and, a day later, the French Communist Party published a telegram from three prominent Mensheviks living in internal exile in Kazan. "We hail with joy the united front pact," ran the message, concluding with a ringing, "Long live mutual understanding between socialists and Communists throughout the world! Long live unity in action and fighting! Long live socialism!"[4]

No one doubted the authenticity of the telegram or the credibility of its signatories: B. N. Ber-Gurevich was a long-standing member of the Menshevik Central Committee; S. O. Ezhov and K. I. Zakharova were Martov's brother and sister-in-law. All three had once belonged to the extreme Menshevik Left, but their party credentials were unimpeachable, and their views appeared to reflect those of other Mensheviks in Russia as well.[5] Whatever questions were raised abroad concerned not the signatories but rather the Soviets' motives in allowing the telegram to reach Paris. As *Vestnik* pointed out, the last Menshevik political statement to come openly out of Soviet Russia dated to 1921, when the RSDRP Central Committee had issued an appeal for famine relief.[6]

If the Soviet purpose in authorizing the Kazan telegram was to solidify the French pact, its immediate effect was to unleash a polemic between the Communist *Humanité* and the socialist *Populaire*. Both approved the message, but they could not agree on much more. *Humanité* saw in it the signatories' admission of their earlier "tragic errors." Léon Blum in *Le Populaire* refuted Communist allusions to Menshevik counterrevolutionary attitudes in 1918 and to the Menshevik trial of 1931. He also put his new Communist allies on guard against believing that socialists would now cease to criticize the Soviet dictatorship.[7]

Exiled Mensheviks of all tendencies were moved and excited by this "voice of menshevism out of the USSR," as *Vestnik* titled the telegram, although Nicolaevsky probably exaggerated in writing that "some of our people are packing their trunks [to return home]."[8] In fact, the Mensheviks' evaluations differed according to political tendencies. Dan's official response expressed deep pride that sufferings long endured by the Kazan signatories had not driven them into political indifference or led them to abandon their ideals. Extrapolating somewhat freely, he declared that the Kazan socialists were in full agreement with the party abroad. They too saw the world as standing before the choice of war and fascism or revolutionary socialism. They too saw that the condition of victory in this decisive struggle against fascism was proletarian unity worldwide, including the Soviet Union. Dan insisted that Russian socialists were not "sacrificing" themselves for the common good but participating in a common effort. He recalled Martov's concept of "agreement," meaning that the RSDRP did not seek hegemony for its ideas but only required the possibility of influencing the course of the Revolution. Dan did wonder whether the Kazan telegram was a Communist maneuver, but even if it was one, he vowed that the socialists would continue to work for unity.[9]

Raphael Abramovitch showed more reserve. The Kazan telegram was undoubtedly the most significant event in party life of the last several years, he declared, though he did not share the optimism of the Kazan comrades, and he did not care to inquire into Communist motives behind the telegram. Moreover, a united front was only a surrogate for true unity. Nevertheless, Abramovitch was convinced that Russian socialists must not put obstacles in the path of unity. This was not an admission of impotence but a moral and political injunction. "Imagine," he wrote, "that such a proposition [in favor of unity] had been made in Germany in early 1933 and we had said no."[10]

Turning to rightist critics who reproached him for his "nod" at the SFIO national conference, Abramovitch emphasized that the French pact implied only that the condition of socialists in the USSR would not be a *preliminary* condition for a united front. Counterattacking, he questioned the good faith of French opponents of the pact who had shown little concern for terror in Russia earlier, and who were now bringing up the issue because they lacked better arguments. As proof of the immediate benefits of the pact for the RSDRP, Abramovitch cited the polemic in the French press that had obliged French socialists to refute Communist calumnies and to reiterate their solidarity with Russian comrades.

Notwithstanding his strident tone, Abramovitch was more sensitive to criticism of the party's policy than was Dan. Both considered the possibility that Communist cooperation was merely an "export product" and emphasized that the only true united front comprised the Soviet Union. Whereas Dan reacted rapturously, however, as if the pact were a *mariage d'amour*, Abramovitch approached it more guardedly, as befitted a *mariage de raison*.[11]

A discussion article in the next issue of *Vestnik* presented the point of view of the Menshevik Right. It was unfortunate, wrote Petr Garvi, that the Kazan comrades had been depicted as the voice of Russian socialism. Given their situation as prisoners of Soviet power, incapable of communicating openly with their own party, and lacking any guarantees that their gesture would not be distorted and exploited, the Kazan trio would have been well advised to restrain their natural impulse to intervene in this question. Of course, socialists everywhere shared the fear of fascism, and there was a spontaneous, often uncontrollable mass drive to unity in countries that were directly threated, such as France. Nevertheless, Dan's alternative, "fascism and war or revolutionary socialism," was simply false. It excluded the possibility of democratic development, whether in countries that were still democractic or in those under fascist influence. "The Marxist palette should have all colors," wrote Garvi, "not merely black and white."[12]

Appealing to the authority of a party father, Garvi recalled the late Pavel Axelrod's guidelines from 1922: in the search for unity it was necessary to have a common understanding of both goals and means, as well as a sincere desire to work together to attain these goals. Such minimal common ground was now lacking as the Communists strove to replace the prospect of fascist dictatorship with their own dictatorship. According to Axelrod, a united front with the Comintern meant a union of socialists with a government that mercilessly persecuted proponents of liberty, democracy, and socialist thought. Nothing had changed in this regard since 1922, declared Garvi. By now treating the united front as a goal in itself rather than a means toward a goal, socialists were choosing not to look at the essence of the Russian Question. This was not merely the matter of imprisoned Russian socialists or the problem of whether socialists should set "preliminary conditions" for negotiation. The fundamental issue was the contradiction between cooperation in the West and repression in the Soviet Union. By ignoring this contradiction, socialists were tacitly sanctioning the Bolshevik experiment as a whole.

In October 1934 French Communist leaders acting in the name of the Comintern addressed an invitation to the LSI Executive to undertake discussions concerning a common campaign on behalf of Spanish miners. The ensuing Brussels meeting proved fruitless. The will to unity at both the grassroots level and the level of some national parties continued unabated, but the movement toward an international united front bore no fruit. Neither the Ethiopian conflict nor even the Spanish civil war, which provided an occasion for exchanges between the two Internationals, brought about the desired result. As division continued, controversy over unity persisted, on the international as well as on the Russian level. The Menshevik debates echoed, in even more passionate form, the discussions raging in other socialist parties.[13]

Abramovitch, the main (and often sole) Russian member in the governing bodies of the LSI, was most heavily engaged in the debate over unity.[14] Copious notes from LSI meetings attest that he followed every twist and turn in this process. He brought to the debate a restless activism, a taste for tactics, and a growing personal ambivalence regarding the prospects for unity.

At the outset Abramovitch urged boldness: "If your house is burning, you have to jump out of the window when there is no other way." This advice against SPD passivity in 1933 applied to jumping into negotiations with the Comintern as well. He agreed with skeptics such as Kautsky that there was no reason to trust the Communists. The question, however, was whether self-interest would drive them to behave "more decently." The only way to find out would be to open full-scale negotiations between the two Internationals. This, too, was the only way to put the Russian Question on the table, since piecemeal negotiations precluded raising general issues. Abramovitch's tactical approach to the question was exemplified by his proposal (vetoed by his own party) that the LSI send a delegation including Mensheviks to Moscow. He confirmed this tactical approach in remarking privately on one of the innumerable breakdowns in negotiations with the Comintern: "Too bad . . . It was a brilliant opportunity to press the Bolsheviks against the wall on the question of terror."[15]

In exasperation, Abramovitch urged Western socialist leaders to answer Soviet press attacks: "Sure, a prolonged polemic may diminish the chances of an agreement between the two Internationals that seems to me the only means of saving the world and the Russian Revolution, but proletarian unity . . . cannot be realized by equivocation and sleight of hand." Bitterly he added: "Bolsheviks only understand and respect force, moral as well as material. 'How many battalions do they have?' was Lenin's first question in November 1917 when Kamenev and others insisted on an agreement with Mensheviks and other socialists."[16]

Abramovitch stated his views formally in the leading journal of the German socialist emigration. Working-class unity, he wrote, could only be the result of a long process. Certainly, unity of action was possible at any moment, and could be profitable, as French experience showed, but it created the risk of raising false hopes. The real obstacle to unity lay in fundamental attitudes toward the proletariat and the proletarian party, differences as fundamental as those between democracy and dictatorship. The Communists seemed to be aware of these differences. They supported moves toward unity only to the extent that these coincided with Soviet foreign policy interests, and they rejected any merger of parties. If the issue was only that of repelling fascism, then a broad popular front, encompassing nonproletarian forces, would suffice. If socialists preferred to work for proletarian unity, however, they would have to ask some hard questions: Were they prepared to endorse the Soviet system, whether in its entirety or with some reservations? Would they wish to reproduce it at home? It was not possible, concluded Abramovitch, to be for democracy at home but for terror in Russia, and the defense of democracy required criticism of the Soviet Union.[17]

Abramovitch's disillusion was no doubt exacerbated by the feeling that some Western comrades considered the Mensheviks an embarrasment in the search for unity. Completely devoted to the International, he chafed at the fact that its organ, *International Information,* called on foreigners such as Bauer and Adler to comment on Russian matters.[18] Gradually, perhaps imperceptibly, Abramovitch was moving toward an anti-unity position.

Another prominent Menshevik who found himself in the anti-unity camp was Boris Nicolaevsky. "Both [Dan and Abramovitch] have gone out of their mind," he grumbled, attributing to his party leaders a belief in a new era of social revolution. According to Nicolaevsky, Dan's radicalism was just a desire "to die a beautiful death," and he was making a fool of himself in the LSI. The French socialist party's move left was one of suicidal capitulation. Nicolaevsky's own answer to fascism was simple: a French-led war against Germany. This option had been discussed and rejected at the LSI Paris Conference in August 1933.[19] Nicolaevsky, however, persisted in his belief and its implication that socialists should ally with any bourgeois party or any state willing to fight fascism.

The anti-unity Menshevik Right, initially a weak minority, thus gained two prominent Foreign Delegation members as allies. By late 1935 Nicolaevsky, Abramovitch, and the Menshevik Right were making comon cause within the delegation and, by 1939, were close enough to present a common platform to the LSI. They insisted on the absolute primacy of democracy, arguing that belief in the transitory character of dictatorship and its spontaneous evolution toward democracy had proved to be an illusion. Experience had discredited the term "dictatorship of the proletariat"; it had lost its original Marxist meaning and now referred only to Russian dictatorship and Stalinist terror. Of course, complete democracy could only be based on socialism, but the error of the working class was to underestimate the value of democracy itself.

The common platform was a plea for socialism to pay attention to the middle classes. In contrast to the slow growth of the proletariat under contemporary capitalism, the social weight of the "middle classes" was increasing. Especially in countries where fascism had triumphed or was on the point of triumphing, the working class had allowed itself to be seduced by the desire for vengeance against the bourgeoisie. Such fascist manipulation (as well as alignment with Communists, argued the platform implicitly) had isolated the proletariat. The task now was to create the broadest-based front possible, whether including peasants as in Scandinavia, bourgeois radicals as in France, or intellectuals and other intermediate social strata as in other countries. After the debacle at Munich there could be no more concessions to totalitarian countries. In the forthcoming war the victory of the antifascist bloc had to be ensured at any price, even that of integrating the most heterogeneous elements.[20]

This platform collided directly with the leftist position of Fedor Dan, and indeed was formulated in opposition to him.[21] In 1933 Dan described the international situation as the result of capitalist class domination that had led humanity into ever deeper misery. The only solution was to orient all the LSI's efforts toward the seizure of political power by the proletariat, and it was unlikely that this could be done peacefully.[22] Of course, Dan stood for democracy, but he insisted that although socialism was unthinkable without democracy, at present democracy could not exist without socialism. Mankind faced the stark choice: socialism or fascism.

All Mensheviks agreed that the most pressing problem was that of war, but it was over this issue that the split in the Foreign Delegation came into the open. Debate began when Dan expressed his views in a controversial international document, L'Internationale et la guerre. Dan and his coauthors declared that military defeat of fascist Germany would unleash proletarian revolution there, whereas defeat of the Soviet Union would hand that country over to bloody counterrevolution. Unlike the situation in 1914, when two imperialist coalitions had faced each other and imposed neutrality on socialists, now international socialism had to take sides. Notwithstanding various concessions to socialist tradition, L'Internationale et la guerre marked a radical break with socialist pacifism. Socialists were urged not only to take sides but to take up arms as well.[23]

An unconditionally defensist attitude toward the Soviet Union and an alliance with capitalist powers were fraught with dangers, admitted Dan and his coauthors. Under pressure from its bourgeois allies, Moscow might dissimulate or even eradicate the proletarian revolutionary character of its policies and foster bonapartism. Moreover, there was a profound contradiction between capitalist and socialist war aims: the former sought to dismember, subject, and exploit Germany; the latter aimed at unleashing the proletarian revolution there. There was no doubt that as Soviet victories multiplied, its bourgeois allies would come to fear Moscow more than their common enemy. As the German revolution gathered strength, bourgeois states would undertake counterrevolutionary intervention, even more energetically than in the aftermath of World War I.

How should socialists proceed in case of war? asked *L'Internationale et la guerre*. Everywhere they should collaborate unconditionally with Communist parties. In Russia they should subordinate all interests to that of victory. In allied countries they should not shirk national defense but transform it into a "revolutionary jacobin" defense. If the proletarian revolution succeeded in Germany before the working class had seized power in allied countries, the Soviet Union should break its alliance and immediately conclude a separate peace fully supported by all socialist parties. In any case, socialists had no interest in concealing the fact that their immediate aim everywhere, even in countries where struggle was normally waged by peaceful means, was the conquest of power and the overthrow of capitalism.

L'Internationale et la guerre was an attempt to define a coherent socialist position in the face of a growing war threat. Its purpose was, above all, to avoid a repetition of the trauma of 1914, when the International had been taken by surprise and immobilized. Moreover, the authors even expressed the paradoxical hope that the bellicose tone of their theses would make adversaries hesitate before embarking on war. Dan, in particular, was moved to dismay by the shortsightedness even of those socialist leaders whom he respected. "Blum told me he is not interested in the question of 'War and the International' since he does not believe in a war and, in any case, nothing can be done about it," Dan wrote to Adler in July 1935. Moreover, he complained, Blum was inconsistent in calling both for defense of Soviet Russia and for disarmament.[24]

Dan, too, was not entirely consistent. As Adler pointed out, he was indulging in self-deception by imagining that war could be waged with *Burgfrieden* practice but without *Burgfrieden* ideology, in other words, that a policy of class conciliation could be applied without any theoretical concessions to conciliation. In fact, although Dan claimed to be the original motor force behind *L'Internationale et la guerre*, Otto Bauer was its main and most radical author. Dan insisted that the document put more emphasis on the revolutionary possibilities inherent in the working classes of the advanced countries rather than on the revolutionary possibilities of the Soviet Union. He also urged that the socialist attitude toward the war be defined "not by the 'democratic' or 'nondemocratic' character of the warring governments but by the revolutionary possibilities of the war against Hitler's Germany."[25] That is, he saw the socialists' most important and most reliable allies not in Moscow but among the workers of western Europe.

Although Bauer accepted a number of these amendments, Dan continued to express reservations, particularly with regard to Bauer's belief in "the unequivocal socialist perspectives" of the Soviet Union.[26] Indeed, their disagreement was such that Bauer turned down Dan's proposal to work out a common set of theses on proletarian unity. It was their common stance on war, however, that led to Dan's eventual loss of leadership within the Foreign Delegation.

In late 1935 the exiled Mensheviks discussed several drafts of a platform on the issue of war. Eventually it was Dan's proposal that obtained a one-vote majority against the proposals of the Right formulated by Aronson, of the rightist pacifist Garvi, and of the extreme Left represented by Domanevskaia. Nicolaevsky, fulminating against Bolsheviks and "vegetarians" (that is, pacifists), joined the Right, as did Abramovitch, who could not bring himself to endorse Bauer's views on the Soviet Union. In fact, all competing drafts (except Garvi's) stressed their points of convergence, so much so that Abramovitch even hoped to obtain a compromise formulation.[27]

Years later, Abramovitch maintained that it was at this point that the "real division of our group took place." Returning to a metaphor already invoked in 1922, he wrote that the Mensheviks had confused the ninth month of pregnancy with the first month. On might conclude from this that one could not invalidate a policy because later events proved it to be ill founded. This, however, was not the conclusion Abramovitch drew. As he later saw it, division within the party, implicit from the outset, had worked itself to the surface by 1935. It could hardly be otherwise because at issue were two incompatible views of the Soviet Union and of the relation between democracy and socialism.[28]

Division and Defeat

In 1940 the Mensheviks were forced to flee Europe for the United States. Their world collapsed, however, even before the fall of France, and perhaps even before the outbreak of war. The Labor and Socialist International faded away with barely a whimper in the course of 1939–40. The fragile unity of the RSDRP organization disintegrated in early 1940 amid recriminations. The two institutional pillars on which Russian social democracy in exile rested thus disappeared almost simultaneously, though *Sotsialisticheskii vestnik* and the Menshevik family survived to embark on their last exile.

It was the evolution of Raphael Abramovitch's views from left to right that eventually tipped the balance within the Foreign Delegation against the Martov Line and its diehard supporters led by Fedor Dan. Abramovitch's reservations concerning his own party's policies began with the discussion over socialist construction in the Soviet Union in the early 1930s. For a time Abramovitch and Dan both sparred against Otto Bauer rather than against each other. Only in 1935, with the publication of Bauer's and Dan's *Internationale et la guerre,* did Abramovitch explicitly demarcate himself from Dan. Even then he sought, unsuccessfully, a compromise which would spare any appearance of rift.

There were solid political reasons for disagreement between Abramovitch and Dan, but personal rivalry also crept in. Both claimed the right to speak on behalf of the party in the councils of the LSI, Dan as party chairman and Abramovitch as RSDRP representative. So long as there was no fundamental disagreement, the matter was merely one of division of labor. In 1933, however, as their rift deepened, Dan imposed a system of rotating representation whereby he and Abramovitch took turns at attending LSI meetings. Abramovitch smarted at being partially removed from the position in which he had excelled.[1] His subordinate status was underscored when Dan forbade him to circulate within the LSI Executive a personal memorandum critical of the RSDRP's resolution on the issue of war.[2]

A comrade who dismissed Abramovitch as "a great conservative, precisely where one should be conservative least of all, in the domain of thought," missed the essence of Abramovitch's personality.[3] Above all, Abramovitch was a man of compromise, convinced that one could always strike a deal. This conviction governed his behavior in party matters, even as differences deepened. It failed him, however, in the most tragic moment of his personal life. When his only son was kidnapped by Communists in Spain during the civil war, Abramovitch unsuccessfully deployed every possible effort to save him. Although Abramovitch's reorientation toward a more pronouncedly anticommunist position had begun earlier, this tragedy, with the light it shed on Communist intransigence and socialist impotence, marked both a personal and a political watershed.

Abramovitch's son, Marc Rein, a twenty-seven-year-old radio engineer, arrived in Barcelona in March 1937 as a volunteer worker in a Catalan munitions factory. He had always been active in German (rather than Russian) socialist circles, particularly in the left wing Paris-based group "Neu Beginnen." In Barcelona he associated with other German emigrants, both socialist and Communist, and his main political preoccupation was that of winning them over to the united front. On the eve of his disappearance, he had succeeded in gathering signatures for a telegram to be sent to a Paris conference of German exiles due to debate this issue. He was also on the point of meeting with German anarcho-syndicalists to enlist them in the unity cause.[4]

A minute reconstitution of the kidnapping offers few clues. Marc Rein left his hotel room late one evening unexpectedly (leaving his typewriter virtually in midsentence), apparently at the request of someone he trusted. He took nothing with him. A few days later, after worried friends had alerted the police and were contacting his father, two letters, postmarked Madrid, arrived from him assuring a friend that he would be back in a few days and asking the hotel manager to hold his room. The search was called off, and only some days later did Friedrich Adler, then traveling in Spain, examine the letters and find the dates on them to be forgeries.[5]

At this point Abramovitch began the fruitless search for his son which was to obsess him for the rest of his life. The speed with which Rein's letters had arrived, uncensored, suggested that official figures may have been involved. German Communists in Barcelona aroused suspicion by expressing distrust of Marc Rein and then either blaming Trotskyists or voicing the hope that he would turn up safe and sound. "My boy was *kidnapped* by the Communists or Bolsheviks (the PSUC-Party in Barcelona)," stated Abramovitch with certainty on the basis of a secret report by the intelligence service of the Catalonian army. No fewer than forty kidnappings had been traced to the International Department of the PSUC, headed by two German Communists. It was this unit which had been charged with conducting the investigation of Marc Rein's disappearance.[6]

"I am paralyzed by the thought that it is too late," wrote Abramovitch as he waited for news. This atypical reaction immediately gave way to a more characteristic but desperate burst of energy. Abramovitch pleaded with every public figure he could reach. "The Bolsheviks must become aware that an international scandal will ensue," he threatened, adding in a cajoling tone, "It is a private 'bargain' which is to be proposed to the Bolsheviks: they release the prisoner in a decent manner and we guarantee that . . . no publicity at all will be made." He demanded that "very prominent people . . . have a very private talk with the appropriate Russians." He even asked whether British double agents could not get proof of GPU involvement.[7]

Most, but not all, of Abramovitch's contacts reacted sympathetically. The international secretary of the British Labour Party responded, "How is it possible for me or anyone else to ask our government to tell Moscow that they ought to advise their agents in Spain to assist in rescuing your son?" With much common sense but little sensitivity he added, "In any case, my dear friend, what is the use of it?" The British government was not saying a word about the ongoing "slaughter of eminent Russian personalities." Soviet ambassador Maiskii had even refused to receive some British women who wanted to plead the case of Eva Broido. As Maiskii put it, "Ten Russian generals have been executed. I am not safe myself."[8]

Marc Rein was thus a distant victim of the terrible Russian year 1937, one victim among many others. Western politicians, unable to enforce the policy of international nonintervention in Spain, did not intervene on behalf of Abramovitch's son so as not to jeopardize their failed policy. A party comrade later complained that Abramovitch had become excessively sensitive, even hysterical, on the question of the Spanish civil war, and argued that Abramovitch's evolution toward the right was at odds with his son's own left wing views.[9] This may be true, but it takes no account of a father's grief.

Abramovitch never gave up the search for his son. Almost twenty years later he traveled to Washington to interview a Soviet defector who had been in Spain; he discovered the truth about the Trotskyist Mark Zborowski, but nothing about his son. Years after the kidnapping Abramovitch would burst into tears when speaking about Marc, and, at the very end of his life, he dedicated his final work, *The Soviet Revolution*, to the memory of his son.[10]

The year 1937 also marked a watershed for the Foreign Delegation. The evolution of the Soviet Union and of the international situation favored a reassessment of policies. Debates over the General Line and the theses on war contained in *L'Internationale et la guerre* crystallized disagreements. By the end of 1937 there was a strong majority (five to three) within the Foreign Delegation in favor of what Dan scornfully called the "Potresov Line," with only Iugov, Schwarz, and himself supporting the official Martov Line.[11]

At this point Dan's strong, even authoritarian, character came to the fore. Dan refused to submit to the new "line" internally or to represent it internationally. He threatened to leave the co-editorship of *Sotsialisticheskii vestnik* rather than accept the reorientation. "It is not a question of majorities for me," he wrote to Adler, "but of factual relations in the world of the working class." Dan did not doubt that he represented "the political attitude of the majority of comrades still attached to social democracy in the USSR." Giving up now would rob the RSDRP of the chance to become the gathering point of all honest socialist elements who were turning away from Stalin. "The fruits of twenty years of work would now be lost as the harvest approaches."[12]

Dan's defiance of the Foreign Delegation majority was based not only on messianic pretensions. It rested on the shrewd observation that the majority was only a majority against him, that there were five political lines for five members. Dan could thus continue as before, making minimal concessions on the wording of resolutions and then intimidating the majority into voting for them.[13]

Division within the Foreign Delegation was matched by division within the LSI. The long-standing rift between reformist and revolutionary parties widened ever further over the issue of the united front with Communists, support for Spanish Republicans, and the attitude toward war. Unable to reconcile its two wings, the LSI Executive canceled, in November 1934, its order of the previous year that member parties refrain from concluding unity pacts with Communists on a national basis.[14] Henceforth, with each party free to define its policy on this key issue, it was difficult for the LSI to maintain even a pretense of authority.

Increasingly, the division between reformists and revolutionaries became one between parties operating at home and those in exile, to the disadvantage of the latter.[15] Abramovitch expressed alarm at this new alignement early on, and his fears proved well founded as, in 1939, the reformist parties of Scandinavia, the Netherlands, and, above all, Great Britain imposed a reorganization of the LSI.[16] Henceforth, parties representing "countries without democracy" were relegated to the margins of the International. The change gave the RSDRP only a consultative vote in the Executive, though a British proposition that members of "illegal" parties should not be admitted into the Bureau was not adopted.[17]

In principle, all parties had been consulted, and there was even sentiment among emigrés, especially right wing ones, for the argument that influence in the LSI should be commensurate with responsibility at home. Nevertheless, the reorganization left a bitter taste in the exiles' mouths. "It is not the illegal parties that are creating difficulties for the International," wrote Fedor Dan, "but the illegal era in which we live."[18] The administrative reorganization was all the more painful as it came amid political paralysis. Never having overcome the division among proponents and opponents of the united front, the LSI was now split between isolationist and interventionist parties with respect to the threat of war. It had confronted—or failed to confront—the Munich crisis in a state of complete disarray that continued unchecked. On top of these woes, Friedrich Adler found himself under criticism from the British for his management of LSI finances. He resigned, declaring, "There is no doubt that the attempt to reconstruct the International to which I devoted twenty years has temporarily failed."[19]

The Mensheviks had not recovered from this blow when the Soviet-German pact destroyed whatever certitudes they still possessed. Vera Alexandrova wrote that when she heard the news, life hardly seemed worth living. The Foreign Delegation reacted more soberly, though not more decisively. It appealed to all Soviet citizens to transform the USSR into an active participant in the anti-Hitler struggle in order to strike a definitive blow to the Stalinist dictatorship. Dan recalled that he had anticipated a Soviet-

German pact as a consequence of Munich, but had predicted that this could take place only after Stalin's forcible removal and replacement by individuals not tied to the revolutionary tradition. The pact proved that Stalin himself incarnated bonapartist-Nazi tendencies. It broke the last threads tying him to proletarian socialism. Whatever Stalin's future zigzags, he was now shutting himself off definitively from all roads leading back to the working-class movement.[20]

The unanimity of the Foreign Delegation's reaction did not stop the search, particularly among the party's Left, for the historical logic of the Soviet-German pact. Olga Domanevskaia argued that this unnatural agreement could not be explained by internal changes in the USSR since there had been none recently. Rather, the pact was a result of the weakness of the West, as demonstrated at Munich and at the Anglo-Franco-Soviet negotiations of summer 1939. The pact did not mean the abandonment of the construction of socialism in the USSR, and in any case, it was more favorable to the USSR than to Germany.[21]

The invasion of Poland sharpened debate over the logic of Soviet behavior. The Left evoked the objectively progressive fact that socially and nationally oppressed regions were being liberated by the Red Army. True, Soviet-German cooperation was repugnant, but Stalin's policies were bringing revolutionary ferment to liberated areas. Although a unanimously adopted resolution of the Foreign Delegation specifically rejected such reasoning, Dan proved susceptible to it. The Soviet-German pact was not a military alliance, he observed. Moreover, Soviet expansion demonstrated the vitality of dynamic forces in the USSR, and it could even have a stimulating effect on the German working class.[22]

Dan set a litmus test for the USSR as a revolutionary state. A Soviet invasion of Finland would cause an insurmountable contradiction, he wrote, since proletarians would then have to assume a defeatist position toward the USSR. Within weeks the Soviet Union did indeed invade, and the Foreign Delegation passed, again unanimously, a ringing resolution "In Defense of Finland." Dan, however, could not bring himself to draw his own conclusions. The Hitlerite and Stalinist regimes were the same, but nazification and sovietization of a country were not the same thing, he now argued. The task of socialists was not to preach unconditional defeatism of the Soviet Union but to bring it (back) into the anti-German alliance and to use the war to further democratization there. Perhaps to escape from an unbearable present, Dan looked to the future, to "a new year and a new world" that would be socialist or, simply, would not be.[23]

The new year brought only further division and defeat. As the international order collapsed, the small world of the Mensheviks shrank still further with the loss of contacts (and financial support) in German-occupied countries and then in the Soviet-occupied Baltic. Still, *Sotsialisticheskii vestnik* persevered, and the Mensheviks, who had survived so much, might have expected to weather this crisis as well.[24] As Lidia Dan put it, "All would be all right in our little world if not for the perfectly animal relations that, little by little, come to dominate among us." In her words, "Kefali is screaming, B.I. [Nicolaevsky] is making vulgar remarks, and R.A. [Abramovich] is trying to find conciliatory formulae." Of course, resolutions were being adopted unanimously, but everyone gave them his or her own interpretation. Lidia Dan added, sadly, that no one was sure any longer that it was worth "gluing and preserving the old house."[25]

The long-brewing revolt within the Foreign Delegation against Fedor Dan's leadership and his politics finally erupted in February 1940. The political events of the previous autumn, from the Soviet-German pact to the invasion of Finland, had made his position untenable. Bickering within the party reached unbearable proportions. Even so, it required a decisive act of political will to turn the Foreign Delegation consciously against its historic leader. The move was made by Abramovitch, but it was orchestrated by Nicolaevsky, and Garvi provided its occasion.

Petr Garvi had been smarting at his exclusion from the Foreign Delegation for seventeen years. When he emigrated in 1923, it had been taken for granted that he was entitled to a place on the Foreign Delegation; his rightist allies thus pressed other demands. Dan acceded to these demands while vetoing Garvi's membership in the delegation.[26] Outmaneuvered, ill, destitute, and cantankerous, Garvi found himself politically isolated, even from other rightists. With the crisis in the party, however, Garvi became a rallying point for the opposition to Dan, precisely because of his previous isolation.

Garvi now lashed out at the culprit responsible for his own and his party's miseries. "You have committed political murder," he wrote to Dan, accusing him of surrounding himself with fainthearted followers, of ruling by ultimatum, of practicing a soulless formalism, of transforming the Martov Line into dead dogma. "Where is your mandate?" asked Garvi, as he enumerated Dan's lost political gambles. "Think of all this and say in conscience whether it is normal that after all these mistakes you continue to represent the party, to head the Foreign Delegation, to put your stamp, the stamp of factionalism, on *Sotsialisticheskii vestnik*."[27]

Garvi rejected Dan's offer of a place on *Vestnik's* editorial board, and Dan in turn refused, on the basis of an old party resolution, to grant him membership in the Foreign Delegation.[28] Pressure in favor of Garvi grew, both within the Paris Menshevik Club and from key American comrades who were subsidizing *Vestnik*. In early 1940 the Foreign Delegation met four times within two weeks. At the third meeting it adopted a unanimous resolution (with only Nicolaevsky abstaining) calling for a review of the party platform and an open discussion in *Vestnik*. At the next meeting the first point on the agenda was a proposition sponsored by Abramovitch calling on Dan to resign from the chairmanship of the Foreign Delegation. It was not debated since Dan (and Iugov) failed to appear at the meeting. Instead they sent their resignations, as party chairman and co-editor of *Vestnik* in the case of Dan, and as party secretary in that of Iugov. Abramovitch was elected party chairman and appointed sole editor of *Vestnik*.[29]

"The activity of the Foreign Delegation and of *Sotsialisticheskii vestnik* has long failed to correspond to what our comrades in the USSR and young generations of the Soviet proletariat are entitled to require of us," wrote Dan and Iugov in their resignation.[30] No one would have disagreed with this assessment, but the move still cast the Mensheviks into turmoil.

Nicolaevsky defended himself halfheartedly against the charge of having engineered a palace coup by not consulting the Paris Menshevik group. "Where did you learn that 2 times 2 is *always* 4?" he bantered, arguing that organizational principles must be adapted to needs. Democracy was necessary for a mass party, but it need not be applied in a "propaganda group" whose task was to express a position and conserve whatever capital it possessed. The fact that there were only eight members in the Foreign Delegation but eighty members in the Paris group did not make the latter group of "widows and orphans" a mass organization, he concluded dismissively. Although Nicolaevsky promised Garvi support for his cooptation into the Foreign Delegation, he did not hide his impatience with Garvi's personal complaints and political outlook. Nicolaevsky's move was clearly dictated not by personal sympathy but by a radically new orientation. In Nicolaevsky's words, with the destruction of the "Kremlin" by the "Liubianka," Martov's wager on internal forces within Russia was lost, and the Mensheviks now had to look to external forces alone. He began by seeking alliance with exiled SRs, as later he was to seek allies in the U.S. State Department. The break with Menshevik exile tradition was so complete that it startled even Garvi.[31]

While Nicolaevsky knew exactly what he wanted and worked at obtaining it, Solomon Schwarz tried to play a mediating role by urging Dan to continue in the Foreign Delegation and in *Vestnik*, as a sort of "leader of the opposition." It is testimony to the affection that Schwarz enjoyed among his comrades that he was allowed to mediate. His efforts were futile, however, as

Dan (even though he did not give up his Foreign Delegation membership) refused to fight within the old structures. Although he identified with Dan politically, Schwarz now concluded that Dan's group was dominated by the ultra-Left, and he gravitated toward *Vestnik*. His wife, Vera Alexandrova, lamented the turn of events. "Somewhere in the depths of my soul I am sorry for Dashen'ko [Dan] that in his late years he let himself be led into such an adventure," she wrote. In her view Dan had allowed obstinacy to overcome passion, exemplifying a generation that had followed rigid principles rather than its instincts, and that was now witnessing the bankruptcy of these principles.[32]

Abramovitch clutched at the very last threads of unity. "It is not yet a split," he wrote to a comrade in New York, contradicting himself in the postscript: "You cannot imagine how long and how stubbornly I opposed a split. I simply ran out of strength." When Dan carried out his threat to found a new journal, Abramovitch insisted stoutly that there were now two journals but still one party. Lidia Dan, too, wrote that her husband's group had no intention of splitting the party. Its aim was simply to unite the left wing of the party and of the LSI and to overcome paralysis within the Foreign Delegation.[33] These assurances were unconvincing, and, in spite of intense pressure from individuals and from party organizations in Paris, New York, and Geneva, the appearance of Dan's new journal, *Novyi mir*, confirmed the split.[34]

The man at the center of the controversy, Fedor Dan, admitted that his nerves had cracked under constant sniping by Nicolaevsky, Garvi, and others. In his last contribution to *Sotsialisticheskii vestnik* Dan reiterated his belief that the essence of the Martov Line lay in the attempt to ensure that the collapse of bolshevism would be followed by a democratic and not by a counterrevolutionary regime. Turning accusations of rigidity and conservatism against his opponents, he declared that he did not want the party to be a church or mausoleum in which to end his days. His new journal would mobilize old and new forces; by clarifying matters it would put an end to old quarrels rather than begin new ones.[35]

Behind this forward-looking approach, Dan could not conceal his concern, shared by his opponents, for the judgment of history. Laboring under the shadow of Martov, he recalled that Martov had saved the proletarian and socialist character of the RSDRP; this was what Dan intended to do now. It was the last chance to rescue the party, he wrote.[36] Dan meant thereby that he wished to go down in history as someone who had never broken faith with the Russian Revolution, just as his opponents wished to be remembered for never having betrayed the principles of democratic socialism. The struggle within the party was now a struggle for dominion over the historical record and over the memory of the party.

The first issue of *Novyi mir* came out in March 1940. Dan denounced his party as a little circle of old men, sometime Marxists and now bourgeois liberals, who were eking out their political lives completely closed to new forces and new ideas.[37] Furious, the targets of his criticism lashed back. "Total impotence," sniffed Nicolaevsky, claiming that even on a literary level *Novyi mir* could not measure up to *Sotsialisticheskii vestnik,* that there was no youth in the new journal, and that it relied on foreigners.[38] In fact, the core of the *Novyi mir* group was made up of talented young Russian-speakers from Latvia, including a future Columbia University professor of mathematics, Lipman Bers, and Edvard Neuschloss, a Chinese art expert and gifted caricaturist, as well as the Menshevik whiz kid Alexander Shifrin. The foreigners, referred to as "Austrians," included genuine Austrians such as Oscar Pollak and left-oriented socialists from other countries. The "Austrian" par excellence, Otto Bauer, had died in July 1938, but he was the spiritual father of *Novyi mir.*[39]

The new journal put out only four issues before the fall of Paris drove the Mensheviks, and so many others, first to the South of France and then out of Europe. Among the mass of refugees the Mensheviks proved particularly fortunate. In distant America a delegation of labor leaders was successfully lobbying Undersecretary of State Sumner Welles to provide some four hundred visas for European comrades in danger. Not only did the delegation include old friends of the Mensheviks, but also the person specifically responsible for drawing up the visa list was one of their own, Samuel Estrine, recently settled in the United States. Estrine would keep a notepad by his bed and wake up in the night to add yet more names, from memory, to his list.[40]

"They are taking all who believe in God," Abramovitch assured his comrades, meaning that they could all count on a visa. Still, he warned against underestimating the hardships to come. Even with visas there was no guarantee of getting out of Europe, as Spain was constantly opening and closing its border. Visas were temporary, and life in America would be difficult.[41] Nevertheless, one by one, through Marseilles, Lisbon, or, in the case of Leo Lande and Boris Sapir, after a year's wait in Cuba, the Menshevik Party made its way to New York.

The Mensheviks did not leave precipitously; perhaps they even went reluctantly. Anna Bourguina took time to bury one hundred boxes of Nicolaevsky's archives in Amboise, thus ensuring they survived the war. She was able to leave the occupied zone by calling on the inspector who had investigated the theft of the Trotsky archives four years earlier. Nicolaevsky refused to leave France until an ailing Fedor Dan had recovered sufficiently to travel; only then did he embark for America, with the protocols of the General Council of the First International and other archival treasures in his baggage.[42] Abramovitch continued to intercede on behalf of individuals who were not on the magic list of visa recipients, no mean task in view of the U.S. consulate's suspicion of any leftists. Even the Petainist minister of the interior and former socialist Adrien Marquet discreetly extended help to the Dans.[43]

Just before they set sail, the Dans received two affectionate letters from Léon Blum. He inquired anxiously about Oreste Rosenfeld, who had enlisted in the French army as perhaps its oldest second lieutenant and was now a prisoner of war somewhere in Germany. "This adieu is not definitive," wrote Blum. "I shall see you again in France, I am sure . . . I am well, calm, and I do not fear the future . . . Remember me to all our common friends in America."[44]

8

Sea Change

New Roads and Old

"Coelum non animum mutant quae trans mare currunt"—"They change their sky but not their spirit who run across the sea," writes Ovid, who might have been speaking of the Mensheviks. The emigrés who arrived in America from various European ports in the course of 1940 and 1941, and even via Cuba in 1942, found themselves in a political and cultural environment completely unlike anything they had known in their distant Russian home or in their previous places of sojourn. This novelty did not make them forget their disputes. On the contrary, they re-created factional alignments and resumed quarrels much where they had left them. Only when these quarrels were exhausted did some Mensheviks turn to other concerns dictated by new conditions.

Upon landing in New York, the Mensheviks—several dozen men, women, and children—were greeted by Samuel Estrine or another member of the Rescue Committee which had provided their visas. Supplied with ten or fifteen dollars as pocket money, they were whisked off to accommodations provided by local sympathizers. One of the first surprises for these new immigrants must have been the number of organizations ready to look after them: the Plekhanoff New York Group of Russian Social Democrats, the New York Group of the Russian Social Democratic Labor Party, the Russian Section of the Social Democratic Federation, the Workmen's Circle, the Jewish Socialist Verband, the Jewish Labor Committee, and a bewildering number of other socialist, labor, and Jewish associations.

Initially the new immigrants may well have been disoriented. Denike and Nicolaevsky spent entire days playing chess in the Brooklyn living room of *New Leader* editor Sol Levitas. Soon, however, the Mensheviks managed to

271

set themselves up. Most rented apartments near one another on the Upper West Side of Manhattan. The Dans, Iugovs, Bienstocks, and Aronsons and Lazar Pistrak all settled at 352 West 110th Street. Lidia Dan taught Russian to unwilling Menshevik children. Neighborly relations somehow survived political differences; for a time, social evenings provided moments of political truce. Soon, however, factionalism triumphed over conviviality as even party-goers congregated according to factional allegiance, each faction in a separate room.[1]

Menshevik "headquarters" lay at the other end of town. The building at 7 East Fifteenth Street housed some of the organizations that had greeted the Mensheviks, as well as the Rand School and the *New Leader*'s editorial offices. This address immediately appeared on the masthead of the revived *Sotsialisticheskii vestnik*. It was here, too, that the Mensheviks first met American comrades such as *New Leader* editorialist Daniel Bell, NYU professor Sidney Hook, Social Democratic Federation chairman Algernon Lee, and *New York Times* labor correspondent Joseph Shaplen. In spite of the Mensheviks' superior attitude—after all, they had made the Russian Revolution, they had been on intimate terms with Kautsky!—relations with American comrades were mutually profitable. Soon, Americans, Russians, and other emigrés were collaborating in a Rand School study group and other projects. Thus began the twenty-some-year-long Menshevik participation in American debate on international affairs and on the Soviet experience.

Materially, too, things were working out. Several older Mensheviks received grants—a new word for them—from a fund set up by the Jewish Labor Committee with trade union money, ostensibly to write their memoirs. Work proved easier to find once war broke out. Lidia Dan worked as a dyer in a factory and then as a typist in a Russia-related office of the U.S. War Ministry which also employed the Iugovs and Dan's new protégé, Adam Kaufman. For the first time in many years Abramovitch's wife felt secure, and even Fedor Dan let it be known that he was generally happy in his new surroundings.[2]

Still, such comforts did not undo the anguish of a new exile. Once again, the Mensheviks were relearning the "science of exile" and "the sociology of defeat," as Garvi put it. *Vestnik*'s first American editorial, titled "Berlin–Paris–New York," recalled past hopes of a short exile, of Soviet evolution, of a truly united proletarian front. Instead, the diminishing Menshevik forces had suffered a European catastrophe which had hurled them across the ocean. In the face of disaster, the Mensheviks could only hope again: "From New York the road is either toward nonexistence along with all European and world democracy or else to Moscow, to a new democratic, social democratic Russia, against the background of a New Europe."[3]

Such common hopes could not reconcile internal divergences. The shift in favor of the Right that had taken place within the Foreign Delegation during the last months in France was decisively confirmed in America. Abramovitch was reelected chairman of the Foreign Delegation and editor of *Vestnik* (with Dan and Iugov abstaining). Indeed, Abramovitch's star had rarely shone brighter. Over six hundred people attended a banquet on his sixtieth birthday (and contributed over $2,000 to the party chest). The American Federation of Labor set up, under Abramovitch's chairmanship, its Labor Conference on International Affairs, which was to serve long and well as a funnel for union support to the Mensheviks and numerous other causes inside and outside the United States. Even a German rival for American attention who had complained about the Mensheviks in the past gave Abramovitch his due: "I admire this man [Abramovitch]. In spite of creeping blindness and constant headaches, he is unfalteringly active and informed about everything. He deals in English, Russian, German, and Yiddish (an important language here); makes excellent speeches, and, moreover, is a truly good friend to us."[4]

At the same time, the gulf grew between the Abramovitch-led Foreign Delegation and its left minority, reduced to Dan and Iugov. The minority held out unsuccessfully against proposals that the Mensheviks join the Russian section of the American Social Democratic Federation and that they participate in the New York All-Socialist Club, which also included SRs. Particularly infuriating for Dan and Iugov was the Foreign Delegation's decision (by a vote of only four of the eight members) to accept among *Vestnik* collaborators Stepan Ivanovich-Portugeis, the extraparty right wing Menshevik who had been Martov's particular bête noire.[5]

By then, however, Dan and Iugov had a new institutional base. The Paris *Novyi mir* (New World) group reconstituted itself under the name *Novyi put'* (New Road), and the first issue of its new journal declared: "We hold in our hands the old party banner only in order to transmit it to those unknown soldiers of the future Rusian social democratic army." *Novyi put'* was founded on the premise that the present era was revolutionary and democracy could now only be socialist; it claimed to look to young working-class generations of the Soviet Union in order to bring them over to "our idea." The *"Novyi put'* Club" also declared that it was not a substitute for or a rival of the official party group or of the Foreign Delegation.[6]

In fact, conflict proved unavoidable and was waged, first, around bureaucratic issues. Dan insisted that the Foreign Delegation had violated party rules by admitting three new members to the party (including Ivanovich). The delegation responded that these were but readmissions of former members. When Dan and Iugov announced that they would not participate in the delegation's regular work, it retorted that Dan's "methods of opposition recalled those of the Bolsheviks on the eve of the split" and retaliated by removing him as the party's alternate representative to the LSI, a punishment lessened by the fact that the LSI no longer effectively existed. The final stage in this bureaucratic bickering was the decision to violate earlier practice in coopting three new Foreign Delegation members—Dallin, Denike, and Garvi—by a majority rather than a unanimous vote. Ignoring derisive remarks about the incompatibility of his revolutionary beliefs and conservative practices, Dan declared that the Foreign Delegation had destroyed its only legal base and had therefore "self-liquidated." In a retaliatory gesture of excommunication, the delegation announced that Dan and Iugov had "removed themselves" from the governing body of the RSDRP.[7]

The conflict was intensely personal as well. *Vestnik* denounced *Novyi put'* contributor Alexander Shifrin for publishing with a quasi-Communist publisher and for writing in the Soviet embassy bulletin. Nicolaevsky accused Dan of defending all of Stalin's behavior, including the pact with Hitler.[8] Dubois attacked Nicolaevsky so viciously that *Vestnik* enlisted the Jewish Labor Committee to make an inquiry and lay charges of calumny. JLC interference provoked indignation, in turn, even among other emigrés.[9] Personalities and principles proved inseparable. Not even the *Novyi put'* group cared much for one of its members, Boris Skomorovskii. Still, when Skomorovskii was denied the floor at a meeting of the entire New York Menshevik Club in 1941, *Novyi put'* members left, and most never returned. Two years later, the Foreign Delegation expelled Skomorovskii from the party for publicly lauding *Mission to Moscow*, the pro-Soviet film based on the memoirs of former U.S. ambassador Joseph E. Davies. Although Skomorovskii had already left *Noyvi put'* for the overtly pro-Communist press, Dan continued to defend him, denying that Skomorovskii had been excluded from *Novyi put'* and insisting that the Foreign Delegation had never been entitled to expel a party member.[10]

The small world of the Mensheviks thus turned into two even smaller ones. The intimate nature of its new offshoot, consisting of about twenty individuals, was underscored by the fact that *Novyi put'* would publish health bulletins about its ailing members. Prominent in the club was Alexander Shifrin (pseudonym Werner), now a self-taught military pundit for the *New Republic* and the New York newspaper *PM*. Among the Menshevik old guard who had followed Dan was Aaron Iugov, doglike in his loyalty; Iugov's pugnacious left wing wife, Olga Domanevskaia; as well as Anatolii Dubois, who combined personal attachment to Dan with passionate Russian patriotism. *Novyi put'* also included Olga Kolbassina, former wife of SR leader V. M.

Chernov; and Sonya Dubnova Erlich (pseudonym Mirskaia), wife (and soon widow) of the Bundist leader. Dan took particular pride in the group's younger members: veterans of the Berlin Martov Club such as Samuel Estrine and the psychologist Anna Gourevitch; and several Baltic and Polish socialists, including Grigorii Kagan (pseudonym A. Lipskii), a former Communist and Comintern functionary in France. The youth reciprocated with heartfelt personal admiration for Dan.[11]

Financially, *Novyi put'* could not count on the largesse of organizations that supported *Sotsialisticheskii vestnik.* Apparently only the Bundist philanthropist S. S. Atran gave money to both journals so they could "fight it out." *Novyi put'*s only regular benefactor was Simon Lieberman, a wealthy ex-Menshevik businessman who had worked in the Soviet forest industry during the early years of the Revolution. Through the efforts of the sculptor Anatolii Dubois and caricaturist Edvard Schloss, the *Novyi put'* Club held auctions for canvases donated by Fernand Léger, Mark Chagall, and lesser artists.[12]

The *Novyi put'* group defined itself as revolutionary. "There exists a clear 2½ International here, consisting of Neubeg[innen], Austrians, and Dan-Russians, with support in academic circles and in the CIO," wrote a German Social Democrat, adding: "These people are resolved in all circumstances to be 25 percent more radical than we."[13] The spectrum within *Novyi put'* ran from left to far left. Fedor Dan was not always able to rule with his usual iron hand, leading *Vestnik* to insinuate that Dan was a prisoner of his own faction.[14] Dan tolerated Shifrin's statement "Stalin knows better than we do," but he would not abide Grigorii Meiksins's accusation that the Mensheviks had committed a crime, not only in deserting the Revolution but also in taking part of the working class with them. Dan exploded when Domanevskaia declared it was fortunate that the Mensheviks had not won the Revolution, given the way most of them had turned out. To Dan's relief (and the unconcealed gloating of the Foreign Delegation), Domanevskaia and Meiksins soon left *Novyi put'* definitively.[15]

The conflict between *Novyi put'* and *Sotsialisticheskii vestnik* was painful to many. Vera Alexandrova, who continued her literary column in *Vestnik,* sent Dan emotional personal letters recalling bygone days and lamenting the turn of events. "The differences between us, Fedor Illich, are not of logic but of the heart," she wrote, adding, "I do not see, or rather I do not feel, anything new in *Novyi put'* and therefore I continue to live in our old house where the memory of old worker-Mensheviks lingers on." Dan, too, might be suspected of personally regretting the split. He wrote a sympathetic obituary for Mark Kefali, one of the original right wing Mensheviks on the Foreign

Delegation, maintaining that Kefali did not see the Bolsheviks' constructive side but saw only the destructive one because they had destroyed the trade union movement that was his life's work. More surprisingly, Dan paid a warm and generous farewell to his former nemesis Petr Garvi: "He remained a socialist to the marrow of his bone . . . the incarnation of menshevism's romantic strivings." Dan could not resist the temptation to polemicize against the party majority, referring to Garvi as "a living reminder that menshevism is not that dwarflike common sense, sobriety, and moderation that its enemies and petty bourgeois members" [would make of it]." Still, one cannot doubt the nostalgia of Dan's remarks.[16]

These Menshevik feuds were taking place in the shadow of the most momentous historical events. As the war gathered fury, the Mensheviks looked anxiously toward the Soviet Union. In a January 1941 lecture Fedor Dan insisted that no effort should be spared to bring the Soviet Union into the war on the Allied side. Dan lashed out at his rivals in *Vestnik,* who saw the Soviet-German pact as durable because of the identity of the two regimes. They were different in their roots and their social structure, he retorted, in spite of Hitler's anticapitalism and Stalin's growing counterrevolutionary degeneration. The obstacles to attracting the Soviet Union into the Allied camp lay, above all, in the West's dogmatic antibolshevism.[17]

Sotsialisticheskii vestnik was much more reserved. "One can only guess at [Stalin's] world-political strategy," it declared in February 1941. Was Stalin wagering on an Axis victory in order to share more booty? Was he counting on a war of attrition that would exhaust both coalitions until only Russia remained as a great power? In early 1941 *Vestnik* maintained that the Soviet-German honeymoon was over; Stalin had obtained all he could in Europe, and Hitler no longer needed him. In June, however, Abramovitch affirmed that it looked as if cooperation between Hitler and Stalin was proceeding smoothly according to a prearranged plan. Were there any circumstances under which Stalin would turn against Hitler rather than support him? Theoretically there was only one such case: if Hitler were losing the war, Stalin might jump in at the last minute, as Mussolini had done in France. As an afterthought Abramovitch added the hypothetical possibility that Hitler would attack Stalin and Stalin would thus have to surrender or seek coalition with the Allies. This was an extremely unlikely possibility, however, a statement with which *Novyi put'* later taunted Abramovitch.[18]

"Operation Barbarossa," the German attack on Russia in June 1941, was the most significant event the Mensheviks had experienced since 1917. It should have united the two Menshevik camps; instead it set them apart even further. Both *Sotsialisticheskii vestnik* and *Novyi put'* took a "defensist" position vis-à-vis the USSR, but the difference between them emerged clearly in their separate resolutions. "By Hitler's will the Soviet Union is at war with Germany," declared *Vestnik*. "Objectively" the Soviet Union had thus become a participant in the world front of democracy. The RSDRP therefore urged "defense of our country against Hitlerite attack, subordinating the struggle for the liquidation of Stalinist despotism to the supreme interests of the war against fascism." *Novyi put'*, by contrast, announced that "the counternatural and perditious pact of Stalin and Hitler has been broken." At this turning point in the Russian Revolution, the antifascist and anticapitalist struggle, paralyzed by the pact, could resume. It was now imperative to oppose all attempts at Allied compromise with Hitler at Soviet expense. The resolution concluded with a call for all comrades of miltary age, wherever they might be, to enter the ranks of the Red Army.[19]

The Foreign Delegation adopted *Vestnik*'s resolution by six votes to one, with one abstention (either Dan or Iugov). All Mensheviks might take satisfaction in the rumor that this resolution had been read on Moscow radio and Muscovites were talking about it appovingly.[20] Menshevik debate over the meaning of and prospects for the war did not abate, however. Abramovitch admitted that he could not imagine why Hitler had broken with Stalin at precisely this moment. But he defended himself against his detractors by reminding them that he had always said Stalin could not remain neutral. Moreover, only the liquidation of the dictatorship could inspire the masses and the Red Army with the will to fight successfully. In an atypically optimistic outburst he speculated that the perspective of a "reform" of the dictatorship, so completely utopian in recent years, was now acquiring shape. Those who had "survived the illusions and failures of the past" were entitled to be skeptical, but this was the perspective worth "fighting and living for."[21]

In the meantime, *Novyi put'* was unreservedly applauding "the day we have all been waiting for," claiming cockily that this moment had been inevitable, that it corresponded to Hitler's original plan, and even that a hidden war had been going on between the two dictators since August 1940. In reply *Vestnik* reminded *Novyi put'* that the latter's military expert (Shifrin) had contended earlier that Russia would attack Germany, and he should therefore now argue that Germany's attack was a defensive one.[22]

Soon the two factions were exchanging escalating accusations of "defeatism" and "capitulationism." Anatolii Dubois, Dan's disciple but still a contributor to *Vestnik*, was the first to accuse the Foreign Delegation of waffling on the question whether Stalin's regime had to be overturned or whether it should be supported until victory. Shifrin explained the Foreign Delegation's attitude in terms of "two antibolshevisms." In addition to Hitlerite antibolshevism, there was a democratic antibolshevism which sought to separate the Anglo-Americans from the Russians. For these "democrats" antibolshevism had become a substitute for politics. Everywhere, even in the planned economy, they saw *totalitarshchina*. Everywhere they saw Bolshevik agents, making De Gaulle, Benes, and the *Times* of London into a Bolshevik version of the Elders of Zion.[23]

Boris Nicolaevsky soon provided a specific focus for disagreements. Arguing against the claim of *Novyi put'* that antibolshevism was incompatible with antifascism, he added that there was no need to make concessions to Communists because they would now be antifascist regardless of democrats' attitudes. Nicolaevsky even maintained, just before the United States entered the war, that the task of social democrats was to inspire the average American's confidence that the fight against Hitler would not strengthen Communist positions. *Novyi put'* attacked these remarks as well as a declaration signed by Nicolaevsky (and other Mensheviks and SRs) stating that "if the Bolshevik regime survives the war, democratic nations will have to consider it a source of danger." Most offensive, however, was Nicolaevsky's thesis, published just after Pearl Harbor, that when the Japanese attacked, they had assurances that Soviet Russia would not move against them, and the simultaneous easing of the German offensive on the Moscow front was no coincidence.[24]

These insinuations of German-Soviet complicity drove the *Novyi put'* group into a fury. Dan raged at Nicolaevsky's "maniac antibolshevism" and diagnosed him as a politically senile accomplice of darkest reaction. The Foreign Delegation's refusal to take a position, as Dan requested, on what he considered the suspect nature of Nicolaevsky's defensism led Dan to complain of disrespect for minority rights, a complaint that must have amused those who remembered only too well their own minority status under Dan's rule.[25] Although there were weightier issues at hand, the question of Nicolaevsky's "defeatist insinuations" was never put to rest. Dan scoffed at Nicolaevsky as organically incapable of understanding that one "can think of political situations and historical processes in categories other than that of the detective novel." Nicolaevsky, for his part, claimed confirmation of his insinuations.[26]

Both *Sotsialisticheskii vestnik* and *Novyi put'* anxiously followed the course of the war. Dan and his friends surveyed the Western Allies suspiciously, minimized Allied aid to Russia, and called repeatedly, almost obsessively, for a second front. They refused to endorse the Foreign Delegation's position on the United States' entry into the war; the Foreign Delegation, they claimed, had turned things upside down in noting that the Soviet Union remained neutral against Japan but failing to acknowledge that the whole burden of the war lay on the Soviet Union. Insisting that opening a second front was a political decision, they refused to accept *Vestnik*'s assurances that, although there were indeed people in the West who wished to put off opening the second front, these were not the people in power. *Novyi put'* reacted lyrically to "the miracle of Stalingrad," dubbing it "the miracle of the Revolution," and chiding those who failed to see that "Stalingrad [was] not just strategy or politics but history," in comparison to which Sedan, which decided the Franco-German war of 1870, had been but a minor skirmish.[27]

The Mensheviks closely analyzed news from the old continent. They reported on the resistance movements, especially in France, whose tragedy, they agreed, was that "events had not brought out one authentically democratic leader abroad."[28] They conveyed their horror at the impending Holocaust. "Mass expulsions into parts unknown [make it] almost impossible to doubt that this means anything other than physical extermination," reported *Vestnik* in autumn 1942. "Rumors of gas chambers . . . though long evoking natural incredulity are now receiving maximally authoritative confirmation . . . These are no longer war pogroms. This is the execution of a whole plan of extermination of European Jewry."[29] *Vestnik*'s concern, however, was too easily diverted to the new sympathy between Communists and Zionists. *Novyi put'*, though it also wrote frequently of the tragedy, concluded characteristically that "socialism is the only historical perspective for saving Jewry."[30]

As the war drew on, the Mensheviks debated the contours of the emerging postwar order. *Vestnik* emphasized that the RSDRP program respected the sovereignty of Russia's neighbors, but this did not exclude (peaceful) revision of unjust treaties, such as that establishing the Polish border, or of unjust amputations, such as that of Bessarabia. It approved Soviet refusal to endorse the prewar Polish borders, scolded the Polish exile government for putting excessive emphasis on its eastern territories, and debated whether the issue should be put to a referendum. As Soviet ambitions in Poland became clearer, however, *Vestnik*'s sympathies moved toward the Polish position, prompting *Novyi put'* to accuse the Foreign Delegation of demanding Stalin's unconditional surrender to the Poles.[31]

On other issues, the divergences between *Sotsialisticheskii vestnik* and *Novyi put'* were pronounced from the outset. Dan reviled the "fetishization" of the "right to national self-determination." True, even *Novyi put'* had difficulty accepting the thesis of its sometime contributor Grigorii Meiksins, according to whom the Baltic states had been created by German intrigue, and numerous Balts had been saved from Hitler by being deported to the Soviet Union. In general, however, Dan's group did not repudiate Meiksins's idea that the only choice facing the Balts was Hitler (death) or Stalin (life), that lasting peace was more important than sovereignty, and that the best solution would be the realization of the old ideal of "a free Latvia, Estonia, and so on in a free Russia."[32]

Both Menshevik factions sought to leapfrog over present problems by looking toward a future European federation. Early in the war Abramovitch painted his vision of this future federal structure that would undo the fragmentation of the Versailles system. There was a danger, he acknowledged, that a united Europe would be a colony of the victors (Great Britain, above all), but even the great powers recognized that this was the only way to avoid World War III. *Novyi put'* retorted that the only possible federation would have to be a socialist one, built on the revolutionary destruction of the capitalist order and inclusion of the USSR.[33]

Instead of a European federation, a divided Europe emerged from the war. The Menshevik majority chafed over the outcome of the Teheran Conference, which, as they saw it, established a Soviet sphere of interest encompassing the Balkans, Poland, the Baltic, and, apparently, Czechoslovakia. It set up a world "directoire" of great powers that would dominate the "heir" to the League of Nations; it ruled out a future peace conference, ensuring that all problems would have to be decided in the course of the war. They grieved over Yalta, where "democracy and international justice [had] been sacrificed to the Moloch of the imperialist interests of the great powers, in the first instance, the USSR." There was no true instrument of collective security, no obstacle to the division of Europe (and perhaps of Asia) into spheres of influence, no barrier to the sovietization of eastern Germany. The only positive note was that Yalta had engaged U.S. responsibility in Europe for the first time. Otherwise, wrote *Vestnik* on the eve of the conference, "The judgment of history will say: what a gigantic war, what heroic nations, and what a miserable, sorry, dangerous, and impermanent peace."[34]

Novyi put' exulted, but only briefly. "The first beams of the future grandeur of a revolutionary country already fall in freedom on the blood-and-tear-soaked soil of Europe," it rhapsodized. Balkan nations might be "reach[ing] out to the Soviet Union," but the earlier fears of *Novyi put'* were being confirmed: the occupation of Germany without a revolution was making the Allies into prison wardens. "Defeatists" in the West were already looking to a World War III, and the Western press was treating the USSR as an inevitable foe. All in all, *Novyi put'* could, for once, agree with *Vestnik* (though for different reasons), that this was an "inglorious end" to the war.[35]

"The war was not carried out along ideological lines, but now the construction of the peace order is taking place along ideological lines," wrote

Abramovitch, fearing a new Europe permeated with nationalist hatreds and Communist temptations. Dan's friends dreaded the atomic menace that could be triggered at any moment by reactionaries seeking revenge for Soviet victory.[36] Above all, reconstruction along old ideological lines meant that the Mensheviks had lost their last wager on the "Martov Line," with its promise of Soviet deradicalization. Lately this wager had been only implicit among the *Vestnik*-centered Menshevik majority, but for Dan's group it was explicit, and it could not be abandoned, even when proven false.

The watershed beyond which Dan could no longer return to an authentically critical view of the Soviet Union was the murder of Henryk Erlich and Viktor Alter. These two old Bundist friends, whose political stance Dan considered unimpeachable, were arrested in the Soviet Union in 1941. Dan was indignant at their arrest, and he was stunned by news of their execution in 1943. His group reacted with passionate outrage at the "nightmarish crime." It rejected all attempts at justification, already rife in the Communist press. Still, the group concluded, this abomination would "not prevent us from serving the cause" or from opposing reactionary efforts to "exploit our righteous indignation."[37]

Henceforth Dan could hardly separate himself from apologia for the Soviet Union—nor did he much care to. Whereas the previous year he had written to the *Nation* to deny its characterization of his group's outlook as one of "growing sympathy for Bolshevism," from now on such disclaimers would sound hollow.[38] His journal's clashes with *Sotsialisticheskii vestnik* were increasingly a dialogue of the deaf, even when they were of a quasi-academic nature. Dan's lieutenant Iugov and *Vestnik*'s Schwarz, with some help from Nicolaevsky, debated the issue of social cleavages in the Soviet Union. Iugov denied that a Soviet governing class or caste was being consolidated in the course of the war, whether composed of the technocracy, as Schwarz argued, or of the party, as Nicolaevsky would have it.[39] After the war, Iugov argued triumphantly that new purges in the USSR were proof that there was no ruling caste, that the spirit of the Revolution was as strong as ever and winning over apparatchik tendencies. In Schwarz's earlier phrase this was again mere "vishful sinking."[40]

Dan himself argued that the process of democratization was taking place "by other routes and much slower than hoped, but it [was] going on." As *Vestnik* pointed out, Dan was inconsistent on whether democratization would come from above or below. Would it follow from what Boris Sapir mockingly called "a change of heart of Communist leaders," or would it be the product of growing egalitarianism, patriotic solidarity, and mass pressure? "The day that bolshevism democratizes, it will die," retorted one newly intransigent *Vestnik* contributor, and another questioned whether Dan's notion of democratization went beyond convoking the Supreme Soviet.[41]

Characteristically, both Dan and his opponents swore fidelity to Martov. "Today, too, Martov is a living participant in our struggle," wrote *Novyi put'* and *Vestnik* claimed as much for itself.[42] *Novyi put'* contrasted the Foreign Delegation's present ambivalence on supporting the Soviet Union with Martov's decisiveness ("he knew which side to choose") during the Civil War. It invoked Martov's authority to denounce "gravediggers of social democracy," such as Abramovitch, who were claiming that the dividing line between SRs and social democrats had been replaced by one between democratic and dictatorial socialism.[43] Dallin and Nicolaevsky responded to the appropriation of Martov by *Novyi put'* by demonstrating that he had been a Soviet defensist only in the first phase of (not throughout) the 1920 Polish-Soviet war, and that Martov's party had never fought with Bolsheviks against SRs.[44]

Both sides accused each other of "liquidationist" tendencies, borrowing a term from distant party history, and both appealed to Marxism. Responding to Dan's stance, Nicolaevsky and Denike contended that bolshevism, like fascism, had neglected a fundamental value within socialism: the free development of the individual. Marx's fundamental concern had been the search for the full and free development of the human personality.[45] Instead, the twentieth century had developed an infinitely more virulent mutation of nineteenth-century bonapartism: totalitarianism. The phenomenon was so novel and so deadly that it invalidated previous comparisons between the French and the Russian revolutions.[46] Even in its fascist variant, totalitarianism could co-opt the workers, maintain their social attainments, even enlist a measure of popular support.[47] It radically transformed the nature of the economy, of the state, and of war. If one imagined, in 1942, that the world was experiencing a capitalist war like any other, it sufficed to put the question to a Jew in the Warsaw ghetto.[48]

Both Menshevik factions read each other's journal avidly. If the early encounter between bolshevism and menshevism has been portrayed (with only partial justification) as a clash of opposites, the confrontation between *Sotsialisticheskii vestnik* and *Novyi put'* really did oppose archetypal visions. So envenomed did this confrontation become that it excluded the prospect of a synthesis or perhaps even of any mutual learning. In its later phases this debate became sterile. One of the few remaining questions was whether *Novyi put'* would eventually go over to the Communist camp, as its opponents predicted. The question was never answered because the death of Fedor Dan in February 1947 suspended the debate.

The Last of the Martov Line

"I am grateful to my father for the first time in my life for having me study medicine," Dan told one of his young comrades during his last illness. "If I were not a doctor I would think I am dying." In fact, Dan was dying, far from home and with diminishing prospects of realizing the tasks he had set himself. The revolutionary process had slowed down in Europe even before the end of the war, and a year later it was static. Dan's optimistic lieutenant, Iugov, was gushing over the prospect of working-class unity opened by the meeting of British socialist Harold Laski with Stalin and by the latest pronouncements of Czechoslovak Communist leader Klement Gottwald.[1] Dan himself, however, was probably more convinced by *Vestnik*'s analysis of Communist confrontational tactics and of the impossibility of reunifying the working class.[2]

Dan was bitter toward his former comrades-in-arms. In 1944 he refused to participate in a Bund banquet where Abramovitch was to speak. He spent his last two summers in Tannersville, New York, without seeing other Menshevik families also vacationing there. When Léon Blum, soon to be restored to power, visited New York after the war, Dan fretted that the visit would be exploited by *Vestnik* Mensheviks. Though disappointed by Blum's postwar political outlook (but consoled by his failure to endorse Abramovitch), Dan found comfort in the affection of this "warm and faithful friend"; he noted with pride that this was Blum's only visit to a private home during his trip.[3]

At the same time, Dan's unshakable Marxism endowed him with renewable reserves of hope. "We two belong today to that small inner circler of the 'elders' whose great luck it has been to have been implanted for life with belief in the triumph of socialism," Friedrich Adler had recently written him. Armed with this faith, Dan feverishly prepared his "political testament to future socialist generations." It was intended, wistfully, for "the average Soviet reader . . . (into whose hands, I hope, it will fall sooner or later)."[4]

This testament, *The Origins of Bolshevism*, was a historical account of the "unique development of democratic ideas in Russia." It was, however, an account strongly marked by Dan's recent thinking. Already during the war Dan had tried to show the historical legitimacy of the two "polar opposites of proletarian-socialist ideology, the reformist-democratic and the revolutionary authoritarian." Now, the world inaugurated by the bourgeois revolutions of 1848 was collapsing, and socialism was no longer a distant goal but an immediate task, the sole historically given antithesis of fascism. It was pointless to regret that communism had proved the only bearer of socialist tendencies of development. Dan maintained that the organizational character of the (future) united wokers' movement was secondary, prompting *Vestnik* to retort that he saw the future RSDRP as an ideological consultant to the Communist Party.[5]

In *The Origins of Bolshevism* Dan turned to the Russian implications of this reasoning. In Russia, he wrote, capitalism and bourgeois democracy had proved nonviable from the very outset because of Russia's belated development; indeed, the "profound peculiarity" of Russian democratic thought lay in its thorough anticapitalism. Bolshevism emerged as an inevitable stage of the liberation struggle. It assumed the burden of the properly Russian contradiction that made it impossible in Russia to realize democracy without socialism, or to realize socialism in freely democratic forms. Dan concluded his book on a lyrical note. Reviving Alexander Herzen's century-old prophecy that Europe and Russia would take different paths—"you to socialism through the proletariat, we [i.e., Russia] through socialism to freedom"— Dan affirmed that not only would Russia attain freedom through socialism, but henceforth the Russian path had every chance of becoming universal. This "Russian idea" would thus become the common good of all humanity.[6]

Dan outlived by a year publication of the book which he now called his "swan song." Physically, he felt like a "horse who had run himself out." Politically, his *Novyi put'* group was maintaining that "outside [U.S.] intervention could not stop the socialization of Europe" but could delay it, condemning the world to a "prolonged period of armed peace with ever present dangers of atomic war." Personally, ties to old friends proved difficult to re-establish: former LSI chairman Louis de Brouckère saw Dan as having capitulated to bolshevism; Jean Zyromsky, coauthor of Dan's theses on war in 1935, had joined the French Communist Party. Dan complained even about Blum: "I have not received any letters from him; I have only received a big photo—a really hideous one." And he grumbled to a comrade in France about the United States: "You will truly never learn to hate capitalism (here they call it 'free enterprise') as 'concretely' as here in America."[7]

Dan's last settling of accounts was with the faithful though manipulative Iugov. In the flush of Soviet victory, Dan and Iugov were seriously considering returning to the Soviet Union, as many patriotic Russian emigrés were doing. They were also entertaining the alternative of moving *Novyi put'* to Paris and publishing it in French, to take advantage of the more propitious political climate in Europe.[8] It was Iugov, already considerably more pro-Soviet than Dan, who promoted these projects with particular zeal until Dan lashed out, whether upset at being pushed beyond his better judgment or at the realization that he no longer had the physical capacity to carry out these plans.

"Why this suspiciousness toward me, after I have been working for years with you, without any pretensions?" wrote the pathetic Iugov. "Why did you consider it indispensable 'in the interests of the cause' to tell me the 'truth' about my limited capacities and even to say that you would make a declaration disclaiming responsibility?" Iugov guessed that Dan was afraid "our position" would be deformed in the direction of "capitulationism." In fact, Dan's fears and his conviction that *Novyi put'* could not outlive him were well founded. The second-to-last issue of the journal was a tribute to Dan on his seventy-fifth birthday. Dan's portrait on the front page shows an ill and aged man, huddled inside in a winter coat. The last issue, put out by Iugov, was a memorial published on the occasion of Dan's death.[9]

At Dan's funeral there was a noticeable gulf between the organizers and the other mourners. Among the many speakers only two belonged to Dan's past, before the *Novyi put'* chapter. Iugov's speech stressed Dan's role in the struggle against intervention in Soviet Russia, against primitive antibolshevism, and against Churchillian democracy. Shifrin declared that Dan had been a pupil not only of Martov but also of Lenin, and from his early days he had succeeded in creating a synthesis of menshevism and Leninism.[10]

Vestnik Mensheviks reacted to Dan's death without generosity. Boris Sapir had commented dourly that Dan's book should be called not "The Origins" but "The Justification of Bolshevism," and he had made Dostoyevsky's *Possessed* the leitmotiv of his review of the book. Abramovitch's obituary article on Dan was a purely political commentary. Two souls were struggling in Dan's breast, he wrote, and until 1940 the first dominated. Thereafter, Dan embarked on the path of those who "nonetheless" see some elements of historical truth and progress in bolshevism. Dan's example showed that even a strong and intelligent man standing on this path inevitably descends to full capitulation. Dan's last service to the party, concluded Abramovitch, was that "his example will serve as a warning to all who vacillate and doubt."[11]

Dan's little group dissolved without a stir. Lidia Dan's old friends suspected that she had never really followed her husband in the political evolution of his last years. Still, this "person of the nineteenth century," as she called herself, was to react much as her husband would have to post-Stalin political events: in the late 1950s she dismissed Khrushchev as a thermidorian who might undo collectivization. Upon Fedor Illich's death, this emotionally strong woman broke down. Lonely and alien, she considered moving back to France: "After six years . . . I feel as foreign as the day I came off the boat.

In some ways it is now much worse, first, because I am alone, and second, because there are no longer the few illusions that there were then." She tried to seek out in the Soviet Union her sisters and the daughter of her first marriage, from whom she had not heard since before the war, but her letters were returned to her. Only fourteen years later did she manage to trace her family: one sister failed to appear for her meeting with Lidia's messenger; another asked to be left in peace; her daughter requested that she not write.[12]

Aaron Iugov quickly moved toward a "capitulationist" position, as if he had only been waiting for Dan's death to do so. He began writing regularly for the pro-Soviet *Russkii golos* in New York, contributing articles such as "The Struggle for Abundance in the USSR."[13] In reprisal the Jewish Labor Committee cut off his stipend for labor movement veterans. "Bolshevik methods," protested Friedrich Adler, explicable only by a "specifically American mentality" which assumed that the basis for the stipends was political good behavior and that the boundary between moral and immoral individuals corresponded to that between members of Communist and socialist parties. Lidia Dan threatened to give up her own stipend, although she had just opposed Iugov's attempt to publish the political conclusion to Dan's last book as a separate brochure. Iugov found work in a factory and died of a heart attack, in dire circumstances, a few years later.[14]

Other members of *Novyi put'* went in different directions. Samuel Estrine returned to the social democratic mainstream and continued to act for many years as an intermediary for the Jewish Labor Committee. Alexander Shifrin never changed his views; a weak heart resulted in his early death in 1951. Boris Skomorovskii sought unsuccessfully to return to the Soviet Union. Sent abroad as a UN employee, he was denied permission to return to the United States; nearly blind, he committed suicide in Geneva in 1965 after the death of his wife.[15]

Among the Mensheviks in both camps, Oreste Rosenfeld succeeded best in avoiding ideological polarization. He harbored no sympathy for the Soviet regime but never discarded the old Martov Line concept of a "deacceleration with brakes." He believed that the USSR was a state capitalist order founded on primitive accumulation and that it could normally develop only toward oriental despotism. Still, this state capitalism had produced significant material results and, with them, internal contradictions. "In Russia, thermidor is in full swing," he wrote in March 1956, using old Menshevik language and expressing Menshevik optimism that the Kremlin would not be able to stop short of a critique of Leninism. Rosenfeld's distance from the quarrels of the New York Mensheviks, his search for a "third way" among French socialists, and the fact that he was the only Menshevik actually to travel to the Soviet Union no doubt influenced his outlook.[16]

The last survivor of the original Menshevik left wing, Olga Domanevskaia, continued to live in New York until 1974, writing for the pro-Communist Toronto *Russkii vestnik*. Alexander Erlich last saw her at a Vietnam demonstration in Washington, D.C., in the late 1960s. This veteran of the Russian Revolution of 1905 was too frail to march, but she had hoisted herself onto the steps of a monument, thus participating in what she undoubtedly considered another chapter of the struggle she and her comrades had been waging since the beginning of the century.[17]

The End of the Foreign Delegation

The postwar world was much more like that anticipated by *Vestnik* Mensheviks than those of *Novyi put'*. Moreover, it offered the RSDRP a last chance at party renewal, though at a cost the Mensheviks could not accept.

In many respects the Menshevik majority might well have felt vindicated. The Soviet Union did not democratize after the war—quite the contrary—and whatever revolutionary stirrings occurred elsewhere soon subsided. Sovietophile public opinion, which had so disturbed the Mensheviks during the war years, soon dissipated, at least in America. Of course, debate about the USSR continued. The *Vestnik* crowd crossed swords with Russian emigrés, especially with their old friend Ekaterina Kuskova. She blamed both the West and the USSR for the cold war and predicted a new generation of Russian "Decembrists," the revolutionaries of 1825, inspired by their experience of the West during the Napoleonic wars. As Nicolaevsky pointed out, the Decembrists took ten years to prepare their revolt, and it failed. Curiously, Kuskova's attitude recalled that of the Mensheviks themselves in the heyday of the Martov Line.[1] As for non-Russians, earlier attacks on fellow travelers and naive peace advocates now alternated with sermons against Westerners who failed to distinguish between Soviet and Russian national interests. "The only national [Russian] policy is a democratic one," asserted *Vestnik*.[2] Notwithstanding their irritation at insufficient appreciation of the Soviet threat, *Vestnik*'s writers could enjoy, for the first time, the satisfaction of representing some sort of mainstream opinion.

The RSDRP did suffer the indignity of being refused admission to the reconstituted Socialist International (whereas its cousin party, the Jewish Labor Bund, was admitted). The Mensheviks had shown understanding for their exclusion from preparatory meetings, and they expressed skepticism about the chances for reconstitution, because of both Soviet domination of eastern European socialist parties and the excessively important role of the British Labour Party within the projected International. Nevertheless, they were offended at being barred from a body with which they identified so closely.[3]

The Mensheviks could find comfort in the close convergence, almost to the point of merger, with remaining SR organizations. More significant than the so-called Joint Bureau of Russian Socialists was the informal symbiosis of the two groups, with individual SRs contributing to *Vestnik* and participating in editorial meetings. Only a few years earlier SRs had been accusing the Mensheviks, especially Nicolaevsky, of slandering some of their comrades in order to bar them from the United States and even to provoke their arrest in occupied France.[4]

Materially, too, the Mensheviks found themselves more secure than they had ever been before. Although most *Vestnik* subscriptions were sent out gratis, as "we have never refused to send *Sv* to anyone who really wanted it," there were funds to pay "outside," mostly European, contributors. The accounts of the journal show subsidies from the Jewish Labor Committee, the American Labor Conference on International Affairs, *Forverts,* and other sources. Periodic fund-raising banquets could fetch as much as $4,000.[5]

Ironically, it was amidst these auspicious circumstances that the Foreign Delegation split and collapsed. It fell victim to an utterly unforeseen and, potentially, welcome development: the birth of a new constituency made up of hundreds of thousands of Soviet citizens—prisoners of war, Reich slave laborers, refugees from the advancing Red Army, and, later, defectors from Soviet occupation forces—all scattered in DP camps throughout the western zones of Germany and Austria. Owing to them, the print run of *Vestnik* shot up and still could not satisfy demand. The prospect of once again becoming a mass party of sorts glowed.[6] Instead of meeting the challenge, however, the Mensheviks were defeated by it, perhaps because it demanded that they abandon the party ethos which was their last possession.

Though physically in America, in their hearts the Mensheviks had never left Europe. They suffered from a sense of guilt, exploited by their critics, at having escaped to safety while so many of their own suffered. "Russian democrats in the United States have experienced the war differently from us in Europe. Their views have remained unchanged, ours have evolved," wrote Kuskova.[7] Of course this was untrue, since both groups had evolved, but in different directions.

Above all, starved for information about Russia, the Mensheviks leaped at news first trickling in from members of Allied missions, then flooding in from the millions of Soviet refugees and soldiers who were overruning Europe. Rumors of the survival of individual comrades or of social democratic sentiment somewhere in the Gulag never ceased to fill the Mensheviks with joy. Personal and political accounts by "nonreturners" *(nevozvrashchentsy)*, casual conversations with Soviet personnel, and travelers' observations all found their way into *Vestnik*. For the first time in years the journal again opened a column of "reports about Russia."[8]

Most news about Russia confirmed the Mensheviks' darkest suspicions, but it was news concerning Russians abroad which particularly alarmed them. Stories of forced repatriation of Russian prisoners of war multiplied. Reports from France drew a terrifying picture of GPU "scalp hunters" operating with impunity on French soil.[9] The Mensheviks immediately publicized the fate of these hapless victims, and rushed to their aid as best they could. Initially content merely to strike a blow at Soviet despotism, gradually the Mensheviks came to reflect on the implications of this new emigration for their party.[10]

It was Boris Nicolaevsky who came out earliest and most emphatically in favor of reaching out to the new emigrés. From the outset he had been interested in them as a source of information and as potential readers of *Vestnik*. He also saw in their passionate anti-Sovietism a vindication of *Vestnik*'s line against those who accused it of "emigré blindness." In 1947, while traveling in Germany to recover his library, removed from France during the war and now held in the American occupation zone, Nicolaevsky came face to face with the new emigrés. His excitement at the recovery of his library—"I can think of nothing but her [that is, the library]"—multiplied several fold upon his discovering this new Russia abroad. "The future belongs to it," he declared in *Vestnik*, "not only because it is younger but also because it is closer than we are to contemporary Russia; it is the flesh of its flesh." Decades of nostalgia and yearning burst forth as he met those "born there, in the world of the humiliated and the oppressed." An observer recalls the usually dour Nicolaevsky weeping openly as he reported on these encounters to New York Mensheviks.[11]

Other Mensheviks followed suit. David Dallin traveled to the occupation zones and established contacts there. Raphael Abramovitch, too frail to travel, also looked toward the emigration. Commenting on one of the first new Soviet defectors, the minor functionary Viktor Kravchenko, Abramovitch expressed delight with this "worker, a pure product of the Soviet system," a natural democrat who defected for selfless motives and who, untainted by any hint of Trotskyism, had "instinctively come to speak Menshevik prose." Abramovitch continued to believe that many new emigrés were speaking socialist prose without realizing it.[12]

The Mensheviks did not shut their eyes to problems posed by the new emigrés. Most were uneducated, depoliticized, and demoralized; all were frightened. Nicolaevsky described them publicly as "plebeians" and recognized privately that there were many antisemites among them. Moreover, the new emigrés were susceptible to manipulation by the Russian Orthodox Church and by the most reactionary elements of the old Russian emigration, transplanted from the Balkans to Germany. But, Nicolaevsky argued, there was a promising stratum among the new emigrés. This was the technical intelligentsia, who represented about a quarter of the total; their skills gave them some independence and qualified them for leadership of the opposition to Stalin, at home and abroad.[13]

Abramovitch fretted at the unprecedentedly difficult position of the Russian emigrés. He complained that never had an emigration been as utterly separated from its homeland, and never had there been anything to compare with the totalitarian state that now rendered all organized opposition impossible. All that the Russian emigration could really do was to represent its country's interests before the public opinion of the free world. Even a radio station, the sole means of penetrating the Iron Curtain, could be established only by a foreign state sponsor. An additional, particular problem for the Mensheviks was the utter discredit of the term "socialism" among new emigrés. In Nicolaevsky's words, the Mensheviks' task was to rehabilitate the concept by showing it to be "inseparable from democracy and from the freedom of human personality"; this could be done only if the emigrés had no grounds for suspecting the Mensheviks "of any inclination toward compromise with the Bolsheviks."[14]

Even so, the task was not easy. As one emigré put it sarcastically, "I thought I had gotten away from socialism, but now I learn that I had only gotten away from inauthentic socialism." What was this "socialism" that has never been realized? he asked rhetorically, comparing it to an unpainted painting or an unwritten poem. He scored the Mensheviks' pride at never having supported attempts to overthrow the Bolsheviks and quoted their own dissident, Stepan Ivanovich, to prove they had been willing to limit universal suffrage in 1919–1921. Reproaching them for caring more for the fate of the Revolution than of Russia, he accused them of simply wanting to make the "SSSR" into the "SSR" (the Union of Socialist Republics) while maintaining *kolhoz*es and all. The Menshevik Party consisted only of leaders, he scoffed, and asked, unfairly, where had the Mensheviks been as Soviet prisoners of war were being repatriated from Fort Dix and elsewhere? Characteristically, this emigré described "Abramovitch and company" as "90 percent Jewish . . . with no ties to the Russian nation." Even though he acknowledged, smirking, that one did not hear much about Marxism from Mensheviks these days, he knew that they and their American ex-Communist friends were plotting a "new Marxist conspiracy against Russia."[15]

None of the Mensheviks would renounce their loyalty to the socialist ideal for the sake of the new emigrés. "We are a tiny island [whose task it is] to preserve for the future the banner of democratic socialism," Abramovitch had written recently, and he now reiterated this position: "We struggle in the name of socialism, however awfully compromised this term is . . . We could throw out our socialist program as unwanted ballast, but we have always refused to sacrifice the sense of our existence for the sake of existence."[16] Still, the Mensheviks differed in the extent to which they were willing to accommodate to the realities of the new emigration, and it was over this issue that the Foreign Delegation collapsed.

Most vocal in arguing the case for rapprochement with new emigrés was Boris Nicolaevsky. He identified two important groups: "Solidarists," (NTS, or Natsional'no Trudovoi Soiuz or National Labor Alliance), a corporatist group founded in Belgrade in 1930, popular among younger emigrés; and the Committee for the Liberation of the Peoples of Russia (KONR, or Komitet Osvobozhdeniia Narodov Rossii). The latter was a continuation of General Andrei Vlasov's Russian Liberation Movement created under German auspices during World War II. According to Nicolaevsky, the specificity of Vlasov's movement lay not in its cooperation with Germans (others had cooperated, too) but in its democratic and federative program. Above all, it was the only new emigré group that identified with the old Russian revolutionary tradition. Who could be surprised, asked Nicolaevsky, that these unguided Soviet youths occasionally lost their way, even as they sought to remain faithful to this noble tradition?[17]

Nicolaevsky's benign view of the Vlasovites aroused controversy. Abramovitch criticized it discreetly in a probably imaginary dialogue with a Vlasovite. He did not blame his interlocutor for "running away from the Soviet hell" or even for defeatist attitudes, but he drew the line at making common cause with aggressors against one's own country. What could have been the calculation of the Vlasovite leaders? Abramovitch inquired. If Hitler were to win, they would merely have been his gauleiters; if Hitler were defeated, they could hardly fail to anticipate the Allies' attitude toward them. In the final analysis it was Hitler, not Stalin, who was the main enemy, and since democracy consisted not only of goals but also of methods, one could not adopt Stalinist tactics to fight Stalin. Ever the conciliator, Abramovitch added that he did not condemn individual Vlasovites, so long as they did not personally have any crimes on their conscience.[18]

Other members of the Foreign Delegation, particularly Grigorii Aronson and Boris Dvinov, criticized Nicolaevsky's indulgence much more stridently. According to Aronson, both Nicolaevsky's judgment and his facts were wrong. It was only as they were losing the war that the Vlasovites experienced their democratic conversion. Moreover, Aronson accused the Vlasovites of outright antisemitism and even speculated about their participation in the extermination of the Jews. This contrasted with Nicolaevsky's verdict that there was no evidence of Vlasovite antisemitism and Abramovitch's view that the Vlasovites had simply followed the line of least resistance.[19]

Controversy soon spilled over beyond the pages of *Vestnik*. Nicolaevsky prepared a response to Aronson, and at a Foreign Delegation meeting in May 1948 a majority voted, over Nicolaevsky's objections, to allow Aronson to publish a reply. Nicolaevsky withdrew his article and resigned from the Foreign Delegation and from *Vestnik*. Almost simultaneously his resignation was followed by that of David Dallin, even more vehemently in favor of "amnestying" the Vlasovites but less involved in the polemic (and not very active in *Vestnik*), as well as by that of Iurii Denike. Iraklii Tsereteli, once again a good friend to the Mensheviks, attempted to bring the dissidents back to the fold.[20] It was not until 1952 and 1954, respectively, that Denike and Nicolaevsky were to publish once more in *Vestnik;* Dallin never wrote for it again.

Raphael Abramovitch, as party chairman and *Vestnik* editor, was torn between his growing disenchantment with the new emigration—"they have no people and no ideas," he wrote privately—and his political instincts. His efforts to mend the rift within the Foreign Delegation by steering a middle course were unsuccessful. Dvinov responded angrily to Abramovitch's plea to consider the "inner tragedy" of the Russians who had marched with Hitler. Others accused Abramovitch of adopting a double standard, of being more critical of Vlasov in his Yiddish articles than in his Russian ones.[21]

In spite of the burden of the unresolved Vlasovite issue, the Mensheviks dived headlong into the buoyant political life of the new Russian emigration. The result was the creation of the League of Struggle for People's Freedom (Liga Bor'by za Narodnuiu Svobodu), which held its first mass meeting in New York in 1949 on the anniversary of the February Revolution, chaired by its president and leading force Boris Nicolaevsky. "That's politics," was one of Nicolaevsky's favorite expressions, and he would not let issues of past behavior shake his determination to be part of the new "Russia Abroad."[22] Among the league's other leaders were Abramovitch, Dallin, Denike, and Dvinov, as well as SR leader Chernov and former prime minister Kerensky. The distinctiveness of the league, as its founders saw it, was its resolutely democratic-republican program, and, one might add, the fact this was the first nonsocialist Russian emigré organization with which the Menshevik leaders were willing to identify their party.[23]

Divisions emerged very early in the league. Memories of 1917 made it difficult for Kerensky to cooperate with the Mensheviks. Pointing from a friend's New York appartment to the opposite side of the street, where Abramovitch and some other Mensheviks lived, Kerensky would repeat, "They, they ruined me." And yet when Kerensky evoked moral considerations at league bureau meetings, Nicolaevsky would grumble, "After the Kornilov Affair I don't see how you have any right to talk of morality." Kerensky's present outlook also grated on the Mensheviks, as it had in 1944, when they accused him of seeking to restore the western borders of the tsarist empire without even holding a referendum in the Baltic states or in eastern Poland. Kerensky eventually left the league, taking several "Great Russian"–oriented personalities with him.[24]

The Vlasovite question refused to go away. Boris Dvinov and his allies in the New York social democratic group demanded that the league eschew any partiality to the Vlasovites. Instead, it seemed to be cooperating ever more closely with the Vlasovite Union of Struggle for the Liberation of the Peoples of Russia (SBONR, or Soiuz Bor'by Osvobozhdeniia Narodov Rossii), as well as with umbrella groups which included monarchists and NTS Solidarists. The situation was aggravated by a marked rightward drift even among those Vlasovites who had originally subscribed to the SBONR's democratic platform, and by the growing Solidarist influence on them. Because of this, and because of the league's rapprochement with separatist forces among non-Russian Soviet exiles, the fiercely anti-Solidarist Dallin also left the league. Abramovitch continued to defend the league's allies, though he complained of SBONR attacks (for which the group apologized) on Solomon Schwartz, who had asked that applicants to the league be screened for antisemitism, as well as attacks on Grigorii Aronson (for which it did not apologize).[25]

Politics within the league, as within the entire Russian emigration, soon focused on the nationality question. Elaborating on their party's twenty-year-old national platform—"a free federation of free nations"—*Vestnik* pointed out that the nationality question was, in fact, a whole series of questions. Emphasis on the right of separation, the focus of emigré controversy, obscured the wider issue and, unfortunately, created an atmosphere uncongenial for arguments against separation. Existing strong separatist feelings, *Vestnik* claimed, were not rooted in fundamental antagonism between Russians and other nations living on Soviet territory; they were a primitive form of protest against Communist dictatorship confusing "Moscow" wth the true enemy, Stalin. To be sure, the will to separation should be tested by free elections under UN control, except for the Baltic states, which, because of the circumstances of their incorporation, must be granted independence first and then asked if they wished to return voluntarily to the Russian Federation. However many cases of separation ensued, numerous national minorities would remain in Russia, if only because "national self-determination" obscured the fact that self-determination was, in fact, not "national" but territorial. After the experience of India and Pakistan, further transfers of populations were unthinkable, and therefore guarantees would have to be found for the minority populations that would inevitably remain. If such guarantees could be assured, the whole issue of separation would lose much of its sharpness.[26]

Underlying emigré quarrels was the life-or-death issue of U.S. support. All emigré organizations competed for Washington's favor; none wished to be seen as carrying out American orders. *Vestnik* called for public assurances that Western powers had no intention of infringing on the territorial integrity of the USSR. It recognized that although there were no "national" contradictions between the interests of the United States and those of free Russia, there could be temporary divergences. Unfortunately, these had come to the fore as well-meaning Americans sought to impose unnatural alliances on Russian democrats. David Dallin complained more bluntly to some league members: "Functionaries in New York want to use us Russians like marionettes."[27]

These matters came to a head with a series of meetings in Germany aimed at uniting Russian emigré organizations. Sponsors were American and, ostensibly, private citizens. These included Spencer Williams, a foreign correspondent and representative of the American Chamber of Commerce in Moscow throughout the 1930s. Williams, "said to have been at one time connected with an official Committee for Political Warfare," now represented the Munich Institute for the Study of the History and Culture of the Soviet Union and was still someone whom "accredited State Department officials do not repudiate." Among other prominent Americans were authors and journalists with close ties to the Mensheviks, including W. H. Chamberlin, Isaac Don Levine, and Eugene Lyons, founder of the so-called American Committee for the Liberation of the Peoples of Russia, Inc., which evolved into the American Committee for Liberation from Bolshevism.[28]

Initially Nicolaevsky's league gained ground. A British report even complained that the State Department favored Mensheviks and SRs, people "who [had] helped to pave the way for the Bolshevik revolution and afterwards found it expedient to leave Russia in great haste." It described these "Marxists" as "wholly discredited" people, stressing that the "Mensheviks and others are Communists, differing only from the Bolsheviks because of their belief that Communism ought to be introduced by graudal [sic] or Fabian methods." Moreover, the report added, these people "certainly are not Russians by race or creed, even if they were ever technically of Russian or Soviet nationality."[29]

American sponsorship proved a thankless task. All emigré groups, including the Mensheviks, sought to manipulate the American Committee for Liberation and related organizations to their own advantage. One committee member complained to its president about the "offensive observations" of David Dallin and several other Mensheviks. Dallin was using his regular column in the *New Leader* not only to denounce other emigré groups but also to expose American innocence (or deviousness, as the case might be) in dealing with them. He was therefore barred from one of the meetings as a "disruptive influence" who practiced "slanderous attacks" on the American committee. Nicolaevsky, when invited to disassociate himself from Dallin, refused, not because he agreed with Dallin (they were at odds over Solidarists and over SBONR) but in protest against outside interference in the league. Abramovitch, too, fulminated from afar against American agents who sought to give instructions to Russians, especially as these agents were increasingly turning to the most recent emigration, consisting of rabidly anti-Marxist defectors from the Soviet occupation army in Germany.[30]

In these circumstances all attempts at emigré unification failed. The league opposed cooperation with Solidarists, whom it considered chauvinists, anti-semites, and reactionaries; Solidarists opposed cooperation with Menshevik Marxists and advocates of Russia's dismemberment. When the Solidarists reversed their "Great Russian" nationalist policy to obtain U.S. support— "Paris is worth a mass," commented Abramovitch—feuding broke out in earnest.[31] After more than two years of effort, a Coordinating Center for Anti-Bolshevik Struggle did come into existence in Munich, including Nicolaevsky's league, the Vlasovite SBONR, and others. Success was of short duration. The center soon broke up into a majority group, reinforced by Solidarists who had not been in the original center, and a minority group, made up of Nicolaevsky's league and most nationality groups. In disgust at the bickering, in August 1953 the American Committee for Liberation withdrew its support from both sides, leaving Radio Liberty as the only fruit of its efforts.[32]

Meanwhile, the Mensheviks continued to quarrel about the emigration. The degeneration of the Vlasovite movement made cooperation, even with individual Vlasovites, into a "capitulation . . . of the democratic revolution of February 1917 before a group compromised by collaboration with Hitler," wrote Aronson in early 1951. Exceptions could be made only for Vlasovites who openly and publicly condemned their Vlasovite past, but of these there were none. Soon Aronson and two other Foreign Delegation members issued an ultimatum: if Abramovitch and Schwarz took the RSDRP, via the league, into a projected emigré council which included Vlasovites and Solidarists, these three members would not "bear responsibility." Abramovitch and Shwartz, unwilling to withdraw from the league, turned for support to the New York Group of the RSDRP. After a number of stormy meetings, the group decided, in June 1951, that it would replace the Foreign Delegation as the institutional center of the party and as publisher of *Sotsialisticheskii vestnik*. Shortly afterwards the group voted in favor of RSDRP participation in the projected emigré council, which, in any case, never came into existence.[33]

Aronson and his allies continued their campaign. They castigated the RSDRP's new "coalition with antidemocratic totalitarian tendencies." They denounced *Vestnik* as the personal organ of its editor, Raphael Abramovitch, and founded a new periodical publication, *Protiv techeniia* (Against the Current). Their objections went beyond the issue of cooperation with nondemocratic groups to encompass the question of foreign involvement in Russia's liberation. "We must stand with 'our face to Russia,'" announced the first of *Protiv techeniia*'s two volumes, meaning that the emigration should not dream of returning to Russia on the coattails of an invading foreign army. *Protiv techeniia*'s denunciation of American-sponsored plans for the "dismemberment of Russia" also made it a spokesman for those Mensheviks opposed to alliance with separatist Soviet nationality organizations in exile.[34]

Shortly before the demise of the Foreign Delegation, Boris Nicolaevsky had written gloomily that he feared "the funeral of Menshevism, or rather the last nail in its coffin." He would have had the party reach out in a completely new direction. For some this direction was unacceptable; others were paralyzed by the prospect of splitting the remains of the party. A few years later, when American interest in emigrés and the prospects of emigré unification had disappeared, the editors of *Protiv techeniia* returned to *Vestnik*, but without much joy on either side.[35] No one, however, had the heart to resuscitate the Foreign Delegation. Who could say whether its death was due to betrayal of its own principles through the excessive hopes that some had placed in the new emigration, or whether it died a natural and, indeed, belated death after three decades of brave survival in the harsh climate of exile?

Waging the Cold War

Upon arriving in America one Menshevik made the paradoxical observation that although socialism did not exist in the new world, "our chances [here] have risen considerably."[1] The reasoning behind this assertion proved correct. When the cold war broke out, the Mensheviks' "chances" did indeed improve. The chances, however, were no longer those of the RSDRP as a party but those of certain individual party members.

Long-standing connections with American labor, particularly through labor leaders of Russian Jewish origin such as David Dubinsky, matured and broadened. Continuing the Rand School projects that had involved several Mensheviks during the early stages of the war, The AFL-founded Labor Conference on International Affairs drew on Mensheviks in sponsoring social democratic reflection on the postwar world. Among these efforts to revive socialist theory was the short-lived *Modern Review*, founded in 1944 and animated largely by Raphael Abramovitch. He and the journal's other Menshevik editor, Iurii Denike, fell out with their American counterparts when one of the latter, Lewis Coser, aroused Abramovitch's ire with a neutralist article on China. Still, *Modern Review* did contribute to relaunching debate on the totalitarian nature of the Soviet Union.[2]

AFL-Menshevik connections also had practical results in helping the AFL establish ties in western Europe and even transfer funds. Such unofficial transactions—sending "fifteen books," for instance, meant sending $15,000—were carried out discreetly and efficiently by Samuel Estrine, acting through the Jewish Labor Committee. The Mensheviks, in turn, called on AFL backing for their own causes, such as the successful defense of Russian DPs in Austria. The Mensheviks' satisfaction at the AFL's growing international involvement in the cold war was therefore understandable; it had been fostered by contact with the Mensheviks themselves.[3]

The Mensheviks branched out beyond the American labor community. Once the party had discarded its self-imposed taboo on publication in the nonsocialist press, Mensheviks wrote frequently for Russian emigré newspapers and journals, such as New York's *Novoe russkoe slovo* and *Novyi zhurnal;* some, like Abramovitch and Aronson, also continued to contribute to the dwindling Yiddish-language press. *Vestnik's* literary critic, Vera Alexandrova, was an editor at the Chekhov Publishing House, set up by the Ford Foundation's East European Fund to promote Russian-language publication abroad. Mensheviks' bylines would appear in wide-circulation American magazines as diverse as the *New Republic* and *Saturday Review*, as well as in academic or government-sponsored publications such as *Problems of Communism*.[4] Most pieces were commentaries on Soviet affairs, and many contributed to ongoing intellectual debates. Official U.S. channels even served to promote some Menshevik writings. Books distributed abroad by American government agencies included several of David Dallin's works and Solomon Schwarz's *Labor in the Soviet Union.*[5]

The Mensheviks came to the forefront in one of the great cold war "affairs," the Kravchenko case. It was David Dallin who elicited Kravchenko's decision to defect. Having quarreled with Dallin's first recommended ghostwriter, Isaac Don Levine, Kravchenko was directed, again by Dallin, to new collaborators, notably Eugene Lyons and Mark Khinoy, the latter a Menshevik printer resident in the United States since 1913 and a *Vestnik* contributor. Lyons rewrote Kravchenko's book, and when differences arose between the acknowledged and the unacknowledged author, Khinoy prepared a translation of Kravchenko's own postscript.[6]

Four years later Kravchenko launched (and won) a famous libel lawsuit in Paris against a French magazine.[7] Among the allegations was that Kravchenko's book had actually been written by Mensheviks; consequently, Dallin and Nicolaevsky were evoked repeatedly in lurid terms throughout the trial, as were *New York Times* correspondent Joseph Shaplen and the SR Vladimir Zenzinov, both also described as Mensheviks. The defense at the trial exploited fully the ambiguities of the manuscript's authorship (Kravchenko refused to identify his editor and translator; Levine wrote that he had never had anything to do with Kravchenko) and of Menshevik involvement (including invocation of the late Fedor Dan as an anti-Kravchenko Menshevik).[8] In light of all this, it is not surprising that an FBI report should have identified Dallin as Kravchenko's "literary agent." Though technically inaccurate, this description nonetheless pointed to their privileged relationship and to the services Dallin rendered the defector (not to mention the more doubtful service of having unwittingly provided Kravchenko with former Soviet agent Mark Zborowski as a companion and bodyguard).[9] Although this was not the Mensheviks' first experience in protecting and promoting a Soviet defector, the tremendous impact of the Kravchenko case—his book sold over 5 million copies in twenty-two languages and his trial was an international cause célèbre—gave it unusual significance.

Less dramatically, the Mensheviks routinely participated in various academic and intellectual gatherings; some were involved in creating one of the characteristic institutions of the times, the Congress for Cultural Freedom. Boris Nicolaevsky and Solomon Schwarz, representing respectively the League of Struggle for People's Freedom and the Foreign Delegation of the RSDRP, attended the congress's founding meeting in Berlin. Nicolaevsky's speech there was much applauded and he was elected to the congress' governing body, but, with few exceptions, the Mensheviks did not write much in the congress' highbrow magazines.[10]

Unquestionably the Mensheviks' American "flagship" was the *New Leader*, put out weekly in New York by the Social Democratic Federation. Criticized even by insiders for being "more anti-Communist than socialist," the *New Leader* displayed unrivaled perseverance and ideological coherence. "If any single feature has consistently distinguished this magazine from all others . . . it is our detailed study of events in the Communist world," stated the *New Leader* in 1962. Moreover, "we have been fortunate in attracting to our pages not merely 'experts' but the very men who participated in modern Russia's birth."[11]

Most of these men (and one woman) were Mensheviks. A reader of *Sotsialisticheskii vestnik* who picked up the *New Leader* sometime in the 1950s could not read long without stumbling upon familiar names. Some, like Vladimir Woytinsky, who wrote sunny forecasts for the American economy, already considered themeselves more American than Russian. Menshevik offspring who cut their teeth on the *New Leader*, such as Alexander Dallin, Leon Gouré (son of Boris Gurevitch-Dvinov), and *New Leader* associate editor Anatol Shub, were genuinely American; they were joined by a recent young defector from Poland adopted by the Mensheviks, Seweryn Bialer.[12] It is not clear whether Boris Souvarine, whose role in France may be compared to that of the Mensheviks in America, was thinking of the *New Leader* when he complained that New York Mensheviks "have absorbed the platitudes and elementary slogans of the most vulgar American press." In any case, Souvarine and other Paris ex-Mensheviks such as Nikolai Valentinov-Volsky and Oreste Rosenfeld also contributed to the *New Leader*, thanks to their New York friends. No longer a powerful political figure, Rosenfeld might well have reflected on the parallel decline of his own star and the ascent of that of his American comrades.[13]

The *New Leader* hosted some rank-and-file Mensheviks, such as its associate editor Simon Wolin, and Lazar Pistrak, who did *Vestnik*'s subscription list in New York and later worked for the Voice of America.[14] The magazine also served as a regular platform for three historic Menshevik leaders who brought with them the past authority of the RSDRP: Raphael Abramovitch, Boris Nicolaevsky, and David Dallin. Their views provide an overall picture of the Menshevik outlook on the cold war world.

Abramovitch, by now the uncontested Menshevik patriarch, was unambiguously pessimistic. Whereas comrades such as Denike reflected on the concept of totalitarianism, Abramovitch invoked it automatically, attributing to it iron laws. Earlier Abramovitch had looked to Russia's internal regime as "the question of all questions."[15] With the end of World War II, however, he turned all his attention to the international scene, effectively abandoning any hope of change within Russia. "The world is moving toward war," he believed, "toward a catastrophe of unseen proportions" sufficiently imminent and apparent for Abramovitch to argue strenuously against his daughter's return to France in the early 1950s. Most alarming and incomprehensible was the West's failure to understand the situation. What madness to sign treaties with Russia, the equivalent of "a united front with polygamists against polygamy," as he titled one of his articles. War need not break out right away since, for as long as they could, the Bolsheviks would simply take advantage of the Allies' distraction and confusion; the clash, however, could not be put off indefinitely.[16]

Positing the identity of Nazi and Bolshevik totalitarianism, Abramovitch was ever on guard for signs that the West was returning to "appeasement." He welcomed the outbreak of the Korean War, lamented the Geneva Conference on Indochina (tantamount to a "second Munich"), and denounced those who spoke of "doing all, short of war." The graybearded fire-eater "Syngman" (as in Syngman Rhee) Abramovitch, wrote the Communist press, thinks of nothing but the atomic bomb and how to crush the Soviet Union. Although Abramovitch stated, regretfully, that it was too late to use the atomic bomb now that the United States had lost its monopoly, he urged that "we must rid ourselves of the fear of A and H bombs." From Abramovitch's perspective, Eisenhower was a "Kerensky on a world scale," with the only difference being that in 1917 the Revolution had perished in an impotent attempt to continue an unnecessary war, whereas now catastrophe loomed because of an equally impotent fear of undertaking the risk of war.[17]

Only once after Stalin's death did Abramovitch depart from his blanket refusal to count on any internal changes in the Soviet leadership. "Was Beria the Great Chance?" he asked wistfully in a *New Leader* article that evoked the long-discarded Menshevik concept of "going downhill on brakes." Since Abramovitch expressed this sentiment only after Beria had been deposed, the Communist press may have been correct in claiming that he was unhappy with Beria's arrest simply because it reduced the struggle within the Kremlin. In any case, Abramovitch never again expressed hope in any of Stalin's successors. He set no store in de-Stalinization, differing even from his closest party comrades in his belief that no Russian thermidor was in sight and merely regretting that the West had lost its opportunity to stop Red imperialism.[18] When *Pravda* mentioned Abramovitch, for the first time in twenty-six years, as an admirer of Soviet sputnik technology, he refused the compliment and replied that he considered it his greatest duty to warn American workers of the Soviet danger.[19]

Boris Nicolaevsky was as harsh as anyone with respect to the Soviet Union. "Revolution is a barbarian form of progress," he wrote, quoting the French socialist Jean Jaurès, and added, "but there are regimes that are a barbarian form of regression . . . Stalin's regime is the most regressive that has ever existed in the history of mankind."[20] Whereas for Abramovitch totalitarianism precluded internal Soviet development and left only the USSR's external dynamism—that is, its international aggressiveness—as an object of study, Nicolaevsky's recognition of the totalitarian nature of the Soviet Union directed his interest from macropolitical to micropolitical considerations.

According to Nicolaevsky, Stalin had destroyed the "independent dukedoms" of the early Soviet years and replaced them with a "service nobility" subordinate to himself. Stalin held absolute power as the ultimate arbiter of rival apparati which checked one another; only the war years had momentarily hindered Stalin in his constant intervention to prevent these apparati from transcending narrowly defined boundaries. Nicolaevsky thus dwelt on divisions and nuances within the Soviet power structure. The Soviet regime was not immobile, he argued, and even a purely formal change in government ministers was significant as a symptom of the evolution of power and as a key to the struggle of elite factions, the surrogate politics of the Soviet Union. Moreover, factional struggles in the Soviet Union not only existed but also had policy significance.[21]

The essence of kremlinology, as conceived and practiced by Nicolaevsky, was the identification of the rising (and falling) stars in the Soviet political firmament. Early on, Nicolaevsky placed his bets on Georgii Malenkov against Andrei Zhdanov. After Stalin's death, he declared Malenkov and Beria allies and, as imminent targets of Stalin's last purge, beneficiaries of the dictator's demise. Beria's liquidation was therefore a triumph of the Stalinists, and, inasmuch as it was Khrushchev's doing, Nicolaevsky concluded that Khrushchev belonged to the Stalinist camp.[22] Although Nicolaevsky had been first to note the disappearance of Stalin's secretary A. N. Poskrebyshev and of Beria, Khrushchev's dramatic denunciation of Stalin at the Twentieth Party Congress caught him off guard (as it did everyone else). He could only explain it, feebly, in terms of Khrushchev's effort to improve relations with Tito.[23]

Nicolaevsky's minute hermeneutical analyses of Soviet sources, claiming to pry open the Byzantine world of the Kremlin leadership, drew criticism both on the left and on the right. "Boris Ivanovich Nikolaevskii has become an inexhaustible supplier of information from the Soviet Union," scoffed Fedor Dan as early as 1946. "Who are those correspondents of Nikolaevskii from whom nothing can be hidden?"[24] Boris Souvarine, convinced that he enjoyed special insight into the workings of the Soviet leadership, doubted whether one could unravel, much less predict, the meaning of events in the Kremlin. He was sure, however, that any talk of factional struggle within the Kremlin was nothing but a dangerous illusion which could lull the West into a false sense of security.[25] "Little Boris" and "Big Boris" (nicknames referring to Souvarine's and Nicolaevsky's comparative physical stature) sparred on specific points, with Nicolaevsky denouncing Souvarine's "know-nothing" position as leading the West to forfeit opportunities.[26]

Nicolaevsky was not always convincing. To his earlier penchant for conspiracy theories he now added a detectivelike approach based on clever but often unverifiable conjecture.[27] He could not help wondering whether Stalin had been murdered or forgo speculating on "Stalin's secret sickness," although he resisted the Souvarine-Volsky thesis that Stalin was simply mad. Nor could he shake off the temptation, familiar from *Sotsialisticheskii vestnik*'s early days, to pronounce the dictatorship in the throes of a major crisis.[28] Notwithstanding such weaknesses, Nicolaevsky's analyses would inspire even his critics' respect. Souvarine called the New York Menshevik colony a "madhouse," and he was merciless with respect to the products of "Rand Corporation kremlinology," but he considered Nicolaevsky's articles required reading.[29] Nicolaevsky's critics would have to resign themselves to the fact that the art of kremlinology, very much Nicolaevsky's trademark, was to become the tool of an entire profession.

The most constant star in the *New Leader*'s firmament was David Dallin. Abramovitch's Cassandra warnings and Nicolaevsky's kremlinological pyrotechnics were frequent features, but Dallin's columns were a weekly staple from his appointment as *New Leader* associate editor in 1945 through 1953; later he continued to contribute almost on a monthly basis. Dallin was also author of a dozen English-language books on the Soviet Union. All attracted attention in their time, and some are still considered classics. In short, Dallin became the ultimate Menshevik pundit.

David Dallin had always been something of a maverick within the party. In the United States his views continued to be idiosyncratic. He reviewed earlier Menshevik hopes in the evolution of bolshevism, emphasized that they had all proven sterile, and yet affirmed, paradoxically, that "we were right then": so long as there was a spark of hope, the Mensheviks were morally obliged to believe in evolution as "the least painful road" for their country. With Soviet entry into the war in 1941, however, Dallin was virtually alone among all Mensheviks in refusing to adopt a defensist policy.[30]

At odds with his comrades and tired of the emigré milieu, Dallin struck out on his own. Within four years he had published four books in English at Yale University Press. The first, *Soviet Russia's Foreign Policy, 1939–1942* (1942), was remembered by the *New York Times* forty-five years later as "remarkably prescient" for having reconstituted some of the secret clauses of the 1939 Soviet-German pact. At the time the same newspaper described Dallin's next book, *Russia and Post-War Europe* (1943), as a "cold-blooded book with a warm-hearted conclusion," thus giving as much importance to Dallin's brief conjecture about an alternative to Soviet isolationism as to his thesis. Historians have since pointed to this book and its sequel, *The Real Soviet Russia* (1944), as the first break in the publishing industry's informal policy of not putting out books critical of Russia during the war years.[31]

Dallin's early wartime writings paid particular attention to the Soviet-German relationship. In *Soviet Russia's Foreign Policy* he was more nuanced than Nicolaevsky (and than he himself was later to be) in affirming that Stalin had always sought an alliance with Hitler. In *Russia and Postwar Europe* Dallin's argument was that since no collective security system was likely to emerge from the war, the German problem, and with it the Russian problem, would return. Suspicious of the unreliable and distant West and fearful of an inevitably resurgent Germany, the USSR was likely to build up its military strength, seize and mobilize eastern Europe, and, if unable to impose itself on Germany, come to terms with it as it had in the past.[32]

As the contours of the postwar world became fixed, and as Dallin's confidence and reputation grew, his message became clearer. "From the optimistic to the ridiculous is only a short step," he warned, disparaging "rosy hopes . . . of universal peace." In spite of superficial similarities, Soviet policy was unlike that of imperial Russia. In contrast to those of its predecessor, the Soviet Union's expansionist ambitions were unlimited, encompassing even the internal order of its victims, and excluding the possibility of lasting cooperation with other powers. Moreover, whatever its twists and turns, Soviet policy had to be seen as perfectly consistent since, as one Communist leader had put it, "bolshevism is not an umbrella which can be opened or closed at will."[33]

Dallin's fellow Russian emigrés were not all enthusiastic about his books. Predictably, *Novyi put'* complained that Dallin had failed to discover the inner logic of the Soviet-German pact, and it dismissed a later book as "a bog of anti-bolshevism." It did make the more valid point that Dallin criticized Stalin both for having betrayed the Revolution and for having successfully promoted it.[34] Less predictably, a *New York Times* review of *The Big Three* by *Novyi Zhurnal* editor and Harvard professor Michael Karpovich was also unenthusiastic. Sniffing at the the mass of "facts and figures," Karpovich commented on Dallin's thesis that Stalin applied Leninism, not nationalism, that it really did not matter whether it was the left foot or the right foot that stomped on people's toes.[35]

American reviewers were more impressed. "He is said to be a political exile from Russia and consequently he cannot be a buddy of Stalin's," wrote the *New York Times,* describing Dallin as a "a hard-headed, tough-minded professional thinker." The *New Republic* thought Dallin wrong, but its reviewer was impressed despite himelf. It was Dallin's ability to combine geopolitical analysis with apparent ideological insight that gave him authority in the eyes of his American readers.[36] Dallin's later books also attracted attention. Reviewers noted *The New Soviet Empire*'s call for a "pro-Russian anti-Communist policy for the West" and sympathized with its protest at new social-anthropological interpretations that branded Russians as naturally aggressive.[37] *The Rise of Russia in Asia* was received more critically. Dallin was told that he should have taken account not only of the Soviet "lust for power" but also of Asian aspirations for a better life as a factor in Soviet expansion, a view which he explicitly combated.[38] Nor did Dallin's biggest and most ambitious book, *Soviet Espionage,* receive the acclaim he wanted. It displeased the FBI at the time, and its sources have since been disparaged as almost worthless.[39] Ironically, *Soviet Espionage* appeared just before Dallin discovered that he and his wife had been associating for years with a former Soviet spy, Zborowski.

Dallin's most noteworthy book was *Forced Labor in Soviet Russia,* published in 1947. Nicolaevsky wrote the chapter on labor camps in the Far East and was listed as coauthor; Boris Sapir recorded his experiences in the Solovetskii camps from 1923 to 1925, stressing the then-novel treatment of political prisoners like common law criminals. As the *New Leader* put it, this was "an account of the return in this century of slave labor as a government institution."[40]

This was not the first account on the subject, even by Mensheviks. *Vestnik* had often hosted reminiscences and revelations.[41] Early studies, such as the duchess of Atholl's, written with the help of Anatolii Baikalov, were now swollen by a growing postwar literature, including Kravchenko's disclosures. Dallin, too, had devoted one chapter of *The Real Soviet Russia* in 1944 to forced labor. As in the early days of emigration when the Mensheviks had made it their business to debunk starry-eyed travelers' reports, Dallin declared that "the serious reader . . . demands something more contemporary than tales of the military prowess of the Russian nation and of Stalinist wisdom." Nothing was more revealing of the nature of the Soviet Union than the Gulag, and to speak of the Soviet Union without mentioning forced labor was like telling "the story of Germany during the last decade without mentioning the fate of the Jews."[42]

Forced Labor in the Soviet Union was painstakingly detailed, containing maps of the camp system, facsimiles of documents, and statistics. Above all, it proposed an overall vision and explanation of the Gulag. Hannah Arendt, then working on her classic *Origins of Totalitarianism,* noted that the book explained the most incomprehensible aspect of totalitarian regimes, their emancipation from economic laws. The *New York Times* called the book "gruesome reading" and predicted it was "certain not to be read."[43]

In fact, *Forced Labor* was read and passionately debated. Pro-Communist public opinion had always denied the nature or the scope of the Soviet camps; Fedor Dan, for instance, claimed that concentration camps had recently existed in America as well, citing internment of Japanese Americans and a camp for Jewish refugees in Oswego, New York.[44] Even more moderate opinion was skeptical. The *Economist,* referring to the long history of Russian serfdom, explicitly questioned Dallin's conclusion that the Soviet Gulag could not be compared to anything in tsarist times. It also published an article on the Kolyma gold fields which followed the account in *Forced Labor* very closely without mentioning the book. When the figures on gold production, originally produced by Nicolaevsky, were contested, the *Economist* backed down, repudiating its anonymous correspondent and agreeing that the figures were "undoubtedly, an exaggeration."[45]

The *New Statesman and Nation* launched the most extensive criticism of the book with an ambivalent review by the popular former Moscow correspondent Edward Crankshaw. After remarking that the "sickening aspects" of "penal servitude *à la russe*" reflected "the difference between Russian and English conceptions," Crankshaw commended this "elaborate and laborious study" for its facts. He also criticized it as dull, imperceptive, and reductionist, "trying for duty's sake to make the flesh creep." Crankshaw concluded with some ambiguous remarks about the human suffering that could have been spared if the West had earlier adopted a more reasonable attitude toward Russia.[46]

Crankshaw's remarks were mild compared to the onslaught that followed. A letter to the *New Statesman and Nation* poked holes in Dallin's calculations of prison population and in his evidence. The letter rather discredited itself by its intemperate tone: "utterly worthless . . . a tissue of distortions and malicious gossip, useful only to professional poisoners of international relations." References to Dallin's Menshevik past were, one must assume, supposed to clinch the argument. The Franco-British journalist and author on Soviet matters, Alexander Werth, also stepped into the fray, moved perhaps by Dallin's disparaging remarks about the ignorance of foreign correspondents in Russia. Werth's language was more moderate, his statistical analysis more complex. He too, however, found that Dallin's "figures and generalizations" made *Forced Labor* one of the most "cockeyed books" he had ever read and that Crankshaw's "applause" (such as it was) was irresponsible.[47]

Virtually all reviewers zeroed in on Dallin's figures, largely inferred from partial information, as the most vulnerable part of his book. Those, such as the *New Statesman* critics, who would have preferred to deny the existence of forced labor, re-counted Dallin's categories or extrapolated from them to show that his figures were inconsistent or incredibly high. Other critics endorsed sources, such as Kravchenko, who gave even higher figures. In fact, Dallin's chapter "How Many Camps and Prisoners?" considered various evidence, ranging from emigré economist S. N. Prokopovitch's estimate of 5 to 7 million political prisoners, through two Polish authors' anecdotally cited figure of 35 million. Dallin concluded that his earlier figures of 7 to 12 million, presented in *The Real Soviet Russia* and drawn from Viktor Alter, were approximately correct.[48] Later Dallin was to cite a slightly higher U.S. Army estimate of 13 million, while his Menshevik comrade Naum Jasny revised the figures sharply downward to 3.5 million.[49] Debate on the issue continues and, indeed, has intensified in recent years.[50]

Forced Labor in Soviet Russia quickly became a political issue. At a meeting of the first committee of the UN General Assembly, the South African delegate held up a copy and quoted from it. The book was immediately denounced before the committee by Ukrainian representative D. Z. Manuilsky, and by former Menshevik and Moscow trial prosecutor A. I. Vyshinsky, now at the UN as Soviet deputy minister. "Gangsters," "idiots," and purveyors of "information from Hitlerite agents" were some of Vyshinsky's epithets, backed by the assertion that the authors claimed there were 20 million political prisoners in the USSR. What is noteworthy is not the fact that Vyshinsky distorted the book's findings but that he was familiar with it and that his main quarrel concerned the size, not the existence, of the Gulag. Dallin's and Nicolaevsky's reaction was to launch a million-dollar slander suit against Vyshinsky, which foundered on the rocks of the latter's diplomatic immunity but served its purpose in publicizing the issue. At the urging of the AFL and the British representative, the UN Economic and Social Council voted to call for an investigation into the Gulag, as Dallin had urged earlier, but the scheduled discussion did not take place.[51]

Another repercussion of *Forced Labor in Soviet Russia* was its part in the establishment of David Rousset's Commission internationale contre le régime concentrationnaire. A survivor of Nazi camps, Rousset launched a movement of former political prisoners against labor camps. Universal in its aspirations, it was directed, in the first instance, against the Soviet camp system. Although critical of Dallin's emphasis on the economic role of the camps and his failure, in Rousset's eyes, to recognize the unprecedented "pattern" shared by Soviet and Nazi camps, Rousset acknowledged *Forced Labor in Soviet Russia* as the empirical cornerstone of his movement.[52] For Rousset's two successful libel suits in Brussels and Paris (similar in many respects to the Kravchenko trial, and not only because the defendant was again *Lettres fran-çaises*), Dallin helped to recruit witnesses. In later years he continued to participate in the work of Rousset's commission and to publish under its sponsorship.[53]

It was Dallin's weekly *New Leader* articles that reflected his perception of the ebb and flow of the cold war. His most passionate pieces were directed against fellow travelers and other Soviet dupes. Prime among these was Henry Wallace, whose presidential platform Dallin referred to as "the Stalin-Wallace Program."[54] Those who misled and distorted public opinion on the question of China incurred Dallin's particular wrath. They included Wallace and, above all, the controversial Asia specialist Owen Lattimore. Even the Alsop brothers, "two of our most intelligent and best informed columnists," were taken severely to task as appeasers for suggesting that the Chinese Communists might be nationalists or that there could be a rift between Moscow and Peking.[55]

Vigilance was the most constant theme of Dallin's articles. This implied not only watchfulness but also self-restraint on the part of the United States. Dallin opposed compulsory registration of Communist front organizations as a measure that would only serve anti-American propaganda abroad, and he argued against State Department plans to sever relations with Soviet satellites. He complained about the "no nationalization" conditions attached by Congress to the Marshall Plan, about U.S. reluctance to seek allies among liberals and socialists in Europe, and about the transformation of the military occupation of Germany into a colonial administration.[56]

Consistency was the first requisite of U.S. policy. Dallin attributed defeat in China directly to the State Department's and specifically Secretary George Marshall's zigzags, and he warned of new zigzags if the myth of Chinese Titoism gained acceptance. Having criticized Allied inconsistency on Berlin just before the blockade began, Dallin found confirmation of his thesis, although he discounted the importance of the blockade itself.[57] Dallin initially hailed George Kennan's article "Sources of Soviet Conduct" as the basis for a coherent approach to the Soviet Union. With time and the emergence of a Republican-inspired alternative, however, he came to believe that "containment was merely an expedient and not a profound policy conception."[58] In Dallin's view, the real goal of American foreign policy, by the very logic of the situation, had to be liberation, at least of the satellite countries. Europe would never be able to lead a peaceful existence so long as the Soviets encroached on its eastern half, and the burdensome American commitments required by this unstable situation would be difficult to sustain.

With U.S. foreign policy on the right track, Dallin's main concern was the fickleness of western Europeans. West Germans distrusted America, understandably in view of the American record of vacillation and unreliability. The French—obsessed with the German problem, influenced by their own Communists, fainthearted in Indochina—could not even be called an ally.[59] In Dallin's view, the pivotal situation in Europe justified support for Tito. To be sure, if it were possible to choose one's allies, one would reject Tito, but "strange bedfellows do not impair the righteousness of our cause." Dallin agreed with his Communist opponents that "the world has entered a decisive period out of which one of two parties must emerge victorious." Like the intermediate classes in Marxist theory, the European states could move either East or West, and it was up to the United States to see that it won this crucial contest.[60]

Only with German rearmament was Dallin reassured that the United States had wrested the initiative from Soviet Russia and the earlier "dangerous mood of relaxation" in Europe had been overcome. Dallin could now afford to be cautiously optimistic. Weakness remained "the greatest of all possible blunders," and the West continued to make mistakes, as at the 1954 Indochina Conference, where it accepted a negotiated settlement (although, unlike Souvarine, Dallin did not rule out all negotiations with Communists). The United States had always been superior to the Soviet Union in military and other potential; now it was finally attaining that potential.[61]

The death of Stalin did make a difference in Soviet foreign policy. The new Soviet leaders were "graduates of the Stalin school of crime," said Dallin, but they were not risk takers as Stalin had been since 1939.[62] In order to win the cold war, America needed only to remember that it had faced the same enemy "at the Yalu, in the valley of the Elbe, on the banks of the Danube, in the hills of Greece, at abortive conferences, demarcation lines, propaganda trials, and UN debates."[63]

Dallin even expressed optimism about Soviet internal evolution. To be sure, there was no political underground in Russia, and although discontent was widespread, it was only a latent force. Antisemitism was spreading, even though it was not the government that was spreading it. Some Western policies, premised on theories of the inherent aggressiveness of the Russian people and banking on the dismemberment of the Soviet Union, were actually counterproductive.[64] Still, there was hope for post-Stalin Russia. A new generation of intellectuals was growing up there, Dallin wrote in 1957, and it yearned for "liberty to live, to think, and to create." This was a "return to the basic ideas of the pre-Soviet democratic revolution of 1917," and it was "perhaps the most important development in present day Russia." This tendency would "not make itself felt immediately in Soviet politics, [but] it augur[ed] well for the future."[65]

Dallin's wistful remarks in 1957, during de-Stalinization, are less lyrical than Fedor Dan's rhapsodic conclusion to *The Origins of Bolshevism* during the heyday of Stalinism. Even so, they are very much an exception to Dallin's usual tone, as are his sympathetic remarks in the same period concerning the attractiveness of communism to third world semi-intellectuals, in which he evokes his own revolutionary past.[66] Yet these lapses from Dallin's habitual pose as a hard-bitten, realistic cold warrior are significant. They demonstrate the lingering, perhaps unconscious, hold of earlier Menshevik hopes over those who appeared to have strayed furthest from them.

The Mensheviks wanted to be foot soldiers of the Revolution but found themselves soldiers in the cold war. They fought this campaign as vigorously as they had all others. They had new allies, new arguments, and even new values, but, like their comrades who had gone off in different directions, they were convinced that their cause remained the same.[67]

The American File

"It appears that the Party [RSDLP] is quite small and exists principally to give the members an opportunity for mental exercise and reminiscing. Long forgotten in Russia and with no real roots in American society, the Party probably represents only the view of its few members. Similarly, its influence is probably neither wide nor deep among non-members."[1] This opinion, expressed by the U.S. Department of Justice in 1942, was reiterated ten years later by another government agency: "The state of complete inactivity and obscurity into which the *Mensheviki* at home and abroad have lapsed since the final triumph of the Soviet power show [sic] that their movement has entirely spent what little force it may ever have had." The author's confused references to Kerensky as a Menshevik did not prevent him or her from confidently asserting that "the *Menshevik* cause is even more dead than that of the *Tsarists*."[2]

In spite of such repeated dismissals, the U.S. government subjected the Mensheviks to persistent investigation, investing countless hours and processing thousands of pages on their activities. All the documents cited here were obtained under the terms of the Freedom of Information Act. Even after the end of the cold war, however, a considerable number of documents on the Mensheviks are still denied to researchers on grounds not only of protection of privacy but also of national security considerations. The picture of the Mensheviks' "American file" presented here is therefore, unfortunately, incomplete.

In 1943 FBI director J. Edgar Hoover confirmed that "the Bureau's files contain considerable information relative to Theodore Dan."[3] The reliability of this information is undermined by subsequent reports of muddled investigators who confide that "J. Martow" is actually Theodore Dan.[4] Among the FBI's early interests is a possible connection between Dan and the German journalist Paul Scheffer, identified as a German agent at the 1938 Moscow trials. The Bureau's New York office, satisfied by its confidential informants' assurances that Dan is not pro-Nazi and that his apparent adherence to the Communist line is merely tactical, deems the connection unlikely inasmuch as investigation of Scheffer has "always been from a Nazi espionage viewpoint."[5] FBI headquarters retorts, however, that Dan "could well have had strong personal and political motives for working with the German Secret Service against Russia."[6] Hoover also notes a recommendation of the U.S. Interdepartmental Visa Committee regarding Dan: "There can be no question but that his political views are opposed to the American form of life. He is unquestionably a dangerous man to have in the United States, and his status should be kept, during the emergency, such that he can easily be deported at the end of the hostilities." Hoover adds, with apparent regret, "It does not appear that testimony in the Moscow trials was made available to the various committees in connection with the subject's visa application."[7]

Dan's group is the subject of a twenty-four-page Office of Strategic Services (OSS) report also addressed to the secretary of state.[8] The author confesses to a personal fondness for the "decent and courageous" *Novyi put'* people, whose views he considers incorrect but "more original and otherwise noteworthy" than those of other Russian groups. In addition to summarizing these views, the report describes the personalities in the group. It dwells on the group's banker, Simon Lieberman, who made and lost at least four fortunes (the most recent one by selling condensed milk to the Spanish Loyalists at a "huge and rather unexpected profit"). It expresses admiration for Dan's clear mind, and it comments indulgently on Anatol Dubois's naïveté.

The report gives considerable coverage to the *Novyi put'* group's resentments against other Mensheviks. Iugov complains that Solomon Schwarz broke his promise to him and to Jacob Marshak to keep politics out of their recently published *Management in Russian Industry and Agriculture.* Dan grumbles about Boris Nicolaevsky's uncompromising antibolshevism, attributing it to Tsereteli's influence, and refuses to be moved by Lidia Dan's intercession on behalf of Nicolaevsky as a sick man. None of the *Novyi put'* people have anything good to say about David Dallin, whom they deride as a "capable man but with no principles," who would hide his prejudices in his scholarly works but was completely unrestrained in his other writings.

The report conveys the *Novyi put'* Mensheviks' concerns, both material and political. After having collapsed while working in a war plant, Aaron Iugov is soon to lose his government job compiling a Russian-English military dictionary, and he has been denied a fellowship at the Institute of Pacific Relations because of Communist influence there (unlike *Vestnik*, the Communists apparently do not see Iugov as having capitulated to them). Even the wealthy Lieberman has cause for concern as much of his fortune is frozen in Britain or marooned in France. Lidia Dan is quoted as saying, "We have changed so many countries in our long years of exile, and have always gotten used to each new country. But we cannot get used to America. I suppose that we are too old." With regard to political developments, however, the group's members are extremely sanguine, buoyed by Soviet successes. In fact, the only thing that mars their confidence is the resurgence of antisemitism, which figures so prominently in the reports they are receiving from Russia.

In its sympathetic tone this OSS report is an utter anomaly among U.S. documents on the Mensheviks. As late as 1952 the successor to the OSS, the Central Intelligence Agency (CIA), states that "[Dan's] group, which calls itself socialist, is today a medium for bolshevik propaganda among Socialists and for Soviet intelligence activity. Many members of this group, particularly in the U.S.A., are used as unwitting agents of the Soviet State." Dan is incorrectly identified here as "a member of the Social Revolutionary Party." More significantly, the CIA is not aware that Dan's group has long since dissolved and Dan himself has been dead for five years (two years, according to this report).[9]

Aaron Iugov and his wife, Olga Domanevskaia, received close FBI attention until the end of their lives. The Bureau notes that the Iugovs' visa application had initially been disapproved for a variety of reasons. These include "possible derogatory information" regarding one of their sponsors, Nahum I. Stone, alleged to be a "satellite of the the New School for Social Reasearch" and an avowed member of the League for Industrial Democracy; sponsorship by future Nobel Prize winner Simon Kuznets does not suffice to dispel doubts. Iugov's "record of socialistic political acitivity" and the undesirability of having people of "that stamp at that time" in the United States also count against him and his wife. Prejudicial, too, is the fact that Iugov "left a brother and two sisters somewhere in Russia, possibly in German-occupied Russia," as well as his statement that "he had been sent in 1922 by the Communist Party in Russia as a socialist to some meeting, which he did not name."[10] In short, there are ample reasons to be suspicious of Iugov. For years the FBI continued to monitor Iugov's and Domanevskaia's publications carefully. As late as 1967 the Bureau was still translating Domanevskaia's numerous articles in the New York *Russkii Golos,* describing her as its "principal editorial writer" and systematically comparing her views to positions taken in the Communist *Daily Worker.*[11]

Boris Nicolaevsky appears in a more favorable light in government files, but the overwhelming impression is that of the investigators' perplexity. The FBI notes an informant's view that Nicolaevsky has been "sort of close" to American diplomat Charles Bohlen and that ambassador "GEORGE KENNAN, when in State Dept., considered NICOLAEVSKY an expert on Soviet Russia and consulted him in important matters related thereto."[12] Nicolaevsky is erroneously quoted as saying that he defected from the Soviets in the 1930s, and the report wonders whether Nicolaevsky might have gotten along with Stalin if there had been a milder regime in Russia. The FBI is much agitated, too, by the question whether Nicolaevsky and Abramovitch are still Marxists. "Honest men but fanatics of Marxism," is an informant's opinion, and the investigator's synopsis conveys this as "NICOLAEVSKY is 'absolute fanatic Marxist.' "[13]

Nicolaevsky's name appears repeatedly in FBI files, particularly on account of his activities in Russian emigré organizations, his very broad contacts, and his involvement with defectors such as Walter Krivitsky and Victor Kravchenko and with the Soviet agent Mark Zborowski. Bureau agents repeat what they hear about Nicolaevsky, usually without verification or evaluation. An informant (whose identity is still concealed in documents released) quotes Walter Krivitsky as saying that Nicolaevsky was "the only so-called Aryan among the Mensheviks" and that his institute in Paris was financed "by one LEON BLUM . . . a French Socialist . . . acquainted with LENIN"; this statement is reproduced verbatim ten years later.[14] Further allegations that Nicolaevsky has been "in virtual control of all U.S. opinion directed behind Iron Curtain" led the FBI to compile, at its director's request, a bulky document which contains all information available about Nicolaevsky, including synopses of his recent writings.[15]

Nicolaevsky had always been fascinated by police agents and one cannot but wonder how he would have reacted to being himself described as one. A U.S. intelligence report recounts that, in Berlin in the 1930s, Nicolaevsky pocketed proceeds from publication of secret prerevolutionary Russian police files, that this brought about his break with his former sponsors, the Soviet authorities, and that he has since been exploiting his knowledge and archives in a financially remunerative anti-Soviet campaign. The same report also cites "pro-Soviet literary circles" that claim Nicolaevsky was "a British agent for financial reasons and . . . since the death of LEON TROTZKY, he [is] his ideological successor."[16]

Several FBI informers surmise that the continued failures of the American Committee for the Liberation of Russia to unite the Russian emigration might be Nicolaevsky's work, although cleverly devised so as not to be attributable to him. One individual paints a sinister scene of Nicolaevsky's financial blandishments (for unspecified purposes) during a dinner at the Russian Tea Room, and another accuses Nicolaevsky outright of trying to bribe him or her.[17] A more measured though hardly friendlier assessment came several months later. A "source" states that Nicolaevsky's constant efforts "to break up any strong anti-Communist group" are due to his ambition to see social democrats rule Russia. The source does not believe that Nicolaevsky is a Soviet agent nor that he is a security risk to the United States even though he is an "intelligent, ruthless, unpleasant person."[18]

Other Mensheviks are also objects of Bureau interest and surveillance. An early report on Abramovitch notes that his "right name" is "Rein," his nationality is "Israelite," and "in June 1923, an individual by this name was listed as a member of the Bolshevist government."[19] The Bureau is soon reassured—"[Abramovitch] is not regarded as inimical to the U.S."—and his name comes up later mainly when he is attacked by the Communist press.[20] The FBI New York office's records also contain "numerous references" to Iurii Denike. There is "some indication (however slight) that DENICKE might be making inquiries on [deleted] at the request of French intelligence," but the office adds in its communication to FBI director Hoover that Denike has "enjoyed a good reputation in his contacts with this office."[21] The "Russian Social Democratic Club, a group described as having as its ultimate objective a Socialist form of government for the U.S." is mentioned occasionally.[22] Many files deal with the Mensheviks' publications. Since "the Director expressed an interest" in Grigorii Aronson's *Soviet Russia and the Jews,* the FBI presents the author and reviews the text, noting that it "contains some of the usual highly colored Nazi atrocity stories and, coming principally from Communist sources, must be discounted to some extent."[23]

David Dallin's FBI file stands out as the only interactive one. Other Mensheviks are passive objects of investigation, only occasionally assuming a more active role, for example, through cooperation in an interview. Dallin, however, engages the FBI in a two-way relationship as he attempts to pry information and to negotiate over the requests the Bureau makes to him. "This is getting 'smellier' all the time but also more intriguing. Keep our wits about us but let us get to the bottom of this" is J. Edgar Hoover's scribbled comment on one of the earliest FBI references to Dallin, a much-excised document apparently dealing with the impending Kravchenko case.[24] "Very worthwhile reading" is his reaction three years later to a scurrilous review of Dallin's books in the Moscow-sponsored *Soviet Russia Today*.[25] Dallin's name and work are threrefore already known to Hoover when he receives a respectful request from Dallin for access to any nonclassified files for a book on Soviet espionage.[26] The request is supported by a cordial personal note from *New Leader* editor Sol Levitas, but it is unconditionally turned down. Indeed, Hoover even rebuffs Levitas's friendly inquiry as to whether he has had a chance to read the *New Leader* by saying he does not think it "wise to specifically answer" that question.[27]

Dallin and his friends tried different approaches. A member of the Senate Internal Security Subcommittee (McCarran Committee) called the FBI to vouch for Dallin as "a very trustworthy, *discreet individual* and might be used as an outlet for any information the Bureau cares to have publicized without showing its hand."[28] Dallin himself assured the Bureau that his book would not deal with espionage in the U.S. and that he was willing to make the book available to the Bureau prior to its general release.[29] None of these efforts bore any fruit, but by the time *Soviet Espionage* appeared, the FBI files contained 350 references to Dallin.[30]

The FBI's initial reaction to *Soviet Espionage* was mildly critical. It noted that only one of ten chapters dealt with operations in the United States and that "there is nothing new in its contents within our jurisdiction." Unimpressed, the Bureau's reviewer notes that only a small part of the book was documented, but Dallin's style "would probably lead the average reader to believe that he is an authority on Soviet espionage." Dallin wrote as if the networks he knew of were the only ones in existence. His case summaries were fragmentary and based merely on newspaper or magazine articles, themselves unreliable. Dallin filled in information gaps with conjecture and comment about what various agents on both sides thought, "as though he were the investigating officer," and he made numerous factual mistakes. Still, the book would "serve the purpose of further alerting the public to the magnitude and clandestine nature of Soviet intelligence operations and their importance in shaping world affairs." References to the FBI were "substantially accurate and [were] not critical of Bureau."[31]

Hoover did not share this benign view of *Soviet Espionage*, and he expressed his displeasure directly to Dallin. It was not true that he, Hoover, had agreed to NKVD-OSS cooperation during the war. There was no proof that William Ullmann made FBI reports available to the Soviets, and had Dallin possessed such proof, Hoover was "certain that you would have furnished it to the

FBI." Finally, Dallin's criticism of FBI "passivity" with regard to atomic espionage was completely unwarranted.[32] Dallin tried to take advantage of Hoover's reaction as a wedge with which to pry open the FBI's secrets. He thus replied very deferentially, without defending himself. Yes, he subscribed entirely to Hoover's statement that "the FBI has had a comprehensive realization over the years of the menace of Communism in the United States." But, Dallin continued, "it appears to me that the FBI was not always free to act and that the White House and the State Department in particular were putting [on] brakes." Dallin did not know that some of his sources were inaccurate, and he would, "of course, change the text" and "make amends" in the second printing of his book. What he really needed, however, he told Hoover, was "a few more details and a more extensive statement from you." He concluded with a request for a personal talk with the director.[33]

Hoover would not allow himself to be lured. "Obviously Dallin is attempting to draw further comment from us which he can use to sensationalize his book and involve us in issues having political implications," wrote a Bureau official, and Hoover added by hand: "Yes. We should not extend any cooperation such as Dallin seeks nor will I see him."[34] Dallin persisted and did meet an FBI official who reported that Dallin requested assistance with his research and "wondered whether there were any specific areas which we [FBI] were interested in seeing developed whereby we might give him some guidance." Using the recent revelations about Zborowski as bait, Dallin said that the *New Leader* was thinking of writing more on this subject, but it occurred to him that perhaps the Bureau was utilizing Zborowski and there might be some reason not to publicize this case. Hoover commented by hand: "It is alright [sic] to find out who Zborowski is but we must not give Dallin anything. He did a vicious job on me in his last book."[35]

At the same time that the FBI was rebuffing Dallin, another branch of the Department of Justice was soliciting his services. The department's Infiltrated Organizations Unit sought Dallin's expert testimony in a case involving the suspected Communist infiltration of the International Union of Mine, Mill and Smelter Workers. The unit invoked the fact that Dallin had been the "outstanding expert employed by the Criminal Division in the Lattimore case" and that his insight into international communism was said to be "equal if not superior, to any man in the field."[36] Indeed, Dallin's services were deemed essential inasmuch as he was not only without peer in his field but also one of the "very few willing to publicly appear in support of his judgement or to take the appreciable time required to study and prepare opinion in this class of cases."[37] The department's hopes were confirmed when it learned of Dallin's proposed approach to the Mine Workers' case;

its only reservations were financial. After some bargaining it raised its offer from twenty-five to fifty dollars a day, which had been the fee in the Lattimore case, while grumbling that Dallin "was anything but modest in his time charges."[38]

Dallin's file continues for several years after his death.[39] Very substantial deletions allow only conjecture, but from a recent book, *Deadly Illusions* by John Costello and Oleg Tsarov, one might infer that the reason for such posthumous interest was accusations against Dallin and his wife by the Soviet NKVD defector Alexander Orlov. In a 1965 debriefing Orlov accused Lolla Dallin (the former Lolla Estrine) of being a Soviet agent and David Dallin of having been one in Berlin, although perhaps not in America.[40]

Orlov's case is preposterous. The grounds for his accusation are the Dallins' reluctance to admit that Mark Zborowski might have been a spy and their purported tardiness in denouncing him. Orlov claims that the Dallins made "a clean breast of things before the Senate Internal Security Committee" only after realizing that Orlov knew about Zborowski's past.[41] In fact, the Dallins had already been interviewed by the FBI before their meeting with Orlov, and well before the affair became public Lolla Dallin had told the FBI that she "found it hard to realize ZBOROWSKI was a Soviet Agent, although the evidence was very clear that he was."[42] In short, the Dallins were candid with the FBI, both before and after meeting Orlov, never hiding their incredulity about Zborowski or Lolla's previous attachment to him.

Orlov's further revelations are farcical. Without any explanation he states that Dallin had run a source in the First Section of the German Foreign Office on behalf of the Soviets. Lolla Dallin's guilt is confirmed by her "flustered and confused" acknowledgment—"Yes, I know him. He comes from the same town as I do"—concerning someone whom Orlov identifies as the NKVD Paris agent for emigré affairs. Such is Orlov's suspiciousness that when Lolla Dallin goes into the kitchen to make tea, Mrs. Orlov accompanies her to make sure they are not poisoned.[43]

The source of these stories itself provides reasons for doubting Orlov's credibility. Indeed, the thesis of the book is that Orlov was never a full-fledged defector. In a devil's pact with his Soviet paymaster, he exchanged safety abroad for concealment of his greatest secrets. One would assume that the conclusion to be drawn is that one should be very careful of Orlov's unsubstantiated allegations. Not only do Costello and Tsarov fail to draw this conclusion, but they irresponsibly present Lola Dallin as a proven Soviet spy.[44] One should perhaps not expect more from Costello, who describes himself as the "first Westerner to set eyes on actual volumes of KGB files" and then cheerfully acknowledges that he does not read Russian.[45]

Most of the other U.S. government files discussed here end with copies of the newspaper obituaries of their subjects. The FBI's last mention of *Sotsialisticheskii vestnik* occurs in July 1964. Whereas fifteen years earlier the Bureau had described the "MECHEVIKS" (sic) or "Socialist Democrats" who published the journal as "people of Russian extraction belonging to the Jewish faith," it now referred to them as "Jewish people of Russian extraction."[46] Apparently the FBI was not really sure to the end whom it was dealing with and it did not notice either the closure of *Vestnik* in 1963 or its re-creation as an annual volume of miscellany in 1964 and 1965.

The Final Campaign

The Mensheviks' last campaign was the struggle over memory. They waged it relentlessly, as if oblivion and distortion of their own history were indignities harder to bear than political defeat. So jealous were the Mensheviks of their own past that some, like Raphael Abramovitch, saw enemies among their benefactors. Others, notably Boris Nicolaevsky, hoarded the past, exploiting only a fraction of their resources. All Mensheviks were suspicious of one another as historians, even more than they had been as politicians. At the same time, they differed not in regard to the importance of transmitting historical records but in the strategies they adopted to do so.

Ever argumentative, the Mensheviks sparred as readily over the past as over the present. Stalin's death did not put an end to polemics over Stalin's sanity. "There were pathological traits in Stalin—who doesn't have them?" wrote Abramovitch to Volsky, arguing that Stalin's policies were a perfectly rational response to the problem posed by the unstable social base of his power. Stalin was ideally suited to be a hangman, and hangmen are often pathological individuals, Abramovitch acknowledged, but added, "It is not they who invented the scaffold." After Khrushchev's secret speech on Stalin's crimes, Souvarine exulted, "If now B. I. [Nicolaevsky] says Stalin was not crazy, it is he who has to be cured." Eventually Nicolaevsky may have come around to the view that Stalin was mad at the end of his life, but, wrote Souvarine in frustration, another incorrigible Menshevik, David Dallin, continued to hold that Stalin was perfectly sane.[1]

The most passionate debates were about the distant rather than the recent past. The question of the intellectual origins of Leninism again pitted Nicolaevsky against Volsky. The latter made much of the influence on Marx, and especially on Lenin, of the nineteenth-century Russian radical Nikolai Chernyshevskii. Nicolaevsky did not deny such influence but emphasized that both Marx's and Lenin's maximalism should be traced to the early Marx of the period of the *Critique of Hegel's "Philosophy of Right."*[2] At issue was the proposition that "the October Revolution led by Lenin could be 'made' without any 'Marxiana' and using only Chernyshevskii's teachings as reworked by Lenin." Ironically, Soviet historians reacted more enthusiatically to Volsky's thesis—"in this case he can be believed regardless of his Menshevik sympathies and Machist philosophical views"—than did Nicolaevsky.[3]

A debate on Lenin's purported Jewish origins was a less worthy subject, and the Mensheviks entered it with distaste. Both Volsky and Anna Bourgina refuted what they considered the irresponsible claims of their erstwhile comrade David Shub, who attributed a Jewish grandfather to Lenin. After Shub had invoked Nicolaevsky's authority, the latter stepped into the fray to deny publicly that a statement made to him by Rykov in Berlin in 1923 about "all the filth that is being dreamed up about Lenin" had anything to do with Lenin's alleged Jewish ancestry. In fact, Nicolaevsky was stonewalling shamelessly. In 1949 he had confided to Volsky that Lenin's grandfather was indeed a converted Jew who had written denunciations of his coreligionists in Astrakhan, much as Shub later alleged (Shub himself maintained that he was the original discoverer of this fact). Nicolaevsky claimed to know details owing to the archives of the Russian Orthodox synod, but as he put it, "It is not seemly to unearth all this filth." Recent findings have confirmed the substance of Nicolaevsky's (and Shub's) discoveries.[4]

It was the Mensheviks' own past that engaged them most passionately. "The party past has value per se—it is a sort of thing in itself," Nicolaevsky had written in a polemic against *Novyi put'* about Martov's attitude toward the SRs. Elsewhere he was even more explicit: "If an emigré party preserves the documents of its illustrious past, this past reflects back upon it and it will be seen as the continuator of its tradition."[5] The Mensheviks pronounced judgment on new publications, including those such as Bertram Wolfe's *Three Who Made a Revolution* in which they had had a hand, and quarreled among themselves about party history and the meaning of menshevism.[6]

"I give up trying to describe that insane asylum," wrote Souvarine on returning from a visit to the New York Mensheviks. He commiserated with Volsky, who complained that David Shub once borrowed the manuscript of his *Encounters with Lenin* under the pretext of finding a publisher, but in fact to check on a rival biographer of Lenin. Nicolaevsky, too, read the manuscript and, according to Valentinov, declared it "unsuitable and unfinished." Instead of helping to publish it, he offered to pay $200 or $300 in exchange for depositing it in the Columbia University archives. Such had been Volsky's need at the time that he had accepted; only at the insistence of his wife did he later show the manuscript to Vera Alexandrova at the Chekhov Press and to Michael Karpovich, who took one look and sent it to press.[7]

Souvarine readily amplified his friend's complaints. Shub's behavior was typically American and his book was vulgar, "like *everything that sells* in the USA," he sniffed. Souvarine cited his own experience: "I have myself been squeezed like a lemon by people who 'make money' [in English in original] with my knowledge and left me to starve. That is their genre." Americans (including, one presumes, Mensheviks in America) "live off crumbs from Europe, magnifying and vulgarizing them, and treating Europeans like natives 'who do not have needs,' whereas they need a lot of dollars." Even Denike, "the most intelligent and the most open of the whole Vestnik group," lost favor for butchering one of Souvarine's *Vestnik* articles.[8]

Souvarine grumbled most vehemently about Nicolaevsky, and no one would deny that Boris Ivanovich was a difficult person. Nicolaevsky refused to allow one of his *Vestnik* articles to be reprinted in the commemorative *Martov i ego blizkie* because the book contained an article about Fedor Dan (who had been dead for over a decade). He killed one of Boris Sapir's publication projects by refusing to share documents. He would abruptly and inexplicably break off relations with old friends such as Volsky or just as abruptly reestablish them, as he did with Lidia Dan. After going years without speaking to her, he arrived without explanation, to gossip for hours, "like two priests' wives," about Lenin's romances and other matters. "A strange almost crazy person," wrote Lidia Dan after Nicolaevsky had once again broken off relations. Moreover, he was someone who had no judgment in present-day matters, viewing them, as she put it, "po suzdal'ski," that is, with a peculiar provincial mentality. Still, she bore him no ill will and did not rule out the possibility that he might one day return to his senses and once again come for tea.[9]

Lidia Dan's good temper explains why she is the only Menshevik who remained on speaking terms with all the others. "It has fallen upon me, in a certain sense, to 'unify society,' in the old days the function of the governor's wife," she wrote with bemusement, and could have added that she had played the same role in 1917 and at other moments in the past. Her equanimity also puts into perspective the Mensheviks' complaints about one another and the reproaches addressed to them. "Though we are odd characters [*chudaki*], we are nonetheless good and kind people," wrote Abramovitch to Volsky, with some justification, over yet another *Vestnik* editorial quarrel. Volsky himself, in spite of complaints, could not deny that New York's Mensheviks had gone out of their way to find him financial support. Souvarine, too, though he ridiculed Nicolaevsky's "obsession" with the

"Letter of an Old Bolshevik" and maintained that "le grand Boris's" reputation was waning, agreed, both privately and publicly, that Nicolaevsky was an excellent historian and a "living encyclopedia of the Russian Social Democratic movement."[10]

Above all, it was grossly unfair to accuse the Mensheviks of exploiting other people's knowledge. Lidia Dan was generous with her memories, as many young scholars of that period can testify. She feigned exasperation at the "boys" who "drink my blood," but she was pleased to be told by John Keep that he had learned a lot from her. She was enthusiastic about Israel Getzler's research—"a fine fellow, he will amount to something, i.e., I hope he writes a not bad biography of Martov"—and she looked forward to her meetings with Joel Carmichael, the translator of Fedor Dan's *Origins of Bolshevism*. Her generosity was anchored in the conviction that her memories were a uniquely precious asset which had to be passed on, to the greatest extent possible. Sharing her impressions of Leonard Schapiro, who was then undertaking his *Communist Party of the Soviet Union*, and whom she had also received well, Lidia Dan confided to Volsky: "He knows a lot, or rather, he has read a great deal, almost everything that can be read, and he understands much quite well, but not all," adding, "who but ourselves can understand all this and absorb that inimitable era?"[11]

Lidia Dan had her memories and Boris Nicolaevsky had his archives. In spite of crankiness and suspicion, he too shared his treasure. Innumerable scholars "all sat at his feet," and Nicolaevsky's posthumous *Festschrift* acknowledged the profound debt of many authors. Unlike Lidia Dan's memories, however, Nicolaevsky's archives were not only his love but his livelihood. He had lost them and reconstituted them at least three times. He had fought over them and worried about them for decades.[12] At the end of his life they allowed him to conclude a business deal which had been thirty years in the making.

In Paris in the 1930s Nicolaevsky had already been negotiating with the Hoover Institution's Merrill Spalding over contracts for historical studies. These plans, which had all the makings of the future Menshevik project, were interrupted by the war. In America, Nicolaevsky continued to collect, correspond, and negotiate, partly under the rubric of his own, largely fictitious, American Labor Research Institute. In 1948, convinced that war would break out again (or invoking this as a pretext), Nicolaevsky tried to have the collections of the Amsterdam Institute of Social History, including those he had tended in Paris on its behalf, transferred to the United States. He confided that he was negotiating with various American universities about this (and, one may assume, other matters) but did not have much hope of success. It was not until 1963 that his plans came to fruition with the Hoover Institution's announcement that it had purchased "fifteen tons of materials" from Nicolaevsky under the auspices of a program that emphasized international communism's threat to free institutions.[13]

Nicolaevsky's deal with the Hoover Institution (and with Indiana University, which took a much smaller part of his collections) relieved him of old worries about finding a home for his archives. The purchase price, reportedly $250,000, also made him, to his own surprise, a relatively wealthy man. He and Anna Bourguina, his right hand for many years, set up house in Menlo Park, close to the institution. Nicolaevsky seemed pleased with his "nice garden, flowers, fruits, and now the grep-frukty ripening," but he could not reconcile himself to the "great wilderness [*glusha*]" of his California surroundings.[14]

While living in New York, Nicolaevsky was surrounded by other exiles; he lectured (in Russian) at Harvard, and kept in direct touch with his European network. Shortly before moving to California, he attended a conference in Geneva and was delighted to find himself in the city which had hosted so many Russian revolutionaries.[15] He had been enchanted by a notice, "This lawn is under the protection of citizens," in front of the institution where I now teach. My colleagues recall Nicolaevsky and Souvarine, "Big Boris" and "Little Boris," walking up and down by the lake, arguing, no doubt, about the past. The move to California removed Nicolaevsky, at the age of almost eighty, one step further not only from Russia but also from his cozy exile ghetto and from the world familiar to him through his archives.

Nor was Nicolaevsky's mind entirely at peace with the arrangements at the Hoover. He was concerned about the fate of his archives after his death and about the institution's treatment of Anna Bourguina. He married Bourguina not only to avoid the "scandal" of their cohabiting out of wedlock but also to reinforce her claim, as Nicolaevsky's wife and, later, widow, to curatorship of the collections. Bourguina outlived Nicolaevsky by sixteen years and carried out her curatorial mission with almost religious dedication. She complained bitterly to me that the director of the Hoover cared about the archives as much as he did about "last year's snows," and it is true that I cannot remember seeing any permanent fellows of the institution working in the Hoover Archives while I was there. At her death Bourguina bequeathed as much as she could to the Hebrew University of Jerusalem, not only to acknowledge her roots but also to spite the Hoover.[16]

With funds from the National Endowment for the Humanities, the Hoover archival staff did take up Bourguina's unfinished and jealously guarded project of cataloguing the entire Nicolaevsky Collection. In the process of doing so it came across such treasures as a seventy-six-box collection of the exile papers of Trotsky and his son Lev Sedov. Some items from the Nicolaevsky Collection have been transferred to the Hoover Library, but the collection as a whole still contains 811 boxes and measures 330 linear feet; the guide to the collection is over 700 pages long.[17]

Among the contents of the Nicolaevsky Collection rest, no doubt, Nicolaevsky's 1,300-page manuscript on Russia in 1908–1912, as well as his unpublished biography of Malenkov and numerous other writings.[18] As Nicolaevsky must have known, however, his greatest contribution to his party would reside not in what he wrote or published but in what he saved. Any serious writer on Russian social democracy, or for that matter on the Russian Revolution and other such subjects, is dependent now and for the foreseeable future on what Nicolaevsky could save and chose to save. Herein lies Nicolaevsky's genius as well as his merit.

Rustic and with only a smattering of foreign languages, Boris Nicolaevsky succeeded in making generations of Western scholars his debtors, whereas the sophisticated polyglot Raphael Abramovitch failed to do so. Both were knowledgeable (although Nicolaevsky was incomparably more so), both cared for the reputation of their party, and both saw history as political capital. The key to Nicolaevsky's success and Abramovitch's failure must be sought in their tactics. Whereas Nicolaevsky made himself indispensable by offering his services to the academic establishment, Abramovitch challenged the establishment head-on and lost.

Abramovitch made no secret of his agenda. In his view the significance of the Bolshevik Revolution was that it had given birth to totalitarianism: "The greatest evil was not that Lenin decided to make a socialist experiment in immature Russia . . . The fundamental misfortune was that Lenin succeeded in creating a totalitarian dictatorship," he wrote. Communism was not a purely Russian illness, nor was the Russian Revolution a belated democratic revolt against backwardness. October 1917 marked the first of a continuing series of totalitarian revolutions, "barbarian forms of regression" utterly different from the "barbarian forms of progress" of earlier revolutions.[19]

In Abramovitch's view it was the Mensheviks' mission to bear witness to these truths, of which Westerners had only an inkling. He and several comrades (though, apparently, not Nicolaevsky) put together a proposal for a one- or two-volume collective study to be carried out under the auspices of the Research Project (later Program) on the History of the CPSU, chaired by Philip Mosely at Columbia University, with Ford Foundation support. To Abramovitch's outrage, his project was rejected in favor of an alternative proposal that eventually came to fruition in Leonard Schapiro's *Communist*

Party of the Soviet Union. It thus fell to an outsider to write what a major sovietologist has recently described as still "the most complete and convincing demonstration of the Leninist origins of Stalinism."[20]

Abramovitch's fury at being robbed, as he saw it, of his own past knew no bounds. He accused Mosely to his face of having plagiarized his project and, behind his back, of "having taken funds intended for us" and given Schapiro "huge sums of money."[21] In language reminiscent of intraparty feuds at the turn of the century, Abramovitch accused "your Committee of Four [of] trying to eliminate our Group." He denounced the injustice of the Ford Foundation's decision, and demanded a veto over the approved project and a division of authority between his Menshevik group and the project's steering committee. Defiantly Abramovitch declared that he and his friends would not give up their original plan. If they did not receive assurances regarding their "active and adequate participation" in the project, they would "go it alone." In that case they would not be available for any advice or contribution.[22] Judging by the acknowledgments to Schapiro's book (where only Nicolaevsky is mentioned), it was a threat they carried out.

Mosely was as conciliatory as possible. True, the emphasis he put on the need to find a native English speaker for the projected study was not entirely convincing, and one suspects, as Abramovitch did, that Mosely's doubts about the Mensheviks' academic credentials were decisive. In the course of their exchanges, however, Mosely proposed that Abramovitch and his friends undertake a "thorough and objective history of the Social Democratic opposition to the Bolshevik regime, especially between October 1917 and September 1918." As Mosely put it, too many accounts of the Russian Revolution ended in October 1917, and "if you and your friends do not undertake to record this important part of the struggle for freedom and progress in Russia, I do not know who will in the future, ever be able to do it." One cannot tell whether this suggestion was merely a consolation prize, offered to make peace and to obtain Menshevik cooperation in the main project. In any case, Abramovitch reacted disdainfully, stretching the period concerned up to 1924 and suggesting that Nicolaevsky would be Mosely's "best bet," but he did not reject the idea outright.[23]

Abramovitch did "go it alone," a proof of his much-admired fortitude in the face of adversity and physical affliction. *The Soviet Revolution,* which appeared the year before his death, turned out to be a history of the Soviet Union rather than of communism, although for Abramovitch the two were merely aspects of totalitarianism. Lidia Dan was relieved to find the book "better than [she] had feared." It read easily, and there was an audience for this sort of book in America, she thought; but, admittedly, it was not a scholarly book, and its readers were not those of whom Abramovitch had dreamed.[24] Abramovitch himself privately described the aim of his book as "deepened propaganda," and the praise it received, including a generous homage from Leonard Schapiro, was tribute to Abramovitch's personal qualities and past merits rather than to the contents of his book.[25]

Although the Mensheviks' bid for a dominant role in the Research Project on the CPSU failed, they succeeded in conquering the field of Menshevik history for themselves, within the project and even beyond it. The moving spirit in this victorious campaign was Lidia Dan, who saw an occasion to bring together her feuding and often demoralized comrades around a common enterprise. Her original request to the Research Project on the CPSU, presented just after the exchange between Mosely and Abramovitch, was for approximately $14,000 to allow the Menshevik group to prepare a card index identifying the three to five thousand individuals active in the "Russian liberating movement" at the end of the nineteenth century. Although the project director turned down her request, he astutely observed that what the Mensheviks were really seeking was "the program's recognition as capable and scholarly collaborators," whereas they now felt that the program was seeking to exploit them "in a cheap and undignified fashion." This feeling could be overcome and the Mensheviks' future collaboration ensured, he suggested, by encouraging them to write down their own experiences with the help of existing documents and by treating their memoir projects "as scholarly undertakings deserving support in the form of stipends comparable to the stipends given to other collaborators."[26]

This suggestion, as well as Mosely's earlier invitation to Abramovitch regarding the post-October period, eventually led to what was to become the Inter-University Project on the History of the Menshevik Movement. Abramovitch announced that although his group had broken relations with Mosely in relation to the CPSU ("formerly our") project, "none of us has broken with him personally and we are all negotiating memoirs, special projects, etc." In 1959 the Ford Foundation agreed to fund separately what Lidia Dan called "our fantasy—the history of menshevism."[27] Leopold Haimson, a young professor at the University of Chicago and former student of Michael Karpovich, took charge of the project and undertook to accumulate the mass of documentation and to coax out the oral and written testimonies from which I have drawn in this book.

Treading carefully among the susceptibilities, hostilities, and vanities of the "fast dwindling Menshevik community," as he put it, Haimson did not succeed in pleasing all his Menshevik collaborators. Haimson's preface to the project's first publication, Solomon Schwarz's *Russian Revolution of 1905*, provoked a bitter reprimand from Boris Sapir, who took it upon himself to speak on behalf of deceased comrades as well.[28] The collective volume, *The Mensheviks from the Revolution of 1917 to the Second World War*, was described by a knowledgeable reviewer as "an invaluable contribution but not a substitute for a full party history." Regarding Haimson's role in the Menshevik Project, however, it was once again Lidia Dan who expressed the soundest judgment. Whatever his faults, she wrote, "I am very well disposed to him and I value him very highly. I think that we Mensheviks have been very fortunate that fate tied us precisely to him."[29]

Conclusion

None of the major actors in this study lived to see the demise of the Soviet Union. The last surviving member of the Foreign Delegation, Boris Sapir, died in December 1989. An announcement stated that his family was "deeply grateful that he lived long enough to witness the onset of the process of the disintegration of Communism in Eastern Europe." Only a few younger Mensheviks outlived the Soviet era. Among them was Columbia University mathematician Lipman Bers, one of Dan's disciples in *Novyi mir* and *Novyi put'*. In his last years he founded a human rights committee at the National Academy of Sciences, and his *New York Times* obituary lauded him as "a champion of human rights who was instrumental in securing exit visas for Soviet mathematicians."[1]

We do not know how the Mensheviks would have reacted to the fall of the regime in which they had invested so much hope, fear, and loathing. We have only a slight inkling of their reaction to its last attempts at transformation. Boris Sapir was "reluctant to accept that Gorbachev was engaged in anything more than cosmetic changes." He circulated a letter of protest against the presence of member parties of the Socialist International at the Twenty-Seventh Congress of the CPSU in 1986, and one can guess what his reaction would have been to Gorbachev as keynote speaker at the Berlin Congress of the International in 1992. Refusing to state whether he still considered himself a Marxist, Sapir would also not let himself be drawn into speculation on how his comrades would have analyzed perestroika. Yet Lipman Bers wrote me, spontaneously and with visible enthusiasm, "I cannot not try to imagine how Dan would have reacted to the Gorbatchev reforms." Evidently the division between right and left Mensheviks persisted unto the end.[2]

We are also not yet able to judge how post-Soviet Russia will react to the

Menshevik heritage. To be sure, the Russian emigration has become an object of utter fascination, both popular and academic. It may be a slight exaggeration that "entire sections of the Russian Academy of Sciences are working only on the emigration," but interest, already nascent in the last years of the Soviet regime, shows no signs of abating and attracts Western scholars, too.[3] Indeed, the concern today must be that the emigration, after having suffered oblivion and scorn for so long, will become the object of an uncritical cult. Myths of a harmonious and immaculate "Russia Abroad" appear as the mirror image of Soviet reality, and it is tempting to seek in the emigration one's legitimate cultural and political ancestors without questioning its values or accepting one's natural parentage.

Let us note, however, the continued validity of my earlier observations concerning scholarly neglect of exile movements and the deplorable lack of historical imagination to which this attests. In many ways the situation of the Russian emigration has now become analogous to that of the German emigration under Hitler. Only with the defeat of its adversaries and the ideological "return home" has the Russian emigration attracted broader attention. In other words, the emigration acquires its *lettres de noblesse* only when it ceases to be "merely" an emigration. Hijacked by new political imperatives, the emigration may now be requisitioned to serve as an instrument of historical legitimation. Politically and psychologically this is understandable; perhaps one cannot avoid resorting to myths to heal the scars left by the disappearance of a regime, especially one of gruesome memory. Such instrumentalization, however, prevents the emergence of the emigration as an object of study in its own right, entitled to dispassionate examination. Still applying a logic of victor and vanquished, new scholars run the risk of approaching the emigration as unimaginatively and unidimensionally as in the past. On the stock exchange of Russian history the value of the emigration's stock has shot upward while other stocks have fallen. Does this mean that the brokers know and understand what they are selling?

The discovery and legitimation of the emigration is but one aspect of a transformation in the view of the Russian past. The most obvious spur to this change is the opening of archives. It is only in the long run, however, that the significance of these archives can be assessed and only in the very long run that their contents can be assimilated. On the one hand, the mass of documents is utterly daunting. On the other hand, continued inaccesibility, reorganization, material shortages, and suspicions create chaotic archival conditions; these merely mirror the chaos of Russian life today. The nature of this subject makes it likely that the most important sources on the Mensheviks after 1921 will continue to be those on which I have drawn here.[4]

A less tangible but more far-reaching revolution in visions of the Russian past must be sought in a change of attitude, among both Russians and Westerners. Already in the Gorbachev years "normalization" of Russian history prompted thinking on neglected historical actors and the alternative courses they represented. Whereas earlier such thinking had been confined to dissidents, by the late 1980s even establishment historians were commenting on the "sudden interest in losers." Ironically, the disappearance of the Soviet Union—a prospect which had remained taboo even among historical alternatives—initially proved a setback to *alternativnost'* as a principle of inquiry. As visions of Russian history return into focus after the shocks of the recent past, however, it is likely that the fashion for *alternativnost'* will mature into a fruitful heuristic device. Perhaps Russian historians will take to heart the warning that "unless we face alternatives of the past, as they were faced at the time, our history is dead too." If they do so, this will set the stage for a truly radical revolution in Russian historiography.[5]

What bearing do these developments have on the history of our Mensheviks? From the point of view of archival findings, it is to be hoped that new materials will make possible a more complete picture of the party's activities in Russia in the first years of the Soviet regime. Materials not specifically related to the Mensheviks may one day make it possible to evaluate systematically *Sotsialisticheskii vestnik*'s information about Soviet Russia; let us note that documents released so far have not put into question the reliability of that information.

It is in the light of these new possibilities that Leopold Haimson has put together a post-Soviet Menshevik Project aimed at publishing a series of documentary materials on the history of the party. The first two volumes, concerning the Mensheviks in 1917, have already appeared. Not only does the project involve Russian historians, but also it has been published in Russia. At the same time, a Russian postdoctoral thesis has, for the first time, presented a sustained comparison of the Mensheviks and the Bolsheviks, including the postrevolutionary period, to the advantage of the former. From a historiographic point of view the Mensheviks have returned home.[6]

Notwithstanding these developments, and some historians' references to the "revenge of the Mensheviks," there is little doubt that the Mensheviks have benefited less than others from the present a priori indulgence toward adversaries of the Bolsheviks.[7] The self-defined socialist dissidents of the late Soviet era hardly ever invoked Menshevik inspiration, although their ideological universe would have been familiar to readers of *Sotsialisticheskii vestnik*.[8] Under Gorbachev it was Bukharin, not Martov or Dan, who incarnated a missed socialist alternative. A 1988 Soviet monograph, "The Crash of Menshevism in Soviet Russia," proved even more uncompromising than the same authors' earlier work, although it confirmed Lenin's interest in exiled

Mensheviks and the resilience of the Menshevik underground.[9] Nor did the founding of a Social Democratic Party of the Russian Federation in 1990 redress the situation. The new Russian Social Democrats displayed no historical consciousness, and perhaps not even a socialist one. Their hero, as it turned out, was the West German liberal Ludwig Erhard.[10]

It is easy enough to explain the neglect of and ignorance about the Mensheviks in today's Russia. Avowedly socialist and Marxist, freethinking and antitraditionalist, antinationalist and even, to use a code term of the past, cosmopolitan, the Mensheviks continue to labor posthumously under familiar handicaps in their homeland. Nor do they find succor among Western intellectuals who fault academic "inheritors of the mantle of Menshevism" or who chide the Mensheviks for their "inertia disguised as submission to the forces of history."[11] They are dismissed for having lost and accused of not even having tried to win. For good measure they are charged with having poisoned the minds of the young by putting into question the inevitability of Soviet history. Evidently the injunction to keep "open, as it were, the options of the past which history as a mere record of fact has closed" has not struck deep roots in Western scholarship either.[12]

Our Mensheviks were, in their origins, barely distinguishable from their counterparts who went on to undertake the Soviet experiment. The continuum at the outset gradually gave way in the course of their long itinerary to a succession of binomial oppositions. These first separated the Mensheviks from the Bolsheviks and then worked their way into the heart of our exile group. The Mensheviks realized that refusal to ride the crest of elemental forces in 1917 meant a final and irreversible split within Russian social democracy; that unwillingness to take up arms against the Bolsheviks in 1918–1921 meant that this abominable regime would perdure; that hopes placed during the 1920s in a "deacceleration with brakes" of the regime were fragile because they depended on an increasingly demoralized working class. The course they advocated—loyal opposition and noncollaboration, pressure from within and criticism from without—was dictated by their refusal to be confined within a single pair of alternatives. The Mensheviks' later split, a sort of scissors crisis whereby some went left and others went right, was prompted by the realization that Stalin's revolution had indeed narrowed their options by obliging them either to discard Marxist verities and past hopes or to come to terms with the regime as it existed. This evolution paralleled that of Western social democrats, but unlike many of the latter, Mensheviks in both factions chose their camp without repudiating their past.

I would submit that the Mensheviks' record deserves our attention for a number of reasons. The analysis of Russian society in terms of social forces, at which they excelled, will continue to yield insight into the new Russia as well. The relation between economic liberalization and political democracy which so preoccupied the Mensheviks, especially during NEP, is again at issue, as is the problem of the mechanisms, agents, and costs of economic progress. The scope of freedom in a fragile society, the compromises to be made with unpalatable realities of a postrevolutionary order—these are to-day's issues, but they echo those that concerned the Mensheviks. The underlying impetus of their ideology, the attempt to define a space "on the left of the right and on the right of the left," the conviction that multiple possibilities lie between destructive solutions of the Right and of the Left, was and will be shared by others.[13] To borrow Alexander Herzen's words, cited in the epigraph to this book, the Mensheviks did not "seek refuge in the almshouse of reaction," but they did not allow themselves "to perish with the Revolution" either, choosing exile to promote its cause.

"Even without us our ideas will arise again in Russia," wrote Fedor Dan to Kautsky in 1932.[14] He was not claiming for his party the honor of being called correct ahead of its time. Dan himself once commented that today's correct tactic may be wrong yesterday as well as tomorrow, and a comrade added that "correctness in politics means being one step ahead of one's followers; being fifty years ahead of one's time is no good."[15] Rather, Dan was expressing his faith in the durability of democratic socialism. One may hope, as the Mensheviks did, that a future Russia will arise where democratic socialists will feel at home. If so, the legacy of the Mensheviks will find a place there.

The Mensheviks' legacy is, however, independent of the course of political development in Russia, and it speaks even to those who do not share their vision. To be sure, their trajectory will not be repeated because it involves a unique configuration of conundrums proper to our century: the futility or fertility of exile, the oppressive or emancipatory potential of Marxism, the hold of ideology over the trauma of experience, the appeal of internationalism over other loyalties, the uniqueness or universality of Russia's fate. Whatever their foibles and frailties, the Mensheviks' final legacy lies in the manner in which they confronted these issues.

The Mensheviks remained mindful of Marx's affirmation that men make their own history though they make it in conditions determined for them. In exile, the "last resort of free men," they freely and unflinchingly accepted responsibility for their actions and the consequences of their choices.[16] Ultimately, the Menshevik experience leads us to ask in what sense the history of our troubled century belongs to those who, through travails and disillusions, have tried to remain true to their conscience and to their ideals.

Biographical Summaries

Italics indicate less used legal or maiden names or, in the case of Shifrin and Volsky, pseudonyms used only occasionally.

Abramovitch, Raphael *Rein* (1880–1963)   Engineering student in Riga. Member Bund Central Committee from 1905 and RSDRP Central Committee from 1906. Abroad 1903–1904, 1910–1917. Liquidator, then internationalist during World War I. Member Central Executive Committee of Soviets 1917–1918, member Moscow Soviet 1919–1920; imprisoned. Leaves Russia with Martov, autumn 1920. Cofounder and editor *Sv* 1921–1963, sole editor 1940–1945. Member of LSI Bureau and Executive 1923–1940. Member of ZD 1920–1951 and chairman from 1940. Originally supporter of Martov Line; moves right after 1931, and especially in post–World War II period. Tries unsuccessfully to maintain Menshevik unity over new emigration issue after World War II. Longtime contributor to New York *Forverts* (Jewish Daily Forward), author *Soviet Revolution* (1962).

Alexandrova, Vera *Schwarz-Monoszon née Mordvinov* (1895–1966) Daughter of tsarist general of peasant origin, wife of Solomon Schwarz. Employed in Moscow after February 1917, exiled in 1922. Joins RSDRP sometime between 1919 and 1921. *Sv*'s cultural and literary critic; also writes for foreign socialist press on literary matters (pseudonyms include W. Friede). After World War II contributor to Russian emigré and English language press; editor U.S. government publication *Amerika*; editor at Chekhov Publishers, New York.

Aronson, Grigorii Iakovlevich (1887–1968)   Son of Petersburg banker, journalist. Bolshevik 1903–1907, then Bundist and Menshevik. Active in Vitebsk social organizations 1914–1916; internationalist, chairman Vitebsk Workers' Soviet 1917. Active in Employees Union and Bund affairs 1918–1922; member Moscow Soviet. Imprisoned, then exiled 1922. Right wing's representative in ZD 1922–1951. Correspondent for Kerensky's *Dni* until party interdiction 1930. After World War II hostile to rapprochement with new Soviet emigration. Author on Soviet Jewish affairs.

Axelrod, Pavel Borisovich (1850–1928)   Son of poor country laborer, initially Bakuninist and populist. Living abroad since 1881, founds with G. V. Plekhanov early Marxist Emancipation of Labor group; co-edits *Iskra;* leading theoretician of menshevism. Liquidator, gradually moving toward internationalism during World War I, opposes Bolsheviks unconditionally and after 1917 puts hopes in "socialist intervention" in Russia. In last years abroad, though ill and politically isolated from ZD, enjoys status of party patriarch. Identified with Menshevik right wing but respected and loved by whole party and many foreign socialist admirers.

Baikalov, Anatolii Vasil'evich (1882–1964)   Of cossack origin, originally Bolshevik; 1905, member of Menshevik Krasnoiarsk committee. After 1917 in England, where active in short-lived right wing London Group of Social Democrats banned by Martov. Writer and consultant on Russian matters to Trades Union Council and duchess of Atholl, Conservative MP and minister. Formally outside the party because of right wing views. After World War II establishes relations with Solidarists and other nonsocialist emigré formations.

Bienstock, Grigorii Osipovich (1884–1954)   Son of Petersburg jurist, culturally German-oriented, graduates from several German universities; lawyer by profession. Bolshevik 1904–1907; orientation as Menshevik varies. On returning to Russia in 1917 edits journal with left wing internationalist Iurii Larin but also commands army regiment. In 1919, abroad with Axelrod to plead for "socialist intervention." Right wing Menshevik in Odessa 1920–1921; arrested, exiled in 1922. Abroad is right wing Russian Menshevik and left wing German Social Democrat. Writes in *Sv* (pseudonym Gr. Osipov) and in right wing *Zapiski sotsialdemokrata.* In 1930s writes several much-translated books on international politics. Mystic, lively intelligence, politically difficult to classify.

Dallin, David Iul'evich *Levin* (1889–1962)   Son of Rogachev merchant, studies law in Russia and economics in Germany. Enters RSDRP between 1907 and 1909. Returning from abroad in 1917, enters Menshevik Central Committee as internationalist. Member Moscow Soviet, arrested, exiled 1921. ZD member 1921–1934 and 1942–1948; co-editor *Sv* 1923–1933. In USA well-known sovietologist, author of twelve books on Russia, including foreign policy classics and the important *Forced Labor in the Soviet Union;* prolific columnist for *New Leader.* Heavily involved in emigré politics after World War II. Breaks with Menshevik majority, first over support for new Russian emigration and then over Russia's territorial integrity. Originally adherent of left wing Martov Line, always inclined toward independent positions.

Dan, Fedor Il'ich *Gurvich* (1871–1947)   Son of Petersburg pharmacist, physician. Activist in Union of Struggle for Emancipation of Labor, arrested during strikes of 1896. Iskrite, co-organizer of Second RSDRP Congress. Leading Menshevik at all party conferences after 1903, active in party politics at home and abroad. During World War I exiled to Siberia; co-founder of Siberian Zimmerwaldism with I. Tsereteli. Revolutionary defensist in 1917, vice-chairman of Soviet Central Executive Committee and Central Executive Committee member after October. Arrested, then exiled 1922; chairman of RSDRP and co-editor of *Sv* 1922–1940. Unyieldingly faithful to left wing Martov Line; closely tied to Austro-Marxists, especially Otto Bauer. Moves steadily left in 1930s because of fascist threat and under impact of Soviet collectivization and industrialization, even as many other Mensheviks move right. Founds own group in 1940 (*Novyi mir* then *Novyi put'*); breaks completely with ZD in 1942 after years of increasing tension. Publishes *Origins of Bolshevism* shortly before death (occasional pseudonym Grekov).

Dan, Lidia Osipovna *née Tsederbaum* (1878–1963)   Sister of Martov, wife of Fedor Dan. Studied in Dorpat. First arrested in 1899, works abroad for *Iskra*, returns illegally to Russia, exiled again. Works in politics and journalism with husband in Geneva, Paris, Petersburg, Siberia until Revolution; exiled with him after 1922. Employed in social organizations after 1917, active in Political Red Cross; Menshevik representative to LSI Women's Commisssion. Never elected to party body but as "grande dame" of menshevism plays key role in keeping factions on friendly terms and, in 1950s, in organizing Menshevik group and recording party history.

Denike, Iurii Petrovich (1887–1964)   Son of Kazan judge with gentry connections. Bolshevik 1904–1906; returns to politics in 1917 as Menshevik vice-chairman of Kazan Soviet. After October Revolution active as Moscow right wing Menshevik, "sets himself outside party" 1918–1919, readmitted only in emigration. Works in Communist Academy and elected to Moscow University chair of history and sociology in 1920. Sent to Soviet trade mission in Berlin, defects in 1926. Joins SPD, assists Hilferding in editing SPD theoretical journal *Die Gesellschaft;* after 1933 acquires reputation as German emigré publicist. Contributor to *Sv* then co-editor 1954–1963; coopted into ZD in 1943. Writes in Russian emigré press after World War II; employed by Voice of America. Supports Menshevik rapprochement with new emigration. (German pseudonym Georg Decker.)

Domanevskaia, Ol'ga Iosifovna (1885–1974)   Journalist and economist, wife of Aaron Iugov. Studies in Petersburg; after 1917 edits journal of Moscow Economic Soviet. Left wing member of Menshevik Moscow organization in 1917, leaves party with A. I. Vishinskii and N. N. Sukhanov in 1920–1921. Rejoins party abroad, contributes to *Sv*, though continuing to write for Soviet economic publications (pseudonym Z. Eber). In 1930s represents extreme Menshevik Left, quits Dan's *Novyi put'* group in 1942. After World War II leading contributor to pro-Communist New York *Russkii golos* and Toronto *Vestnik*.

Dubois, Anatolii Eduardovich (1881–1958)   Petersburg lawyer, becomes prizewinning sculptor late in life. Bolshevik deputy chairman of Soviet of Unemployed in 1905; then Menshevik liquidator and trade union organizer. Defensist in

World War I, volunteers for military service; in 1917 political commissar on front and deputy minister of labor. Sympathetic to anti-Soviet Constituent Assembly front on Volga, arrested, exiled to Siberia, then abroad in 1923. Right wing Menshevik, moves left for nationalist reasons, joining Dan's *Novyi put'* (pseudonym A. Gorskii.)

Dvinov, Boris L'vovich *Gurevitch* (1886–1968)   Son of Vitebsk merchant, studies commerce. Bundist, then Menshevik from 1903. Imprisoned in 1905; active in Vilno party organization and Kiev student social democratic press; functionary in legal Moscow Union of Shop Clerks after 1913. Member Moscow soviet until 1922 and member of its executive in 1917–1918. Internationalist, in Moscow Menshevik organization 1917; member Central Committee Bureau in 1921; first *Sv* coordinator in Moscow. Exiled in 1923, becomes a successful businessman. ZD member 1923–1951, adherent of Dan's faction until 1940. After World War II writes on emigré politics and against Menshevik rapprochement with new emigration.

Estrine, Lilia Iakovlevna *née Ginzburg* (1898–1981)   Born in Libau, studies law in Saratov. Accompanies husband to Moscow, then in exile abroad. In 1920s works in Soviet trade mission in Berlin. In 1930s Nicolaevsky's secretary at Paris office of IISG. Active Trotskyist in 1930s, contributes to Trotsky's *Biulleten' oppozitsii* (pseudonyms L. Iakovlev, Paulsen). Later marries David Dallin.

Estrine, Samuel Efimovich (1893–1976)   Son of modest Orsh confectioner, Moscow law graduate 1922. Works in Saratov socialist student collective, elected to local soviet in 1918 but not allowed to take seat. Arrested with other Mensheviks during Kronstadt Uprising in 1921. Heads economic division of Moscow Mosselprom until again arrested. Later employed in cultural-educational division of Tsektran while engaged in illegal work. Leaves Russia 1923, active in SPD youth organization until 1933. Works in Paris for International Trade Unions during Spanish civil war. Emigrates to America 1939, international secretary of Jewish Labor Committee 1946–1976. Joins *Novyi put'* but returns to *Sv* after Dan's death.

Garvi, Petr Abramovich *Bronshtein* (1881–1944)   Son of Odessa accountant, Petersburg University law graduate in 1911. Social democrat since 1899–1900, participates in organization of 1905 Moscow uprising, later trade union activist. Early Menshevik, liquidator after 1905, moves from extreme internationalism to moderate defensism during World War I. Militantly antibolshevik, refuses to enter unified RSDRP Central Committee in 1910; serves in Menshevik Organizational Committee from 1912 and in Menshevik Central Committee in 1917 but leaves in protest after October Revolution. Journalism and party work in Odessa 1918–1921; arrested, then exiled in 1923. Contributor to *Sv* and foreign socialist press; Russian expert for SPD Secretariat. Leader of intraparty Menshevik right wing; member of RDSRP delegation to LSI congresses but not member of ZD until 1942. On poor terms politically with Dan and isolated in party until arrival in America. Also writes poetry under pseudonyms (Karelin and others).

Garvi, Sofia Samoilovna *née Fichman* (1881–1958)   Daughter of prosperous Odessa family, enters social democratic circle in Kishinev in 1900. First arrest in 1902, followed by internal and foreign exile intertwined with party work at husband's side. After World War II opposes Menshevik rapprochement with new emigration. (Pseudonym Sylvia.)

Grinfeld, Iudif' Aronovna (1888–?)   Tübingen economics doctorate 1913. Social democrat since 1905, arrested and flees abroad, lives in Copenhagen during World War I. After Revolution, party work in Odessa. Exiled in 1922, writes for German social democratic press and *Sv* (pseudonym Braginskaia). First wife of G. Bienstock.

Ingerman, Sergius Mikhailovich (1868–1943)   Physician, resident in USA from 1891. Originally populist, flees Russia for Switzerland and enters Emancipation of Labor group. Co-founder of Russian Social Democratic Society in New York (1891) and Socialist Party of America. Always hostile to bolshevism, defensist in World War I and co-founder of New York Plekhanov Group. In 1920s and 1930s supports extraparty Menshevik right wing and its publications.

Iudin, Isaia L'vovich *Aizenstadt* (1867–1937)   Born in Vilno. Originally populist, one of first Marxists in Jewish labor movement and leader of first mass strike of Jewish workers 1893–1894. Bund Central Committee member from 1902. At one time sympathetic to bolshevism, defensist during World War I. Exiled 1922, ZD member and secretary as well as *Sv* business manager in Berlin and Paris.

Iugov, Aaron Abramovich *Frumson* (1886–1954)   Native of Rostov, Petersburg law and economics graduate 1911. Enters revolutionary movement 1903, several times arrested and exiled. Active in Samara social democratic organization 1915–1916, defensist then internationalist. After October Revolution heads Moscow Mosselprom. Member of Menshevik Central Committee 1918 and of its Executive Committee 1920. Arrested, exiled abroad 1923. ZD member 1923–1942 and its secretary-treasurer 1937–1942. Publishes several books on economic matters, articles in *Sv* and in German socialist press. Left Menshevik, devoted to Dan, becomes Dan's closest collaborator on *Novyi put'*. After 1947 writes for pro-Communist New York *Russkii golos*. Husband of Olga Domanevskaia.

Ivanovich, Stepan *Portugeis, Semen Osipovich* (1880–1944)   Son of Kishinev artisan, journalist. Enters social democratic work in Kishinev 1900; liquidator, then defensist during World War I; antibolshevik work in Odessa during Civil War. Moving spirit of extraparty Menshevik right wing after Revolution. Publishes *Zaria* in Berlin and *Zapiski sotsialdemokrata* in Paris; leads campaign against *Sv*'s Martov Line. Readmitted into party and coopted into ZD in 1942.

James, Iakov Markovich *Lupolov* (1868–1943)   Apprenticeship in Perm. In revoutionary movement from 1891, flees to London and USA. In Boston founds Russian section of Socialist Party of America 1893, then Society of Russian Social Democrats; later co-founds New York Plekhanov Group. After party work in Russia 1900–1907, returns permanently to New York as longtime secretary of New York Russian Social Democrats.

Jasny, Naum Mikhailovich (1883–1967)   Son of wealthy Kharkov entrepreneur, economist. Enters revolutionary movement 1899–1900. Petersburg Menshevik in 1905, drifts away from politics until reentering Menshevik group in Berlin in 1925. Employed in Zemstvo organization in 1916, member of All-State Food Soviet, consultant to Higher Economic Soviet and land ministry. Works for Soviet trade mission's grain branch in Hamburg, then joins German research institution. In USA from mid-1930s; prolific academic economist specializing on USSR. Moderately right orientation, also writes in *Sv.*

Kefali, Mark Samoilovich *Kammermacher* (1882–1943)   Son of Vilno printer, himself a printer. Bundist, first arrested 1901, at one time a Bolshevik. Active in Printers' Union after 1905, abroad as Menshevik 1909–1917, defensist during World War I. A leader of All-Russian Union of Printers, head of its Moscow branch. After arrest in 1920 flees to Siberia and then abroad. Enters ZD in 1924 as its only authentic worker and as representative of right wing. Also writes in *Sv.*

Khinoy, Mark Samoilovich (1884–1968)   Son of Chernigov wood dealer, typesetter. RSDRP member 1901, flees from renewed arrest to Paris, then to USA in 1913. Writes in socialist press in Russian (including *Sv*), Yiddish, and English.

Lande, Leo Semenovich (1901–1976)   Son of Warsaw merchant, member of a Moscow socialist Zionist organization during World War I, then co-founder of Menshevik Youth Union. Student, later employed in Chemists' Union 1920–1921, arrested during Kronstadt Uprising, illegal party work in Moscow and Ukraine after release. Flees abroad in 1923; economics student and later assistant in Social Science Institute of Heidelberg University where co-organizes Menshevik group. Moves to Netherlands in 1933, then Cuba and USA during World War II. Adheres to Martov Line, writes in *Sv.*

Martov, L. *Tsederbaum, Iulii Osipovich* (1873–1923)   Born into well-to-do Petersburg bourgeois family which produces several revolutionaries (S. Ezhov, V. Levitskii, F. Dnevnitskii, L. Dan), co-founder with Lenin in 1895 of Union of Struggle for Emancipation of Labor. After arrest and exile, works abroad as an *Iskra* editor. Menshevik leader after 1903, mostly abroad, combats both liquidators and Bolsheviks. Internationalist in World War I, succeeds in moving Menshevik majority leftward after October Revolution and imposes his view on the party. Leaves Russia in 1920 to head ZD and found *Sv*, contributing actively until premature death. Outstanding theoretician and charismatic personality, much loved by Russian and Western socialists, respected even by Bolsheviks. After 1917 defines Martov Line which guides party until 1940.

Nicolaevsky, Boris Ivanovich (1887–1966)   Son of Ufa province village priest, historian. Enters revolutionary movement 1903, arrested 1904; experiences 1905 as Bolshevik in Samara. Menshevik by 1907, party work alternates with internal exile until 1917. Irkutsk Zimmerwaldist during World War I, Menshevik Central Committee member from 1918. Petrograd soviet member, enters commission for supervison of Okhrana files; although not even high school graduate, is director of Central Archives for History of the Revolutionary Movement in Moscow 1919–1921. Under arrest 1921–1922, then exiled, becomes Berlin representative of Moscow's Marx-Engels Institute and in 1930s director of IISG's Paris branch. Does research, accumulates materials, writes academic and journalistic pieces in USA for English and Russian publications, moves to Hoover Institution 1964–1965 as curator of his own collection. Knowledgeable and infatigable collector of historical materials and founder of kremlinology, a uniquely invaluable resource person on Soviet Russia. ZD member from 1923, moves away from Martov Line during 1930s. Breaks with Menshevik majority in 1948 over his involvement with emigré politics but returns to *Sv* as co-editor 1954–1963. Frequent contributor to *Sv* from earliest days, long in charge of *Sv* correspondence from Russia (occasional pseudonym B. Andreev).

Potresov, Aleksandr Nikolaevich (1869–1934)   Of gentry stock, co-founder with Lenin and Martov in 1895 of Union of Struggle for Emancipation of Labor, an editor of *Iskra* before the RSDRP Second Congress. A Menshevik from the outset, liquidator after 1905, defensist during World War I. Ideological leader of extraparty right wing Menshevik *Zaria* group (effectively led by S. Ivanovich) after Revolution. Leaves Russia in 1925 but proves impossible to collaborate with Menshevik party abroad because of ideological divergences.

Rosenfeld, Oreste Ivanovich (1891–1964)   Son of Astrakhan functionary, studies law in Moscow and already Menshevik in 1914. In France in 1917 as officer with Russian unit, remains abroad and may have served in French Foreign Legion. Works with Axelrod on *Echos de Russie* 1918–1919, joins staff of Léon Blum's socialist daily *Populaire* as its Russian expert, becomes managing editor in 1936. Mobilized in 1939, prisoner of war 1940–1945. Editor of Sunday *Populaire* and SFIO member of Assembly of French Union after World War II; expelled from SFIO for criticism of its colonial policy.

Sapir, Boris Moiseevich (1902–1989)   Son of Lodz merchant. Before entering Menshevik Party in 1919, participant in pupils' movement in 1917 and chairman of Moscow Union of Jewish Pupils in 1918. Mobilized into Red Army 1919–1920. Member of Central Bureau of Union of Social Democratic Youth 1921–1922; underground secretary of Kharkov Menshevik Committee 1922–1923. Arrested in 1921, Solovetskii Isles prisoner 1923–1925; flees abroad. Law graduate Heidelberg University, employed by IISG in 1930s, works in New York Jewish welfare organizations after 1944, returns to IISG in 1960s as Russian curator and publishes on Russian revolutionary movement. Menshevik representative on Executive of Socialist Youth International

1926–1940; ZD member 1944–1951, contributor to *Sv.* Moderately right wing inclination, leaves *Sv* 1951–1954 over quarrel about new emigration.

Schwarz, Solomon Meerovich *Monoszon* (1883–1973)   Son of prosperous
Vilno family, Heidelberg law graduate 1911. Bolshevik in 1903; liquidator, trade
union journalist from 1905. Defensist, secretary of workers' group of War Industries
Committee 1916; assistant to head of labor division of Petrograd soviet, then head
of social insurance division of Ministry of Labor, 1917. After Revolution, organizer of
Petrograd civil servants' strike; employed in Moscow health insurance administration.
Mobilized into Red Army; employed in Red Cross, legal work in Revnosovet. Arrested
during Kronstadt Uprising and exiled 1922. Abroad, writes on labor for international
socialist press and International Labor Organization. In USA also associated with New
School of Social Research and publishes on Soviet economic and social subjects, including *Labor in the Soviet Union.* Longtime regular *Sv* contributor (pseudonyms include Strannik), co-editor of German-language *RSD* 1925–1932 and of *Sv* 1945–1963;
ZD member 1922–1951. Adheres to Martov Line, breaks reluctantly with Dan in
1940. Emigrates to Israel shortly before death.

Shifrin, Aleksander Mihailovich *Max Werner* (1901–1951)   Native of
Kharkov, obtains social science doctoratate there and teaches economics. Underground Menshevik party work and member Ukraine Menshevik Party Committee;
arrested in 1922 and exiled. Abroad, SPD member and an editor of Mannheimer *Volk-
stimme* as well as collaborating with Hilferding's *Gesellschaft.* After 1933 prominent in
left wing of German socialist emigration; becomes military expert. Writes several
well-known books on strategy; regular contributor to *New Republic* and (New York)
PM. Always left wing Menshevik, active in *Novyi put'* (occasional pseudonym A. Mihailov).

Skomorovskii, Boris Alekseevich (1894–1965)   Native of Kishinev, secretary Menshevik Central Committee in Moscow in 1920. Later member and secretary
Paris Menshevik group. Menshevik delegate to LSI congresses. Extreme left wing orientation. Rare case of expulsion from the party abroad in 1942 after he has already
quit *Novyi put'.* Later works for UN and contributes to Toronto procommunist *Vestnik.*

Stein, Aleksandr Nikolaevich *Rubinstein* (1881–1949)   Native of Riga,
studies at Polytechnic there. Bolshevik member of Riga RSDRP Committee 1905.
Flees to Germany 1906, active in SPD; publishes bulletin on Russia, works on committee to help political prisoners in Russia. Interned during World War I, co-founder of
USPD and editor of its *Freiheit.* After World War I edits SPD *Sozialistische Bildung und
Bücherwarte;* as German citizen pro forma editor of *Sv,* acts as patron to Berlin Mensheviks. Exiled to Prague and New York after 1933.

Volsky, Nikolai Vladislavovich *Valentinov* (1879–1964)   Of Tambolsk
gentry, studies in Kiev and enters revolutionary movement there. Arrested 1902,
hunger strike, released and goes abroad. Member of Lenin's Geneva Bolshevik group

1903–1904, thereafter Menshevik. Liquidator after 1905, contributes to Menshevik and nonparty press including *Russkoe slovo,* writes on social and philosophical matters. Not involved in party work in 1917. Under Soviet regime becomes assistant editor of Sovnarkhom journal under F. Dzerzhinskii. Sent to Paris trade mission as editor of *Vie des soviets,* defects in 1931. Writes in Russian emigré press, including, after World War II, in *Sv* (pseudonyms include Iur'evskii). Right wing in orientation but aloof from party organization abroad, contributes historical reminiscences, especially the popular *Encounters with Lenin.*

Vulikh, Tatiana Ivanovna (1886–1959)   Graduate of Tiflis Gentry *(dvorianskii)* Institute. Social democrat in Caucasus, belongs to L. Kamenev's circle, participates in Moscow uprising 1905. Abroad, breaks with Bolsheviks 1911. After 1917 a Menshevik, lives in Egypt and Greece.

Wolin, Simon Iul'evich *Levin* (1892–197?)   David Dallin's brother. Studies law abroad. Defensist 1917, employed in trade union organizations until arrested during Kronstadt Uprising. Flees from internal exile to Berlin 1927. Enlists in French army 1940. In USA works for *New Leader* and Voice of America. Contributes to *Sv* and writes on Soviet system. Right wing Menshevik.

Woytinsky, Vladimir Savel'evich (1885–1960)   Son of Petersburg professor, studies economics there and publishes well-received academic monograph in 1905. Bolshevik chairman of Soviet of Unemployed in 1905; imprisoned and exiled to Siberia. Close to Iraklii Tsereteli during World War I, returns to Petrograd as Irkutsk Zimmerwaldist and becomes Menshevik. In 1917, member of Central Executive Committee of Soviets, editor of *Izvestiia,* commissar at front. After release from Bolshevik imprisonment, represents independent Georgia abroad 1919–1921. Researcher, then research director, German Federation of Trade Unions 1929–1933, and International Labor Organization employee 1933–1935. In USA after 1935, employed in Central Statistical Board and Social Security Board and instrumental in setting up U.S. social security system. Writes prolifically, including memoirs, and lectures on economic matters. Right wing Menshevik in emigration, keeps distance from ZD and later from Russian emigration as a whole.

Abbreviations

AA   Abramovitch Archive, IISG
BP   Baikalov Papers, Columbia University Archives
[Ed]   Editorial
FOIA   (U.S. government documents released under the terms of the) Freedom of Information Act
GARF   Gosudarstvennyi Arkhiv Rossiiskoi Federatsii, Moscow
IISG   Internationaal Instituut voor Sociale Geschiedenis, Amsterdam
[IP]   Iz Partii (*Sv* reports on Menshevik Party matters)
KA   Kautsky Archive, IISG
KD   Constitutional Democrats (Russian liberal party)
LSI   Labor and Socialist International
MP   Inter-University Project on the History of the Menshevik Movement
NC   Nicolaevsky Collection, Hoover Institution, Stanford (note: file numbers given according to original classification; new classification is in parentheses)
NEP   New Economic Policy (1921–1927)
NL   *New Leader* (weekly publication of Social Democratic Federation, New York)
Np   *Novyi put'*
NYT   *New York Times*
PBO   *Protokoly berlinskoi organizatsii* (transcripts of discussions of Berlin Menshevik Club, available at YIVO, IISG, MP)
PMP   Philip E. Mosely Papers, University of Illinois, Urbana-Champaign
[PR]   Po Rossii (*Sv* reports and correspondence from Russia)
RSD   *Russische Sozial Demokratie* (Menshevik German-language bulletin)
RSDLP   Russian Social Democratic Labor Party (=RSDRP)
RSDRP   Rossiiskaia Sotsial Demokraticheskaia Rabochaia Partiia (=RSDLP)
RTsKhIDNI Rossiiskii Tsentr Khraneniia i Izuchaniia Dokumentov Noveishei Istorii, Moscow (former Party Archives)

SAI	Sozialistische Arbeiter International (=LSI) Archives, IISG
SC	Souvarine Collection, Hoover Institution, Stanford
SFIO	Section française de l'Internationale ouvrière (French Socialist Party)
SPD	Sozialistische Partei Deutschlands
SR	Socialists-Revolutionaries (Party)
Sv	*Sotsialisticheskii vestnik*
TUC	Trades Union Council (Great Britain)
USPD	Unabhängige Sozialistische Partei Deutschlands
VC	Volsky Collection, Hoover Institution, Stanford
YIVO	YIVO Institute for Jewish Research, New York
ZD	Zagranichnaia Delegatsiia (Foreign Delegation of RSDRP)

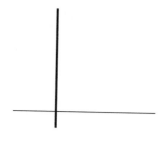

Notes

Introduction

1. This point was made forcefully long ago by Edinger, *German Exile Politics,* viii. Ironically, it no longer holds true for Edinger's specific subject, but it remains all the more valid as a general observation.
2. Abramowitsch to Mehr, 5 October 193[3?], AA I/3. The letter continues: "When Iu. O. [Martov] in 1922 criticized the SPD for its policy during the war, a 'devastating' note appeared in *Vorwärts* about emigrés who practice politics in cafés. Now the author of these lines is himself sitting in a café in emigration and I am almost sure he has changed his mind."
3. Exiles are their own severest critics, for example, Bauer, *Illegale Partei,* 141–142, who cites his predecessors in exile, including Friedrich Engels.
4. On exile as a modern predicament, see Arendt, *Origins of Totalitarianism.* On the influence of exiles, see Fleming and Bailyn, eds., *Intellectual Migration,* as well as Radkau, *Deutsche Emigration in den USA.* The few studies on the general phenomenon of political exile, however, are either provocative but sketchy (Williams, "European Political Emigrations"), superficial (Tabori, *Anatomy of Exile*), or schematic (Shain, *Frontiers of Loyalty*).
5. Hobsbawm, *Revolutionaries,* viii.
6. The theoretical literature on power is at a loss in dealing with this sort of phenomenon. For representative views, Champlin, ed., *Power.* As a counter to the mainstream tendency, compare Barry, ed., *Power and Political Theory,* and Lukes, *Power;* above all, see Mokken and Stokman, "Power and Influence as Political Phenomena."
7. This point, made years ago by Keep, "From the Finland Station," and noted (ruefully) by Croan, "Politics of Marxist Sovietology," has now been reiterated by Laqueur, *Dream That Failed,* 120: "All serious sovietology came out of the mantle of Menshevism, including those practitioners who were not aware of it."
8. For example, Carr, *Socialism in One Country,* 2:448, refers to *Sv* as an "influential and often well-informed anti-Soviet journal," but is so ill acquainted with the source that he mistakes its frequency of publication. Some exceptions to this

neglect are Brovkin, "Mensheviks and NEP Society in Russia," and Filtzer, *Soviet Workers and Stalinist Industrialization*.

9. For example, Service, *Bolshevik Party in Revolution*, 4, mentions but does not pursue the question of the "profound influence over later generations of writers outside the Soviet Union" exercised by "four individuals: Martov, Stanislav [presumably Stepan] Ivanovich, Fyodor Dan, R. Abramowitch." All were Mensheviks.

10. See R. Abramowitsch, "Geschichte fun Lenin's Tsavoye," *Forverts*, 23 May 1956, for an account of the scoop.

11. Fischhoff, "Hindsight: Thinking Backward?" and Fischhoff and Beyth, " 'I Knew It Would Happen.' "

12. Cohen, citing Dwight MacDonald in "Bolshevism and Stalinism," 6. Daniels, *Conscience of the Revolution*, 8, makes the same point forcefully.

13. "Brillant premonitions" is the term used by Wolfe, *Three Who Made a Revolution*, 366. On other prophetic statements, see ibid., 293; Baron, *Plekhanov*, 360; and Ascher, *Axelrod*, 201–202. On the example given here, see Deutscher, *Prophet Armed*, 90. The title of Deutscher's trilogy says everything there is to say about assigning prophetic attributes.

14. The Menshevik influence on historiography is particularly difficult to treat analytically. For example, Wolfe's *Three Who Made a Revolution* has been enormously successful—5 editions, 64 printings, 23 translations, 800,000 copies sold—and therefore (one is inclined to presume) influential. Four of the first eight individuals acknowledged in the book are members of the Menshevik group discussed here (Schwarz, Alexandrova, Nicolaevsky, and Abramovitch). What can one infer about their influence?

1. The Menshevik Family

A GROUP PORTRAIT

1. The term is Sapir's, interview 1.

2. For the party background in the early years, see Keep, *Rise of Social Democracy in Russia*, and Wildman, *Making of a Workers' Revolution*.

3. On these early deviations, see Keep, *Rise of Social Democracy*, and Kindersley, *First Russian Revisionists*.

4. Former Bolsheviks include Aronson, Baikalov, Bienstock, Denike, Nicolaevsky, Schwarz, Valentinov-Volsky, and Woytinsky.

5. Dan, *Origins of Bolshevism*, 235. Compare this account with the one in Frankel, *Prophecy and Politics*, 226.

6. The depth of Dan's antipathy to revisionism can be gauged from one example. In 1947, when plans were afoot for a French translation of *Origins of Bolshevism*, it was suggested to Dan that he might rectify a statement he had mistakenly attributed to the revisionist and future liberal Petr Struve. Dan vehemently refused, stating he would not have the French translation of his work more in-

dulgent toward Struve than the Russian original. L. O. Dan Archive VI/23 (IISG).

7. D. Dalin, "Proch illiuzii," *Sv* 8, 20 May 1921, and *Posle voin i revoliutsii.*

8. The most impressive account of this stratum is Frankel, *Prophecy and Politics.*

9. On Martov, see Getzler, *Martov,* 58. On Petliura, see Abramovich to Goldman, 11 June 1926, AA V/1.

10. Abramovich to Levitas, 6 April 1936, AA IV/2; Aronson, *Revoliutsionnaia iunost',* 90; Aleksandrova to F. Dan, 24 October 1941, L. O. Dan Archive VII/26.

11. For instance, although Aronson refused to have any dealings with that part of his family that had emigrated to Palestine/Israel, he left money to the Jewish National Fund. Turim, interview.

12. On Schwarz's last years, see Bialer, interview. Wolfe, interview, adds that Schwarz was intensely disappointed to find in Israel not a socialist society but, as he put it, "just another capitalist state."

13. These nationalities included the Georgians, whose independence the Mensheviks had once defended. See R. Abramovich, "Opasnyi put'," *Sv* 156, 18 July 1927, and "Dve taktiki," *Sv* 163/164, 10 November 1927. Discussed in Roobol, *Tsereteli,* 235–242.

14. See Nicolaevsky's interviews with Leopold Haimson, partially translated as Haimson, ed., *Making of Three Russian Revolutionaries.* On language, see Bourguina, interview 1.

15. See Nikolaevskii to Baikalov, 11 March 1934, BP; also Bialer, interview.

16. Vulikh to Nikolaevskii, 26 February 1932, NC 134(207).

17. Kristof, "B. I. Nicolaevsky," 20, and Mosely, "Boris Nicolaevsky."

18. On Ukraine, see Dan to Kautsky, 5 May 1929, *Pis'ma,* 371–380. On the Tsereteli-Dan break in 1930, see Roobol, *Tsereteli,* 246–248.

19. Woytinsky's Americanization involved so thorough a downplaying of his Russian and socialist past that his closest friend, Tsereteli, broke with him on reading his English-language memoirs (published as *Stormy Passage*); see Roobol, *Tsereteli,* 251. At Woytinsky's funeral his wife forbade the use of any language other than English; Bourguina, interview 2. For a review of the relevant literature on the intelligentsia, see Scherrer, *Petersburger religiösphilosophische Vereinigungen,* 25–39.

20. Garvi, *Vospominaniia sotsial demokrata,* 3, discussed in Wildman, "Russian and Jewish Social Democracy," 83.

21. See Bohachevsky-Chomiak and Rosenthal, eds., *Revolution of the Spirit,* and Read, "New Directions in the Russian Intelligentsia."

22. Wildman, "Russian and Jewish Social Democracy," 83.

23. Kristof, "B. I. Nicolaevsky," 9.

24. Wildman, "Russian and Jewish Social Democracy," 77.

25. See Nikolaevskii, "Pamiati S. O. Portugeisa (St. Ivanovich)."

26. On the concept of a workers' intelligentsia, see Ascher, *Axelrod,* esp. 101–109.

27. For a corrective to the traditional stress on "alienation," see Brym, *Jewish Intelligentsia and Russian Marxism.*

28. Ivanovich, "Aforizmy (dlia S. Ingermana): 1938," NC 23(65).

29. For an application of this policy, see Viliatser to Abramovich, 25 January 1934, and "Rezoliutsiia Zagranichnoi Delegatsii RSDRP," 2 February 1934, NC 75(130).

30. Sapir, "Shtrikhi k kharakteristike," in Garvi, *Vospominaniia.*

A PORTRAIT GALLERY

1. Sapir, "Theodor Dan und sein letztes Buch"; Dvinov, "F. I. Dan"; L. Dan, interviews, and Haimson, ed., *Making of Three Russian Revolutionaries;* Liebich, "Menshevik Origins."

2. D. Anin, "F. I. Dan," *Unser Shtime,* 9–10 February 1947. Compare Garvi, *Vospominaniia,* 422, who attributes the quotation to Lenin's wife.

3. "A Note on Theodore Dan," in T. Dan, *Origins of Bolshevism,* vii.

4. Haimson, ed., *Making of Three Russian Revolutionaries,* 181.

5. Sapir, "Theodor Dan und sein letztes Buch," 17–18.

6. Haimson, *Russian Marxists and the Origins of Bolshevism,* 216, cites Berdyayev's characterization of the Russian *intelligent* as someone who all his life remains a student youth. The same image is used with regard to Martov by the Bolshevik luminary Lunacharskii, "Iulii Osipovich Martov (Tsederbaum)," 64. Getzler's invaluable biography of Martov has been criticized as "hopelessly dry" for not presenting a vivid picture of Martov, "the restless chain-smoker, the inventive bohemian, the warm-spirited comrade, the humane and not very disciplined revolutionist." See Howe, "Authority of Failure," 460. Such a picture emerges more clearly from L. Dan interviews.

7. Valentinov, *Encounters with Lenin,* 114; Krupskaya, *Reminiscences of Lenin,* 99; Shishkin, *Iz vospominanii kooperativnykh i politicheskikh,* 35.

8. Dan was sent away to school by his stepfather. His first marriage ended in divorce after years of estrangement. One of his two sons from this marriage died in 1917. The other, Viktor Gurvitch, remained in the Soviet Union, and Lidia Dan recounts that in the 1940s, at the New York Public Library, Dan came across a copy of a volume of Tadzhik poems translated by his son. Sapir, "Theodor Dan und sein letztes Buch"; see also Sapir, *Martov i ego blizkie,* and L. Dan, interviews.

9. Sapir, "Theodor Dan und sein letztes Buch," 17. Sapir perhaps exaggerates the unanimity between Martov and Dan in previous periods. Compare Getzler, *Martov,* 105, 120–121. Historians hostile to Dan's orientation, whether in 1917 (as too far right) or in exile (as too far left), have argued that Dan dominated Martov. Nikolaevskii, interview 21, adds for good measure that Martov probably never really liked Dan and refers to a letter from Trotsky in 1904 citing Martov as shouting at Dan: "How many times have I told you, it is not a question of outarguing [*peresporit'*] but of convincing [*perebedit'*]."

10. Reproduced in Getzler, *Martov,* 92.

11. Abramowitsch to Adler, 1 November 1934, SAI 2623, and Ivanovich to Ingerman, 16 July 1928, NC 23(63).

12. Nove, interview, recounting Dan's conversation with Nove's father, Iakov Nova-kovskii, an old Menshevik.

13. Bienstock to Kautsky, 3 May 1929, KA G 16.

14. Cited in Wolfe, *Three Who Made a Revolution*, 386. The same certitude was noted in Lenin, mostly by the latter's political opponents, such as Valentinov.

15. L. Dan, interview 22.

16. Compare the withering remarks of Kerensky's secretary and future Harvard sociologist Sorokin, *Leaves from a Russian Diary*, 36.

17. A. Koralnik, "Ilich—der getreyer: de F. I. Dan, der serzijährigen," *Tag*, 15 November 1931.

18. Garvi to Dan, 25 September 1939, NC 18(53).

19. Shvarts, "Biograficheskii ocherk," in Aleksandrova, *Literatura i zhizn'*, 4. On Iugov, see "Ideologicheskaia liniia 'Sv,'" *Sv* 692, April 1956. It might be noted that Iugov had had a similarly servile attitude toward Martov. According to Denike, interview 15, Iugov would always state, " 'I'm in complete agreement with Iulii Osipovich [Martov],' and Martov would ask, 'Didn't I say something stupid?' "

20. Lewin, *While Messiah Tarried*, 306.

21. Tobias, *Jewish Bund in Russia from Its Origins to 1905*, 309, cites Abramovitch's nostalgic recollections of "those Bund towns [where] I used to feel like the representative of a great power that was well-loved and supported by the working masses and the intelligentsia alike." He could not express similar feelings for the RSDRP, given that the 1903 congress which witnessed the Bolshevik-Menshevik split also saw the temporary withdrawal of the Bund in protest. On the condescending attitude toward the Bund, see L. Dan, interviews.

22. Zetkin, *Trotzkis Verbannung und die Sozialdemokratie*, 13. Compare Trotsky's description of Abramovitch as "a conservative pedant whose every instinct had been outraged by the Revolution," in *History of the Russian Revolution*, 2:28. Lenin, too, harbored a strong antipathy to Abramovitch; see Lenin to Molotov, 10 June 1921, in Lenin, *Polnoe sobranie sochinenii*, 52:263.

23. On cowardice, see Medvedev, *Let History Judge*, 279. On courage, see Stampfer to the Sopade, 10 February 1943, in Stampfer, *Mit dem Gesicht nach Deutschland*, 582.

24. Compare Abramowitsch to Mehr, 5 October 193[3?], AA I/3, with Dan to Kautsky, 10 June 1929, *Pis'ma*, 381: "We are dealing with emigré groups which, in my conviction, are far more the rejects of an already historical process rather than the kernels of any fruitful future development." To be sure, Dan was referring not to his own group but rather to his extraparty right Menshevik opponents around Potresov.

25. Abramovitch's importance was sometimes telescoped backwards. W. H. Chamberlin, in his review of Abramovitch's *Soviet Revolution*, *NL*, 25 June 1962, speaks of Martov, Abramovitch, and Dan as the most important figures of the Menshevik group in 1903!

26. Nikolaevskii, interview 1.

27. Abramowitsch to Adler, 5 February 1927, SAI 2623.

28. Sedov to Nikolaevskii, esp. 25 January 1936 and 23 August 1937, Trotsky Ar-

chives, Houghton Library, Harvard University. See also Reed and Jakobson, "Trotsky Papers at the Hoover Institution."

29. Rabinowitch, "Foreword," in *Revolution and Politics in Russia,* and Mosely, "Boris Nicolaevsky."

30. "Au sujet du cambriolage du 7 novembre, 7 rue Michelet," protocols dated 8–21 November 1936, Paris, Archives de la Préfecture de Police, BA 1626.

31. In 1940 Nicolaevsky refused to leave Paris until Dan, by then a political opponent, had sufficiently recovered from an operation to be able to travel. Schapiro, interview. In his last days Nicolaevsky sought to strengthen Mme. Bourguina's formal claims on the archives, fearing that the collection would be neglected and Bourguina would be mistreated by the Hoover Institution after his death. Haimson, Wolfe, interviews.

32. L. Fischer, review of Nicolaevsky, *Power and the Soviet Elite, NYT Book Review,* 21 November 1965, writes: "Nicolaevsky is without doubt the greatest authority in the world on Soviet politics . . . He is our master, the master Kremlinologist."

33. Getzler, *Martov,* vii. Rabinowitch, "Foreword," quotes similar tributes by A. Dallin, G. Kennan, L. Schapiro, and R. C. Tucker.

34. Nicolaevsky himself wrote: "If an emigré party preserves the documents of its glorious past, that past reflects back on it and it will be seen as the guardian of its tradition." Letter to P. Hertz, 18 April 1934, cited in Mayer, "Geschichte des sozialdemokratischen Parteiarchivs."

35. Those who knew the Mensheviks abroad may ask why individuals who stood at the very center of the group and who have left vivid memories have been passed over in these portrait sketches. For example, David Dallin, as associate editor of the *New Leader,* author of hundreds of articles and twelve major English-language books on Soviet policy, was the Menshevik most widely read in the United States. Similarly, from a human point of view, Solomon Schwarz deserves recognition. In many conversations and interviews he is the only individual Menshevik of whom I have heard no ill. Dallin, Schwarz, and others will figure fully later in this account.

2. Mensheviks and Bolsheviks

A PHENOMENOLOGY OF FACTIONS

1. For example, see Dan, *Origins of Bolshevism,* 242.
2. Compare Baron, *Plekhanov,* 231–253, and Getzler, *Martov,* 63–95. On the original use of "hard"/"soft," see Dan et al., eds., *Pis'ma P. B. Aksel'roda i Iu. O. Martova,* 88–91.
3. Valentinov, *Encounters with Lenin,* 128.
4. Compare Fainsod's noted textbook *How Russia Is Ruled,* 48, which contains a sanitized version of such traits listed in Abramovich's introduction to Garvi, *Vospominaniia,* x; and Dalin, "Obryvki vospominanii," 113.
5. Over seven thousand pages of Lenin's works refer to Mensheviks, usually negatively, often scurrilously.

6. The Bolshevik P. Lepeshinskii, "Partiinaia likhoradka," 43–44, wryly suggests that factional attributes are interchangeable: "respect for parents, legal marriages, educating children" versus "disrespect for parents, deflowering virgins, breaking youths' heads against stones."

7. Baron, *Plekhanov*, 269, points out that Plekhanov's charges against the Bolsheviks repeat those he made against Narodnaia Volia two decades earlier.

8. Keep, *Rise of Social Democracy*, 301. Compare Wolfe, *Three Who Made a Revolution*, 160–161.

9. Valentinov, "Rozhdenie men'shevizma," 267, unpublished ms, VC 1,

10. For example, see W. H. Chamberlin, review of Abramovitch, *Soviet Revolution*, NL, 25 June 1962; Ascher, introduction to Garvy, *Zapiski sotsial demokrata*, xx; Kamenka, review of Getzler, *Martov;* Carr, review of Schwarz, *Russian Revolution of 1905*.

11. This may imply a certain admiration for Lenin's qualities, as in [Ed], "Smert' V. I. Lenina," *Sv* 72, 25 January 1924. Valentinov admits to being "infatuated" with Lenin; see *Figaro littéraire*, 19 February 1964. Aronson, *Revoliutionnaia iunost'*, 219, sees Lenin as physically unimpressive ("you do not feel in looking at Lenin that he is of the . . . gentry"), but insists on Lenin's iron character. Compare the contemptuous assessment of Lenin by Pitrim Sorokin in his *Leaves from a Russian Diary*, 47.

12. See B. Sapir, "Bol'shevizm i men'shevizm," *Sv* 587/588, 20 August 1946;. G. Aronson, "Men'shevizm: opyt kharakteristiki," *Sv* 635, 31 October 1949. Continuity is a major issue in Western historiography of the Soviet period. See the essays in Tucker, ed., *Stalinism,* esp. Cohen, "Bolshevism and Stalinism," 3–29.

13. Soviet historiography shows remarkable continuity in this respect. Compare Bystranski, *Menschewiki und Sozial-Revolutioniire* (1922), and Podbolotov, "K voprosu o srokakh okonchatel'noi politicheskoi gibeli mel'koburzhuaznykh partii v SSSR."

14. Compare Ascher, introduction to Ascher, ed., *Mensheviks in the Russian Revolution,* 8; Keep, *Rise of Social Democracy,* esp. 265–304; Schapiro, *Communist Party of the Soviet Union,* 72–103. Among Mensheviks themselves, see Schwarz, *Russian Revolution of 1905;* Aronson, "Bolchèviks et menchèviks."

15. Compare Dan, *Origins of Bolshevism,* 330.

16. See especially Haimson, *Russian Marxists and Origins of Bolshevism.*

17. Compare Haimson, editor's preface to Wildman, *Making of a Workers' Revolution,* xiii

18. Dan, *Origins of Bolshevism,* 258–260.

19. Ibid., 259.

20. Compare Daniels, *Conscience of the Revolution,* 434–438. Note also [Ed], "Smert' V. I. Lenina," *Sv* 72, referring to Lenin and Martov as "two poles of the same movement."

21. Compare Valentinov-Volsky, who notes that *Sv* criticized NEP and the position of right Communists "from the left" and adds, "Obviously, it would be unpleas-

ant to remind these Mensheviks of this now." Vol'skii to Souvarine, 24 May 1960, SC.

THE SECOND CONGRESS AND ITS AFTERMATH

1. Compare Malov, "Protiv fal'sifikatsii istorii II s'ezda"; Zlobin, *Vtoroi' s'ezd RSDRP*, 3 and passim; Baron, *Plekhanov*, 234; B. Nikolaevskii, "K 80-letiu L. O. Tsederbaum-Dan," *Sv* 718, June 1958; Wolfe, *Three Who Made a Revolution*, 248.

2. Schapiro, *Communist Party of the Soviet Union*, 54, and Souvarine, *Staline*, 73, put the decisive break later. Treadgold, *Lenin and His Rivals*, 33, traces the cleavage back to 1898; compare Keep, *Rise of Social Democracy*, 105, and Wildman, *Making of a Workers' Revolution*, 181. Sources as diverse as Valentinov, "Rozhdenie men'shevizma," 268, unpublished ms., VC; the official *History of the Communist Party of the Soviet Union (Bolsheviks): Short Course*, 55–75; and Ulam, *Bolsheviks*, 176–193, attribute equal significance to the appearance of Lenin's *What Is To Be Done?*

3. See also Ascher, *Axelrod*, 182; Berlin, "Political Ideas in the Twentieth Century," 364.

4. Wolfe, *Three Who Made a Revolution*, 239 and 248, plays down the congress as a "congregation of somnambulists" but concludes that it produced "hopeless" division. Keep, *Rise of Social Democracy*, 105 and 128, minimizes its importance, though his chapter is titled "The Great Schism." Compare Zlobin, *Vtoroi s'ezd RSDRP*, 3 and 74.

5. Dan, *Origins of Bolshevism*, 243, points out that unanimity reigned on virtually all resolutions at the congress. See also Keep, *Rise of Social Democracy*, 125 and 129.

6. Ascher, *Axelrod*, 194; Wolfe, *Three Who Made a Revolution*, 250. Souvarine, *Staline*, 73, describes Lenin's efforts to prevent a split without endorsing them. For a contrary view, insisting on Lenin's desire *ab initio* for a split, see Valentinov, *Encounters with Lenin*, 136. For one leader's tergiversations on this issue, Baron, *Plekhanov*, 282 and 286.

7. Bystranski, *Menschewiki und Sozial-Revolutionäre*, 11, speaks of a "kernel"; Wolfe, *Three Who Made a Revolution*, 249, of a "germ," to take two examples from opposite ends of the historiographic spectrum.

8. This criticism was raised earlier by Lenin in 1903; see Getzler, *Martov*, 85. Compare Malov, "Protiv fal'sifikatsii istorii II s'ezda," 107. Keep, *Rise of Social Democracy*, 143, considers the logic which makes Marxists seek out "objective" factors.

9. The aura of inevitability of the final split pervades all the literature. Compare Wolfe, *Three Who Made a Revolution*, 249; Ascher, introduction to *Mensheviks in the Russian Revolution*, 11; Chamberlin, review of Abramovitch, *Soviet Revolution*. Dan, *Origins of Bolshevism*, 250, cautions that this perspective is based on hindsight

10. For example, Isaiah Berlin, quoted earlier. Wolfe, *Three Who Made a Revolution*, 249, rightly criticizes Bolshevik historians for imputing "brilliant anticipation"

to Lenin, but such anticipations are just as ubiquitous among Western commentators, not least Wolfe himself.

11. Keep, *Rise of Social Democracy*, 143, speaks of "fateful dichotomy" and "remorseless logic," although his meticulous study does not support such terms.

12. See Aronson, "Mysli o revoliutsii" (lecture of 1937), in *Bol'shevistskaia revoliutsiia i men'sheviki*, 14–18. Keep, *Rise of Social Democracy*, 147, writes of the factional differences as being "ethical" as much as "political."

13. Martow, *Geschichte der russischen Sozialdemokratie*, 79.

14. For example, see Keep, *Rise of Social Democracy*, 107–111; Getzler, *Martov*, 75; Zlobin, *Vtoroi s'ezd RSDRP*, 15–16; Malov, "Protiv fal'sifikatsii istorii II s'ezda RSDRP," 103.

15. Note the warm comments of the anti-Iskrite and foe of the Martov line Garvi, *Vospominaniia*, 387.

16. Getzler, *Martov*, 60–61, 56, 82.

17. The German socialist Rudolf Hilferding was referring to Martov when he stated that "between socialism and Bolshevism there is not only an ideological but also a moral gulf," cited by Getzler, *Martov*, 211. See also articles in *Sv*'s commemorative issue for Martov (*Sv* 54/55, 24 April 1923) by foreign socialist leaders.

18. Former Menshevik (and future Soviet ambassador) Ivan Maiskii writes that the Mensheviks "were incapable of setting up any sort of successful party intrigue" (a backhanded compliment perhaps). Maiskii, *Demokraticheskaia kontr-revoliutsiia*, 106.

19. Valentinov, *Encounters with Lenin* portrays him as engaging until crossed. L. Dan, interview 6, assesses Lenin's human qualities positively—including that old chestnut of Soviet hagiography, Lenin's love for children.

20. "Long live the honest revolutionary Martov!" exclaimed Trotsky in 1917. See Lunacharskii, *Revoliutsionnye siluety*, 65, and Getzler, *Martov*, 55 and 218–219. On Lenin's attitude, see Valentinov, *Encounters with Lenin*; Krupskaya, *Reminiscences of Lenin*; Shishkin, *Iz vospominanii kooperativnykh i politicheskikh*.

21. For example, see Keep, *Rise of Social Democracy*, 127.

22. Even agreement was sometimes illusory. For example, Martow, *Geschichte der russischen Sozialdemokratie*, 82, shows that Lenin and Plekhanov favored centralization for different reasons.

23. Baron, *Plekhanov*, stresses Plekhanov's theoretical contributions and downplays his character. Compare personal accounts such as L. Dan in Haimson, ed., *Making of Three Russian Revolutionaries*, 125–131, and Valentinov, *Encounters with Lenin*, 178 and passim. Dan et al., eds., *Pis'ma P. B. Aksel'roda i Iu. O. Martova*, contains, even after the rift with Lenin, far more complaints about Plekhanov than about Lenin. Ulam, *Bolsheviks*, 184–185, is more indulgent.

24. L. Dan, interview 1, claims that Potresov's gentry origins and marriage to a "plebeian" (though social democratic) woman with "some sort of nervous disorder" put him "outside our milieu entirely." Whereas other Iskrites lived practically communally, "one could not come late to Potresov's or visit without writing a note." Moreover, "Potresov would spend time with very distinguished people in whose company we would probably have been bored."

25. Lenin, *Leninskii sbornik*, 286. Letter invoked by Dan, *Origins of Bolshevism*, 238. Frankel, *Vladimir Akimov*, 68, calls Potresov's quibbles "a major reservation;" but compare Keep, *Rise of Social Democracy*, 112.
26. Frankel, *Vladimir Akimov*, 61–73. Schapiro, *Communist Party of the Soviet Union*, 68, attributes differences between the Bolsheviks and Mensheviks to disputes between Lenin and Plekhanov over the party program. Plekhanov, however, took a Bolshevik stance at the Second Congress.
27. Getzler's powerful arguments in favor of a growing rift are largely based on retrospective accounts by interested third parties such as Potresov and Trotsky. See Getzler, *Martov*, 64–67.
28. L. Dan, interview 7, and *Iz arkhiva L. O. Dan*, 34–50.
29. See Frankel, *Prophecy and Politics*, 181, and *Vladimir Akimov*, 58.
30. See L. Dan, interview 6, on Martov's *vykhodki* (outbursts).
31. This is the view of L. Dan, ibid. Lenin's claims at the Second Congress that Martov knew of his plans caused Martov embarrassment, and he denied them.
32. Denike, interview 18.
33. See *1903: Second Ordinary Congress of the RSDLP*. A non-Iskrite delegate's critique is Frankel, *Vladimir Akimov*, 99–182.
34. Frankel, *Vladimir Akimov*, 104, and Wolfe, *Three Who Made a Revolution*, 232.
35. Berlin, "Political Ideas," 364. Compare D. Bell, "On the Trail of Posadovsky," *NL*, 27 November 1950. Posadovskii (=Mandelberg), a Menshevik deputy to the Second Duma, died in Palestine around 1945 as chairman of a society for friendship with the Soviet Union. Bell, interview.
36. *History of the Communist Party*, 72–74.
37. Frankel, *Vladimir Akimov*, 180.
38. Compare Schapiro, *Communist Party of the Soviet Union*, 50, and Getzler, *Martov*, 68–69, on whether there had previously been any real differences between Lenin and Martov on the proposed party statutes.
39. On the murky past—and future—of Lenin's protégés N. Bauman and G. Krasikov, see Getzler, *Martov*, 66–67, 74. Krasikov may have been as much Plekhanov's protégé as Lenin's. The personal file on Martov which Lenin tried to communicate to Dan after the congress (see Chapter 1) involved Martov's protégée E. Aleksandrova.
40. Among the most vivid descriptions is still Wolfe, *Three Who Made a Revolution*, 230–248; also Keep, *Rise of Social Democracy*, 117–133; regarding specific protagonists, Baron, *Plekhanov*, 230–245; and Getzler, *Martov*, 75–83. The harshest judgment on the Mensheviks here by a historian sympathetic to them is Schapiro, *Communist Party of the Soviet Union*, 54.
41. Lenin's nerves were badly frayed before and after the congress, though he maintained his composure there; Martov, previously calm, became quite hysterical. See Krupskaya, *Reminiscences of Lenin*, 86, and Keep, *Rise of Social Democracy*, 127.
42. L. Dan, interview 11.
43. Getzler, *Martov*, 83. See cite in Frankel, *Vladimir Akimov*, 180: "The motto of the 'hards' [Bolsheviks] leads, by necessity and with logical consistency, to 'Nechaevism [Nechaevshchina]. Today, Comrade Martov is indignant about it. A pity he

has only just come to see it; but, of course, better late than never. However, Comrade Martov ought to take the trouble to discover the facts and the principles at the root of this Nechaevism in our Party. It is much too superficial to explain it by the fact that Lenin is an obstinate blockhead. Lenin is a Blanquist, and nothing Blanquist is alien to him."

44. Krupskaya, *Reminiscences of Lenin*, 98; Ulam, *Bolsheviks*, 194–197.

45. Keep, *Rise of Social Democracy*, 133, citing Trotsky's "Vtoroi s'ezd RSDRP." L. Dan, in Haimson, ed., *Making of Three Russian Revolutionaries*, 124, has complained about the frequently used "bolt out of the blue" image but herself suggests it (163).

46. Ermanskii, *Iz Perezhitogo*, 69: "The explanations of the split by Martov, Lenin, and Plekhanov did not explain anything. Sincere Iskrites were most distraught . . . among the less sincere, decisions were made on the basis of personal relations."

47. Garvi, *Vospominaniia*, 107–114; L. Dan, interview 9.

48. L. Dan, interview 9; compare Garvi, *Vospominaniia*, 432–433.

49. Garvi, *Vospominaniia*, 365, citation, 379.

50. Ibid., 424.

51. Ibid., 422.

52. Valentinov-Volsky, the target of the mug, gallantly remarks, "It served me right"; see his *Encounters with Lenin*, 36.

53. Abramovich, interview fragment.

54. Frankel, *Prophecy and Politics*, 247–251.

55. Dvinov, interview.

56. Aronson, *Revoliutsionnaia iunost'*, 16–99 passim.

57. Nikolaevskii, interviews 3 and 4. For Plekhanov's importance, see L. Dan, interviews, and Haimson, ed., *Making of Three Russian Revolutionaries*, 99–100, 110, 161–162 and passim; Dvinov, interview; Garvi, *Vospominaniia*, 9.

58. Haimson, ed., *Making of Three Russian Revolutionaries*, 241–242.

59. Nikolaevskii, interview 4, and Haimson, ed., *Making of Three Russian Revolutionaries*, 265; Valentinov, *Encounters with Lenin*, 28.

60. L. Dan, interviews 9, 10, 6; Haimson, ed., *Making of Three Russian Revolutionaries*, 163, 178–180.

61. This point is emphasized by Kristof, "B. I. Nicolaevsky."

62. See Haimson, "Yu. P. Denicke"; Denike, interviews, in *Erinnerungen*, 49–65; and Haimson, ed., *Making of Three Russian Revolutionaries*, 342–351.

63. Denicke, *Erinnerungen*, 55; L. Haimson, preface to Schwarz, *Russian Revolution of 1905*, ix; Woytinsky, *Stormy Passage*, 16; Valentinov, *Encounters with Lenin*, 34.

64. Baikalov, *I Knew Stalin*, viii. This did not prevent him from moving to the extreme Menshevik Right and even beyond after 1917.

65. Compare Aronson's "unreserved adherence to the cult of Lenin" in 1903 and his impression of Lenin in 1917, in *Revoliutsionnaia iunost'*, 16 and 219.

66. Apparently *What Is To Be Done?* was influential only among young social democrats. Compare Keep, *Rise of Social Democracy*, 93, and Haimson, ed., *Making of Three Russian Revolutionaries*, 127.

67. Valentinov, *Encounters with Lenin*, 29–34, on I. Isuv, later a prominent Menshevik liquidator close to Garvi. Cf. Garvi, *Revoliutsionnye siluety*, 8–13.

68. Valentinov, *Encounters with Lenin*, 26. Compare Garvi, *Vospominaniia*, 590–592, and *Revoliutsionnye siluety*, 16–18.

69. Ermanskii, *Iz Perezhitogo*, 72. L. Dan, interview. 7, by the way, describes Ermanskii as deceitful and a "repulsive" personality.

70. Piatnitsky, *Memoirs of a Bolshevik*, 58.

71. Garvi, *Vospominaniia*, 391.

72. Ulam, *Bolsheviks*, 194–195, and Keep, *Rise of Social Democracy*, 133–134, give the evidence in favor of Lenin as both distressed by the split and as determined to push it to the end. Compare Valentinov, *Encounters with Lenin*, 110–317; Garvi, *Vospominaniia*, 381.

73. L. Dan, interview 13, emphasizes that there were more widespread and longer-lived illusions about unity among the Bolsheviks than among the Mensheviks, and Lenin had more illusions than Martov or Dan.

74. L. Dan, interview 13, and Haimson, ed., *Making of Three Russian Revolutionaries*, 213, on the Economists; on Chicherin, L. Dan, interview 18, and Getzler, *Martov*, 129.

75. Garvi, *Vospominaniia*, 427.

REVOLUTIONARY REHEARSAL

1. Ascher, *Axelrod*, 192.

2. P. Aksel'rod, "Ob'edinenie rossiiskoi sotsialdemokratii i eia zadachi," *Iskra* 55, 57, trans. (with excisions) in Ascher, ed., *Mensheviks in the Russian Revolution*, 48–52.

3. See Valentinov-Vol'skii, "Men'shevizm i problema vlasti," VC. On Trotsky's related thesis of substitutionism, see Knei-Paz, *Social and Political Thought of Leon Trotsky*, 192–199.

4. Dan, *Origins of Bolshevism*, 259 and passim.

5. P. Garvi, "P. B. Aksel'rod i men'shevizm," *Sv* 109/110, 18 August 1925, cited in Ascher, *Axelrod*, 202.

6. Martov, *Istoriia rossiiskoi sotsialdemokratii*, 88, also cited in Schwarz, *Russian Revolution of 1905*, 31n4.

7. See Ascher, ed., *Mensheviks in the Russian Revolution*, 11, citing Valentinov, *Encounters with Lenin*, 115, 120.

8. Martynov, *Dve dikatury*, 1.

9. Valentinov-Vol'skii, "Men'shevizm i problema vlasti," VC, makes Martynov's brochure the linchpin of his argument. Martynov's emphasis on Lenin's populist deviation coincides with Volsky's view.

10. See Schwarz, *Russian Revolution of 1905*, 8–10.

11. Valentinov-Vol'skii, "Men'shevizm i problema vlasti," VC 27–30.

12. Ascher, *Axelrod*, 219, attributes the conception of the *zemstvo* campaign to Axelrod. L. Dan, interview 11, credits Fedor Dan with the plan.

13. Aronson, *Men'shevizm v 1905 g.*, 10.

14. Dan, *Origins of Bolshevism*, 131, makes claims on behalf of Petersburg's Mensheviks, but see Ascher's authoritative *Revolution of 1905*, 1:150.
15. Aronson, *Men'shevizm v 1905 g.*, 40. Other Mensheviks and scholars refute such claims. See Dan, *Origins of Bolshevism*, 361; Schwarz, *Russian Revolution of 1905*, 171–189; Schapiro, *Communist Party of the Soviet Union*, 69; and even Ascher, *Revolution of 1905*, 1:218.
16. Participants and historians agree on this point. For example, see Aronson, *Men'shevizm v 1905 g.*, 34, and *Revoliutsionnaia iunost'*, 40; Dan, *Origins of Bolshevism*, 345; Garvi, *Vospominaniia*, 518; Keep, *Rise of Social Democracy*, 283; Wolfe, *Three Who Made a Revolution*, 339. Exceptions are Martow, *Geschichte der russischen Sozialdemokratie*, and, in part, Schwarz, *Russian Revolution of 1905*.
17. The apposite term "floundering" is Ascher's, in *Mensheviks in the Russian Revolution*, 15.
18. On Martov, see Schwarz, *Russian Revolution of 1905*, 11. On Lenin, see Ulam, *Bolsheviks*, 217.
19. On permanent revolution, see Schwarz, *Russian Revolution of 1905*, 246–254.
20. Vol'skii to Aronson, 19 June 1961, SC, writes that he took part only in order to avoid being called a coward. Garvi, *Vospominaniia*, 584.
21. Dan, *Origins of Bolshevism*, 345, and *Pis'ma*, 165.
22. S. Ivanovich, "Aforizmy," NC 23(61).
23. Sapir to Haimson, 24 September 1967, MP Archives.
24. For instance, although M. Zborovskii, chairman of the 1905 Petersburg Soviet, played no party role in exile, he was elected as Menshevik delegate to LSI congresses.
25. See Ascher, *Revolution of 1905*, 1:1; also Strada, "Polemica tra bolscevichi e menscevichi sulla rivoluzione del 1905," 445.
26. On Menshevik remorse, see Wolfe, *Three Who Made a Revolution*, 340.
27. Henri de Man, cited by Edinger, *German Exile Politics*, 50, with reference to the German SPD in 1933.

AFTER THE REVOLUTION (1905)

1. See Schapiro, *Communist Party of the Soviet Union*, chap. 5, 86–100; Getzler, *Martov*, 119–124 passim.
2. Dan in Martow, *Geschichte der russischen Sozialdemokratie*, 242, and in Dan, *Origins of Bolshevism*, 395.
3. Dan in Martow, *Geschichte der russischen Sozialdemokratie*, 247; Ulam, *Bolsheviks*, 283; Daniels, *Conscience of the Revolution*, 27.
4. See Wolfe, *Three Who Made a Revolution*, 535–558.
5. Stalin was among those Bolsheviks least willing to recognize the ineluctable character of the split, in 1912 and even in 1917; see Medvedev, *Let History Judge*, 34–44 passim. Dan, "Ende der Opposition," 1–2, argues that the Bolsheviks were still sound social democrats in 1917, communist ideology being only an outcome of the Civil War.
6. "When you read documents of those days you often wonder what people were

fighting over . . . Their fights are over shades yet from these shades arise different movements." Nikolaevskii, *PBO,* 17 February 1931.

7. Lane, *Roots of Russian Communism,* 21–39.

8. L. Dan, interview 13. Volsky affirms that Mensheviks tended to be married men (hence supposedly more responsible), whereas Bolsheviks were single. Vol'skii to Haimson, 6 January (?) 1964, VC, confirmed by Swain, *Russian Social Democracy and the Legal Labour Movement, 1906–1914,* 59.

9. Nikolaevskii to Vol'skii, 25 January 1961, VC, and Vol'skii to Haimson, 23 January 1961, MP Archives.

10. Sapir to Haimson, 27 September 1967, MP Archives.

11. More Menshevik than Bolshevik delegates to the Party Congress of 1907 belonged to the underground; Vol'skii to Haimson, 3 July 1961, VC. Swain, *Russian Social Democracy,* maintains that everyone agreed with the "struggle on two fronts" and that debates dealt rather with different images of party structure and questions of committeemen versus worker activists.

12. See Haimson, "Problem of Social Stability in Urban Russia, 1905–1917" (1), 631–632.

13. See Schapiro, *Communist Party of the Soviet Union,* chaps. 5 and 6; Elwood, *Russian Social Democracy in the Underground,* 176.

14. *Resolutions and Decisions of the Communist Party of the Soviet Union,* 2:53–72; 1:93–94.

15. Elwood, *Russian Social Democracy,* provides a guide through the alignments within and without both factions. On 1905, see Getzler, *Martov,* 129; for the period after 1905, see Daniels, *Conscience of the Revolution,* 15–24.

16. For example, Schapiro, *Communist Party of the Soviet Union,* 114–116. Compare Schapiro's more nuanced pupil Swain, *Russian Social Democracy,* 86 and 188, who admits that "liquidationism" in the sense of "Economism" existed but denies that it had any influence, and that liquidationism in the strict sense of the term was on the defensive by 1909 and defeated by 1911. Note that Volsky dates the birth of liquidationism to 1908; Vol'skii to Haimson, 7 March 1961, VC.

17. Menshevik liquidators claim that they only drew conclusions from the practical dissolution of the underground party. See Nikolaevskii in Garvi, *Vospominaniia,* xxiii; reiterated in Elwood, *Russian Social Democracy,* ix. See also Swain, *Russian Social Democracy.*

18. Garvi, *Zapiski,* 43.

19. Getzler, *Martov,* 122.

20. Dan's notes in Dan et al., eds., *Pis'ma P. B. Aksel'roda i Iu. O. Martova,* 103.

21. L. Dan, interviews 13 and 19. Compare Elwood, *Russian Social Democracy,* 33.

22. Getzler, *Martov,* chap. 6, "The Missed Opportunity," and Swain, *Russian Social Democracy,* 93.

23. Compare Dan in Martow, *Geschichte der russischen Sozialdemokratie,* 242–245, and Dan, *Origins of Bolshevism,* 395. In the former, Dan writes that the refusal of the three liquidators served as an occasion for Lenin and Zinoviev to intensify their agitation against liquidationism in spite of the intention of the Bolshevik Central Committee members in Russia who were prepared to name other liquidator can-

didates to the Central Committee. In the latter, Dan writes that the decision of the Central Committee was broken by the refusal of the three liquidators to accept the posts offered them.

24. Ermanskii, *Iz Perezhitogo*, 77; Nikolaevskii, interview 21.

25. "Dan: daty biografii," *Np*, 64/65, 2 April 1947; Ermanskii, *Iz Perezhitogo*, 91; Souvarine, *Staline*, 94; Ascher, *Mensheviks in the Russian Revolution*, 19.

26. Lenin, *Pol'noe sobranie sochinenii*, 15:293.

27. Compare L. Dan, interview. 18, and Dan, *Origins of Bolshevism*, 394. See also Getzler, *Martov*, 120–128.

28. Abramovich, *In tsvey revoliutsy*, 1:123.

29. Abramovich to Vol'skii, 27 January, 16 January, and 8 May 1961, VC.

30. Garvi, *Zapiski*, 6. This is confirmed in many other sources, for example, Voitinskii, *Gody pobed i porazhenii*, 2:15; L. Dan, interview 13.

31. Garvi, *Zapiski*, 166.

32. Ibid., 171, 154.

33. Voitinskii, *Gody pobed i porazhenii*, 41.

34. Nikolaevskii, interview 4.

35. Garvi, *Zapiski*, 96. On Martynov's hostility to liquidationism, see L. Dan, interview 17.

36. E. Kuskova, "Fedor Il'ich Dan," *Novoe russkoe slovo*, 5 February 1947.

INTO THE GREAT WAR

1. A classical statement is Gerschenkron, "Problems and Patterns of Russian Economic Development," 60, challenged in Haimson, "Social Stability," 622.

2. See Woytinsky, *Stormy Passage*, xiv; more elaborately, Valentinov-Vol'skii, "Rossiia v predvoennye gody (1908–13)," NC 164(224); Compare Dan in Martow, *Geschichte der russischen Sozialdemokratie*, 252–259.

3. Abramovitch, *Soviet Revolution*, 1.

4. Abramovich to Vol'skii, 14 July 1957, VC.

5. See Abramovich to Vol'skii, 9 June 1960. Volsky also convinced L. Dan, *Iz arkhiva L. O. Dan*, 169–170.

6. Rather ungraciously, Nicolaevsky expresses this view in his introduction to Garvi, *Vospominaniia*, xxx.

7. Nikolaevskii to Vol'skii, 25 January 1961, VC.

8. See Haimson, "Social Stability."

9. Elwood, *Russian Social Democracy*, 82; Swain, *Russian Social Democracy*, 184–187.

10. Aronson, *Bol'shevistskaia revoliutsiia i men'sheviki*, 16; Diubua (and Abramovich's vigorous rebuttal), *PBO*, 23 April 1931.

11. See Ascher, *Axelrod*, and Geyer, *Kautskys Russisches Dossier*. For an overall study, see Donald, *Marxism and Revolution*.

12. Axelrod to Kautsky, (?) February 1925, KA KC.10.

13. Abramowitsch, "Karl Kautsky und der Richtungsstreit in der russischen Sozialdemokratie."

14. See the conclusion to Geyer, *Kautskys Russisches Dossier*.

15. See Elwood, "Lenin and the Brussels 'Unity Conference' of July 1914." Compare Schapiro, *Communist Party of the Soviet Union,* 139–142, and Geyer, *Kautskys Russisches Dossier,* 238–241.

3. From Exile to Exile

WAR

1. Dan, *Origins of Bolshevism,* 398; Aronson, *Revoliutsionnaia iunost',* 107. Dan viewed events from Petersburg, Aronson from Vitebsk. Politicians cited in Dvinov, *Pervaia mirovaia voina,* 17–19.
2. Compare Aronson, *Rossiia nakanune revoliutsii,* 188; Lenin, *Polnoe sobranie sochinenii,* 49:64.
3. Dvinov, *Pervaia mirovaia voina,* 23, 67, 97–98. Compare Dan in Martow, *Geschichte der russischen Sozialdemokratie,* 273.
4. Melancon, *Socialist Revolutionaries,* 172, has refuted Soviet and even some Menshevik claims that the Mensheviks favored the war.
5. Contested by Schapiro, *Communist Party of the Soviet Union,* 143; confirmed by Melancon, *Socialist Revolutionaries,* 37.
6. Kollontai cited in Aronson, *Rossiia nakanune revoliutsii,* 185.
7. Dvinov, *Pervaia mirovaia voina,* 25. Among the Mensheviks who became Bolsheviks were V. Antonov-Ovseenko, I. Maiskii, M. Uritskii, I. Larin, G. Chicherin, and A. Troianovskii.
8. Lenin, *Polnoe sobranie sochinenii,* 49:14; Dvinov, *Pervaia mirovaia voina,* 14; but compare Getzler, *Martov,* 139.
9. Nikolaevskii in Garvi, *Vospominaniia,* xxxii. Melancon, *Socialist Revolutionaries,* 2 and 167–189 passim, stresses the formation of joint party organizations throughout the war, encompassing not only social democrats but SRs as well
10. Dan, *Origins of Bolshevism,* 400; but compare Aronson, *K istorii pravogo techeniia,* 3.
11. Abramovich, *In tsvey revoliutsy,* 2:44.
12. See Aronson, *Revoliutsionnaia iunost',* 227.
13. Some 3,400 individuals, including Bolsheviks, Mensheviks, SRs, and anarchists, signed up at the Russian Social Democratic Club in Paris. Dvinov, *Pervaia mirovaia voina,* 27, and Aronson, *Rossiia nakanune revoliutsii,* 184.
14. See Zeman and Scharlan, *Merchant of Revolution,* and Bjorkegren, *Ryska Posten,* 207–209, 284. L. Dan to Vol'skii, 21 May 1956, VC. Reluctance to discuss this episode is due not only to the murky nature of Parvus's enterprise but also to his reprehensible behavior toward several Menshevik women. None of the exiled Mensheviks in Berlin in the 1920s ever sought Parvus's help. Sapir, Erlich, interviews.
15. Voitinskii, *Gody pobed i porazhenii,* 2:392. Woytinsky's confusion comes through in his confession that although he was a firm opponent of the war, he yearned to acquaint himself with "the face of war" and desisted from volunteering because for an exile the only way to go to the front was to appeal to the tsar himself. On 1917, see Nicolaevsky, "Revolutionary and Writer in Russia," 42.

16. L. Dan, interview 21. Galili y Garcia, "Origins of Revolutionary Defensism," and Dan in Martow, *Geschichte der russischen Sozialdemokratie*, 281. One might note that none of our future exiled Mensheviks appear to have joined the Mezhraionka, whose most prominent member was to be Trotsky.

17. Dan, *Origins of Bolshevism*, 398. Compare Dvinov, *Pervaia mirovaia voina*, 20.

18. See Dvinov, *Pervaia mirovaia voina*, 98.

19. See Siegelbaum, *Politics of Industrial Mobilization in Russia, 1914–1917*, esp. chap. 7, and Melancon, *Socialist Revolutionaries*, 98–100.

20. Compare Martynov, *O men'shevizme i bol'shevizme.* and Nikolaevskii, in Garvi, *Vospominaniia*, xxxiii. Martynov is incorrect in claiming that not one Menshevik in Russia resisted the temptation to participate in the war industries' committees.

21. Siegelbaum, *Politics of Industrial Mobilization in Russia*, 164–165, misconstrues the positions of the Foreign Secretariat and of the Organizational Committee by confusing their respective bulletins.

22. It was in this capacity that Schwarz met his future wife, who was then working on the newspaper of the Moscow war industries committee. Her memoirs emphasize the "progressive" atmosphere she encountered among the committee's staff, Aleksandrova, *Perezhitoe.*

23. See Siegelbaum, *Politics of Industrial Mobilization in Russia,*155, and Schapiro, *Communist Party of the Soviet Union*, 153.

24. Nikolaevskii, in Garvi, *Vospominaniia*, xxxiii. Compare Anweiler, *Soviets*, 99–101.

25. Schapiro, *Communist Party of the Soviet Union*, 153–154, attributes overriding significance to the Central Workers' Group in triggering the events of February–March 1917 and comments on the ironic fact that moderate Menshevik defensists should have unleashed the Revolution. Compare Anweiler, *Soviets*, 104, who agrees that the "decisive step" in forming the Petrograd soviet was taken by members of the Central Workers' Group but differs in his account of events.

REVOLUTION

1. Nikolaevskii, *Men'sheviki v gody revoliutsii*, would seem to be exaggerating in claiming that the first provisional Executive Committee of the Petrograd soviet consisted only of Mensheviks. Compare Schapiro, *Russian Revolution of 1917*, 46.

2. This view is accepted by many, Communist and non-Communist, observers: Carr, *Bolshevik Revolution*, 1:81 who cites Lenin for support; Bystranski, *Menschewiki*, 17; and Trotsky, *History of the Russian Revolution*, 1:168–170.

3. The Menshevik Organizational Committee voted against participation, but a week later its decision was overwhelmingly reversed, contrary to party statutes, by the Menshevik members of the Soviet Central Executive Committee. Abramovitch, *Soviet Revolution*, 39.

4. Aronson, *Rossiia v epokhu Revoliutsii*, 42.

5. Trotsky, *History of the Russian Revolution*, 1:289. As F. Dan, "K istorii russkoi revoliutsii," *Sv* 248, 23 May 1931, points out, this deflects the accusation of menshevism so often directed against Trotsky. Note that Trotsky was not yet a Bolshevik in the spring of 1917.

6. Chamberlin, *Russian Revolution,* 1:320, cites the figure of 390; Schapiro, *Origins of the Communist Autocracy,* 66, cites 300; Pipes, *Russian Revolution,* 498, cites 338; Anweiler, *Soviets,* 193, speaks of a bare majority.

7. Lande, "Mensheviks in 1917," in Haimson, ed., *Mensheviks,* 8.

8. Nikolaevskii, *Men'sheviki v gody revoliutsii.*

9. Compare Sukhanov, *Zapiski o revoliutsii,* 3:134–139; Sorokin, *Leaves from a Russian Diary,* 63.

10. L. Dan, interview 23, dates his change of attitude to September. See Dan, "K istorii poslednikh dnei Vremennogo pravitel'stva."

11. L. Dan, interviews 21 and 22.

12. Reed, *Ten Days That Shook the World,* 79. Lidia Dan, in Haimson, ed., *Making of Three Russian Revolutionaries,* 189, comments that at meetings in 1905 and 1917 people often did not hear what was being said but knew the speaker's position in advance and thus knew how to react.

13. Woytinsky, *Stormy Passage,* 254 and 377.

14. Ibid., 365. Scarlet Pimpernel–like anecdotes and a curiously naive tone of self-satisfaction weaken the memoirs' credibility. Compare Trotsky, *History of the Russian Revolution,* 2:23–72.

15. Sukhanov, *Zapiski o revoliutsii,* 2:291. Trotsky, *History of the Russian Revolution,* 1: 229–230.

16. MP biographical summaries; Jasny, *To Live Long Enough,* 26–37.

17. For reminiscences, see Aronson, *Revoliutsionnaia iunost';* Denicke, *Erinnerungen;* Dvinov, *Moskovskii sovet rabochikh deputatov;* Aleksandrova, *Perezhitoe,* 29.

18. On the congress, see Haimson, "Mensheviks after the October Revolution" (2).

19. Anniversaries were an occasion for reflection, for example, [Ed], "K iubileiu revoliutsii;" and F. Dan, "Desiat' let revoliutsii," *Sv* 147/148, 12 March 1927, and "Iubilei diktatury," *Sv* 163/164, 10 November 1927. Also, reacting to Trotsky's history, Dan, "K istorii russkoi revoliutsii," *Sv* 248, and "Eshchë o istorii russkoi revoliutsii," *Sv* 286/287, 27 January 1933.

20. For example, Diubua, *PBO,* 23 April 1931, and Abramovich, *PBO,* 26 February 1931. Galili, *Menshevik Leaders in the Russian Revolution,* takes issue with such stereotypes.

21. The distinction between a "right" and "left" critique sometimes collapses. The Trotskyist Isaac Deutscher, *Ironies of History,* 219, applies a "rightist" critique in calling the Mensheviks " 'men of the Formula,' the doctrinaires who in the name of an abstract principle or constitutional dogma turned a deaf ear on life's realities."

22. For example, Domanevskaia, *PBO,* 26 February 1932 and 23 April 1931: "Our tragedy in 1917 was that we renounced our socialist doctrines in the name of democratic ones." And: "I am surprised that Abramovich blames our party in 1917 for revolutionary maximalism, for doctrinairism. On the contrary, it was precisely the policy of small deeds that . . . lost our party."

23. *PBO,* 23 April 1931, with Abramovitch, Dallin, Dan, Domanevskaia, Iugov, Kefali, and Woytinsky participating. Abramovitch, for example, practically accuses Dubois of both right wing and left wing deviation. He argues that the

Bolsheviks also thought the Revolution would be bourgeois, and they too had an incoherent agrarian program. According to Abramovitch, it was a myth that the Mensheviks had lost the masses because they failed to tie themselves to "elemental forces." The masses did not abandon the Mensheviks; the proletarian masses followed the Mensheviks after October as well. Abramovitch's conclusion is that the Mensheviks lost not because their philosophy was wrong but because they did not know how to solve the problem of the war.

24. For example: "There are moments in the development of revolutions where the most clever and sensible *logical* constructions are insufficient and where one must take account not of logic but of the *psychology* of the masses. Unfortunately, this is what our party came to perceive very clearly in the autumn of 1917." Abramowitsch to Louise Kautsky, 14 August 1923, KA D I.

25. See Denike, "Men'sheviki v 1917 g.," which also argues that the "psychology" of menshevism differed from that of bolshevism even though they shared the same concept of revolution.

26. As Dubois, *PBO,* 23 April 1931, puts it, "We went into government with a feeling of sin and guilt," but one cannot trust the ex-Menshevik renegade and Soviet ambassador Ivan Maiskii, *Demokraticheskaia kontr-revoliutsiia,* 110, when he says that he "often heard Mensheviks from Tsereteli to Martov complain bitterly, 'If only someone would take power away from us.'" Compare Getzler, "Marxist Revolutionaries and the Dilemma of Power."

27. See Aronson, *Revoliutsionnaia iunost'?* 192, and his *Rossiia v epokhu revoliutsii.* The counterargument, that the Mensheviks overestimated the threat from the right, has been made by right wing historians.

28. For Dan's defense of this position, see *PBO,* 17 February 1931.

29. For example, Schapiro, *Origins of the Communist Autocracy,* 209; his *Russian Revolution of 1917,* 50, poses the issue in terms of a means-end dilemma. Deutscher, *Ironies of History,* 219, applies Carlyle's description of the Girondins to the Mensheviks.

30. "I would not want us in 1955 to present ourselves as failures, sluggards, and good-for-nothing embarrassed *intelligents* . . . We too had our quite crafty lads who were capable of anything . . . Why should we keep up the myth that the Bolsheviks are crafty fellows, that they know how to do anything, and that their opponents are . . . useful for nothing except chattering?" Abramovich to Vol'skii, 10 November 1955, VC.

31. The further implication is that the October events were not inevitable; see, for example, Abramovitch, *Soviet Revolution,* 98. In a spirit of contradiction Nicolaevsky affirms that February was accidental but October was inevitable; see Nikolaevskii to Vol'skii, 23 February 1950, VC.

32. "Let Lenin end up in a stinking corner of history," states Abramovitch, and Dan adds, "If all comes down to a bad democracy, we don't want anything of it." *PBO,* 17 February 1931.

33. Ulam, "Uses of Revolution," 334. The combination of factors I have evoked may not be specific to the Mensheviks. As Daniels, *Conscience of the Revolution,* 69, points out, the same attributes—"literal Marxism, political caution, and demo-

cratic scruple"—can be evoked to explain the defeat of the Bolshevik Right Opposition in 1917.

34. As Trotsky puts it, "The Socialists took upon themselves a third of the power and the whole of the war." Cited in Wolfe, *Strange Communists I Have Known,* 198.

35. Dan, in Martow *Geschichte der russischen Sozialdemokratie,* 298–304.

36. See Dan's responses to Trotsky, *Sv* 248, 286/287.

37. Diubua, *PBO.* Compare Kingston-Mann, *Lenin and the Problem of Marxist Peasant Revolution,* 92 and 112.

38. See Kingston-Mann, *Lenin and the Problem of Marxist Peasant Revolution,* 197 and 167. Diubua, *PBO,* points out that it took the Bolsheviks thirteen years after 1917 to put a definitive solution to the land issue on their agenda, yet critics would have the Mensheviks find a solution in the course of the February Revolution.

39. Woytinsky, *Stormy Passage,* 264. On subsidies, see Aronson, *Rossiia v epokhu revoliutsii,* 70–73. Abramovitch sensibly states that the Mensheviks, too, received subsidies, and the SRs received even more than the Bolsheviks, but this did not save them from defeat. Abramovich to Vol'skii, 10 November 1955, VC. Nicolaevsky's file titled "Bolsheviks and German money," NC 152(216), contains only press clippings.

40. Jasny, *To Live Long Enough,* 37, describes the pathetic sight of Martov riding in a motorcycle sidecar in 1917, concentrating his energy on the struggle for abolition of the death penalty.

41. Woytinsky, *Stormy Passage,* 334, defends the reintroduction of the death penalty at the front but argues that this was of little practical consequence since it was unenforceable. Abramovich to Vol'skii, 2 November 1953, VC, maintains that he was the only Soviet Executive Committee member in favor of both the death penalty and withdrawal from the war. Dan, "Eshche o istorii russkoi revoliutsii," *Sv* 286/287, makes a point of refuting Trotsky's contention that Dan voted against recall of the death penalty; but see Pipes, *Russian Revolution,* 444.

42. See Suny, "Towards a Social History of the October Revolution." Compare Rosenberg, review of Haimson, ed., *Mensheviks.*

43. Haimson, "Mensheviks after the October Revolution," 462.

44. Dan himself sometimes slides toward "accidentalist" explanations. His insistence (*PBO,* 23 April 1931) that if it were not for the war, which armed the peasantry, Menshevik tactics would have been correct evoked an aphoristic reply from right wing Menshevik Stepan Ivanovich, "Aforizmy," NC 23(65): "All revolutionaries, having lost their revolution, complain that the revolution occurred in extremely unfavorable conditions. This is like a shipwrecked sailor who complains that the storm developed in very nasty weather. It is well known that in good weather one can have a storm only in a glass of water."

FACING BOLSHEVIK POWER

1. Nikolaevskii, *Men'sheviki v gody revoliutsii,* docts. 1, 5, 10.

2. Ibid., docts. 10, 11.

3. Ibid., docts. 5, 6.
4. Lande, "Mensheviks in 1917," 47–53.
5. Neither Abramovitch, *Soviet Revolution*, nor Nikolaevskii, *Men'sheviki v gody revoliutsii*, mentions the committee, although Aronson does in *K istorii pravogo techeniia*, 22.
6. Lande, "Mensheviks in 1917," 71; Abramovitch, *Soviet Revolution*, 112–119.
7. Nikolaevskii, *Men'sheviki v gody revoliutsii*, 2, and Getzler, *Martov*, 169, consider the Vikzhel episode a Bolshevik ploy to gain time. Brovkin, *Mensheviks after October*, 33, writes that the defensist minority on the Menshevik Central Committee could effectively veto any agreement with the Bolsheviks by threatening a split in the party. In fact, the defensists had left the Central Committee in protest against the perspective of negotiations and returned only when the negotiations collapsed.
8. Abramovich to Vol'skii, 30 June 1960, VC, is incensed that Schapiro's *Origin of the Communist Autocracy*, 70–79 passim, misrepresents the nature of Vikzhel. In fact, Schapiro's account corresponds largely to Abramovitch's. See also L. Dan, interview 24.
9. See Aronson, *Divzhenie upolnomochennykh*, as well as Bernshtam, ed., *Nezavisimoe rabochee dvizhenie v 1918 godu*.
10. Compare Aronson, *Dvizhenie upolnomochennykh*, 5, who sees the movement as originating in demands for freedom of the press and Brovkin, *Mensheviks after October*, 162—176, who explains it in terms of fear aroused among workers by the withdrawal of the Soviet government from Petrograd to Moscow in the face of German advances in February 1918 and by the generally chaotic conditions at the time.
11. Dan declined the invitation with the fatuous excuse that his wife had obtained flour to make blini, so he could not miss dinner. Denike, a factory representatives movement activist, also adds that Dan, like Martov, was suffering from depression (interview 15).
12. Brovkin, "Mensheviks' Political Comeback in 1918."
13. Haimson, "Mensheviks after the October Revolution," and Denicke, "From Dissolution of the Constituent Assembly to Outbreak of Civil War"; but compare Brovkin, *Mensheviks after October*, 46, who contests this view.
14. Denicke, "From Dissolution of the Constituent Assembly to Outbreak of Civil War," 107–108.
15. Getzler, *Martov*, 185. Compare Brovkin, *Mensheviks after October*, 72
16. Denike, interview 16.
17. Western commentators fail to appreciate the Mensheviks' reservations concerning bourgeois parliamentarianism. Billington, "Six Views of the Russian Revolution," 454, assumes that Abramovitch's chapter "Point of No Return" in *Soviet Revolution* refers to the Constituent Assembly. In fact, it deals mostly with Vikzhel.
18. Abramovitch, *Soviet Revolution*, 90 and 99n19, attributes this solicitude to an unnamed internationalist Menshevik who turns out to be himself.
19. Aleksandrova, *Perezhitoe*, 37.

20. Haimson, "Mensheviks after the October Revolution," 452.
21. Martov to Aksel'rod, 19 November 1917, in Dallin, "War Communism and Civil War," 103.
22. Nikolaevskii, *Men'sheviki v gody revoliutsii*, 54–55.
23. Dallin, "War Communism and Civil War," 161, cites a description of Martov's expulsion in Gethsemene-like language: "Martov, shouting curses against dictators and Bonapartist usurpers in his sickly tubercular voice, grabbed his coat and tried to put it on, but his shaking hands could not find the sleeves. Lenin, very pale, stood looking at Martov . . . Pointing at Martov, a Left SR burst into loud laughter . . .'You have no reason to be so jolly, young man,' croaked Martov, turning to him. 'Before three months are out, you will follow us.' " Martov calls the expulsion a "mini coup d'état," but it is not clear whether the accent is on the adjective or on the noun. Martov to Stein, 16 July 1918, *Sv* 125/126, 25 April 1926.
24. Dvinov, *Moskovskii sovet rabochikh deputatov*, 61–67.
25. "Tsirkularnoe pis'mo no. 5, 1 June 1920," published as "Rukovodstvo dlia shpikov," *Sv* 5, 21 April 1921.
26. Dvinov, *Ot legal'nosti k podpoliu*, 28.
27. Ibid., 25.
28. Dvinov, *Moskovskii sovet rabochikh deputatov*, 102, and *Ot legal'nosti k podpoliu*, 58.
29. Martov, in *Sozialistische Revolution*, 128; in 1919 there were 225 Menshevik deputies in the Kharkov soviet, 120 in Ekaterinoslav, 45 in Tula, and more than 30 in Kiev, Samara, and Irkutsk. "Martov o partii v 1918/1919 godakh," *Sv* 149, 4 April 1927. See also Leggett, *Cheka*, 319.
30. *Izvestiia* reported that Dan's speech was applauded by Lenin and Trotsky. Dan, *Dva goda skitanii*, 85.
31. Ibid., 92
32. Ibid., and Dvinov, *Ot legal'nosti k podpoliu*, 47.
33. Dvinov, *Moskovskii sovet rabochikh deputatov*, 103–108.
34. Hilger and Meyer, *Incompatible Allies*, 60, provides a vivid eyewitness description of Lenin's last live confrontation with the Mensheviks in December 1920. He even sparred with absent Mensheviks. See Lenin, *Polnoe sobranie sochinenii*, 45: 89.
35. Brovkin, *Mensheviks after October*, 106–108.
36. Nikolaevskii, *Men'sheviki v gody revoliutsii*, 15.
37. Martov to Stein, 16 July 1918, *Sv* 125/126.
38. G. Aronson, "Stalinskii protsess protiv Martova," *Sv* 435/436, 28 April 1939.
39. Martov to Aksel'rod, 23 January 1920, in *Sozialistische Revolution*, 126, and Dan, *Dva goda skitanii*, 58.
40. Aronson, "Anglichane v Moskve," and Dan, *Dva goda skitanii*, 13–14.
41. Dallin, "War Communism and Civil War," 228.

WITHIN THE PARTY

1. Getzler, *Martov*, 201. For Martov's lament, see Dallin, "War Communism and Civil War," 212.

2. "Tsirkularnoe p'is'mo," *Sv* 5, 21 April 1921.

3. Daniels, *Conscience of the Revolution*, 86 and 107–130 passim.

4. See Dalin, "Obryvki vospominanii," 103. An editorial note in *Sv* 54/55, 24 April 1923, emphasizes that the job of foreign commissar had been only privately discussed.

5. In a Menshevik journal a party official announced: "For matters concerning the business of local organizations, my office hours are from 12 to 6. For matters concerning unlawful searches and arrests, I receive comrades with no waiting in line." Brovkin, *Mensheviks after October*, 174.

6. Brovkin, "Mensheviks' Political Comeback."

7. Lande, "Appendix A," in Haimson, ed., *Mensheviks*, 389. Brovkin, *Mensheviks after October*, 201, argues that these figures underestimate Menshevik Party membership.

8. For example, V. G. Groman lost his faith in Marxism and left the Mensheviks to become a leading Soviet planner without becoming a Bolshevik. See Dvinov, *Ot legal'nosti k podpoliu*, 93, and Jasny, *Soviet Economists of the Twenties*, 89–123.

9. Dvinov, interview, and his *Ot legal'nosti k podpoliu*, 124. Vyshinskii represented a left wing Menshevik tendency which favored "waiting out" Bolshevik power rather than opposing it.

10. Martynov, still a Menshevik Central Committee member, reappeared in Moscow after four years' absence and went straight to the influential Bolshevik leader Karl Radek, avoiding any contact with other Mensheviks. The extreme left Menshevik Ermanskii, also a Central Committee member, left the party "temporarily" and rose to prominence in the Soviet movement for the scientific organization of work. Dvinov, *Ot legal'nosti k podpoliu*, 151 and 40.

11. Aronson, *K istorii pravogo techeniia*, 62.

12. Maiskii, *Demokraticheskaia kontr-revoliutsiia*, 14–17 and 39; L. Martov, "Vospominaniia renegata," *Sv* 45/46, 9 December 1922, and "Po povodu odnogo prevrashcheniia," *Sv* 11, 8 July 1921. See also Liebich, "Diverging Paths."

13. Dvinov, *Ot legal'nosti k podpoliu*, 40–44, and *Moskovskii sovet rabochikh deputatov*, 103.

14. Denike, interview 19.

15. Dvinov, interview.

16. Martov was particularly shaken by Martynov's defection. Dallin, taking it more lightly, quipped that Martynov's behavior proved that his intellectual capacities were in inverse proportion to his baldness. Dvinov, *Ot legal'nosti k podpoliu*, 151.

17. "Chto takoe men'shevistskaia programma?," *Pravda*, 23 April 1921, co-signed by future academician and Soviet planner G. Strumilin and O. Domanevskaia, who later returned to the Mensheviks.

18. "Ob ukhodiashchikh (nadgrobnoe slovo)," *Sv* 12, 22 July 1921.

19. Dvinov, *Ot legal'nosti k podpoliu*, 151; F. Dan, "Lekhkomyslennyi akusher," *Sv* 52 and 56, 1 April and 12 May 1923.

20. On Larin, see Martov to Stein, 16 July 1918. On "foul times," see "Ob ukhodiashchikh," *Sv* 12.

21. L. Dan, interview 7; Dvinov, *Ot legal'nosti k podpoliu*, 40.

22. Communists condemned this formula as a hypocritical unwillingness to sanction

party members who pursued anti-Soviet policies. Bystranski, *Menschewiki und Sozial-Revolutionäre*, 24.

23. Aronson, *Bol'shevistskaia revoliutsiia i men'sheviki*, 3; Denike, interviews 15, 16, and 18.

24. Garvi to Tsereteli, 30 June 1925, NC 15(29).

25. Dallin, "War Communism and Civil War," 211.

26. Ibid.

27. L. Dan, interview 24.

28. Ascher, ed., *Mensheviks*, 107–124; *Sozialistische Revolution*, 73–116.

29. Aleksandrova, *Perezhitoe*, 38, writes that workers defined themselves as "Bolshevik" because they wanted more *(bol'she)* rather than less *(men'she)*.

30. "Bonapartism" gained currency over its Roman alternatives. F. Dan, "Bol'shevistskii bonapartizm," *Novaia zaria*, 20 May 1918, already suggests that bonapartism marks the transition of Soviet power from petty bourgeois plunder to bourgeois capitalism.

31. Stishov, "Opyt periodizatsii," 36.

32. *Martov i ego blizkie*, 48–50, quoted by Dallin and Denike in Haimson, ed., *Mensheviks*, 104 and 107; Getzler, *Martov*, 172; Burbank, *Intelligentsia and Revolution*, 19–20.

33. Martov, "Diktatura i demokratii," translated in Ascher, ed., *Mensheviks*, 125.

34. Martov, "Konets odnoi dvusmyslennosti," translated in Ascher, ed., *Mensheviks*, 119.

35. Published as *Bol'shevizm v Rossii i v Internatsionale.* and in U.S. *Congressional Record*, Committee to Investigate Communist Propaganda, 17 June 1930.

36. Martov to Aksel'rod, 5 April 1921, in *Martov i ego blizkie*, 52–60.

37. L. Martov, "Po povodu pis'ma tov. P. B. Aksel'roda," *Sv* 8, 20 May 1921.

38. Ibid.

39. Ibid. A Menshevik contribution to this task is the 1919 party program, titled "What Is To Be Done?" prepared, according to Denike, interview 17, partly at the behest of Bolshevik leaders. Selections in Ascher, ed., *Mensheviks*, 111–117.

40. Wolin, "Mensheviks under NEP and in Emigration," 448–449. Compare Ivanovich to James, 5 April 1923, NC 1(1).

41. Dalin, "Obryvki vospominanii," 118. Compare Aronson, "Kak zhil i rabotal Iu. O. Martov," 100–102.

42. B. Nikolaevskii, "K pred'istorii *Sotsialisticheskogo vestnika*," *Sv* 690/691, February–March 1956.

43. Nikolaevskii, interview 18, affirms that there was an Odessa variant of the April theses closer to Martov's views.

44. Getzler, *Martov*, 224.

45. L. Martov, "Nasha platforma," *Sv* 41, 4 October 1922.

46. L. Martov, "Liberal'nyi sotsializm," *Sv* 47, 1 January 1923. Martov harbored a particular antipathy to Ivanovich, whom he called a "complete swine," Anan'in, *Iz vospominanii revoliutsionera*, 74.

47. L. Martov, "Otvet kritikam," *Sv* 48, 17 January 1923. His critics were G. Aronson and G. Kuchin.

48. D. Dalin, "Proch illiuzii," *Sv* 8, 20 May 1921, and his *Posle voin i revoliutsii.*

49. Whatever his doubts, Dallin supported the Martov Line publicly: "Our revolution is bloody and terrible, but it is our native Russian revolution and one should not damn it but correct it." D. Dalin, "Bol'shevizm i revoliutsiia," *Sv* 176, 18 May 1928.

50. Comparing those views with those emanating from Communist commentators, one finds both the theory that Martov had deserted to the counterrevolutionary camp and the theory that he was the prisoner of right wing intellectuals such as Dan, of all people, within his own party. Compare *Pravda* articles by Radek, Vardin, and others, 5, 10, 20, 23 April, 5 June 1921, and Humbert-Droz, *Origines et débuts des partis communistes des pays latins,* 20–21.

51. See Avrich, *Kronstadt, 1921,* and Getzler, *Kronstadt.*

52. NEP was decided on before Kronstadt. See Carr, *Bolshevik Revolution,* 2:271, and Narkiewicz, *Making of the Soviet State Apparatus,* 13.

53. Denike, interview 15.

54. Dvinov, *Ot legal'nosti k podpoliu,* 30.

55. D. Dalin, "Aufstand in Kronstad," [*Wiener*] *Arbeiter-Zeitung,* 17 March 1921.

56. [Ed], "Groznoe predosterezhenie," *Sv* 4, 18 March 1921.

57. Dan, *Dva goda skitaniia,* 111.

58. [L.M.], "Kronshtadt," *Sv* 5, 5 April 1921.

PERSONAL ITINERARIES

1. A sympathetic fictionalized account, E. Kazakevich, "Vragi" [Enemies], *Izvestiia,* 21 April 1962, aroused the ire of Lidia Dan, who insisted that Lenin did not "save" Martov. L. Dan to Vol'skii, 1963 [?], VC. On Lenin's obituary, Denike, interview 15; on rations, L. Dan, interview 24. Denike, interview 17, claims that of all the Bolshevik leaders only Lenin favored allowing Martov (and Abramovitch) to leave.

2. Dan, *Dva goda skitaniia,* 15–20.

3. Ibid., 21–22.

4. Ibid., 43, 80. Dan cites a remark typical of an officer corps ripe for bonapartism: "Trotsky would be a perfectly good dictator; too bad he's a Jew." Also pro-Communist were Jewish handicraft workers who felt liberated as Jews and whose low standard of living had improved by direct trading with the state. Ibid., 67.

5. Ibid., 102.

6. Curiously, a purported autobiographical sketch in the archives of the Soviet society of former tsarist political prisoners asserts that Denike was never a Menshevik, though in 1917 he "moved to Martov's group." Both statements are untrue. Denike I. P., "avtobiografia," fond 533 opis 1 delo 1287, GARF. Denike was readmitted to the party in 1927.

7. Denike, interviews 16, 17, 18.

8. Dvinov, *Moskovskii sovet rabochikh deputatov,* 79.

9. G. Aronson, "Kefali v bor'be s diktaturoi nad proletariatom," *Sv* 531/532, 8 November 1943.

10. Estrin, "Vospominaniia," NC 136(208).

11. Aleksandrova, *Perezhitoe,* 65, 57–63.

12. Dvinov, *Ot legal'nosti k podpoliu,* 57.

13. Denike, interview 17.

14. Dan, *Dva goda skitaniia,* 107.

15. Denike, interview 16; Dvinov, *Ot legal'nosti k podpoliu,* 90.

16. Dan, *Dva goda skitaniia,* 59; Leggett, *Cheka,* 316.

17. Their fears were well founded, since Petrograd's Bolshevik chief Zinoviev favored shooting Dan as a hostage for Kronstadt. Dan, *Dva goda skitaniia,* 136; Leggett, *Cheka,* 424n122; L. Dan, interview 24.

18. Leggett, *Cheka,* 314, and Aronson, *Na zare krasnogo terrora,* 87.

19. Aronson, *Na zare krasnogo terrora,* 81–87.

20. Ibid., 192, recounts this exchange between a Cheka interrogator and a Menshevik: Q. "So your father is a doctor, consequently, a bourgeois?" A. "What is more to the point is that your father has a son who is a scoundrel."

21. Dvinov, *Ot legal'nosti k podpoliu,* 25.

22. Dan, *Dva goda skitaniia,* 192, 198. Dorothea Hanson has drawn my attention to a more recent variation. At a UN committee meeting a Soviet delegate was addressed as "Mr. Menshevik." He replied, "My name is Menshikov. And I am a Bolshevik, not a Menshevik." *NYT,* 23 September 1985.

23. Leggett, *Cheka,* 321.

24. Dan, *Dva goda skitaniia,* 250.

25. Denike, interview 16, also recounts how offended his interrogator (Troianovskii's former wife) was at being compared to an Okhrana interrogator.

26. Dan, *Dva goda skitaniia,* 123.

27. Rubin to ZD, 25 November 1921, NC 25(686).

28. Aronson, *Na zare krasnogo terrora,* 91, and Dan, *Dva goda skitaniia,* 165.

29. Aronson, *Na zare kransnogo terrora,* 122.

30. Ibid., 88, 89.

31. Ibid., 101, and Dan, *Dva goda skitaniia,* 228.

32. Aronson, *Na zare krasnogo terrora,* 88, 181.

33. Dan, *Dva goda skitaniia,* 177: "The better the external conditions of prison, the more one feels the strictly psychological oppression connected to prison."

34. Dan, review of Melgunov, *Rote Terror in Russland.* Abramovich to Vol'skii, 18 June 1957, VC, wrote that even lower-level Cheka personnel were not bloodthirsty or cruel, and the masses were just simpleminded, easily misguided, and tragically indifferent.

35. Dan, *Dva goda skitaniia,* 250.

36. Ibid., 253.

37. [Anon], "Iz khroniki semii Tsederbaum," in *Martov i ego blizkie,* 41.

38. [PR], "Moskva," *Sv* 26, 23 February 1922.

39. Dvinov, *Ot legal'nosti k podpoliu,* 85.

40. Ibid., 155, and sources cited.

41. [PR], "Moskva: likvidatsiia tiuremnoi golodovki," *Sv* 26, 23 February 1922; Dan, *Dva goda skitaniia,* 267.

4. Inside and Outside

SETTLING INTO EXILE

1. "When I left [Russia] I intended to come back in the spring but now they will simply not allow it; we must wait until the terror weakens." Martov to Khinoy, 12 June 1921, Khinoy Papers, YIVO.
2. In early 1922 Dan wrote: "I do not believe the sojourn abroad will be especially long. The accursed contemporary regime is saturated to such a degree from top to bottom with contradictions that it can hardly hold in its present form for any length of time . . . [T]he Bosheviks will cease controlling the government or— in one sense or another—stop being 'Communists.' " Cited by A. Ascher, introduction to Garvi, *Zapiski.* xix–xx.
3. D. Dalin, "Iz vospominanii," *Sv* 100, 4 April 1925. Inflation worked in favor of the Mensheviks and other Russians in Germany.
4. Biographical details from published sources supplemented by interviews with L. and P. Andler, A. Dallin, B. Sapir, and M. Turim. Liebich, *Marxism and Totalitarianism.*
5. Gul', *Ia unes Rossiiu,* 1:91–95; Wolin, "NEP and Emigration," 321.
6. According to Garvi to Kautsky, 30 April 1930, KA 16, he wrote all articles on the Soviet Union in the SPD Werbeabteilung's (Propaganda Division) *Parteikorrespondenz.*
7. Woytinsky, *Stormy Passage,* 460–462. Jacob Marshak, more marginal as a Menshevik but more prominent as an economist, was employed in the SPD-sponsored Forschungsstelle für Wirtschaftspolitik. Arrow, "Jacob Marschak."
8. See Nikolaevskii, "Pamiati S. O. Portugeisa."
9. "Lola Dallin (1898–1981)," *Cahiers Léon Trotsky* 9 (1982): 3–4; Stenzel, interview 4; V. Broido-Cohn to author, 6 August 1987.
10. Denike, interview 19.
11. Jasny, *To Live Long Enough,* 59–62.
12. Income from Gosizdat', arranged by Riazanov, eventually dried up. Thereafter the Mensheviks collected money among themselves for Axelrod but, to spare his pride, pretended that it came from his author's royalties in the Soviet Union. L. Dan to Tsereteli, 17 March 1926, NC 15(30), and 19 December 1926, *Iz Arkhiva L. O. Dan,* 137; Abramowitsch to Adler, 17 December 1926, SAI 2623.
13. Fleischman et al., eds., *Russkii Berlin,* 355; Woytinsky, *Stormy Passage,* 446.
14. Dan to L. Kautsky, 5 December 1927, *Pis'ma,* 366.
15. Gourevitch correspondence, MP Archives.
16. L. Dan to Tsereteli, 20 November 1925, NC 15(30). On Garvi, see Ivanovich to Ingerman, 27 June 1928, NC 23(63).
17. Anna Gourevitch's recollections have been translated and edited by her son Victor Gourevitch in an unpublished volume. I am most grateful to him for having lent me this invaluable document.

18. Jasny, *To Live Long Enough*, 62.
19. Gourevitch correspondence, letter dated September 1932.
20. Woytinsky, *Stormy Passage*, 449.
21. Dan to Branting, 10 October 1923, NC 23(683).
22. Note, for example, the Dans' solicitude for Axelrod (noted by him) and for Potresov, with both of whom the Dans disagreed. Aksel'rod to Tsereteli, 21 October 1927, NC 15(29), and L. Dan to Tsereteli, 22 February 1925, NC 15(30).
23. Ivanovich to Ingerman, 21 March 1928, NC 23(63).
24. For example, see D. Dalin, "Pod znakom restavratsii," *Sv* 115, 14 November 1925. The Mensheviks also seem to have believed that they could immunize themselves against the Bolsheviks' preposterous labeling of them as "White Guards" and "bourgeois counterrevolutionaries" by avoiding any contamination with the rest of the emigration.
25. Garvi to Tsereteli, 4 July 1927, NC 15(29).
26. See D. Dalin, "O samom glavnom," *Sv* 470, 11 March 1941. Garvi, suspected of having been indulgent toward interventionists during the Civil War in Odessa, was pointedly reminded of this twenty years later. Nikolaevskii to Garvi, 15 April 1940, NC 18(53).
27. Fitzpatrick, "Civil War as a Formative Experience."
28. E. Broido, "Na zare 'Sotsialisticheskogo vestnika,' " *Sv* 100, 4 April 1925.
29. Poretsky, *Our Own People*, 62. That Lenin read *Sv* is confirmed by his letter to Gorky, 7 September 1922, cited in Fleishman et al., eds, *Russkii Berlin*, 350, as well as by Podbolotov and Spirin, *Krakh men'shevizma*, 161.
30. Reported by the former Polish Communist and later contributor to *Sv* Waclaw Solski in *Moje Wspomnienia*, 250–251.
31. Fragmentary evidence in LSI Congress reports and correspondence between the Foreign Delegation and LSI Secretariat, 20 February 1928, 21 October 1931, NC 25. Also, Abramowitsch to Adler, 24 March 1933, AA I/1.
32. [IP], "N'iu-iorkskii banket v chest' tov. Abramovicha," *Sv* 218, 25 February 1930. Some of these funds were destined for relief purposes in Russia, and thus only part could be used for specifically party needs.
33. L. Martov, "Otvet londonskoi gruppe RSDRP," 13 November 1920, NC 53(87).
34. Arcane distinctions among "meetings," "general sittings," and "individual sittings" had the practical purpose of excluding the Menshevik Right. ZD to Parizhskaia gruppa, 8 March 1924, and Skomorovskii, Paris secretary, to Iugov, 30 September 1926, NC 25(683?). Aronson, Woytinsky, Wolin, Garvi, Grunfeld, and Kefali to ZD, 10 November 1929, NC 44(84), protested restrictions on the Right's access to *Sv*.
35. For example, Lidia Dan herself had been "deprived of party political rights" and was reinstated in 1924. Three years later Iurii Denike was also reinstated, although with restrictions. "Protokoly Zagranichnoi Delegatsii," 29 January 1924 and 28 October 1928, MP Archives.
36. ZD to Parizhskaia gruppa, 20 July 1927, NC 45(683?).
37. Martov, "Otvet londonskoi gruppe RSDRP," states categorically: "The Central Committee does not consider it possible to have any initiatives [*vystupleniia*]

abroad either directly or indirectly in the name of the party from anyone other than those specifically mandated by the Central Committee. These are Abramovitch and myself." The group was still in existence in late 1923 but was not considered an official party group. Ivanovich to Baikalov, president of the London group, 9 October 1923, BP.

38. Latvian Social Democrats published in 1922–23 *Svobodnaia mysl'*, described as "organ oblastnogo komiteta" of the Latvian Social Democratic Party, with Dan and Shchupak on the editorial board, and later *Trudovaia mysl.*' See also Kalnins, "Social Democratic Movement in Latvia."

39. The Geneva auxiliary group announced the renewal of its activities "interrupted in 1917" in *Sv* 45/46, 9 December 1922. Reports on the Geneva group's polemics against the Sovietophile Parti socialiste genevois appear in NC 25, and in SAI.

40. Wolin, "NEP and Emigration," 320; Chicago in *Sv* "funds received" column. Members of the student groups interviewed by me include Sapir (Heidelberg) and Schapiro and A. Kisselgoff (Toulouse).

41. Lupolov-James founded the first Russian socialist group in America in Boston in 1893–94. See "75-letie Ia. M. Dzhemsa," *Sv* 531/532, 8 November 1943.

42. Viliatser to Iugov, 14 March 1926, NC 25(688), explains that the Plekhanoff Club is in the hands of the Zaristy (that is, the extraparty right wing), "otherwise, we could collect ten times as much money as is now the case."

THE POLITICAL ECONOMY OF NEP

1. For a summary characterization of NEP, see Lewin, *Political Undercurrents.*

2. Trifonov, *Klassy v nachale NEPa*, 32. The Mensheviks contested Lenin's claim, remarking that Bolshevik prestige among Western workers resided in the fact that they had favored an immediate transition to socialism. R. Abramovich, "Otstuplenie ili vypriamlenie linii?" *Sv* 11, 8 July 1921.

3. See Volin, *Century of Russian Agriculture*, 166.

4. A foreign eyewitness stresses that only Lenin's personal charisma persuaded congress delegates after they had initially been convinced by Dan's arguments. Hilger and Meyer, *Incompatible Allies*, 60–62.

5. Getzler, *Martov*, 198, describes the program as a response to a request from Iurii Larin and intended to appeal to moderate Bolsheviks. Among its authors was V. G. Groman. Extracts in Ascher, ed., *Mensheviks*, 114.

6. Burbank, *Intelligentsia and Revolution*, 274; "Lenin otstupaet," *Sv* 4, 18 March 1921.

7. For example, Burbank, *Intelligentsia and Revolution*, 62.

8. For periodization, see Klimov, "K voprosu o periodizatsii novoi ekonomicheskoi politiki," but also Jasny, *Soviet Economists of the Twenties*, 4–20.

9. D. Dalin, "Opiat' perelom," *Sv* 29, 3 April 1922, "Ekonomicheskie zigzagi," *Sv* 72, 25 January 1924, and "Nazad," *Sv* 80, 10 May 1924; A. Iugov, "Pered XIII s'ezdom RKP," *Sv* 81, 28 May 1924; [Ed], "XIII s'ezd RKP," *Sv* 82/83, 20 June 1924.

10. [Ed], "Neo-NEP," *Sv* 104, 29 May 1925.

11. [PR], "Pered s'ezdom RKP," *Sv* 117/118, 21 December 1925. For Dallin's prediction, see "Ekonomicheskie zigzagi," *Sv* 72.

12. Yugoff, *Economic Trends in Soviet Russia*, 344. Also Dalin, "Ekonomicheskie zigzagi," *Sv* 72, "Opiat' perelom," *Sv* 29, and "Nazad," *Sv* 80; as well as Jugow, " 'Die sozialistische Akkumulation' und die Zukunft der Industrie in Russland."

13. I. Osipov [= Binshtok], "Sudorogi," *Sv* 38, 2 August 1922.

14. On Soviet "planlessness" and *Sv*'s contribution to it, see Filtzer, "Translator's Afterword." Some relevant articles include A. Iugov, "Kto vinovat?" *Sv* 97, 18 February 1925, and "Planovoe khoziaistvo i ocherednaia reorganizatsiia," *Sv* 146/147, 12 March 1927; Jugow, "Grundprobleme der russischen Wirtschaft"; also B. Dvinov, "Plan i zhizn'," *Sv* 139, 1 November 1926.

15. Jugow, "Grundprobleme," 425–426.

16. Yugoff, *Economic Trends*, 304, also 332; Jugow "Grundprobleme," 422.

17. Yugoff, *Economic Trends*, 302.

18. As of 1923 *Sv* was speaking of the first crisis of a purely capitalist type in Soviet Russia. [Ed], "Promyshlennyi krizis v Rossii," *Sv* 69/70, 17 December 1923. See also Z. Eber, "Bolezni tovarooborota," *Sv* 143, 15 January 1927.

19. Citation from Wolff, *Peasant Wars of the Twentieth Century*, 97; D. Dalin, "Derevnia," *Sv* 90, 22 October 1924.

20. Yugoff, *Economic Trends*, 115.

21. Jasny, *Soviet Economists*, 16. Problems of the tax in kind had been noted early on by both Bolshevik and Menshevik commentators. See D. Dalin, "Finansy novogo kursa," *Sv* 23, 1 January 1922.

22. Volin, *Russian Agriculture*, 176, and Yugoff, *Economic Trends*, 145.

23. [Ed], "Krest'aianstvo i krizis diktatury," *Sv* 96, 31 January 1925; D. Dalin, "Vokrug muzhika," *Sv* 98, 5 March 1925, and "Sotsialdemokratiia i novoe krestianskoe dvizhenie," *Sv* 99, 19 March 1925.

24. Volin, *Russian Agriculture*, 184.

25. P. Garvi, "Kommunisty i derevianskaia bednota," *Sv* 132, 26 July 1926.

26. Dalin, "Ekonomicheskie zigzagi."

27. Volin, *Russian Agriculture*, 184–186; Yugoff, *Economic Trends*, 132; A. Iugov, "Tseny, industrializatsiia i lzhekooperatsiia," *Sv* 146, 26 February 1927.

28. Yugoff, *Economic Trends*, 135.

29. [PR], *Sv* 142, 24 December 1926.

30. D. Dalin, "Ekonomicheskaia platforma RSDRP," *Sv* 84, 6 July 1924.

31. See, for example, Dalin, *Posle voin i revoliutsii*, 106, and his "Bezdorozhe," *Sv* 50, 21 February 1923; [Ed], "Bor'ba za sovety," *Sv* 93/94, 1 December 1924; Jugow, "Sozialistische Akkumulation."

32. Dalin, "Ekonomicheskie zigzagi"; Jugow, "Grundprobleme," 434, and Yugoff, *Economic Trends*, 52.

33. S. Shvarts, "Proizvoditel'nost' truda i zarabotnaia plata," *Sv* 87, 1 September 1924; Jugow, "Grundprobleme," 434.

34. Jasny, *Soviet Economists*, 25; Jugow, "Grundprobleme," 436.

35. A. Iugov, "Nalogovoe oblozhenie v sovetskoi Rossii," *Sv* 99, 19 March 1925, estimates that in spite of all the productive economic resources under its control,

the Soviet state was obliged to cover 90 percent of its normal expenses through taxes.

36. D. Dalin, "Pod'em, urozhai, i politicheskii krizis," *Sv* 111/112, 28 September 1925.

37. Yugoff, *Economic Trends,* 101–103, and Dalin, *Posle voin,* 46. Over seven years only 163 concessions were granted for lack of candidates; Yugoff, *Economic Trends,* 220.

38. Private trading accounted at one time for two-thirds of total trade, but private industry employed only 2 percent of the industrial labor force. Yugoff, *Economic Trends,* 183, and Narkiewicz, *Making of the Soviet State Apparatus,* 146.

39. On excessive nationalization, see Yugoff, *Economic Trends,* 99. On industrialization, see Jugow, "Sozialistische Akkumulation," 563.

40. D. Dalin, "Mnogo shumu," *Sv* 150, 23 April 1927, and A. Iugov, "Litsemernaia politika," *Sv* 140, 20 November 1926. On squandering capital, see Dalin, "To o chem molchit kazennaia pechat'," *Sv* 97, 18 February 1925.

41. Yugoff, *Economic Trends,* 224, 271, 228.

42. F. Dan, "Pervyi shag," *Sv* 49, 31 January 1923. Compare W. Woytinsky, "Le bolchèvisme et les concessions," *République russe* 4, no. 2 (1921).

43. [Ed], *Russisches Bulletin* 2, 14 February 1922. Yugoff, *Economic Trends,* 346.

44. Quoted from Iugov, "Lenin otstupaet." See also Dalin, "Nazad," *Sv* 80; Iugov, "Litsemernaia politika," *Sv* 140.

THE NATURE OF NEP RUSSIA

1. Cited in Dan, "Geist und Geschichte des Bolschewismus," 76, and Abramowitsch, "Stalinismus oder Sozialdemokratie," 144. [Ed], "Pravo na samoupravlenie," *Sv* 3, 1 March 1921.

2. Dalin, *Posle voin,* 7, and "15 let," *Sv* 266, 12 March 1932.

3. G. Kuchin, "O revoliutsionnykh elementakh bol'shevizma," *Sv* 84, 6 July 1924.

4. L. Martov, "Dialektika diktatury," *Sv* 25, 3 February 1922.

5. Dalin, *Posle voin,* 7; Yugoff, *Economic Trends,* 320.

6. L. Martov, "Nasha platforma," *Sv* 42, 20 October 1922; "Dialektika diktatury," *Sv* 25.

7. S. Sumskii, "O national bol'shevizme," *Sv* 21, 2 December 1921.

8. [Ed], "10 let revoliutsii," *Sv* 147/148, 12 March 1927.

9. Dalin, *Posle voin,* 161, and "Krizis Nepa," *Sv* 37, 2 August 1922.

10. Briefly discussed in Kolakowski, *Main Currents of Marxism,* 2:332–336.

11. Dalin, *Posle voin,* 217, 247–248.

12. See Liebich, *Marxism and Totalitarianism.*

13. Lenin, *Polnoe sobranie sochinenii,* 36:295; also 45:279.

14. Brin, *Gosudarstvennyi kapitalizm v SSSR;* Lewin, *Political Undercurrents,* 86.

15. Ball, "Lenin and the Question of Private Trade in Soviet Russia," 406. See Lenin, *Polnoe sobranie sochinenii,* 45:296–297.

16. Compare Trifonov, *Klassy v nachale NEPa,* 24 and 39.

17. D. Dalin, "Gosudarstvennyi kapitalizm," *Sv* 58, 1 July 1923.

18. D. Dalin, "Denationalizatsiia," *Sv* 47, 1 January 1923.

19. Martov, "Nasha platforma," *Sv* 42, and Dalin, "Gosudarstvennyi kapitalizm," *Sv* 58.
20. D. Dalin, "Pod'em, urozhai i politicheskii krizis," *Sv* 111/112, 28 September 1925.
21. Trifonov, *Klassy v nachale NEPa*, 7; D. Dalin, "Ekonomicheskaia platforma RSDRP," *Sv* 84, 6 July 1924, and "Kapitalizm ili sotsializm?" *Sv* 117/118, 21 December 1925.
22. "Zadachi i metody bor'by," *Sv* 23, 1 January 1922.
23. Martov, "Dialektika diktatury"; Dalin, "Gosudarstvenyyi kapitalizm."
24. Dalin, "Pod'em, urozhai, politicheskii krizis," *Sv* 111/112.
25. Martov, "Otvet londonskoi gruppe," 13 November 1920, NC 53(87).
26. L. Martov, "Problema edinogo fronta v Rossii," *Sv* 35/36, 20 July 1922.
27. Dan, *Nouvelle politique économique*, 47–51, 57–66.
28. Yugoff, *Economic Trends*, 261.
29. Narkiewicz, *Making of the Soviet State Apparatus*, 152.
30. D. Dalin, "Politicheskie sud'by krest'ianstva," *Sv* 223, 17 May 1930; Dan, *Gewerkschaften und Politik in Sowjetrussland*, 30.
31. Compare Martov, "Dialektika diktatury," *Sv* 25, and "Nasha platforma," *Sv* 42.
32. Abramowitsch, "Entwicklung Sowjetrusslands," 323.
33. Ibid., 335.
34. [Ed], "Bor'ba za sovety," *Sv* 93/94, 1 December 1924; D. Dalin, "V sovremennoi derevne," *Sv* 66, 3 November 1923, and "Rassloenie novoi derevni," *Sv* 71, 10 January 1924.
35. [L. Martov], "Soglashenie s krest'ianstvom," *Sv* 6, 20 April 1921.
36. Dalin, "Politicheskie sud'by krest'ianstva," *Sv* 223
37. Dallin's definition of *meshchanstvo* illustrates the Mensheviks' moral outlook: "Pettiness, extreme spirit of calculation, passion for the commonplace, absorption in present-day matters, attention to what is superficial, concern about 'standing,' household geraniums in the window, a boulevard newspaper, light novels, boxing, dancing, gossip, easy betrayals, sordid jokes, talk about 'love.' And above all this stands the ruling, all-absorbing concern with the price of potatoes and eggs, with new soles and with darning torn stockings." Dalin, *Posle voin*, 172.
38. D. Dalin, "Novaia burzhuaziia," *Sv* 18, 15 October 1921.
39. Ibid., and Dalin, *Posle voin*, 161, 158.
40. Dalin, *Posle voin*, 159, and Abramowitsch, "Entwicklung Sowjetrusslands," 339; [Ed], "10 let revoliutsii," *Sv* 147/148.
41. [Eds], "Ekonomika i politika," *Sv* 1, 1 February 1921; "Puti revoliutsii," *Sv* 2, 16 February 1921; and "K iubileiu revoliutsii," *Sv* 147/148, 12 March 1927.
42. Dan, "Pervyi shag"; [Eds], "Ekonomika i politika"; Yugoff, *Economic Trends*, 99.
43. Dan, *Sowjetrussland wie es wirklich ist*, 34; [L. Martov] "Lenin protiv kommunizma," *Sv* 10, 19 June 1921.
44. Dalin, *Posle voin*, 45.
45. D. Dalin, "RKP na shestom godu revoliutsii," *Sv* 60, 16 August 1923.
46. Quoted by Miliband, "Bonapartism," 53.

47. Lenin, *Polnoe sobranie sochinenii*, 34:48–52.
48. Abramowitsch to Kautsky, 24 May 1925, KA D1, credits Kautsky with introducing the concepts into debate on Soviet Russia. In fact, the Mensheviks were using the concept before Kautsky did in 1921. See D. Dalin, "Griadushchaia epoka," *Mysl'* 11 (May 1919) trans. in Dallin, *From Purge to Coexistence*, 147–160. Also R. Abramovich, "Termidor i krest'ianstvo," *Sv* 197/198, 12 April 1929. Compare Salvadori, *Kautsky and the Socialist Revolution*, 281–284.
49. [Ed], *Russisches Bulletin* 1, 18 January 1922. Also Abramowitsch, "Entwicklung Sowjetrusslands," 344.
50. Dalin, *Posle voin revoliutsii*, 67, and Dallin, *From Purge to Coexistence*, 160.
51. Compare the editorials "Puti revoliutsii," *Sv* 2, 16 February 1921; "V trekh sosnakh," *Sv* 103, 14 May 1925; "Iubileinyi razgrom," *Sv* 163/164, 10 October 1927; D. Dalin, "O sushchnosti rezhima," *Sv* 171, 6 March 1928.
52. Compare Kuchin, "O revoliutsionnykh elementakh bol'shevizma."
53. P. Garvi, "Bonapartizm ili demokratsiia?" *Sv* 69/70, 17 December 1923, and "Pod znakom termidora," *Sv* 160, 22 September 1927, also published in the SPD's *Vorwärts* and criticized in *Pravda*. See P. Garvi "Ot sud'by ne uidësh." *Sv* 161, 7 October 1927.
54. These obstacles were stressed even in the face of deepest pessimism. In 1928 Dan, "Ende der Opposition," stated that there was no way except toward thermidor, but because of the origins of the communists, the road would not be easy.
55. D. Dalin, "NEP i anti-NEP," *Sv* 171, 6 March 1928. Dallin never completed his book on the "Russian thermidor and the degeneration of communism." An extract, "O termidore," *Sv* 165, 1 December 1927, takes issue with a *Pravda* discussion of thermidor.
56. A late defense of their views is L. Dan, *Iz Arkhiva L. O. Dana*, 151.

THE PARTY UNDERGROUND

1. Deliberations on the decision to go underground in "Chernovik konspekta B. L. Gurevicha-Dvinova" [n.d., late 1922], NC 25(685). See also B. Dvinov, *Ot legal'nosti k podpoliu* and its appendix, G. Kuchin-Oranskii, "Zapiski," as well as Til', "Sotsial-demokraticheskoe dvizhenie molodezhi 1920-kh godov."
2. Podbolotov, "K voprosu o srokakh," 391. Usually Mensheviks and SRs are mentioned together. Podbolotov and other Soviet scholars recognized that SRs ceased to present any danger earlier than did the Mensheviks.
3. Lenin, *Polnoe sobranie sochinenii*, 45:89 and 189. The latter document, first published in 1937, was not included in the first four editions of Lenin's works.
4. Ibid., 43:64, 241.
5. See Pethybridge, "Concern for Bolshevik Ideological Predominance at the Start of NEP," and Podbolotov, "Istoricheskaia literatura pervoi poloviny 20-kh godov o krakhe partii men'shevikov."
6. G. Osipov (=Binshtok), "Sudorogi," *Sv* 38, 2 August 1922, and Dvinov, *Ot legal'nosti k podpoliu*, 107. Also Broido, *Lenin and the Mensheviks*, 137.

7. L. Martov, "Ko vsem sotsialisticheskim partiiam i professional'nym organizatsiiam," *Sv* 9, 5 June 1921.

8. See F. Dan, "Vnutrennyi men'shevizm," *Sv* 59, 26 July 1923. Abramovitch's working notes to *Soviet Revolution* contain an interesting file on "[Bolshevik] opposition as a variant of menshevism." Bakhmeteff Archives. Compare Carr, *Socialism in One Country,* 2:22–23.

9. Referring to Zinoviev's statement that "every criticism, regardless of whether it is from the Right or the Left, is nothing but hidden menshevism," Dan, "Vnutrennyi men'shevizm," *Sv* 59, comments, "In a sense he is right."

10. See F. Dan, "Na ushcherbe," *Sv* 39, 8 September 1922, and the report on the Eleventh Congress, [PR], "Moskva: usilenie terrora," *Sv* 30, 20 April 1922. On the Soviet side, see Trifonov, *Lenin i bor'ba s burzhuaznoi ideologiei v nachale NEPa.* The Mensheviks' importance in Soviet eyes is amply confirmed by the fact that *Sv* is by far the most frequently cited journal in the digest of the emigré and foreign press, prepared biweekly and then monthly by the Communist Party Central Committee staff from 1927 to 1934 for the use of party leaders (f. 17 op. 86 d. 229–231, RTsKhIDNI).

11. Podbolotov, "Bor'ba RKP(b)," 37; [PR], "Moskva: Kak v luchshikh semeistvakh," *Sv* 28, 21 March 1922. The campaign to "liquidate" the Menshevik Party by means of the *byvshie* movement (rather than delegalizing the party outright) is recorded in f. 17 op. 84 d. 310, 500, 517, 640–642, RTsKhIDNI; Molotov's circular, f. 17 op. 84 d. 641, RTsKhIDNI.

12. A. Bubnov, "Razval partii gospodina Dana," *Pravda,* 17 August 1923, cited in Podbolotov, "Bor'ba RKP(b)," 41; M. Stishov, "Opyt periodizatsii," and B. Astrov, "Chetvert' chasa v men'shevistskoi kukhne," *Pravda,* 29 March 1927.

13. Abramowitsch to Kautsky, 25 December 1923, KA; Dan to Adler, 24 December 1927, *Pis'ma,* 367; Kuchin to ZD, cited in Broido, *Lenin and the Mensheviks,* 147. For some reports from Russia up to 1920, see Brovkin, ed., *Dear Comrades.*

14. ZD to Russia, 21 February 1929, NC 25.

15. 1925, LSI, *Second Congress,* 184. Organizations existed in Moscow, Leningrad, Kharkov, Kiev, Ekaterinoslav, Odessa, Rostov, Aratov, Sormovo, and the Don Basin. ZD to Secretariat LSI, 20 February 1928, NC 25.

16. These intercepted communications are available as "Pis'ma chlenov ZD RSDRP(m) iz Berlina v TsK RSDRP(m) v Rossiiu," f. 275 op. 1 d. 83. See also f. 17 op. 84 d. 641, RTsKhIDNI.

17. Woytinsky, *Stormy Passage,* 282. Sukhanov, *Russian Revolution,* 454, described Kuchin on the same occasion as "martial, 'trench-like.'"

18. Sapir, "Notes and Reflections," 380–382; Til', "Sotsialdemokraticheskoe divizhenie," 201–203. On Kuchin's hunger strike, see correspondence in Labour Party Archives. Kuchin, like many other political prisoners, received help from the Political Red Cross, headed by Gorky's former wife. See file dated 30 November 1925 under E. P. Peshkova, pomoshch' politicheskim zakliuchënnym, f. 8409/74, GARF.

19. Broido, *Lenin and the Mensheviks,* 116. Til', "Sotsialdemokraticheskoe dvizhenie," is the richest source and unique testimony on the movement. See also Wolin, "Mensheviks under NEP and in Emigration," 264–265.

20. Til', "Sotsialdemokraticheskoe dvizhenie," 192; Sapir, "Andrei Kranikhfeld."

21. Til', "Sotsialdemokraticheskoe dvizhenie," 206–207, 223; also Broido, *Lenin and the Mensheviks*, 103, 147.

22. Kuchin, "Zapiski," 171, 178–179; Dvinov, *Ot legal'nosti k podpoliu*, 144.

23. Gul', *Ia unes Rossiiu*, 1:250.

24. Boris Sapir, last surviving member of the Menshevik Foreign Delegation, wrote me on 31 January 1987: "In my opinon, it is not appropriate to enlarge upon this subject even now."

25. B. Dvinov, " 'Sotsialisticheskii vestnik' v Moskve," *Sv* 690/691, February–March 1956.

26. Kalnins, "Social Democratic Movement in Latvia," 155–157; Dan to Bruno Pavlovich [Kalnins?], 9 August 1927, NC 25(685): "In September we intend to send a comrade through Riga and further. A Jewish woman aged about 50. Most convenient and simple would be if we could have an appropriate document of some Latvian citizen and equip it with a photo of our comrade."

27. Affirmed by Hilger, longtime member of the German embassy, but not mentioned in Hilger, *Incompatible Allies*. A. Dallin, interview.

28. D [Dan] to Russia, 21 August 1927, NC 25(685?).

29. [PR], "Moskva," *Sv* 156, 18 July 1927; some letters with their secret messages between the lines are in NC 25(685?).

30. Dvinov, " 'Sotsialisticheskii vestnik' v Moskve," *Sv* 690/691, cites one thousand copies of early issues. In *Ot legal'nosti k podpoliu*, 75, Dvinov cites two hundred copies until the Latvian channel added several hundred more.

31. Dvinov, " 'Sotsialisticheskii vestnik' v Moskve," *Sv* 690/691; ZD to Secretariat LSI, 20 February 1928, NC 25.

32. Dvinov, *Ot legal'nosti k podpoliu*, 65, 75; Russia to ZD, 8 March 1926, NC 25(685?). In 1924 *Sv* ceased giving names of individuals arrested or interrogated because this intensified the repression against them and their kin, but it still reported on individuals sentenced. [PR], *Sv* 82/83, 20 June 1924.

33. Dvinov, *Ot legal'nosti k podpoliu*, 53.

34. Dvinov, " 'Sotsialisticheskii vestnik' v Moskve," *Sv* 690/691.

35. Kuchin to ZD, 16/17 October 1922, NC 25(685). Designation adopted in April 1923 and maintained until the last issue in December 1963. Numerous but irregular Menshevik publications in Russia inventoried in Bourguina, *Russian Social Democracy*, 357–360. Samples of underground press available in NC 6(7).

36. Sergei (?) to Kharkov Committee and Bureau of RSDRP Central Committee, 29 December 1928, NC 25(685).

37. Kuchin to ZD, 16/17 October 1922, and "Zapiski," 174.

38. Lenin quoted in Dan, *Origins of Bolshevism*, 238.

39. Kuchin to ZD, 25 January 1923, NC 25(685); Til', 243, citing B. O. Bogdanov. Note the recently published memoir by Bogdanov's daughter N. B. Bogdanova, *Men'shevik*, which gives the unique perspective of a child on these times and people.

40. Aronson, *Bol'shevistskaia revoliutsiia*, 1; ZD [Iugov] to Russia, 5 March [1928?], NC 25(685). See also Ivanovich to Ingerman, 3 May 1928, NC 23(63).

41. Kuchin, "Zapiski," 175.

42. G. Kuchin, "Ot starogo k novomu," *Sv* 47, 1 January 1923; Kuchin to ZD, 25 January 1923. See also Sapir, "Notes and Reflections," 380–388.

43. Bureau RSDRP to ZD, September–October 1923, NC 25; Kuchin to ZD, 14 October 1922, NC 25(685).

44. [PR], "Moskva: oppozitsiia i 'spetsy'; spetsy iz 'byvshikh' i prosto spetsy," *Sv* 160, 22 September 1927.

45. Cited from Valentinov (Vol'skii), *Novaia ekonomicheskaia politika*, 23; also 115–116, as well as idem, "De Boukharine au stalinisme," 69–71.

46. Valentinov, *Novaia ekonomicheskaia politika*, 4, and "De Boukharine au stalinisme," 72.

47. Valentinov, *Novaia ekonomicheskaia politika*, 74, 79.

48. Abramovich to Vol'skii, 30 January 1957, VC.

49. Valentinov's *Novaia ekonomicheskaia politika* also registers Moscow rumors so numerous that the Thirteenth Party Congress adopted a resolution against spreading them. Although Valentinov rejects the most lurid of these rumors (that Stalin poisoned Lenin, 36–50), and casts doubt on others (that Lenin suffered from syphilis, 46), he recounts those conerning Stalin's disdain for Lenin after Lenin's stroke (205) and his theft of Lenin's documents (61–64).

50. Ibid., 65, 195, 213.

51. Valentinov, "De Boukharine au stalinisme," 70, and *Novaia ekonomicheskaia politika*, 101, 130–133, 111, 157.

52. Valentinov, *Novaia ekonomicheskaia politika*, 1–23. In the manuscript of this work Valentinov did not name the members of the Liga; even in 1956 he did not wish to compromise any who might still be alive. The names of its nine members were added to the published version in 1970 with the permission of Valentinov's widow.

53. Ibid., 202–205.

54. Abramovich to Vol'skii, 30 January 1957, and Valentinov, *Novaia ekonomicheskaia politika*, 134.

55. Valentinov, *Novaia ekonomicheskaia politika*, 251.

56. Til', "Sotsial-demokraticheskoe dvizhenie," 218; Broido, *Lenin and Mensheviks*, 102.

57. Til', "Sotsial-demokraticheskoe dvizhenie," 226. In reply to the charge that the Mensheviks did not seek an amnesty for nonsocialist political prisoners, Abramovitch was able to make only a convoluted and unconvincing reply. Abramowitsch to Adler, 26 November 1927, SAI 2623.

58. For example, the Menshevik press campaign against mistreatment of prisoners in the Solovetskii monastery prison in 1924 and that unleashed by Kuchin's hunger strike. See correspondence in Labour Party Archives and Abramowitsch-Adler correspondence, February 1924, SAI 2623/2632.

59. Til', "Sotsial-demokraticheskoe dvizhenie," 224–238.

60. Ibid., 228. On complaints that the GPU treated "Whites" more leniently than social democrats, see [PR], "V tiurme i ssylke," *Sv* 182/183, 5 September 1928.

61. Broido's *V riadakh RSDRP* was published with a favorable introduction by a Communist editor, a fact which drew the ire of *Pravda*, "Vrednaia kniga," 10 March 1929.

62. S. Tsederbaum-Ezhov received the *Daily Herald*. His wife mentions to a correspondent that Andrei [Kranikhfeld?] would be happy to receive *Rote Fahne* (a German Communist publication) and the *Vossische Zeitung* as well as an economic journal. She also requests Aldous Huxley's *Those Barren Leaves* (in a specific edition) and adds: "They say that we shall be able to return to Moscow in November. I do not particularly believe this. Moscow both tempts me and it does not. Life will be very different there materially and morally. In any case, wherever we live we shall have the company of books." Zakharova-Tsederbaum to L. Estrin, 5 May 1927. Later letters, December 1927 through March 1928, are more pessimistic (NC 20 [59]).

63. [PR], "V tiurme i ssylke," *Sv* 182/183.

64. Valentinov, *Novaia ekonomicheskaia politika*, 30–31; Aronson, *Na zare krasnogo terrora*, 187; Dvinov, *Ot legal'nosti k podpoliu*, 89; [PR], "Moskva: torgovlia i RKP," *Sv* 28, 21 March 1922;. S. Dvinov, "Grandioznaia zhizn'," *Sv* 33, 3 June 1922.

65. [PR], "Moskva," *Sv* 23, 1 January 1922; [PR], "Smolensk: 'Rasprava s rabochimi,'" *Sv* 27, 5 March 1922; [PR], "Moskva: stachka i lokaut," *Sv* 28, 21 March 1922; [Ed], "Neizbezhnoe," *Sv* 71, 10 January 1924, referring to *Pravda*, 31 December 1923. See also F. Dan, "Samoorganizatsiia rabochego klassa," *Sv* 107, 10 July 1925.

66. [PR], "Moskva: tipografia Kominterna," *Sv* 38, 16 August 1922.

67. For the intervention, see "Smolensk: 'Rasprava s rabochimi,'" *Sv* 27, 5 March 1922. At Kiev University in 1927, however, law students still defied the local Communist cell in elections for a faculty elder. See [PR], "V Vuz'akh—Iz Kieva," *Sv* 163/164, 10 November 1927. On wage hikes, see [PR], "Moskva," *Sv* 82/83, 20 June 1824.

68. S. Semkovskii, "Vospominaniia o men'shevikakh i bol'shevikakh v Sovetskoi Rossii," [n.d.], NC 25. Reference is to the "Pervaia Tipografiia," Kharkov.

69. [PR], "Moskva: terror, bezrabotnitsa," *Sv* 156, 18 July 1927.

70. Diadia Tom [!], "V stolitse bol'shevikov (pis'mo iz Moskvy)," *Sv* 101/102, 25 April 1925.

71. Ibid.

72. "Nakanune desiatiletiia (Pis'mo iz Moskvy)," *Sv* 163/164, 10 November 1927. Another report explained that antisemitism was perceived as the only possible form of protest against the authorities; see [PR], "Moskovskie nastroeniia," *Sv* 161, 17 October 1927; [PR], "Nastroenie naseleniia," *Sv* 149, 4 April 1927. On the unease, see also [PR], "Moskva," *Sv* 170, 21 February 1928.

73. [PR], "Moskva: terror, bezrabotnitsa," *Sv* 156; quote from [PR], "Moskva," *Sv* 186, 28 October 1928; [Ed], "Predosterezhenie," *Sv* 191, 9 January 1929. For rations, see [Ed], "Nesostoiatel'nost' zlostnaia," and [PR], "Moskva," *Sv* 196, 22 March 1929.

WATCHING THE KREMLIN

1. Valentinov, *Novaia Ekonomicheskaia politika*, 203, acknowledges, begrudgingly, the excellent quality of the information published in *Sv* in 1923–24 and calls on the surviving editors, Dallin and Abramovitch, to reveal their sources. There is

no indication that they ever did so. On Troianovskii in the Kremlin Archives, see Denike, interview 17.

2. Nicolaevsky, "K 80-letiu L.O. Tsederbaum-Dan (2)," Sv 719/720, July–August 1958, writes that Rykov told him (after he had left Russia) that the Politburo debated the question of helping Martov financially. See also Nikolaevskii to Vol'skii, 19 July 1956, VC, and Gul', Ia unes Rossiiu, 1:153–154.

3. Nicolaevsky's brother Vladimir, also once a Bolshevik, later a Menshevik, was married to Rykov's sister and lived with Rykov from 1920 until both were arrested in 1937. Kristof, "B. I. Nicolaevsky," 342n2.

4. For humbler contacts, note that Abramovitch's brother-in-law Abram Gert was in charge of Pravda's technical division. Sapir, interview 2.

5. "Appréciation des chefs bolchéviques sur le danger représenté pour eux par les divers groupes de l'émigration russe," Paris, Archives de la préfecture de police, 1928[?], BA/1708. Some issues of Sv, however, were withheld even from high officials. See Valentinov, Novaia ekonomicheskaia politika, 203–205.

6. See Bajanov, Bajanov révèle Staline.

7. Nikolaevskii to Vol'skii, 20 April 1956, VC, adds that Iugov's informers tended to be Trotskyists.

8. Among the most important documents: Lenin's memorandum on the national question, 30 and 31 December 1922; Lenin's letter, 5 March 1923, asking Trotsky to take up the Georgian case against Stalin and Dzerzhinskii, on "whose objectivity I [Lenin] cannot rely"; Lenin's letter to the Georgians Midvani Makharadze and others, March 6 1923, expressing indignation at the "connivances of Stalin and Dzerzhinskii"; letter from Fotieva (Lenin's secretary), April 16 1923, to Kamenev with copy to Trotsky confirming Lenin's request of March 5. All in "Nelegal'naia bol'shevistskaia literatura," Sv 69/70, 17 December 1923, announced previously in [PR], "Na s'ezde RKP Pis'mo iz Moskvy," Sv 61, 1 September 1923. A summary of Lenin's critical views of the party leaders, December 1922, constituting the core of his "Testament," appeared in "Pis'mo iz Moskvy: S'ezd RKP i zaveshchanie Lenina (vokrug s'ezda RKP)," Sv 85, 24 July 1924. Trotsky's letter to the Politburo, 8 October 1923, the Politburo reply, and Trotsky's second letter, 24 October 1923, were announced in [PR], Sv 72, 25 January 1924, and printed in "Za kulisami diskussii ('sovershenno sekretnye' dokumenty)," Sv 81, 28 May 1924. Also "Obrashchenie gruppy 'Rabbochaia Pravda,'" Sv 65, 18 October 1923; and "Vozzvanie gruppy 'Rabochaia Pravda,'" Sv 49, 31 January 1923. Most were first published in the Soviet Union during the Gorbachev era, Izvestiia TsKom KPSS 5 (1990): 165–174.

9. For instance, Populaire, 28 January 1924, reported and quoted Lenin's notes on the nationality question from Sv 69/70. "Zametki," Sv 67/68, 27 November 1923, revealed a secret circular signed by Lenin's wife, Krupskaia, containing a list of books banned from public libraries; this was reported in Populaire, 2 February 1924. Wolfe, "Krupskaia Purges the People's Libraries," identifies the source of the revelation as Maksim Gorky, who was so horrified by the circular that he showed a copy to an exiled Menshevik, S. Sumskii-Kaplun (no doubt expecting the document to find its way into Vestnik).

10. Lewin, Lenin's Last Struggle.

11. Lewin, *Political Undercurrents*, 18 and 24.

12. Daniels, *Conscience of the Revolution*, 472n29; Schapiro, *Communist Party of the Soviet Union*, 300.

13. Eastman, *Since Lenin Died*, 26, and *NYT*, 18 October 1926. Trotsky and Krupskaia both publicly denied the existence of Lenin's "Testament."

14. "French See Stalin Downing Trotsky," *NYT*, 16 October 1926. The article also speaks of the opposition as one between the "Russian Communist, such as Trotsky is, with the added strength of his Jewish race, and the German kind of Communist as Stalin has shown himself, plodding, unimaginative, careful and strong."

15. Carr, *Interregnum*, 279, referring to *Sv* 61, and *Foundations of a Planned Economy*, 2:62, referring to *Sv* 186, 28 October 1928. Carr, *Interregnum*, 259 and 263, cites *Sv* as a source for Lenin's notes on the nationalities question and acknowledges that summaries, which he calls "inaccurate in some details," of Lenin's "Testament" first appeared in *Sv*.

16. Cohen, *Bukharin and the Bolshevik Revolution*, 277–291.

17. For example, Kamenev's "pilgrimage" to Bukarin in July 1928, revealed by German Trotskyists, picked up as "Bol'sheviki o samikh sebe: zamechatel'nyi razgovor," *Sv* 196, 22 March 1929, and completed by further details in *Sv* 199, 4 May 1929. None of the major historical accounts of this episode (Carr, Daniels, Cohen, Reiman) gives the German Trotskyist source. See also Fel'shtinskii, "Dva epizoda." For other examples, see "Dokumenty mezhduusobitsy: listovka o mezhduusobnoi bor'be v riadakh bol'shevistkoi partii," *Sv* 167, 12 January 1928, and [A. G.], "Zhalkii dokument (avtobiograpfia Trotskogo)," *Sv* 186, 28 October 1928.

18. F. Dan, "Novyi fazis mezhduusobitsy," *Sv* 135/136, 18 September 1926; "Razgrom trotskistov," *Sv* 193, 9 February 1929. Also, on mutual accusations of menshevism among Bolshevik leaders, see Daniels, *Conscience of the Revolution*, 195–245 passim, esp. 236; Carr, *Socialism in One Country*, 18; and [Ed], "Komintern na rasputi," *Sv* 65 18 October 1923.

19. Examples from Daniels, *Conscience of the Revolution*, and from Abramovitch papers, Bakhmeteff Archives. Daniels let himself be convinced by these accusations as he concludes his book (409) with the statement that "the Menshevik character of the Opposition pervades their whole history."

20. Lerner, *Karl Radek*, 143; F. Dan, "Tuchi c vostoka," *Sv* 150, 23 April 1927.

21. *NYT*, 29 May 1924.

22. [Ed], "Raskol v VKP," *Sv* 2, 16 February 1921.

23. D. Dalin, "Nado podumat' do kontsa," *Sv* 65, 18 October 1923. See also [PR], "Moskva: vnutri RKP," *Sv* 66, 3 November 1923.

24. [Ed], "Smert' V. I. Lenina," *Sv* 72, 25 January 1924. Abramowitsch to Adler, 22 January 1924, SAI 2623, remarks: "In spite of everything, it is a pity about the old man [Lenin]. He was certainly a colossal figure." P. Garvi, "Bonapartizm ili demokratiia," *Sv* 69/70, 17 December 1923.

25. [PR], "Moskva: krizis-voiennaia partiia," *Sv* 66, 3 November 1923; Abramowitsch to Adler, 22 January 1924.

26. F. Dan, "Konets Trotskogo," *Sv* 93/94, 1 December 1924. The *NYT* conveyed

reports of Trotsky's arrest on 30 December 1924. On December 24 it "confirmed" reports of Stalin's arrest.

27. R. Abramovich, "Krizis diktatury," *Sv* 71, 10 January 1924; Dan, "Konets Trotskogo." Also D. Dalin, "Fel'febel' v Vol'terakh," *Sv* 56, 12 May 1923.

28. Dan, "Konets Trotskogo," and D. D. [Dalin], "Kavkazskoe lecheniie," *Sv* 94, 24 December 1924.

29. G. Weiss, "Trotskii front," *Sv* 96, 31 January 1925, declared that "Trotsky has gone and is not going to return," describing Trotsky as the first victim of the diversion he himself had created. [PR], "Moskva," *Sv* 76, 24 March 1924.

30. [PR], "Na kommunisticheskikh verkhakh," *Sv* 100, 4 April 1925; [PR], "Pis'mo iz Moskvy: stabilizatsiia VRKP," *Sv* 107, 10 July 1925, reported the first version. The second, also mentioning the rumor that Trotsky would replace Dzerzhinskii as head of the Supreme Economic Council, appeared in [PR], "Moskva: Na verkhakh partii i profsoiuzov," *Sv* 105/106, 20 June 1925.

31. [PR], "Moskva: Plenum TsK-ta VKP," *Sv* 128, 22 May 1926; [PR], "Pis'mo iz Moskvy: Sumerki bogov," *Sv* 133/134, 25 August 1926; [PR], "Moskva: bor'ba na bol'shevistskom Olimpe," *Sv* 187, 14 November 1928.

32. "S'ezd RKP i zaveshchanie Lenina" *Sv* 85; [PR], "Trevozhnye dni (pis'mo iz Moskvy)-slukhi o voine-vozrozhdenie populiarnosti Trotskogo," *Sv* 154, 20 June 1927; [PR], "Moskovskie nastroeniia," *Sv* 168/169, 6 February 1928. [PR], "Moskva," *Sv* 191, 9 January 1929, reported that "Trotsky is winning admiration for his persistence and bravery," (From whom? one might ask.)

33. [PR], I. "Moskva," *Sv* 138, 16 October 1926; [PR], 5. "Moskva," *Sv* 160, 22 September 1927, reported that a resolution excluding Trotsky and Zinoviev had been adopted and then withdrawn at the last Central Committee plenum. [PR], "Moskva," *Sv* 140, 20 November 1926; [PR], I. "Moskva," *Sv* 204, 15 July 1929.

34. Abramovich, "Krizis diktatury" *Sv* 71; F. Dan, "Nachalo kontsa," *Sv* 72, 25 January 1924; A. Iugov, "Pered XIII s'ezdom RKP," *Sv* 81, 28 May 1924; [PR], "Posles'ezdovskaia bor'ba s oppozitsiei," *Sv* 124, 31 March 1926.

35. See Liebich, "Mensheviks in the Face of Stalinism."

36. "Pis'mo iz Moskvy: Stabilizatsiia VRKP," *Sv* 107. [PR], "Moskva: krushenie oppozitsii," *Sv* 139, 1 November 1926, reemphasized Stalin's search for compromise and reported on his inability to make the Moscow party organization retract its insistence on punitive measures against the opposition, even though the previous year he had been successful in this same attempt.

37. F. Dan, "Bol'shevistskii opyt i sotsializm," *Sv* 122, 25 February 1926. Citation from [Ed], "Posle s'ezda," *Sv* 119, 16 January 1926.

38. "Moskva: Na verkhakh partii i profsoiuzov," *Sv* 105/106.

39. "Stabilizatsiia VRKP," *Sv* 107; [PR], "Moskva," *Sv* 113, 15 October 1925; "Posle s'ezda," *Sv* 119; [PR], "Moskva: Plenum TsK-ta VKP," *Sv* 128; [PR], "Moskva," *Sv* 151, 9 May 1927.

40. "Moskva: Plenum TsK-ta VKP," *Sv* 128, and "Pis'mo iz Moskvy: Sumerki bogov," *Sv* 133/134; Dan, "Novyi Fazis mezhdusobitsy," *Sv* 135/136; R. Abramovich, "Gde vykhod?," *Sv* 133/134, 25 August 1926.

41. [PR], "Moskva: krushenie oppozitsii," and "Moskva: konferentsiia VKP," *Sv* 140,

20 November 1926. A letter from Moscow remarked that "of course" Stalin himself did not engage in antisemitism, but it was invoked at local levels in the struggle with the opposition. [PR], "Moskovskie nastroeniia," *Sv* 168/169.

42. "Konferentsiia VKP," and "Posle konferentsii," *Sv* 140.

43. D. D., "Kavkazskoe lecheniie," *Sv* 94.

44. Cited from "Posle s'ezda," *Sv* 119, and "Posle konferentsii," *Sv* 140.

45. "Pered XIII s'ezdom RKP"; [Ed], "Pravaia oppozitsiia," *Sv* 186.

46. [PR], "Leningradskie nastroeniia," *Sv* 154.

47. Dan, "Programma pravykh," *Sv* 199; [PR], "Moskva," *Sv* 186. D. Dalin, "NEP i anti-NEP," *Sv* 195, 8 March 1929, "Pravyi uklon v VKP," *Sv* 187, and [Ed], "Pravaia oppozitsiia," *Sv* 186.

48. Quoted from Dan, "Programma pravykh," *Sv* 199, and I. Grekov [=Dan], "Biurokratizatsiia diktatury," *Sv* 200/201, 25 May 1929.

49. [PR], "Moskva," *Sv* 192, 24 January 1929; [PR], "Moskva," *Sv* 197/198, 12 April 1929.

50. D.D. [= Dalin], "Shtrikhi k pravomu uklonu," *Sv* 190, 19 December 1928. A correspondent wrote, "As for the right wing tendency, it is nowhere and everywhere." [PR], "Moskva," *Sv* 192, 24 January 1928.

51. [PR], "Vokrug plenuma TsK VKP," *Sv* 188/189, 5 December 1928; [PR], "Moskva," *Sv* 193, 9 February 1929; [PR], "Moskva," *Sv* 195, 8 March 1929; [PR], "Moskva," *Sv* 202, 14 June 1929; [PR], "Moskva," *Sv* 200/201, 25 May 1929.

52. [PR], "Moskva," *Sv* 202; [A.V.], "Dve otstavki," *Sv* 206/207, 11 September 1929; [PR], "Moskva," *Sv* 191, and "Moskva," *Sv* 199, 4 May 1929; "Bol'sheviki o samikh sebe," *Sv* 196, 22 March 1929.

53. [PR], "Moskva," *Sv* 202; [A.V.], "Dve otstavki," *Sv* 206/207; [PR], "Moskva," *Sv* 191, 9 January 1929, and "Moskva," *Sv* 199.

54. "Bol'sheviki o samikh sebe zamechatel'nyi razgovor," *Sv* 196, 22 March 1929. This report accompanied the transcripts of Bukharin's secret conversations with Kamenev the previous summer. In fact, Bukharin was not removed from the Politburo until November 1929, Rykov in December 1930, and Tomskii in June 1930.

55. [PR], "Moskva: ideologicheskii obstrel Bukharina," *Sv* 211, 7 November 1929.

56. [Ed], "Na vershine," *Sv* 228, 26 July 1930; A. Shifrin, "Poslednii bol'shevistskii teoretik," *Sv* 231/232, 27 September 1930.

57. [Ed], "Po lezviiu nozha," *Sv* 227, 12 July 1930; [PR], "S'ezd VKP," *Sv* 226, 26 June 1930.

58. [Ed], "Na vershine."

59. [PR], "Moskva," *Sv* 203, 1 July 1929; *Sv* 208, 27 September 1929; *Sv* 210, 24 October 1929. Compare [PR], "Moskva," *Sv* 186.

60. [PR], "Moskva," *Sv* 236, 22 November 1930; for "Genghis Khan" see D.D., "Shtrikhi k pravomu uklonu," *Sv* 190.

61. Dan, "Ende der Opposition," 6; Abramovich to RSDRP in Russia, 21 June 1925, NC 25(685).

62. Abramowitsch to Adler, 26 January and 12 February 1926, SAI 2623; Aksel'rod

to Tsereteli, 11 August 1926, NC 15(29). Horthy's Hungary tolerated, within strict limits, a tamed Social Democratic Party.

63. [Ed], "Politika vykhodit na ulitsu," *Sv* 155, 2 July 1927; I. Grekov [= Dan], "Velikii kanun," *Sv* 157, 1 August 1927.

64. [Ed], "Neotlozhnaia zadacha," *Sv* 165, 1 December 1927.

65. "K partiinoi platforme: tezisy F. Dana, D. Dalina, Kefali i Aronsona," [n.d.], NC 18; internal evidence points to 1929. "Instruktsiia dlia redaktsii 'Sotsialisticheskogo vestnika,' " [1928], NC 18(54).

5. Mensheviks and the Wider World

INTO THE INTERNATIONAL ARENA

1. See Abramovich, "Men'sheviki i sotsialisticheskii internatsional, 1918–1940," 253, and Wolin, "NEP and Emigration," 278–294.

2. Although the party repudiated Axelrod's "socialist intervention," the concept remained at the heart of Menshevik strategy. See Ascher, *Axelrod,* 343–380 passim, and Getzler, *Martov,* 204–217.

3. Compare Ascher, *Axelrod,* 359, and Abramovich, "Men'sheviki i sotsialisticheskii internatsional," 264–265; also Getzler, *Martov,* 205–209. The historian's (Getzler's) account would seem to be more accurate than the participant's (Abramovitch's).

4. Nicolaevsky cites Bukharin's statement to an unnamed friend (possibly Denike): "The majority was opposed; the Mensheviks are going to put spokes in the wheels of all the Comintern's work. But we couldn't do anything with Il'ich [Lenin], who is in love with Martov and wants to help him go abroad at any price." B. Nikolaevskii,"K 80-letiu L. O. Tsederbaum-Dan" (2), *Sv* 719/720, July–August 1958. Compare Volkogonov, *Lenin,* 86–88.

5. As Getzler, *Martov,* 207, remarks "This must have been one of the few occasions when he [i.e., Martov] crossed the Russian border legally." Years later Abramovitch invoked this passport episode to defend himself against American Communist insinuations concerning his departure from Russia; see his "Open Letter," *Veker,* 28 March 1928.

6. See Braunthal, *History of the International,* 2:213–223.

7. Getzler, *Martov,* 211, writes that the majority vote of 236 to 150 (in fact, 237 to 156) at Halle in favor of the Comintern was "much greater than Martov seems to have expected." Abramovich, "Men'sheviki i sotsialisticheskii internatsional," 266, writes that the USPD was divided into "two almost equal parts," an assessment which corresponds more to Menshevik hopes than to reality.

8. In addition to the Abramovitch, Getzler, and Braunthal sources cited in notes 1, 2, and 6, see Sapir, "Notes and Reflections," 376–377; Naarden, *Socialist Europe and Revolutionary Russia,* 410–415.

9. Lazitch and Drachkovitch, *Lenin and the Comintern,* 419–425, complain that at an earlier national meeting the USPD had voted overwhelmingly against joining the

Comintern and that it reversed itself at Halle. See also Abramovich, "Men'sheviki i sotsialisticheskii internatsional," 267. In fact, the earlier meeting brought together only party functionaries whose preference was overturned by a pro-Bolshevik tide at the grass-roots level; corrected by Wheeler, "21 Bedingungen und die Spaltung der USPD."

10. Braunthal, *History of the International*, 222.
11. Sapir, "Notes and Reflections," 376. Compare. Lösche, *Bolschewismus im Urteil der deutschen Sozialdemokratie*, 265.
12. Naarden, *Socialist Europe and Revolutionary Russia*, 415.
13. Cited from R. Gil'ferding, "Martov i Internatsional," *Sv* 54/55, 24 April 1923; and Abramovich, "Men'sheviki i sotsialisticheskii internatsional," 268.
14. Cited in Naarden, *Socialist Europe*, 415.
15. L.M. [=Martov], "Na puti k Internatsionalu," *Sv* 1, 1 February 1921. On the mood of European socialism, see Lindemann, *Red Years.*
16. Naarden, *Socialist Europe*, 375.
17. Ibid., 416, and Donneur, *Histoire de l'Union des partis socialistes*, 35–36.
18. For instance, Lenin declared that "eradication of Menshevism" was the central task of *Italian* socialists; cited in Lazitch and Drachkovitch, "Third International," 163.
19. Abramovich, "Men'sheviki i sotsialisticheskii internatsional," 270.
20. [Ed], "K venskoi konferentsii," *Sv* 4, 18 March 1921; Donneur, *Histoire de l'Union des partis socialistes*, 54–59. Meeting at Bern were the French, Swiss, and Austrian Socialist parties as well as the German USPD, British Independent Labour Party, German Social Democratic Party of Czechoslovakia, and the RSDRP. Also represented but not present were the Latvian socialists.
21. Donneur, *Histoire de l'Union des partis socialistes*, 90, 98–99, and 128; also Steiner, "Internationale Arbeitsgemeinschaft Sozialistischer Parteien." Abramovitch's opposition to Poale Zion, based formally on the principle that only national organizations could be admitted to the Union, was an expression of his own and the Mensheviks' anti-Zionist position. The Mensheviks contested granting two votes to Left SRs (against six votes for the RSDRP) on the grounds that the Mensheviks still had local soviet representation in Russia.
22. See Radek, *Theorie und Praxis der 2½ Internationale.*
23. [Ed], "K venskoi konferentsii," *Sv* 4; Donneur, *Histoire de l'Union des partis socialistes*, 127.
24. Donneur, *Histoire de l'Union des partis socialistes*, 152–162.
25. Abramovich, "Men'sheviki i sotsialisticheskii internatsional," 283–294; Donneur, *Histoire de l'Union des partis socialistes*, 187–224; Sukiennicki, "Abortive Attempt at International Unity of the Workers' Movement," 206–238.
26. From a comparison of Donneur, *Histoire de l'Union des partis socialistes*, 203, with Abramovich, "Men'sheviki I sotsialisticheskii internatsional," 288–290, it appears that it took several meetings involving Martov, Abramovitch, Dan, Bauer, and others to wrest this concession from the Second International.
27. See Jansen, *Show Trial under Lenin.* In *Soviet Revolution*, 71, Abramovitch credits

Mensheviks with raising the issue of the arrested SRs. See also Dvinov, *Ot legal'nosti k podpoliu*, 114–115. The principal statement by an exile Menshevik, but published by SRs, is Voitinskii, *Dvenadtsat' smertnikov*.

28. Sukiennicki, "Abortive Attempt," and Donneur, *Histoire de l'Union des partis socialistes*, 243–249.

29. Wolin, "NEP and Emigration," 278, recalls references to the merger as a "loveless marriage." See also Donneur, *Histoire de l'Union des partis socialistes*, 292–310.

30. Martow, "Problem der Internationale," 2–3; D. Dalin, "Mezhdu Londonom i Moskvoi," *Sv* 34, 18 June 1922.

31. Martow, "Problem der Internationale," 3.

32. On Left SRs and other Vienna Union parties which continued outside both the Social Democratic and Communist mainstreams, see Dreyfus, "Bureau de Paris et bureau de Londres."

33. On the "twenty-one conditions," see Hulse, *Forming of the Communist International*, 205–211. The Vienna Union made its decisions binding on all members, as did the Comintern, but did not adopt anything like the infamous twenty-first condition calling for expulsion of those who voted against acceptance of the conditions. See Donneur, *Histoire de l'Union des partis socialistes*, 398.

34. See the reports "K ob'edineniu Internatisionalov," *Sv* 47, 1 January 1923; "Na puti k edinstvu," *Sv* 48, 17 January 1923; "Pered gamburgskim kongresom," *Sv* 54/55, 24 April 1923. Also Abramovich, "Men'sheviki i sotsialisticheskii internatsional" (2).

35. The French consul-general in Hamburg wrote: "A socialist congress is to be held in Hamburg in a fortnight or two. No one is doing anything about it." Allemagne 319, Archives du Ministère des affaires étrangères, Paris. See "V sotsialisticheskom Internatsionale—posledniaia konferentsiia Venskogo ob'edineniia," *Sv* 57, 12 June 1923.

36. Abramovitch, *Soviet Revolution*, 272. Neither Beatrice Webb's *Diaries* nor a report on the Hamburg Congress in Labour Party Archives, LSI 12/1/10 (1923, n.d.) makes any mention of this incident. Note, however, that Abramovitch is speaking from personal experience as a member of the credentials committee (not the political subcommittee, as he states) and that the account is entirely consistent with Webb's expressed opinions regarding Russian emigré socialists.

37. Ivanovich-Portugeis, "Appeal to the Executive Committee of the Second International," 4 May 1923, BP; D. Dalin, "Za bortom," *Sv* 57, 12 June 1923; also, NC 25(679).

38. Proceedings published as *Protokoll des ersten Internationalen Sozialistischen Arbeiterkongresses*. [Ed], "Gamburgskii kongress," *Sv* 57, 12 June 1923. On the Curzon ultimatum, see Carr, *Interregnum*, 168–173.

39. The Mensheviks seemed particularly indignant that the book was being sold for 100 marks instead of the usual price of 3,000 to 4,000 marks. G.A. "V sotsialisticheskom Internatsionale: Ob'edinitel'nyi kongress," *Sv* 57, 12 June 1923.

40. *Protokoll*, 20–21. The Mensheviks claimed that the protests took place at their initiative. [Ed], "Gamburgskii kongress," *Sv* 57; also R. Abramovich, "Pod damoklovym mechom," *Sv* 57, 12 June 1923.

41. Most openly Italian delegate Giuseppe Modigliani, who stated that the Bolsheviks had the merit of "having toppled tsarism in Russia." The Labour Party report cited in note 36 refers to "the effect of a declaration of war against Moscow," but the British did not engage the Mensheviks in debate. Others, including a close Menshevik ally, Otto Bauer, kept their distance from the Menshevik position implicitly. *Protokoll*, 37–38 and 24.

42. Braunthal, *History of the International*, 269–270, also refers to the violent "arguments about this resolution" in the commission.

43. "Russian émigré socialists, backed by Poland and other hostile neighbours, rammed through and carried a resolution," Webb, *Diaries*, 239. The Labour Party report (see note 36) explains that the British were adverse to "placing the New International in a relation of special hostility to the Soviet government."

44. Elections to these positions were personal but, in practice, took account of national quotas. Adler to Abramowitsch, 8 March 1926, SAI 2623. The other Russian member of the Executive, the SR V. V. Sukhomlin, was also a consultative member of the Bureau.

MENSHEVIK FOREIGN RELATIONS

1. See Abramovitch in *Protokoll*, 30–35, and his *Zukunft Sowjetrusslands;* also Dan's similar statements for foreigners: *Politique économique* and *Arbeiter in Sowjetrussland*.

2. [Anon], "Po povodu odnogo nedoumeniia," *Sv* 1, 1 February 1921.

3. [Ed], "Mirnye dogovory i zadachi proletariata v Rossii," *Sv* 5, 5 April 1921.

4. Abramowitsch, *Zukunft Sowjetrusslands*, 40–44.

5. Ibid., 45. Dalin, *Posle voin i revoliutsii*, 280–286, argued that normalization of relations between Germany and Russia would diminish the danger which a militaristic Poland posed to its eastern neighbor.

6. Dalin, *Posle voin I revoliutsii*, 278–279. The Menshevik stance on the "national question" clearly shares some of the ambiguities of the Bolshevik position.

7. "Londonskaia konferentsiia i vosstanovlenie razrushennykh oblastei," *Sv* 4, 18 March 1921; Dalin, *Posle voin i revoliutsii*, 278–279.

8. See, for example, Dan, "Programm der sozialen Revolution."

9. Abramovich to Vol'skii, 9 July 1959, VC. He added, "I appeared more often and more successfully than Martov with his hoarseness and illness of the throat . . . and nonetheless the hoarse Martov had one hundred times more influence than the unknown Abramovich."

10. Collotti, "Appunti su Friedrich Adler."

11. For example, Abramowitsch to Adler, 5 April 1924 [1923 in original], SAI 2623. Even a key Soviet study of the LSI does not manage to connect the Mensheviks to its anti-Marxist policies. Krivoguz, *Rabochii sotsialisticheskii internatsional*, 36.

12. O. Bauer, "K marsel'skomu kongressu," *Sv* 109/110, 18 August 1925. Compare Garvi to Viliatser, 16 November 1925, NC 75(130).

13. F. Dan, "Itogi smotra," *Sv* 182/183, 5 September 1928. See also [Ed], "Russkii vopros v Internatsionale," *Sv* 111/112, 28 September 1925.

14. Dogliani, "Ricostituzione della Internazionale socialista," 227.
15. Panaccione, "Presupposti e linee di sviluppo," 338.
16. See Abramowitsch-Adler correspondence, SAI 2623.
17. Salvadori, *Kautsky and the Socialist Revolution*, 251–318.
18. For example, see Abramowitsch to K. and L. Kautsky, 31 January 1928, KA 15.
19. Bauer to Kautsky, 16 July 1921, KA. On Bauer, see Löw, *Bauer und die Russische Revolution;* Marramao, "Tra bolscevismo e socialdemocrazia"; Croan, "Politics of Marxist Sovietology"; and Bourdet, ed. *Bauer et la Révolution.*
20. O. Bauer, "Socialism and Soviet Russia," *International Information*, 31 December 1925. Abramowitsch to Adler, 28 March 1925, SAI 2623, described Bauer as "the only foreign socialist who understands Russian and knows the situation there."
21. [P. Aksel'rod], "Tov. P. B. Aksel'rod o bol'shevizme i bor'be s nim," *Sv* 6 and 7, 20 April and 7 May 1921, trans. in Ascher, ed., *Mensheviks*, 130–136.
22. See, though, F. Dan, "Bol'shevistskii opyt i sotsializm," *Sv* 122, 25 February 1926.
23. *Second Congress of the LSI*, pt. 1:32–37; also Abramowitsch to Adler, 29 August 1924, SAI 2623; and Abramovitch's interview, "La lumière doit se faire sur la terreur bolcheviste," *Populaire*, 7 April 1927. Aksel'rod to Tsereteli, 23 September 1927, NC 15(29), compared the commission to the Sacco and Vanzetti defense committees.
24. "The International and the So-Called Soviet Government," KA I 28, later published in Russian, German, and French. Panaccione, "Presupposti e linee di sviluppo," 342–346.
25. Dan to Kautsky, 19 December 1924, *Pis'ma*, 322–329; Abramowitsch to Kautsky, 21 November 1924, KA G 15; Dan, "Kautsky über den russischen Bolshevismus."
26. Fears expressed in Dan to Kautsky, 19 December 1924, but not in Dan's "Kautsky über den russichen Bolshevismus." On rightists' intiatives, see Garvi and Bienstock to Kautsky, 14 December 1924, "on behalf of the opposition within the party." Also Aksel'rod to Kautsky, 23 December 1924, KA G 15.
27. Adler to Kautsky, 23 December 1924, KA G 15; "Internatsional v Briussele," *Sv* 95, 17 January 1925.
28. On SRs, see Koons, "Histoire des doctrines politiques de l'émigration russe," 124–135, and Iugov to Viliatser, 5 September 1928, NC 75(130). See also Weill, "Mencheviks et Socialistes Révolutionnaires en exil."
29. *Second Congress of the LSI*, pt. 2:268–276 and 287–288; also Abramovich, "Men'sheviki i sotsialisticheskii internatsional" (2), 103–112.
30. *Troisième Congrès*, 9:6 and 2:6–7; Dan, "Itogi smotra," *Sv* 182/183; also Sokolova, *Internationale socialiste entre deux guerres mondiales*, 89–101.
31. See, for example, "Avstriiskaia rabochaia delegatsiia v Rossiiu?" *Sv* 96, 31 January 1925; [Ed], "Gosti," *Sv* 109/110, 18 August 1925; Strannik [=Nikolaevskii], "Vokrug delegatsii," *Sv* 114, 29 October 1925. These and other delegations are discussed in Löw, *Bauer*, 117–124.
32. BTU Delegation, *Russia Today.* A German version was also published.
33. The principal refutation was a book-length "guide"; see Dan, *Sowjetrussland wie*

es wirklich ist. Reactions from Russia in [PR], "V Biuro Internatsionala i Amsterdamskogo Ob'edineniia," *Sv* 91, 10 November 1924; [IP], "Dokladnaia zapiska Biuro TsKRSDRP germanskoi delegatsii," *Sv* 109/110, 18 August 1925; [IP], "Obrashchenie biuro tsentralnogo komiteta k avstriiskim tovarishcham," *Sv* 128, 22 May 1926. LSI condemnation reported in "Internatsional v Briussele," *Sv* 95.

34. [IP], "Protiv klevety," *Sv* 95, 17 January 1925. The article in the Communist *Rote Fahne*, 31 December 1924, titled "Mercenary Scoundrels against Ben Tillett," described the Menshevik Foreign Delegation as "counterrevolutionary swine in the keep of international capital."

35. Adler to Dan, 9 March 1925, SAI 2597, and "Otkrytoe pis'mo: ispolnitel'nomu komitetu angliiskoi rabochei partii i general'nomu sovetu tred-iunionov," *Sv* 94, 20 December 1924. Adler's rebuttal, prepared for *Kampf,* came out in several languages, with a preface by Dan to the Russian version. *Vestnik*'s critique of the report is [Ed], "Nechestnaia kniga," *Sv* 99, 19 March 1925.

36. Adler, *Anglo-Russian Report,* 18.

37. Dan, *Sowjetrussland wie es wirklich ist,* 19–23. At least one delegation, that of the Mining Workers' International, canceled its planned trip; see "Vokrug delegatsii." Even the (London) *Times,* 28 Februrary 1925, picked up the suggestion that delegates should have submitted their "worthless [and] prejudiced report to unbiased anti-Bolshevik Russian emigrés for verification." Nonetheless, the report sold ten thousand copies. See Calhoun, *United Front,* 122–124.

FRATERNAL PARTIES

1. *Sv* 616/617, 15 February 1949; Williams, *Culture in Exile,* 189–193; Papanek, "Alexander Stein."

2. For example, see Abramowitsch to Mehr, 5 October 193(3?), AA I/3.

3. Haimson, ed., *Making of Three Russian Revolutionaries,* 423. On Denike, see B. Nikolaevskii, "Opyt politicheskoi biografii," and S. Shvarts, "Ne proiznesennaia rech'," both in *Sv: sbornik* 3 (1965). Also Decker, *Erinnerungen;* Liebich, *Marxism and Totalitarianism,* 42–45.

4. S. Shvarts, "Pamiati G. O. Binshtoka," *Novoe russkoe slovo,* 21 December 1954. Sapir to author, 2 January 1989; F. Heine to author, 24 February 1989; also Liebich, *Marxism and Totalitarianism,* 47–49. Bienstock's brochure *Kampf um die Macht,* calling for an offensive socialist policy in 1932, created a stir.

5. R. Abramovich, "Krizis v Germanii i ob'edinenie sotsialisticheskoi partii," *Sv* 41 and 42, 4 and 19 October 1922. On SPD antibolshevik culture, see Lösche, *Bolschewismus im Urteil der deutschen Sozialdemokratie.*

6. For example, see Abramowitsch to Adler, 7 September 1923, LSI 2623.

7. For example, in their attitude toward German delegations to Russia: [V tiurme i ssylke (in prison and exile)], "Nemetskaia delegatsiia v russkoi tiurme," and [PR], "Delegatsiia germanskikh rabochikh v Khar'kove," *Sv* 117/118, 21 December 1925, and S. Shvarts, "Dlia chego germanskiie delegaty ezdili v Rossiiu?" *Sv* 111/112, 28 September 1925.

8. "Tragediia germanskogo sotsializma," *Sv* 2 and 4, 16 February and 18 March 1921.

9. R. Abramovich, "Nakanune pobedy fashizma," *Sv* 67/68, 27 November 1923; also S. Shvarts, "Germanskii krizis," *Sv* 96, 31 January 1925.

10. *Sv* covered German events thoroughly, and Abramovitch even reported on German party politics to Adler; see Abramowitsch to Adler, 10 December 1923, SAI 2623.

11. Bauer, *"Neuer Kurs" in Russland.*

12. Abramowitsch to Adler, 10 July 1924, 24 October 1924, 26 November 1927, SAI Archive 2623; Dan to Adler, 10 November 1927, SAI 25997; ZD RSDRP to Austrian Social Democratic Party, 5 April 1926, NC 25B.

13. Abramowitsch to L. Kautsky, 25 November 1927, KA 15; Dan to Adler, 10 November 1927, *Pi'sma*, 363–364.

14. See Braunthal, *History of the International*, 216; Collotti, "Friedrich Adler," 91; and Löw, *Bauer und die russische Revolution*, 126.

15. On SFIO, see Abramowitsch to Adler, 21 December 1924, SAI 2623. See Dan to Adler, 10 November 1927, and Dan, "Programm der sozialen Revolution."

16. Even Axelrod thought that Bauer was coming around to a more moderate position. Aksel'rod to Tsereteli, 4 December 1926, NC 15(29). For instance, under Menshevik pressure Bauer warned that the Austrian workers' delegation to Russia should go only "if it were possible to do so without damanging our links of solidarity with the Russian socialists" and without "forfeit[ing] anything of one's own self-respect." O. Bauer, "Socialism and Soviet Russia," *International Information*, 31 December 1925. The Austrian theoretical journal *Kampf* was also more open to the Mensheviks than the daily press. On the tenth anniversary of the Revolution it published Abramowitsch, "Zwei Revolutionen und eine Diktatur."

17. See Braunthal, *History of the International*, 192–198, and Wohl, *French Communism in the Making*, 193–207.

18. But see the moving obituary for Axelrod in *Populaire*, 18 April 1928. Some of Tsereteli's extensive correspondence with French socialist leaders such as Alexandre Bracke, Paul Faure, and Pierre Renaudel is in NC 15(31). On the divergences and break between Tsereteli and Dan and the ensuing polemics, see Roobol, *Tsereteli*, 220–248.

19. Duhamel and Racine, "Léon Blum."

20. Cited in Racine, "Parti socialiste devant le bolchevisme," 315.

21. Verdier, "Oreste Rosenfeld."

22. F. Dan, "X_e anniversaire de la dictature bolcheviste," *Populaire*, 7 November 1927.

23. [IP], "Kak priniali Dana v Parizhe," *Sv* 51/52, 16 March 1923.

24. [IP], "F. Dan v Parizhe," *Sv* 94, 24 December 1924; Dan to Adler, 25 January 1925, *Pis'ma*, 333.

25. Aksel'rod to Tsereteli, 16 September 1924, NC 15(29).

26. Dan to Rozenfel'd, 26 April 1926. Rosenfeld had written on behalf of "our French comrades," NC 25(688?).

27. Parizhskaia gruppa RSDRP to ZD, 17 September 1924, NC 25(688).

28. See the report "Vopros o terrore protiv russkikh sotsialistov vo frantsuskom par-lamente," *Sv* 87, 1 September 1924.

29. Abramowitsch to Adler, 29 August and 10 September 1924, SAI 2623. Adler could only reiterate what he had already written to Abramovitch, 7 April 1924, regarding the Austrians: "Bolshevism is very much out of fashion, but antibol-shevism cannot arouse enthusiam among the people who count."

30. Adler to Abramowitsch, 7 April 1924, and reply, 3 May 1924, SAI 2623. Adler, 11 September 1924, advised that Abramovitch's "speech[es] should be in the English manner, condensed to the maximum degree, if possible in point form . . . [S]aving time assures great sympathy in advance here." He added: "It is very important that you speak *Russian* [presumably as opposed to German]. This formal aspect is more important than the content. As for the content I would not say one word of polemics against bolshevism." Adler to Abramowitsch, 24 September 1924, SAI 2623.

31. A major study, John F. Naylor's *Labour's International Policy,* (1969) does not even mention the LSI. Is it significant, too, that Beatrice Webb even got Adler's name wrong in her diary entries at the Hamburg Congress? Webb, *Diaries,* 239.

32. "If only the thick-skinned English spoke a human language," wrote Aksel'rod to Tsereteli, 16 September 1924, NC 15(29). It is a measure of the Mensheviks' alienation from the British that Adler did not know where to send one hundred copies of the English edition of the Menshevik *RSD.* Adler to Abramowitsch, 24 February 1924, SAI 2623.

33. See Graubard, *British Labour and the Russian Revolution,* 289.

34. Beatrice Webb, *Diaries,* 298, evoked the "soul" of the Soviet constitution and added: "We don't quite like that soul; still it seems to do the job."

35. Whereas the Mensheviks criticized Kautsky for advocating that conditions be imposed on loans to Russia, they insisted that the British make the improvement of the situation of socialist prisoners in Russia a condition for loans. Abramo-witsch to Adler, 3 May 1924, 24 June 1926, 29 August 1924, SAI 2623.

36. Even when the British did stop to consider the question, their conclusions only drove the Mensheviks to despair. The indomitable Mrs. Webb wrote to Labour Party International secretary William Gillies, 12 May 1932 (Gillies Papers, Labour Party Archives): "Stories about the treatment of prisoners are very difficult to test; but I assume there is a good deal of brutality in Russia as elswhere with regard to political prisoners as it is difficult even with the best intentions to get the right people as wardens."

37. Adler to Abramowitsch, 15 April 1924; also 15 June 1927, both SAI 2623.

38. Baikalov to Citrine, 20 August 1934, BP, and his *I Knew Stalin.* Other Mensheviks in England, notably Iakov S. Novakovskii, were politically inactive.

39. Baikalov, "Ekonomicheskaia platforma," *Zaria* 9/10 (1922). See Slonim to Bai-kalov, 24 May 1922, BP.

40. Baikalov's books ranged from the sensationalist *I Knew Stalin,* which described Stalin as of "doubtful inheritance from the eugenic point of view" (3–4), to the merely popular, such as *In the Land of Communist Dictatorship.* On his press connec-tions, see Baikalov to Nikolaevskii, 7 October 1933, BP. Doubts about his English

are raised by turns of phrase such as "fragrant crimes against humanity," Baikalov to Lansbury, 1 April 1932, Labour Party Archives.

41. For example, see Keynes to Baikalov, 22 November 1928, BP.

42. Webb did extend an invitation to Baikalov, later canceled because, he said, of a cold. Webb's letter also reads: "We have both read the book you sent us as affording a sample of the contents of the Soviet press. I could not help wondering what England would look like to a Russian workman if you made the same kind of analysis of the contents of some of our widely circulating Sunday newspapers with their police news and labour disputes etc." Webb to Baikalov, 24 March and 11 April 1934, and Baikalov to Nikolaevskii, 29 March 1934, BP.

43. Citrine to Baikalov, 10 February, 14 February, 4 April, and 25 May 1928, BP.

44. Citrine to Baikalov, 19 April 1929 BP; Baikalov to Kerensky, 15 January 1928, BP. In fact, Baikalov's work was intended for members of the General Council and not for publication.

45. Baikalov accompanied his boast with a nasty portrait of Gillies: "He has no views of his own. He is a typical party man, always following the line of his center," Baikalov to Nikolaevskii, 29 March and 10 June 1934, BP.

46. See Baikalov's extensive correspondence with the duchess of Atholl, 1932–1948, BP, and the duchess's memoirs, *Working Partnership,* 183.

47. "Londonskii shtab interventov," *Pravda,* 2 July 1932. Nikolaevskii to Vol'skii, 17 October 1950, reports rumors that Baikalov organized the meeting between emigré General (and Soviet agent) N. V. Skoblin and Marshall M. N. Tukhachevskii which led to Tukhachevskii's demise in 1937.

48. Kautsky to Baikalov, 10 September 1931, BP, described the book as "good and useful" but invoked the "different political mentality in Germany and England."

49. Baikalov to Craigavon, 18 September 1950, BP. Correspondence with "Dear Healey" dating from 1948 suggests the two had met.

50. On 28 August 1948, BP, Baikalov confided to Malcolm Muggeridge, one of his longtime correspondents, that reliable sources informed him the Soviet invasion of Iran, Pakistan, and India was to take place as soon as the conquest of China had been completed.

51. M. Borukhov, "Povorot v amerikanskom rabochem dvizhenii," *Sv* 88, 20 September 1924.

52. "Iubileiskii s'ezd Arbeiter ringe v Amerike," *Sv* 105/106, 20 June 1925; Epstein, *Jewish Labor in USA, 1882–1914,* 309; "Nastroeniia rabochikh v Amerike," *Sv* 51/52, 16 March 1923.

53. R. Abramovich, "Tri mesiatsa v Amerike," *Sv* 105/106, 20 June 1925, and 107; also Epstein, The *Jew and Communism.*

54. Abramovich, "Tri mesiatsa v Amerike," *Sv* 105/106; Abramowitsch to Adler, 5 and 28 March 1925, SAI 2623; and "An Ofener Brief," *Veker,* 28 March 1925.

55. Abramovich, "Tri mesiatsa v Amerike," *Sv* 105/106, and Abramowitsch to Adler, 28 March 1925.

56. Abramowitsch to Adler, 28 March 1925, described the intercession of Roger Baldwin, New York City ACLU chairman.

57. *NYT,* 19 February 1925. The *Nation,* 4 March 1925, 238, also published a pro-Soviet article by Louis Fischer describing Mensheviks as "special offenders in lies

about Soviet Russia." Compare L. Fischer's encomiums for Nicolaevsky forty years later, *NYT Book Review,* 21 November 1965.

6. Stalin's Revolution

THE GREAT TURN

1. Reiman, *Birth of Stalinism,* 40. Contrast Schapiro, *Communist Party of the Soviet Union,* 365: "Not even the shrewdest observer at the Fifteenth Party Congress in December 1927 could have concluded that the Soviet Union was on the eve of a new social revolution." Also Ulam, *Stalin,* 293, who describes the program of the Fifteenth Congress as "reasonable."
2. Jasny, *Soviet Industrialization,* 51; Abramovitch, *Soviet Revolution,* 329. Compare *History of the CPSU (b),* 286–288.
3. D. Dalin, "Ot 'burnogo rosta' k promyshelennomu krizisu," *Sv* 124, 31 March 1926. Compare A. Iugov, "Litsemernaia politika," *Sv* 140, 20 November 1926.
4. [PR], "Moskovskiie nastroeniia," *Sv* 161, 7 October 1927.
5. [Ed], "Bor'ba s 'termidorom,'" *Sv* 165, 1 December 1927.
6. See for example, the appeal "Ko vsem sotsial-demokraticheskim rabochim Sovetskogo soiuza!" *Sv* 154, 20 June 1927.
7. Quoted from [PR], "Pis'mo provintsiala," *Sv* 165, 1 December 1927. [Ed], "Neotlozhnaia zadacha," ibid. On elite attitudes, see [PR], "Na kommunisticheskikh verkhakh," *Sv* 143, 15 January 1927.
8. *Pravda,* 14/15 September 1928, cited in [Ed], " 'Aktivizatsiia' kapitalizma," *Sv* 184, 27 September 1928; [Ed], "Politika kontsessii," *Sv* 186, 28 October 1928; F. Dan, "Osnovnoi vopros," *Sv* 188/189, 5 December 1928.
9. D. Dalin, "Na tom zhe meste," *Sv* 180, 23 July 1928; [Ed], "Politika primechanii," *Sv* 185, 13 October 1928. Also D. Dalin, "NEP i Anti-NEP," *Sv* 195, 8 March 1929, and "Itogi," *Sv* 200/201, 22 May 1929.
10. D. Dalin, "Bezrabotnost'," *Sv* 217, 8 February 1929. Compare A. Iugov, "Nazad k prodrazverstke," *Sv* 168/169, 6 February 1928.
11. See for example, Lewin, "Immediate Background of Soviet Collectivization," and Davies, "Socialist Market." On Trotsky, see Day, "Trotsky on Problems of Smychka and Forced Collectivization."
12. See Lewin and Davies essays cited in note 11 and Carr, "Revolution from Above." For an "intentionalist" critique of "functionalists," see Tucker, "Stalinism as Revolution from Above."
13. [PR], "Nakanune desiatiletiia (pis'mo iz Moskvy)," *Sv* 163/164, 10 November 1927. For the aftermath of the Fifteenth Congress, see [PR] "Stolpotvorenie vavilonsuoe," *Sv* 172, 21 March 1928; [Ed], "Anti-NEP," *Sv* 171, 6 March 1928. Day, Deutscher, Tucker, and Merl, *Agrarmarkt und Neue Okonomische Politik,* argue that Stalin's program was a travesty rather than an application of the left opposition's ideas. Contrast V. Voitinskii, "Ekonomicheskaia platforma oppozitsii," *Sv* 165, 1 December 1927.
14. [PR], *Sv* 172; [PR], *Sv* 185, 13 October 1928; and [PR], *Sv* 197/198, 12 April 1929. See Liebich, "Mensheviks in the Face of Stalinism."

15. R. Abramovich, "Sfinks Stalin," *Sv* 353, 10 November 1935, and *Soviet Revolution,* 320. Also [Ed], "Potselui Lamuretta," *Sv* 158/159, 20 August 1927.
16. Abramovich, untitled ms., 6–7, MP Archives.
17. Abramovitch, *Soviet Revolution,* 329, and N. Valentinov, "Iz proshlogo," *Sv* 752, April 1961.
18. A. Iugov, "Ot prodrazverstki k glavkam," *Sv* 206/207, 11 September 1929, and "Ekonomicheskie posledstviia otmeny NEPa," *Sv* 211, 7 November 1929.
19. [PR], "Moskva," *Sv* 215, 11 January 1930; [PR], "Moskva," *Sv* 211, 7 November 1929.
20. D. Dalin, "Neurezannyi kommunizm," *Sv* 216, 25 January 1930; [Ed], "Znamenitel'nyi s'ezd," *Sv* 151, 9 May 1927.
21. [Ed], "Pokazatel'nyi protsess," *Sv* 172, 21 March 1928; Dalin, "NEP i Anti-NEP," *Sv* 195.
22. [PR], "Moskva," *Sv* 142, 24 December 1926; [Ed], "Krest'ianskii orekh," *Sv* 167, 12 January 1928. The latter article claims that the Georgian insurrection of 1924 had forced the regime to give up its plans to de-kulakize at that time.
23. [Ed], "Pokazatel'nyi protsess," *Sv* 172, and Dalin, "Anti-NEP," *Sv* 195.
24. [PR], "Moskva," *Sv* 174/175, 3 May 1928, and *Sv* 181, 3 August 1928; [Ed], "Terror snizu," *Sv* 188/189, 5 December 1928. [PR], "Moskva," *Sv* 202, 14 June 1929, reports that Bukharin cited a figure of 270 Communists killed in the countryside during the month of March alone.
25. [PR], "Moskva," *Sv* 199, 4 May 1929; O. Domanevskaia, "Ot khlebnoi monopolii k meshechniku," *Sv* 200/201, 25 May 1929, and "Iubilei bez iubiliara?" *Sv* 204, 14 June 1929.
26. O, Domanevskaia, "Kollektivizatsiia sovetskoi derevni," *Sv* 210, 24 October 1929. Note that the Mensheviks never confused the problem of agricultural production with procurement, a confusion that fuels much of the Western debate about collectivization. See Liebich, "Russian Mensheviks and the Famine."
27. Domanevskaia, "Kollektivizatsiia sovetskoi derevni," *Sv* 210; O. Domanevskaia, "Piatiletnii plan v deistvii," *Sv* 215, 11 January 1930. Quote from [PR], "Moskva," *Sv* 211, 7 November 1929.
28. [Ed], "Malaia grazhdanskaia voina," *Sv* 211, 7 November 1929. Circular in [PR], "Moskva," *Sv* 218, 25 February 1930.
29. [PR], *Sv* 220/221, 12 April 1930.
30. [PR], *Sv* 233, 17 May 1930. Compare Viola, "Campaign To Eliminate the Kulak as a Class."
31. [PR], *Sv* 220/221, 12 April 1930; [Ed], "Okulachivanie i raskulachivanie," *Sv* 219, 15 March 1930; O. Domanevskaia, "Sud'by kollektivizatsii," *Sv* 228, 26 July 1930; S. Shvarts, "Sovkhoznaia metamorfoza," *Sv* 222, 26 March 1930; [Ed], "Voina za khleb," *Sv* 230, 30 August 1930.
32. [Ed], "Malaia grazhdanskaia voina," *Sv* 211. Quote from [Ed], "Po kraiu propasti," *Sv* 246, 25 October 1930; A. Iugov, "Sdvig psikhologii," *Sv* 195, 8 March 1929; A. Iugov, "Vsia vlast' direktoru," *Sv* 208, 27 September 1929.
33. Quote from [PR], "Moskva," *Sv* 212, 21 November 1929; [PR], signed "G.A.," *Sv* 208, 27 September 1929.

34. Quote from [Ed], "Bez perspektiv," *Sv* 170, 21 February 1928; O. Domanevskaia, "V prochnom krugu," *Sv* 167, 12 January 1928.
35. "G.A.," *Sv* 208; Domanevskaia, "V prochnom krugu," *Sv* 167.
36. [Ed], "Desiatiletie NEPa," *Sv* 244/245, 3 April 1931.

SOCIALIST DEBATES

1. A. Iugov, "Nekotorye itogi piatiletki," *Sv* 235, 11 November 1930.
2. "Darling, what more do you want?" Abramowitsch to L. Kautsky, 14 February 1926, KA, with reference to the German writer Emil Ludwig.
3. Kautsky, *Bolschewismus in der Sackgasse*, 7. See Salvadori, *Kautsky and the Socialist Revolution*, 251–318; Weber, "Russie soviétique et le 'pape du marxisme' Karl Kautsky"; the appeal "Maiskoe vozzvanie RSI," *Sv* 222, 26 April 1930; and "Sotsialisticheskii Internatsional sovetskim rabochim," *Sv* 223, 17 May 1930.
4. Garvi to Kautsky, 24 May 1930, KA G 15.
5. Kautsky, *Bolchevisme dans l'impasse*, v. Garvi to Kautsky, 16 July 1930, KA G 16. Kautsky heeded Garvi's advice and dropped these remarks. Woytinsky was also advising Kautsky.
6. Kautsky, *Bolchevisme dans l'impasse*, 17. See also Kautsky to Axelrod, 5 January 1925, in Dan, *Pis'ma*, 577.
7. Dan to Kautsky, 7 April 1930, *Pis'ma*, 394–396. Compare Tsereteli to Kautsky, 10 June 1930, KA 16.
8. Dan to Kautsky, 5 May 1929, 8 May and 24 August 1930, *Pis'ma*, 370–380, 403, 405–408.
9. Dan, "Probleme der Liquidationsperiode"; Abramowitsch, "Revolution und Konterrevolution in Russland."
10. Kautsky, "Sozialdemokratie und Bolschewismus," "Aussichten des Sozialismus in Russland," "Bolschewistische Kamel," "Aussichten des Fünfjahresplanes," "Demokratie und Diktatur." R. Abramovich, "Na tu zhe temu," *Sv* 242, 28 February 1931.
11. Adler, "Was täte ein Lenin heute zur Rettung der russischen Revolution?" and "Zur Diskussion über Sowjetrussland."
12. Kautsky to the Garvis, 1 May 1937, NC 18(53). On Potresov, see Dan, "Tua res agitur," 284. On relations with Bauer, see Dan, "Perspektivy general'noi linii." Compare Aksel'rod to Rozenfel'd, 7 January 1926, NC 15(498)
13. See Bauer, "Evropa i men'shevizm," *Sv* 100, 4 April 1925. On 1917, see Löw, *Otto Bauer*, 10.
14. Dan, "Perspektivy general'noi linii," 159. See also Kautsky to Tsereteli, 20 January 1928, NC 15(31).
15. Bauer, *Kapitalismus und Sozialismus nach dem Weltkrieg*, 1:204, 223. On the debate unleashed by Bauer, see Croan, "Politics of Marxist Sovietology"; Marramao, *Austromarxismo e socialismo di sinistra fra le due Guerre*, 32–38; and Gardoncini, "Sistema sovietico nel dibattito degli Austromarxisti."
16. R. Abramovich, "Piatiletka plius inkvizitsiia," *Sv* 246, 25 April 1931.
17. Abramowitsch, "Fünfjahresplan und Sozialdemokratie."

18. Dan, "Perspektivy general'noi linii," 156; Abramowitsch, "Fünfjahresplan und Sozialdemokratie," 39.

19. D. Dalin, "Vokrug piatiletki," *Sv* 249, 13 June 1931.

20. Bauer, "Zukunft der russischen Sozialdemokratie." Unattractive personal traits noted by Sturmthal, *Democracy under Fire*, 62, 174.

21. Adler, "Stalinsche Experiment und der Sozialismus."

22. Dan, "Zur sozial-ökonomishcen Entwicklung Russlands."

23. Abramowitsch, "Stalinismus oder Sozialdemokratie," 145.

24. Dan, "Neue Phase der Bolschewistichen Diktatur," and "Zur sozial-ökonomischen Entwicklung Russlands."

25. Bauer to Kautsky, in Bourdet, "Bauer et la Russie soviétique," 478.

26. [IP], "K 60-letiu F. I. Dana," *Sv* 259, 14 November 1931. E. Kuskova, "Fedor Il'ich Dan," *Novoe russkoe slovo*, 5 February 1947, recalled Dan's telling her in the 1930s that what was terrible about young Russian workers was that they did not care about freedom; indeed, they imagined that the sports and cultural parks with which the Bolsheviks had filled their heads were freedom.

27. Abramowitsch to Adler, 22 February 1930, SAI 2623.

28. Abramowitsch to Adler, 1 January 1926, SAI 2623.

29. Abramowitsch, "Revolution und Konterrevolution in Russland."

30. The Mensheviks continued to polemicize against foreign socialists. See, for example, Jugow, "Ergebnisse des Fünfjahresplans," and Abramowitsch, *Wandlungen der Bolschewistischen Diktatur*.

31. *PBO*, 17 February 1931. Abramovitch still considered failure more likely than success, but he considered only partial success (even a 10 percent survival rate for the *kolkhoz*es) enough. Note that Abramovitch is speaking even before Bauer's challenge.

32. Ibid.

33. "Tezisy oppozitsii," *Sv* 230, 30 August 1930, resuscitating Axelrod's old idea of "socialist intervention." Dan's reply in *PBO*, 17 February 1931.

34. G. Aronson, "Na novom etape," *Sv* 268, 16 April 1932; A. Potresov, "R. Abramovich protiv K. Kautskogo," *Dni*, 9 November 1930; S. Ivanovich, "Aforizmy," NC 23(65).

35. F. Dan, "K itogam diskussii," *Sv* 289/290, 4 March 1933; see also his "K problemam sotsial'no-ekonomicheskogo razvitiia SSSR," *Sv* 267, 26 March 1932, as well as "K mezhdunarodnoi diskussii o russkoi sotsial-demokratii," *Sv* 262/263, 23 January 1932.

36. S. Ivanovich, "Gosudarstvennyi kapitalizm i russkaia demokratiia," *Zapiski sotsial-demokrata* 14 (May 1932); and G. Aronson, "O mirovom goskapitalizme i o russkom krestianstve," *Sv* 280, 15 October 1932. Dan, too, had invoked this argument against Bauer.

37. Quote from *PBO*, 17 February 1931; Dvinov, *PBO*, 28 January 1932, pointed out that it was contradictory for Alexandrova to support the five year plan and to fight for the economic interests of the workers: "Any Red director can . . . fulfill the five year plan by violating the interests of the workers."

38. See G. Aronson, "Osnovnye linii nashikh raznoglasii," *Sv* 289/290, 4 March 1933.

39. See Liebich, *Marxism and Totalitarianism*.

THE MENSHEVIK TRIAL

1. Jansen, *Show Trial*, 153, 51, 58.

2. Cited in Berman, *Justice in the USSR*, 36.

3. D. Dalin, "Sotsial'nyi zakaz," *Sv* 208, 27 September 1929; [Ed], "Budni pala-chei," *Sv* 204, 14 June 1929.

4. A. Iugov, "Odin iz urokov," *Sv* 180, 23 July 1928. I. Grekov [=Dan], "Ekonom-icheskii espionazh," *Sv* 180, recalls Iugov's warning in 1925. On specialists, see [PR], *Sv* 214, 21 December 1929; [Ed], "Vreditel'skii navet," *Sv* 219, 15 March 1930.

5. [PR], "Aresty i ssylka," *Sv* 206/207, 11 September 1929. An anonymous socialist-Zionist to L. Dan, [1929/1930?], NC 25(688).

6. [Ed], "Posledniaia povestka," *Sv* 231/232, 27 September 1930. Trial predicted in [PR], "Moskva," *Sv* 235, 8 November 1930.

7. N. Popov, "Na reshaiushchim etape likvidatsii kulachestva," *Pravda*, 15 September 1930.

8. *Pravda*, 17 December 1930; M. Gorky in *Izvestiia*, 17 December 1930. Bitter retorts by R. Abramovich, "Klevetnikam sotsializma," *Sv* 238, 20 December 1930, and F. Dan, "Velichaishee prestupleniie," *Sv* 239, 9 January 1931.

9. F. Dan, "Velichaishee prestupleniie," *Sv* 239, 9 January 1931. Medvedev, *Let History Judge*, 270; [PR], "Moskva," *Sv* 239. Archival sources suggest that Stalin may have decided on the trial as late as February 1931. See the Politburo minutes dated 25 February 1931, f. 17 op. 3 d. 814, RTsKhIDNI.

10. On Garvi, see [Ed], "Gnusnaia zateia," *Sv* 241, 9 February 1931; LSI *Bulletin*, 21–23 February 1931; "Soviet Plans New 'Sabotage Trial,'" *NYT*, 25 January 1931; [PR], *Sv* 239, *Sv* 241, and *Sv* 242, 9 January, 9 February, 28 February 1931.

11. Braude described by Cummings, *Moscow Trial*, 19. During the "Industrial Party" trial Abramovitch ironically suggested that if the prosecutor wanted information on Menshevik policy during the Civil War, he should call on Vyshinskii as witness. R. Abramovich, "Klevetnikam sotsializma," *Sv* 238, 20 December 1930. See also Medvedev, *Let History Judge*, 378.

12. Lenin himself often mentioned Sukhanov, sometimes positively; see Jasny, *Soviet Economists*, 181. Gul', *Ia unes Rossiiu*, 1:289, cites reports by the writer Konstantin Fedin that confiscation of Sukhanov's diaries launched the Menshevik trial.

13. See Jasny, *Soviet Economists*, and above all, *Protsess kontrrevoliutsionnoi organizatsii men'shevikov*.

14. Solzhenitsyn, *Gulag Archipelago*, 1:400, is not convincing. Why would a twelve-year-old boy have read the records "line by line" if "the whole performance" was a "yawning bore"? How could he tell that the "actors spoke their lines with-

out enthusiasm," given that the Menshevik trial, unlike others, was not transmitted by radio?

15. Ibid., 113.
16. Ibid., 29.
17. Ibid., 30–35, summarizes these charges, detailed in the testimony.
18. Ibid., 355. On Groman, see Jasny, *Soviet Economists*, 89–90. For a critical view of Jasny's claims on Groman's behalf, see Schlesinger, "Context of Early Soviet Planning."
19. Cited in Jasny, *Soviet Economists*, 99. Groman was then in charge of consumer goods distribution in Petrograd.
20. Jasny, *Soviet Economists*, 34, 110, and 49. Denunciation of the theory of the declining growth rate curve was encouraged by the fact that, initially, statistics disproved it. V. A. Bazarov, Groman's close associate, corrected the theory to state that growth rate curves would begin to decline when the Soviet economy had reached prewar output, not prewar capacity.
21. Jasny, *Soviet Economists*, 116–118, 90.
22. *Protsess*, 355–360.
23. Least punished were Teitelbaum, because of ill health, and Volkov, the only defendant of working-class origin. Finn-Enotaevskii, presented as a woolly academic, was the only defendant to express reservations about his own guilt, and his sentence was harsher than the prosecutor's recommendation.
24. On Kondratiev, father of long-term cycle theory, see Jasny, *Soviet Economists*, 65 and 158–178. Ikov testified that letters were written in invisible ink on the margins of German newspapers sent to him at his office. "Chto oni 'vypuskaiut'?" *Sv* 243, 14 March 1931.
25. *Protsess*, 66 and 103.
26. *Protsess*, 38, and Jasny, *Soviet Economists*, 82.
27. A. Shifrin, "Sudebnaia lozh'," *Sv* 244/245, 3 April 1931.
28. *Protsess*, 59, 21, 67, 89.
29. R. Abramovich, "Moia poezdka v Moskvu i 'Protsess 14,'" *Sv* 243, 14 March 1931.
30. After three years in the *politisolator* of Suzdal, Eva Broido was sent to Tashkent and, on the expiration of her term, exiled to the Mongolian border. She was rearrested, tried twice by a military tribunal, and shot in September 1941 in Orlov prison. In the 1930s the LSI led a vigorous but unsuccessful campaign to obtain the release of this revolutionary grandmother, whose health had been terribly affected by her travails. See "Case of Eva Broido," *International Information*, 24 January 1936; the William Gillies Papers, Labour Party Archives; V. Broido-Cohn to author, 22 June 1996. Eva Broido's memoirs are *V riadakh RSDRP*.
31. [Ed], "Gde M. A. Braunshtein?" *Sv* 243, 14 March 1931, and "Sudebnaia lozh'." See also Jasny, *Soviet Economists*, 78. [PR], "K protsessu '14,'" *Sv* 246, 25 April 1931, reported conflicting accounts as to whether Braunshtein was still alive. V. Broido, *Lenin and the Mensheviks*, 105, writes that Eva Broido was brought to Moscow during the preparations for the trial, but the dates she gives do not tally.

32. [PR], "K protsessu '14,'" *Sv* 246, and [PR], "Protsess men'shevikov," *Sv* 259, 14 November 1931.

33. Abramovich to Vol'skii, 24 December 1954, VC; *Protsess,* 229.

34. [PR], "Protsess men'shevikov," *Sv* 259.

35. Interviewer is B. Wolfe, "D'authentiques mencheviks au procès menchevik" (1956), Bertram Wolfe Papers 51, Hoover Institution. Iugov to Abramovich, 29 March 1930, AA, identifies Dallin and Nicolaevsky as the skeptics blocking such initiatives.

36. Nikolaevskii to Vol'skii, 28 January 1956, VC; [PR], "Moskva," *Sv* 235, 8 November 1930.

37. Schwarz cited in Wolfe, "D'authentiques mencheviks," 59. Jasny, *Soviet Economists,* 3, sees the menshevism of the defendants as simply "a mode of thought" but describes the 1920s (Menshevik) economic opposition within Russia as the domestic equivalent of the (Menshevik) political opposition abroad.

38. *Protsess,* 362.

39. *Protsess,* 115–120. Some of the defendants challenged Dan and Abramovitch to come before the Moscow court, a proposition which the Foreign Delegation actually considered but rejected. "Postanovlenie ZD RSDRP," *Sv* 243, 14 March 1931.

40. Iakubovich in Medvedev, *Let History Judge,* 274–279. Solzhenitsyn, *Gulag Archipelago,* 404, notes acidly that Iakubovich hated Abramovitch but praised Krylenko. Medvedev, *Let History Judge,* 273, defends Iakubovich against this charge.

41. Medvedev, *Let History Judge,* 280–284. [PR], "K protsessu '14,'" *Sv* 246, reports rumors of hypnosis. N. V. Valentinov, "Iz proshlogo," *Sv* 752 (April 1961).

42. Medvedev, *Let History Judge,* 279, 277. Was it out of consideration for the defendants' sensitivity that indictments claimed that money from abroad was spent on non-Mensheviks who could not be politically motivated? *Protsess,* 37.

43. L. Blum, "L'odieux procès de Moscou," *Populaire,* 5 March 1931.

44. [Ed], "Udar po rabochemu klassu," *Sv* 242, 28 February 1931.

45. Jasny, *Soviet Economists,* 5, writes of the trial's extremely valuable information.

46. [PR], "Koe chto o men'shevistskom protsesse 1931g," *Sv* 405/406, 25 January 1938; *Protsess,* 30–33; [PR], "Moskva," *Sv* 238, 20 December 1930.

47. [PR], "Moskva," *Sv* 238; *Protsess,* 68.

48. On specialists, see A. Shifrin, "Konets reformistskoi linii," *Sv* 239, 9 January 1931; [PR], "Moskva," *Sv* 214, 21 December 1931. Old Bolshevik in "Protsess men'shevikov," *Sv* 259, 14 November 1931. *Protsess,* 362 (syntax is the defense counsel's).

49. K. Radek, "Puti men'shevizma," *Izvestiia,* 9 March 1931; *Protsess,* 368.

50. N. Popov, "Na reshitel'nym etape" *Pravda,* 15 September 1930; *Protsess,* 86.

51. On Strumilin, see Jasny, *Soviet Economists,* 71. On the exchange of insults between Stalin and Riazanov at the Fourth Congress of Trade Unions in 1921, see Medvedev, *Let History Judge,* 34; Denike, interview 19. Wolfe, who knew Riazanov, writes in "D'authentiques mencheviks," 52, that Krylenko did not dare confront Riazanov's "imposing stature, thundering voice, fiery temperament and irresistible irony." Politburo discussion of Riazanov, dated 5 February 1931, in f. 17 op. 3 d. 814, RTsKhIDNI.

52. Medvedev, *Let History Judge*, 132–139. Rubin told the court he had given Riazanov incriminating documents in a *sealed* envelope, and when asked to confirm that there was an organizational tie between them, he replied that there was "only great personal trust." Rubin's *History of Economic Thought* and *Essays on Marx's Theory of Value* have recently been republished in English translation.

53. See Ginzburg's testimony about Lidia Kantsel's (= L. Dan) planned trip to Moscow to hand over Martov's archive. The Soviet interlocutor he refused to name could only have been Riazanov. See also *Protsess*, 79. *Vestnik's* political obituary for Riazanov called him "an honest man, although a political opponent." L-ch, "Prestuplenie i nakazanie," *Sv* 243, 14 March 1931.

54. "Prigovor prinesen," *Izvestiia*, 10 March 1931. A. Semenov, "Russkie men'sheviki. Interventsiia 1918 g.," *Krasnaia zvezda*, 28 February 1931.

55. *Protsess*, 70, 43, 345.

56. Telegram in *Protsess*, 115. "Protiv fashizma i bol'shevistskoi klevety," *Sv* 243, 14 March 1931; also, *Sv* 244/245, 3 April 1931; note that the Berlin meeting was against fascism as well.

57. L. Trotskii, "Problemy razvitiia SSSR," *Biulleten' oppozitsii* 20 (April 1931), and note to "B.S.," "Iz pis'ma tovarishcha," *Biulleten' oppozitsii* 51 (July–August 1936).

58. "Istina vostorzhestvovala," *Sv* 256, 26 September 1931; "Soviet Plot Charge Branded as False," *NYT*, 28 February 1931.

59. Two defendants were members of a committee in memory of Dzerzhinskii at the time of their arrest. G. Aronson, "Posle protsessa," *Sv* 244/245, 3 April 1931.

60. Solzhenitsyn, *Gulag Archipelago*, 406. Iakubovich presents the theory of a triptych-like operation for the sake of balance. See Medvedev, *Let History Judge*, 274.

61. "Da zdravstvuet sotsialdemokratiia." This theory would account for the failure to hold the "Toiling Peasant Party" trial. Some questions may find answers in the Commissariat of Justice's extensive files on the trial, "Delo kontr revoliutsionnoi orgnizatsii soiuznoe biuro RSDRP (men'sheviki)," f. 9474 op. 7 d. 448–461, GARF. These files have been transferred to the Supreme Court, however, presumably in connection with a rehabilitation procedure, and, as of August 1995, were still unavailable.

62. "Da zdravstvuet sotsialdemokratiia", [IP], "Iskliuchenie iz partii," *Sv* 257, 10 October 1931.

63. "Truth Will Out," *International Information*, 5 May 1934. Wolfe, "D'authentiques mencheviks," 54.

64. On boycott and application, see [PR], "V sovetskoi tiur'me i ssylke," *Sv* 365, 10 May 1936; "Sud'ba V. G. Gromana, I. I. Rubina i N. N. Sukhanova," *Sv* 696 (August 1956).

65. [PR], "Iz pis'ma," *Sv* 244/245, 3 April 1931, reports a pamphlet distributed by the RSDRP in Tiflis. Rumors in "T.A.," "O sud'be A. Gotsa i M. Gendel'mana," *Sv* 637 (October 1950).

66. Even finding writing supplies was impossible: they could be obtained only by

theft from one's workplace, and this was the least hazardous part of the operation. [PR], "Moskva," *Sv* 250, 2 July 1931.

7. Hard Times

LIFE IN FRANCE

1. Dan to Adler, 7 August 1932, SAI 2597; Nikolaevskii to Vulikh, 22 July and 11 August 1932, NC 134(207); Iugov to Viliatser, 14 December 1932, NC 75(130).
2. Estrin, "Vospominaniia" (3), 11, NC 136(208). Headline in *Sv* 289/290. Aleksinskii, "Transfer de centre menchévik russe de Berlin à Paris," 7 March 1933, F 13505, Archives nationales, Paris. Dan had advanced his departure after learning that the Nazi *Völkische Beobachter* had referred to him several times as a "harmful personality." Dan, *Pis'ma*, 440.
3. Sandvoss, *Wiederstand in einem Arbeiterbezirk*, 27; Haimson, ed., *Making of Three Russian Revolutionaries*, 396.
4. Iugov to Viliatser, 9 February 1933, NC 75(130); Dan to Kautsky, 17 September 1937, *Pis'ma*, 494; Abramowitsch to Adler, 26 December 1933, AA 1. On Schwarz's arrest and release, see Abramowitsch to Adler, 24 March 1933 and 12 April 1933, AA 1. Dalin to Abramovich, 3 January 1936 AA 4/1.
5. ZD to Russia, 26 February 1932, NC 25; Iugov (treasurer) to Viliatser, 21 September and 14 December 1932, NC 75(130).
6. *Izvestiia*, 22 February 1932. Compare F. Dan, "Withdrawal of Civil Rights," *International Information*, 27 February 1932. Vulikh to Nikolaevskii, 26 February 1932, NC 134(207). The Mensheviks' Soviet passports had not been renewed since 1927.
7. Iugov to Viliatser, 20 March 1931, NC 75(130).
8. Abramovich to Dalin, 7 July [1931?], AA 1; Nikolaevskii to Vulikh, 11 March 1932, NC 134(207).
9. Quoted from Strauss, *Jewish Immigrants*, 126. On Raeff, see Dan, *Pis'ma*, 443n5, and *Sv* 637, October 1950. On DOSSE (Documentation de statistique sociale et économique), see *International Information*, 28 December 1937. On Gurland, who also translated some of Domanevskaia's and Iugov's books, see Emig and Zimmerman, "A. Gurland."
10. Dan, *Pis'ma*, 504n1; Abramovich to Viliatser, 6 April 1936, AA 4/2; Nikolaevskii to Vulikh, 11 June 1934, NC 134(207).
11. Abramovich to Hillquit, 30 March 1933, AA 1/1; Nikolaevskii to Vulikh, 6 December 1935, NC 134(207); G. Aronson, "Anatolii Dubya," *Novoe russkoe slovo*, 11 November 1958; Nikolaevskii to Baikalov, 6 June 1934, BP, and to Vulikh, 19 January 1934, NC134(207).
12. Abramovich to ?, 19 December 1933, AA 1/1; Dan to Garvi, 22 February 1937 NC 18(53).
13. Abramovich to Stein, 6 August 1936, AA 4/2; to Shaw, 20 April 1934, Gillies Papers, Labour Party Archives; to Jasny, 13 July 1933, AA 4/1.

14. Nikolaevskii to Vulikh, 6 December 1935, NC 134(207); idem to Spalding, 14 May 1937 and others, Spalding Collection, Hoover Institution. Ivanovich to Ingerman, 1 February 1928, NC 23(63).

15. On Jasny, see Voitinskii to the Garvis, June 1938, NC18(53); Estrin, "Vospominaniia"; Voitinskii to the Garvis, 31 August 1936, 30 June 1937, June 1938 NC 18(53).

16. Abramowitsch, correspondence with Danish party, 15 November to 21 December 1933, AA 1/1; Abramowitsch to Adler, 14 June 1933, AA 1/1; Nikolaevskii to Vulikh, 11 June 1933, NC 134(207). Rumors circulated that Nicolaevsky had kept the best books for himself. A. and L. Kisselgoff, interview.

17. Quoted from Abramowitsch to the Kautskys, 7 January 1935, KA DI; Hillquit to Abramovich, 21 April 1933, AA 1/1; Abramowitsch to Adler, 24 December 1934, AA 2/1.

18. Abramowitsch to the Kautskys, 9 November 1935, KA DI; and to Levitas, 6 April 1936, AA 4/1. On Zionism, see Abramowitsch to the Kautskys, 7 January 1935; and to Viliatser, 17 July 1936, AA 1/1. Also R. Abramovich, "Amerika 1935," *Sv* 343, 10 June 1935, and "Amerika v 1935-om godu," *Sv* 345, 10 July 1935.

19. Nikolaevskii to Vulikh, 31 July 1934.

20. Quoted from Abramowitsch to Adler, 1 November 1934, AA; Dan to L. Kautsky, 22 January 1934, *Pis'ma*, 443. Garvi found himself repeatedly forced to justify his behavior in Odessa, Garvi to Rozenfel'd, n.d. [end 1934], NC 18(53).

21. Dan's adoption of a "Great Russian" position occasioned the break with Tsereteli, See Roobol, *Tsereteli*, 242–249. Quotes from Nikolaevskii to Vulikh, 11 June 1933, 1 February 1935; also 23 October, 20 December 1933, 19 January 1934, NC 134(207).

22. Dalin to Abramovich, 11 May 1934; and to Nikolaevskii and Abramovich, 3 January 1936, AA 4/1. As late as March 1934 Dallin still seems to have been undecided whether to move right or left. Nikolaevskii to Vulikh, 30 March 1934, NC134(207). Dallin did not contribute to *Sv* after January 1933 (until 1940), and he resigned sometime before mid-September 1935, but his resignation does not appear to have been publicized. See Abramovich to Levitas, 14 September 1935, AA 4/2.

23. Abramowitsch to Adler, 1 November 1934, AA 2/1; Nikolaevskii to Vulikh, 11 June and 23 October 1933; Dan to Adler, 12 and 20 December 1937, *Pis'ma*, 500–503.

24. Nikolaevskii to Vulikh, 1 February 1935; Edinger, *German Exile Politics*, 54; Breitscheid in Stampfer, *Mit dem Gesicht nach Deutschland*, 226. The Mensheviks did use offices in the *Populaire* building.

25. Abramowitsch to Kautsky, 7 January 1935. German accounts consider these Russians full-fledged German socialists. See *Biographisches Handbuch der deutschsprachigen Emigration*.

26. Scholing, "Georg Decker"; and see Freyberg, *Sozialdemokraten und Kommunisten*.

27. In addition to numerous articles in the SPD's *Zeitschrift für Sozialismus*, note Bienstock, *Struggle for the Pacific*; Schifrin, *Aufmarsch zum zweiten Weltkrieg* and (as "Max Werner") *Military Strength of the Fighting Powers*.

28. Verdier, "Oreste Rosenfeld," recounts that Rosenfeld was a social democrat at thirteen, that he was expelled from school and imprisoned for political agitation at fifteen, and that he was set to be deported to Siberia when war broke out. There is no separate confirmation of this information, which is plausible as far as it goes, except that a political deportee was not likely to have been commissioned as an officer in the tsarist army in 1914. See also Rozenfel'd to L. Dan, 20 May 1958, L. Dan Archive VI/22; Aksel'rod to Tsereteli, 18 February 1925, NC 15(29).

29. Verdier, "Oreste Rosenfeld"; Rozenfel'd to Iugov, 18 March 1926, NC 25(688); Aksel'rod to Tsereteli, 18 November 1926 NC 15(29). Verdier places the appointment as editor in 1932, but *International Information*, 20 June 1936, confirms it took place when Blum resigned his editorship to become prime minister.

30. L. Blum, "L'odieux procès de Moscou," *Populaire*, 5 March 1931. Jean Longuet, Marx's grandson and Rosenfeld's predecessor as foreign editor at *Populaire*, wrote to Rosenfeld, "I suppose that Blum has returned to Hasségur but that he calls you every evening from there?" Longuet to Rosenfeld, 30 August 1938, NC 21(60). See also Duhamel and Racine, "Léon Blum," 136–137, and Ziebura, *Léon Blum*, 252.

31. Nikolaevskii to Vulikh, 16 June 1934, NC 134(207), continues, "But he is still working as before, carrying the whole editorial work on his shoulders."

32. Tirade cited in Colton, *Leon Blum*, 144. B. Souvarine, "Léon Blum," *L'Express*, 10 July 1981, is at pains to state that Rosenfeld was "Greek Orthodox, as his Greek baptismal name indicated, contrary to what one might think because of his Germanic surname." Lacouture, *Léon Blum*, 572, also feels compelled to state that Rosenfeld was not Jewish.

33. On Rosenfeld as chameleon, see Bourguina, interview 2; Aksel'rod to Tsereteli, n.d. 1926, NC15(29). On "Dan's double," see Kerenskii, "Tainy Danovskogo men'shevizma," cited in *Sv* 203, 1 July 1929.

34. Dan, *Pis'ma*, 486.

CONTACTS

1. Abramovich to Vorriuk, 6 February 1936, AA 4/1; Viliatser to Dubinskii, 30 April 1939, NC 75(130).

2. G. Aronson, "Agenty NKVD v emigratsii," *Novoe russkoe slovo*, 30 March 1964.

3. Ibid.

4. ZD to Russia, 26 September 1937, NC 25(687).

5. Aronson, "Agenty NKVD," refers to a commendation of Semon Grigorevich Godes in *Pravda*, 27 April 1940. Correspondence with Nikolai Petrovich, in code and invisible ink, in NC 25(687).

6. Dan to Adler, 20 December 1937, *Pis'ma*, 503. Citation from Voytinskii to the Garvis, June 1938, NC 18(43); on attitudes toward Mensheviks, see Poretsky, *Our Own People*, 258.

7. Corrections to Krivitsky's claims by Reiss's widow in Poretsky, *Our Own People*, 148; and L. Dan, "Begstvo Krivitskogo," *in Iz Arkhiva L. O. Dan*, 122. According

to L. Dan, Krivitsky was indignant at the "general" title, claiming this had been inserted, like many other details, by an unscrupulous translator, probably Isaac Don Levine, but possibly Eugene Lyons.

8. Krivitsky, *I Was Stalin's Agent;* Dan, "Begstvo Krivitskogo," 117. See V. Krivitskii, "Begstvo ot Stalina," *Sv* 403/404, 24 December 1937, and "Dvoinaia bukhalteriia," *Sv* 409, 18 March 1938.

9. A. Tsiliga, "Stalinskie repressii v SSSR," *Biulleten' Oppozitsii* 47 (January 1936); [Ed], "Po povodu statei tov. Tsiliga," *Biulleten' Oppozitsii* 51 (July–August 1936); A. Tsiliga, "Pis'mo v redaktsiiu," *Sv* 387/398, 27 April 1937. Ciliga's first article, "Po sovetskim tiurmam i ssylkam," *Sv* 366, 27 May 1936, was prefaced with the editorial statement that "Comrade Tsiliga is a communist. His general evaluation therefore does not correspond with ours . . . [A]ll the more precious is his testimony about Soviet terror and the call for unity."

10. Fox, "Ante Ciliga, Trotskii, and State Capitalism," 132. On the meeting with Trotsky, see Pierre Broué to author, 9 December 1985. On Alexandrova, Garvy and Schapiro, interviews, and Schapiro, communication to author, 7 June 1984. On Lolla Estrine, see *Cahiers Léon Trotsky,* no. 9 (January 1982).

11. "Arkhiv Trotskogo u GPU," *Sv* 378, 25 November 1936; L. Yakovlev (=L. Ginzberg-Estrine), "Léon Sedov," *Cahiers Léon Trotsky,* no. 13 (March 1983), 56–61. See also Deutscher, *Prophet Outcast,* 347–349. Paris police files indicate that the initial suspect was Boris Souvarine, B A/1626, Préfecture de Police, Paris.

12. In an oral deposition given to Pierre Broué in 1980, Lolla Estrine did not mention her brother, R. I. Ginsburg, an active right wing Menshevik, but attributed Sedov's transfer to her sister-in-law, Fanny Trachtenberg, also a physician. Yakovlev, "Léon Sedov."

13. FBI-NY, 23 May 1956, NY 105–7490, FOIA.

14. H. Kasson (=David Dallin), "Zborowski Case," *NL,* 21 November 1955, and Dallin, "Mark Zborowski, Soviet Agent," *NL,* 19 and 26 March 1956. Margaret Mead, who sponsored Zborowski's professional career in the United States as a specialist on the east European Jewish shtetl, was equally skeptical of Zborowski's guilt. See S. Estrin, "Vospominaniia" (3), NC 136(208), 11, and *Cahiers Léon Trotsky,* no. 9 (January 1982). The biographical blurb to a recent edition of Zborowski's classic work actually introduces him as a victim of American McCarthyism. Zborowski and Herzog, *Olam.*

15. F. Dan, "Eshchë o istorii russkoi revoliutsii," *Sv* 286/287, 27 January 1933; Trotsky, *History of the Russian Revolution,* 144. See also McNeal, "Trotskyist Interpretations of Stalinism"; Lovell, *Trotsky's Analysis of Soviet Bureaucratization.*

16. D. Dalin, "Trotskii i Trotskiizm," *Sv* 192, 24 January 1929. A. Shifrin, "Trotskii i Trotskiizm," *Sv* 310, 10 January 1934. Shifrin was then active in the left wing German RSD.

17. P. Garvi, "Oppozitsiia nakanune parts'ezda," *Sv* 227, 12 July 1930. See also A. Potresov, "Lettre ouverte au camarade Vandervelde," supplement to *Zapiski Sotsialdemokrata* 18 (n.d.), provoked by the LSI president's expression of regret at the Belgian authorities' refusal to let Trotsky ashore in Antwerp, "knowing how you would have loved to see Rubens and early Flemish masters." *International Information* 7 (January 1933).

18. Dan, "Eshchë o istorii russkoi revoliutsii," *Sv* 286/287. "Trying to outdo Trotsky" was Nicolaevsky's reproach against Dan. Nikolaevskii to Vulikh, 2 March 1934, NC 134(207).

19. Quoted, respectively, from Souvarine, "Une controverse avec Trotski;" and Fox, "Ante Ciliga, Trotskii, and State Capitalism."

20. Trotskii to Sedov, 3 October 19(36?), B A/1626, Archives de la Préfecture de Police, Paris.

21. Van Heijenoort, *With Trotsky in Exile*, 39, writes that Trotsky's comunications with Russia ceased altogether in spring 1933, earlier with Moscow and Leningrad.

22. According to Estrin, "Vospominaniia" (3), 5, it was he himself (and his wife, Lolla) who persuaded Trotsky's son, Sedov.

23. Nikolaevskii to Vulikh, 7 August 1934, NC 134(207). On Sereni, see Boffa, interview. Three years later PCI leader Togliatti was barely able to rescue Sereni from the wrath of a Comintern commissar sent to Paris over this incident.

24. Souvarine to Volsky, n.d. [probably ca. 1959], SC, and the anonymous introduction, probably by Souvarine, to L. Dan's article "Boukharine, Dan et Staline," which credits French minister and Russophile Anatole de Monzie, and Souvarine himself, as the one who suggested the operation to de Monzie. It seems more likely that the plan was Nicolaevsky's and that Souvarine intervened with de Monzie at Nicolaevsky's request.

25. Mayer, "Geschichte des sozialdemokratischen Parteiarchivs." My account is based on this excellent source. It is not clear, however, that Mayer is correct in assuming that the 50.000 francs paid the Mensheviks (allowing them to cover their move from Berlin to Paris) refers to the Berlin library rather than the Menshevik Paris library on the rue des Gobelins, sold in this same period.

26. L. Czech [Czechoslovak social affairs minister] to Tsereteli, 8 May 1933, NC 15(29).

27. Directeur de la Bibliothèque-musée de la Guerre to Ministre de l'éducation nationale, 11 September 1933, L. Dan Archives VI/23.

28. Nikolaevskii to Vulich, 24 November 1933, 16 June 1934, 7 July 1934, NC 134(207). This "institution" was probably the École normale supérieure on the rue d'Ulm, or perhaps the Institut d'études slaves on the rue Michelet, where the archives later came to rest. In the interim, the archives had lodged in an international office of trade unions and in Nicolaevsky's own apartment.

29. Nicolaevsky to Hertz, 16 August 1935, cited by Mayer, "Geschichte des sozialdemokratischen Parteiarchivs," 104. Dan to Bauer, 25 September 1935, *Pis'ma*, 461. The Soviets proposed to exchange Dan's archive held by the Germans for Bismarck's letters in French hands and to return his archive without reading it. Why either France or Germany should have agreed to such a proposition or why the Soviets should have been considered appropriate intermediaries is not clear.

30. Dan to Bauer, 25 September 1935, *Pis'ma*, 461.

31. Dan to Adler, 18 January 1936, *Pis'ma*, 483.

32. Y.Z., "Kak podgotovlialsia moskovskii protsess? (Iz pis'ma starogo bol'shevika)," *Sv* 379/380, 22 December 1936, and *Sv* 381/382, 17 December 1937; trans. in Nicolaevsky, *Power and the Soviet Elite*. See Conquest, *Great Terror*, and *Stalin and the Kirov Murder*.

33. "Zaiavlenie redaktsii 'S.v.,' " *Sv* 736, December 1959. Among skeptical historians, see Slusser "Role of the Foreign Ministry," 221–222, and review of *Power and Soviet Elite*. For Nicolaevsky's admission, see *Novoe russkoe slovo*, 6 December 1959, and his *Power and the Soviet Elite*, 2–25.
34. L. Dan, "Boukharine, Dan et Staline," 200.
35. Boukharina, *Boukharine*, 275. Other challengers are Medvedev, *Let History Judge* and *Bukharin*; Getty, *Origins of the Great Purges*. Medvedev's challenge rests entirely on Bukharina's testimony. Getty confuses dates as well as the issue of the "Letter's" authenticity with that of Nicolaevsky's later assertion that Stalin had Kirov murdered. See Liebich, "I Am the Last."
36. For "gossip," see Rykov, cited by Boukharina, *Boukharine*, 112. For confirmations, see Reswick, *I Dreamt Revolution*, 325, and Malraux, *Chênes qu'on abat*, 216.
37. *Iz Arkhiva L. O. Dan*, 109n, 160.
38. The incongruous baptism was undertaken in a tsarist prison so that Larin could have an Orthodox marriage entitling him to take his bride into exile. See *Iz Arkhiva L. O. Dan*, 54–58.

THE TOTALITARIAN NEXUS

1. Quoted from Abramovich to Hillquit, 30 March 1933, AA 1/1. On secret channels, see Abramowitsch to Adler, 24 March 1933 AA 1/1.
2. Dan, "Vormarsch der deutschen Konterrevolution"; D. Dalin, "Serioznyi krizis," *Sv* 235, 8 November 1930. See also F. Dan "Krizis germanskogo gosudarstva," *Sv* 273, 26 June 1932; A. Shifrin, "Fashizm i Germania," *Sv* 227 12 July 1930, and his "Internationale und deutsche Krise."
3. Quip from Nolte, "Vierzig Jahre Theorien über den Faschismus," 15. Quote from V. Shvarts (Aleksandrova), *PBO*, 28 January 1932. For Italian contributions, see Zibordi, "Faschismus als antisozialistische Koalition"; Turati, "Faschismus, Sozialismus und Demokratie"; Kautsky, "Force and Democracy."
4. S. Sumskii, "Fashizm," *Sv* 59, 27 July 1923, drawing on. Olberg, "Ist der Faschismus eine Klassenbewegung?" Compare Menshevik economist Marschak, "Korporative und hierarchische Gedanke im Fascismus."
5. D. Dalin, "Fashistskaia volna," *Sv* 239, 240, 241, 9 and 24 January and 28 February 1931. Traits such as antisemitism and racism, claimed Dallin, were transitory aspects of fascism, and Abramovitch agreed that antisemitism was merely a form of anticapitalism. R. Abramovich, "Antisemitizm i fashizm," *Sv* 297, 10 July 1933.
6. B. Sapir, "Sotsialdemokratiia pered problemoi fashizma," *Sv* 294, 10 June 1933, published as Irlen, *Marx gegen Hitler*, with an introduction by Bienstock, who may well have been its inspiration. For critical reaction, see Dan to L. Kautsky, 22 January 1934, *Pis'ma*, 442.
7. The main spokesperson for the left wing was Olga Domanevskaia, whose "Na Putiakh reformizma," *Sv* 248, 23 May 1931, and "Bor'ba za sotsializm," *Sv* 297, 10 July 1933, crossed swords with *Vestnik*'s moderately left editorial board, [Ed],

"Ot redaktsii," *Sv* 248, and the right wing, P. Garvi, "Krizis mezhdunarodnoi sotsialdemokratii," *Sv* 295/296, 25 June 1933.

8. F. Dan, "O Zadachakh russkoi sotsialdemokratii," *Sv* 340, 25 April 1935; Schifrin, "Revolutionäre Sozialdemokratie," 81.

9. Dalin, "Fashistskaia volna," *Sv* 239; R. Abramovitch, "Meeting of the Commission of Enquiry into the Conditions of Political Prisoners," *International Information,* 23 August 1933; Irlen, *Marx gegen Hitler,* 9.

10. F. Dan, "Germanskaia katastrofa," *Sv* 293, 25 May 1933, replying to A. Potresov, "Revoliutsiia reaktsionnogo plebsa i germanskaia sotsial-demokratiia," *Zapiski sotsialdemokrata* 19 (1933), and Dan's reply to Turati's speech at the 1928 LSI Brussels Congress. For early right wing views, see I. Talin (=S. Ivanovich), "Lenin, Horti, Mussolini," *Zaria* 8 (1922): 248. The theme of bolshevism as a model for Italian fascism appeared regularly, even among mainstream Mensheviks, for example, Abramowitsch, *Politische Gefengenen in der Sowjetunion,* 9.

11. Bauer, "Gleichgewicht der Klassenkräfte."

12. Schmitt, "Weiterentwicklung des totalen Staats in Deutschland"; Radkau, *Deutsche Emigration in den USA,* 226. Fisichella, *Analisi del totalitarismo,* 18–19.

13. Irlen, *Marx gegen Hitler,* 25–26.

14. F. Dan, "Puti vozrozhdeniia," *Sv* 370/371, 14 August 1936; Bauer, *Zwischen zwei Weltkriegen,* 207; Trotsky, *Revolution Betrayed,* 100.

15. Weber, "Théorie du stalinisme," 63, incorrectly states that "the concept of totalitarianism is then [in the mid-1930s] current in the Marxist literature." He quotes Trotsky and Bauer but without quotation marks and, in the latter case, inaccurately.

16. R. Gil'ferding, "Gosudarstvennyi kapitalizm ili totalitarnoe gosudarstvennoe khoziaistvo?" *Sv* 460, 25 April 1940. Weber, "Théorie du stalinisme," 75, erroneously attributes to Kautsky's texts of the 1930s the influence of Hilferding's article written in 1940, after Kautsky's death. Schlangen's excellent study *Totalitarismus Theorie* misdates Hilferding's article by three years. A judicious evaluation is Jänicke, *Totalitäre Herrschaft.*

17. R. Worrall, "USSR: Proletarian or Capitalist State?" *Left* 39 (December 1939), translated in *Sv* 459, 11 April 1940.

18. As his article, published under the pseudonym R. Kern, put it, "Totaler Staat, totaler Bankerott," *Neuer Vorwärts* 7, 30 July 1933. Hilferding's doubts were expressed in the posthumously published "Das historische Problem." His disappointment at the lack of democratic passion among German workers is emphasized by his intimate associate A. Shifrin, "Rudolf Gil'ferding," *Np* 11/12, 26 October 1941. See also Gottschalch, *Strukturveränderungen der Gesellschaft und politisches Handeln in der Lehre von Rudolf Hilferding,* and Stein, *Rudolf Hilferding und die deutsche Arbeiterbewegung.*

19. Sapir to author, 24 June 1985. The title of Hilferding's journal was *Die Gesellschaft* (The Society).

20. On Shifrin in the exiled SPD left wing, see Freyberg, *Sozialdemokraten und Kommunisten;* Decker (=Denike), "Aufstand der Gescheiterten."

21. Matthias, *Sozialdemokratie und Nation,* 176–178.

22. Nikolaevskii to S. Garvi, 16 March 1940, NC 18(53). Hilferding was the most frequent visitor to Nicolaevsky's lodgings. "Au sujet du cambriolage du 7 novembre," B A/ 1626, Archives de la Préfecture de Police, Paris.

23. B. Nikolaevskii, "O klassovoi strukture totalitarnykh gosudarstv," *Sv* 471, 26 March 1941 and *Sv* 471 (sic), 12 April 1941; "Teoreticheskoe zaveshchanie R. Gil'ferdinga," *Sv* 593/594, January–February 1947; B. Goldenberg, "Kriticheskie zamechaniia k statee R. Gil'ferdinga," *Sv* 587/588, 20 April 1946; and B. Dvinov, "Sosial'naia baza komfashizma," *Sv* 590, 23 October 1946.

24. Hilferding's article reprinted in *Sv* 585, 22 May 1946. English version in *Modern Review* 1, no. 4 (1947). Extracts in Hook, *Marx and the Marxists*. French version in *Revue socialiste*, 16 December 1947, with translation of Nikolaevskii's "Teoreticheskoe zaveshchanie." See also Liebich, *Marxism and Totalitarianism*.

PURGES AND POLITICS

1. P. Garvi, "Demokraticheskoe obnovlenie," *Sv* 391, 12 June 1937.

2. For the "intentionalist" interpretation, stressing Stalin's person and initiative, see Conquest, *Great Terror*. For the revisionist or "functionalist" challenge, see Getty, *Origins of the Great Purges,* insisting on lower-level, discrete, and unplanned bureaucratic processes.

3. The "Letter," first published in *Sv* 1936–37, has been discussed earlier in this chapter. Contrary to the now established consensus among Russian and Western historians, Adam Ulam argues authoritatively that there is simply no proof of Stalin's guilt, as the chairman of the Soviet special commission into the matter under Mikhail Gorbachev had to confess. Ulam to author, 31 August 1992

4. Nicolaevsky, *Power and the Soviet Elite*, 34, 44.

5. On Riutin, see [Ed], "Pravil'no," *Sv* 217, 8 February 1930; P. Garvi, "Sluchai Riutina," *Sv* 234, 25 October 1930; [PR], "Pis'mo 18 bol'shevikov," *Sv* 278/279, 26 September 1932. *Sv* apparently had access to the appeal "Ko vsem chlenam VKP(b)" rather than to the longer and more problematic document attributed by some to Riutin alone; see Borshchagovskii, "Martemian Riutin—sotsialn'nyi myslitel'." On foreign policy, see [PR], *Sv* 311, 25 January 1934. On the congress, see [PR], *Sv* 313, 25 February 1934; also Conquest, *Stalin and Kirov Murder*, 27–30.

6. [Pis'mo iz Moskvy], "Blizhaishee okruzhenie diktatora," *Sv* 308, 25 November 1933; [PR], *Sv* 317, 25 April 1934. Conquest, *Stalin and Kirov Murder,* 26, cites the same issue of *Sv* as saying that Kirov had become more conciliatory, but the only reference to Kirov there says the opposite. D'Agostino, *Soviet Succession Struggles*, 143, points out the hard-liberal discrepancy.

7. [PR], *Sv* 330, 10 November 1934, and [PR], *Sv* 332, 20 December 1934. The only reference to a period of liberalism before the Kirov murder, as argued by Getty, *Origins of the Great Purges,* comes in a retrospective remark about "optimists who could see evidence of a softening of the regime," contained in a letter from Russia, 19 November 1935, NC 25(687), probably written by the provocateur Nikolai Petrovich, discussed earlier.

8. [PR], *Sv* 332.

9. L.T. [=Trotskii], "Vse stanovitsia postepenno na svoe mesto," *Biulleten' Oppozitsii* 42 (February 1935); [PR], *Sv* 431, 17 February 1939.

10. Nikolaevskii to Baikalov, 13 January 1935, BP. B. Nikolaevskii, "Stalin i ubiistvo Kirova," *Sv* 693, 698, 700 (May, October, December 1956); "Stalin i Kirov: eshche raz o konflikte 1932–4 gg.," *Sv* 704 (April 1956); and "Eshche o Staline i Kirove," *Novoe russkoe slovo*, 6 December 1959. See also Nicolaevsky, *Power and the Soviet Elite*, 69–104.

11. *Sv* 333, 10 January 1935; "New Wave of Terror in Soviet Union," *International Information*, 26 January 1935.

12. *Sv* 333; [PR], *Sv* 337/338, 23 March 1935; *International Information*, 7 December 1935; Abramowitsch to Adler, 8 May 1936, with manuscript "Immer wieder Terror gegen Sozialisten in Russland," LSI 2623. On Broido, see *International Information*, 24 January and 11 February 1936.

13. On Stalin, see [PR], *Sv* 337/338; and *Sv* 348, 25 August 1935. On attitudes, see [PR], *Sv* 351, 10 October 1935, and [PR], *Sv* 376, 28 October 1936.

14. [PR], "Neobkhodimo perestroit'sia." *Sv* 387/388, 27 April 1937. Compare Thurston, "Fear and Belief in the USSR's 'Great Terror,' " dating generalized fear from August 1937. On odiousness, see [PR], *Sv* 374/375, 10 October 1936. On "no-goods," [PR], *Sv* 386, 25 March 1937.

15. R. Abramovich, "Zagadka moskovskogo protsesa," *Sv* 372, 30 August 1936; L. Brouckère, *International Information*, 21 August 1936; Adler, *Witchcraft Trial in Moscow*. Dan wanted an LSI protest demonstration against the Zinoviev trial of August 1936; see Bauer to Dan, 19 August 1936, SAI 2616.

16. F. Adler, "Another Witchcraft Trial," *International Information*, 3 February 1937; "Protest against Moscow Slanders," *International Information*, 10 March 1938.

17. Abramovich to Viliatser, 11 September 1936, AA 4/2; Abramowitsch to SOPADE, 3 September 1936. AA 4/1.

18. [Ed], "Na vershine," *Sv* 228, 26 July 1930; [PR], *Sv* 307, 10 November 1933.

19. S. Schwarz, "Destruction of Old Bolshevism," *International Information*, 12 February 1937; F. Dan, "Politicheskii krizis Sovetskogo Soiuza," *Sv* 384, 25 February 1937; Abramowitsch to Sopade, 3 September 1936. At the time of the Riutin Platform, Trotsky was indeed in contact with former opposition leaders of all tendencies in the Soviet Union with a view to creating a "bloc," as shown by Broué, "Trotsky et le bloc des oppositions de 1932." Broué adds, "What would it have served to recognize in 1938 the existence of an ephemeral bloc in 1932? Historical truth perhaps, but it could wait" (29). See also Joubert, "L'affaire Kirov commence en 1934."

20. For example, Balticus (=V. Sukhomlin), "Russian Mystery;" explained the Tukhachevskii purge in terms of the army's pro-German orientation and supported his argument by drawing heavily on the "Letter of an Old Bolshevik" and quoting *Sv*. In fact, his quotation is nowhere to be found in the issue of *Vestnik* cited. Rather, the Mensheviks invoked Voroshilov's (and Stalin's) rivalry with Tukhachevskii dating from the Civil War, as well as the Red Army's identification with the peasantry and other factors. See [PR], *Sv* 394/395, 11 August

1937. [PR], *Sv* 339, 10 April 1935, suggests that war anxiety may have been greater among the general population than among the elite.

21. Abramowitsch to Kautsky, 25 February 1937, KA D/1. [PR], *Sv* 211, 7 November 1929, speaks of "nepreryvnaia chistka" (the uninterrupted purge).

22. [PR], *Sv* 372, 30 August 1936, reiterated in [Ed], "Prisiaga Stalinu," *Sv* 389, 14 May 1937. R. Abramovich, "Pered novym protsessom?" *Sv* 377, 10 November 1936. P. Garvi, "Udar na levo i na pravo," *Sv* 381/382, 17 January 1937, predicted a trial involving an "amalgamation of right and left." Aronson to Lesin, 11 March 1938, YIVO, predicted a trial for Jews.

23. [Ed], "Prigovor bol'shevizmu," *Sv* 383, 11 February 1937, and "Novaia boinia v Moskve," *Sv* 409, 18 March 1938.

24. Souvarine and Volsky were the main partisans of the "mad Stalin" thesis. See Liebich, "Mensheviks in the Face of Stalinism."

25. Quoted from Abramowitsch to Kautsky, 25 February 1937, KA D/1. On the future "Koestler explanation," see Abramowitsch to Adler, 8 May 1936, LSI 2623; and Schwarz, "Destruction of Old Bolshevism." Also Löw, *Bauer und die Russische Revolution*, 270–271.

26. S. Grammatikopulos, "K Zagadkakh moskovskikh protsessov," *Sv* 431; 17 February 1939. Kolakowski, *Main Currents of Marxism*, 3:84, attributes the first variant regarding Vyshinskii to Isaac Deutscher; for the second variant, see Berger, *Shipwreck of a Generation*.

27. For "prophylactic," see [PR], *Sv* 379/380, 22 December 1936; Dan to Adler, 30 August 1936, *Pis'ma*, 486. As Stalin's illusion, see [PR], *Sv* 379/380. Compare Getty, "State and Society under Stalin," who argues that the "democratic" constitutional project was a "trial balloon" burst by social reality, but not until late 1937.

28. Dan to Bauer, 25 September 1935, SAI 2616; [PR], *Sv* 367, 11 June 1936. See also F. Dan, "Terror i konstitutsiia," *Sv* 410, 31 March 1938.

29. [PR], *Sv* 367; F. Dan, "Perspektivy sotsialdemokraticheskoi raboty," *Sv* 381/382, 17 January 1937.

30. F. Dan, "Puti vozrozhdeniia," *Sv* 370/371, 14 August 1936.

31. P. Garvi, "Novaia sovetskaia konstitutsiia," *Sv* 369, 10 July 1936.

32. Abramovich to Dan, 19 July 1936, AA 4/1; accusations in *Pravda*, 13 July 1936.

33. [ZD], "Vsesoiuznomu S'ezdu Sovetov," *Sv* 376, 28 October 1936, translated in *International Information*, 3 November 1936.

34. [Ed], "K stalinskomu plebistsitu," *Sv* 401, 17 November 1937. For analyses, see A. Iugov, "Klassy v sovetskoi Rossii," *Sv* 368, 26 June 1936, and "O sovetskom sluzhashchem," *Sv* 378, 25 November 1936; S. Shvarts, "Pervye shagi," *Sv* 411, 15 April 1938; [Ed], "Stavka na intelligentsiiu," *Sv* 426, 25 November 1938. For the left argument, see O. Domanevskaia, "K sotsializmu ili k termidoru?" *Sv* 381/382, 17 January 1937.

35. [Ed], "Pered s'ezdom," *Sv* 432/433, 15 March 1939. On the new elite, see [PR], "Iuliliary i triumfatory," *Sv* 359, 10 February 1936; S. Schwarz, "New Trend of Soviet Population Policy," *International Information: Women's Supplement* (October 1936); V. Aleksandrova, "Vtoroe rozhdenie," *Sv* 446, 19 October 1939. Compare Shatz, *Stalin, Great Purge, and Russian History*, 18.

36. [Ed], "Pered s'ezdom." *Sv* 432/433; Nikolaevskii to Garvi, 16 March and 5 April 1940, NC 18(53).

37. R. Abramovich, "Sfinks Stalin," *Sv* 353, 10 November 1935, and "Dzhingis Khan 20-go veka," *Sv* 627, 30 December 1949.

SEARCH FOR UNITY

1. See Braunthal, *History of the International*, 415–447; Tartakovsky, "SFIO et fascisme dans les années trente"; Donneur, *Alliance fragile*, 73–160.

2. F. Dan, "Krizis frantsuzskoi sotsialisticheskoi partii," *Sv* 295/296, 26 June 1933. On the underestimation of Hitler by Blum and *Le Populaire*'s German expert, the Menshevik Oreste Rosenfeld, see Köller, *Frankreich zwischen Faschismus und Demokratie*.

3. F.I. [Dan], "Edinyi front vo Frantsii," *Sv* 322, 10 July 1934; S. Ivanovich, "Indul'-gentsiia," *Posledniie novosti*, 19 August 1934.

4. *Populaire*, 12 August 1934; *Humanité*, 13 August 1934; "Mensheviks and United Front in France," *International Information*, 8 September 1934; "K voprosam mezhdunarodnogo rabochego edinstva," *Sv* 324/325, 29 August 1934.

5. *International Information*, 26 January 1935, published a communication to the RSDRP Foreign Delegation "from Social Democratic party organizations working in the Soviet Union" approving the Kazan telegram.

6. R. Abramovich, "Kazanskaia telegramma i kommunisticheskie manevry," *Sv* 324/325, 29 August 1934. More or less at the same time, exiled Russian SRs in Prague heard rumors that their Central Committee members in Russia had been freed and that one of them, A. R. Gots, had been seen in the Lenin Library and at the Moscow Art Theater. The rumors turned out to be disinformation, probably concocted to forestall a demonstration in favor of socialist prisoners in Russia. V. M. Zenzinov note [autumn 1940], NC 232(377).

7. "Frantsuzskaia sotsialisticheskaia pechat' o kazan'skoi telegrame," *Sv* 324/325, 29 August 1934.

8. Nikolaevskii to Vulikh, 21 August 1934, NC 134(207).

9. F. Dan, "Golos men'shevizma iz SSSR," *Sv* 324/235, 29 August 1934.

10. Abramovich, "Kazanskaia telegramma i kommunisticheskie manevry," *Sv* 324/325.

11. Privately, Abramovitch was even more guarded. See his letters to Kautsky and Adler, both 27 August 1934, LSI 2623.

12. P. Garvi, "Edinyi front i russkii vopros," *Sv* 326, 12 September 1934.

13. The record of relations between Comintern and LSI, from the socialist perspective, is to be found in *International Information*. Sources sympathetic to the LSI are Braunthal, *History of the International*, and Donneur, *L'Internationale socialiste*. Mildly critical is Mancini, "L'IOS e la questione del fronte unico negli anni trenta," and extremely critical is Kalicka, *Problemy jednolitego frontu w miedzynarodowym ruchu robotniczym*, which contains a detailed chronology. Note that the French unity pact was followed by one between exiled Italian parties.

14. SRs were also represented in the LSI Executive, but internal squabbles left them inactive for long periods. Only the RSDRP represented Russia in the Bureau,

but from 1933 Abramovitch and Dan alternated as party representatives, with Abramovitch retaining the title of official representative. Abramowitsch to Adler, 27 August 1934.

15. Abramowitsch to Hedtoft-Hansen (a Scandinavian socialist), 4 December 1935, AA 4/1; R. Abramovich, "V Rabochem Sotsialisticheskom Internatsionale," *Sv* 301/303, 10 September 1933. See also Abramowitsch to the Kautskys, 9 November 1935, KA D1; Dan to Adler, 3 September 1935, *Pis'ma*, 458–459.

16. Abramovitch to Brouckère, 2 September 1936, AA 4/1.

17. Abramowitsch, "Einheitsfront und Einheitspartei."

18. Abramovitch to Brouckère, 2 September 1936. "What would German comrades say if a special issue of I.I. [*International Information*] on Germany were confided to Russian comrades, although some of us are as well informed on Germany as Bauer is on Russia?" German comrades complained precisely about this with respect to *Le Populaire*.

19. Nikolaevskii to Vulikh, 2 March 1934 and 16 June 1934, NC 134(207). See Buschak, *Londoner Büro*.

20. "Theses on the International Discussion on the Fight for Democracy and Peace. Draft by Abramovitch, Nicolajevski, Aronson. For the Meeting of the LSI Executive, January 14–16, 1939," LSI 22, Labour Party Archives. Only Garvi, "Pis'mo v redaktsiu," *Sv* 358, 25 January 1936, held out against accusing other rightists of promulgating *Burgfrieden*, or class truce tendencies. The right wing's platform was guided by Kautsky, who devoted his last letter to it; see Kautsky to Garvy, 27/30 August 1938, KA-C.

21. "Struggle for Democracy. Thesis by Theodor Dan," [prepared for LSI Executive meeting, 14–16 January 1939], LSI 22, Labour Party Archives. Previously discussed as "K mezhdunarodnoi diskussii o bor'be za demokratiiu," with contributions by Dan, Abramovich, Garvi, Domanevskaia, and Aronson, in *Sv* 419/20, 28 August 1938, *Sv* 421, 15 September 1938, and *Sv* 422, 30 September 1938.

22. [Draft of Dan and Grimm resolution for LSI Bureau Session, 19, 20 November 1933], Bureau Documents, LSI 649; F. Dan, "Kautsky on the War Problems of Socialism," *International Information*, 15 December 1937.

23. *L'Internationale et la guerre. Thèses de Bauer, Dan, Dunois, et Zyromski.* Compare F. Dan, "K voprosam mezhdunarodnogo sotsialisticheskogo kongressa: bor'ba i mir," *Sv* 252, 18 July 1931.

24. Dan to Adler, 29 July 1935, *Pis'ma*, 457.

25. Adler to Dan, 7 February 1936, LSI 2597. Quoted from Dan to Bauer, 6 June 1935. Perhaps Dan was simply expressing solidarity with his coauthors when he wrote to Kautsky, 23 December 1935, *Pis'ma*, 473, "I must insist that I am not the victim of Z[yromsky's] and B[auer's] seduction but rather the seducer."

26. Dan to Bauer, 5 December 1935, *Pis'ma*, 466–468. On amendments, see Dan to Bauer, 6 June 1935, *Pis'ma*, 452–455.

27. O. Domanevskaia et al., "K mezhdunarodnoi diskussii o voine," *Sv* 354, 26 November 1935; R. Abramovich and G. Aronson, *Sv* 355/356, 28 December 1935. [ZD], "Voina i sotsializm: Tezisy Zagranichnoi Delegatsii RSDRP"; and [IP], "Zaiavleniia k motivam golosovaniia," *Sv* 357, 10 January 1935.

28. Quoted from R. Abramovich, "Ideologicheskaia liniia *Sv*," *Sv* 692, April 1956. For the pregnancy metaphor, see R. Abramovich, "Nashi raznoglasiia," *Sv* 460, 25 April 1940.

DIVISION AND DEFEAT

1. Dan to K. Adler, 5 November 1933, SAI 2597. See also Abramowitsch to F. Adler, 27 August 1934, SAI 2623.
2. Dan argued that the resolution had already made concessions to Abramovitch's view in return for his abstention. See Dan to Adler, 29 December 1935, *Pis'ma,* 476.
3. Nikolaevskii to S. Garvi, 8 March 1940, NC 18(53).
4. *International Information*, 22 September 1937 and 4 October 1937.
5. "Summary of the Facts and Hypotheses in the Case of Mark Rein in Barcelona," Gillies Papers, Labour Party Archives.
6. Abramowitch to Morrison, 24 July 1937, Gillies Papers.
7. Abramowitsch to Adler, 29 April 1937, SAI 2623. Abramowitch to Gillies, 29 April 1937, Gillies Papers.
8. Gillies to Abramowitsch, 15 June 1937, Gillies Papers. Maiskii was a former Menshevik Party comrade.
9. Skomorovskii to Dan, 14 April 1941, NC 136(209).
10. Poretsky, *Our Own People,* 259. No clues to the disappearance ever turned up. Broué was denied the Marc Rein file in the French National Archives in 1988; see Broué, *Trotsky,* 874.
11. The majority was now made up of the old rightists Aronson and Kefali, plus Abramovitch, Dvinov, and Nicolaevsky. Dan to Adler, 12 December 1937, *Pis'ma,* 500–501.
12. Ibid.
13. Dan to Adler, 20 December 1937, *Pis'ma,* 503.
14. *International Information*, 17 November 1934.
15. See Kautsky to Garvi, 11 January 1935, NC 18(53). Also Löw, *Bauer und die russische Revolution,* 206.
16. Abramovich to Dalin, 7 May 1934, AA 2/1.
17. *International Information*, 24 May 1939.
18. R. Abramovich, "Reforma Internatsionala?" *Sv* 437/438, 27 May 1939; F. Dan, "V Rabochem Sotsialisticheskom Internatsionale," *SV* 440, 30 June 1939.
19. F. Adler, "The Position of the LSI" [memorandum, spring 1939], SAI 688. See Steiner, "Internationale socialiste à la veille de la Seconde Guerre mondiale"; Rapone, "Crisi finale dell'Internazionale Operaia e Socialista"; and, for a bitter account by an insider, Braunthal, *History of the International,* 468–492.
20. V. Aleksandrova, "Starye spory i novye fakty," *Sv* 449/450, 2 December 1939, and "Ko Vsem chlenam partii [31 August 1939]," *Sv* 444, 9 September 1939; F. Dan, "Pod grom pushek: II," *Sv* 445, 29 September 1939.
21. O. Domanevskaia, "Germano-sovetskii pakt," *Sv* 446, 19 October 1939.

22. Ibid; "Rezoliutsiia ZD," *Sv* 445, 29 September 1939; F. Dan, "Pod grom pushek: III," *Sv* 446, 19 October 1939.

23. F. Dan, "Pod grom pushek: IV," *Sv* 447/448, 12 November 1939; [RSDRP], "V zashchitu Finlandii," *Sv* 449/450, 2 December 1939; F. Dan, "Pod grom pushek: V," *Sv* 453/454, 24 January 1940; [Ed], "Novyi god i novyi mir," *Sv* 451/452, 25 December 1939.

24. The Mensheviks no longer had privileged contacts within Russia, and in 1935 Stalin forbade even polemical mention of *Sv*. See G. Aronson, "Sotsialisticheskii vestnik 1921–1963," *Russkaia mysl'*, 19 January 1964. Still, *Vestnik* remained an authoritative source, even for diplomatic chancelleries. See, for example, "Further Correspondence re the Soviet Union," Confidential Print 1, 14 March and 2 April 1938, Foreign Office 418, Great Britain.

25. L. Dan to Estrin, 27 December 1939, NC 136(209).

26. See Wolin, "Mensheviks under NEP," 291–292.

27. Garvi to Dan, 25 September 1939, NC 18(53).

28. Iugov to Garvi, 27 September 1939, and Garvi to Iugov, 28 September 1939, NC 18(53). Iugov acted as Dan's emissary.

29. Iugov to Estrin, 16 December 1939, NC 136(209); Dan to Estrin, 19 February 1940, *Pis'ma*, 515–518.

30. "Zaiavlenie tov. Dana i Iugova," *Sv* 455/456, 15 February 1940.

31. Nikolaevskii to S. Garvi, 10 February 1940 and 15 April 1940; to P. Garvi, 16 March and 5 April 1940, NC 18(53). On alliance with SRs, see R. Abramovich, "O soglashenii s s-rami," *Sv* 461, 10 May 1940.

32. S. Shvarts, "Vsem chlenam zagranichnoi organizatsii RSDRP," 17 February 1940, Khinoy Archive, YIVO; Aleksandrova to Estrin, 25 April 1940, NC 136(209).

33. Abramovich to Viliatser, 18 February 1940; L. Dan, postscript to F. Dan to Estrin, 20 March 1940, NC 136(209); Bers, interview.

34. Dan to Estrin, 20 March 1940, *Pis'ma*, 518–521; Minkov to Nikolaevskii, 25 March 1940, NC 25; "Zaiavlenie Zhenevskoi grupy," *Sv* 462, 1 June 1940; "Rezoliutsiia N'iu-iorkskoi gruppy," *Sv* 460, 25 April 1940.

35. Dan, "Pod grom pushek," *Sv* 455/456, 15 February 1940; Dan to Estrin, 19 February and 20 March 1940, *Pis'ma*, 515–521. Accusations in Garvi to Dan, 25 September 1939 NC 18(53).

36. F. Dan, "Pamiati P. B. Aksel'roda i Iu. O. Martova," *Novyi mir* 2, 10 April 1940.

37. F. Dan, "Neobkhodimoe ob'iasnenie," *Novyi mir* 1, 20 March 1940; also Dan to Estrin, 25 May 1940, *Pis'ma*, 524–525.

38. Nikolaevskii to S. Garvi, 26 March 1940, NC 18(53).

39. Other "Latvians" were Grigorii Meiksins and Azrach Anin, later involved in Radio Liberty. Shifrin wrote as "A. Mikhailov." Bers and A. and L. Kisselgoff, interviews.

40. Estrin, "Vospominaniia" (2), NC 136(208). See also Levenstein, *Escape to Freedom*.

41. Abramovich to "Dorogiie druz'ia," 18 July 1940, L. O. Dan Archive 1.

42. Bundist Richard Ryba, interview, recalls that Fedor Dan sent Lidia to congratulate him on his decision to remain in France. On the archives, see Mayer, "Ge-

schichte des sozialdemokratischen Parteiarchivs,'' 153; Bourguina, interview 2; Estrin, ''Vospominaniia'' (2), 42, NC 136(208). Other archives were brought to America on Nicolaevsky's behalf by Ambassador William Bullitt. Rabinowitch and Rabinowitch, ed., *Revolution and Politics*, ix.

43. See Fry, *Surrender on Demand;* Poretsky, *Our Own People*, 259; on Marquet, Schapiro, interview.

44. Blum to the Dans, August 1940, L. O. Dan Archive 8. Rosenfeld had taken advantage of a provision allowing Allied officers of World War I to obtain a French commission.

8. Sea Change

NEW ROADS AND OLD

1. Estrin, ''Vospominaniia'' (3), 33. There were soon fifty-nine newly arrived Mensheviks and SRs, including children, in New York. A smaller number arrived later. Garvi to Spalding, 28 October 1940, Spalding Collection; interviews with Levitas, Andler, Turim, Bers.

2. Braunthal to F. Dan, 13 November 1941, L. O. Dan Archive 8/26; Dan to Mering, 17 January 1945, *Pis'ma*, 531; Andler, interview.

3. P. Garvi, ''O 'bankrotstve demokratii,' '' *Sv* 466/467, 19 January 1941; [Ed], ''Berlin–Paris–Niu Iork,'' *Sv* 463, 15 November 1940.

4. Stampfer to Sopade, 10 February 1943, *Mit dem Gesicht nach Deutschland*, 581–582. For Abramovitch's reelection, see [ZD], ''Zasedanie ot 8 dekabria 1940,'' *Sv* 489, 24 January 1942; [IP], ''Banket v chest' R. A. Abramovicha,'' *Sv* 468, 10 February 1941. On ALCIA, Bell, interview.

5. [ZD], ''Zasedanie ot 9 noiabria 1940,'' and [ZD] ''Zasedanie ot 10 marta 1941,'' both in *Sv* 489, 24 January 1942; Ingerman to Abramovich, 25 February 1941, NC 23(63). On Ivanovich, see [ZD], ''Zasedanie ot 30 noiabria 1941,'' *Sv* 489; also F. Dan and A. Iugov, ''Partiinye dela,'' *Np* 14, 3 January 1942.

6. Quoted from [Ed], ''Nashi zadachi,'' and F. Dan, ''Sud'by demokraticheskogo sotsializma,'' *Np* 1/2, 22 April 1941; ''Klub 'Novogo Puti','' *Np* 4, 7 June 1941.

7. On readmission, see [Partiinye dela], ''V zagranichnuiu delegatsiiu RSDRP,'' *Np* 14, 3 January 1942; [ZD], ''Rezoliutsiia ZD RSDRP ot 20 ianvaria 1942,'' *Sv* 489, 24 January 1942. On the quarrel, see [ZD], ''K chlenam Niu iorkskoi gruppy RSDRP,'' *Sv* 490/491, 24 February 1942; [IP], ''V zagranichnuiu delegatsiiu RSDRP,'' *Sv* 505/506, 3 October 1942, and F. Dan, ''V tsarstve tenei,'' *Np* 21, 6 September 1942; [IP], ''V Zagranichnoi delegatsii RSDRP,'' *Sv* 519/520, 8 May 1943; [IP], ''Smeshnye pretenzii,'' *Sv* 523/524, 8 July 1943, and ''Samolikvidatsiia Z-D RSDRP,'' *Np* 31, 6 June 1943; [IP], ''O Samoustranenii tt. Dana i Iugov iz ZD RSDRP,'' *Sv* 505/506, 3 October 1942.

8. [IP], ''70-letie F. I. Dana,'' and [Pis'mo v redaktsiiu], B. Nikolaevskii, ''Po povodu odnogo interv'iu (otvet F. Danu),'' *Sv* 484, 31 October 1941. The accusation appeared in the *New York Post*, 6 September 1941. Nicolaevsky promised to retract the accusation but did not; see F. Dan, ''Neostorozhnaia entsiklopedia,'' *Np* 11/12, 26 October 1941.

9. Regarding Shifrin, see R.A., "Kuda chlen plyvet?" *Sv* 494/495, 12 April 1942; and the response, M. Werner [=Shifrin], "Pis'mo v redaktsiiu," *Np* 18, 3 May 1942. Regarding Dubois, see his "Pis'mo v redaktsiiu," *Np* 16, 8 March 1942. And see Friedrich Adler's protest that the JLC lacked competence in the matter, "Po povodu odnoi intrigi," *Np* 43, 23 July 1944.

10. [IP], "Iskliucheniie iz partii Borisa Skomorovskogo," *Sv* 527/528, 8 September 1943, and [IP], "*Novyi Put'* na leninskom puti," *Sv* 531/532, 8 November 1943; F. Dan and A. Iugov, "Vynuzhdennoe zaiavlenie," *Np* 34, 10 October 1943, and "Zlostnaia vydumka," *Np* 36, 12 December 1943. Estrin, "Vospominaniia," 19, describes the 1941 meeting, adding that he left only later, when Abramovitch defended Admiral François Darlan, the French Vichy leader seen by some as an alternative to both Pétain and DeGaulle.

11. Estrin, "Vospominaniia," 23–29 passim, and Bers, interview.

12. On Atran, Erlich, interview, not confirmed in *Novyi put*'s acknowledgments, and Lieberman's memoirs, *Dela i liudi* and *Building Lenin's Russia*. See also *Np* 57/58, 10 February 1946. On the auctions, see "Khudozhniki—na pomoshch *Novomu Puti*," *Np* 21, 6 September 1942; Dan to Mering, 30 April 1946, *Pis'ma*, 565. A Chagall canvas fetched $500 at the time.

13. Stampfer to SOPADE, 14 July 1943, *Mit dem Gesicht nach Deutschland*, 613.

14. Mihailov (=Shifrin) has triumphed over Dan, wrote Aronson, "Poputchiki poslednego rozryva (po stranitsam 'Novogo Puti')," *Sv* 529/530, 9 October 1943.

15. O. Domanevskaia, "Pis'mo v redaktsiu," *Np* 21, 6 September 1942; [IP], "Konets odnogo nedorazumeniia (Ukhod iz partii O.I. Domanevskoi)," *Sv* 505/506, 3 October 1942. See Bers, interview, and, on Meiksins, Estrin, "Vospominaniia," 23–24.

16. Aleksandrova to Dan, 24 and 28 October 1941, L. O. Dan Archive 7/26; F. Dan, "Pamiati Kefali," *Np* 35, 14 November 1943. Dan, like other Mensheviks, was also sensitive to the fact that Kefali was the only genuine worker on the Foreign Delegation. See Dan, "Pamiati Garvi," *Np* 39, 19 March 1944, and Dan's review of Garvi, *Vospominiia Sotsial-Demokrata, Np* 57/58, 10 February 1946.

17. F. Dan, "Sovetskii Soiuz i Voina," *Np* 1/2, 22 April 1941; Iu. Grinfeld, "Gitler—chempion 'mirovoi revoliutsii,' " *Sv* 466/467, 19 January 1941.

18. R. Abramovich, "Strakh plokhoi sovetnik (O tezisakh F. I. Dana)," *Sv* 476, 12 June 1941. Even a year later *Vestnik* was arguing that Balkan operations in the spring of 1941 could just as easily have been preparation for a joint Russian-German strike against the British Empire. See Iu. Denike, "God russkoi voiny," *Sv* 499/500, 30 June 1942. For taunts, see [Ed], "Zertsalo liubomudrosti," *Np* 43, 23 July 1944.

19. [ZD], "RSDRP o sovetsko-germanskoi voine," *Sv* 477, 30 June 1941; F. Dan and A. Iugov, "O Germano-sovetskoi voine," *Np* 5/6, 5 July 1941.

20. [PR], "Iz moskovskikh nastroenii," *Sv* 481, 20 September 1941.

21. Quoted from R. Abramovich "Kharakter nashego oboronchestva," *Sv* 481, 20 September 1941; see also his "Istoricheskii povorot," *Sv* 477, 30 June 1941; "Voina i politicheskie rezhimy," *Sv* 479, 4 August 1941; "Strela ili bumerang?" *Sv* 513/514, 5 February 1943.

22. A. Kober, "Vozvrashchenie v Evropu," and F. Dan, "Voina i Sovetskii soiuz,"

Np 15, 8 February 1942; [Ed], "Otechestvo v opasnosti," *Np* 7, 23 July 1941; [Ed], "Istoricheskii den'," and A. Mikhailov (=Shifrin), "Nachalo voiny," *Np* 5/6, 5 July 1941, idem, and "Chem byli germano-sovestskie otnosheniia?" *Np* 7, 23 July 1941. On the thesis of a German defensive attack, see recently Suvorov, *Icebreaker*. And see Iu. Denike, "Chitat', tak vsë chitat'," *Sv* 507/508, 3 November 1942.

23. A. Diubua, "Voina i oppozitsiia," *Sv* 481, 20 September 1941. A. Mikhailov (=Shifrin), "Dva anti-bol'shevizma," *Np* 36, 12 December 1943.

24. B. Nikolaevskii, "O roli kommunistov i o pugale 'antibol'shevizma," *Sv* 485/486, 24 November 1941; F. Dan, "Porazhencheskaia podderzhka," *Np* 13, 30 November 1941; G. Golosov (=Nikolaevskii), "Itogi i uroki," *Sv* 487, 15 December 1941, and "Axis Starts a New Front—Why?" *NL* 20, December 1941.

25. V. Ivlev (=Dan), "Po ves'ma ser'eznomy povodu," *Np* 14, 3 January 1942; [Partiinye dela], "Zaiavlenie v ZD RSDRP," *Np* 15, 8 February 1942.

26. F. Dan, "Ne slishkom li?" *Np* 41, 28 May 1944; B. Nikolaevskii, "Itogi odnogo spora," *Sv* 551/552, 23 September 1944.

27. On Allied aid, see M. Veinbaum, "Po povodu doklada F.I. Dana," *Novoe russkoe slovo* 29 March 1944. On U.S. entry into the war, see [Ed], "Odna voina—odno komandovanie," *Sv* 487, 15 December 1941, and "Partiinye dela," *Np* 14, 3 January 1942. On the second front, see A. Mikhailov, "Vozmozhen li vtoroi front?" *Np* 13, 30 November 1941; [Ed], "Vtoroi front," *Sv* 501/502, 31 July 1942. On Stalingrad, see Mikhailov, "Dva anti-bol'shevizma."

28. See [Ot redaktsii], "K frantsuzskoi probleme," *Sv* 525/526, 8 August 1943, which chides Garvi for his uncritical admiration of De Gaulle.

29. G. Aronson, "Za poslednei chertoi (tragediia evropeiskogo evreistva)," *Sv* 505/506, 3 October 1942. A *Vestnik* editorial provided confirmation: "There is no doubt about the existence of a plan of physical extermination of the Jews. It could have been guessed early . . . but it was thought to be demagogic exaggeration." [Ed], "Karfagen dolzhen byt' razrushen," *Sv* 509/510, 3 December 1942.

30. G. Aronson, "Sionizm i stalinizm," *Sv* 523/524, 8 July 1943, and "Roman sionistov s kommunistami," *Sv* 559/560, 23 January 1945; F. Dan, "Martirologia evreistva," *Np* 25, 10 January 1943.

31. P. Garvi, "Vtorzhenie v Rossiiu i natsional'naia problema," *Sv* 478, 17 July 1941; S. Shvarts, "Sovetskii Soiuz i Pol'sha," *Sv* 494/495, 12 April 1942, and B. Sapir, "Pol'skii vopros," *Sv* 547/548, 20 July 1944. See also R. Abramovich, "Mezhdunarodnyi sotsializm i germanskaia problema," *Sv* 551/552, 23 September 1944.

32. F. Dan, "K sovetskim problemam mira—tezisy F. Dana," *Np* 30, 1 May 1943. Meiksins, *Baltic Riddle*, is discussed in B.L., "Baltiiskii vopros," *Np* 38, 13 February 1944, and S. Shvarts, "Baltiiskii uzel," *Sv* 535, 10 January 1944. Even Meiksins did not claim that the 1940 plebiscites had been free.

33. R. Abramovich, "Voina i mir," *Sv* 470, 11 March 1941, and *Sv* 471, 12 April 1941; [Ed], "Evropeiskaia federatsiia, kakaia?" *Np* 16, 8 March 1942.

34. [Ed], "Moskva–Kair–Tegeran," *Sv* 533/534, 10 December 1943; R. Abramovich, "Ialta i griadushchii mir," *Sv* 561/562, 27 February 1945; [Ed], "Russkoe nastuplenie i konferentsiia Trëkh," *Sv* 559/560, 23 January 1945.

35. Quoted from [Ed], "Vozvrashchenie domoi," *Np* 49, 1 April 1945. See A. Iugov,

"SSSR i slavianskie narody," *Np* 50, 13 May 1945; F. Dan, "Mir na shtykakh," *Np* 26/27, 14 February 1943; Dan, "Besslavnyi konets," *Np* 49, 1 April 1945.

36. Quoted from R. Abramovich, "Voina i ideologiia," *Sv* 545/546, 20 June 1944; also his "Posle Gitlera," *Sv* 565/566, 28 April 1945. A. Mikhailov, "Filosofiia tret'ei voiny," *Np* 59, 28 April 1946.

37. [Ed], "Khuzhe chem prestuplenie," *Np* 14, 3 January 1942; F. Dan, "Kak mozhno skoree," *Np* 15, 8 February 1942; F. Dan, "60-ie Erlikha," *Np* 19, 3 June 1942; "Eshchë ob Erlikhe i Altere," *Np* 26/27, 14 February 1943; "K rasstrelu tt. Erlikha i Altera," and [Ed], "U mogily druzei," which asked (incorrectly), "Why for the first time are socialists killed in the Soviet Union?" *Np* 28/29, 4 April 1943. The Menshevik majority had no problem explaining the murder; see [ZD], "K ubiistvu Genrikha Erlikha i Viktora Altera," *Sv* 513/514, 5 February 1943. Erlich's son Alexander left the *Novyi put'* group after the murder, considering its reaction inadequate; Erlich's widow remained.

38. See Dan's letter and editorial apology, *Nation*, 15 August 1942.

39. S. Shvarts, "Problemy sovetskoi ekonomii," *Sv* 494/495, 12 April 1942, and "O sotsialnykh protsessakh v SSSR (otvet t. Iugovu)," *Sv* 511/512, 5 January 1943; B. Nikolaevskii, "O klassovoi strukture totalitarnykh gosudarstv," *Sv* 473/474, 22 May 1941; A. Iugov, "O praviashchikh gruppakh v SSSR," *Np* 24, 6 December 1942, and "Eshchë o praviashchikh gruppakh v SSSR," *Np* 26/27, 14 February 1943. Dan joined the debate in "S knizhnoi polki," *Np* 41, 28 May 1944. Much of the debate was prompted by *Management in Russian Industry and Agriculture*, to which Bienstock, Iugov, Marschak, and Schwarz contributed.

40. A. Iugov, "Smysl chistkov v SSSR," *Np* 62/63, 17 October 1946; S. Shvarts, "Problemy sovetskoi ekonomii," *Sv* 494/495, 12 April 1942.

41. Quoted from F. Dan, "Puti demokratsii (3)," *Np* 40, 23 April 1944. Dan claimed that according to the Martov Line, democratization occurred from the top down, by way of agreement between Communists and other parties. Moiseev (=Sapir), "O 'tret'ei sile," *Sv* 539, 17 March 1944, and S. Shvarts, "Nashe Oboronchestvo i ego kritika," *Sv* 489, 24 January 1942, contrasted this view with Dan's of democratization from below in "Puti demokratsii (2)," *Np* 39, 19 March 1944. On bolshevism dying, see B. Dvinov (recently Dan's ally), "Svidanie na mostu," *Sv* 497/498, 31 May 1942. On Supreme Soviet, see S. Sh[varts], "Na novom puti," *Sv* 490/491, 24 February 1942.

42. Quoted from F. Dan, "Dvadtsataia godovshchina (ob Iu. O. Martove)," *Np* 28/29, 4 April 1943; R. Abramovich, "Osnovopolozhniki mirovogo men'shevizma (pamiati P.B. Aksel'roda i Iu. O. Martova)," *Sv* 515/516, 7 April 1943.

43. A. Iugov, "Pererozhdenie ideologii," *Np* 33, 5 September 1943; F.D., "Mogilshchiki sotsialdemokratii," *Np* 40, 23 April 1944.

44. D. Dalin, "Politika Martova v pol'sko-sovetskoi voine," *Sv* 515/516, 7 April 1943; B. Nikolaevskii, "Iu. O. Martov i s.-r. (istoricheskaia spravka)," *Sv* 543/544, 15 May 1944. Both these issues were highly topical, given the state of Polish-Soviet relations and the prospects for unification between SRs and Mensheviks.

45. B. Nikolaevskii, "Chto takoe sotsializm," *Sv* 497/498, 31 May 1942, and "O sotsializme i fashizme," *Sv* 503/504, 31 August 1942; Iu. Denike, "Problemy sotsializma," *Sv* 482/483, 15 October 1941.

46. B. Nikolaevskii, "Termidor russkoi revoliutsii," *Sv* 573/574, 6 September 1942; R. Abramovich, "Bonapartizm i russkaia revoliutsiia," *Sv* 523/524, 8 July 1943.

47. B. Sapir, "Sotsialdemokratiia prered problemoi fashizma," *Sv* 513/514, 5 February 1943; S. Shvarts, "Chto zhe dal'she?" *Sv* 592, 27 December 1946. Shvarts was taken to task for affirming that Communist, unlike fascist, ideology was built on an emancipatory and humanist idea. See A. Bronshtein, "Chto delat'?" *Sv* 593/594, 3 February 1947.

48. B. Nikolaevskii, "Sovremennaia voina i kapitalizm," *Sv* 509/510, 3 December 1942.

THE LAST OF THE MARTOV LINE

1. Dan quoted from Bers, interview. A. Kober, "Puti revoliutsii," *Np* 48, 25 February 1945, and "Pered novymi boaiami," *Np* 57/58, 10 February 1946; A. Iugov, "Puti k sotsializmu," *Np* 62/63, 17 October 1946.

2. R. Abramovich, "Perspektivy rabochego dvizheniia v Evrope," *Sv* 555/556, 25 November 1944; [Ed], "V povoennoi Evrope," *Sv* 567/568, 29 May 1945. See also Abramovich, "Novaia volna illiuzii," *Sv* 529/530, 9 October 1943.

3. Dan to Kurskii, 25 January 1944, Bund Archives; Andler, interview; Dan to Mering, 22 June 1945, and 24 April 1946, *Pis'ma*, 540, 564. Sapir's editorial note, *Pisma* 564, claims that Dan mistook Blum's attitude toward Abramovitch.

4. Adler to Dan in Braunthal, *Victor und Friedrich Adler*, 180; Dan, *Origins of Bolshevism*, 3; Dan to Mering, 24 April 1946.

5. Dan, *Origins of Bolshevism*, 2; idem, "Vozrozhdenie sotsializma," *Np* 20, 5 July 1942; [Ed], "Novyi mir k novomu puti," *Np* 28/29, 4 April 1943; F. Dan, "Puti demokratii," *Np* 38, 13 February 1944, and "Vozrozhdenie ili likvidatsiia," *Sv* 501/502, 31 July 1942.

6. Dan, *Origins of Bolshevism*, 10, 435, 30, 440.

7. On America and old friends, see Dan to Mering, 11 February and 21 March 1946, *Pis'ma*, 556, 559; on health and Blum, see Dan to Mering, 17 May 1946, *Pis'ma*, 567, and "Ocherednaia zadacha (deklaratsiia gruppy 'Novogo Puti')," *Np* 60/61, 30 June 1946.

8. Dan to Mering, 3 March 1945, *Pis'ma*, 533.

9. Iugov to Dan, 4 July 1946, Bund Archives. The portrait is on the front page of *Np* 62/63, 17 October 1946; "Prekrashchenie izdaniia *Novyi Put'*," *Np* 64/65, 2 April 1947.

10. "Pokhorony F. I. Dana," *Novoe russkoe slovo*, 25 January 1947.

11. B. Sapir, "Bol'shevizm i Mens'shevizm: po povodu knigi F. I. Dana," *Sv* 587/588, 20 August 1946; R. Abramovich, "Put' F. I. Dana," *Sv* 593/594, 3 February 1947.

12. G. Aronson, "Pamiati L. O. Dan," *Novoe russkoe slovo*, 3 March 1963. On collectivization, see Ladis Kristof, communication to author, 16 July 1987. L. Dan to N. Starobinskaia, 24 February 1947, L. O. Dan Archive, 6/23; L. Dan to Vol'skii, 1 May 1961, VC.

13. A. Iugov, "Bor'ba za obilie v SSSR," *Russkii golos*, 9 July 1947. Thirty-five years

later Alexander Erlich, who spoke well of Iugov, still recalled this title with particular irritation and distaste. Erlich, interview.

14. Adler to Estrine, 29 June 1947; L. Dan to Estrin, 2 February 1949, NC 136(208). On Iugov's death, Erlich, interview.

15. Estrin, "Vospominaniia." On Skomorovskii, see Nikolaevskii to Estrin, 9 April 1965, NC 136(209).

16. Rozenfel'd to L. Dan, 24 March 1958, L. O. Dan Archive III; to Tsereteli, 22 January 1957, NC 15; to Estrin, 31 March 1956, NC 136(209). On Rosenfeld's experiences in the USSR in 1947, 1956, and 1959, see his "Déstalinisation et le Nouveau Programme du PC de l'URSS," *Nouvelle revue marxiste*, February–March 1962. A member of the SFIO Central Committee, he was suspended from the party in June 1954 over colonial policy and left the party in 1958 to found the Parti socialiste autonome and direct the *Nouvelle revue marxiste*.

17. Erlich, interview.

THE END OF THE FOREIGN DELEGATION

1. Kuskova-Nicolaevsky exchange in *Sv* 575/576, 579/580, 10 October and 10 December 1945. See also B. Dvinov, "Russkii narod i Kreml'," *Sv* 603, 26 December 1947; R. Abramovich, "Slepaia tochka E. D. Kuskovoi," "Sushchnost' dela," and "Ob osnovnom," *Sv* 628/629, 631, 633, 20 February, 27 April (June 1950).

2. R. Abramovich, "Natsional'nye interesy Rossii i vneshnaia politika Stalina," *Sv* 567/568, 29 May 1945. See, typically, the letter to *NYT*, 8 July 1951, signed by Abramovitch, Nicolaevsky, Shwartz, and several SRs, elaborated in "Politika Kremlia—ne natsional'naia politika Rossii," *Sv* 645 (June–July 1951).

3. R. Abramovich, "Vosstanie sotsialistichekogo internatsionala," *Sv* 559/560, 23 January 1945; D. Dalin, "Sotsializm i komunizm," *Sv* 596, 15 April 1947; B. Sapir, "Problema Internatsionala," *Sv* 607/608, 20 May 1948. On exclusion, see Abramovitch's bitter letter to the secretary of the new International, J. Braunthal, 6 November 1951, Labour Party Archives. With excessive optimism, Angelika Balabanov, the Russian-Italian head of the Italian delegation to a Socialist International congress (probably Copenhagen in 1950), wrote to Lidia Dan (undated letter, L. O. Dan Archive) that the "next bureau meeting, I imagine, will rule in favor of acceptance . . . Spaak and Huysmans are for it." On reconstitution, see Braunthal, *History of the International*, 3, 133–142 and 182–212.

4. NC 232; "Na puti k edinoi sotsialisticheskoi partii," *Sv* 651, March 1952. Vishniak, *Gody emigratsii*, 261. On SR accusations, see Sukhomlin to New York SR group, 10 November 1941, and Chernov's testimony concerning M. Slonim, 25 October 1941, NC 232; also Gul', *Ia unes Rossiu*, 2:177.

5. Quoted from Abramovich to Dune, 20 June 1950, NC 181(235); and Abramovich to Vol'skii, 30 March 1951, VC. See "Vypiski schëtov," Wolin Papers, Bund Archives; "Vecher *Sotsialisticheskogo vestnika*," *Sv* 595, 12 March 1947.

6. *Sv* estimated the new Russian emigration in western Germany alone at 800,000 to 1 million. See "Novaia emigratsiia v Germanii," *Sv* 584, 18 April 1946. Demand for *Sv* quadrupled in a single year and was constrained only by the diffi-

culty of transferring funds to Europe for printing and distribution there. See "K nashim chitateliam," *Sv* 592, 27 December 1946. In 1951, after resettlement of refugees, *Vestnik*'s greatest readership was still in Germany and Austria, followed closely by the United States, France, and Israel. There were special thin paper copies for distribution behind the Iron Curtain. Reply (by Abramovitch) to questionnaire (sent by Socialist International) of 13 September 1951, Labour Party Archives.

7. E. Kuskova, "Psikhologiia i ubezhdeniia," *Sv* 575/576, 10 October 1945. Compare "Golos neslomlënnoi Evropy," *Sv* 498, 31 May 1942.

8. On survival, see Berger, *Shipwreck of a Generation*, and *Protiv techeniia* 2 (1954); Abramovitch in *Forverts*, 21 March 1956. In contrast to the earlier "Iz Rossii," "Vesti o Rossii" did not suggest that the Mensheviks had their own correspondants. It was precious news nonetheless.

9. "Russkie voenno-plennye na zapadnom fronte (iz pis'ma)," *Sv* 565/566, 28 April 1945; "Sud'by russkoi emigratsii: eshchë ob okhotnikakh za cherepam vo Frantsii (svodka po pis'mam)," *Sv* 584, 18 April 1946.

10. Dallin lobbied the State Department and publicized the repatriation issue in *NL*. See "V zashchitu Di-Pi," *Sv* 607/608, 20 May 1948, and Dallin's ironically titled article about repatriation from Italy, "Outstanding Military Successes," *NL*, 28 June 1947. In Britain, Baikalov was "trying to create as big a stir as possible" over the same repatriation cases. Baikalov to Nikolaevskii, 20 May 1947, BP.

11. On "blindness," see B. Nikolaevskii, "Novaia emigratsiia i zadachi russkikh sotsialistov," *Sv* 584, 18 April 1946. On library, see Nikolaevskii to Vulikh, 14 January 1947, NC 134(207). On emigration, see Nikolaevskii, "O novoi i staroi emigratsii," *Sv* 604, 26 January 1948. Vishniak, *Gody Émigratsii*, 219.

12. R. Abramovich, "Sluchainost' ili zakonomernost' (o dele Kravchenko)," *Sv* 541/542, 15 April 1944, and "O platforme RSDRP: 'filosofiia epokhi v nashei programe," *Sv* 605, 28 February 1948.

13. Nikolaevskii, "O 'novoi' i 'staroi' emigratsii," *Sv* 604; Nikolaevskii to Vulikh, 1 September 1946, NC 134(207).

14. R. Abramovich, "Problemy russkoi emigratsii," *Sv* 619, 30 April 1949, and "Dela emigrantskie," *Sv* 658 (January 1953); Nikolaevskii to Vulikh, 1 September 1946; Nikolaevskii, "Novaia emigratsiia i zadachi russkikh sotsialistov," *Sv* 584.

15. Bashilov, *Zapiski sbezhavshego ot 'nenastoiashchego sotsializma*.

16. Abramovich, "Chetvert' veka," *Sv* 581, 18 January 1946; and "O platforme RSDRP," *Sv* 605.

17. Nikolaevskii, "O 'staroi' i 'novoi' emigratsii (II)," *Sv* 605. See Andreyev, *Vlasov and the Russian Liberation Movement*.

18. R. Abramovich, "O chem my vsë-taki sporim?" *Sv* 607/608, 20 May 1948.

19. G. Aronson, "Chto nado znat' o vlasovskom divezhenii?" *Sv* 606, 29 March 1948. See also Aronson, *Pravda o vlasovtsakh*, and Dvinov, *Vlasovtsy v svetle dokumentov*.

20. [IP], *Sv* 650 (February 1952). The Vlasovite polemic continued in *Novyi Zhurnal* and *Novoe russkoe slovo*. B. Dvinov, "Nekotorye utochneniia," *Sv* 640 (January 1951).

21. "U nikh niet liudei i niet idei," Abramovich to Vol'skii, 16 July 1951; R.A., "K

voprosu o 'vlasovskom dvizhenii,' " *Sv* 637 (October 1950); Dvinov, "Nekotorye utochneniia." On double standard, see Estrin, "Vospominaniia," (3), 25.

22. "Eto politika," Schapiro, interview.

23. "Liga Bor'by za narodnuiu svobodu," *Sv* 618, 25 March 1949.

24. Quoted from Gul', *Ia unes Rossiu*, 2:38 and 47. R. Abramovich, "Dve Pravdy," *Sv* 543/544, 15 May 1944; S. Shvarts, "Cherchil', Stalin i Pol'sha," *Sv* 557/558, 27 December 1944. For a more favorable view of Kerensky's activities in the league, one that presents him as a victim of nationalists, see Abraham, *Alexander Kerensky*, 378.

25. Dvinov, "Rezoliutsiia" [prepared for ZD], 25 February 1951, NC 75(130), refers to a resolution of the New York group dated 7 January 1950. R.A., "Zametki," *Sv* 630, March 1950, and "Neprilichnaia isterika," *Sv* 625, 31 October 1949.

26. S. Shvarts, "K natsional'nomu voprosu v Rossii," *Sv* 645 (June–July 1951).

27. R. Abramovich, "Narody SSSR—soiuzniki mirovoi demokratii," *Sv* 643 (April 1951); D. Dalin to *mezhpartiinoe soveshchanie*, 19 December 1950, NC 236.

28. "USA State Department and the Free Russia Movement" [confidential and anonymous document], March 1951, NC 235(404). The report is accompanied by a note from Lyons to Nicolaevsky describing it as a "British report—allegedly intelligence." Lyons's organization, it claimed, was supported by David Dubinsky, the head of the International Ladies Garment Workers' Union, "who is notorious in well-informed American quarters for his manipulation of elections in Marxist interests." Moreover, Lyons had allegedly persuaded the State Department to send several "Marxist Harvard professors" to misrepresent the views of the Russian emigration.

29. Ibid.

30. Complaint, Levine to Lyons, memorandum, 31 July 1951, NC 241(424). D. Dallin, "The Wrong Russians Again," *NL*, 12 February 1951, and "Russian Emigré Talks Hit Snag," *NL*, 31 December 1951. On Nicolaevsky and Dallin, see Nikolaevskii to L. Estrin, n.d. [summer 1951], VC. R. Abramovich, "Komu nuzhny takie fal'shivki?" *Sv* 657 (November–December 1952).

31. R. Abramovich, "Fiussen i Shtutgart," *Sv* 647 (September–October 1951). Abramovich was particularly irritated by the Solidarists' claim that they possessed a vast underground network in the Soviet Union. If this was the case, he remarked, Stalinist repression was understandable. The NTS also claimed credit for the Kirov murder in 1934. See Abramovich, "Opasnyi avantiurizm," *Sv* 613, 30 October 1948; R.A. "Nepriiatnyi razgovor," *Sv* 636 (September 1950); and his "Russia's Underground: Facts and Fancy," *American Federationist* (September 1951); 28–30. See also S. Shvarts, "O solidarizme i solidaristakh," *Sv* 646 (August 1951).

32. R. Abramovich, "Tegernsee, Miunkhen, Parizh," *Sv* 664 (September 1953); Chamberlin, "Emigré Anti-Soviet Enterprises and Splits."

33. G. Aronson, "Pis'mo v redaktsiiu," *Sv* 640 (January 1951); Aronson, Dvinov, and Sapir to Abramovich and Shvarts, 8 March 1951, NC 75(130). See "Zaiavleniie Gr. Aronsona, B. Dvinova, B. Sapira," *Sv* 649 (December 1951), and [IP], *Sv* 666 (January 1954), which first gave the details of what had transpired over two years earlier.

34. "Zaiavleniie Gr. Aronsona, B. Dvinova, B. Sapira," *Sv* 649 (December 1951). B.D. [=Dvinov], "Protiv techeniia," *Protiv techeniia* 1 (1952). Opposed to separatism were Dalin, L. Dan, L. Lande, and S. Garvi; see their "Zaiavlenie gruppy russkikh sotsialistov," *Novoe russkoe slovo,* 1 December 1954, reprinted with a reply by Abramovitch and Shwarz in *Sv* 666 (January 1954). See also G. Aronson, "K natsional'nomu voprosu," *Protiv techeniia* 2 (1954).

35. Nikolaevskii to Vol'skii, 20 May 1951, VC. "High time," commented Abramovitch to Vol'skii, 24 February 1956, VC, on the return of the three: Sapir, "a man who reads and thinks but who writes with difficulty"; Aronson, a " 'glib' but uncommonly empty journalist, who does not read and who thinks little"; and Dvinov, "who reads and thinks but who writes in a shallow way and is ill."

WAGING THE COLD WAR

1. G. Aronson, "Neotlozhnaia zadacha," *Sv* 468, 10 February 1941.

2. Bell, interview; Brick, *Daniel Bell and the Decline of Intellectual Radicalism,* 150–153; and Bell, "Modern Review." See also Liebich, *Marxism and Totalitarianism.*

3. Estrine, "Correspondence with French Socialists," especially Verdier to Dubinsky, 19 October 1948 and 17 August 1951, NC 136(208); "Amerikanskaia federatsiia truda v zashchitu rossiiskikh bezhentsev v Avstrii; memorandum redaktsii 'Sotsialisticheskogo vestnika,' " *Sv* 682 (May 1955). The Mensheviks achieved their goal of having the deportation clause removed from the Austrian State Treaty. D. Dallin, "A Great Beginning: AFL and International Affairs," *NL,* 3 January 1948.

4. For bibliograhies of individual Mensheviks' writings, see Rabinowitch and Rabinowitch, eds., *Revolution and Politics,* (Nicolaevsky); Dallin, *From Purge to Coexistence;* Woytinsky, ed., *So Much Alive;* Degras and Nove, eds., *Soviet Planning* (Jasny).

5. The number distributed is modest in comparison with the 4,500 presentation copies of David Shub's *Lenin.* Shub, a longtime *Forverts* editor and contributor to the right wing Menshevik *Zaria* in 1923, was not an insider in the Menshevik group. See "Books Distributed Abroad by the Government," *NL,* 3 August 1953.

6. FBI, letter to SAC, New Haven, "Re: Viktor Andreevich Kravchenko, David J. Dallin, internal security-R," 25 March 1944, and FBI, memo, 1 April 1944, FBI 100–59596, 13 and 24. On Kravchenko's contact with Levine, see FBI, memo, "Re: Viktor Andreevich Kravchenko, internal security—C," 7 April 1944, and "internal security—R," 10 April 1944, 100–59596. For Khinoy's sheltering of Kravchenko, see FBI, memo, "Re: Victor Kravchenko, special inquiry," 15 August 1949, 100–59596, 436. All FOIA. See also Malaurie, *Affaire Kravchenko,* 32–41.

7. S. Thomas, "Comment fut fabriqué Krawchenko," *Lettres françaises* (November 1947). See also Berberova, *Affaire Kravtchenko,*

8. One defense lawyer stated: "I knew them all very well! Nikolaevski is simply a madman [*un possédé*]! Their antibolshevism has driven them half crazy. In the whole world only Franco and the Mensheviks have not yet recognized Soviet power . . . Nikolaevski told me in 1945 that De Gaulle was a Bolshevik." Another

defense lawyer fastened on Kravchenko's statement that the only people he had seen while writing his book were Zenzinov, Dallin, and Nicolaevsky, whom this lawyer identified as "professionals of anti-Soviet propaganda, who have all been unmasked during the war as agents of Goebbels and Hitler." Berberova, *Affaire Kravtchenko*, 222, 117–118, 162–163, 216. I. D. Levine's memoirs, *Eyewitness to History*, repeatedly mention Krivitsky but never Kravchenko.

9. Director, FBI, to SAC, New York, "Espionage—R," 7 February 1948, 100–59596, 310, FOIA. H. Kassen (=Dallin), "Zborowski Case," *NL*, 21 November 1955; D. Dallin, "Mark Zborowski, Soviet Agent," *NL*, 19 and 26 March 1956.

10. S. Shvarts, "Na berlinskom kongresse," *Sv* 634 (July 1950). On the congress, see Grémion, *Intelligence de l'anticommunisme*. Note Laqueur's claim in "Pokhval'noe slovo men'shevikam" that the strongest influence on the congress was Menshevik.

11. For criticism, see Estrine to J. Moch, 27 April 1954, NC 136(208). *NL* quotation from obituary for Dallin, 5 March 1962.

12. V. Woytinsky, "Another Depression on the Way?" *NL*, 19 July 1947; "Will There Be a Depression?" *NL*, 1 December 1952; and "Economic Forecast for 1954," *NL*, 7 December 1953. See L. Gouré's review article, *NL*, 18 January 1947; A. Dane (=A. Dallin), "New Fascists at Work," *NL*, 5 April 1947 and others; S. Bialer, "Three Schools of Kremlin Policy," *NL*, 29 July 1957. Bialer was also a *Vestnik* contributor; Bialer, interview.

13. Souvarine to Volsky, n.d . [ca. 1957], VC; E. Yourevsky (=Volsky), "What's Next in France?" *NL*, 16 July 1951, and "Death of the Stalin Myth," *NL*, 23 August 1954. B. Souvarine, "Failure Is Assured," *NL*, 25 January 1954. O. Rosenfeld, "From Paris," *NL*, 25 January 1947, and "Last Empire," *NL*, 18 January 1954.

14. Wolin, David Dallin's brother, wrote an *NL*-sponsored publication, *Communism's Postwar Decade*. Pistrak wrote *Grand Tactician: Khrushchev's Rise to Power*. Information also from Bell, interview.

15. R. Abramovich, "Totalizatsiia bol'shevizma," *Sv* 646 (August 1951), and "Vopros vsekh voprosov," *Sv* 573/574, 6 September 1945.

16. Quoted from R. Abramovich, "1938 i 1948," *Sv* 606, 29 March 1948, and "Rozhdestvennye kolokola," *Sv* 592, 27 December 1946. On "polygamy," see *NL*, 6 January 1945. Andler, interview.

17. R. Abramovich, "Otvergnutyi Miunkhen i opasnost' voiny," *Sv* 634, July 1950; "After Geneva," *NL*, 2 August 1954; and "Does the U.S. Have a Policy?" *NL*, 17 May 1954. On the H bomb, see also idem, "Outlook at Bermuda," *NL*, 7 December 1953. For Communist attacks, see "Abramovich wunder harmat," *Morning Frayhayt*, 29 June 1950; also *Neie Presse*, 8 October 1954. On the 1917 analogy, see Abramovich to Vol'skii, 14 June 1954, VC.

18. R. Abramovitch, "Was Beria the Great Chance?" *NL*, 20 July 1953; compare corroborating remarks by R. Pikhoia cited in Sudoplatov, *Special Tasks*, 346. Abramovitch, "Behind the Moscow Shifts," *NL*, 14 March 1955; on lost opportunity, see I. Trotskii, "SSSR na novom etape; doklad R. A. Abramovicha," *Novoe russkoe slovo*, 31 May 1956. Communist attacks in "Afardinter Atestat," *Morning Frayhayt*, 16 July 1953.

19. R. Abramovich, "Pravda zitert tsve artiklen fun Forverts," *Forverts,* 26 November 1957; reference to *Forverts* of 9 and 16 October and *Pravda,* 30 October 1957.
20. Nikolaevskii to Vulikh, 1 September 1946, NC 134(207).
21. B. Nikolaevskii, "Na komandnykh vysotakh Kremlia," *Sv* 585 and 586, 22 May and 21 June 1946, and "Novoe pravitel'stvo Stalina," *Sv* 584, 18 April 1946. On policy significance, Nicolaevsky wrote that the Kirov affair might have meant that "Soviet Secret Policy Turned Pro-Nazi in 1934," *NL,* 23 August 1941. On Kremlinology, see D'Agostino, *Soviet Succession Struggles,* chap. 8.
22. B. Nikolaevskii, "Na komandnykh vysotakh Kremlia. G. M. Malenkov i 'malenkovtsy,'" *Sv* 586, 21 June 1946; "How Did Stalin Die?" *NL,* 20 April 1953; "Strange Death of Mikhail Ryumin," *NL,* 4 October 1954; "Russia Purges the Purgers," *NL,* 28 December 1953; "For What Did Beria Die?" *NL,* 4 January 1954; "Return to Stalinism," *NL,* 19 April 1954. Compare L. Pistrak, "Malenkov: Man and Myth," *NL,* 16 March 1953, who found a Trotskyist past for Malenkov and called Khrushchev Malenkov's "young cohort." See also Knight, *Beria,* 180–184, 245n6, 258, 283, who comes down on Nicolaevsky's side, although she questions his view that Beria's ministry was instrumental in bringing about the 1939 Soviet-German pact.
23. For a more cautious view of Malenkov's primacy, contradicting both Abramovitch's and Nicolaevsky's, see Denicke, "Russia—No Monoliths," *NL,* 27 July 1953. See D'Agostino, *Soviet Succession Struggles,* 189.
24. F. Dan, "Znai meru," *Np* 57/58, 10 February 1946.
25. Souvarine owed his influential position to his reputation as Stalin's biographer and to his editorship of *Contrat social,* for which several Mensheviks, including Alexandrova, Dallin, Jasny, Nicolavsky, and Pistrak, wrote, as well as to his numerous contributions to *Est et Ouest* and other French publications. See Panné, *Boris Souvarine.*
26. Cited from B. Nikolaevskii, "O sushchestve spora (otvet B. K. Suvarinu)," replying to B. Souvarine, "Ot neozhidannosti k neozhidannosti," both *Sv* 783/784 (November–December 1963). See also their letters in *Contrat social* 3 (January 1959): 61–62.
27. Nicolaevsky's first and most important book was *Aseff the Spy.* In the 1930s he dealt with the "Protocols of the Elders of Zion." See Cohn, *Warrant for Genocide,* 221.
28. D'Agostino, *Soviet Succesion Struggles,* 172, 181–182, cites B. Nicolaevsky, "Stalin's Secret Sickness," *This Week Magazine,* 7 November 1948; Nicolaevsky, "How Did Stalin Die?" See also Abramovich to Vol'skii, 28 November 1953, VC, and Souvarine to Volsky, n.d. [probably late 1957], VC. For "major crisis," see Nicolaevsky, "The Abakumov Case," *NL,* 10 January 1955.
29. On "madhouse," see Vol'skii to Souvarine, 21 September 1959, SC. Only Denike received praise from Souvarine. On Rand Corporation, see Souvarine, "Kremlinologie," 121–125.
30. D. Dalin, "O samom glavnom," *Sv* 470, 11 March 1941, and on defensism, idem, "Zhestokii ekzamen," *Sv* 478, 17 July 1941.
31. [Editorial Notebook], K. Meyer, "Russia's Worst Kept Secret," *NYT,* 29 August

1988; review by John Chamberlain, *NYT,* 7 January 1944. O'Neill, *Better World,* 78, writes that the books were published by Yale because commercial publishers feared a boycott.

32. "Riga, Hankö and Kishinev seemed a better defense than Paris and London," wrote Dallin in *Soviet Russia's Foreign Policy,* xix and 54. Cf. his "Stalin and Molotov, 1939–1941 and 1945–1948," *NL,* 31 January 1948, and *Russia and Postwar Europe,* 220–223.

33. Dallin, *Real Soviet Russia,* vii, and *Russia and Postwar Europe,* 4–5.

34. "Iz predistorii soveto-germanskoi voiny," *Np* 25, 10 January 1943, and A. Iugov, "V triasine anti-bol'shevizma" *Np* 37, 16 January 1944. See also Iugov, "Prekratite revoliutsiiu," *Np* 48, 25 February 1945.

35. M. Karpovich, review of *Big Three and World Peace, NYT,* 12 August 1945.

36. F. Hackett, review of *Real Soviet Russia, NYT,* 25 November 1944; R. Bates, "Challenge of History," *New Republic,* 17 January 1944, cited in O'Neill, *Better World,* 78.

37. Reviews by P. Mosely, "A Pro-Russian, Anti-Stalin Policy," *NL,* 21 May 1951; A. Berle, "Beyond the Kremlin Are the People," *NYT,* 25 February 1951.

38. T. Durdin, "Russia and the East," review of *Rise of Russia in Asia, NYT,* 12 June 1949.

39. Dallin's relations with the FBI are discussed later in this chapter. On sources, see Navasky, "Transformation of Historical Ambiguity into Cold War Verity."

40. Dallin and Nicolaevsky, *Forced Labor in Soviet Russia.* In addition to the impact of the book, there were a number of popular spin-offs, B. Nicolaevsky, "Stalin's Eldorado," *Fortune* (August 1947); D. Dallin, "'Slave Empire within the Soviet Empire, *NYT Magazine,* 14 October 1951. See *NL* editorial comment in "Challenge to Vyshinsky," 8 November 1947.

41. Accounts included in Dallin and Nicolaevsky, *Forced Labor;* B. Sapir's memoir, "19-oe dekabria (k godovshchine Solovetskoi tragedii 1923)," *Sv* 141, 6 December 1926; and B. Nicolaevsky's rendition of a sailor's story, "Krov'iu omytoe sovetskoe zoloto ('Dal'stroi—sovetskaia katorga v Kolymskom krae)," *Sv* 579/580, 10 December 1945. Early accounts include A. Tsiliga, "Po sovetskim tiurmam i ssylkam," *Sv* 366, 27 May 1936; "Po sovetskim izoliatoram," *Sv* 391, 12 June 1937; and other articles. Duchess of Atholl, *Conscription of a People,* mentions Baikalov's help; his book *In the Land of the Communist Dictatorship* is one of her fundamental sources. See annotated bibliography in Dallin and Nicolaevsky, *Forced Labor,* and Zorin, *Soviet Prisons and Concentration Camps.*

42. Dallin and Nicolaevsky, *Forced Labor,* ix. Compare D. Dalin, "Gulag," *Sv* 587/588, 20 August 1946.

43. Arendt, "Totalitarian Terror"; O. Prescott, review of *Forced Labor, NYT,* 26 August 1947.

44. Dan, "Znai meru," *Np* 57/58.

45. Dallin, "Préface à l'édition française," in Dallin and Nicolaevsky, *Travail forcé en URSS;* "Russian Gold (By a Correspondent)" and D. Keswick, letter to the editor, *Economist,* 29 May and 28 June 1948.

46. E. Crankshaw, "Forced Labour in Russia," *New Statesman and Nation,* 15 May 1948.

47. A. Rothstein, correspondence, *New Statesman and Nation,* 27 May 1948. On this prominent Communist, see Caute, *Fellow Travellers,* 137, 342; A. Werth, correspondence, *New Statesman and Nation,* 19 June 1948.

48. B. Atkinson, "Penal Servitude, Russian Model," *NYT,* 31 August 1947; Dallin and Nicolaevsky, *Forced Labor,* 84–86.

49. D. Dallin, "An Unfinished Task," *NL,* 8 January 1949; Jasny, "Labour and Output in Soviet Concentration Camps."

50. Robert Conquest, who relied on *Forced Labor* as a source for the first edition of his *Great Terror,* lowered the estimates in the revised edition without repudiating *Forced Labor.* Compare N. Werth, "Goulag: Les vrais chiffres," *Histoire* 169 (September 1993), whose figure of 2–2.5 million Gulag inmates on the average over fifteen years is, coincidentally, very close to his father's figures (1.5–2 million) in the *New Statesman* letter of 1948 cited in note 47. On A. Werth's defense of these figures in 1967, see Caute, *Fellow Travellers,* 103. Compare Getty, Rittersporn, and Zemskov, "Victims of the Soviet Penal System," who tend to confirm Jasny's figures.

51. "Million Dollar Slander Suit against Vyshinsky," *NYT,* 2 November 1947; "Soviet Exiles Urge Slave Labor Study," *NYT,* 17 February 1950; D. Dallin, "Bad Habits," *NL,* 1 November 1947, and "Poimannye s polichnym," *Sv* 622, 29 July 1949.

52. David Rousset, "Le sens de notre combat," in Barton, *Institution concentrationnaire en Russie,* 22. See also "Nazi Victims Join Slave Labor Fight," *NYT,* 26 March 1950. On Rousset, see Caute, *Communism and the French Intellectuals,* esp. 182–185.

53. "French Open Libel Trial," *NYT,* 26 November 1950, and Daix, *J'ai cru au matin,* 256–261. See also R. Abramovich, "Fiussen i Shtutgart," *Sv* 647 (September–October 1951); and Levine to Lyons, 31 July 1951, NC 241(424). Compare Judt, *Past Imperfect,* 113–115; Dallin, *From Purge to Coexistence,* 3–116.

54. D. Dallin, "Stalin-Wallace Program," *NL,* 22 May 1948.

55. D. Dallin, "Henry Wallace and Chinese Communism," *NL,* 22 October 1951; "Lattimore on China," *NL,* 11 June 1949; and "Mao No Tito; US Must Act," *NL* 7 May 1949. The Lattimore case is discussed later, but note there is no mention of Dallin in Lattimore's *Ordeal by Slander.* On the Alsops, see Dallin, "Myth of Chinese 'Titoism' Revived," *NL,* 27 August 1951.

56. D. Dallin, "The Mundt-Nixon Bill," *NL,* 8 May 1948, and "How To Deal with the Satellites," *NL,* 18 February 1952. On the Marshall Plan, see his "Capitalism in One Country," *NL,* 23 August 1947. On Europe, idem, "Europe's New Anti-Americanism," *NL,* 30 May 1953, and on Germany, "We Are Staying Too Long," *NL,* 11 September 1948.

57. D. Dallin, "The Debacle in China," *NL,* 27 November 1948; "More Zigzags or Consistency? Need for a Dynamic Policy for America," *NL,* 22 March 1947; and on Berlin, "Either-Or," *NL,* 17 April 1948.

58. D. Dallin, "Sources of Soviet Conduct," *NL,* 19 July 1947, and "Liberation or Containment?" *NL* 29 September 1952. For earlier criticism of Kennan for seeking to spare Soviet loss of prestige, see Dallin, "Russia's Iron Hoop," *NL,* 16 July 1949.

59. D. Dallin, "West Doesn't Exist," *NL,* 8 October 1951, and "Why Germans Dis-

trust America," *NL*, 2 June 1952. See also "Is France our Ally? No, says David Dallin," and the reply (yes) by A. Shub, *NL*, 26 July 1954; and, previously, Dallin, "France—The West's Weakest Link," *NL*, 18 December 1950.

60. Cited from D. Dallin, "With Whom and For What," *NL*, 14 August 1948. Aee also his "Problem of Tito: Should We Accept Undemocratic Allies?" *NL*, 11 August 1952. For his "intermediate classes" analogy, see "Evolution of Stalin's Communism," *NL*, 17 January 1948.

61. On relaxation and superiority, see D. Dallin, "World Ike Faces," *NL*, 19 January 1953, and "Europe Comes First," *NL*, 3 January 1955. In Indochina nothing less than complete victory was acceptable, and Dallin urged recruitment of an expeditionary force of South Koreans, Chinese nationalists, and German volunteers; see his "How To Win in Indochina," *NL*, 22 February 1954. Compare B. Souvarine, "Failure Is Assured," *NL*, 25 January 1954. For potential U.S. superiority, see Dallin, "Repercussions," *NL*, 8 October 1949.

62. D. Dallin, "Moscow's Strategic Retreat," *NL*, 5 April 1953, and "What Malenkov Wants," *NL*, 25 January 1954.

63. Dallin, "How To Win in Indochina," and "Europe Comes First."

64. D. Dallin, "Ukrainian Army Myth," *NL*, 3 December 1951; "Anti-Semitism in Russia," *NL*, 6 March 1948; "Our Enemy Is Not the Russian People," *NL*, 26 November 1951; and "Europe after Stalin Falls," *NL*, 17 December 1951.

65. Dallin, "Soviet Revolution: Shattered Hopes" (1957), in *From Purge to Coexistence,* 174. Compare O. Rosenfeld's similar sentiments, cited earlier, acknowledging specifically, as Dallin did not, that he was no longer counting on the working class.

66. Dallin, "Social Change and Soviet Foreign Policy" (1960), in *From Purge to Coexistence,* 181.

67. See further Liebich, "Mensheviks Wage the Cold War."

THE AMERICAN FILE

1. Vera Turin, "Memorandum for Mr. James R. Sharp, Chief, Foreign Agents Registration Act Section, Re: The Russian Social Democratic Labor Party," Department of Justice, 5 November 1942, 144-1163.

2. "A Brief History of the Menshevik Party" [document of unspecified origin attached to] Wendell G. Johnson to Asst. Chief of Staff, G-3, Intelligence, "Subject: The Menshevik Dvinow (Boris Gurevich), Saphier, G. J. Aronson," 16 November 1951, 105-0-4429.

3. J. Edgar Hoover, Director, FBI, to SAC, NY, "THEODORE GOURVITCH-DAN, with aliases Theodor Gourvitch-Dan, Theodore Dan, Theodor Dan," 5 October 1943, 100-236199-1–5.

4. FBI, NY, "THEODORE GOUREVITCH-DAN, with aliases," 11 and 13 December 1943, NY 100-54462; "NOVY PUT, a.k.a.: The New Road, The New Way," 8 [month deleted] 1945, FBI, NY 100-60093.

5. FBI, NY, "Title [deleted] with alias," 12 October 1944 [ref: Teletype from Chicago to Bureau, Washington Field and NY], 16 September 1944, NY 100-61198-21.

Paul Scheffer was a correspondent in Moscow in the 1920s whose *Sieben Jahre Sowjetunion* had impressed the Mensheviks at the time.

6. As summarized in FBI, NY, 12 October 1944.

7. Hoover to SAC, NY, "THEODORE GOURVITCH-DAN," 5 October 1943, 100-236199.

8. Quotations are from DeWitt Poole, "Some Notes on the Russian Community in New York [Memorandum for the Director of Strategic Services, Secretary of State]," 11 October 1944, OSS Foreign Nationalities Branch, FN no. S-119, introducing report titled "My Russian Week in New York," whose author is described as "an American citizen of Russian background who is well known to the Branch as a competent and sympathetic political interpreter." The cover page also bears a handwritten file number 100-7826-30.

9. Frank G. [illegible], Dep. Director, Plans, to Director, FBI, att. Mr. S. J. Papich, "Subject: [deleted]," internal security, Bureau File no. [deleted], 23 December 1952, CIA.

10. FBI, Washington, D.C. [case originated at New York], "OLGA YUGOW, 7 April 1955, WFO 105-11169.

11. FBI, NY, "RUSSKY GOLOS PUBLISHING CORPORATION," 9 November 1955 and 12 August 1957, 100-39588-100 and NY 100-4123. The latter file goes up to 1967.

12. FBI, NY, "BORIS IVAN NICOLAEVSKY," 28 January 1955, NY 105-7278.

13. FBI, NY, "BORIS IVAN NICOLAEVSKY, 6 April 1955, NY 105-7278.

14. SAC, NY, to Director, FBI, "WALTER G. KRIVITSKY, with aliases," 16 November 1944, letter to Director, NY 100-59589; FBI, NY, "BORIS I. NICOLAEVSKY," 9 June 1954, NY-105-7278.

15. FBI, NY, "*CHANGED* BORIS IVAN NICOLAEVSKY, was: Boris Nikolayevsky, Boris Nicolajewsky, N. Borisov, Gregory Golosov, Barton, Nicholas, 'Ivanov,' " 17 September 1954, NY-105-7278.

16. Col. S. V. Constant, GSC, Dir., Sec. & Intel. Div. [for the commanding general], "Boris NIKOLAEVSKY [illegible]," Intelligence Report no. 2176, Sec. & Intel. Div Hq., 2nd S.G., Governors' Island, NY, 30 April 1946 [document released by Department of the Army].

17. FBI, NY, 9 June 1954 and 17 September 1954.

18. FBI, Richmond, "BORIS IVAN NICOLAEVSKY," 23 November 1954, RH 105-396.

19. FBI, "Re: R. ABRAMOWITSCH (Abramovich, Abramovitch)," 8 March 1941, 40-0-1462.

20. FBI, NY, "Title: RAPHAEL REIN-ABRAMOVITCH, was Raphael Abramovitch, R. A. Abromovitch," 20 June 1944, 100-244021-3.

21. FBI, SAC, NY, to Director, FBI, "Subject: CINRAD," 12 February 1952, 100-190625-3726.

22. FBI, Boston, "Title: VERA MORDVINOV (Pen name Alexandroff Monsosshohn-Schwarz) aka Mrs. Solomon Monsosshohn-Schwarz," 22 May 1948, file no. 123-81, reference: bureau file 123-426 [extended file number illegible].

23. [Name deleted] to D. M. Ladd, "Subject: 'SOVIET RUSSIA AND THE JEWS' BY GREGORY ARONSON, 1949," 20 July 1949, 94-39917.

24. FBI, MEMORANDUM FOR THE DIRECTOR, Re [deleted] David J. Dallin [deleted], 14 March 1944, 100-275683-46.

25. FBI [routing slip with negative photocopy of article], stamped 30 October 1947, 105-35817-81.
26. Dallin to Hoover, 27 September 1951, 105-35817-X9 [or 5].
27. Levitas to Hoover, 28 September 1951, 105-35817-X9 [or 5].
28. [Name deleted; Hoover?] to Mr. A. H. Belmont, "Subject: DAVID DALLIN, INFORMATION CONCERNING," 11 April 1952, 105-35817-X6. The name of the committee member is deleted as well.
29. SAC, NY (94-0) to Director, FBI, "Subject: RESEARCH MATTER DAVID J. DALLIN," 26 February 1954, 105-35817-X13.
30. W. A. Branigan to A. H. Belmont, "Subject: REVIEW OF BOOK 'SOVIET ESPIONAGE' BY DAVID J. DALLIN," 2 November 1955, 105-35817-4.
31. A. H. Belmont to L. V. Boardman, "Subject: 'SOVIET ESPIONAGE' BY DAVID J. DALLIN. MISCELLANEOUS INFORMATION CONCERNING (ESPIONAGE)," 9 November 1955, 105-35817.
32. Hoover to Dallin, 23[5?] November 1955, 105-35817-9. These allegations appear on pp. 427, 442, and 474 of *Soviet Espionage.*
33. Dallin to Hoover, 5 December 1955, 105-35817-8.
34. A. H. Belmont to L. V. Boardman, "Subject: DAVID J. DALLIN MISCELLANEOUS-INFORMATION CONCERNING (ESPIONAGE)."
35. [Name deleted] to Mr. Tolson, 16 January 1956, "Subject: DAVID J. DALLIN," 105-35817-12.
36. Joseph Alderman, Chief, Subversive Organizations Section, to William E. Foley. Executive Assistant, "Subject: David J. Dallin, Expert Witness; International Union of Mine, Mill and Smelter Workers," 30 September 1955. Thomas A. Daly to A. Warren Littman, Head, Infiltrated Organizations Unit, "Subject: Expert Witness, David J. Dallin," 30 August 1955.
37. William F. Tompkins, Asst. Attorney General, Internal Security Dvision, to S. A. Andretta, Asst. Attorney General, Administrative Division, "David J. Dallin, Expert Witness; International Union of Mine, Mill and Smelter Workers," 11 October 1955.
38. [Name illegible] to Joe Warren, "Subject, MINE, MILL expert: DAVID J. DALLIN" [date illegible]. The remark is attributed to "Miss Helen Hundhausen."
39. SAC, NY, to Director, FBI, 11 January 1967, "Subject: [excised], re. Bulet," 30 November 1966, 100-59596.
40. Costello and Tsarov, *Deadly Illusions;* 1965 debriefing, app. 3 (406–411). It is not clear who carried out the briefing; Costello claims to have obtained the text from an anonymous source in French counterintelligence.
41. Ibid., 409. The book is confused about dates, even though it claims that this is the essence of the matter. It refers to "Christmas 1953 [sic—should be 1955]." In fact, by Christmas 1955 Dallin had already written his first article about the Zborowski case *(NL,* 21 November 1955).
42. Report of FBI interview with the Dallins, 16 December 1953, and L. Dallin, 23 May 1954, in FBI, NY [summary], 23 May 1956, "Title: Changed LYDIA DALLIN, aka: Mrs. David J. Dallin, nee LILIA GINZBERG, was: Lilia Estrin, Lilly Estrin, Lola Estrin, Mrs. Samuel Estrin," NY 105-17490.

43. Costello and Tsarov, *Deadly Illusions,* 409–410.
44. Ibid., 322. "Lola Estrine [Dallin] reported to the NKVD that the 'Stein' letters [to Trotsky] were postmarked from San Francisco." The information was Lola's, but the report was Zborowski's, gleaned by him in conversation with her. Compare L. Dallin's memorandum of Zborowski's confessional visit to her, 3 October 1955. SAC, NY to SA [deleted], "Subject: MARK ZBOROWSKI, was ESP-R," 18 May 1956, 105-17490-3.
45. Costello and Tsarov, *Deadly Illusions,* 488. This section is written in the first person by Costello, presumably the overall author, as attested to by howlers resulting from his ignorance of Russian; see, for example, p. 320, illustration facing p. 414, p. 470n53. His coauthor, Tsarov, who translated the documents, worked for the KGB and, one presumes, is still working for its successor.
46. FBI, NY, "Socialist Courrier," 28 July 1964, 100-123986-8180 and 5 May 1949, NY 65-14900.

THE FINAL CAMPAIGN

1. Abramovich to Vol'skii, 28 November 1953, VC. Cited from Souvarine to Volsky, n.d. [1957], VC; Souvarine to Volsky n.d. [ca. 1958], SC. See also Liebich, "Mensheviks in the Face of Stalinism."
2. E. Iur'evsksii [=Volsky], "Dva marksizma" (also in *Contrat social* 3 [1959]) and "K kharakteristike N. G. Chernyshevskogo," *Sv* 684/685 (July–August 1955) and 686 (September 1955); B. Nikolaevskii, "Marks i Chernyshevskii," *Sv* 687 (October 1955), and "Lenin mezhdu Marksom i Chernyshevskim," *Sv* 688 (December 1955). The announced second part of the last article never appeared. See also Vol'skii to Souvarine, 22 August 1962, SC; Nikolaevskii to Vol'skii, 25 July 1962, VC.
3. R.A., "Lenin i marksizm. Po povodu knigi N. Valentinova: 'Vstrechi s Leninym,'" *Sv* 664 (September 1953); Belik, "O vliianii Chernyshevskogo," 74.
4. Shub, "O predkakh Lenina"; A. Burgina, "K sporu o rasovom proiskhozhdenii deda Lenina," *Novoe russkoe slovo,* 30 April 1961; N. Valentinov, "Eshchë o Lenine i ego predkakh," *Sv* 753 (May 1961); B. Nikolaevskii, "Pis'mo v redaktsiiu," *Sv* 753 (May 1961); Nikolaevskii to Vol'skii, 19 February 1949, VC. Volkogonov, *Lenin,* 8–9, confirms but dates discovery to the period after 1924.
5. B. Nikolaevskii, "Iu. O. Martov i s-r (istoricheskaia spravka)," *Sv* 543/544, 15 May 1944; Nicolaevsky to P. Herz, 18 April 1934, cited in Mayer, "Geschichte des sozialdemokratischen Parteiarchivs," 99.
6. B. Sapir, "Bol'shevizm (po povodu knigi Bertrama Vol'fa 'Troe kotorye sdelali revoliutsiiu: Lenin–Trotskii–Stalin)," *Sv* 614, 30 November 1948, and "Men'-shevizm," *Sv* 616/617, 15 February 1949. Rebuttals in G. Aronson, "Neopravdannaia reviziia," *Sv* 623/624, 23 September 1949, and "Men'shevizm," *Sv* 625, 31 October 1949.
7. Souvarine to Volsky, 21 September 1959, and Vol'skii to Souvarine, 29 July 1960, SC.

8. Souvarine to Volsky, n.d. [1960], and n.d. [1957], SC. On Denike, see Souvarine to Volsky, 21 September 1959 and 16 April 1960, SC.

9. On the Martov book, see L. Dan to Estrin, 1 October 1958, NC 136(209). On Sapir's projects, see L. Dan to Vol'skii, 19 April 1960, and Sapir's note in *Iz Arkhiva L. O. Dan*, 159. See also Vol'skii to Souvarine, n.d. [1964], SC. Cited from L. Dan to N. and V. Vol'skii, 28 October 1956, *Iz Arkhiva L. O. Dan*, 152; and L. Dan to N. Vol'skii, 19 April 1960.

10. Cited from L. Dan to Vol'skii, 28 May 1959; editor's introduction, *Iz Arkhiva L. O. Dan.*, xxix and 154. See also Abramovich to Vol'skii, 27 October 1958, VC; Nikolaevskii to Vol'skii, 28 January 1956, and Abramovich to Vol'skii, 3 October and 18 December 1957, VC; Souvarine to Volsky, 29 January 1957, SC. Cited from Souvarine, "Viol de Clio," 119.

11. L. Dan to V. and N. Vol'skii, May 1962, *Iz Arkhiva L. O. Dan*, 178; also Liebich, "Mensheviks, Then and Now." On Schapiro, see L. Dan to V. and N. Vol'skii, 28 October 1956.

12. Cited from Louis Fischer, in A. Rabinowitch, "Foreword" to the commemorative volume *Revolution and Politics in Russia*, vii. On the archives, see Mosely, "Boris Nicolaevsky: American Years."

13. Nikolaevskii to Spalding, 26 August 1933, Spalding Collection, Hoover Institution. See also Nicolaevsky to H. Hirsch, 19 April 1948, Leo Beck Library, Tamiment Institute, New York; "Hoover Institute Gets Russia File," *NYT*, 22 December 1963.

14. Epstein, "Nikolaevskii Collection at Indiana"; Bourguina, interview 2. Cited from Nikolaevskii to Estrin, 30 September 1965, NC 136(209).

15. Bourguina, interview 2. Conference proceedings edited as Keep, ed., *Contemporary History in the Soviet Mirror*.

16. Bourguina, interview 2; Wolfe, interview. See also *Novoe russkoe slovo*, 28 October 1982.

17. Reed and Jakobson, "Trotsky Papers at the Hoover Institution"; Palm, *Guide to the Boris I. Nicolaevsky Collection in the Hoover Institution Archives*, ii.

18. Nikolaevskii to Vol'skii, 24 April 1951, VC.

19. Abramovich to Vol'skii, 16 September 1957 and 11 January 1956, VC.

20. Abramovich to Vol'skii, 25 September 1957, VC; "inkling" refers to M. Fainsod and B. Wolfe. On Schapiro, see Carrère d'Encausse, "URSS ou le totalitarisme exemplaire," 211.

21. Mosely to Abramovitch, 1 September 1955, PMP, referring to a letter from Abramovitch to him, dated 15 August 1955; Abramovitch to Vol'skii, 13 March 1957, VC.

22. Abramovitch to Mosely, 10 November 1955, PMP.

23. Mosely to Abramovich [sic], 20 October 1955; Abramovitch to Mosely, 10 November 1955, PMP.

24. L. Dan to Vol'skii, 8 August 1960; for her view of the book, see L. Dan to Vol'skii, n.d. [1963], VC. See also Mosely to Abramovich, 20 October 1955; Abramovich to Vol'skii, 14 April 1956, VC.

25. Sidney Hook, "Introduction," in Abramovitch, *Soviet Revolution*, vii–xii; L. Schapiro, review of Abramovitch, *Soviet Revolution, Listener*, 21 March 1963.

26. L. Dan to Vol'skii, 28 May 1959, *Iz Arkhiva L. O. Dan*, 154; L. Dan to A. Meyer, 6 December 1955, PMP; Meyer to Messers. Fainsod, Fischer, Mosely, and Robinson, 8 December 1955, PMP.

27. Abramovich to Vol'skii, 15 December 1955, VC; L. Dan to Vol'skii, 28 May 1959, *Iz Arkhiva L. O. Dan*, 154.

28. Haimson, "Preface," in *Mensheviks*, xi; Sapir to Haimson, 24 September 1967, MP Archives.

29. Rosenberg, review of Haimson, ed., *Mensheviks*, 731; L. Dan to N. Vol'skii, 28 May 1959, *Iz Arkhiva L. O. Dan*, 154. See also Liebich, "Mensheviks, Then and Now."

Conclusion

1. Sapir announcement in posession of author. Bers obituary, *NYT*, 4 February 1993.

2. Sapir's letter, for publication, in *Novoe russkoe slovo*, transmitted through the kindness of SPD veteran F. Heine to author. Citation on Gorbachev, D. Abulafia's obituary of Sapir, *Independent*, 14 December 1989. On perestroika, see Sapir to author, 2 January 1989; and Bers to author, 31 May 1988. On Sapir's Marxism, see M. Jansen, "Ideeën zijn blijkbaar niet definitief te doden," *NRC Handelsblad*, 5 January 1986.

3. Citation from J. Hellbeck, "Zweimal Russland," *Frankfurter Allgemeine Zeitung*, 22 June 1994, reporting on a conference which drew almost forty paper presenters and an equal number of researchers on the emigrations; published as Schlögel, ed., *Russische Emigration in Deutschland*. Among relevant recent Western monographs anticipating this interest are Johnson, *New Mecca, New Babylon;* Raeff, *Russia Abroad;* and Stephan, *Russian Fascists* (the latter two now translated into Russian), as well as Andreyev, *Vlasov*. See also Schlögel, " 'Andere Russland,' " and Schlögel, ed., *Grosse Exodus*.

4. See Werth, "De la soviétologie," 127–144, and discussion in *Slavic Review* 52 (1993): 87–106. Note Pipes's remarks in *Russia under the Bolshevik Regime*, xviii.

5. Schapiro, "Soviet History Writing"; Osharov, "To Alien Shores," 294. For "losers," see Emmons, "Recent Developments," 150. On facing alternatives, see H. Trevor-Roper, "Lost Moments of History," *New York Review of Books*, 27 October 1988.

6. Galili, Haimson, and Nenarokov, eds., *Men'sheviki v 1917 g*. The thesis is Tumarinson, *Men'sheviki i bol'sheviki*.

7. On "revenge," see Volobuev and Klokov, "Noveishie amerikanskie publikatsii po istorii men'shevizma," 209.

8. On socialist dissidents, I am indebted to Boris Weil of Copenhagen. See materials collected by Radio Liberty in "Arkhiv samizdata," notably *Sotsialist 82*, and the anonymous "Retsenziia 'o zhurnale "Levyi povorot" ' " (1982), among the very few to mention *Sv*, if only cursorily. The most representative work of this current, Kagarlitsky, *Thinking Reed*, passes over the Mensheviks entirely.

9. Podbolotov and Spirin, *Krakh men'shevizma v sovetskoi Rossii*.

10. Alexander Dallin, who attended the inaugural Social Democratic Congress, has

kindly conveyed his impressions. On Erhard, see interview with the party's Soltan Dzarasanov, *Wirtschaftswoche,* 11 May 1990.

11. Citations from Odom, "Pluralist Mirage," 101, and Pipes, *Russian Revolution,* 557.

12. Trevor-Roper, "Lost moments of History."

13. The citation regarding longtime *New Leader* editor Sol Levitas and Daniel Bell, the self-described American Menshevik, is from Healey, *Time of My Life,* 201.

14. Dan, *Pism'a,* 402.

15. Dan cited in Sapir, "Theodor Dan," 16; D. Dalin, "O samom glavnom," *Sv* 470, 11 March 1940.

16. Citation from Umberto Eco, *NYT Book Review,* 12 March 1989.

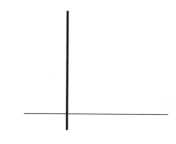

Sources

Archives

Amsterdam
Internationaal Instituut voor Sociale Geschiedenis.

Cambridge, Mass.
Houghton Library, Harvard University.

London
Labour Party Archives (now at National Museum of Labour History, Manchester).

Moscow
Gosudarstvennyi Arkhiv Rossiiskoi Federatsii.
Rossiiskii Tsentr Khraneniiia i Izuchaniia Dokumentov Noveishei Istorii.

New York
Archives of the Inter-University Project on the History of the Menshevik Movement, Columbia University.
Archives of Russian and East European History (Bakhmeteff Archives), Columbia University.
Archives of the YIVO Institute for Jewish Research.
Columbia University Archives.
Federal Bureau of Investigation, field office.
Jewish Labor Bund Archives.
Tamiment Library, New York University.

Paris
Archives du Ministère des Affaires étrangères.
Archives nationales.
Archives de la Préfecture de Police.

Stanford
Hoover Institution Archives.

Urbana
University Archives, University of Illinois at Urbana-Champaign.

Washington, D.C.
Department of Justice, Criminal Division.
Federal Bureau of Investigation.

Interviews

AUTHOR INTERVIEWS

Andler, Pierre and Lia [née Rein]. Paris, 26 May 1982.
Bell, Daniel. Cambridge, Mass., 31 March 1984.
Bers, Lipman. New York, 2 April 1984.
Bialer, Seweryn. New York, 27 October 1981.
Boffa, Giuseppe. New York, 2 April 1984.
Bourguina, Anna. Stanford, (1) 21 and 31 July 1980; (2) 29 April and 8 May 1981.
Dallin, Alexander. Stanford, 5 May 1981.
Erlich, Alexander. New York, 29 October 1981.
Garvy, George. Manhasset, N.Y., 25 October 1981.
Gourevitch, Victor. New York, 6 April 1984.
Haimson, Leopold. New York, 28 October 1981.
Kisselgoff, Avran and Lila. New York, 28 October 1981.
Levitas, Esther. New York, 6 April 1984.
Nove, Alec. London, 2 June 1982.
Ryba, Richard. Montreal, 15 September 1984.
Sapir, Boris. Amsterdam, (1) 16 and 17 January 1980; (2) 2 March 1982.
Schapiro, Leon. New York, 4 April 1984.
Turim, Marie [née Aronson]. Washington, D.C., 28 August 1984.
Wolfe, Ella. Stanford, 18 August 1983.

MENSHEVIK PROJECT (L. H. HAIMSON, TRANSCRIPTS, 1960–1963)

Abramovich, Rafael Rein.
Dan, Lidia Osipovna.
Denike, Iurii Petrovich.
Dvinov, Boris L'vovich.
Nikolaevskii, Boris Ivanovich.
Stenzel, Sigmund Simonovich.

(Parts of the Dan, Denike, and Nikolaevskii interviews were translated and published in *Making of Three Russian Revolutionaries*.)

Publications

Abraham, Richard. *Alexander Kerensky: The First Love of the Revolution*. New York: Columbia University Press, 1987.

Abramovich, Rafael. "Men'sheviki i sotsialisticheskii internatsional, 1918–1940." MP paper in *Men'sheviki*, ed. Iu. G. Fel'shtinskii. Benson, Vt.: Chalidze Publications, 1988.

——— "Men'sheviki i sotsialisticheskii internatsional, 1918–1940." Pt. 2, "Ot Gamburga k Marseliu." MP paper, n.d.

Abramovitch, R. *The Soviet Revolution, 1917–1937*. New York: International Universities Press, 1962.

——— *In tsvey revoliutsy*. Vol. 1. New York: Workman's Circle, 1944.

Abramowitsch, R. "Einheitsfront und Einheitspartei." *Zeitschrift für Sozialismus* 33 (1936): 1050–58.

——— "Die Entwicklung Sowjetrusslands." *Die Gesellschaft* 1 (1926): 322–345.

——— "Fünfjahresplan und Sozialdemokratie." *Die Gesellschaft* 8 (1931): 24–39.

——— "Julius Martow and das russische Proletariat." *Der Kampf* 16 (1923): 180–188.

——— "Karl Kautsky und der Richtungsstreit in der russischen Sozialdemokratie." *Der Kampf* 17 (1924): 27–33.

——— *Die Politische Gefangenen in der Sowjetunion*. Berlin: J. H. W. Dietz, 1930.

——— "Revolution und Konterrevolution in Russland: Das neue Kautsky-Buch über Russland." *Die Gesellschaft* 7 (1930): 532–540.

——— "Stalinismus oder Sozialdemokratie." *Die Gesellschaft* 9 (1932): 133–147.

——— *Wandlungen der Bolschewistischen Diktatur*. Berlin: J. H. W. Dietz, 1931.

——— *Die Zukunft Sowjetrusslands*. Jena: Thüringer Verlaganstalt, 1923.

——— "Zwei Revolutionen und eine Diktatur." *Der Kampf* 20 (1927): 492–498.

Abramowitsch, R., V. Suchomlin, and I. Zeretelli. *Der Terror gegen die sozialistischen Parteien in Russland und Georgien*. Berlin: J. H. W. Dietz, 1925.

Adler, Friedrich. *The Anglo-Russian Report: A Criticism of the Report of the British Trades Union Delegation to Russia from the Point of View of International Socialism*. London: P. S. King & Son, 1925.

——— "Das Stalinsche Experiment und der Sozialismus." *Der Kampf* 25 (1932): 14–16.

——— "Was täte ein Lenin heute zur Rettung der russischen Revolution?" *Der Kampf* 22 (1929): 57–60.

——— *The Witchcraft Trial in Moscow*. London: Commission of Enquiry into the Conditions of Political Prisoners, 1936.

——— "Zur Diskussion über Sowjetrussland: Ein Briefwechsel mit Karl Kautsky." *Der Kampf* 31 (1933): 58–68.

Adler, F., et al. *The Moscow Trial and the LSI*. London: Labour Party, 1931.

Agurskii, M. S. *Ideologiia natsional bol'shevizma*. Paris: YMCA Press, 1980.

Aleksandrova, Vera. *Literatura i zhizn': ocherki sovetskogo obshchestvennogo razvitiia do kontsa vtoroi mirovoi voiny*, ed. S. Shvarts. New York: Russian Institute of Columbia University, 1969.

——— *Perezhitoe (1917–1921)*. MP Paper 12. New York, 1962.

Anan'in, E. A. *Iz vospominanii revoliutsionera*. MP Paper 7. New York, 1961.

Andreyev, Catherine. *Vlasov and the Russian Liberation Movement: Soviet Reality and Emigré Theories*. Cambridge: Cambridge University Press, 1987.

Anin, D. *Revoliutsiia 1917 goda glazami eë rukovoditelei*. Rome: Ed. Aurora, 1971.

Anweiler, Oskar. *The Soviets: The Russian Workers', Peasants', and Soldiers' Councils, 1905–1921*. New York: Random House, 1974.

Arendt, Hannah. *The Origins of Totalitarianism*. New York: Harcourt, Brace & Co., 1951.

———— "Totalitarian Terror." *Review of Politics* 12 (1949): 112–115.

Aronson, Grigorii. "Anglichane v Moskve." *Novyi Zhurnal* 11 (1945): 330–341.

———— "Bolchèviks et menchèviks." *Le Contrat social* 8 (1964): 271–281.

———— *Bol'shevistskaia revoliutsiia i men'sheviki: stat'i i materialy k istorii sotsialisticheskoi mysli v emigratsii*. New York, 1955.

———— *Dvizhenie upolnomochennykh ot rabochikh fabrik i zavodov v 1918 godu*. MP Paper. New York, 1960.

———— *K istorii pravogo techeniia sredi men'shevikov*. MP Paper 4. New York, 1960.

———— "Kak zhil i rabotal Iu. O. Martov." In *Martov i ego blizkie*. 100–102.

———— *Men'shevizm v 1905 g.* N.p., n.d.

———— *Na zare krasnogo terrora*. Berlin: Hirschbaum, 1929.

———— *Pravda o vlasovtsakh: problemy novoi emigratsii*. New York, 1949.

———— *Revoliutsionnaia iunost': Vospominaniia, 1903–1917*. MP Paper 6. New York, 1961.

———— *Rossiia nakanune revoliutsii: istoricheskie etiudy-monarkhisty, liberaly, masony, sotsialisty*. New York, 1962.

———— *Rossiia v epokhu revoliutsii*. New York, 1966.

———— *Soviet Russia and the Jews*. New York: American Jewish League against Communism, 1949.

Arrow, Kenneth. "Jacob Marschak." In *International Encyclopaedia of the Social Sciences*. Biographical Supplement, ed. David L. Sills. New York: Free Press, 1979. 500–507.

Ascher, Abraham. *Pavel Axelrod and the Development of Menshevism*. Cambridge, Mass.: Harvard University Press, 1972.

———— *The Revolution of 1905*. 2 vols. Stanford: Stanford University Press, 1988, 1992.

Ascher, Abraham, ed. *The Mensheviks in the Russian Revolution*. Ithaca: Cornell University Press, 1976.

Atholl, Duchess of. *Conscription of a People*. London: Philip Allan, 1931.

———— *Working Partnership*. London: Arthur Barker, 1958.

Avrich, Paul. *Kronstadt, 1921*. Princeton: Princeton University Press, 1970.

Baikalov, A. V. *I Knew Stalin*. London: Burns Oates, 1940.

———— *In the Land of Communist Dictatorship: Labour and Social Conditions in Soviet Russia Today*. London: Jonathan Cape, 1929.

Bajanov, Boris. *Avec Staline dans le Kremlin*. Paris: Ed. de France, 1930.

———— *Bajanov révèle Staline*. Paris: Gallimard, 1979.

Ball, Allan. "Lenin and the Question of Private Trade in Soviet Russia." *Slavic Review* 43 (1984): 399–412.

Balticus (= V. Sukhomlin), "The Russian Mystery: Behind the Tukhachevsky Plot." *Foreign Affairs* 16 (October 1937): 44–63.

Baron, Samuel H. *Plekhanov: The Father of Russian Marxism*. Stanford: Stanford University Press, 1963.

—— Review of L. Haimson, *Russian Marxists and the Origins of Bolshevism.* *American Historical Review* 61 (1956): 968–969.

Barry, Brian, ed. *Power and Political Theory: Some European Perspectives.* London: Wiley, 1976.

Barshchagovskii, A. M. "Martemian Riutin, sotsial'nyi myslitel'." *Vestnik akademii nauk SSSR,* no. 1 (1991): 80–106; no. 2 (1991):96–113.

Barton, Paul. *L'institution concentrationnaire en Russie (1930–1957).* Paris: Plon, 1959.

Bashilov, Boris. *Zapiski sbezhavshego ot 'nenastoiashchego sotsializma'.* Buenos Aires, 1951.

Basil, John D. *The Mensheviks in the Revolution of 1917.* Columbus, Ohio: Slavica 1984.

Bauer, Otto. "Das Gleichgewicht der Klassenkräfte." *Der Kampf* 16 (1924): 57–67.

—— *Die Illegale Partei.* Paris: Editions de la lutte socialiste, 1939.

—— *Kapitalismus und Sozialismus nach dem Weltkrieg.* Vol. 1, *Rationalisierung-Fehlrationalisierung.* Vienna: Wiener Volksbuchhandlung, 1931.

—— "Der Kongress in Marseilles." *Der Kampf* 18 (1925): 281–285.

—— *Der "neue Kurs" in Russland.* Vienna: Wiener Volksbuchhandlung, 1921.

—— "Die Zukunft der russischen Sozialdemokratie." *Der Kampf* 24 (1931): 1–7.

—— *Zwischen zwei Weltkriegen: die Krise der Weltwirtschaft, der Demokratie und des Sozialismus.* Bratislava: E. Praeger, 1936.

Belik, A. P. "K voprosu o vliianii tvorchestva N. G. Chernyshevskogo na formirovanie revoliutsionnykh vzgliadov V. I. Lenina." *Voprosy filosofii* (1958): 73–76.

Bell, Daniel. "At a Vecherinka" [letter from New York]. *Encounter* 7 (July 1956): 65–68.

—— "The Modern Review: An Introduction and Appraisal." *Labor History* 9 (1968): 380–383.

Berberova, Nina. *L'affaire Kravtchenko.* Paris: Actes Sud, 1990.

Berger, Joseph. *Shipwreck of a Generation.* London: Harvill Press, 1971.

Berlin, Isaiah. "Political Ideas in the Twentieth Century." *Foreign Affairs* 28 (1950): 351–385.

Berman, Harold J. *Justice in the USSR: An Interpretation of Soviet Law.* Rev. ed. Cambridge, Mass.: Harvard University Press, 1966.

Bernshtam, Mikhail, ed. *Nezavisimoe rabochee dvizhenie v 1918 godu.* Paris: YMCA Press, 1981.

Bienstock, G. *Deutschland und Frankreich: eine Europäische Auseinandersetzung.* Berlin, 1932.

—— *Europa und die Weltpolitik.* Karlsbad: Graphia Verlag, 1936.

—— *Kampf um die Macht: zur neuen Politik der Sozialdemokratie.* Berlin: E. Laubsche, 1932.

—— *Struggle for the Pacific.* London: Macmillan, 1936.

Bienstock, G., S. Schwarz, and A. Yugow. *Management in Russian Industry and Agriculture,* ed. Arthur Feiler and Jacob Marschak. New York: Oxford University Press, 1944.

Billington, James H. "Six Views of the Russian Revolution." *World Politics* 18 (1965/1966): 452–473.

Biographisches Handbuch der deutschsprachigen Emigration nach 1933. ed. Institut für Zeitgeschichte (Munich) and Research Foundation for Jewish Immigration (New York). Munich: K. G. Saur, 1980.

Bjorkegren, Hans. *Ryska Posten: De ryska revolutionarerna i Norden, 1906–1917.* Stockholm: Bonniers, 1985.

Bogdanova, N. B. *Moi otets-men'shevik.* St. Petersburg: Nauchno informatsionnyi tsentr "Memorial," 1994.

Bohachevsky-Chomiak, Martha, and Bernice Glatzer Rosenthal, eds., *Revolution of the Spirit: Crisis of Value in Russia, 1890–1918.* Newtonville, Mass.: Oriental Research Partners, 1982.

Boukharina, Anna Larina. *Boukharine, ma passion.* Paris: Gallimard, 1989.

Bourdet, Yvon. "Otto Bauer et la Russie soviétique: quatre lettres inédites d'Otto Bauer à Karl Kautsky." *International Review of Social History* 15 (1970): 468–478.

Bourdet, Yvon, ed. *Otto Bauer et la Révolution.* Paris: Études et documentation internationales, 1968.

Bourguina, A. M. *Russian Social Democracy—The Menshevik Movement: A Bibliography.* Stanford: Hoover Institution, 1968.

—— "The Writings of B. I. Nicolaevsky: A Selected Bibliography." In *Revolution and Politics,* ed. A. And J. Rabinowitch. 322–341.

Braunthal, Julius. *History of the International.* Vol. 2, *1914–1943.* New York: Praeger, 1967. Vol. 3, *World Socialism, 1943–1968,* Boulder, Colo.: Westview, 1980.

—— *Victor und Friedrich Adler: Zwei Generationen Arbeiterbewegung.* Vienna: Wiener Volksbuchhandlung, 1965.

Brick, Howard. *Daniel Bell and the Decline of Intellectual Radicalism: Social Theory and Political Reconciliation in the 1940s.* Madison: University of Wisconsin Press, 1986.

Brin, I. D. *Gosudarstvennyi kapitalizm v SSSR v perekhodnyi period ot kapitalizma k sotsializmu.* Irkutsk: Irkutskoe knizhnoe izd., 1959.

British Trades Union Delegation to Russia and Caucasia, 1924. *Russia Today: The Official Report of the British Trades Union Delegation.* New York: International Publishers, 1925.

Broido, Eva. *V riadakh RS-DRP.* Moscow: Izd. vsesoiuznogo obshchestva politkatorzhan i ssyl'no poselentsev, 1928.

Broido, Vera. *Lenin and the Mensheviks: The Persecution of Socialists under Bolshevism.* Boulder, Colo.: Westview Press, 1987.

Broué, Pierre. *Trotsky.* Paris: Fayard, 1988.

—— "Trotsky et le bloc des oppositions de 1932." *Cahiers Léon Trotsky,* no. 5 (1980): 5–37.

Brovkin, Vladimir N. "The Mensheviks and NEP Society in Russia." *Russian History* 9 (1982): 347–377.

—— *The Mensheviks after October: Socialist Opposition and the Rise of the Bolshevik Dictatorship.* Ithaca: Cornell University Press, 1987.

—— "The Mensheviks' Political Comeback in 1918: The Elections to the Provincial City Soviets in Spring 1918." *Russian Review* 42 (1983): 1–50.

Brokvin, Vladimir N., ed. And trans. *Dear Comarades: Menshevik Reports on the Bolshevik Revolution and the Civil War.* Stanford: Hoover Institution Press, 1991.

Brym, Robert J. *The Jewish Intelligentsia and Russian Marxism: A Sociological Study of Intellectual Radicalism and Ideological Divergence.* New York: Schocken Books, 1978.

Burbank, Jane. *Intelligentsia and Revolution: Russian Views of Bolshevism, 1917–1922.* New York: Oxford University Press, 1986.

Buschak, Willy. *Das Londoner Büro: Europäische Linkssozialisten in der Zwischenkriegszeit.* Amsterdam: Stichting IISG, 1985.

Bystranski, W. *Die Menschewiki und die Sozial-Revolutionäre.* Hamburg: Verlag der Kommunistischen International, 1922.

Calhoun, Daniel F. *The United Front: The TUC and the Russians, 1923–1928.* Cambridge: Cambridge University Press, 1976.

Carr, E. H. *The Bolshevik Revolution.* 3 vols. London: Macmillan, 1950, 1952, 1953.

―――― *Foundations of a Planned Economy, 1926–1929.* Vol. 2. London: Macmillan, 1971.

―――― *The Interregnum, 1923–1924.* London: Macmillan, 1954.

―――― Review of S. Schwarz, *The Russian Revolution of 1905. History* 54 (1968): 118.

―――― "Revolution from Above: Some Notes on the Decision to Collectivize Soviet Agriculture." In *The Critical Spirit: Essays in Honor of Herbert Marcuse,* ed. Kurt H. Wolff and Barrington Moore, Jr. Boston: Beacon Press, 1967. 313–327

―――― *Socialism in One Country, 1924–1926.* 2 vols. London: Macmillan, 1958, 1959.

Carrère d'Encausse, Hélène. "L'URSS ou le totalitarisme exemplaire." In vol. 2 of *Traité de science politique,* ed. Madeleine Grawitz and Jean Leca. Paris: Presses universitaires de France, 1985, 210–236.

Caute, David. *Communism and the French Intellectuals, 1914–1960.* London: André Deutsch, 1964.

―――― *The Fellow Travellers: A Postscript to the Enlightenment.* London: Weidenfeld and Nicolson, 1973.

Chamberlin, W. H. "Emigré Anti-Soviet Enterprises and Splits." *Russian Review* 13 (1954): 91–98.

―――― *The Russian Revolution, 1917–1921.* 2 vols. New York: Macmillan, 1935.

Champlin, John R., ed. *Power.* New York: Atherton Press, 1971.

Ciliga, Anton. *The Russian Enigma.* London: Labour Book Service, 1940.

Cohen, Stephen F. "Bolshevism and Stalinism." In *Stalinism,* ed. Robert Tucker. 3–29.

―――― *Bukharin and the Bolshevik Revolution: A Political Biography, 1888–1938.* New York: Random House, 1971.

Cohn, Norman. *Warrant for Genocide: The Myth of the Jewish World Conspiracy and the Protocols of the Elders of Zion.* New York: Harper & Row, 1967.

Cole, G. D. H. *History of Socialist Thought.* Vol. 4, pt. 2, *Communism and Social Democracy, 1914–1931.* London: Macmillan, 1958.

Collotti, Enzo. "Appunti su Friedrich Adler segretario della Internazionale Operaia Socialista." In *L'Internazionale Operaia e Socialista* ed. Enzo Collotti. 65–103.

Collotti, Enzo, ed. *L'Internazionale Operaia e Socialista tra le due guerre. Annali Feltrinelli* 23 Milan: Feltrinelli Editore, 1983–84.

Colton, Joel. *Leon Blum: Humanist in Politics.* New York: Knopf, 1966.

Conquest, Robert. *The Great Terror: A Reassessment.* Rev. ed. London: Hutchinson, 1990. Orig. pub. as *The Great Terror: Stalin's Purge of the Thirties.* London: Macmillan, 1968.

——— *Stalin and the Kirov Murder.* Oxford: Oxford University Press, 1989.

Costello, John, and Oleg Tsarov. *Deadly Illusions.* London: Century, 1993.

Croan, Melvin. "The Politics of Marxist Sovietology: Otto Bauer's Vision." *Journal of Politics* 21 (1959): 575–591.

Cummings, Arthur John. *The Moscow Trial.* London: Victor Gollancz, 1933.

D'Agostino, Anthony. *Soviet Succession Struggles: Kremlinology and the Russian Question from Lenin to Gorbachev.* Boston: Allen & Unwin, 1988.

Daix, Pierre. *J'ai cru au matin.* Paris: Laffont, 1976.

Dalin, David. "Obryvki vospominanii." In *Martov i ego blizkie.* 103–119.

——— *Posle voin i revoliutsii.* Berlin: Izd. "Grani," 1922.

Dallin, David J. *The Big Three.* New Haven: Yale University Press, 1945.

——— *The Changing World of Soviet Russia.* New Haven: Yale University Press, 1956.

——— *From Purge to Coexistence: Essays on Stalin's and Khrushchev's Russia.* Chicago: Henry Regnery, 1964.

——— *The New Soviet Empire.* New Haven: Yale University Press, 1951.

——— "The Period of War Communism and the Civil War." In *The Mensheviks,* ed. Leopold Haimson. 95–240.

——— "The Policy of Containment." *Annals of the American Academy of Political and Social Science* 283 (1952): 22–30.

——— *The Real Soviet Russia.* New Haven: Yale University Press, 1944.

——— *The Rise of Russia in Asia.* New Haven: Yale University Press, 1949.

——— *Russia and Postwar Europe.* New Haven: Yale University Press, 1943.

——— *Soviet Espionage.* New Haven: Yale University Press, 1955.

——— *Soviet Russia's Foreign Policy, 1939–1942.* New Haven: Yale University Press, 1942.

——— *Soviet Foreign Policy after Stalin.* New Haven: Yale University Press, 1961.

——— *Soviet Russia and the Far East.* New Haven: Yale University Press, 1945.

Dallin, D., and B. Nicolaevsky. *Forced Labor in Soviet Russia.* New Haven: Yale University Press, 1947.

——— *Le travail forcé en URSS.* Paris: Aimery Smogy, 1949.

Dan, F. *Dva goda skitanii (1919–1921).* Berlin: Russische Bücherzentrale Obrazowanje, 1922.

——— *Fedor Il'ich Dan: Pis'ma (1899–1946),* ed. Boris Sapir. Amsterdam: Stichting IISG, 1985.

——— "K istorii poslednikh dnei Vremennogo pravitel'stva." *Letopis' revoliutsii* 1 (1923): 161–176.

——— "Perspektivy general'noi linii." Afterword to A. Iugov, *Piatiletka.* Berlin: Izd. "Sv" [1931?].

——— "Predislovie" to F. Adler, *Ob otchete angliiskoi delegatsii.* Berlin: Izd. "Sv," 1925.

Dan, F., B. Nikolaevskii, and L. Tsederbaum-Dan, eds. *Pis'ma P. B. Aksel'roda i Iu. O. Martova.* Berlin: Russkii revoliutsionnyi arkhiv, 1924.

Dan, L. O. "Boukharine, Dan et Staline." *Le Contrat social* 8 (1964): 196–202.

——— *Iz arkhiva L. O. Dan,* ed. Boris Sapir. Amsterdam: Stichting IISG, 1987.

Dan, Th. *Der Arbeiter in Sowjetrussland.* Berlin: J. H. W. Dietz, 1923.

——— "Aus dem Nachlass J. Martows." *Der Kampf* 18 (1925): 166–170.

——— "Das Ende der Opposition." *Der Kampf* 21 (1928): 41–49.

——— "Geist und Geschichte des Bolschewismus." *Der Kampf* 20 (1927): 76–80.

——— *Gewerkschaften und Politik in Sowjetrussland.* Berlin: J. H. W. Dietz, 1923.

——— "Kautsky über den russischen Bolshevismus." *Der Kampf* 18 (1925): 241–250.

——— "Die Neue Phase der Bolschewistischen Diktatur und die Sozialistische Arbeiter-Internationale." *Der Kampf* 21 (1928): 4–11.

——— *La nouvelle politique économique et la situation de la classe ouvrière en Russie soviétique.* Brussels: L'Eglantine, 1923.

——— *The Origins of Bolshevism.* London: Secker and Warburg, 1964. Orig. pub. as *Proiskhozhdenie bol'shevizma: k istorii demokraticheskikh idei v Rossii posle osvobozhdeniia krest'ian.* New York: Izd. "Novaia Demokratia," 1946.

——— "Probleme der Liquidationsperiode." *Der Kampf* 23 (1930): 504–519.

——— "Das Programm der sozialen Revolution." *Der Kampf* 19 (1926): 470–480.

——— Review of S. P. Melgunov, *Der rote Terror in Russland, 1918–1923. Gesellschaft* 2 (1925): 185–187.

——— *Sowjetrussland wie es wirklich ist: Ein Leitfaden für Russlanddelegierte.* Prague: Parteivorstand der Deutschen Sozialdemokratischen Arbiterpartei in der Tchechoslowakischen Republik, 1926.

——— "Tua res agitur." *Der Kampf* 18 (1925): 59–71.

——— "Der Vormarsch der deutschen Konterrevolution." *Der Kampf* 25 (1932): 329–337.

——— "Zur sozial-ökonomishcen Entwicklung Russlands." *Die Gesellschaft* 9 (1932): 310–324.

Daniels, Robert V. *The Conscience of the Revolution: Communist Opposition in Soviet Russia.* Cambridge, Mass.: Harvard University Press, 1960.

——— Review of R. Abramovitch, *Soviet Revolution. Commentary* 35 (1963): 84–86.

Davies, R. W. " 'Drop the Glass Industry': Collaborating with E. H. Carr." *New Left Review* 145 (1984): 57–70.

——— "The Socialist Market: A Debate in Soviet Industry, 1932–33." *Slavic Review* 43 (1984): 201–223.

Day, Richard B. "Leon Trotsky on the Problems of the Smychka and Forced Collectivization." *Critique* 13 (1981): 55–68.

Decker, G. "Aufstand der Gescheiterten." In G. Decker, *Revolte und Revolution: Der Weg zur Freiheit.* Karlsbad: Graphia, 1934; rpt. in Georg Denicke, *Erinnerungen und Aufsätze.* 173–178.

Degras, Jane, and Alec Nove, eds. *Soviet Planning: Essays in Honour of Naum Jasny.* Oxford: Basil Blackwell, 1964.

Denicke, G. "From the Dissolution of the Constituent Assembly to the Outbreak of Civil War." In *The Mensheviks,* ed. Leopold Haimson. 107–155.

Denicke, Georg/Decker, Georg. *Erinnerungen und Aufsätze eines Menshewiken und*

Sozialdemokraten, ed. Werner Plum. With biographical contributions by Fritz Heine, Kurt Lachmann, Boris Nikolajewski, and Solomon Schwarz. Bonn: Friedrich Ebert Stiftung, 1980.

Denike, I. "Men'sheviki v 1917 g. (v strane)." MP Paper, n.d.

Deutscher, Isaac. *Ironies of History: Essays on Contemporary Communism.* Berkeley: Ramparts Press, 1957.

———— "Mr. E. H. Carr as Historian of the Bolshevik Regime." In *Heretics and Renegades and Other Essays.* London: Hamish Hamilton, 1955. 91–110.

———— *The Prophet Armed: Trotsky, 1879–1921.* New York: Oxford University Press, 1954.

———— *The Prophet Outcast: Trotsky, 1929–1940.* New York: Oxford University Press, 1963.

Dogliani, Patrizia. "La ricostituzione della Internazionale socialista nel primo decennio postbellico (1918–1928): Le caratteristiche nuove di quadri e organizzazioni." In *L'Internazionale Operaia e Socialista,* ed. Enzo Collotti. 225–278.

Donald, Moira. *Marxism and Revolution: Karl Kautsky and the Russian Marxists, 1900–1924.* New Haven: Yale University Press, 1993.

Donneur, André. *L'Alliance fragile: socialistes et communistes français* (1922–1983). Montreal: Nouvelle Optique, 1984.

———— *Histoire de l'Union des partis socialistes pour l'action internationale (1920–1923).* Sudbury, Ontario: Librairie de l'université laurentienne, 1967.

———— *L'Internationale socialiste.* Paris: Presses universitaires de France, 1983.

Dreyfus, Michel. "Bureau de Paris et bureau de Londres: le socialisme de gauche en Europe entre les deux guerres." *Mouvement social* 112 (1980): 25–55.

Duhamel, Olivier, and Nicole Racine. "Léon Blum: les socialistes français et l'Union soviétique." In *L'URSS vue de gauche,* ed. Lilly Marcou. 121–156.

Dvinov, B. "F. I. Dan." In *Martov i ego blizkie.* 119–137.

———— *Moskovskii sovet rabochikh deputatov, 1917–1922.* MP Paper 1. New York, 1961.

———— *Ot legal'nosti k podpoliu (1921–1922).* Supplement by G. Kuchin-Oranskii, "Zapiski." Stanford: Hoover Institution, 1968.

———— *Pervaia mirovaia voina i Rossiiskaia sotsialdemokratia.* MP Paper 10. New York, 1962.

———— *Politics of the Russian Emigration.* Santa Monica, Calif.: Rand Corporation, 1955.

———— *Vlasovtsy v svetle dokumentov.* New York, 1951.

Eastman, Max. *Since Lenin Died.* New York: Boni and Liveright, 1925.

Edinger, Lewis J. *German Exile Politics: The Social Democratic Committee in the Nazi Era.* Berkeley: University of California Press, 1956.

Elwood, R. C. "Lenin and the Brussels 'Unity Conference' of July 1914." *Russian Review* 39 (1980): 32–49.

———— *Russian Social Democracy in the Underground: A Study of the RSDRP in the Ukraine.* Assen: Van Gorcum, 1974.

Emig, Dieter, and Rüdiger Zimmerman. "Arkadij Gurland (1904–1979)." In *Vor dem Vergessen Bewahren,* ed. Peter Lösch, Michael Scholing, and Franz Walter. 81–98.

Emmons, Terence. "Recent Developments on the Historical Front: Excerpts from an Interview with Viktor Petrovich Danilov." *Slavic Review* 50 (1991): 150–156.

Epstein, Fritz T. "The Nikolaevskii Collection at Indiana." *Library News Letter: Indiana University,* no. 1 (April 1966): 1–12.

Epstein, Melech. *The Jew and Communism, 1919–1941: The Story of Early Communist Victories and Ultimate Defeats in the Jewish Community, USA.* New York: Trade Union Sponsoring Committee, n.d.

———— *Jewish Labor in USA: An Industrial, Political, and Cultural History of the Jewish Labor Movement, 1882–1914.* 2d ed. N.p.: Ktav Publishing House, 1969.

———— *Jewish Labor in USA, 1914–1952: An Industrial, Political and Cultural History of the Jewish Labor Movement.* 2d ed. N.p.: Ktav Publishing House, 1969.

Ermanskii, O.A., *Iz Perezhitogo.* Moscow: Gosudarstvennoe izd., 1927.

Fainsod, Merle. *How Russia Is Ruled.* Rev. ed. Cambridge, Mass.: Harvard University Press, 1963.

Fel'shtinskii, Iu. G. "Dva epizoda iz istorii vnutripartiinoi bor'by: konfidentsial'nye besedy Bukharina." *Voprosy istorii* no. 2/3 (1991): 182–189.

Filtzer, Don. *Soviet Workers and Stalinist Industrialization: The Formation of Modern Soviet Production Relations, 1928–1941.* Armonk, N.Y.: M. E. Sharpe, 1986.

———— Translator's Afterword to C. Rakovsky, "The Five Year Plan in Crisis." *Critique* 13 (1981): 53.

Fischhoff, Baruch. "Hindsight: Thinking Backward?" *Psychology Today* 8 (1975): 1–19.

Fischhoff, Baruch, and Ruth Beyth. " 'I Knew It Would Happen': Remembered Probabilities of Once-Future Things." *Organizational Behaviour and Human Performance* 13 (1975): 1–16.

Fisichella, Domenico. *Analisi del totalitarismo.* Messina: G. D'Anna, 1976.

Fitzpatrick, Sheila. "The Civil War as a Formative Experience." In *Bolshevik Culture: Experiment and Order in the Russian Revolution,* ed. A. Gleason, P. Kenez, and R. Stites. Bloomington: Indiana University Press, 1985. 57–76.

Fleischman, Lazar, Robert Hughes, and Olga Raevsky-Hughes, eds. *Russkii Berlin, 1921–1923.* Paris: YMCA Press, 1983.

Fleming, Donald, and Bernard Bailyn, eds. *The Intellectual Migration: Europe and America 1930–1960.* Cambridge, Mass.: Harvard University Press, 1969.

Fonst, C. M. Review of R. Abramovitch, *The Soviet Revolution. American Historical Review* 68 (1962): 226.

Fox, Michael S. "Ante Ciliga, Trotskii, and State Capitalism: Theory, Tactics, and Re-evaluation during the Purge Era, 1935–1939." *Slavic Review* 50 (1991): 127–143.

Frankel, Jonathan. "The Polarization of Russian Marxism (1833 [sic, 1883]–1903): Plekhanov, Lenin, and Akimov." Introduction to *Vladimir Akimov on the Dilemmas of Russian Marxism, 1895–1903: Two Texts in Translation,* ed. Jonathan Frankel. Cambridge: Cambridge University Press, 1969. 3–73.

——— *Prophecy and Politics: Socialism, Nationalism, and the Russian Jews.* Cambridge: Cambridge University Press, 1981.

Freyberg, Jutta v. *Sozialdemokraten und Kommunisten: Die Revolutionären Sozialisten Deutschlands vor dem Problem der Aktionseinheit, 1934–1937.* Cologne: Pahl Rugenstein, 1973.

Friedman, Saul S. *Pogromchik: The Assassination of Simon Petlura.* New York: Hart, 1976.

Friedrich, Carl J., ed. *Totalitarianism: Proceedings of a Conference Held at the American Academy of Arts and Sciences, March 1953.* Cambridge, Mass.: Harvard University Press, 1953.

Fry, Valerian. *Surrender on Demand.* New York: Random House, 1945.

Galili, Ziva. *The Menshevik Leaders in the Russian Revolution: Social Realities and Political Strategies.* Princeton: Princeton University Press, 1989.

Galili y Garcia, Ziva. "The Origins of Revolutionary Defensism: I. G. Tsereteli and the 'Siberian Zimmerwaldists.' " *Slavic Review* 41 (1982): 455–476.

Galili, Z., L. Kheimson, and A. Nenarokov, eds. *Men'sheviki v 1917 godu.* Vol. 1, *Ot ianvaria do iul'skikh sobytii.* Moscow: Izd. Progress-Akademiia, 1994.

Gardoncini, Giovanni Battista. "Il sistema sovietico nel dibattito degli Austromarxisti." *Mondoperaio* 31 (1978): 77–82.

Garvi, P. A. *Revoliutsionnye siluety.* MP Paper. New York, 1962.

——— *Vospominaniia sotsial demokrata: stat'i o zhizni i deiatel'nosti P. A. Garvi.* New York: Fond po izdaniiu literaturnogo nasledstva P. A. Garvi, 1946.

Garvi, P. A. *Zapiski sotsial demokrata (1906–1921).* Newtonville, Mass.: Oriental Research Partners, 1982.

Gerschenkron, Alexander. "Problems and Patterns of Russian Economic Development." In *The Transformation of Russian Society,* ed. C. E. Black. Cambridge, Mass.: Harvard University Press, 1960. 42–71.

Getty, J. Arch. *Origins of the Great Purges: The Soviet Communist Party Reconsidered, 1933–1938.* Cambridge: Cambridge University Press, 1985.

——— "State and Society under Stalin: Constitution and Elections in the 1930s." *Slavic Review* 50 (1991): 18–35.

Getty, J. Arch, Gabor Rittersporn, and Viktor N. Zemskov. "Victims of the Soviet Penal System in the Pre-War Years: A First Approach on the Basis of Archival Evidence." *American Historical Review* 98 (1993): 1017–49.

Getzler, Israel, *Kronstadt, 1917–1921: The Fate of a Soviet Democracy.* Cambridge: Cambridge University Press, 1983.

——— *Martov: A Political Biography of a Russian Social Democrat.* Cambridge: Cambridge University Press, 1967.

——— "Marxist Revolutionaries and the Dilemma of Power." In *Revolution and Politics,* ed. A. and J. Rabinowitch. 88–112.

Geyer, Dietrich. *Kautskys Russisches Dossier: Deutsche Sozialdemokraten als Treuhänder des russischen Parteivermögens, 1910–1915.* Frankfurt: Campus Verlag, 1981.

Gottschalch, Wilfried. *Strukturveränderungen der Gesellschaft und politisches Handeln in der Lehre von Rudolf Hilferding.* Berlin: Duncker und Humblot, 1962.

Graubard, Stephen. *British Labour and the Russian Revolution, 1917–1924.* Cambridge, Mass.: Harvard University Press, 1956.

Grémion, Pierre. *Intelligence de l'anticommunisme. Le Congrès pour la liberté de la culture à Paris (1950–1975).* Paris: Fayard, 1995.

Gul', Roman. *Ia unes Rossiiu: apologiia emigratsii.* 2 vols. New York: Most, 1981, 1984.

Gurian, Waldemar. Review of T. Dan, *Proiskhozhdenie bol'shevizma. Review of Politics* 11 (1949): 106–107.

Haimson, Leopold H. "The Mensheviks after the October Revolution." 3 pts. *Russian Review* 38 (1979): 457–473; 39 (1980): 181–207, 462–483.

———— "The Problem of Social Stability in Urban Russia, 1905–1917." Pt. 1. *Slavic Review* 23 (1964): 619–642.

———— *The Russian Marxists and the Origins of Bolshevism.* Cambridge, Mass.: Harvard University Press, 1955.

———— "Yu. P. Denicke (1887–1964)." *Slavic Review* 24 (1965): 370–375.

Haimson, Leopold H., ed. *The Making of Three Russian Revolutionaries: Voices from the Menshevik Past.* In collaboration with Ziva Galili y Garcia and Richard Wortman. Cambridge: Cambridge University Press, 1987.

———— *The Mensheviks from the Revolution of 1917 to the Second World War.* With contributions by David Dallin, George Denicke, Leo Lande, Boris Sapir, and Simon Wolin. Chicago: University of Chicago Press, 1974.

Healey, Denis. *The Time of My Life.* London: Penguin Books, 1990.

Hilferding, Rudolf. "Das historische Problem." *Zeitschrift für Politik* 1 (1954): 293–324.

Hilger, Gustav, and Alfred G. Meyer. *The Incompatible Allies.* New York: Macmillan, 1953.

History of the Communist Party of the Soviet Union (Bolsheviks): Short Course, ed. Commission of the Central Committee of the CPSU (B). Moscow: Foreign Languages Publishing House, 1951.

Hobsbawm, Eric J. *Revolutionaries: Contemporary Essays.* New York: Random House/ Pantheon Books, 1973.

Hook, Sidney. *Marx and the Marxists: The Ambiguous Legacy.* Princeton: D. Van Nostrand, 1955.

Howe, Irving. "The Authority of Failure" [review of I. Getzler, *Martov*]. *Dissent* 16 (1969): 459–462.

Hulse, James W. *The Forming of the Communist International.* Stanford: Stanford University Press, 1964.

Humbert-Droz, Jules [Archives]. *Origines et débuts des partis communistes des pays latins (1919–1923),* ed. Siegfried Bahne. Dordrecht: D. Reidel, 1970.

L'Internationale et la guerre. Thèses de Otto Bauer, Théodore Dan, Amédée Dunois, et Jean Zyromski. Paris: Nouveau Prométhée, 1935.

Irlen, B. (= B. Sapir). *Marx gegen Hitler.* Vienna: E. Prager, 1933.

Jänicke, Martin. *Totalitäre Herrschaft: Anatomie eines politischen Begriffes.* Berlin: Duncker und Humblot, 1971.

Jansen, Marc. *A Show Trial under Lenin: The Trial of the Socialist Revolutionaries, Moscow, 1922.* The Hague: Martinius Nijhoff, 1982.

Jasny, Naum. "Labor and Output in Soviet Concentration Camps." *Journal of Political Economy* 69 (1951): 405–419.

——— *To Live Long Enough: The Memoirs of Naum Jasny, Scientific Analyst,* ed. Betty A. Laird and Roy D. Laird. Lawrence: University Press of Kansas, 1976.

——— *Soviet Economists of the Twenties: Names To Be Remembered.* Cambridge: Cambridge University Press, 1972.

——— *Soviet Industrialization, 1928–1952.* Chicago: University of Chicago Press, 1961.

——— "A Soviet Planner—V. G. Groman." *Russian Review* 13 (1954): 52–58.

Jelenski, K. A. "The Literature of Disenchantment." *Survey,* no. 41 (1962): 109–119.

Johnson, Robert H. *New Mecca, New Babylon: Paris and the Russian Exiles, 1920–1945.* Montreal: McGill–Queen's University Press, 1988.

Joubert, Jean-Paul. "L'affaire Kirov commence en 1934." *Cahiers Léon Trotsky,* no. 20 (1984): 79–97.

Judt, Tony. *Past Imperfect: French Intellectuals, 1944–1956.* Berkeley: University of California Press, 1992.

Jugow, A. "Ergebnisse des Fünfjahresplans." *Die Gesellschaft* 10 (1933): 141–154.

——— "Grundprobleme der russischen Wirtschaft." *Die Gesellschaft* 4 (1927): 419–454.

——— "Die sozialistische Akkumulation und die Zukunft der Industrie in Russland." *Die Gesellschaft* 2 (1925): 546–563.

Kagarlitsky, Boris. *The Thinking Reed: Intellectuals and the Soviet State, 1917 to the Present.* London: Verso, 1988.

Kalicka, Felicja. *Problemy jednolitego frontu w miedzynarodowym ruchu robotniczym (1933–1935).* Warsaw: Książka i Wiedza, 1962.

Kalnins, Bruno. "The Social Democratic Movement in Latvia." In *Revolution and Politics,* ed. A. and J. Rabinowitch. 134–156.

Kamenka, E. Review of I. Getzler, *Martov. Historical Studies* 13 (1969): 561–562.

Kautsky, Karl. "Die Aussichten des Fünfjahresplanes." *Die Gesellschaft* 8 (1931): 255–264.

——— "Die Aussichten des Sozialismus in Russland." *Die Gesellschaft* 8 (1931): 420–444.

——— *Le bolchevisme dans l'impasse.* Paris: "La Russie opprimée," 1931.

——— *Der Bolschewismus in der Sackgasse.* Berlin: J. H. W. Dietz, 1930.

——— "Das bolschewistische Kamel." *Die Gesellschaft* 8 (1931): 342–356.

——— *Bol'shevizm v tupike.* Berlin: Izd. "Sv," 1930.

——— "Demokratie und Diktatur." *Der Kampf* 26 (1933): 48–58.

——— "Force and Democracy" [extract from *The Materialist Conception of History,* 1927]. In *Marxists in the Face of Fascism: Writings by Marxists on Fascism from the Inter-War Period,* ed. David Beethan. Manchester: Manchester University Press, 1984. 244–250.

——— *L'Internationale et la Russie des Soviets.* Paris: Libraire populaire, éditions du parti socialiste [SFIO], 1925.

——— "Sozialdemokratie und Bolschewismus." *Die Gesellschaft* 8 (1931): 54–71.

Keep, John. "From the Finland Station" [review of R. Abramovitch, *The Soviet Revolution*]. *Survey,* no. 46 (1963): 162–164.

———— *The Rise of Social Democracy in Russia.* Oxford: Clarendon Press, 1963.

Keep, John, ed. *Contemporary History in the Soviet Mirror.* New York: Praeger, 1964.

Kindersley, Richard. *The First Russian Revisionists: A Study of ''Legal Marxism'' in Russia.* Oxford: Clarendon Press, 1962.

Kingston-Mann, Esther. *Lenin and the Problem of Marxist Peasant Revolution.* New York: Oxford University Press, 1983.

Klimov, N. ''K voprosu o periodizatsii novoi ekonomicheskoi politiki.'' *Voprosy istorii KPSS,* no. 11 (1966): 61–66.

Knei-Paz, Baruch. *The Social and Political Thought of Leon Trotsky.* Oxford: Clarendon Press, 1978.

Knight, Amy. *Beria: Stalin's First Lieutenant.* Princeton: Princeton University Press, 1993.

Kolakowski, Leszek. *Main Currents of Marxism,* Vols. 2 and 3. Oxford: Clarendon Press, 1978.

———— ''Marxist Roots of Stalinism.'' In *Stalinism,* ed. Robert Tucker. 283–298.

Köller, Heinz. *Frankreich zwischen Faschismus und Demokratie (1932–1934).* Berlin: Akademische Verlag, 1978.

Koons, Tilghman B. ''Histoire des doctrines politiques de l'émigration russe 1919–1939.'' Litt.D. thesis, University of Paris, 1952.

Kristof, Ladis K. D. ''B. I. Nicolaevsky: The Formative Years.'' In *Revolution and Politics,* ed. A. and J. Rabinowitch. 3–32.

Krivitsky, Walter. *I Was Stalin's Agent.* London: Hamish Hamilton, 1939.

Krivoguz, I. M. *Rabochii sotsialisticheskii internatsional (1923–1940).* Moscow: Vysshaia shkola, 1979.

Krupskaya, N. *Reminiscences of Lenin.* New York: International Press, 1970.

Lacouture, Jean. *Léon Blum.* Paris: Seuil, 1977.

Lande, Leo. ''The Mensheviks in 1917.'' In *The Mensheviks,* ed. Leopold Haimson. 1–92.

Lane, David. *The Roots of Russian Communism: A Social and Historical Study of Russian Social Democracy, 1898–1907.* Assen: Van Gorcum, 1969.

Laqueur, Walter Z. *The Dream That Failed: Reflections on the Soviet Union.* New York: Oxford University Press, 1994.

———— *The Fate of the Revolution: Interpretations of Soviet History.* London: Weidenfeld and Nicolson, 1967.

———— (=W. Laker). ''Pokhval'noe slovo men'shevikam.'' *Novoe vremia* 45 (1992): 38–40.

Lattimore, Owen. *Ordeal by Slander.* Boston: Little, Brown, 1950.

Lazitch, Branko, and Mitorad M. Drachkovitch. *Lenin and the Comintern.* Stanford: Hoover Institution Press, 1972.

———— ''The Third International.'' In *The Revolutionary Internationals, 1864–1943,* ed. M. Drachkovitch. Stanford: Stanford University Press, 1966. 159–202.

Leggett, George. *The Cheka: Lenin's Political Police.* New York: Oxford University Press, 1981.

Lenin, V. I. *Leninskii sbornik,* ed. L. B. Kamenev. Institut Lenina pri tsentral'nom Komitete RKP(b). Moscow: Gosudarstvennoe izd., 1925.

———— *Polnoe sobranie sochinenii*, ed. Institut marksizma-leninizma pri tsentral'nom komitete KPSS. 5th ed. Moscow: Izd. politicheskoi literatury, 1970.

Lepeshinskii, P. N. "Partiinaia likhoradka 20 let tomu nazad." *Proletarskaia revoliutsiia*, no. 25 (1924): 23–46.

Lerner, Warren. *Karl Radek: The Last Internationalist.* Stanford: Stanford University Press, 1970.

Levenstein, Aaron. *Escape to Freedom: The Story of the International Rescue Committee.* Westport, Conn.: Greenwood Press, 1983.

Levine, Isaac Don. *Eyewitness to History: Memoirs and Reflections of a Foreign Correspondent for Half a Century.* New York: Hawthorn Books, 1973.

Lewin, Moshe. "The Immediate Background of Soviet Collectivization." *Soviet Studies* 17 (1965): 162–180.

———— *Lenin's Last Struggle.* New York: Random House, 1968.

———— *Political Undercurrents in Soviet Economic Debates: From Bukharin to the Modern Reformers.* Princeton: Princeton University Press, 1974.

Lewin, Nora. *While Messiah Tarried: Jewish Socialist Movements, 1871–1917.* New York: Schocken, 1977.

Liberman, S. I. *Dela i liudi: na sovetskoi stroike.* New York: New Democracy Books, 1944.

Lieberman, S. I. *Building Lenin's Russia.* Chicago: University of Chicago Press, 1945.

Liebich, André. "Diverging Paths: Menshevik Itineraries in the Aftermath of Revolution." *Revolutionary Russia* 4 (1991): 28–37.

———— "Eine Emigration in der Emigration: Die Menschewiki in Deutschland 1921–1933." In *Russische Emigration in Deutschland, 1918–1941*, ed. Karl Schlögel. 229–241.

———— "I Am the Last: Memories of Bukharin in Paris." *Slavic Review* 51 (1992): 767–781.

———— *Marxism and Totalitarianism: Rudolf Hilferding and the Mensheviks.* Kennan Institute of Advanced Russian Studies, Washington, D.C. Occasional Paper 217, 1987. [Shorter version in *Dissent* 34 (1987): 223–240].

———— "I Menscevichi di fronte alla costruzione dell'URSS (1924–1945)." In *Storia del marxismo*, ed. Eric J. Hobbawm et al. Vol. 3, tome 2. Turin: Einaudi, 1981. 132–166.

———— "Menshevik Origins: The Letters of Fedor Dan." *Slavic Review* 45 (1986): 724–728.

———— "The Mensheviks in the Face of Stalinism." *Ripensare il 1956*, Annali della Fondazione Giacomo Brodolini. Rome: Lerici, 1987. 184–200.

———— "Mensheviks, Then and Now" [review of *Iz Arkhiva L. O. Dan; Making of Three Russian Revolutionaries;* V. Broido, *Lenin and the Mensheviks;* and V. Brovkin, *Mensheviks after October*]. *Russian Review* 48 (1989): 67–80.

———— "Mensheviks Wage the Cold War." *Journal of Contemporary History* 30 (1995): 247–264.

———— "The Russian Mensheviks and the Famine of 1933." In *Famine in Ukraine, 1932–1933*, ed. Roman Serbyn and Bohdan Krawchenko. Edmonton: Canadian Institute of Ukrainian Studies, 1986. 97–108.

——— "Why NEP Would Not Work: The Menshevik View." In *L'URSS il mito le masse*. Annali della Fondazione Giacomo Brodolini. Milan: Franco Angeli. 1991: 667–688.

Lindemann, A. S. *The Red Years: European Socialism vs. Bolshevism, 1919–1921*. Berkeley: University of California Press, 1974.

Lösche, Peter. *Der Bolschewismus im Urteil der deutschen Sozialdemokratie, 1903–1920*. Berlin: Colloquium Verlag, 1967.

Lösche, Peter, Michael Scholing, and Franz Walter, eds. *Vor dem Vergessen Bewahren: Lebenswege Weimarer Socialdemokraten*. Berlin: Colloquium Verlag, 1988.

Lovell, David W. *Trotsky's Analysis of Soviet Bureaucratization*. London: Croom Helm, 1985.

Löw, Raimund. *Otto Bauer und die Russische Revolution*. Vienna: Europa Verlag, 1980.

Lukes, Steven. *Power: A Radical View*. London: Macmillan, 1974.

Lunacharskii, A. "Iulii Osipovich Martov (Tsederbaum)." In *Revoliutsionnye siluety*. Moscow: Deviatoe ianvaria, Transposektsia, 1923. 63–70.

Maiskii, Ivan. *Demokraticheskaia kontr-revoliutsiia*. Moscow: Gosudarstvennoe izd., 1923.

Malaurie, Guillaume. *L'affaire Kravchenko. Paris 1949. Le Goulag en correctionnelle*. Paris: Robert Laffont, 1982.

Malov, Iu. K. "Protiv fal'sifikatsii istorii II s'ezda RSDRP v sovremennoi anglo-amerikanskoi burzhuaznoi istoriografii." *Voprosy istorii KPSS*, no. 7 (1973): 102–113.

Malraux, André. *Les chênes qu'on abat*. Paris: Gallimard, 1971.

Mancini, Mario. "L'IOS e la questione del fronte unico negli anni Trenta." In *L'Internazionale Operaia e Socialista*, ed. Enzo Collotti. 177–198.

Marcou, Lilly, ed. *L'URSS vue de gauche*. Paris: Presses universitaires de France, 1982.

Marramao, Giacomo. *Austromarxismo e socialismo di sinistra tra le due guerre*. Milan: La Pietra, 1977.

——— "Tra bolscevismo e socialdemocrazia: Otto Bauer e la cultura politica dell'austro-marxismo." *Storia del marxismo*, ed. Eric J. Hobsbawm et al. Vol. 3, *Il marxismo nell'età della Terza Internazionale*. Pt. 1, *Dalla rivoluzione d'Ottobre alla crisi del '29*. Turin: Einaudi, 1979. 241–298.

Marschak, J. "Der korporative und der hierarchische Gedanke im Fascismus." *Archiv für Sozialwissenschaft und Sozialpolitik* 52 (1924): 695–728 and 53 (1924): 81–140.

Martov i ego blizkie: sbornik. With contributions by G. Ia. Aronson, L. O. Dan, B. L. Dvinov, and B. M. Sapir. New York, 1959.

Martov, L. *Le bolchévisme mondial*. Paris: Nouveau Promethée, 1934.

——— *Bol'shevizm v Rossii i v Internationale*. Berlin: Izd. *Sv*, 1923.

——— *Istoriia rossiiskoi sotsialdemokratii*, 2d ed. Moscow: Kniga, 1923.

——— *Mirovoi bol'shevizm*. Berlin: Iskra, 1923.

——— *Das Problem der Internationale und die Russische Revolution: Rede auf dem Parteitage in Halle*. Magdeburg: Magdeburger Volkszeitung, 1920.

———— *Zapiski sotsialdemokrata.* Rpt. Newtonville, Mass.: Oriental Research Partners, 1975.

Martow, J. *Geschichte der russischen Sozialdemokratie.* Appendix, Th. Dan, "Die Sozialdemokratie Russlands nach dem Jahre 1908." Berlin: J. H. W. Dietz, 1926.

———— "Das Problem der Internationale." *Der Kampf* 16 (1923): 1–9.

Martynov, A. S. (Piker). *Dve dikatury.* Geneva: Tipografia partii, 1905.

———— *O men'shevizme i bol'shevizme: doklad na kutaiskoi konferentsii byvshikh men'shevikov, 9 July 1923.* 2d rev. ed. Moscow: Izd. Krasnaia noch', 1923.

———— *Vom Menschewismus zum Kommunismus.* Hamburg: Kommunistische Internationale, 1923.

Matthias, Erich. *Sozialdemokratie und Nation: Ein Beitrag zur Ideengeschichte der sozialdemokratischen Emigration in der Prager Zeit des Parteivorstandes, 1933–1938.* Stuttgart: Deutsche Verlags-Anstalt, 1952.

Mayer, Paul. "Die Geschichte des sozialdemokratischen Parteiarchivs und das Schicksal des Marx-Engels-Nachlasses." *Archiv für Sozialgeschichte* 6/7 (1966–67): 5–133.

McNeal, Robert H. "Trotskyist Interpretations of Stalinism." In *Stalinism,* ed. Robert Tucker. 30–52.

Medlin, V. Review of *The Mensheviks,* ed. Leopold Haimson. *American Historical Review* 81 (1976): 910–911.

Medvedev, Roy A. *Let History Judge: The Origins and Consequences of Stalinism.* New York: Knopf, 1971. Rev. ed. New York: Columbia University Press, 1989.

———— *Nikolai Bukharin: The Last Years.* New York: W. W. Norton, 1980.

Meiksins, Gregory. *The Baltic Riddle: Finland, Estonia, Latvia, Lithuania—Key Points of European Peace.* New York: L. B. Fischer, 1944.

Melancon, Michael. *The Socialist Revolutionaries and the Russian Anti-War Movement, 1914–1917.* Columbus: Ohio State University Press, 1990.

Mendelsohn, Ezra. Review of A. Ascher, *Axelrod. Problems of Communism,* no. 6 (1967): 95.

Men'sheviki interventy, sbornik statei. Moscow: Gosudarstvenno-sotsial'no-ekonomicheskoe izd., 1931.

Merl, Peter. *Der Agrarmarkt und die Neue Ökonomische Politik: Die Anfänge staatlicher Lenkung der Landwirtschaft in der Sowjetunion, 1925–1928.* Munich: R. Oldenbourg, 1981.

Miliband, Ralph. "Bonapartism." In *A Dictionary of Marxist Thought,* ed. Tom Bottomore et al. 53–54. Oxford: Basil Blackwell, 1983.

Mokken, R. J., and F. N. Stokman. "Power and Influence as Political Phenomena." In *Power and Political Theory,* ed. Brian Barry. 33–54.

Moore, Barington, Jr. *Terror and Progress: Some Sources of Change and Stability in the Soviet Dictatorship.* Cambridge, Mass.: Harvard University Press, 1954.

Mosely, Philip E. "Boris Nicolaevsky: The American Years." In *Revolution and Politics,* ed. A. and J. Rabinowitch. 33–38.

Naarden, Bruno. *Socialist Europe and Revolutionary Russia: Perception and Prejudice, 1848–1923.* Cambridge: Cambridge University Press, 1992.

Nahirny, Vladimir C. *The Russian Intelligentsia: From Torment to Silence.* New Brunswick, N.J.: Transaction Books, 1983.

Narkiewicz, Olga A. *The Making of the Soviet State Apparatus.* Manchester: Manchester University Press, 1970.

Navasky, Victor. "Weinstein, Hiss, and the Transformation of Historical Ambiguity into Cold War Verity." In *Beyond the Hiss Case: The FBI, Congress, and the Cold War,* ed. Athan G. Theoharis. Philadelphia: Temple University Press, 1982. 215–245.

Nicolaevsky, Boris I. *Aseff the Spy. Russian Terrorist, and Police Stool.* New York: Doubleday, 1934.

——— *Power and the Soviet Elite: "The Letter of an Old Bolshevik" and Other Essays,* ed. Janet D. Zagoria. New York: Federick A. Praeger for the Hoover Institution, 1965.

——— "Revolutionary and Writer in Russia." In *So Much Alive,* ed. Emma Woytinsky. 39–51.

Nicolaievsky, B. *Karl Marx. Eine Biographie.* Hanover: J. H. W. Dietz Nachf., 1933.

Nikolaevskii, B. *Men'sheviki v gody revoliutsii.* MP Paper, n.d.

——— "Pamiati S. O. Portugeisa (Stepan Ivanovich)." *Novyi Zhurnal* 8 (1944): 394–403.

Nikolajewsky, B. "Der neuzeitliche Antisemitismus und die 'Protokolle der Weisen von Zion.'" *Zeitschrift für Sozialismus* 22/23 (1935): 725–733.

Nolte, Ernst. "Vierzig Jahre Theorien über den Faschismus." In *Theorien über den Faschismus,* ed. Ernst Nolte.

Nolte, Ernst, ed. *Theorien über den Faschismus.* Cologne: Kiepensheur und Witsch, 1967.

Nove, Alec. Review of I. Getzler, *Martov. English Historical Review* 83 (1968): 871.

Olberg, Oda. "Ist der Faschismus eine Klassenbewegung?" *Der Kampf* 17 (1924): 390–398.

Odom, William. "The Pluralist Mirage." *National Interest* 31 (Spring 1993): 99–108.

O'Neill, William. *A Better World. The Great Schism: Stalinism and the American Intellectuals.* New York: Simon & Schuster, 1982.

Osharov, M. "To Alien Shores: The 1922 Expulsions of Intellectuals from the Soviet Union." *Russian Review* 32 (1973): 294–298.

Palm, Charles. "Introduction." In *Guide to the Boris I. Nicolaevsky Collection in the Hoover Institution Archives.* Pt. 1, comp. Anna M. Bourgina and Michael Jakobson; pt. 2, comp. Michael Jakobson. Stanford: Hoover Institution, Stanford University, 1989.

Panaccione, Andrea. "Presupposti e linee di sviluppo del dibattito nella IOS sul bolscevismo e sull'URSS." In *L'Internazionale Operaia e Socialista,* ed. Enzo Collotti. 315–360.

Panné, J.-L. *Boris Souvarine: le premier désenchanté du communisme.* Paris: Robert Laffont, 1993.

Papanek, Hanna. "Alexander Stein (Pseudonym: Viator), 1881–1948, Socialist Activist and Writer in Russia, Germany, and Exile: Biography and Bibliography." *IWK. Internationale wissenschaftliche Korrespondenz zur Geschichte der deutschen Arbeiterbewegung,* no. 3 (1994): 344–379.

Peter, Hartmut Rudiger. "Die Parteiplatform der Menschewiki 1924." *Beiträge zur Geschichte der Arbeiterbewegung,* no. 3 (1995): 83–88.

———— "Die russische Exilsozialdemokratie 1956: Zwischen Resignation und Hoffnung." In *Tauwetter ohne Frühling: Das Jahr 1956 im Spiegel blockinterner Wandlungen und internationaler Krisen,* ed. Inge Kircheisen. Berlin: Berliner Debate/GSFP, 1995. 219–229.

———— "Theodore Dan (1871–1947)." In *Lebensbilder europäischer Sozialdemokraten des 20. Jahrhunderts,* ed. Otfried Dankelmann. Vienna: Verlag für Gesellschaftskritik, 1995. 161–174.

Pethybridge, Roger. "Concern for Bolshevik Ideological Predominance at the Start of NEP." *Russian Review* 41 (1982): 445–453.

Piatnitsky, O. *Memoirs of a Bolshevik.* New York: International Publishers, 1930[1931?].

Pipes, Richard. *The Formation of the Soviet Union: Communism and Nationalism, 1917– 1923.* Rev. ed. Cambridge, Mass.: Harvard University Press, 1964.

———— *Russia under the Bolshevik Regime.* London: Harville, 1994.

———— *The Russian Revolution.* New York: Knopf, 1990.

Pistrak Lazar. *The Grand Tactician: Khrushchev's Rise to Power.* London: Praeger, 1961.

Podbolotov, P. A. "Bor'ba RKP(b) s krontrerevoliutsionnoi ideologiei men'shevizma (1923–1925)." *Vestnik leningradskogo universiteta: seriia istoriia, iazyk, literatura,* no. 4 (1971): 35–44.

———— "Istoricheskaia literatura pervoi poloviny 20-kh godov o krakhe partii men'shevikov." *Vestnik leningradskogo universiteta: seria istorii,* no. 4 (1980): 16– 21.

———— "K voprosu o srokakh okonchatel'noi politicheskoi gibeli mel'koburzhuaznykh partii v SSSR." *Vestnik leningradskogo universiteta: seriia istoriia, iazyk, literatura,* no. 1 (1979): 19–24.

Podbolotov, P. A., and A. M. Spirin. *Krakh men'shevizma v sovetskoi Rossii.* Leningrad: Lenizdat, 1988.

Ponthus, René. "Tendances et activités de la social démocratie allemande émigrée, 1933–1941." *Le Mouvement social,* no. 84 (1973): 63–86.

Poretsky, Elisabeth K. *Our Own People: A Memoir of "Ignace Reiss" and His Friends.* London: Oxford University Press, 1969.

Potresov, A. N. "Lenin." *Die Gesellschaft* 4 (1?7): 405–418.

———— *Posmertnyi sbornik proizvedenii.* With an "opyt literaturno-politicheskoi biografii" by B. Nikolaevskii. Paris, 1937.

Protokoll des ersten Internationalen Sozialistischen Arbeiterkongresses, 21–25. 5. 1923, ed. Secretariat of the Labour and Socialist International. Berlin: J. H. W. Dietz, 1923.

Protsess kontrrevoliutsionnoi organizatsii men'shevikov (1 marta-9 marta 1931 g.): stenogramma sudebnogo protsessa, obvinitel'noe zakliuchenie i prigovor. Moscow: "Sovetskoe zakonodatel'stvo," 1931.

Rabinowitch, Alexander, and Janet Rabinowitch, eds., with Ladis K. D. Kristof. *Revolution and Politics in Russia: Essays in Memory of B. I. Nicolaevsky.* Bloomington: Indiana University Press, 1972.

Racine, Nicole. "Le parti socialiste (SFIO) devant le bolchevisme et la Russie soviétique, 1921–1924." *Revue française de science politique* 21 (1971): 281–315.

Radek, Karl. *Les questions de la revolution mondiale à la lumière du menchèvisme.* Petrograd: Editions de l'Internationale communiste, 1921.

—— *Theorie und Praxis der 2 1/2 Internationale.* Petrograd: Kommunistische Internationale, 1921.

Radkau, Joachim. *Die deutsche Emigration in den USA: Ihr Einfluss auf die amerikanische Europapolitik, 1933–1945.* Dusseldorf: Beretelsmann Universitätsverlag, 1971.

Raeff, Marc. *Russia Abroad: A Cultural History of the Russian Emigration, 1919–1939.* New York: Oxford University Press, 1990.

Rapone, L. "La crisi finale dell'Internazionale Operaia e Socialista." In *I Socialisti e l'Europa.* Annali della Fondazione Giacomo Brodolini. Milan: Franco Angeli, 1989. 37–94.

Read, Christopher. "New Directions in the Russian Intelligentsia: Idealists and Marxists in the Early Twentieth Century." *Renaissance and Modern Studies* 24 (1981): 1–17.

Reed, Dale, and Michael Jakobson. "Trotsky Papers at the Hoover Institution: One Chapter of an Archival Mystery Story." *American Historical Review* 92 (1987): 363–375.

Reed, John. *Ten Days That Shook the World.* Rpt. London: Lawrence & Wishart, 1961.

Reiman, Michal. *The Birth of Stalinism: The USSR on the Eve of the "Second Revolution."* Bloomington: Indiana University Press, 1987.

Reisser, Thomas. *Menschewismus und NEP (1921–1928): Diskussion einer demokratischen Alternative.* Munster: LIT, 1996.

Resolutions and Decisions of the Communist Party of the Soviet Union. Vol. 1, *The Russian Social Democratic Labour Party, 1898–October 1917,* ed. R. C. Elwood. Toronto: University of Toronto Press, 1974.

Resolutions and Decisions of the Communist Party of the Soviet Union. Vol. 2, *The Early Soviet Period,* ed. Richard Gregor. Toronto: University of Toronto Press, 1974.

Reswick, William. *I Dreamt Revolution.* Chicago: Henry Regnery, 1952.

Roobol, W. H. *Tsereteli—A Democrat in the Russian Revolution: A Political Biography.* The Hague: Martinius Nijhoff, 1976.

Rosenberg, W. G. Review of *The Mensheviks,* ed. Leopold Haimson. *American Political Science Review* 72 (1978): 730.

Rossiiskaia Sotsial-Demokraticheskaia Rabochaia Partiia. *Second Ordinary Congress of the RSDLP, 1903: Complete Text of the Minutes.* Trans. and annotated Brian Pierce. London: New Park Publications, 1978.

Salvadori, Massimo. *Karl Kautsky and the Socialist Revolution, 1880–1938.* London: New Left Books, 1979.

Sandvoss, Hans Rainer. *Widerstand in einem Arbeiterbezirk.* Berlin, 1983.

Sapir, Boris. "Andrei Kranikhfel'd." In *Martov i ego blizkie.* 138–147.

—— "Boris Ivanovic Nikolaevskij." In *Over Buonarroti: Internationale avant-gardes,*

Max Nettlau en het verzamelen van boeken, anarchistische ministers, de algebra van de revolutie, shilders en schrijvers. Voor Arthur Lehning, ed. Maria Hunink, Jaap Kloosterman, and Jan Rogier. Baarn: Wereldvenster, 1979. 367–375.

——— "Notes and Reflections on the History of Menshevism." In *Mensheviks,* ed. Leopold Haimson. 349–388.

——— "Theodor Dan und sein letztes Buch." Introduction to F. I. Dan, *Ursprünge des Bolshevismus: Zur Geschichte der demokratischen und sozialistischen Ideen in Russland nach der Bauernbefreiung.* Hanover: J. H. W. Dietz, 1968. 9–18.

Schapiro, Judith. "Soviet History Writing: Towards Normalization." *Slavonic and East European Review* 68 (1990): 516–520.

Schapiro, Leonard. *The Communist Party of the Soviet Union.* 2d rev. ed. New York: Random House, 1971.

——— *The Origin of the Communist Autocracy: Political Opposition in the Soviet State. First Phase, 1917–1922.* 2d ed. Cambridge, Mass.: Harvard University Press, 1977.

——— *The Russian Revolution of 1917: The Origins of Modern Communism.* New York: Basic Books, 1984.

Scheffer, Paul. *Sieben Jahre Sowjetunion.* Leipzig: Bibliographisches Institut, 1930.

Scherrer, Jutta. *Die Petersburger religiösphilosophische Vereinigungen: Die Entwicklung des religiösen Selbstverständnisses ihrer Intelligencija-Mitglieder (1901–1917).* Wiesbaden: Harrasowitz, 1973.

Schifrin, A. *Der Aufmarsch zum zweiten Weltkrieg.* Strasbourg: S. Brant, 1938.

——— "Die Internationale und die deutsche Krise." *Die Gesellschaft* 8 (1931): 204–213.

——— "Revolutionäre Sozialdemokratie," *Zeitschrift für Sozialismus* 1 (1933): 81–91.

Schlangen, Walter. *Die Totalitarismus Theorie: Entwicklung und Probleme.* Stuttgart: Kohlhammer, 1976.

Schlesinger, Rudolf. "A Note on the Context of Early Soviet Planning." *Soviet Studies* 16 (1964): 22–44.

Schlögel, Karl. "Das 'andere Russland': Zur Wiederentdeckung der Emigrationsgeschichte in der Sowjetunion." In *Die Umwertung der sowjetischen Geschichte,* ed. Dietrich Geyer. Göttingen: Vandenhoeck und Ruprecht, 1991. 238–256

Schlögel, Karl, ed. *Der Grosse Exodus. Die russische Emigration und ihre Zentren.* Munich: C. H. Beck, 1994.

——— *Russische Emigration in Deutschland, 1918–1941: Leben im europäischen Bürgerkrieg.* Berlin: Akademie Verlag, 1995.

Schmitt, Carl "Weiterentwicklung des totalen Staats in Deutschland." *Europäische Revue* 9 (1933): 65–70.

Scholing, Michael. "Georg Decker, 1887–1964." In *Vor dem Vergessen Bewahren,* ed. Peter Lösch, Michael Scholing, and Franz Walter. 57–80.

Schwarz, Solomon M. *Labor in the Soviet Union.* New York: Praeger, 1951.

——— *The Russian Revolution of 1905: The Workers' Movement and the Formation of Bolshevism and Menshevism.* Chicago: University of Chicago Press and Hoover Institution, 1967.

Second Ordinary Congress of the Labour and Socialist International at Marseilles, 22nd to 27th August 1925. London: Labour Party, 1925.

Service, Robert. *The Bolshevik Party in Revolution: A Study in Organizational Change, 1917–1923.* London: Macmillan, 1979.

Shain, Yossi. *The Frontiers of Loyalty: Political Exiles in the Age of the Nation-State.* Middletown, Conn.: Wesleyan University Press, 1989.

Shatz, Marshall. *Stalin, The Great Purge, and Russian History: A New Look at the "New Class."* Carl Beck Papers in Russian and East European Studies, no. 305. Pittsburgh: University of Pittsburgh, 1984.

Shishkin, M. D. *Iz vospominanii kooperativnykh i politicheskikh.* MP Paper 5. New York, 1960.

Shub, David. *Lenin: A Biography.* New York: Doubleday, 1948.

——— "Po povodu pism'a 'Istorika' i stat'i N. Valentinova o predkakh Lenina." *Novyi Zhurnal* 63 (1961): 288–291.

Siegelbaum, Lewis H. *The Politics of Industrial Mobilization in Russia, 1914–1917: A Study of the War-Industries Committees.* London: Macmillan, 1983.

Slusser, Robert M. Review of B. Nicolaevsky, *Power and the Soviet Elite. Slavic Review* 25 (1966): 529–531.

——— "The Role of the Foreign Ministry." In *Russian Foreign Policy. Essays in Historical Perspective,* ed. Ivo J. Lederer. New Haven: Yale University Press, 1962. 197–239.

Sokolova, Maria. *L'Internationale socialiste entre deux guerres mondiales.* Paris: Ed. Sokolova, 1954.

Solski, Waclaw. *Moje Wspomnienia.* Paris: Instytut literacki, 1977.

Solzhenitsyn, Aleksandr I. *The Gulag Archipelago, 1918–1956: An Experiment in Literary Investigations.* Vol. l. New York: Harper & Row, 1973.

Sorokin, Pitrim. *Leaves from a Russian Diary.* New York: E. P. Dutton, 1924.

Souvarine, Boris. "Une controverse avec Trotski (1929)." In *Contributions à l'histoire du Comintern,* ed. Jacques Freymond. Publications de l'IUHEI 45. Geneva: Droz, 1965. 141–211.

——— "Kremlinologie." *Le Contrat social* 3 (1959): 121–125.

——— *Staline: Aperçu historique du bolchévisme.* Rpt. Paris: Ed. Champ Libre, 1977.

——— "Le viol de Clio." *Le Contrat social* 5 (1961): 117–119.

Sozialistische Revolution in einem unterentwickelten Land? Texte der Menscheviki zur russischen Revolution und zum Sowjetstaat aus den Jahren 1903–1940. Hamburg: Junius Verlag, 1981.

Stampfer, Friedrich. *Mit dem Gesicht nach Deutschland: Eine Dokumentation über die sozialdemokratische Emigration. Aus dem Nachlass von Fr. Stampfer,* ed. Erich Matthias. Dusseldorf: Droste Verlag, 1968.

Stein, Alexander. *Rudolf Hilferding und die deutsche Arbeiterbewegung.* Hanover: SPD, 1946.

Steiner, Herbert. "Die Internationale Arbeitsgemeinshaft Sozialistischer Parteien (2½ Internationale) 1921–1923." In *L'Internazionale Operaia e Socialista,* ed. Enzo Collotti. 45–64.

——— "L'Internationale socialiste à la veille de la Seconde Guerre mondiale, juillet-août 1939. Documents de Friedrich Adler." *Mouvement social*, no. 58 (1967): 95–112.

Stephan, John. J. *The Russian Fascists: Tragedy and Farce in Exile, 1925–1945*. New York: Harper & Row, 1978.

Stishov, M. I. "Opyt periodizatsii istorii bor'by bol'shevizma s mel'koburzhuaznymi partiiami." *Vestnik moskovskogo universiteta: seriia istorii*, no. 8 (1977): 20–40.

Strada, Vittorio. "La polemica tra bolscevichi e menscevichi sulla rivoluzione del 1905." In *Storia del marxismo*, ed. Eric J. Hobsbawm et al. Vol. 2, *Il Marxismo nell'età della Seconda Internazionale*. Turin: Giulio Einaudi, 1979. 441–492.

Strauss, Herbert A. ed. *Jewish Immigrants of the Nazi Period in the USA*. New York: K. G. Saur, 1978.

Sturmthal, Adolf. *Democracy under Fire: Memoirs of a European Socialist*, ed. Suzanne Sturmthal Russin. Durham, N.C.: Duke University Press, 1989.

Sudoplatov, Pavel, and Antolii Sudoplatov. *Special Tasks: The Memoirs of an Unwanted Witness—A Soviet Spymaster*. With Jerrold L. and Leona P. Schechter. Boston: Little, Brown, 1994.

Sukhanov, N. N. *The Russian Revolution 1917*. Ed., abridged, and trans. Joel Carmichael, with new addendum by the editor. Princeton: Princeton University Press, 1983.

Sukhanov, Nikolai N. *Zapiski o revoliutsii*. 3 vols. Berlin: Izd. Z. I. Grzhebina, 1922.

Sukiennicki, Wiktor. "An Abortive Attempt at International Unity of the Workers' Movement (The Berlin Conference of the Three Internationals, 1922)." In *Revolution and Politics*, ed. A. and J. Rabinowitch. 206–238.

Suny, Ronald Gregor. "Towards a Social History of the October Revolution." *American Historical Review* 88 (1983): 31–52.

Suvorov, V. *Icebreaker: Who Started the Second World War?* London: Hamilton, 1990.

Swain, Geoffrey. *Russian Social Democracy and the Legal Labour Movement, 1906–1914*. London: Macmillan, 1983.

Tables de la revue russe: Le messager socialiste, 1921–1963. Ed. La Bibliothèque russe Tourguénev. Paris: Institut d'études slaves, 1992.

Tabori, Paul. *The Anatomy of Exile: A Semantic and Historical Study*. London: Harrap, 1972.

Tartakovsky, Danielle. "La SFIO et le fascisme dans les années trente." In *L'Internazionale Operaia e Socialista*, ed. Enzo Collotti. 725–745.

Thurston, Robert W. "Fear and Belief in the USSR's 'Great Terror': Response to Arrest, 1935–39." *Slavic Review* 45 (1986): 213–244.

Til', T. I. "Sotsial-demokraticheskoe dvizhenie molodezhi 1920-kh godov." *Pamiat'* 3. Moscow, 1978/Paris, 1980. 165–286.

Tobias, Henry J. *The Jewish Bund in Russia from Its Origins to 1905*. Stanford: Stanford University Press, 1972.

Treadgold, Donald W. *Lenin and His Rivals: The Struggle for Russia's Future, 1898–1906*. New York: Praeger, 1955.

Trifonov, I. Ia. *Klassy i klassovaia bor'ba v SSSR v nachale NEPa*. Leningrad: Izd. Leningradskogo universiteta, 1969.

——— *V. I. Lenin i bor'ba s burzhuaznoi ideologiei v nachale NEPa*. Moscow: Znanie, 1969.

Troisième Congrès de l'Internationale Ouvrière Socialiste, Bruxelles, août 1928. Zurich: Secretariat of the LSI, 1928.

Trotsky, Leon. *The History of the Russian Revolution.* 2d ed. 2 vols. Trans. Max Eastman. Ann Arbor: University of Michigan Press, 1957.

—— *The Revolution Betrayed: What Is the Soviet Union and Where Is It Going?* Rpt. London: New Park Publications, 1973.

Tucker, Robert C. *Stalin as Revolutionary, 1879–1929: A Study in History and Personality.* New York: W. W. Norton, 1973.

—— "Stalinism as Revolution from Above." In *Stalinism,* ed. Robert Tucker. 77–110.

Tucker, Robert C., ed. *Stalinism: Essays in Historical Interpretation.* New York: W. W. Norton, 1977.

Tumarinson, V. Kh. *Men'sheviki i bol'sheviki: nesostoiavshiisia konsensus.* Moscow: "Luch," 1994.

Turati, Filippo. "Faschismus, Sozialismus und Demokratie." In *Theorien über den Fascismus,* ed. Ernst Nolte. 143–155.

Ulam, Adam B. *The Bolsheviks: The Intellectual and Political History of the Triumph of Communism in Russia.* New York: Macmillan, 1965.

—— *Stalin: The Man and His Era.* New York: Viking, 1973.

—— "The Uses of Revolution." In *Revolutionary Russia,* ed. Richard Pipes. Cambridge, Mass.: Harvard University Press, 1968. 333–354.

Valentinov, N. (Vol'skii). "De Boukharine au stalinisme." *Le Contrat social* 7 (1963): 69–78.

—— *Encounters with Lenin,* London: Oxford University Press, 1968.

—— *Novaia ekonomicheskaia politika i krizis partii posle smerti Lenina: Gody raboty v VSNKh vo vremia NEP, Vospominaniia.* Stanford: Hoover Institution Press, 1971.

Van Heijenoort, Jan. *With Trotsky in Exile: From Prinkipo to Coyoacàn.* Cambridge, Mass.: Harvard University Press, 1978.

Verbatim Report of the Negotiations between the Second and Third Internationals on the Question of Suppporting the Heroic Struggle of the Spanish Workers. London: Modern Books, 1934.

Verdier, Robert. "Oreste Rosenfeld." *Le Populaire et le premier plan quinquennal soviétique, Cahiers Léon Blum,* no. 10 (1981): 33–38.

Viola, Lynn. "The Campaign to Eliminate the Kulak as a Class: Winter, 1929–30: A Reevalutation of the Legislation." *Slavic Review* 45 (1986): 503–525.

Vishniak, Mark. *Gody emigratsii, 1919–1969: Parizh–Niu Iork (Vospominaniia).* Stanford: Hoover Institution Press, 1970.

Voitinskii, Vladimir. *Dvenadtsat' smertnikov: Sud' nad sotsialistami-revoliusionerami.* Berlin: Izd. zagranichnoi delegatsii PSR, 1922.

—— *Gody pobed i porazhenii.* Vol. 2, *Na ushcherbe revoliutsii.* Berlin: Izd. Z. I. Grzhebina, 1924.

Volin, Vladimir. *A Century of Russian Agriculture: From Alexander II to Khrushchev.* Cambridge, Mass.: Harvard University Press, 1970.

Volkogonov, Dimitrii. *Lenin: A New Biography,* trans. and ed. Harold Shukman. New York: Free Press, 1994.

Volobuev, O. V., and V. A. Klokov. "Noveishie amerikanskie publikatsii po istorii men'shevizma." *Otechestvennaia istoriia,* no. 5 (1992): 209–216.

Webb, Beatrice. *Diaries, 1912–1924,* ed. Margaret I. Cole. London: Longman's, 1952.

Weber, Henri. "La Russie soviétique et le 'pape du marxisme' Karl Kautsky." In *L'URSS vue de gauche,* ed. Lilly Marcou. 14–40.

—— "La théorie du stalinisme dans l'oeuvre de Kautsky." In *Les interprétations du stalinisme,* ed. Evelyne Pisier-Kouchner. Paris: Presses universitaires de France, 1983. 61–90.

Weill, Claudie. "Mencheviks et Socialistes révolutionnaires en exil." In *De Russie et d'ailleurs: feux croisés sur l'histoire: pour Marc Ferro.* Ed. Martine Godet with Muriel Carduner-Loosfelt and Hélène Coq-Lossky. Paris: Institut d'études slaves, 1995. 417–426.

Werner, Max (= A. Shifrin). *Attack Can Win in '43.* Boston: Little, Brown, 1943.

—— *Battle for the World: The Strategy and Diplomacy of the Second World War.* New York: Modern Age Books, 1941.

—— *The Military Strength of the Fighting Powers.* New York: Modern Age Books, 1939.

Werth, Nicolas. "De la soviétologie en général et des archives russes en particulier." *Le Débat,* no. 77 (1993): 127–144.

Wheeler, Robert F. "Die 21 Bedingungen und die Spaltung der USPD im Herbst 1920." *Vierteljahreshefte für Zeitgeschichte* 23 (1975): 117–154.

Wildman, Allan K. *The Making of a Workers' Revolution: Russian Social Democracy, 1891–1903.* Chicago: University of Chicago Press, 1967.

—— "Russian and Jewish Social Democracy." In *Revolution and Politics,* ed. A. and J. Rabinowitch. 75–87.

Williams, Robert C. *Culture in Exile: Russian Emigrés in Germany, 1881–1941.* Ithaca: Cornell University Press, 1972.

—— "European Political Emigrations: A Lost Subject." *Comparative Studies in Society and History* 12 (1970): 140–148.

Wohl, Robert. *French Communism in the Making, 1914–1924.* Stanford: Stanford University Press, 1966.

Wolfe, Bertram D. "Krupskaia Purges the People's Libraries." *Survey,* no. 72 (1969): 141–155.

—— *Strange Communists I Have Known.* New York: Stein and Day, 1965.

—— *Three Who Made a Revolution: A Biographical History.* New York: Dial Press, 1948.

Wolff, Eric R. *Peasant Wars of the Twentieth Century.* New York: Harper & Row, 1969.

Wolin, S. *Communism's Postwar Decade: Gains and Losses of Communist Parties in the Free World since 1945.* New York: New Leader, 1955.

—— "The Mensheviks under the NEP and in Emigration." In *The Mensheviks,* ed. Leopold Haimson. 241–348.

Woytinsky, Emma S., ed. *So Much Alive: The Life and Work of Wladimir S. Woytinsky.* New York: Vanguard Press, 1962.

Woytinsky, W. *Stormy Passage: A Personal History Through Two Russian Revolutions to Democracy and Freedom.* New York: Vanguard Press, 1961.

Yugoff, A. *Economic Trends in Soviet Russia.* London: George Allen & Unwin, 1930.

Zborowski, Mark, and Elizabeth Herzog. *Olam: dans le shtetl d'Europe centrale avant la Shoah.* Paris: Plon, 1992.

Zeman, Z. A. B., and W. B. Scharlan. *The Merchant of Revolution: The Life of Alexander Israel Helphand (Parvus), 1867–1924.* London: Oxford University Press, 1965.

Zetkin, Klara. *Trotzkis Verbannung und die Sozialdemokratie.* Berlin: Internationaler Arbeiter Verlag, 1928.

Zibordi, Giovanni. "Der Faschismus als antisozialistische Koalition." In *Theorien über den Fascismus,* ed. Ernst Nolte. 143–155.

Ziebura, Gilbert. *Léon Blum et le parti socialiste, 1872–1934.* Paris: Armand Colin, 1967.

Zlobin, V. I. *Vtoroi' s'ezd RSDRP: istoriografiia.* Moscow: Izd. Moskovskogo universiteta, 1980.

Zorin, Libushe. *Soviet Prisons and Concentration Camps: An Annotated Bibliography.* New York: Oxford University Press, 1980.

Index

Abramovich, R. *See* Abramovitch, R.

Abramovitch, R., 17, 100, 219, 262; on Soviet experience, 8, 118–119, 164–165, 191–197 passim, 246–248 passim, 250, 299–300, 398n31; in Menshevik exile group, 10, 24–25, 60, 197, 218, 222–223, 226, 260–261, 266–268 passim, 273, 282, 285, 296, 319; as intermediary, 13, 23–24, 104, 180–181, 220, 221, 269, 270, 273, 382n4; in LSI, 23, 160–163 passim, 212–213, 261–262, 392n10, 388n36, 413n14; attacks on, 24, 180–181, 201, 212–213, 246, 261, 282, 349n22, 362n22, 401n40; as Bundist, 24, 26, 40, 52–53, 59–60, 157, 171, 180–181, 349n21, 387n21; on Marxism, 24, 186, 194, 198–199, 312; *Soviet Revolution*, 24, 55, 187, 323–324, 363n31; in 1917, 59, 64, 65, 69; and socialist unification, 60, 157–158, 160, 254, 256–257; opposition to Soviets, 71–74, 77, 91, 166, 168, 203, 206–208 passim, 212, 213; and foreign socialist parties, 77, 99, 152–153, 176, 177, 235, 250, 252, 254, 262; in USA, 104, 180–181, 221, 263, 272, 273, 293, 296, 297, 313, 386n5; on situation in Soviet Russia, 125, 208, 225, 246–247; as historian, 133, 135, 166, 183, 214, 317, 322n4, 349n25, 362–363n23, 364nn39,41, 365nn8,18, 386nn7,9;

on Soviet leadership struggle, 144, 149–150, 197, 246–247, 300, 317; on international politics, 276, 277, 280–281; *bio*, 333

Abramowitsch, R. *See* Abramovitch, R.

ADGB (Allgemeine Deutsche Gewerkschafts Bund), 101

Adler, F., 158, 166–167, 232, 259, 264; relations with Mensheviks, 150, 166, 171, 173, 177, 262–264 passim, 283, 286, 418n9; and Russian Question, 193, 194–195, 257

AFL, 273, 297, 306. *See also* Labor Conference on International Affairs

Aizenstadt, I. *See* Iudin, I.

Aksel'rod, P. *See* Axelrod, P.

Aleksandrova, E., 42, 354n39

Aleksandrova, V. *See* Alexandrova, V.

Alexandrova, V.: in USA, 13, 297, 319; in Russia, 17, 23, 66, 73, 90, 361n22, 368n29; in Menshevik exile group, 198, 227, 264, 268, 275; *bio*, 333

Alexinsky, G., 58

Alsop, J. and S., 307

Alter, V., 281, 306

American Committee for Liberation, Inc. (of the Peoples of Russia; later, from Bolshevism), 294, 295, 313

American Labor Conference on International Affairs. *See* Labor Conference on International Affairs

American Labor Research Institute, 320